Illustrated
QUICK
COOK

Illustrated
QUICK
COOK

Editor-in-Chief **Heather Whinney**

Penguin Random House

Written by Heather Whinney

Additional recipe contributors
Guy Mirabella, Kate Titford

Photography William Reavell,
William Shaw, Jon Whitaker

Project Editor Laura Nickoll
Art Editor Anne Fisher
Managing Editor Dawn Henderson
Managing Art Editor Christine Keilty
Senior Jacket Creative Nicola Powling
Production Editor Ben Marcus
Production Controller Alice Holloway
CTS Sonia Charbonnier

DK INDIA
Editor Alicia Ingty
Designer Neha Ahuja
Design Manager Romi Chakraborty
Editorial Manager Glenda Fernandes
DTP Designer Tarun Sharma
DTP Coordinator Balwant Singh
Head of Publishing Aparna Sharma

NOTE: Every effort has been made to include sustainable foods in this book. Food sustainability is, however, a shifting landscape. We encourage readers to keep up to date on the subject so they are equipped to make their own ethical choices.

First American Edition, 2009
This paperback edition published in 2015

First published in the United States by
DK Publishing
375 Hudson Street
New York, NY 10014

Published in Great Britain by
Dorling Kindersley Limited

A catalog record for this book is available from the Library of Congress.
ISBN 978-1-4654-3008-3

DK books are available at special discounts when purchased in bulk for sales promotions, premiums, fund-raising, or educational use. For details, contact:
DK Publishing Special Markets,
375 Hudson Street, New York, NY 10014
or SpecialSales@dk.com.

Printed and bound in China

All images © Dorling Kindersley Limited
For further information see:
www.dkimages.com

A WORLD O F IDEAS:
SEE ALL THERE IS TO KNOW

CONTENTS

INTRODUCTION

My obsession started many years ago—cookbooks by the side of the bed and stacked high on bulging shelves. I constantly daydreamed about the next meal and the need to be stirring a big pot of something on the stovetop. I'm not sure if this constitutes being a "foodie" or whether it just means I am plain greedy! However, it certainly filled me with enough enthusiasm, 20 years ago, to embark upon a career in food.

I have always enjoyed cooking from scratch. Making something to eat just seems a more natural process than opening a package of food that someone else has made, and waiting for the microwave to "ping." That said, I have never enjoyed cooking complicated or time-consuming meals, so I am certainly not about to start writing about them. All my culinary training has come from bringing up two children and being a home economist, not a chef, so complicated techniques and long ingredient lists are not really my thing. I love eating at restaurants, but consider myself a home cook. If I were to describe my cooking, I would say it is "no frills." My food is simple but hearty, and the recipes in the book reflect this.

I worked for many years on women's magazines as a food editor, which has given me precious insight into what people really want from recipes. Above all, they want simple and straightforward steps, and familiar ingredients. Confident and adventurous cooks want new ideas and inspiration, and beginners want clear and concise recipes to boost their confidence in the kitchen. This book is for the inexperienced cook to learn from, and the experienced cook to learn more from, and for both to enjoy!

This book was an ambitious undertaking, as it had to be many things—practical and inspirational, simple but instructive, easy yet creative, and, most importantly, full of quick meals. It certainly delivers this, and more. It guides you effortlessly through hundreds of recipes that are easy to make, and all take 30 minutes or less of your full attention. Using familiar ingredients, it covers all the bases, from Speedy Suppers—meals you can cook when you come home from work—to All-in-One Roasts, perfect for the weekend cook. For those of us who don't like the heat of the kitchen, the No Cook chapter has delicious flavors running through it, and for those of you who crave sugar, Cakes and Bakes and Indulgent Desserts will more than satisfy your sweet tooth.

The Everyday section has hundreds of recipes to feed the family, and for entertaining, there is the second section, Food for Friends. I hope you will dip in and out of chapters in both sections, and mix and match—the Recipe Choosers at the start will help you choose, as will the Menu Planners. Each chapter is full of time-saving tips and shortcuts, all of which aim to minimize stress and time in the kitchen.

Making time to cook isn't all about time spent in the kitchen. It's also about shopping and planning. The way we shop affects the way we eat, and the secret is in the planning. This can simply be a scribbled note of meals for the week and a budget in mind.

I have learned the art of efficient shopping over the years. Making the right choice at the butcher's, farmers' market, and supermarket all helps to ease the pressure of providing meals from scratch every day. Buying organic vegetables and good-quality fish and meat might be expensive, but you can cancel out this extra cost by shopping seasonally, and buying cheaper (often tastier) cuts of meat. In my experience, an hour spent at the market on a Saturday morning is far more enjoyable and useful than a late night dash at the grocery store. That said, supermarket food and stored goods are invaluable for busy people, so keep your pantry well stocked at all times. You can then concentrate on buying fresh foods, which make up the main ingredients of most of the recipes in this book. If your fridge is bare, however, a well-stocked cupboard can be a lifesaver. The Store Cupboard chapter makes good use of all those packages, cans, and jars, offering meal solutions for when there simply isn't time to shop.

I hope this book becomes a trusty and reliable resource in your kitchen—one that you will turn to again and again, whether to check the quantities for a crêpe, whip up a quick supper, or revisit a favorite chocolate cake. With over 700 foolproof tried-and-tested recipes, this book is a brilliant selection of quick and easy meals that cater to any palate and any occasion. Most importantly, it's the food that my family, friends, and I really love to eat!

Heather Whinney

USEFUL INFORMATION

These guidelines are here to help you in the kitchen with measurements, ingredient information, and equipment tips, and to introduce you to symbols that accompany every recipe in the book. All recipes have been tested on a gas cooktop or in a conventional electric oven. If using a convection oven, reduce the temperature by 25°F. If in doubt about the accuracy of your oven, invest in an oven thermometer.

Linear measures

⅛in	(3mm)	1in	(2.5cm)	4in	(10cm)	8in	(20cm)	12in	(30cm)
¼in	(5mm)	2in	(5cm)	5in	(12cm)	9in	(23cm)	18in	(46cm)
½in	(1cm)	2½in	(6cm)	6in	(15cm)	10in	(25cm)	20in	(50cm)
¾in	(2cm)	3in	(7.5cm)	7in	(18cm)	11in	(28cm)	24in	(61cm)
								30in	(77cm)

Weights

¼oz	(10g)	3oz	(85g)	9oz	(250g)	1lb 10oz	(750g)	4½lb	(2kg)
½oz	(15g)	3½oz	(100g)	10oz	(300g)	1¾lb	(800g)	5lb	(2.25kg)
¾oz	(20g)	4oz	(115g)	12oz	(350g)	2lb	(900g)	5½lb	(2.5kg)
scant 1oz	(25g)	4½oz	(125g)	14oz	(400g)	2¼lb	(1kg)	6lb	(2.7kg)
1oz	(30g)	5oz	(140g)	1lb	(450g)	2½lb	(1.1kg)	6½lb	(3kg)
1½oz	(45g)	5½oz	(150g)	1lb 2oz	(500g)	2¾lb	(1.25kg)		
1¾oz	(50g)	6oz	(175g)	1¼lb	(550g)	3lb	(1.35kg)		
2oz	(60g)	7oz	(200g)	1lb 5oz	(600g)	3lb 3oz	(1.5kg)		
2½oz	(75g)	8oz	(225g)	1½lb	(675g)	4lb	(1.8kg)		

Volume measures

1 tsp		2½fl oz (75ml)	8fl oz (240ml)	16fl oz (500ml)	2½ pints (1.4 litres)
2 tsp		3fl oz (90ml)	8fl oz (250ml)	1 pint (600ml)	2¾ pints (1.5 litres)
1 tbsp (which is		3½fl oz (100ml)	10fl oz (300ml)	1¼ pints (750ml)	3 pints (1.7 litres)
equivalent to 3 tsp)		4fl oz (120ml)	12fl oz (360ml)	1½ pints (900ml)	3½ pints (2 litres)
2 tbsp		5fl oz (150ml)	14fl oz (400ml)	1¾ pints (1 litre)	5¼ pints (3 litres)
3 tbsp		7fl oz (200ml)	15fl oz (450ml)	2 pints (1.2 litres)	
4 tbsp or 2fl oz (60ml)					

Oven temperatures

250°F (130°C)	375°F (190°C)	250°F—very cool oven
275°F (140°C)	400°F (200°C)	275°F–300°F—very low oven
300°F (150°C)	425°F (220°C)	325°F—low oven
325°F (160°C)	450°F (230°C)	350°F–375°F—moderate oven
350°F (180°C)	475°F (240°C)	400°F–425°F—hot oven
		450°F–475°F—very hot oven

Measurements

- Always use the measurements stated, especially when baking—a few extra pinches of spice, herbs, or seasoning in a stew is down to personal taste, but a few extra pinches of something in a cake could end up in failure.
- Always use measuring spoons. The recipes refer to a level spoon, unless otherwise stated.
- Use a measuring cup for liquids, and take the measurement looking at it from eye level.
- Never mix metric and imperial.
- A good old-fashioned pair of balancing scales with weights are the most accurate, will last forever, and won't suddenly run out of batteries!
- There are so many variables in cooking, from the intensity of the heat to the type of pan used, so certain recipes may take less time or longer. All recipes have been tested, and the cooking times given are as accurate as possible, but learn to rely on your instincts for doneness, and check as you go.

Ingredients

Eggs
Use large eggs, which weigh 2¼–2½oz (65–75g) unless otherwise stated, and choose free-range where possible. If preparing a recipe using raw eggs, make sure they are really fresh. It is advisable not to serve raw eggs to children, pregnant women, or the elderly.

Ingredients
Use humanely reared free-range meats if you can, and always use free-range chicken—the finished dish will taste far better and you will have made an ethical decision about the life of an animal or bird.

Seasoning
This brings out the flavor of the food and is an important part of cooking. Use sea salt if you can as this is more natural and tastes so much better. Season at the beginning of cooking, then taste at the end and correct the seasoning. You must keep tasting as you cook, so you can adjust and perfect the flavor of your food.

Equipment

A small selection of good-quality, basic equipment makes life so much easier, and cooking so much more pleasurable.

Pots and pans
- A few heavy-bottomed pans, which conduct heat well.
- A nonstick frying pan, a small one for omelets, and a large one for pan-frying.
- A heavy cast-iron pan for cooking casseroles and stews. They need to retain heat well.

Knives
- A large cook's knife.
- A small vegetable knife.
- A sharp vegetable peeler, such as the swivel-head style, will reduce preparation time by half.

Thick wooden cutting board
For fruit and vegetable food preparation.

Plastic board for meat and fish.

Hygiene in the kitchen

Food poisoning occurs when food has been contaminated by bacteria. This can be easily avoided by taking a little care in the kitchen. Wash your hands before and after handling foods, and thoroughly clean boards, knives, and utensils used in the preparation of raw meat and fish before using them again.

A guide to symbols

Special equipment and essential marinating or chilling times are listed at the top of the recipe, so you start a recipe armed with all the information you need.

 Prep time—this is an average time, as some people chop and peel far quicker than others, but it's a pretty good guide.

 Cook time—this is as accurate as possible, but many variable factors are involved, so check your food just before the cook time is up.

 Indicates a dish, or part of a dish, can be frozen.

 Indicates a dish is "healthy"—either low in fat and saturated fat, or low GI. Healthy recipes are not high in salt, sugar, or saturated fat.

RECIPE CHOOSERS

An instant visual reference to a selection of super-fast recipes for meat, fish, vegetarian dishes, and desserts—15 minutes from start to finish or 30 minutes from start to finish, including both preparation and cooking time.

MEAT IN UNDER 15 MINUTES

Beef with beets and spinach p241

PREP 15 MINS

Smoked chicken salad with papaya fruit salsa p45

PREP 15 MINS

The perfect steak p124

PREP 2 MINS COOK 10 MINS

Quesadilla with ham, gherkin, and smoked cheese p191

PREP 5 MINS COOK 5 MINS

Chicken Caesar salad p47

PREP 15 MINS

Sliced beef and arugula salad with green olive and raisin salsa p41

PREP 15 MINS

Chicken salad with carrot and apple relish p225

PREP 15 MINS

Chicken with aduki beans and herbs p53

PREP 10 MINS

Thai-style beef salad p240

PREP 15 MINS

MEAT IN UNDER 30 MINUTES: STARTERS

Grilled asparagus and pancetta
p356

PREP 15 MINS | COOK 5 MINS

Lemon-soy skewered chicken with hot dipping sauce p114

PREP 15 MINS | COOK 10 MINS

Lamb and mint burgers
p60

PREP 10 MINS | COOK 20 MINS ❄

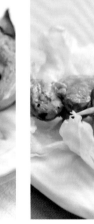

Chicken satay
p361

PREP 15 MINS | COOK 10 MINS

Smoked chicken with basil mayonnaise on cucumber rounds p320

PREP 20 MINS

Chorizo with peppers p335

PREP 10 MINS | COOK 10 MINS

Ham with pears p337

PREP 10 MINS | COOK 15 MINS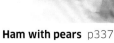

MEAT IN UNDER 30 MINUTES: MAIN MEALS

Pasta carbonara with pancetta and cream p173
PREP 10 MINS COOK 15 MINS

Filet mignon with horseradish cream p442
PREP 10 MINS COOK 10 MINS

Pad Thai p381
PREP 15 MINS COOK 15 MINS

Beef tacos p64
PREP 15 MINS COOK 15 MINS

Pork scallops with bread crumb and parsley crust p69
PREP 15 MINS COOK 15 MINS

Pork and spring greens p233
PREP 10 MINS COOK 10 MINS

Seared duck with five-spice and noodles p70
PREP 10 MINS COOK 20 MINS

Chicken scallops with chiles and parsley p117
PREP 10 MINS COOK 10 MINS

MEAT IN UNDER 30 MINUTES: MAIN MEALS continued

Thai-style ground pork with noodles p66

PREP 10 MINS · COOK 15 MINS

Wasabi beef and bok choy p443

PREP 10 MINS · COOK 10 MINS

Pan-fried ham with pineapple salsa p68

PREP 5 MINS · COOK 20 MINS

Pork steaks with tomato and fava bean sauce p66

PREP 5 MINS · COOK 25 MINS

Turkey burgers p71

PREP 15 MINS · COOK 15 MINS

Quesadilla with spiced beef and tomato p188

PREP 5 MINS · COOK 20 MINS

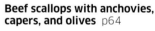

Beef scallops with anchovies, capers, and olives p64

PREP 10 MINS · COOK 20 MINS

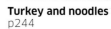

Turkey and noodles p244

PREP 15 MINS · COOK 15 MINS

14

Caramelized pork tenderloin with pecans and apricots p70

PREP 10 MINS · COOK 15 MINS

Pizza bianca with prosciutto, arugula, and mozzarella p185

PREP 10 MINS · COOK 10 MINS

Corned beef hash with horseradish p65

PREP 10 MINS · COOK 20 MINS

Beef with soy and lime with grapefruit and ginger salsa p63

PREP 10 MINS · COOK 15 MINS · ♥

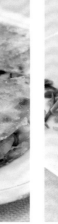

Quesadilla with chicken and sweet onion p191

PREP 5 MINS · COOK 15 MINS

Chicken stir-fried with scallions, basil, and lemongrass p110

PREP 10 MINS · COOK 15 MINS · ♥

Steak and oyster mushroom salad p126

PREP 5 MINS · COOK 15 MINS

Hot and sour beef stir-fry with green beans p63

PREP 10 MINS · COOK 20 MINS

Chicken with noodles and basil p108

PREP 5 MINS · COOK 15 MINS · ♥

FISH IN UNDER 15 MINUTES: STARTERS

Smoked trout with beet, apple, and dill relish
p40

PREP
15
MINS

Smoked mackerel pâté
p363

PREP
5
MINS

Smoked salmon with radishes and spiced yogurt dressing p52

PREP
15
MINS

Chile shrimp with cilantro and lime p45

PREP
15
MINS

Smoked trout with chile and lime dressing p366

PREP
10
MINS

Smoked salmon with mustard and dill dressing p365

PREP
5
MINS

Smoked trout with pickled cucumber and minted yogurt p42

PREP
15
MINS

FISH IN UNDER 15 MINUTES: MAIN MEALS

Niçoise-style salad p47

PREP 15 MINS

Crab salad with grapefruit and cilantro p360

PREP 10 MINS

Baked salmon with salsa verde and cucumber p236

PREP 15 MINS

Pasta with crab and lemon p166

PREP 5 MINS COOK 10 MINS

Crayfish and crisp lettuce panini with herbed mayonnaise p319

PREP 15 MINS

Smoked fish, fennel, and mango salad p52

PREP 15 MINS

Tuna and white beans with olives p277

PREP 10 MINS

Seafood and fennel salad with anchovy dressing p49

PREP 15 MINS

FISH IN UNDER 30 MINUTES: STARTERS

Salt and pepper shrimp
p362

PREP **10** MINS   COOK **10** MINS

Mixed tikka fish kebabs with mango salsa and lime raita p84

PREP **15** MINS   COOK **15** MINS

Scallops skewered with prosciutto p327

PREP **10** MINS   COOK **8** MINS

Battered fish with lemon mayonnaise p338

PREP **20** MINS   COOK **10** MINS

Skewered swordfish with capers p344

PREP **15** MINS   COOK **10** MINS

Thai fish cakes
p361

PREP **15** MINS   COOK **15** MINS

Crab balls
p363

PREP **10** MINS   COOK **15** MINS

Smoked salmon and cream cheese roulades p360

PREP **30** MINS

Sesame shrimp toasts p326

PREP 15 MINS **COOK 10 MINS** **Shrimp cocktail-style wraps with avocado and red pepper mayonnaise** p42 **PREP 20 MINS**

Grilled shrimp with hot pepper sauce p74 **PREP 10 MINS** **COOK 10 MINS**

Grilled squid with arugula salad p434 **PREP 15 MINS** **COOK 2 MINS**

Sautéed scallops with pancetta and wilted spinach p77 **PREP 5 MINS** **COOK 15 MINS**

Tuna, tomato, and zucchini skewers p81 **PREP 10 MINS** **COOK 10 MINS**

Fish sticks with chunky tartar sauce p80 **PREP 15 MINS** **COOK 10 MINS**

FISH IN UNDER 30 MINUTES: MAIN MEALS

White fish with spinach and pine nuts p81
 PREP 10 MINS COOK 15 MINS

Sweet and sour stir-fried fish with ginger p80
PREP 10 MINS COOK 20 MINS

Pasta with clams and parsley p175
PREP 10 MINS COOK 15 MINS

Teriyaki fish with noodles p83
PREP 10 MINS COOK 15 MINS

Butterflied sardines stuffed with tomatoes and capers p73
 PREP 15 MINS COOK 10 MINS

Mussels in fennel broth p76
PREP 10 MINS COOK 20 MINS

Pan-fried shrimp, olives, and tomatoes p79
PREP 5 MINS COOK 15 MINS

Olive and anchovy open tart p206
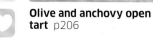 PREP 10 MINS COOK 15 MINS ❄

Baked white fish in wine and herbs p73
PREP 5 MINS COOK 20 MINS

Pasta with seafood and tomatoes
p169

Pan-fried clams with parsley and garlic
p83

Spiced haddock with coconut, chile, and lime p82

Roasted squid and potatoes with cilantro pesto p76

Tuna with sweet shallots p74

Pasta with tuna and roasted onion p172

Lemon sole with herbs p78

PREP 10 MINS COOK 20 MINS

VEGETARIAN IN UNDER 15 MINUTES: STARTERS

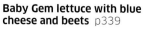

Bruschetta with tomato and basil
p324

PREP 10 MINS

Hummus p323

PREP 10 MINS

Beet-topped mini-rye breads
p327

PREP 15 MINS

Arugula, ricotta, and black olive dip p317

PREP 15 MINS

Quesadilla with cheese and chiles p189

PREP 5 MINS COOK 5 MINS

Baby Gem lettuce with blue cheese and beets p339

PREP 15 MINS

Chilled tomato and red pepper soup p41

PREP 15 MINS

Grilled goat cheese with honey
p335

PREP 10 MINS | COOK 5 MINS

Quesadilla with avocado, scallions, and chiles
p189

PREP 10 MINS | COOK 5 MINS

No-cook pea and mint soup
p48

PREP 10 MINS

Mixed mushroom, scallion, and orange salad p44

PREP 15 MINS

Feta and pea salad with watercress mayonnaise p49

PREP 15 MINS

Artichoke and fennel dip
p316

PREP 20 MINS

Quesadilla with mushrooms and Gruyère cheese p190

PREP 5 MINS | COOK 10 MINS

23

VEGETARIAN IN UNDER 20 MINUTES: SIDE DISHES

Tomato, red onion, and mozzarella salad
p48

PREP 10 MINS

Spinach, pine nuts, and raisins p338

PREP 5 MINS COOK 10 MINS

Chickpeas in olive oil and lemon p342

PREP 10 MINS COOK 5 MINS

Asparagus with lemony dressing p364

PREP 10 MINS COOK 10 MINS

Green beans with toasted hazelnuts
p427

PREP 5 MINS COOK 5 MINS

Bread salad with Gorgonzola
p51

PREP 15 MINS

24

VEGETARIAN IN UNDER 15 MINUTES: MAIN MEALS

Pasta with no-cook tomato sauce p160

PREP 5 MINS | COOK 10 MINS

Lentil, fava bean, and feta salad p40

PREP 15 MINS

Carrot salad with cabbage and peanuts p50

PREP 15 MINS

Goat cheese, beet, and pistachio salad p46

PREP 15 MINS

The perfect omelet p144

PREP 2 MINS | COOK 1 MIN

Bulgur with mixed peppers, mint, and paprika p43

PREP 15 MINS

VEGETARIAN IN UNDER 30 MINUTES: STARTERS

Crêpes with peppers and basil p195 PREP 10 MINS COOK 20 MINS

Mushrooms in garlic sauce p340 PREP 10 MINS COOK 15 MINS

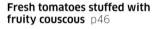

Fresh tomatoes stuffed with fruity couscous p46 PREP 30 MINS

Vegetable tempura with chile dipping sauce p362 PREP 15 MINS COOK 15 MINS

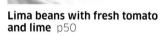

Lima beans with fresh tomato and lime p50 PREP 20 MINS

Zucchini stuffed with raisins, red onion, and pine nuts p91 PREP 10 MINS COOK 20 MINS

Mushrooms on toast with Manchego cheese p336 PREP 10 MINS COOK 20 MINS

Grilled asparagus and Gorgonzola p454 PREP 20 MINS COOK 10 MINS

Baked eggs with tomatoes p146 PREP 5 MINS COOK 15 MINS

VEGETARIAN IN UNDER 30 MINUTES: MAIN MEALS

Grilled pepper and leek couscous p453
PREP 15 MINS COOK 15 MINS

Asparagus, broccoli, ginger, and mint stir-fry p92
PREP 15 MINS COOK 15 MINS

Bean burgers p280
PREP 15 MINS COOK 10 MINS

Halloumi with garlic, chili, and cilantro p341
PREP 10 MINS COOK 15 MINS

Pasta with mushroom sauce p167
PREP 10 MINS COOK 20 MINS

Rice and peas p95
PREP 5 MINS COOK 25 MINS

Tomato and harissa tart p210
PREP 10 MINS COOK 15 MINS

Spicy garlic green vegetable medley p93
PREP 15 MINS COOK 15 MINS

Tomato bulgur wheat with capers and olives p277
PREP 15 MINS COOK 15 MINS

Baked eggs with tomato and peppers p95
PREP 10 MINS COOK 20 MINS

DESSERTS IN UNDER 15 MINUTES

Peaches with meringue and raspberry sauce p470
`PREP 15 MINS`

Apricots with Amaretti cookies and mascarpone p471
`PREP 15 MINS`

Mixed berry cake p472
`PREP 10 MINS`

Middle Eastern oranges with honey p466
`PREP 15 MINS`

Fresh figs with cassis cream p469
`PREP 15 MINS`

Mixed berries with white chocolate sauce p500
`PREP 5 MINS` `COOK 5 MINS`

Easy banoffee pie p466
`PREP 15 MINS`

Knickerbocker glory p467
`PREP 15 MINS`

Vanilla ice cream with coffee drizzle p468
`PREP 10 MINS`

Chocolate biscuit cake p487
`PREP 10 MINS`

DESSERTS IN UNDER 30 MINUTES

Mini summer puddings
p482

 PREP 30 MINS

Mocha pots
p480

PREP 30 MINS

Chilled black cherry cheesecake p497

PREP 30 MINS

Melon with vodka, orange, and mint p467

PREP 15 MINS

Melting-middle chocolate fudge puddings p495

PREP 15 MINS COOK 12 MINS

SAVORY

Quick techniques and shortcuts

Beef stock, make p220

Broil p59

Chicken
> **flatten** p103
>
> **poach** p103
>
> **roast** p103
>
> **skewer** p103
>
> **steam** p103
>
> **stuff** p103

Chicken stock, make p220

Dressings, make p38

Fish, marinate p39

Gravy, make p405

Grill p59

Mayonnaise, make p313

Meat, score p432

No-cook meal, assemble p37

Pancakes, make p183

Pan-fry p58

Pasta, make p159

Pizza dough, make p181

Quesadillas, make p182

Shortcrust pastry, make p199

Spanish omelet, make p331

Spatchcock birds p432

Stir-fry p58

Tart pan, line p200

Assemble a no-cook meal p37

Make your own pasta p159

Make perfect quesadillas p182

Make beef stock p220

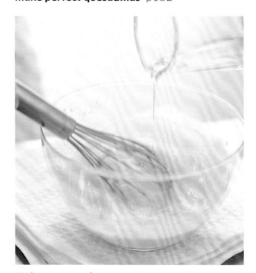

Make mayonnaise p313

Stir-fry p58

SWEET

Quick techniques and shortcuts

Cake pan, line p507

Cheesecake, make p461

Cookie dough, make p508

Fruit fool, make p460

Fruit sorbet, make p479

Ice cream, make without a machine p478

Mangoes, prepare p459

Oranges, prepare p459

Passion fruit, prepare p459

Peaches, prepare p459

Pineapple, prepare p459

Pomegranates, prepare p459

Soft fruit, freeze p477

Sponge cake, make p506

Prepare passion fruit p459

Make fruit fool p460

Make cheesecake p461

Make easy ice cream without a machine p478

Make fruit sorbet p479

Make basic sponge cake p506

Make basic cookie dough p508

EVERYDAY

NO COOK

Instant food—no heat required.

NO COOK

When time is short, there are plenty of ingredients around that can be eaten as they are, with no cooking necessary. With a little imagination and clever shopping, meals can be whipped up in minutes, saving not just time, but clean up and fuel bills, too.

Psst...

To pep up smoked fish, add a handful of basil leaves and flat-leaf parsley to a mortar and pestle and grind with a clove of garlic, drizzle of olive oil, and a splash of vinegar. Refrigerate until ready to use. Drizzle over the fish just before serving.

Best fresh no-cook ingredients
Grab a meal from the deli or salad counter.

CHOOSE	USE	STORE
 **COOKED AND CURED MEAT** Choose cooked meats that are whole and sliced to order at the deli counter, as these will be fresher than ready-sliced and packaged cooked meats. Cured meats are raw meats that have been salted, dried, or smoked, and usually sliced paper-thin.	**Ham** is fabulous served with chutneys and pickles, or chopped and stirred into a salad of beets and fresh corn. **Cured ham** pairs well with delicate sweet flavors such as melon or figs, or mozzarella and arugula. **Beef** slices make a tasty sandwich: beef, watercress, and mustard is a great combination; or, try it sliced and tossed with spinach and an Asian dressing (see p38). **Chicken** can be mixed with mayonnaise, a pinch of curry powder, and cayenne pepper, for the timeless classic, coronation chicken. **Salami** makes a hearty salad: combine with sliced mushrooms and scallions and a fruity dressing. **Chorizo** can be eaten raw or cooked. Toss with nutty chickpeas and chopped red pepper, or served as part of a meat platter with rustic bread.	• Ready-cooked and cured meats in the refrigerator for 3–5 days. Keep them well away from any raw meats.
 **SMOKED AND PICKLED FISH** Hot or cold smoking is an old preserving method, and imparts a delicious woody flavor to fish such as salmon, trout, and mackerel. Try pickled herring (rollmops) cured in brine, or succulent cured anchovies in olive oil, a tasty alternative to the jarred, salted variety.	**Smoked salmon** is fairly rich and fatty, so it needs foods to cut through this, such as beets, horseradish, or citrus fruit. Serve as part of a seafood salad with chopped pickles, or with a soy and lime juice dressing. **Mackerel** is the ultimate no-cook superfood. Blend with Greek yogurt or cream cheese and lemon juice for an instant pâté, or flake and stir into rice or couscous. **Trout** can be bought hot or cold smoked.	It makes a great inexpensive alternative to smoked salmon. It has a more delicate taste and texture, and is lower in calories. Serve with peppery salad leaves, such as chicory or arugula, as part of a salad. **Pickled herring** is most often served with brown or rye bread, and a simple potato salad. **Anchovies**, salty or oily, add a real punch to a crisp green salad, tossed with a light creamy dressing.	• In the refrigerator. If vacuum-packed, eat within 2 days of opening. If bought loose, eat within 4 days of purchase. • Smoked salmon and trout can be frozen for up to 3 months. • Pickled fish will keep for up to 6 months, unopened.
 **CHEESE** Choose traditionally-made cheeses, and keep the cheaper packaged cheese for cooking. Buying cheese from the deli is perfect as you can buy as little or as much as required, and you can try different varieties. For the perfect cheeseboard, serve a hard cheese, a soft cheese, and a blue cheese.	**Hard and semi-hard cheese** such as Cheddar, Cheshire, Wensleydale, Gruyère, and Emmentaler are all good sliced or grated. Cheddar teams perfectly with seasonal fruits such as apple or pears, and nutty cheeses like Gruyère are better suited to chutneys and earthy spinach leaves. **Soft cheese** such as Brie or Camembert works well with sharp fruits such as red currants or cranberries, or sweet fruits such as figs or pears. Enjoy as part of a salad, or blend with walnuts into a pâté.	**Goat cheese** can be paired with some bitter leaves, sweet beets and apple, with a drizzle of balsamic vinegar. **Blue cheese** comes in three types: mild and creamy (eg. Gorgonzola), mature (eg. Stilton) or super-sharp (eg. Roquefort or Danish blue). Try crumbling your favorite type into a dressing, and drizzle it over bitter leaves, or blend with some Greek yogurt for a dip, and serve with crisp raw red pepper strips.	• Wrap hard cheese, goat cheese, and blue cheese in wax paper or foil. Don't wrap in plastic wrap, or it will sweat. Keep cool. If refrigerating, allow to come to room temperature, before serving. • Store soft cheese in the refrigerator. Eat within 3–4 days.
 **SALAD AND HERBS** Buy salad leaves and lettuce loose rather than packaged if possible, as they will last longer and taste better. Herbs are best bought in the pot or—better still—home-grown. Choose blemish-free leaves.	**Romaine lettuce** is the perfect ingredient for the classic Caesar salad. **Iceberg** is good for shredding and tucking into pita pockets with barbecued lamb and mint yogurt, or used in the classic shrimp cocktail. **Arugula** or **wild arugula** is hot and peppery, and ideal for adding to a mixed salad, or serving with cured meats, carpaccio, or a strong cheese. **Chicory** or **endive** are bitter leaves, best paired with sweet or salty foods such as ham, orange, and beets.	**Watercress** has a clean peppery taste. Use instead of, or alongside, salad leaves. It goes particularly well with smoked fish or salty cheeses such as Parmesan or Pecorino. **Scallions** are perfect for slicing and stirring into a leafy salad, or tossing with dressed cucumber before serving with smoked fish. **Soft leafy herbs** such as cilantro, basil, mint, and dill can be added to a mixture of salad leaves, a fresh tomato salad, or a platter of smoked fish.	• All (except basil—place on your windowsill) keep well in the bottom of the refrigerator, which is the coldest part. They will keep for longer if wrapped in damp parchment paper. Give them plenty of room, and remove any plastic to prevent them from sweating.
VEGETABLES When using vegetables raw they need to be very fresh. Baby varieties of vegetables, such as zucchini, carrots, or leeks, are often sweeter, and can be easier to digest.	**Fennel** has a unique liquorice flavor that will perk up any salad, and works as a good digestive aid when eaten raw between meals. Reserve the feathery fronds to use as a garnish. Add to coleslaw, toss with grated raw carrot, apple, and mayonnaise, or serve with a simple drizzle of lemon juice. **Red**, **yellow**, and **orange bell peppers** are deliciously sweet—finely dice or slice, to add color and texture to a salad of leaves, olives, capers, anchovies, tomatoes, and avocado.	**Avocado** can be tossed with cooked shrimp and crayfish and a hot wasabi dressing, or try mashing the flesh for an instant dip with lime or lemon juice, chile, Tabasco, and cilantro. **Spinach leaves** make excellent salads, and team well with smoked fish, ham, cheese, and nuts. **Carrots** add sweetness and vitamins to any salad. Try grated carrot with plump raisins, tossed in a poppy seed dressing, or spiced up with a pinch of paprika and cinnamon, and fresh mint and parsley.	• In the refrigerator. Eat as soon as possible. If storing in plastic, make sure it is perforated so the vegetables don't sweat, or store in a paper bag. • Avocado has a short shelf life. Refrigerate ripe ones and eat within 2 days. Store unripe ones at room temperature, out of sunlight.

Assemble a no-cook meal
These quick and simple "1, 2, 3" preparation steps will turn your raw ingredients into a delicious meal. Experiment with your own combination of ingredients listed in the chart opposite.

1 Slice 3 baby zucchini, or the vegetable of your choice, thinly using a vegetable peeler, and add them to a bowl. Season with salt.

2 Mix together 3 tbsp extra virgin olive oil, 1 tablespoon cider vinegar, ½ a red chile, seeded and finely chopped, and 1 tablespoon chopped mint leaves. Add to the zucchini and gently toss together using your hands.

3 Serve Season the mixture with salt and freshly ground black pepper and pile it onto a serving plate. Sprinkle with some shaved Parmesan cheese and a few torn fresh mint leaves.

Perfect pairings
A mixture of classic and the more unusual—the key to marrying flavors is to experiment!

- Combine **fresh peaches** or **apricots** with **prosciutto**.
- Crumble some **feta cheese** over **fresh figs**.
- Dish up juicy **strawberries** with a drizzle of **balsamic vinegar**.
- Serve **cured meats** with **melon**.
- Team **smoked salmon** with **horseradish**.
- Toss **cooked shrimp** with **lemongrass** and **fresh ginger**.
- Try **smoked mackerel** with **beets** and **fresh dill** or **fresh tarragon**.
- Try **raw shredded red cabbage** with freshly grated **ginger** and **fresh dill** or a **blue cheese dressing**.

- Enjoy **goat cheese** with **honey**.
- Serve **raw fennel** with **sliced oranges** and finely chopped **rosemary leaves**.
- Pair **radicchio** with **blue cheese** and **walnuts**.
- Toss **spinach** with **pomegranate seeds** and **pine nuts**.
- Drizzle **soy sauce**, **chiles**, and **lime juice** over **smoked salmon**.

the raw facts

Lots of precious nutrients are lost in the cooking process, so eating raw foods such as fruit and vegetables, nuts, seeds, grains, pulses, and dried fruits is extremely nutritious. Raw foods are packed with antioxidants: eating them increases energy levels, helps with digestion, and the high levels of vitamins B, C, and E are beneficial to both skin and hair. A good rule of thumb when preparing a raw dish is to use as many different colored fruits and vegetables as possible for optimum health benefits.

Deli salad A fresh and filling salad can be made up in minutes with salad and deli ingredients.

Pantry ingredients
A few lifesavers in the cupboard will help perk up meals in minutes (see also p270).

Scatter **mixed olives** over salad leaves. Serve **capers** with cooked meats and pâtés. **Pickles** and **chutneys** enhance cheese. **Horseradish sauce** goes well with smoked meats and fish. **Mustards**, **honey**, sweet and hot **chili sauces**, and **soy sauce** all make great dressing ingredients. A jar of **mayonnaise** is a must. **Canned pulses** and **beans**, **tuna**, **crab**, or **sardines** make an instant meal, as do **canned corn**, **bulgur wheat**, or **easy-soak noodles**. **Dried fruits**, **nuts**, and **seeds** enhance salads.

STEP-BY-STEP

EVERYDAY

Dressings
Making your own dressing is easy and quick and, once mastered, you can customize it to suit your dish and experiment with flavored oils and vinegars. Double up the quantities if using for large salads or a number of meals, and store in the refrigerator.

Basic technique
From a classic French or Italian dressing, to a blue cheese one, the preparation method remains the same. Remember to taste as you go, tweaking it by adding a little more vinegar, or a little more oil.

1 Measure out your basic ingredients— 3 parts oil to 1 part vinegar.

2 Combine the vinegar and oil, together with other ingredients, if using.

3 Whisk or shake to emulsify.

French
Good for: drizzling over green salads, avocados, or shredded vegetables.

2 tbsp white wine vinegar
2 tsp Dijon mustard
6 tbsp extra virgin olive oil
sea salt and freshly ground black pepper

1 Add the vinegar and mustard to a small bowl or screw-top jar with lid and mix together or shake until well combined.

2 Add the oil, and either whisk until combined, or put the lid on the jar and shake well.

3 Taste and add more vinegar, mustard, or oil if needed. Season to taste with salt and pepper, and whisk or shake again.

Asian
Good for: drizzling over noodles, seafood, and Thai-style salads.

2 tbsp white wine vinegar
juice of ½ lime
pinch of superfine sugar
6 tbsp extra virgin olive oil
1 red chile, seeded and finely diced
1in (2.5cm) piece of fresh ginger, peeled and grated
2 garlic cloves, peeled and grated
2 lemongrass stalks, trimmed and outer hard leaves removed
sea salt and freshly ground black pepper

1 Add the vinegar, lime, and sugar to a small bowl or screw-top jar with lid. Whisk.

2 Add the oil and either whisk until combined, or put the lid on the jar and shake well. Add the remaining ingredients, whisk or shake, and season to taste with salt and pepper.

Blue cheese
Good for: drizzling over crisp leaves, or a chicory and pear salad.

2 tbsp white wine or cider vinegar
juice of ½ lemon
2 tsp mayonnaise
6 tbsp extra virgin olive oil
2½oz (75g) Gorgonzola cheese, crumbled
sea salt and freshly ground black pepper

1 Add the vinegar, lemon juice, and mayonnaise to a small bowl or screw-top jar with lid, and mix together until well combined.

2 Add the oil, and either whisk until combined, or put the lid on the jar and shake well until it has emulsified. Add the cheese and whisk or shake again. Season to taste with salt and pepper.

Marinate fish
Marinating raw fish, such as finely sliced salmon, trout, sea bass, or tuna in an acidic marinade, such as lemon or lime, will basically "cook" the fish (known as ceviche). Uncooked vegetables also benefit from being marinated. You can also use raw marinades as a base for salad dressings. Make sure your fish is very fresh.

Marinating technique
This step-by-step method will suit most firm fresh fish.

1 Place all the ingredients for the marinade in a shallow bowl.

2 Slice your fish fillet paper-thin, making sure all the bones have been removed.

3 Add the fish to the marinade of your choice, making sure it is well covered.

4 Stir it occasionally to make sure all the fish is marinating. Leave for 30 minutes to 1 hour in the refrigerator, until the fish has turned opaque.

5 Remove with a slotted spoon and transfer to a serving plate. Serve with a squeeze of lemon or lime and a fresh leaf salad.

TIP: Put the fish in the freezer for 10 minutes before slicing it paper-thin. This will firm it up, and make slicing much easier.

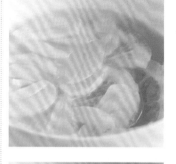

Lemon marinade
Great with: Tuna, sea bass, and salmon.

juice of 4 large lemons, plus 1 lemon sliced and finely quartered
2 garlic cloves, peeled and finely sliced
pinch of sea salt

Lime and cilantro
Great with: Swordfish, tuna, and sea bass.

juice of 4 limes, plus 1 lime finely sliced and quartered
handful of fresh cilantro, leaves only, finely chopped
2 garlic cloves, peeled and finely sliced
pinch of sea salt

Lime and chile
Great with: Swordfish, scallops, sea bass, and tuna.

juice of 4 limes, plus 1 lime finely sliced and quartered
1 red chile, seeded and finely sliced
2 garlic cloves, peeled and finely sliced
1in (2.5cm) piece of fresh ginger, peeled and finely sliced
pinch of sea salt

More marinade ideas
There are many variations that can be used, as long as the base is citrus. Try these with scallops, sea bass, trout, or turbot:

• Juice of 3 limes and 2 lemons with finely sliced **scallions**, a pinch of **paprika**, and a pinch of sugar.

• Juice of 1 lime with torn **fresh basil** leaves, and a pinch of salt.

• Juice of 2 limes, 2 lemons, and 1 orange, with a handful of **fresh thyme** leaves.

• Juice of 2 lemons with 1 teaspoon of **capers** and 1 tablespoon of **fresh dill**, finely chopped.

• Juice of 2 lemons with a handful of **scallions** and 1 clove of **garlic**, crushed.

storing marinades and dressings

Marinades: Keep covered in the refrigerator for a couple of days. If using for fish, discard after use.

Dressings: Can be stored, covered in the refrigerator, for about 3 days. Remember to remove from the refrigerator at least one hour before using, to bring to room temperature, and shake or stir before use.

EVERYDAY

Lentil, fava bean, and feta salad

  PREP 15 MINS

SERVES 4

½ cup frozen shelled fava beans
1 x 14oz (400g) can of green or brown
    lentils, drained and rinsed,
    or 2 cups drained cooked lentils
1 bunch of scallions, finely chopped
1 fresh green chile, finely chopped
6oz (175g) feta cheese,
    cut into cubes
handful of fresh flat-leaf parsley,
    finely chopped
sea salt and freshly ground
    black pepper

For the dressing
3 tbsp olive oil
1 tbsp white wine vinegar
1 x 1in (2.5cm) piece fresh ginger,
    peeled and grated
pinch of sugar (optional)

1 Cover the fava beans with boiling water and let sit for 5 minutes. Drain.

2 Put the lentils in a serving bowl and season with a pinch of salt and some black pepper. Stir in the drained fava beans, scallions, and chile.

3 To make the dressing, combine the oil, vinegar, and ginger in small bowl. Season with salt and pepper and a pinch of sugar (if using), and whisk until well blended. Drizzle over the salad and let stand for 10 minutes to allow the flavors to develop.

4 When ready to serve, stir in the feta and parsley.

 VARIATION
Goat cheese, or any smoked or blue cheese, can be used instead of the feta. For a colorful twist, toss in some peeled orange segments.

COOK'S NOTES

Canned lentils are an excellent pantry standby that will keep up to 1 year. They tend to be salty, so be sure to rinse them with cold water.

Smoked trout with beet, apple, and dill relish

PREP 15 MINS

SERVES 4

3–4 tsp creamed white horseradish
½ red onion, finely diced
1–2 heads curly endive or frisée,
    leaves separated
2 large cold-smoked trout fillets,
    about 8oz (225g) each, flaked
drizzle of olive oil
juice of ½ lemon
sea salt and freshly ground
    black pepper
2–3 eating apples
2 beets, cooked, peeled, and diced
handful of fresh dill, finely chopped

1 In a small bowl, mix the horseradish with half of the onion. Set aside.

2 Arrange the curly endive and flaked trout on a serving plate and drizzle with the oil and lemon juice. Season with salt and some black pepper.

3 Peel, core, and chop the apples into bite-sized pieces. Combine with the beet and dill in a separate bowl and mix together to make the relish.

4 To serve, spoon the relish over the salad. Sprinkle with the remaining red onion and serve the horseradish-onion mixture on the side.

 VARIATION
Crisp lettuce leaves, such as romaine, can be used instead of curly endive.

Chilled tomato and red pepper soup

 PREP 15 MINS

Special equipment • blender

SERVES 4

3 slices white bread, crusts removed
1 garlic clove, coarsely chopped
1 tbsp sherry vinegar or red wine vinegar
1 tbsp olive oil
6 very ripe tomatoes, coarsely chopped
2 red bell peppers, halved, seeded, and coarsely chopped
1 fresh red chile, seeded and coarsely chopped
sea salt and freshly ground black pepper

For the garnish
1 tomato, finely diced
¼ cucumber, seeded and finely diced
1 scallion, finely chopped

1 Using a blender, purée the bread, garlic, and vinegar until smooth. With the motor running, gradually pour in the oil until incorporated. Add the tomatoes, peppers, and chile and blend until well combined.

2 With the motor running, slowly add about 2 cups ice water to the mixture, checking the consistency of the soup as you go–it should resemble gazpacho. Season to taste with salt and pepper. Add a splash more vinegar if the soup needs it. Refrigerate until needed.

3 Make the garnish just before serving. Put the tomato, cucumber, and scallion in a small bowl and stir to combine.

4 Serve the soup chilled, topped with the tomato and cucumber garnish.

VARIATION
For a fiery kick, add a few drops of hot pepper sauce (such as Tabasco), chili sauce, or even a splash of vodka, and serve chilled in shot glasses.

EVERYDAY

COOK'S NOTES

To peel tomatoes, cut a cross on the bottom of each. Place them in a bowl and cover with hot water; count to 10, and drain. Return the tomatoes to the bowl and cover with ice water. The skins will peel off easily.

Sliced beef and arugula salad with green olive and raisin salsa

 PREP 15 MINS

SERVES 2
For the salsa
8–10 green olives, pitted and sliced
handful of plump dark raisins
2 tsp capers, rinsed and gently squeezed dry
drizzle of olive oil
sea salt and freshly ground black pepper
small handful of fresh flat-leaf parsley, finely chopped

handful of fresh arugula
6oz (175g) thinly sliced pastrami or other cooked beef from the deli

1 To make the salsa: In a bowl, mix together the olives, raisins, capers, oil, and parsley. Season to taste with salt and pepper.

2 Arrange the arugula and pastrami in a shallow serving bowl. Spoon the salsa over the top and serve at room temperature.

VARIATION
Top the salad with some freshly shaved Parmesan cheese, if you wish.

Smoked trout with pickled cucumber and minted yogurt

PREP 15 MINS

SERVES 4

1 avocado, halved, pitted, and peeled
juice of 1 lemon
2 tbsp white wine vinegar
2 tsp sugar
1 fresh red chile, seeded and finely
    chopped
½ large cucumber, peeled
    and halved lengthwise,
    seeded, and sliced
4 tbsp Greek-style yogurt
handful of fresh mint leaves,
    chopped
2 large handfuls of mixed lettuce
    leaves
12 green olives, pitted
2 cold-smoked trout fillets, about 7oz
    (200g) each, flaked
sea salt and freshly ground
    black pepper

1 Slice the avocado and sprinkle with the lemon juice to prevent discoloration. Set aside.

2 To make the pickled cucumber, whisk together the vinegar, sugar, and chile in a medium bowl. Add the cucumber and toss to mix. In a separate bowl, mix together the yogurt and mint.

3 Arrange the lettuce and olives in a large bowl or on 4 individual plates. Top with the flaked trout and avocado. Season with salt and pepper. Spoon some of the cucumber mixture over the top and reserve the rest in a bowl to serve on the side along with the minted yogurt.

COOK'S NOTES

Slightly bitter leaves such as curly endive are perfect for this salad. Try to buy salad leaves loose, rather than already packaged in bags, as they will keep for much longer.

Shrimp cocktail-style wraps with avocado and red pepper mayonnaise

PREP 20 MINS

Freeze • Mayonnaise and shrimp mixture
Special equipment • food processor

SERVES 4

3 red bell peppers: 2 coarsely
    chopped; 1 diced
4 tbsp mayonnaise
pinch of paprika
12 cooked shrimp, peeled and
    deveined
sea salt and freshly ground
    black pepper
4 x 8in (20cm) flour tortillas,
    cut in half
handful of crisp lettuce leaves, such
    as romaine, cut into thin strips
1 avocado, halved, pitted, peeled, and
    diced (toss with a little lemon juice
    to prevent discoloration)

1 Pulse the 2 chopped peppers in a food processor until finely chopped. Process in the mayonnaise and paprika to mix well. Coarsely chop 4 of the shrimp and stir into the mayonnaise. Season with salt and pepper.

2 Lay the tortilla halves flat on a clean work surface with the rounded edges facing you. Gently roll each tortilla into a cone shape, folding in a bit of the rounded edge on your first roll, so the filling will be enclosed.

3 To fill the wraps, pack half of the lettuce into the 8 tortilla "cones." Top the lettuce with the shrimp-mayonnaise mixture, the diced avocado and bell pepper, and then the remaining lettuce. Garnish each wrap with 1 whole shrimp. Allow two wraps per person and serve immediately.

VARIATION

To jazz up the flavor profile, add some chopped fresh mango.

COOK'S NOTES

To cut a pepper with minimal effort, slice off the top and bottom. Make 1 lengthwise cut and "unroll" the pepper, skin-side down. Scrape away the exposed seeds and membrane, then cut into strips or chop.

Prosciutto with pear, nectarine, and endive

PREP 15 MINS

SERVES 4

For the dressing

⅓ cup extra virgin olive oil

2 tbsp unsweetened apple juice

1 tbsp balsamic vinegar

sea salt and ground black pepper

2–3 small heads curly endive or frisée, leaves separated

12 thin slices prosciutto

3 firm but ripe pears, cored and sliced

3 firm but ripe nectarines, halved, pitted, and sliced

handful of almonds (skins on)

1 To make the dressing: In a small bowl, whisk together the oil, apple juice, and vinegar. Season well with salt and pepper. Scatter the curly endive over a large serving platter and drizzle with some of the dressing.

2 Top with the prosciutto, pears, and nectarines and toss gently to mix. Sprinkle with the almonds, then drizzle with a little more dressing, as desired. Taste and season if needed. Serve immediately with fresh crusty bread.

VARIATION Substitute radicchio for all or some of the curly endive—it adds an amazing color to the salad.

Bulgur with mixed peppers, mint, and paprika

PREP 15 MINS

SERVES 4

1½ cups fine bulgur (cracked wheat)

about 2 cups low-salt vegetable stock, heated until hot

sea salt and freshly ground black pepper

1 bunch of scallions, finely chopped

1 orange bell pepper, seeded and diced

1 yellow bell pepper, seeded and diced

pinch of paprika

handful of mint leaves, finely chopped

juice of 1 lemon

4–4½oz (125g) soft goat cheese, crumbled (about 1 cup)

drizzle of fruity extra virgin olive oil

1 Put the bulgur in a large heatproof bowl and pour in just enough hot stock to cover. Let stand for 15–20 minutes, until the grains are swollen and the liquid is absorbed. Stir with a fork to fluff up the bulgur. Season well with salt and pepper.

2 Stir in the scallions, peppers, paprika, mint, and lemon juice. Taste and season again if needed.

3 To serve, top with the goat cheese and a generous drizzle of olive oil.

VARIATION Substitute peeled chopped tomatoes for the peppers.

Mixed mushroom, scallion, and orange salad

PREP 15 MINS

SERVES 4

For the dressing

⅓ cup extra virgin olive oil

3 tbsp cider vinegar

pinch of sugar

1 tsp whole grain mustard

sea salt and freshly ground
   black pepper

9oz (250g) mushrooms, such as
   cremini and shiitake, stemmed
   and sliced

pinch of crushed red pepper flakes

1 bunch of scallions, sliced

1-2 oranges, depending on size,
   peeled, cut into segments
   (reserving the juices for the
   dressing), pith and seeds discarded

2 handfuls of fresh baby spinach
   leaves

handful of fresh basil leaves, torn or
   cut into thin strips (see Cook's Notes)

1 To make the dressing: Combine
the olive oil and vinegar in a small
bowl and whisk until blended. Add
a little of the reserved orange juice
along with the sugar and mustard.
Season with salt and pepper; whisk
again and taste. Add a little more
orange juice if needed. Let the
dressing stand for a few minutes
to blend the flavors.

2 To make the salad, put the
mushrooms in a large bowl. Add
the pepper flakes and drizzle in a
little of the dressing. Toss to coat
lightly. Let stand for 10 minutes,
then gently mix in the scallions and
orange segments.

3 When ready to serve, toss in the
spinach and basil leaves and more of
the dressing. Taste and season again,
if needed. Serve immediately.

COOK'S NOTES

*Basil leaves are best torn, rather
than chopped, as they tend to
bruise easily. Alternatively, stack
several leaves and roll tightly like
a cigar; then, with a sharp knife,
cut crosswise into thin strips.*

Flageolet bean and smoked cheese salad

PREP 15 MINS

SERVES 4

1 x 14oz (400g) can flageolet or
   small white beans, rinsed and
   drained

½ red onion, finely chopped

1 tsp Dijon mustard

handful of fresh flat-leaf parsley,
   finely chopped

sea salt and freshly ground
   black pepper

2 large handfuls of watercress,
   coarsely chopped

1 lemon, halved

4-4½oz (125g) lightly smoked cheese,
   such as Gouda, cubed

1 Put the beans in a large bowl. Stir
in half of the chopped onion, the
mustard, and the parsley. Season with
salt and pepper.

2 Arrange the watercress on a large
serving platter or 4 individual plates.

Squeeze the lemon juice over
the top and season with a pinch
of salt to taste. Sprinkle with the
remaining onion, top with the cheese,
and serve.

VARIATION Thin slices of boiled or smoked
ham, or prosciutto, are fabulous
with this, and pecorino makes
a delicious alternative to the
smoked cheese.

COOK'S NOTES

*Crisp, fresh watercress makes
all the difference. Wrap the cress
in a damp paper towel and place
inside an open plastic bag in
the refrigerator.*

Smoked chicken salad with papaya fruit salsa

PREP
15
MINS

SERVES 4
For the dressing
3 tbsp extra virgin olive oil
1 tbsp white wine vinegar
1 tbsp mango or orange juice
sea salt and ground black pepper

1 firm but ripe papaya, halved, seeded, peeled, and chopped
1 fresh red chile, seeded and finely chopped
juice of 1 lime
pinch of sugar
1lb (450g) boneless smoked chicken, sliced
2 handfuls of fresh baby spinach
handful of fresh basil leaves

1 To make the dressing: In a small bowl, whisk together the oil, vinegar, and mango juice. Season well with salt and pepper and set aside.

2 To make the salsa: In a bowl, toss together the papaya, chile, lime juice, and sugar. Season to taste with salt and pepper.

3 In a large bowl, toss the spinach and basil with the dressing, then divide among 4 individual plates and arrange the smoked chicken over the top. Spoon the salsa over the chicken, or serve on the side.

VARIATION
If you cannot find a perfectly ripe papaya, then use a fresh mango instead.

EVERYDAY

Chile shrimp with cilantro and lime

PREP
15
MINS

SERVES 4
16 cooked shrimp, peeled and deveined, tails left on
handful of fresh cilantro, finely chopped
1–2 fresh red chiles, seeded and finely chopped
1 x 14oz (400g) can lima beans or cannellini beans, drained and rinsed
2 handfuls of arugula
juice of 1 lime
sea salt and freshly ground black pepper
splash of Asian hot-sweet chili sauce, such as Sriracha

1 Put the shrimp in a large bowl. Mix in half of the cilantro and the fresh chiles. Add the beans and toss to mix again.

2 Place the arugula in a large serving bowl or on 4 individual plates.

Sprinkle with some of the lime juice, salt, and pepper. Stir the remaining lime juice into the shrimp mixture and adjust the seasonings as needed.

3 Spoon the shrimp mixture over the arugula, then drizzle with the hot-sweet chili sauce and sprinkle the remaining cilantro over the top. Serve immediately.

VARIATION
Use finely chopped fresh flat-leaf parsley instead of cilantro if you wish.

COOK'S NOTES

If the lima beans seem tough, put them in a bowl and cover with hot water before using. Let stand for 10 minutes to soften, then drain well.

EVERYDAY

Fresh tomatoes stuffed with fruity couscous

PREP
30
MINS

SERVES 4

4 large beefsteak tomatoes
⅔ cup tomato juice
¾ cup couscous
½ cup golden raisins
handful of fresh basil leaves
handful of flat-leaf parsley
sea salt and freshly ground
   black pepper

1 Slice the tops off the tomatoes and reserve. Working over a bowl, scoop out the seeds and flesh so you are left with only a "shell." Stir the tomato juice into the tomato flesh mixture. Set the tomato shells upside down on paper towels to drain.

2 Put the couscous in a separate bowl and pour in just enough hot water to cover, about ⅔ cup. Let stand for 10 minutes. Use a fork to fluff up the grains, then mix in the tomato mixture. Let stand for another 10 minutes.

3 Stir the couscous well, breaking up any large bits of tomato. Stir in the raisins, basil, and parsley. Taste and season with salt and pepper as needed. To serve, spoon the mixture into the tomato shells and cover with the reserved tops. Any leftover couscous can be served on the side.

VARIATION For a more savory dish, try substituting pine nuts for the raisins.

COOK'S NOTES

When preparing couscous, it can be a little tricky to perfect the amount of water you need. It is best to add the water slowly, and stop just as soon as it stands on top of the grains.

Goat cheese, beet, and pistachio salad

PREP
15
MINS

SERVES 4

For the dressing
3 tbsp extra virgin olive oil
1 tbsp white wine vinegar
2 shallots, finely chopped
1 tsp coarse-grain mustard
pinch of sugar
sea salt and freshly ground
   black pepper

2 handfuls of arugula
5–6oz (175g) goat cheese, cut into
   slices
4–6 large beets, cooked, peeled, and
   coarsely chopped
handful of shelled pistachios, coarsely
   chopped

1 First, make the dressing. In a small bowl, whisk together the oil and vinegar until well blended. Whisk in the shallots, mustard, and sugar, and season well with salt and pepper. Let the dressing stand for a few minutes to develop the flavors, then taste and adjust the seasonings as needed.

2 Arrange the arugula on a large serving platter or 4 individual plates, then top with the beets and goat cheese. Drizzle with a little of the dressing, then sprinkle with the pistachios. Drizzle with more dressing, if desired. Serve with fresh crusty bread.

Cheat...
If you don't have time to make the dressing, drizzle with a bit of balsamic vinegar instead.

Chicken Caesar salad

PREP 15 MINS

SERVES 4

For the dressing
- 2 egg yolks
- 2 tbsp lemon juice
- pinch of English mustard powder, such as Colman's
- ½ tbsp Worcestershire sauce
- ½ tbsp hot pepper sauce, such as Tabasco
- ⅔ cup vegetable oil
- ¼ cup olive oil

- 2 large handfuls of crisp lettuce leaves, such as romaine hearts
- 1 cup prepared croutons
- ½ cup freshly grated Parmesan cheese
- 2 cooked boneless chicken breast halves (12oz/350g), sliced
- 10 flat anchovies in oil, drained

1 First, make the dressing. In a bowl, whisk together the egg yolks, lemon juice, mustard powder, Worcestershire sauce, and pepper sauce. Whisking continuously, gradually add in the vegetable oil and then the olive oil, a little at a time, until the dressing forms an emulsion. If it is too thick, whisk in a little cold water.

2 Place about half of the dressing in a large bowl, then add the lettuce leaves, croutons, and half of the Parmesan. Toss gently to coat the leaves. Lay out the leaves on serving plates or a platter, and top with the chicken and anchovies. Sprinkle with the remaining Parmesan, drizzle with some more of the dressing, and serve.

VARIATION Instead of chicken, use large shrimp, cooked and peeled, with tails left on.

Cheat... If you don't have time to make your own Caesar dressing, some good varieties can be found on supermarket shelves.

EVERYDAY

Niçoise-style salad

PREP 15 MINS

SERVES 4

For the dressing
- 6 tbsp extra virgin olive oil
- 3 tbsp white wine vinegar
- 2 garlic cloves, finely grated or crushed through a press
- 1–2 tsp Dijon mustard
- sea salt and freshly ground black pepper

- 1 cup frozen fava beans or baby lima beans
- 2 x 6oz (175g) cans tuna in olive oil, drained
- 10 cherry tomatoes, halved
- handful of flat-leaf parsley, finely chopped
- bunch of fresh chives, finely chopped
- 12 black olives, pitted
- 12 salt-packed anchovies, rinsed, or flat anchovies in oil, drained
- 1 head of crisp lettuce, such as romaine, leaves separated
- 2–3 scallions, thinly sliced

1 First, make the dressing. Put all the dressing ingredients in a screw-top jar, seasoning well with salt and pepper, cover with the lid, and shake to blend.

2 Cover the beans with hot water and let stand for 5 minutes. Drain

3 Put the tuna and tomatoes in a bowl and drizzle with half the dressing. Sprinkle in half of the fresh herbs and season with salt and pepper. Toss together. Add the beans, olives, and anchovies, and mix gently.

4 Line a bowl with the lettuce leaves and arrange the tuna mixture on top. Drizzle with the remaining dressing and sprinkle with the remaining herbs.

VARIATION Add some cooked green beans, some boiled new potatoes, and a few hard-boiled eggs, shelled and quartered.

Tomato, red onion, and mozzarella salad

PREP 10 MINS

SERVES 4

8 small ripe plum tomatoes, sliced
6 cherry tomatoes, halved
1 small red onion, thinly sliced
handful of fresh basil leaves, torn
generous drizzle of extra virgin
   olive oil
2 handfuls of arugula
good splash of balsamic vinegar
8oz (2 balls) fresh mozzarella, drained
   and torn into pieces
sea salt and freshly ground
   black pepper

1 Put the tomatoes, red onion, and half of the basil leaves in a bowl. Drizzle generously with olive oil, season well with salt and pepper, and toss gently to blend.

2 Arrange the arugula on a serving platter; drizzle with a little olive oil and balsamic vinegar and season with salt and pepper. Spoon the tomato mixture over the top. Scatter with the torn mozzarella and the remaining basil leaves. Drizzle again with olive oil and balsamic vinegar and serve.

COOK'S NOTES

Consider investing in a good-quality fruity extra virgin olive oil and an aged balsamic vinegar that is both deliciously sweet and thick.

No-cook pea and mint soup

PREP 10 MINS

Special equipment • blender

SERVES 4

2 cups frozen peas
2 cups hot vegetable stock
handful of fresh mint leaves, coarsely
   chopped
leaves from a few sprigs of fresh
   thyme
sea salt and freshly ground
   black pepper
1–2 tbsp crème fraîche (optional)
pinch of freshly grated nutmeg

1 Cover the peas with hot water and let stand for 5 minutes. Drain.

2 Working in batches if needed, process the peas, stock, mint, and thyme in a blender until smooth. Add more stock if the soup is too thick. Season well with salt and pepper and process again.

3 To serve, stir in the crème fraîche and top with a pinch of nutmeg. Serve hot or cold with crusty bread.

VARIATION

Use frozen fava beans or lima beans instead of the peas, or use a combination of peas and beans.

Feta and pea salad with watercress mayonnaise

PREP 15 MINS

Special equipment • food processor

SERVES 4
handful of watercress, chopped
3-4 tbsp good-quality mayonnaise
1 tsp prepared white horseradish
6oz (175g) feta cheese, cut into ½in (1cm) cubes
⅓ cup fresh peas
2 handfuls of baby spinach leaves
small handful of fresh mint leaves
sea salt and black pepper
lemon wedges

1 In a food processor, combine the watercress, mayonnaise, and horseradish. Process until well blended. Season with salt and pepper.

2 Combine the feta, peas, spinach, and mint in a bowl, and season with pepper. Toss gently to mix. Transfer to a serving bowl and pass the watercress mayonnaise and lemon wedges at the table.

VARIATION
Instead of the feta, use a good-quality fresh ricotta cheese and omit the mayonnaise.

COOK'S NOTES

Use frozen peas when fresh are out of season. Cover frozen peas with hot water and let stand for 5 minutes. Drain; refresh with cold water, and drain again. This will retain the vibrant color of the peas.

EVERYDAY

Seafood and fennel salad with anchovy dressing

PREP 15 MINS

SERVES 4
For the dressing
3 tbsp extra virgin olive oil
1 tbsp white wine vinegar
6 flat anchovies in oil, drained and finely chopped
pinch of sugar
handful of flat-leaf parsley, finely chopped
sea salt and freshly ground black pepper

handful of crisp lettuce leaves, such as romaine
1 fennel bulb, thinly sliced
1lb (450g) assorted cooked seafood, such as shelled shrimp, mussels, or squid rings, rinsed and dried
6 flat anchovies in oil, drained
1 fresh hot green chile, seeded and finely chopped
handful of fresh cilantro, coarsely chopped

1 First, make the dressing. In a large bowl, whisk together the oil and vinegar. Add the chopped anchovies, sugar, and parsley, and season well with salt and pepper. Whisk again until well blended.

2 Add the lettuce, fennel, seafood, whole anchovies, chile, and cilantro, tossing gently to coat with the dressing. Pile into a shallow serving bowl. Serve with rice stick noodles and lemon wedges.

COOK'S NOTES

Rice stick noodles are simple to prepare: just soak them in hot water for 5–10 minutes, then drain well and serve.

Carrot salad with cabbage and peanuts

PREP 15 MINS

SERVES 4

For the dressing
1 tbsp light soy sauce
1 tbsp Asian fish sauce (*nam pla*)
1 fresh green chile, seeded and chopped
1 garlic clove, finely grated
juice of 2 limes
1–2 tsp granulated sugar
handful of cilantro, finely chopped
sea salt and freshly ground
    black pepper

2 Fuji or other sweet apples
4 carrots, coarsely grated
1 small white cabbage, cored and
    shredded
handful of roasted sunflower seed
    kernels
handful of cocktail peanuts or
    dry-roasted peanuts

1 First, make the dressing. Put all the dressing ingredients in a small bowl and mix thoroughly until the sugar has dissolved. Taste and season with salt and pepper as needed, then check the seasoning again. If it needs sweetening, add more sugar; if it needs salt, add a little more fish sauce.

2 Quarter and core the apples, then chop into bite-sized pieces. Put in a large bowl with the carrot, cabbage, and sunflower seed kernels. Toss well. Drizzle with the dressing and toss to coat. Transfer to a serving dish or bowl and scatter the peanuts over the top.

VARIATION Use prepared rice stick noodles instead of the cabbage if you prefer.

Lima beans with fresh tomato and lime

PREP 20 MINS

SERVES 4

1 x 14oz (400g) can lima beans,
    rinsed and drained
8 small tomatoes, peeled and chopped
2 limes, cut into segments and
    coarsely chopped (see Cook's Notes)
generous drizzle extra virgin olive oil
sea salt and freshly ground
    black pepper

1 Combine the beans, tomatoes, and lime in a bowl and season with salt and pepper. Toss gently to mix. Drizzle with the olive oil. Serve with crusty bread and a selection of sliced cooked meats.

COOK'S NOTES

To segment a lime, slice off the top and bottom of the lime. Using a sharp knife or vegetable peeler, carefully slice around the entire lime to remove the skin and pith. Using a small serrated knife, slice away one segment at a time, leaving behind the thin membrane that separates them.

Bread salad with Gorgonzola

PREP 15 MINS

SERVES 4

3 thick slices ciabatta or other rustic
   country-style bread, toasted and
   cut into bite-sized chunks
sea salt and freshly ground
   black pepper
handful of fresh basil leaves, torn
2–3 tbsp olive oil
½ x 7oz (200g) jar roasted red
   peppers, drained and sliced
4 tomatoes, coarsely chopped
handful of toasted pine nuts
4oz (115g) Gorgonzola or blue cheese,
   cut into small cubes

1 Put the bread in a large bowl and
drizzle with the olive oil. Add the
basil and season with salt and pepper.
Toss together, then let stand for about
10 minutes to develop the flavors.

2 Add the peppers, tomatoes, pine
nuts, and cheese, and toss gently to
mix. Serve with cold cooked meats.

Curried chickpeas with mango

PREP 20 MINS

SERVES 4
For the dressing
3 tbsp extra virgin olive oil
1 tbsp cider vinegar
pinch of granulated sugar
pinch of curry powder
sea salt and freshly ground
   black pepper

1 x 14oz (400g) can chickpeas,
   rinsed and drained
1 mango, cut into cubes (see Cook's
   Notes)
1 red onion, finely chopped
handful of whole natural almonds
   (skins on), very coarsely chopped
handful of fresh mint, finely chopped

1 First, make the dressing. Whisk
together the oil and vinegar, add the
sugar and curry powder, season with
salt and pepper, and whisk until blended.

2 Add the chickpeas, mango, red
onion, and almonds. Toss gently
to mix. Just before serving, stir in
the mint.

VARIATION

For a more substantial
salad, add boneless
cooked chicken.

COOK'S NOTES

*To cut up a mango, lay it
down on its side and slice
it lengthwise along one side
as near to the pit as possible.
Turn the sliced piece over, slice
a crisscross pattern in the flesh,
and turn the pieces out. Repeat
with the other side (see p459).*

EVERYDAY

Smoked fish, fennel, and mango salad

  PREP 15 MINS

SERVES 4

For the dressing

⅓ cup extra virgin olive oil

3 tbsp red wine vinegar

2 garlic cloves, finely grated or
    crushed through a press

pinch of sugar

handful of fresh dill, finely chopped

10oz (300g) smoked mackerel

5½oz (150g) smoked trout

1 fennel bulb, trimmed and peeled
    into thin strips using a mandoline
    or vegetable peeler

1 mango, sliced

seeds of 1 pomegranate
    (about ½ cup)

1 First, make the dressing. Put all the
ingredients in a small bowl and whisk
together until well blended.

2 Flake the mackerel into bite-sized
chunks, and slice the trout into chunky
strips. Arrange the fish on a platter,
top with the fennel and mango slices,
and scatter the pomegranate seeds
over the top.

3 When ready to serve, drizzle with
some of the dressing. Serve with
whole wheat or other dark bread.

 VARIATION
Use raspberry vinegar instead
of the red wine vinegar.

Smoked salmon with radishes and spiced yogurt dressing

  PREP 15 MINS

SERVES 4

3 tomatoes, peeled, seeded, and diced
    (see Cook's Notes)

1 tbsp capers, rinsed, gently squeezed
    dry, and chopped

handful of radishes, diced

1 orange bell pepper, seeded
    and diced

4 scallions, finely chopped

1 fresh red chile, seeded and
    finely chopped

juice of 1 large orange

juice of 1 lime

4–6 tbsp Greek-style yogurt

juice of 1 lemon

pinch of Asian five-spice powder

sea salt and freshly ground
    black pepper

8oz (225g) sliced smoked salmon,
    chopped into bite-sized pieces

1 In a large bowl, combine the
tomatoes, capers, radishes, bell
pepper, scallions, and chile. Add the
orange and lime juices and season
with salt and pepper. Toss gently
to mix, then let stand for about
10 minutes to develop the flavors.

2 To make the spiced yogurt dressing,
mix together the yogurt, lemon juice,
and five-spice powder in a small bowl.
Season with salt and pepper.

3 When ready to serve, add the
smoked salmon pieces to the salad
mixture and toss again. Serve with the
yogurt dip on the side.

 VARIATION
For a less rich version, use
fresh crabmeat instead of the
smoked salmon.

COOK'S NOTES

Once you have peeled the tomatoes,
cut them in half, scoop out the
seeds, and chop the flesh into dice.

Chicken with aduki beans and parsley

PREP 10 MINS

SERVES 4

½ large red onion, finely diced
1 x 15oz (425g) can aduki beans,
    rinsed and drained
1 tsp coarse-grain mustard
white wine vinegar
extra virgin olive oil
handful of flat-leaf parsley, chopped
12oz (350g) skinless cooked chicken,
    shredded (about 2 cups)
sea salt and freshly ground
    black pepper

1 Set aside 1–2 tablespoons of the onion to garnish the salad. Combine the remaining onion, beans, and mustard in a bowl. Add a splash of vinegar and a drizzle of olive oil, and season with salt and pepper. Add the parsley and toss gently to mix.

2 Spoon the bean mixture into a serving bowl, then top with the chicken. Sprinkle with the remaining onion. Serve with crusty bread and arugula, if desired.

VARIATION
Use cooked brown or green lentils instead of aduki beans, or smoked chicken instead of plain roasted or poached chicken.

EVERYDAY

Lentils with artichokes and peppers

PREP 15 MINS

SERVES 4

1 x 14oz (400g) can green or brown
    lentils, drained and rinsed,
    or 2 cups drained cooked lentils
1 x 14oz (400g) can artichoke hearts,
    drained and sliced
4 or 5 roasted red peppers from a jar
    or the deli counter
leaves from 1–2 fresh thyme sprigs
handful of flat-leaf parsley, chopped
4 scallions, finely chopped
2–3 tbsp walnut oil
1 tbsp cider vinegar
4 or 5 thin slices prosciutto, chopped
handful of arugula

1 Put the lentils, artichoke hearts, peppers, thyme, parsley, and scallions in a bowl. Drizzle the oil and vinegar over the top and toss gently to mix.

2 Toss in the prosciutto and arugula. Transfer to a serving dish and serve with a green salad.

SPEEDY
SUPPERS

30 minutes or less, from start to finish.

SPEEDY SUPPERS

Time is everything, especially when you are home late from work, or cooking for a family. Preparing something quick shouldn't mean it's not tasty, good food—simply choose cuts of meat and fish that require little attention and minimal cooking. Along with some quick-prep vegetables, you can have a meal made from scratch in minutes.

Psst...

To speed things up in the kitchen, marinate your meat the night before cooking. Even a simple combination of olive oil and lemon juice will add that extra edge to your dish. Always remember to season your meat, too.

Quick-cook meat cuts The best quick-cook cuts for meals in minutes.

EVERYDAY

CHOOSE / USE / COOK

STEAKS

Beef—rump, sirloin, minute, rib-eye, fillet

Pork—tenderloin, scallop, fillet

Lamb—leg, loin, shoulder, fillet

Turkey—steak

These cuts come from the middle fleshy part of the animal, which produces the most succulent quick-cook cuts. Because these muscles are used infrequently, the meat is very tender.

Although steaks can cost more than more muscley cuts, there is very little waste. They are best suited to dry cooking methods, such as frying or grilling. Beef steaks should be at least 1in (2.5cm) thick; pork, lamb, and turkey steaks about ¾in (2cm) thick, and scallops about ½in (1cm) thick. Brush with oil before adding to the pan or grill, and turn them once during cooking.

	Fry/grill/broil	Rest
Rare	beef 1–2 mins per side	6 mins
Medium	beef 3 mins per side	4 mins
	lamb 6–8 mins per side	
Well done	beef 4–5 mins per side	1 min
	pork (scallops) 2–4 mins per side	1 min
	pork (tenderloin/fillet) 3–5 mins per side	1 min
	turkey steaks 6–8 mins per side	1 min

CUTLETS

Lamb

Veal

Cutlets are cut from a rib of lamb (sometimes veal). They are thinner than a chop, with only one rib bone. The meat has an intense flavor, and they suit quick cooking.

Cutlets benefit from being marinated and seasoned well with salt and black pepper, or a pinch of herbs. Cutlets are usually ¾–1¼in (2–3cm) thick, and are best eaten when they are still a little pink in the middle. Brush with a little oil before adding to the pan or grill.

	Fry/grill/broil	Rest
Rare	lamb 3–4 mins per side	2–3 mins
	veal 1–2 mins per side	
Medium	lamb 4–5 mins per side	1–2 mins
	veal 3–4 mins per side	
Well done	lamb 6–8 mins per side	2–3 mins
	veal 5 mins per side	

CHOPS

Lamb—blade, rib, loin

Pork—rib, loin, tenderloin

Chops are cut from the loin of an animal, usually lamb or pig. You can buy them with or without the bone.

Chops are tender and succulent, and great for a quick meal. Pork chops need to be cooked all the way through, but it is important not to overcook them, or the meat will dry out. An oil-based marinade will help to both tenderize and add flavor. The thickness of a chop varies but they are usually about 1in (2.5cm) thick. Cook for longer if using thicker cuts.

	Fry/grill/broil	Rest
Rare	lamb 5 mins per side	3 mins
Medium	lamb 8 mins per side	2 mins
Well done	lamb 10 mins per side	1 min
	pork 8–10 mins per side	

BREAST FILLETS

Chicken

Duck

This boneless cut is ideal for fast cooking with little effort, and is both versatile and economical.

Chicken and duck breasts are about the same size, and are both well suited to high heat and quick, dry cooking methods. Chicken breasts can be pounded to an even thickness, which speeds up the cooking process. Pound them thin for scallops. Another way to speed up cooking is to slash the breast a few times diagonally. Duck, which has a richer meat, can be cooked with no added fat, as it produces a lot of its own.

	Fry/grill/broil	Rest
Rare	duck 3–4 mins per side	2 mins
Medium	duck 5–6 mins per side	1 min
Well done	chicken 4–5 mins per side	2 mins
	scallop 2–3 mins per side	2 mins
	duck 4–5 mins per side	2 mins

keeping meat fresh

Look at the color of the flesh, as this is the best indication of freshness. It should be bright, and have no odor at all. It's important to be careful when storing raw meat, in order to avoid food poisoning. Keep it well sealed so that it doesn't drip, either securely wrapped in plastic wrap or in a sealed container, and store it in the bottom of the refrigerator, away from other foods, particularly cooked meats. Use before the use-by date.

Quick-cook fish
Fish requires very little cooking; in fact the less you do to it, the better it will taste. It is the ultimate fast food.

CHOOSE

WHOLE FISH
To cook whole fish quickly, choose fish that aren't too large, and make sure the fish is cleaned, gutted, and trimmed before you start cooking. Whole cooked fish are moist and succulent, and the skin will crisp up beautifully. For added flavor, slash the fish a few times, and rub with some seasoned oil or herbs. The fish will easily flake away from the bone when ready.

COOK

	Fry/grill/broil
Mackerel	1–2 mins each side
Sardine	1–2 mins each side
Trout	4–5 mins each side
Sea bass	4–5 mins each side

STEAKS
This is a fleshy cut, ideally suited to fast cooking methods. It is meaty, rich, and delicious, particularly if marinated before cooking. Cooking time really depends on thickness; the time guidelines here are for steaks about 1in (2.5cm) thick. As a rule, allow about 10 minutes cooking time per extra inch.

	Fry/grill/broil
Salmon	4–5 mins each side
Halibut	4–5 mins each side
Tuna	3–5 mins each side

FILLETS
This fish portion is probably the most widely used for quick cooking, as it is the easiest to handle, and will cook in minutes. Cook with the skin on, as it will protect the delicate flesh from the heat. The time guidelines here are for fillets about ½–¾in (1–2cm) thick. Delicate fish tends to break up when grilled, so it is better suited to frying and broiling.

	Fry/grill/broil
Sea bass	2–3 mins each side
Mackerel	2–3 mins each side
Trout	2–3 mins each side
Salmon	2–3 mins each side
Cod/ haddock	2–3 mins each side

SHELLFISH
For an instant satisfying meal, shellfish can't be beat. It can be bought already cooked, and makes a nutritious low-fat supper dish. You can cook shrimp with or without their shells, but they remain meatier and far more succulent if cooked in the shell. Both shrimp and scallops will turn rubbery if overcooked.

	Fry/grill/broil
Shrimp	2–3 mins each side
Scallops	3–4 mins each side

keeping fish fresh
Look for fish that is ultra fresh. The flesh should be firm, and it should have no "fishy" smell. Ideally, use fish on the day of purchase, but it will store in the refrigerator for 1–2 days, depending on its sell-by date. Wrap in foil or wax paper, and store away from other foods in the refrigerator.

Quick-cook veg
Low maintenance vegetables, like the ones listed below, add flavor, color, and texture.

PEAS
Cook fresh from the pod, or cook from frozen, for about 3 minutes. Mix with fresh mint, tarragon, or chives before serving. Shelled fresh peas are also great raw, in salads.

SPINACH
Baby or young spinach can be eaten raw, tossed with other vegetables such as scallions and radishes. Older spinach should be cooked for a minute or two in a pan, with a little water, or steamed. Try seasoning with nutmeg, or stir-frying with garlic.

BROCCOLI
Versatile and available all year round, broccoli responds well to high heat and quick cooking such as stir-frying, or it can be cooked for a few minutes in boiling salted water, or steamed. Try purple sprouting broccoli when it's in season.

MUSHROOMS
Available in several varieties, from the button mushroom to the earthy cremini mushroom, which adds depth of flavor to a dish. Slice, chop, or grate, and serve raw, or cook in a little melted butter.

CARROTS
Extremely good value, and full of vitamins. Can be eaten raw, if peeled and sliced or grated, in a salad. To cook, sauté in a little melted butter, or steam.

ASPARAGUS
A delicious spring vegetable that livens up any dish. It's delicate, though, and can easily be overcooked. Trim, toss in oil, season, and cook in a hot frying pan; or steam for 4 minutes.

BEANS
All beans, from French to fava beans, can be cooked quickly in a pan of boiling salted water (or steamed) for 3–4 minutes. Delicious served alone, or tossed with a piquant dressing.

ZUCCHINI
These require no peeling. Just trim the ends and slice or dice. They are best pan-fried in a little olive oil, salt and black pepper, and cooked until they soften and turn golden.

LEEKS
A member of the onion family, with a more subtle taste. Cut off the root end and trim away the outer leaves, and wash well (see p404). To cook, slice thinly and pan-fry in a little olive oil or butter until soft.

FENNEL
This vegetable has a slight anise-like taste that complements fish well. It can be shredded and eaten raw, or sliced/quartered, tossed in olive oil, and cooked in a hot frying pan or under a hot broiler.

Speedy cooking Four essential quick cooking methods.

Pan-fry
This quick cooking method is best suited to lean cuts of meat, fish, or tender vegetables. We've used a fish fillet here because it best illustrates the technique. With meat and vegetables, follow the same basic steps. Use a shallow frying pan, preferably non-stick, and a little oil or butter.

1 Pat two fish fillets dry with paper towels and season with salt and freshly ground black pepper. Heat 1½ teaspoons of olive oil or sunflower oil in a nonstick frying pan until hot, but not smoking. Carefully add the fish, skin-side down, and leave to cook for 2–3 minutes, depending on thickness (see chart on p57).

2 Turn the fish over using a metal spatula, and cook the other side for another 2–3 minutes, or longer if the fish fillet is thick. Keep the heat at medium-high.

3 Turn the fish over again, to serve. It should be an even golden color. To check if the fish is cooked, use a fork or knife to gently move the flesh away from the bone down the middle at the thickest part; if cooked, it will come away with ease.

Stir-fry
Stir-frying is a quick and healthy cooking method, and can be used to cook meat and fish, as well as vegetables (demonstrated here): in all cases, chop your ingredients to the same size, keep the heat high, stir constantly, and use very little oil. If you don't have a wok, use a large frying pan.

1 When stir-frying, you need to prepare everything ahead of time, so it can be added to the pan in an instant. If you prepare as you go, the time between adding ingredients will mean those already cooking in the pan will cook for too long. Slice or dice your vegetables to a similar size, and thinly slice the chile, fresh ginger, and garlic (if using).

2 Heat the wok over medium-high heat, then add 1½ teaspoons of vegetable or sunflower oil. Heat until hot and sizzling. Add the spices first, and stir-fry vigorously for a minute, making sure they don't brown. If you want to add meat or seafood to your stir-fry, add it to the pan now.

3 Add the vegetables in order of firmness (firmest first), adding the garlic last, as it burns easily. Continue stirring all the time so the vegetables don't stick to the wok and burn. Stir-fry for 4–5 minutes, until the vegetables are cooked. Season well, and serve immediately.

Grill

Grill This is a fast and low-fat cooking method. Use a heavy ridged cast-iron pan (this type of pan gets very hot), and add oil to the ingredient, not the pan. Grill vegetables and meaty fish using this technique (demonstrated below with pork), brushing with oil *before* adding to the pan.

1 Brush 2–3 pork steaks with a little olive oil and season well with salt and freshly ground black pepper. Retain the fat on the meat, as this will add flavor when cooking. You can always remove it before eating.

2 Heat the grill pan over high heat until it's very hot and begins to smoke. Add the oiled pork steaks, leaving room between them in the pan, and cook undisturbed for 2–3 minutes, depending on thickness (see chart on p57).

3 Once the underside is cooked, it will move freely when you try to turn it over. Turn it, and cook the other side for 2–3 minutes, depending on thickness, until it is golden and cooked through. Pierce with a sharp knife, and if no pink is visible, it is cooked through. Let it rest for a couple of minutes before serving.

Broiler

Broiler The fierce direct heat of the broiler is a fast way of cooking, and is particularly healthy, as there is no addition of oil, unless it is added to the ingredient. For meat and fish, follow steps 1 and 2, and make sure they are cooked through before removing from the broiler.

1 Line the broiler pan with aluminum foil, then replace the wire rack. Turn the broiler to high. Brush the peppers evenly with olive oil, and sit them on the rack.

2 Cook the peppers under the hot broiler for 5–8 minutes, until they begin to blacken slightly, and the skin starts to blister. Carefully turn, and cook for another 5–8 minutes, until blistered all over.

3 Remove the peppers from the heat and put them in a plastic bag. Seal and leave to cool. The steam will help the removal of the skins. To prepare, remove the peppers from the bag, pull away the stem, remove the seeds, and peel away the skin.

EVERYDAY

Pan-fried lamb with green chiles

PREP 5 MINS | COOK 30 MINS

SERVES 4

1 tbsp olive oil
1 onion, finely chopped
1 bay leaf
pinch of cumin seeds
pinch of sea salt
2 garlic cloves, finely chopped
1 fresh jalapeño chile pepper, seeded and finely chopped
2lb (900g) lean lamb, cut into bite-sized pieces
1 tbsp all-purpose flour
2¼ cups hot vegetable or chicken stock
3–4 green bird's-eye (Thai) chiles, left whole
juice of ½ lemon

1 Heat the oil in a large, deep frying pan. Add the onion, bay leaf, cumin seeds, and a pinch of sea salt, and sauté gently until soft. Stir in the garlic and chopped chile and cook for a few seconds more.

2 Now add the lamb and cook until nicely browned on the outside, then stir in the flour. Pour in a little of the stock and increase the heat.

3 Bring to a boil. Add the remaining stock and the whole chiles. Simmer for 20 minutes, or until the lamb is cooked and the sauce has thickened. Stir in the lemon juice and serve.

COOK'S NOTES

This is a good dish to prepare in advance, as the flavors will only get better. To reheat and eat, cook in the microwave on high for about 3 minutes, or reheat in a pan until piping hot.

Lamb and mint burgers

PREP 10 MINS | COOK 20 MINS

SERVES 4

1 tbsp olive oil
1 tbsp butter
1 onion, finely chopped
2 garlic cloves, finely chopped
1in (2.5cm) piece of fresh ginger, finely grated
sea salt and freshly ground black pepper
1½lb (675g) ground lamb
handful of fresh mint leaves, finely chopped
vegetable oil for cooking

1 In a large frying pan, heat the oil and butter over low heat. Add the onion and cook for 5 minutes, or until soft. Add the garlic, ginger, a pinch of salt, and black pepper to taste. Remove from the heat and let cool.

2 Put the lamb in a large bowl and add the cooled onion mixture and the mint. Season with salt and pepper, then mix together until well combined—this is best done using your hands. Form large balls with the mixture and flatten to make burgers. Place the burgers on a plate and refrigerate until firm, if time permits.

3 Heat 1½ tablespoons of vegetable oil in a large frying pan. Cook the burgers for 5–6 minutes on each side until cooked through and no longer pink. Alternatively, grill on a hot griddle, ridged cast-iron grill pan, or barbecue grill. Serve hot. These are delicious with roasted butternut squash and arugula.

Marinated lamb chops with broccoli in lemon juice

PREP 5 MINS **COOK 30 MINS**

Marinating • 5 minutes

SERVES 4

For the marinade
2 tbsp sherry vinegar, cider vinegar, or white wine vinegar
pinch of sugar
splash of soy sauce

4 lean lamb loin chops, excess fat removed
sea salt and freshly ground black pepper
handful of fresh rosemary sprigs
1 head broccoli, about 1lb (450g), florets and stems chopped small
juice of 1 lemon
pinch of crushed red pepper flakes
mint jelly, to serve

1 First, prepare the marinade. Mix together the vinegar, sugar, and soy sauce, then pour over the lamb. Let marinate at room temperature for 5 minutes, or up to 2 hours, if time permits.

2 Preheat the oven to 400°F (200°C). Place the lamb chops in a roasting pan, season well with salt and pepper, and add the rosemary sprigs. Roast in the oven for 20–30 minutes until cooked to your liking.

3 While the lamb is cooking, add the broccoli to a pan of boiling salted water and cook for about 10 minutes until soft. Drain, keeping the broccoli in the pan, then mash gently with a fork. Now squeeze in the lemon juice and stir in the pepper flakes, a pinch of salt, and some black pepper. Serve immediately with the lamb chops and a dollop of mint jelly on the side.

Cheat...
Use a ready-made paste to coat the lamb, such as a pesto or a tapenade.

Skewered lamb with crispy rosemary potatoes

PREP 15 MINS **COOK 30 MINS**

Special equipment • wooden skewers

SERVES 4

1½lb (675g) all-purpose potatoes, peeled and cut into small cubes
1–2 tbsp olive oil, plus extra for coating lamb
handful of fresh rosemary sprigs
sea salt and freshly ground black pepper
2lb (900g) lean lamb, cut into cubes
juice of 1 lemon
2 tsp paprika

1 Preheat the oven to 400°F (200°C). Combine the potatoes, 1–2 tablespoons olive oil, and rosemary in a roasting pan. Season with salt. Using your hands, toss gently so the potatoes are evenly coated. Roast in the oven for 20–25 minutes until golden and crispy at the edges.

2 Meanwhile, put the lamb in a bowl and toss with a little olive oil, the lemon juice, paprika, salt, and plenty of pepper. Thread the pieces of lamb onto small skewers until they are tightly packed.

3 Place the lamb skewers on top of the potatoes in the roasting pan, turning them after 5–8 minutes, and roast until they are cooked through. Serve with the potatoes and a green salad.

Lamb with chickpeas, green peppers, and couscous

   PREP 10 MINS **COOK 30 MINS**

SERVES 4
2–3 tbsp olive oil
1 onion, finely chopped
2 garlic cloves, finely chopped
2lb (900g) lamb, cut into small pieces
1 tsp ground cinnamon
1 tsp paprika
sea salt and freshly ground
    black pepper
2–3 green bell peppers, seeded and
    coarsely chopped
1 x 15½oz (440g) can chickpeas,
    drained and rinsed
3½ cups hot vegetable stock
1 cup couscous
½ cup pine nuts, toasted
handful of flat-leaf parsley, chopped

1 Heat 1 tablespoon of the oil in a frying pan over low heat. Add the onion and cook for 5 minutes until soft. Add the garlic, lamb, cinnamon, and paprika, and season with salt and pepper.

2 Add the peppers and chickpeas and cook, stirring occasionally, until the meat is no longer pink. Pour in 2 cups of the hot stock, cover the pan, and simmer gently for 20 minutes. Add a little hot water if the mixture appears dry.

3 Meanwhile, combine the couscous and 1–2 tablespoons of olive oil in a heatproof bowl, then stir in enough of the remaining hot stock just to cover. Cover tightly with aluminum foil and leave for about 5 minutes, then use a fork to fluff up and separate the grains. Season with plenty of salt and pepper.

4 To serve, sprinkle the pine nuts and parsley over the lamb and serve immediately with the warm couscous.

 VARIATION You could sprinkle toasted sesame seeds over the top instead of pine nuts.

Deviled lamb cutlets with crushed potato and mustard seed salad

  PREP 10 MINS **COOK 30 MINS**

SERVES 4
9oz (250g) new potatoes, halved
1 tbsp olive oil
1 tbsp mustard seeds
1 bunch of scallions,
    finely chopped
8 lamb cutlets
sea salt and freshly ground
    black pepper

For the coating
2 tbsp English mustard powder
2 tbsp tomato ketchup
1 tsp cayenne pepper (or less, to taste)
2 tbsp finely chopped onion
1 tbsp olive oil

1 Preheat the oven to 400°F (200°C).

2 Cook the potatoes in a large pan of boiling salted water for about 15 minutes or until tender, then drain. Pour in the olive oil and crush the potatoes gently with a fork. Stir in the mustard seeds and scallions and season with salt and pepper. Set aside.

3 While the potatoes are cooking, make the coating for the lamb. In a bowl, mix together all the ingredients and season well with salt and pepper. Coat the lamb cutlets evenly, lay them flat in a roasting pan, and roast for 20–30 minutes until cooked to your liking. Serve hot with the crushed potato salad.

Beef with soy and lime with grapefruit and ginger salsa

 PREP 10 MINS **COOK** 15 MINS

Special equipment • wok

SERVES 4

For the grapefruit and ginger salsa
2 grapefruit, peeled, segmented, and chopped (see Cook's Notes)
1in (2.5cm) piece of fresh ginger, finely grated
1 red jalapeño chile pepper, seeded and finely chopped
pinch of sugar (optional)

1 tbsp peanut or sunflower oil
1 red onion, cut into 8 wedges
1½lb (675g) boneless sirloin (rump) steak, cut into strips
1 red jalapeño chile pepper, seeded and cut into thin strips
splash of soy sauce
juice of 1 lime
1 tbsp honey
7oz (200g) mushrooms, sliced
handful of fresh cilantro, to serve
rice or noodles, to serve

1 First, make the salsa. Put all the ingredients in a bowl, stir, and taste. Add a little freshly ground black pepper if you wish. Set aside.

2 Heat the oil in a wok over high heat until hot. Add the onion and stir-fry for about 5 minutes until tender, then add the beef and chile strips. Continue to stir-fry for another 5 minutes or so, keeping everything moving in the wok. Add the soy sauce, lime juice, and honey, and continue stirring and tossing.

3 Add the mushrooms and stir-fry for a few minutes until they are tender and begin to release their juices.

4 To serve, transfer the beef mixture to a platter and pile the cilantro on top. Serve with rice or noodles and the grapefruit salsa on the side.

COOK'S NOTES

To segment a grapefruit, cut a slice from each end, then cut away the peel and pith, following the shape of the fruit. Now cut away each segment, leaving behind the thin layer of membrane between them.

Hot and sour beef stir-fry with green beans

 PREP 10 MINS **COOK** 20 MINS

SERVES 4

For the hot and sour sauce
2 garlic cloves, finely grated
1 tsp dark brown sugar
6 anchovy fillets, drained and chopped
3 red jalapeño chile peppers, seeded and finely chopped
splash of Chinese rice wine
juice of 1 lime

1 tbsp honey
generous splash of Asian fish sauce (*nam pla*)
675g (1½lb) boneless sirloin (rump) steak, sliced into thin strips
handful of small green beans, trimmed
1 tbsp sesame oil

1 First, make the hot and sour sauce. Using a mortar and pestle, pound all the ingredients, except for the rice wine and lime juice, into a smooth paste. Then add the lime juice a little at a time, tasting as you go, and season with salt. Set aside.

2 In a bowl, mix together the honey and fish sauce. Add the steak strips, stirring to coat. Blanch the beans in a pan of boiling water for a few minutes, then drain and refresh in cold water.

3 Heat the oil in a wok or large frying pan over medium-high heat. Add the steak and stir-fry, tossing the meat constantly, for 3–5 minutes until it is nicely browned. Remove with a slotted spoon, and set aside.

4 Add the hot and sour sauce to the wok and stir for a couple of minutes. Return the meat to the pan and stir in the beans. Increase the heat to high, add the rice wine, and let bubble for a minute or two. Serve immediately with noodles or rice.

Cheat...
Use a store-bought hot and sour sauce, or a sweet and sour sauce, and toss it with the meat and vegetables.

COOK'S NOTES

Refreshing the beans in cold water will stop the cooking process and help the beans keep their vibrant green color.

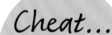 **EVERYDAY**

EVERYDAY

Beef scallops with anchovies, capers, and olives

  PREP 10 MINS · COOK 20 MINS

SERVES 4

2 sirloin (rump) steaks, 6–8oz (175–225g) each, cut in half
6 anchovies, drained and chopped
2 tsp capers, rinsed and drained
handful of pitted black olives
3 tbsp olive oil
2 handfuls of arugula
juice of ½–1 lemon
sea salt
small handful of fresh basil leaves, torn

1 First, prepare the scallops. Working with one piece of steak at a time, sandwich them between two sheets of plastic wrap and pound with a meat mallet or the side of a rolling pin until they are paper-thin.

2 In a bowl, pound together the anchovies, capers, and half of the olives to form a coarse paste—it shouldn't need seasoning, as the anchovies will be salty enough. Now smear the paste evenly over each beef scallop.

3 Heat 1 tablespoon of the oil in a large nonstick frying pan over high heat. Cook the scallops two at a time, adding another tablespoon of the oil for the second batch. Cook for 2–4 minutes on each side.

4 Dress the arugula with the remaining 1 tablespoon olive oil, the lemon juice, and a pinch of salt. Toss with the remaining olives. To serve, top the steak with the torn basil leaves and serve alongside the salad.

Use veal if you wish, instead of the beef.

COOK'S NOTES

Pounding the meat tenderizes it; because it becomes so thin, it cooks in no time. You can also do this with other meats such as pork, chicken, or turkey.

Beef tacos

 PREP 15 MINS · COOK 15 MINS

SERVES 4

1 tbsp olive oil
1 onion, finely chopped
pinch of sea salt
1 garlic clove, finely chopped
1 fresh hot green chile pepper, seeded and finely chopped
1½lb (675g) lean ground beef
1 cup hot vegetable stock
4 ripe tomatoes, peeled and chopped
handful of fresh cilantro, finely chopped
8 taco shells, store-bought or homemade
½ cup shredded sharp Cheddar cheese

1 Position the oven rack 6 inches from the broiler, and preheat to high.

2 Heat the oil in a frying pan over medium heat. Add the onion and salt and cook for a few minutes, stirring occasionally, until soft. Add the garlic and chile and cook briefly before adding the beef. Cook, stirring, until no longer pink, adding just enough of the stock to prevent the meat from sticking, but not so much that it appears wet.

3 When the beef is cooked, stir in the tomatoes and cilantro. Spoon the mixture into the taco shells, and top with cheese. Place upright tacos under the broiler until the cheese has melted. Serve hot.

Indian spiced beef curry

 PREP 15 MINS **COOK 30 MINS**

Special equipment • food processor

SERVES 4

2lb (900g) lean beef, cut into bite-
sized pieces
1 tsp ground coriander
1 tsp ground cumin
1 tsp turmeric
1 tsp garam masala
1 tbsp sunflower or vegetable oil
1 onion, coarsely chopped
2 garlic cloves
1in (2.5cm) piece of fresh ginger,
peeled
4 tomatoes, peeled and coarsely
chopped
2 fresh red jalapeño chile peppers,
seeded and finely chopped
⅔ cup heavy whipping cream
handful of fresh cilantro, finely
chopped (optional)

1 Combine the beef, ground coriander, cumin, turmeric, garam masala, and oil in a bowl, and mix well to coat. Heat a large frying pan over medium heat. Add the beef and cook for about 10 minutes or until cooked through. Remove from the pan, and set aside.

2 In a food processor, combine the onion, garlic, ginger, tomatoes, and chiles. Process until finely chopped. Add to the same frying pan used for the beef, and cook, stirring, for about 5 minutes over medium heat. Stir in the cream, add ⅔ cup water, and bring to a boil. Return the meat to the pan, reduce the heat slightly, and simmer for 15–20 minutes.

3 Stir in the chopped cilantro and serve immediately.

COOK'S NOTES

If you want to watch the calories, swap the cream for Greek-style yogurt. To reheat and eat, heat in the microwave on high for about 3 minutes, or reheat in a frying pan until piping hot.

Corned beef hash with horseradish

 PREP 10 MINS **COOK 20 MINS**

SERVES 4

1 tbsp olive oil
1 onion, finely chopped
sea salt and freshly ground
black pepper
1 garlic clove, finely chopped
1½lb (675g) potatoes, peeled,
quartered, and boiled
3 carrots, peeled and finely diced
1 x 14oz (400ml) can of beef stock,
heated
1 x 12oz (450g) can corned beef,
chopped
2–3 tsp cream-style white horseradish
splash of Worcestershire sauce
pickled red cabbage, to serve

1 Heat the oil in a large frying pan over low heat. Add the onion and a pinch of salt and cook for about 5 minutes until soft. Next, add the garlic, potatoes, and carrots, and cook for about 5 minutes. Pour in a little of the stock and bring to a boil. Stir in the corned beef and mix well.

2 Add the remaining stock, reduce the heat slightly, and simmer gently for about 15 minutes, stirring occasionally to prevent sticking and to break up the chunks of corned beef, until the potatoes and carrots are tender. Taste and season if needed. Stir in the horseradish and Worcestershire sauce. Serve hot with pickled red cabbage.

 VARIATION
Use extra-hot horseradish if you prefer more of a kick.

Pork steaks with tomato and fava bean sauce

PREP 5 MINS · COOK 25 MINS

SERVES 4

4 pork steaks (blade chops), about
    5½oz (150g) each, trimmed
2 tbsp olive oil
generous pinch of dried oregano
sea salt and freshly ground
    black pepper
1 onion, finely chopped
2 garlic cloves, finely chopped
1 x 14oz (400g) can whole peeled
    plum tomatoes with juices, chopped
4½oz (125g) fresh or frozen fava beans
handful of flat-leaf parsley,
    very finely chopped

1 Preheat the oven to 400°F (200°C). Brush the meat with 1 tbsp of the oil and sprinkle with the oregano. Season well with sea salt and black pepper. Place in a shallow roasting pan without crowding and roast in the oven for 10–15 minutes or until golden on the outside and cooked through.

2 Meanwhile, heat the remaining oil in a frying pan over low heat and add the onion and a pinch of salt. Cook

for 5 minutes until soft, then stir in the garlic and cook for a couple of seconds.

3 Pour in the tomatoes, including any juices, and bring to a boil. Reduce the heat slightly and simmer for about 15 minutes. Stir in the fava beans and cook for another 10 minutes, adding a little water if the mixture dries out.

4 When ready to serve, taste the sauce and season if needed. Stir in the parsley. Place the chops in the sauce and serve hot.

VARIATION
Use fresh or frozen peas instead of fava beans.

Cheat...
If time is limited, use a store-bought tomato sauce, and simmer gently before adding the beans.

Thai-style ground pork with noodles

PREP 10 MINS · COOK 15 MINS

SERVES 4

1 tbsp vegetable oil
1½lb (675g) ground pork
4 garlic cloves, finely grated
pinch of sea salt
2 fresh hot red chile peppers,
    finely chopped
juice of 1 lime
splash of Asian fish sauce (*nam pla*)
splash of soy sauce
handful of fresh cilantro, finely
    chopped
medium rice noodles or rice,
    to serve

1 Heat the oil in a wok or large frying pan over medium-high heat.

Add the pork, garlic, and salt. Cook, stirring and tossing, until the pork is no longer pink.

2 Add the chiles, lime juice, fish sauce, and soy sauce, and stir-fry for 5 minutes longer.

3 Just before serving, stir in the cilantro. Serve hot with noodles or rice.

VARIATION
Add some finely chopped vegetables to the pork if you wish.

EVERYDAY

Sticky pork ribs

PREP 10 MINS · COOK 30 MINS

SERVES 4
For the sauce
1 tbsp honey
1 tbsp Dijon mustard
1 tbsp tomato ketchup
generous splash of soy sauce
1 tsp paprika
drizzle of olive oil
sea salt and freshly ground
    black pepper

2lb (900g) meaty pork spare ribs

1 Preheat the oven to 400°F (200°C). To make the sauce, combine the honey, mustard, tomato ketchup, soy sauce, paprika, and oil in a bowl. Season generously with salt and pepper and mix well.

2 Slather the sauce all over the ribs, then place them in a shallow roasting pan without crowding, and cook for 25–30 minutes, or until the ribs are no longer pink on the inside and well charred on the outside. Serve with pita bread and a crisp green salad.

EVERYDAY

Pork fillet stuffed with olives and jalapeño peppers, wrapped in bacon

PREP 15 MINS · COOK 30 MINS

SERVES 4
1½lb (675g) pork tenderloin, trimmed
    (see Cook's Notes)
⅓ cup finely chopped black olives
½ of a 4oz (50g) can diced jalapeño
    chile peppers, finely chopped
handful of flat-leaf parsley,
    finely chopped
5½oz (150g) thinly sliced bacon
    (about 10 slices)

1 Preheat the oven to 400°F (200°C). Slice the pork lengthwise, about ¾ of the way through, so that it opens up like a book; take care not to slice all the way through. In a bowl, mix together the olives, jalapeño peppers, and parsley, then spoon onto one half of the pork and fold the top piece over.

2 Now wrap the bacon around the pork, tightly and evenly, then place the wrapped pork on a rack in a roasting pan. Roast in the oven for 20–25 minutes until the bacon is crisp and the pork is cooked through. Leave to rest for a few minutes.

3 To serve, cut the pork into thick slices and serve hot with spinach and a tomato salad.

COOK'S NOTES

To prepare the pork tenderloin, use a sharp knife to trim the white membrane from the meat.

EVERYDAY

Pan-fried ham with pineapple salsa

 PREP 5 MINS COOK 20 MINS

SERVES 4
1 tbsp olive oil
4 ham steaks
1 tbsp honey
1 x 8oz (225g) can pineapple slices, drained and juice reserved
1 tbsp butter
3 tomatoes, peeled and chopped
½ red onion, finely diced

1 Heat the oil in a large nonstick frying pan over high heat. Add the ham and cook for 3–4 minutes on each side, depending on thickness, until golden and warmed through. Remove from the pan and set aside to keep warm.

2 Slather the honey over the pineapple slices. Melt the butter in the same frying pan. Add the pineapple and cook for a couple of minutes, turning once, until golden and lightly charred. Remove from the pan, cool slightly, and chop into small pieces.

3 To make the salsa, combine the pineapple, tomato, and red onion in a bowl, and toss gently to mix.

4 To serve, pour the reserved pineapple juice into the same pan used for cooking the pineapple and cook over high heat until hot. Pour over the warm ham steaks, and serve with the salsa on the side, perhaps along with some thick fried potatoes.

Pork and butter beans with mint

 PREP 10 MINS COOK 25 MINS

SERVES 4
1 tbsp olive oil
1 onion, finely chopped
handful of fresh rosemary sprigs, leaves finely chopped
2 garlic cloves, finely chopped
1½lb (675g) pork tenderloin, cut into small, bite-sized cubes
½ cup dry white wine
2 x 14oz (400g) cans butter beans or lima beans, drained and rinsed
2 cups hot chicken stock
sea salt and freshly ground black pepper
handful of fresh mint leaves

1 Heat the oil in a large deep frying pan over low heat. Add the onion, rosemary, and a pinch of salt. Cook for about 5 minutes until soft, then add the garlic and pork. Continue cooking for a few minutes, stirring from time to time, until the pork is no longer pink. Increase the heat to high, add the wine, and cook for a couple of minutes until the alcohol evaporates.

2 Add the butter beans, pour in the stock, and allow to simmer for about 20 minutes. Add a little more stock if needed, but be careful not to make the mixture too soupy.

3 Crush some of the beans with a fork, taste, and season the dish with salt and pepper if needed. Stir in the mint, and serve hot.

COOK'S NOTES

Pork tenderloin is reasonably priced and is well suited to high-heat cooking. If you buy it whole, cut the tenderloin into bite-sized pieces or into slices.

Pork scallops with bread crumb and parsley crust

PREP 15 MINS **COOK 15 MINS**

SERVES 4

2½oz (75g) bread crumbs, toasted
handful of fresh parsley, chopped
sea salt and freshly ground
    black pepper 2 boneless center cut
    pork chops,
    6–8oz (175–225g) each
1–2 eggs, beaten
1–2 tbsp all-purpose flour
1–2 tbsp olive oil
½ cup dry white wine

1 In a bowl, mix together the bread crumbs and parsley and season well with salt and pepper. Halve each piece of pork, then sandwich each one between two sheets of plastic wrap. Pound firmly with a meat mallet or the side of a rolling pin until paper-thin. Season well with salt and pepper.

2 Put the egg(s), flour, and bread crumbs each on separate plates. Coat each piece of pork first in the flour, then the egg, and lastly the bread crumbs. Heat half of the oil in a large nonstick frying pan over high heat. Add 2 of the pork scallops, and cook for 2–4 minutes on each side until golden on the outside and no longer pink inside. Remove from the pan, drain on paper towels, and set aside to keep warm while you cook the 2 remaining scallops. Keep warm while making the sauce.

3 Pour the wine into the same pan and scrape up all the crispy bits from the bottom with a wooden spoon. Let simmer until the smell of alcohol has disappeared, then drizzle over the pork. Serve immediately with a spinach and tomato salad, or arugula drizzled with a little lemon juice.

EVERYDAY

Pilaf with chorizo, pancetta, and cranberries

PREP 10 MINS **COOK 25 MINS**

SERVES 4

1 tbsp olive oil
1 tbsp butter
1 onion, finely chopped
2 garlic cloves, finely chopped
3 celery stalks, finely chopped
4½oz (125g) chorizo, sliced
4½oz (125g) pancetta, cubed
1½ cups rice
2½ cups hot vegetable stock, or more
    as needed
¼ cup dried cranberries
handful of flat-leaf parsley, chopped
sea salt and freshly ground
    black pepper

1 In a large nonstick frying pan, melt the oil and butter over low heat. Add the onion and cook for about 5 minutes until soft. Add the garlic

and celery and cook for a few seconds more. Now add the chorizo and pancetta, and cook for another 5 minutes. Stir in the rice.

2 Pour in half of the stock and bring to a boil. Next, pour in the remaining stock, reduce the heat slightly, and simmer gently for about 15 minutes. Stir in the cranberries.

3 Cook until the liquid has been absorbed and the rice is tender, adding a little more stock or water if the mixture appears dry. Taste and season with salt and pepper if needed. Stir in the chopped parsley and serve.

VARIATION
Use chopped dried apricots instead of the cranberries.

Caramelized pork tenderloin with pecans and apricots

PREP 10 MINS **COOK 15 MINS**

SERVES 4

1–2 tsp brown sugar
1½lb (675g) pork tenderloin
   (in one piece)
1 tbsp olive oil
1 tbsp butter
handful of pecan halves and pieces
handful of dried apricots, halved
splash of whiskey (optional)
1 cup heavy whipping cream

1 Rub the brown sugar all over the pork, then slice the pork crosswise into thick medallions.

2 Melt the oil and butter in a frying pan over medium-high heat. Brown the pork for 6–8 minutes, turning once, until golden on the outside and no longer pink inside. Add the pecans and apricots, and cook for a few more minutes.

3 Increase the heat to high and add the whiskey. Let simmer for a couple of minutes until the smell of alcohol has disappeared. Reduce the heat to medium, stir in the cream, and let simmer for a few minutes longer. Serve hot with mashed potatoes.

COOK'S NOTES

This recipe would work just as well with turkey or chicken breast. Cook in 1 tablespoon of olive oil for 8 minutes until golden, then cook as per recipe above.

Seared duck with five-spice and noodles

PREP 10 MINS **COOK 20 MINS**

SERVES 4

4 boneless duck breasts, about 5½oz
   (150g) each, skin on and scored in
   a crisscross pattern
2 tsp Asian five-spice powder
1 tbsp butter
1 x 9oz (250g) package thick or
   medium dried udon noodles
2 tbsp fresh orange juice
1 tsp light or dark brown sugar
handful of fresh cilantro,
   finely chopped

1 Rub the duck breasts all over with the five-spice powder. Melt the butter in a frying pan over high heat. Add the duck breasts, skin-side down, and cook for about 10 minutes, until the skin is golden and crisp. Carefully pour away the fat from the pan, then turn the breasts over and cook on the other side for 8 minutes. Meanwhile, cook the noodles according to the package directions and drain well.

2 Remove the duck from the pan and let stand 3 minutes. Cut into diagonal slices and arrange on a warm plate. Pour away any remaining fat, then add the orange juice to the pan along with the sugar. Let simmer for a minute or two, scraping up any bits from the bottom of the pan with a wooden spoon.

3 Add the drained noodles and toss them in the sauce for a couple of minutes to coat. Remove from the heat and stir in the cilantro. Serve immediately with the warm duck breasts.

Turkey burgers

 PREP 15 MINS **COOK 15 MINS**

SERVES 4

1½lb (675g) ground turkey
handful of fresh thyme leaves, chopped
grated zest and juice of 1 lemon
1 fresh red jalapeño chile pepper,
    seeded and finely chopped
sea salt and freshly ground
    black pepper
1 tbsp butter, melted and cooled slightly
2 tbsp all-purpose flour, for dusting
olive oil or vegetable oil for cooking

To serve

4 hamburger or other bread buns
crisp iceberg lettuce leaves
tomato slices
good-quality mayonnaise

1 Combine the turkey, thyme, lemon zest and juice, and jalapeño in a bowl. Season well with salt and pepper. Mix together until well blended.

2 Add the melted butter and, using your hands, work the mixture until it is cohesive. Divide the mixture into four, then scoop up each portion and form into a ball. Press gently with your hands to form a patty. Dust with the flour, then refrigerate for 5–10 minutes, or until firm.

3 Heat a little oil in a nonstick frying pan over medium-high heat. Cook the burgers for about 4 minutes on each side, or until golden on the outside and no longer pink inside. Serve in a bun with crisp lettuce, tomato slices, and a dollop of mayonnaise.

COOK'S NOTES

The butter in the turkey mixture helps to bind the ingredients together.

EVERYDAY

Duck with pink grapefruit and chicory salad

 PREP 10 MINS **COOK 25 MINS**

SERVES 4

1 tbsp butter
4 boneless duck breasts, about 5½oz
    (150g) each, skin on and scored in
    a crisscross pattern
handful of fresh rosemary sprigs
2 tbsp balsamic vinegar
2 pink grapefruits, peeled and
    segmented
1 small head chicory (curly endive),
    leaves separated
1 fennel bulb, trimmed and
    thinly sliced
sea salt and freshly ground
    black pepper

1 Preheat the oven to 400°F (200°C). Melt the butter in a large nonstick frying pan over high heat, then add the duck breasts, skin-side down, and the rosemary. Cook the breasts for 2–3 minutes on each side until golden all over. Increase the heat, add half of the balsamic vinegar, and let simmer for a few minutes, scraping up any bits from the bottom of the pan with a wooden spoon.

2 Transfer everything to a roasting pan and roast in the oven for 15–20 minutes or until cooked to desired doneness.

3 Meanwhile, prepare the salad. Combine the grapefruit segments, chicory, and fennel in a bowl. Toss gently to mix. Drizzle in the remaining balsamic vinegar, season with salt and pepper, and toss again.

4 To serve, divide the salad equally among 4 plates. Cut each duck breast in half, then slice diagonally. Place sliced duck on top of each salad.

Poached turkey with sticky noodles and chili cashews

PREP 15 MINS · COOK 30 MINS

Special equipment • wok

SERVES 4

10oz (300g) boneless turkey breast, cut in half
3 tbsp soy sauce
1 cup unsalted roasted cashews
¼ tsp chili powder
sea salt
1 tbsp sesame oil
1 bunch of scallions, coarsely chopped
1 tbsp honey
2 garlic cloves, finely grated
1in (2.5cm) piece of fresh ginger, finely grated
juice of 1 lemon
1 x 9oz (250g) package thick or medium dried udon noodles, cooked as package directs, and drained

1 Combine the turkey breasts and 1 tablespoon of the soy sauce in a large saucepan and add enough water to cover. Bring to a boil, then reduce the heat slightly and simmer gently for 15–20 minutes until the turkey is cooked through. Remove with a slotted spoon and, when cool enough to handle, shred the meat and set aside.

2 In a small dry frying pan, toss together the cashews, chili powder, and some sea salt. Cook for a few minutes over medium-high heat, stirring and shaking the pan, until the nuts are golden. Set aside.

3 Meanwhile, while the turkey is cooking, heat the sesame oil in a wok over high heat. Add the scallions and toss for 1–2 minutes. Add the remaining 2 tablespoons of soy sauce, honey, garlic, ginger, and lemon juice, and cook for 1 minute longer.

4 Add the noodles, and toss until they separate, stirring all the time so they soak up the sauce. Pile the noodles into a serving bowl, then top with the shredded turkey and the chili nuts. Drizzle any excess sauce over the top. Serve immediately.

VARIATION Omit the turkey to serve up a vegetarian version.

Chicken livers with shallots and arugula

PREP 15 MINS · COOK 20 MINS

SERVES 4

½ cup hazelnuts
1 tbsp olive oil
9 small shallots, peeled but left whole
sea salt
1–2 tbsp demerara (raw) sugar
1 tbsp butter
250g (9oz) chicken livers, tossed in a little seasoned flour
2 handfuls of arugula
generous drizzle of good-quality balsamic vinegar

1 Spread hazelnuts on a baking sheet. Place under a hot broiler and shake the pan frequently to turn them until they are golden brown. Enclose the hazelnuts in a clean dish towel. Rub to loosen and remove the skins. Chop coarsely, and set aside.

2 Heat the oil in a large frying pan over medium heat. Add the shallots and cook for 5 minutes until they start to color slightly, then sprinkle with some salt and the sugar. Move the shallots around in the pan and cook for another 15 minutes or until they soften and begin to caramelize.

3 In a separate frying pan, heat the butter over medium-high heat. When melted and foaming, add the chicken livers. Cook for 3–5 minutes, turning once, until browned on the outside and just cooked through.

4 Cut the cooked shallots in half and arrange with the livers on a bed of arugula. Top with the toasted hazelnuts and drizzle with the balsamic vinegar. Serve at once with thick slices of whole wheat toast.

COOK'S NOTES

Liver can easily be overcooked and become tough. Be careful to cook only until just cooked through.

Butterflied sardines stuffed with tomatoes and capers

PREP 15 MINS · COOK 10 MINS

SERVES 4

4–6 tomatoes, peeled and finely chopped
2 tsp capers, rinsed and gently squeezed dry
handful of flat-leaf parsley, finely chopped, plus extra, for garnish
2 garlic cloves, crushed
sea salt and freshly ground black pepper
12 fresh sardines, butterflied
a little olive oil
juice of 1 lemon

1 Preheat the oven to 400°F (200°C). Stir together the tomatoes, capers, parsley, and garlic. Season well with salt and pepper and stir again.

2 Lay the sardines flat, skin-side down, and spoon on the tomato mixture. Either roll the sardines lengthwise, or just fold them over to enclose the filling, then place them all on a baking sheet without crowding. Drizzle with a little olive oil and the lemon juice.

3 Bake in the oven for 10 minutes or until the sardines are cooked through and the filling is warm. Garnish with extra parsley, if you wish, and serve with a crisp green salad.

VARIATION
You could use mackerel in place of the sardines.

COOK'S NOTES

Ask your fishmonger to butterfly the sardines for you. To do this, they need to be scaled and the backbone removed before being flattened.

EVERYDAY

Baked white fish in wine and herbs

PREP 5 MINS · COOK 20 MINS

SERVES 4

1½lb (675g) white fish, such as haddock, skinned and cut into 4 pieces
sea salt
¾ cup dry white wine
12 cherry tomatoes
handful of flat-leaf parsley, finely chopped

1 Preheat the oven to 375°F (190°C). Season the fish with salt, then lay in a single layer in an ovenproof dish. Pour in the wine and top with the tomatoes and parsley.

2 Cover the dish tightly with foil, then bake for 15–20 minutes until the fish is cooked through and the wine has evaporated. Serve with a salad and fresh crusty bread for a summery dish, or creamy mashed potatoes for winter.

VARIATION
Use any white fish for this, such as pollack, turbot, or sustainable cod.

COOK'S NOTES

Salting the fish before it is cooked helps to keep the flesh firm during the cooking process.

EVERYDAY

Tuna with sweet shallots

PREP 10 MINS · COOK 20 MINS

Special equipment • food processor • ridged cast-iron grill pan

SERVES 4

6 shallots, peeled
2 garlic cloves, peeled
a few sprigs of fresh thyme, leaves only, plus extra sprigs, for garnish (optional)
sea salt and freshly ground black pepper
3 tbsp olive oil
3 tbsp balsamic vinegar
4 tuna steaks, about 5½oz (150g) each

1 Combine the shallots, garlic, and half of the thyme in a food processor. Process, pulsing the machine on and off, until evenly chopped, making sure the mixture doesn't become mushy. Season with salt and pepper.

2 Heat 1 tablespoon of the olive oil in a nonstick frying pan over low heat. Add the shallot mixture and cook gently until soft and translucent. Increase the heat slightly, add the balsamic vinegar, and continue cooking for about 15 minutes.

3 Meanwhile, heat a ridged cast-iron grill pan until hot. Drizzle the remaining olive oil over the tuna steaks, turning them to cover completely. Season with salt and pepper and sprinkle with the remaining thyme leaves. Cook the steaks, two at a time, for 3–5 minutes on each side, depending upon the thickness and your preference of doneness.

4 To serve, divide the shallot mixture among 4 serving plates. Place a tuna steak on top of each and garnish with thyme sprigs. Serve with tender green beans or an arugula salad.

VARIATION
Use a small red onion instead of the shallots.

Grilled shrimp with hot pepper sauce

PREP 10 MINS · COOK 10 MINS

SERVES 4

9oz (250g) large raw shrimp in the shell, deveined
2 tbsp olive oil
1 fresh red hot chile pepper, seeded and finely chopped

For the hot pepper sauce
1 garlic clove, finely grated
1 tsp hot chili powder
1 tsp paprika
pinch of ground cumin
juice of 1 lime
4–5 tbsp mayonnaise
sea salt and freshly ground black pepper

1 In a bowl, combine the shrimp with 1 tablespoon of the olive oil and the chile pepper. Toss well to coat and set aside.

2 To make the hot pepper sauce, in another bowl, stir together the remaining olive oil, garlic, chili powder, paprika, cumin, lime, and mayonnaise until well blended. Taste and season accordingly.

3 Heat a heavy frying pan or ridged cast-iron grill pan over high heat. Add the shrimp and cook for 3–4 minutes, turning once, until they turn pink and begin to curl. Serve with the hot pepper sauce, a salad, and fresh crusty bread.

VARIATION
Use a pinch of hot red pepper flakes instead of the fresh chile if you're short on time.

COOK'S NOTES

The shrimp can be threaded onto skewers before cooking; allow 2–3 per person.

Smoked fish and anchovy gratin

PREP 10 MINS **COOK 30 MINS**

SERVES 4
For the sauce
1 tbsp butter
1 onion, finely chopped
1 garlic clove, finely chopped
1 tbsp all-purpose flour
1¼ cups whole milk
sea salt and freshly ground
   black pepper
handful of curly parsley, finely
   chopped

4½oz (125g) smoked mackerel, thinly
   sliced or broken into small chunks
4½oz (125g) smoked salmon, thinly
   sliced or broken into small chunks
8–12 anchovies in oil, drained
4 all-purpose waxy potatoes, peeled,
   boiled, and sliced
1–2 tbsp butter, melted

1 Preheat the oven to 400°F (200°C).

2 To make the sauce, melt the butter in a saucepan over low heat. Add the onion and cook gently for about 5 minutes until soft, then add the garlic and cook for a few seconds longer. Remove from the heat and stir in the flour with a wooden spoon, then beat in a little of the milk until smooth.

3 Return the pan to the heat, and slowly add the rest of the milk, whisking until thickened. Season with salt and pepper and stir in the parsley.

4 Layer the fish and anchovies in an ovenproof dish, then cover with the sauce. Top with an even layer of potatoes, brush with melted butter, and bake in the oven for 15–20 minutes or until the potatoes are golden and crispy and the fish is heated through. Serve with a green salad.

COOK'S NOTES

For lump-free sauce every time, once you've beaten in the first amount of milk with a wooden spoon, switch to a balloon whisk while adding the remaining milk.

EVERYDAY

Salmon fish cakes

PREP 15 MINS **COOK 30 MINS**

SERVES 4
2lb (900g) baking potatoes, peeled
   and cut into chunks
1 tbsp butter
2lb (900g) skinless boneless salmon
handful of curly parsley, finely
   chopped
sea salt and freshly ground
   black pepper
flour for dusting
vegetable oil for cooking

To serve
tartar sauce
lemon wedges

1 First, make the mashed potatoes. Boil the potatoes in a saucepan of salted water for about 15 minutes or until soft, then drain well and mash. Add the butter and mash again until smooth. Set aside and keep warm.

2 Put the salmon in a large frying pan and cover with water. Simmer for 5–8 minutes until the fish turns opaque. Remove and cool on a plate for 2–3 minutes. Using your fingers, flake the fish into pieces.

3 Gently mix the fish with the mashed potatoes. Stir in the parsley and season well with salt and pepper. Form the mixture into 8 equal balls, then flatten them lightly into patties. Dust the fish cakes with a little flour.

4 Over medium heat, warm just enough oil to cover the bottom of a nonstick frying pan. Working in batches, cook the fish cakes for about 10 minutes, turning once, until golden. Serve hot with tartar sauce and lemon wedges.

 VARIATION
You can always substitute white fish for the salmon.

Mussels in fennel broth

PREP 10 MINS COOK 20 MINS

SERVES 4

1 tbsp olive oil

1 onion, finely chopped

1 fennel bulb, trimmed and finely chopped

sea salt

2 garlic cloves, finely chopped

2 all-purpose waxy potatoes, peeled and finely diced

1¼ cups hot vegetable stock or light fish stock

1 x 14oz (400ml) can unsweetened coconut milk

3lb (1.35kg) fresh mussels, cleaned (see Cook's Notes)

handful of fresh basil leaves, torn

1 Heat the oil in a medium saucepan over low heat. Add the onion, fennel, and salt, then cook for 5 minutes until softened. Stir in the garlic and potatoes and cook for another 2 minutes until well coated.

2 Pour in the stock and bring to a boil. Stir in the coconut milk, reduce the heat slightly, and simmer gently for about 10 minutes. Bring back to a boil, add the mussels, and cover the pan. Cook for about 5 minutes until the mussels are open (discard any that do not open).

3 To serve, stir in the basil, taste the broth, and season if needed. Serve hot.

COOK'S NOTES

To clean the mussels, turn them into the sink and cover with plenty of cold water. Scrape them one by one to remove any barnacles or hairy "beards" and scrub the shells. Throw away any that are open or badly cracked, and cook at once.

Roasted squid and potatoes with cilantro pesto

PREP 10 MINS COOK 20 MINS

Special equipment • food processor

SERVES 4

For the pesto

large handful of fresh cilantro

large handful of fresh basil leaves

2 garlic cloves, chopped

large handful of pine nuts

½ cup freshly grated Parmesan cheese

pinch of crushed red pepper flakes

⅔ cup extra virgin olive oil (use more or less as required)

sea salt and freshly ground black pepper

2½lb (1.1kg) waxy potatoes, peeled and cubed

2 tbsp olive oil

12oz (350g) squid, cleaned, and scored (ask your fishmonger to do this)

pinch of crushed red pepper flakes (optional)

1 Preheat the oven to 400°F (200°C).

2 To make the pesto, combine the cilantro, basil, garlic, and pine nuts in a food processor and process until the nuts are ground. Add most of the Parmesan and the pepper flakes and process again. With the machine on, slowly add the oil in a slow, steady stream, until the pesto forms a smooth paste. Stir in the remaining Parmesan, taste, and season with salt and pepper as needed. Set aside.

3 Put the potatoes in a roasting pan. Drizzle with 1 tablespoon of the olive oil and toss to coat. Season with salt and pepper. Roast for 15–20 minutes or until tender and golden.

4 Meanwhile, in a bowl, mix together the squid with the remaining olive oil and the pepper flakes. Add to the potatoes for the last 10 minutes or so of cooking. Cook until the squid is slightly charred. Toss the squid and potatoes together and serve hot with the cilantro pesto.

Cheat...

Use a store-bought pesto, such as basil or sun-dried tomato.

Roasted salmon with Swiss chard and herb butter

SERVES 4
For the herb butter
8 tbsp butter, at room temperature
handful of curly parsley, finely chopped
handful of fresh dill, finely chopped
juice of 1 lemon
pinch of crushed red pepper flakes

4 salmon fillets, 5½oz (150g) each
1 tbsp olive oil
sea salt and freshly ground black pepper
2 handfuls of Swiss chard, trimmed, rinsed, and drained

1 To make the herb butter, combine the butter, parsley, dill, lemon juice, and crushed pepper flakes in a mixing bowl and beat well until blended. Spoon the butter onto a piece of parchment paper, then roll into a log shape. Twist the edges of the paper and refrigerate the roll until needed.

2 Preheat the oven to 400°F (200°C). Place the salmon in a nonstick roasting pan, drizzle with the olive oil, and season with salt and pepper. Bake in the oven for 15–20 minutes or until the salmon is cooked through.

3 Meanwhile, cook the chard in a pan of boiling salted water for 5–8 minutes until it tender yet still firm to the bite. Drain well and transfer to a serving dish. Squeeze the lemon juice over the top and add a pinch of pepper flakes. Serve hot, with a slice of herb butter over both the salmon and the chard.

VARIATION Prepare curly kale or spinach instead of chard.

Sautéed scallops with pancetta and wilted spinach

SERVES 4
12 fresh sea scallops
sea salt and freshly ground black pepper
1–2 tbsp olive oil
4oz (115g) pancetta, cut into cubes
generous splash of good-quality balsamic vinegar
2 handfuls of fresh baby spinach, rinsed and drained
juice of 1 lemon

1 Pat the scallops dry with paper towels and season with salt and pepper. Heat the oil in a nonstick frying pan over medium-high heat. When hot, add the scallops, positioning them around the edge of the pan. Sear for 1–2 minutes on one side, then turn them over, starting with the first one you put in the pan. Once you have completed the circle, remove the scallops from the pan (starting with the first), and set aside to keep warm.

2 Add the pancetta to the same pan and cook, stirring occasionally, until crispy. Splash in a generous amount of balsamic vinegar, increase the heat to high, and let bubble for a couple of minutes, stirring to scrape up any bits from the bottom of the pan. Drizzle the balsamic glaze over the reserved scallops.

3 Still using the same pan, add the spinach. Cook for 2–3 minutes, stirring, until just wilted. Squeeze in the lemon juice and serve immediately with the scallops.

EVERYDAY

EVERYDAY

Lemon sole with herbs

 PREP 10 MINS COOK 20 MINS

SERVES 4
3 tbsp extra virgin olive oil
1 tbsp white wine vinegar
1 tsp Dijon mustard
small handful of fresh mixed herbs, such as parsley, thyme, and dill
sea salt and freshly ground black pepper
4 lemon sole or other sole fillets, or other flat white fish fillets such as plaice, about 6oz (175g) each

1 Preheat the oven to 400°F (200°C). To make the dressing, whisk together the oil and vinegar in a small bowl. Mix in the mustard and herbs to blend. Season well with salt and pepper.

2 Lay out the fish in a roasting pan, then add enough water to cover by about ¼in (5mm). Season well with salt and pepper. Bake in the oven for 10–15 minutes until the fish is cooked through and the water has nearly evaporated.

3 Using a spatula, carefully lift the fish onto a serving dish or individual plates. Spoon some of the herb dressing over each fillet. Serve hot with sautéed potatoes and broccoli.

 VARIATION

When possible, serve Dover sole–it is far superior in taste and can be prepared as either fillets or a whole fish. It will, however, be far more costly.

COOK'S NOTES

To check whether the fish is cooked, poke it to make sure that the flesh lifts away from the bone easily. The flesh should be opaque with no traces of pink.

White fish, green beans, and artichoke paella

 PREP 15 MINS COOK 30 MINS

SERVES 4–6
1 tbsp olive oil
1 onion, finely chopped
sea salt and freshly ground black pepper
pinch of turmeric
2 garlic cloves, finely chopped
7oz (200g) fresh green beans, trimmed
1 x 13¾oz (390g) can artichoke hearts, drained and rinsed
4 tomatoes, peeled and chopped
generous pinch of hot or regular paprika
2 cups rice
5 cups hot vegetable stock
1½lb (675g) skinless white fish, such as haddock or sustainable cod, cut into boneless chunks
handful of fresh dill or flat-leaf parsley, finely chopped
juice of 1 lemon

1 Heat the oil in a large heavy frying pan over medium heat. Add the onion and a pinch of sea salt and sauté for about 5 minutes until soft. Stir in the turmeric, then the garlic, beans, and artichokes. Cook gently for about 5 minutes until the beans begin to wilt, adding a little more oil if needed.

2 Now add the tomatoes and paprika and cook for 5 minutes. Stir in the rice. Pour in half of the hot stock. Bring to a boil, then reduce the heat slightly and simmer for about 15 minutes. Add the remaining stock and the fish, cover the pan, and cook over low heat until the rice and fish are cooked through.

3 Keep the lid on the pan until ready to serve, then stir in the fresh dill and lemon juice. Taste and season with salt and pepper. Serve with crusty bread.

Cheat...
Use instant rice instead of the basmati rice—it will speed things up.

Quick fish pie with peas

SERVES 4

2lb (900g) russet or other baking potatoes, peeled and quartered

1 tbsp butter, plus extra for topping, if desired

1½lb (675g) skinless boneless white fish, such as haddock, hake, sustainable cod, or pollack, cut into chunks (see Cook's Notes)

⅔ cup whole milk

1 cup frozen peas

4 hard-boiled eggs, peeled and chopped (optional)

For the sauce

2 tbsp butter

3 tbsp all-purpose flour

1¼ cups whole milk, or as needed

1 tbsp Dijon mustard

sea salt and freshly ground black pepper

1 Preheat the oven to 400°F (200°C), or the broiler to high. Peel and quarter the potatoes, then boil or steam in a pan of salted water for about 15 minutes, or until soft. Drain well and mash. Add the butter, and mash again. Set aside and keep warm.

2 Put the fish in a shallow frying pan. Season well with salt and pepper. Pour in just enough of the milk to cover and poach over medium heat

for 3–4 minutes. Remove the fish with a slotted spoon and transfer to a baking dish.

3 To make the sauce, melt the butter in a saucepan over medium heat. Remove from the heat and stir in the flour with a wooden spoon until smooth. Return the pan to the heat and gradually add the milk, stirring constantly. Keep cooking and stirring for 5–6 minutes until the sauce has thickened. Add more milk if needed. Stir in the mustard and season with salt and pepper. Gently stir in the peas and eggs.

4 Spoon the sauce over the fish and stir gently. Top with the reserved mashed potatoes, swirling the surface with a spoon to form peaks. Dot with extra butter if desired, then bake or cook under the broiler for about 10 minutes, or until the top is crisp and golden and the mixture is heated through.

COOK'S NOTES

If the fish needs to be skinned, lay it skin-side down on a work surface and slice crosswise along the tip of the tail. Now hold on to the end of the tail and use a filleting or boning knife to slice under the skin until it pulls away from the flesh.

Pan-fried shrimp, olives, and tomatoes

SERVES 4

1 tbsp olive oil

1 onion, finely chopped

2 garlic cloves, finely chopped

12 large raw shrimp, peeled and deveined, but with tails left intact

splash of dry sherry

6 tomatoes, peeled

large handful of mixed olives, pitted

handful of fresh basil leaves and flat-leaf parsley, chopped

sea salt and freshly ground black pepper

1 Heat the oil in a large frying pan over medium heat. Add the onion, and sauté for about 5 minutes until soft. Add the garlic, and cook for a few

seconds, then add the shrimp and cook over high heat just until the shrimp begin to turn pink.

2 Add the sherry, and cook for 5 minutes, stirring, until the smell of alcohol disappears, then add the tomatoes and olives. Cook for 2 minutes longer, stirring occasionally, until the tomatoes start to break down. Season well with salt and pepper, and stir in the basil. Serve with fresh crusty bread.

VARIATION If you prefer, use a splash of white wine instead of the sherry.

Fish sticks with chunky tartar sauce

PREP 15 MINS

Special equipment • food processor

SERVES 4

1½lb (675g) thick-cut skinless white
  fish fillets, such as haddock,
  sustainable cod, or pollack
1–2 tbsp all-purpose flour
1 large egg, lightly beaten
1 cup toasted homemade bread
  crumbs (see Cook's Notes)
½ cup freshly grated fresh Parmesan
  cheese
sea salt and freshly ground
  black pepper
about 3 tbsp prepared tartar sauce
1 tsp capers, rinsed, drained, and
  chopped
3 gherkins, drained and finely chopped

1 Preheat the oven to 400°F (200°C).
Cut the fish fillets into thick, even
strips about 1in (2.5cm) wide–you
should end up with about 20 "sticks."

2 Put the flour and egg onto
separate plates. Mix the bread
crumbs with the Parmesan and
season with salt and pepper. Dredge
the fish in the flour, then dip in the
egg to coat. Use the bread crumb
mixture to coat each of the fish
sticks. Coat them well, because this
protects the fish while it's cooking.

3 Place the fish sticks on a lightly
oiled baking sheet without crowding
and bake for 10–15 minutes, turning
once, until golden on the outside and
opaque throughout. (Alternatively, fry
the fish sticks, a few at a time, in a
little peanut oil.)

4 Spoon the tartar sauce into a bowl
and stir in the capers and gherkins.
Serve with the hot fish sticks.

COOK'S NOTES

To make the bread crumbs, process
about 3 slices of firm-textured
white bread slices in a food processor
to make coarse crumbs. Spread out
the crumbs on a baking sheet and
toast in a preheated 400°F (200°C)
oven for 5 minutes until golden.
Pour them back into the processor
and process again until finely
ground. Use at once or freeze in an
airtight container until needed.

Sweet and sour stir-fried fish with ginger

PREP 10 MINS **COOK 20 MINS**

Special equipment • wok

SERVES 4

For the sweet and sour sauce
2 tbsp pineapple juice
1 tbsp white wine vinegar
1 tbsp tomato purée
1 tbsp granulated sugar
2 tsp soy sauce
1 tsp cornstarch

1–2 tbsp cornstarch
sea salt and freshly ground
  black pepper
1½lb (675g) thick-cut skinless white
  fish fillets, cut into strips
1–2 tbsp vegetable or sunflower oil
1 onion, coarsely chopped
2 garlic cloves, finely chopped
1in (2.5cm) piece of fresh ginger,
  finely grated
large handful snow peas or sugar
  snap peas, sliced into strips

1 First, make the sauce by whisking
together the pineapple juice, vinegar,
tomato purée, sugar, soy sauce, and
1 teaspoon cornstarch. Set aside.

2 Put 1–2 tablespoons cornstarch on
a plate and season with salt and
pepper. Toss the fish in this seasoned
mixture to coat.

3 In a wok, heat about half of the
oil until hot, then add the fish. Stir-
fry for about 5 minutes until golden.
Remove with a slotted spoon and
set aside to keep warm. Carefully
wipe out the wok with paper towels
and add a little more oil. When hot,
add the onion and stir-fry until it
begins to soften, then add the garlic
and ginger and stir-fry for a few
minutes longer.

4 Pour in the sweet and sour sauce
and let simmer for a few minutes,
stirring constantly. Reduce the heat to
medium, add the peas, and stir-fry for
1 minute. Return the fish to the wok,
quickly toss together to combine, and
serve hot with rice.

White fish with spinach and pine nuts

SERVES 4

4 turbot fillets or other white fish
    fillets, such as haddock, sustainable
    cod, or pollack, 5½oz (150g) each
sea salt and freshly ground
    black pepper
2 tbsp olive oil
1 onion, finely chopped
handful of plump raisins
handful of pine nuts, toasted
1–2 tsp capers, rinsed and gently
    squeezed dry
2 large handfuls of fresh spinach
    leaves, rinsed and drained

1 Season the fish with salt and pepper. Heat 1 tablespoon of the oil in a large nonstick frying pan over medium heat. Add the fish and cook gently for 10–12 minutes, turning once, until opaque throughout. This will depend on the thickness of the fish, but be careful not to overcook. Remove the fillets from the pan and set aside to keep warm.

2 Carefully wipe out the pan with paper towels, then add the remaining oil. Cook the onion, stirring occasionally, for about 5 minutes until soft. Add the raisins, pine nuts, and capers and cook for a few minutes longer, breaking up the capers with the back of a fork. Stir in the spinach and cook until just wilted. Taste and season with salt and pepper if needed. Serve the fish on a bed of the wilted spinach mixture.

COOK'S NOTES

Salting the fish helps keep it firm while cooking.

EVERYDAY

Tuna, tomato, and zucchini skewers

Special equipment • 8 wooden skewers
• ridged cast-iron grill pan

SERVES 4

2 large tuna steaks, 4–5½oz (115–150g)
    each, cut into large chunks
juice of 1 lemon
1 tsp Asian five-spice powder
olive oil
sea salt and freshly ground
    black pepper
1 red onion, quartered and separated
12 cherry tomatoes
2 small zucchini, sliced
handful of fresh cilantro, chopped

1 Soak the bamboo skewers in cold water for 30 minutes. Combine the tuna, lemon juice, five-spice, and oil in a bowl, and toss well to coat. Season with salt and pepper.

2 Thread the tuna, onion, tomato, and zucchini onto skewers. Cook on a very hot grill pan for 3–5 minutes on each side until the tuna is seared and the tomatoes begin to blister. Sprinkle with cilantro and serve at once.

EVERYDAY

Spiced haddock with coconut, chile, and lime

PREP 10 MINS COOK 20 MINS

SERVES 4
For the spice mixture
1 tbsp cornstarch
1-2 tsp cayenne pepper, to taste
1 tsp paprika
1 tsp ground cinnamon
1 tsp ground coriander

4 haddock fillets, about 6oz (175g) each
sea salt and freshly ground
    black pepper
1 x 14oz (400ml) can unsweetened
    coconut milk
1 fresh red jalapeño chile pepper,
    seeded and finely chopped
juice of 1 lime
splash of Asian fish sauce (*nam pla*)
pinch of sugar (optional)
6oz (175g) fresh green beans
1 tbsp peanut or sunflower oil

1 To make the spice mixture, stir together the cornstarch, cayenne, paprika, cinnamon, and coriander. Season the haddock fillets well with salt and pepper, then coat well with the spice mixture. Set aside.

2 Pour the coconut milk into a wide saucepan, add the chile, and bring to a boil. Reduce the heat to a simmer and add the lime juice, fish sauce, and sugar. Stir in the green beans and simmer for about 5 minutes.

3 Meanwhile, heat the oil in a large nonstick frying pan over high heat. Add the fish and cook for about 10 minutes, turning once, until golden.

4 To serve, add the fish to the sauce and serve hot. Alternatively, serve the sauce on the side.

VARIATION
Use salmon fillets instead of haddock.

COOK'S NOTES
Use low-fat coconut milk if you prefer; but, as with most reduced-fat ingredients, watch that it doesn't separate during cooking.

Mackerel with garlic and tomatoes

PREP 10 MINS COOK 25 MINS

SERVES 4
24 cherry tomatoes on the vine,
    snipped with a bit of the stem left on
4 peeled garlic cloves
few sprigs of fresh thyme
grated zest of 1 lemon
pinch of crushed red pepper flakes
1-2 tbsp olive oil
sea salt and freshly ground
    black pepper
4 mackerel fillets, 4-5½oz
    (115-150g) each

1 Preheat the oven to 400°F (200°C). Combine the tomatoes, garlic, and thyme sprigs in a roasting pan. Sprinkle with the lemon zest and pepper flakes. Drizzle with the oil and season with salt and pepper. Roast in the oven for 10 minutes, until the tomatoes begin to soften and shrivel.

2 Remove from the oven, place the mackerel on top of the tomatoes, then cover the pan with foil. Return to the oven for 10-15 minutes, until the fish is cooked through. Serve hot with a salad and fresh bread.

VARIATION
When sardines are in season, use them instead of the mackerel.

Teriyaki fish with noodles

PREP 10 MINS COOK 15 MINS

SERVES 4
For the teriyaki sauce
1–2 tbsp soy sauce
1 tbsp honey
1in (2.5cm) piece of fresh ginger, finely grated
1 tbsp mirin (rice wine) or dry sherry
pinch of granulated sugar

4 thick-cut skinless sustainable cod fillets, about 5½oz (150g) each
9oz (250g) thick or medium fresh udon noodles
4 scallions, sliced
handful of fresh cilantro, leaves only
lime wedges, for serving

1 Preheat the oven to 400°F (200°C). To make the teriyaki sauce, mix together the soy sauce, honey, ginger, mirin, and sugar. Pour over the fish and leave to marinate for about 10 minutes.

2 Place the fish pieces in a roasting pan and bake for 10–15 minutes until the fish is cooked through.

3 Meanwhile, put the noodles in a bowl and cover with boiling water. Leave for few minutes, then drain and toss with the scallions and cilantro. Serve with the fish and lime wedges for squeezing.

VARIATION
Thin rice noodles can be used instead of the udon noodles.

Cheat...
Use store-bought teriyaki sauce—you'll find it with other Asian ingredients in most supermarkets.

Pan-fried clams with parsley and garlic

PREP 10 MINS COOK 20 MINS

SERVES 4
1 tbsp olive oil
1 onion, finely chopped
pinch of sea salt
2 garlic cloves, finely chopped
1–2 green bell peppers, seeded and finely chopped
¾ cup dry white wine
1lb (450g) fresh clams in the shell, well rinsed (see Cook's Notes)
handful of flat-leaf parsley, finely chopped
lemon wedges, for serving

1 Heat the oil in a large frying pan over medium heat. Add the onion and salt and cook for about 5 minutes until soft. Add the garlic and peppers and cook gently until the peppers begin to soften. Increase the heat to high and add the wine. Cook for a couple of minutes until the wine begins to evaporate.

2 Add the clams and cook, covered, shaking the pan occasionally, for 5–6 minutes or until the clams open. (Discard any clams that do not open.) Stir in the parsley. Serve hot with fresh crusty bread to sop up the juices and lemon wedges for squeezing.

VARIATION
Meat is often paired with seafood in Portuguese cooking. Try adding small cubes of chorizo to this dish, cooking the meat just before you add the clams.

EVERYDAY

Quick fish stew

PREP 10 MINS · COOK 30 MINS

Special equipment • blender

SERVES 4

1 tbsp olive oil
1 onion, finely chopped
3 garlic cloves, finely chopped
5 celery stalks, chopped
2 carrots, chopped
sea salt
sprig of fresh thyme, leaves only
spoonful of tomato purée
½ cup dry white wine
4 ripe tomatoes, peeled
3¾ cups light fish stock or bottled
  clam juice mixed with water
2 haddock fillets, about 12oz (350g)
  each, cut into chunks
8oz (225g) raw shrimp, peeled
  and deveined
handful of flat-leaf parsley,
  finely chopped

1 Heat the oil in a saucepan over low heat and add the onion, garlic, celery, and carrots, along with some salt and the thyme. Cook gently, stirring occasionally, for about 10 minutes.

2 Stir in the tomato purée, increase the heat to high, and add the wine. Let it bubble for a couple of minutes, then add the tomatoes (squashing them with a fork) and a little of the stock, and cook a few minutes longer. Pour in almost all of the remaining stock and bring to a boil. Reduce the heat slightly and simmer for 10 minutes. At this point, you can puree the sauce with a hand-held blender until smooth, or leave it as is. Add the remaining stock if the mixture is too thick.

3 Add the fish and shrimp, cover the pan, and cook for 5–10 minutes until the fish is cooked through. Serve hot with fresh crusty bread.

Cheat...
Add cooked shrimp to the soup instead of fresh. Just before serving, simply stir in to reheat.

Mixed tikka fish kebabs with mango salsa and lime raita

PREP 15 MINS · COOK 15 MINS

Special equipment • 8 skewers

SERVES 4
For the salsa
1 fresh mango, pitted, peeled,
  and diced
1 cucumber, halved lengthwise,
  peeled, seeded, and finely chopped
½ red onion, finely chopped
1 fresh red hot chile pepper, seeded
  and finely chopped
1in (2.5cm) piece of fresh
  ginger, grated

1–2 tbsp medium-hot tikka masala
  curry paste, or other curry paste
4 tbsp Greek-style whole-milk yogurt
sea salt
2½lb (1.1kg) mixed skinless fish
  fillets, such as swordfish and
  salmon, cut into chunks
handful of fresh mint leaves, finely
  chopped
½ cucumber, seeded and diced
juice of 1 lime

1 If using bamboo skewers, soak them in cold water for 30 minutes to prevent burning. Preheat the oven to 400°F (200°C) or the broiler to high.

2 To make the mango salsa, mix together the mango, cucumber, onion, chile, and ginger in a bowl. Set aside to allow the flavors to develop. In another bowl, mix together the curry paste and 2 tablespoons of the yogurt. Season with salt. Spread the paste all over the fish, making sure that each piece is well coated. Let marinate for a few minutes while you prepare the raita dip.

3 Mix together the remaining yogurt with the mint, cucumber, and lime. Taste and season with salt.

4 Thread the fish onto skewers to make kebabs. Line a baking sheet with foil, coat with nonstick cooking spray, then place the kebabs on it. Put in the oven or under the broiler and cook, turning several times, for 5–8 minutes or until the fish is opaque throughout and slightly charred on the outside. Serve hot with the salsa and raita.

COOK'S NOTES

Use whole-milk yogurt, as it is far more stable than the low-fat versions, which can curdle when heated.

Roasted monkfish with chiles, tomatoes, anchovies, and capers

PREP 20 MINS **COOK** 30 MINS

SERVES 4

about 2¼lb (1kg) monkfish, halved (see Cook's Notes)
drizzle of olive oil
sea salt and freshly ground black pepper
2 fresh mild to medium red chile peppers, seeded and finely chopped
6–8 salted anchovies, finely chopped
2–3 tsp capers, rinsed, gently squeezed dry, and chopped
12 cherry tomatoes

1 Preheat the oven to 400°F (200°C). Place the monkfish in a roasting pan and drizzle with olive oil. Season well with salt and pepper and set aside.

2 Using a mortar and pestle, pound together the chiles, anchovies, and capers until they form a paste. Alternatively, mash into a paste with a fork. Using your hands, smear the paste all over the monkfish.

3 Put the fish in a roasting pan and roast in the oven for 10 minutes. Add the tomatoes and roast for another 5–10 minutes, until the fish is cooked through.

4 Leave to rest for 5 minutes, then slice and serve immediately with either a green salad or roasted new potatoes.

VARIATION
Use crushed red pepper flakes instead of fresh

COOK'S NOTES
Buy the monkfish in one piece and cut it in half, or purchase two tails.

EVERYDAY

Pan-fried scallops with chile, ginger, and anchovy dressing

PREP 10 MINS **COOK** 30 MINS

SERVES 4

3 tbsp olive or vegetable oil
1½lb (675g) all-purpose waxy potatoes, peeled and thinly sliced
12 fresh sea scallops
1 fresh red hot chile, seeded and finely chopped
1in (2.5cm) piece of fresh ginger, finely grated
juice of 1 lemon
handful of flat-leaf parsley, finely chopped

For the anchovy dressing
3 tbsp extra virgin olive oil
1 tbsp white wine vinegar
8 anchovies in oil, drained and finely chopped
pinch of sugar (optional)
sea salt and freshly ground black pepper

1 Heat 1–2 tablespoons of the olive oil in a large nonstick frying pan over medium-high heat. Add the potatoes and cook for 15–20 minutes or until tender and golden. Drain on paper towels and set aside to keep warm.

2 Meanwhile, make the anchovy dressing. In a bowl, whisk together the oil, vinegar, and anchovies until well blended. Taste and add a pinch of sugar if needed. Season with pepper.

3 Next, pat the scallops dry with paper towels and season with salt and pepper. Put the remaining tablespoon of olive oil in frying pan over high heat. When hot, add the scallops. Sear for about 1 minute on one side, then turn them over. Add the chile and ginger and squeeze in the lemon juice (being careful, as it may spatter). Remove the pan from the heat and sprinkle with the parsley.

4 Serve immediately with the sautéed potatoes and a drizzle of the anchovy dressing.

Tomato and tarragon pilaf

PREP 10 MINS COOK 25 MINS

SERVES 4

1 tbsp olive oil
1 tbsp butter
1 onion, finely chopped
sea salt and freshly ground
  black pepper
2 cloves garlic, peeled and crushed
1½ cups instant rice
1½ cups hot vegetable stock
1lb (450g) tomatoes, quartered
2 or 3 sprigs of fresh tarragon,
  leaves picked and torn

1 Heat the oil and butter in a large frying pan over low heat. Add the onion and a pinch of salt and cook for about 5 minutes until soft. Stir in the garlic and rice, making sure the rice is well coated with butter.

2 Now pour in the hot stock, and stir again. Bring to a boil, cover, and remove from heat. Let stand for 5 minutes. Uncover and stir to fluff the rice. If the pilaf seems dry, add a little more hot stock or water.

3 Season well with salt and pepper, then stir in the tomatoes and tarragon. Serve hot with a crisp green salad.

VARIATION
Tarragon isn't everyone's favorite herb, so substitute thyme or rosemary, if you wish.

Cheesy potato and mushroom gratin

PREP 10 MINS COOK 30 MINS

SERVES 4

1 tbsp butter
4½oz (125g) mushrooms, sliced
2 garlic cloves, finely chopped
a few sprigs of fresh thyme,
  leaves picked
2lb (900g) all-purpose waxy potatoes,
  peeled and thinly sliced
1 cup Gruyère cheese, shredded
sea salt and freshly ground
  black pepper

1 Preheat the oven to 400°F (200°C). Heat the butter in a frying pan, then add the mushrooms and cook for a few minutes until soft. Add the garlic and thyme and cook for 1 minute longer.

2 Arrange a layer of potatoes in the bottom of a baking dish, then top with some of the cheese and mushrooms.

Season each layer with a pinch of salt and pepper as you go. Continue layering until you have used all of the ingredients, finishing with potatoes and a sprinkling of cheese on top.

3 Bake in the oven for 25 minutes, or until golden on top and bubbly-hot. Serve with a green salad.

VARIATION
Use a smoked or sharp Cheddar cheese.

COOK'S NOTES

If you are cooking for strict vegetarians, be sure to check that the cheese is made with vegetarian rennet. The package should specify this.

EVERYDAY

Chickpea and vegetable stew

SERVES 4

1 tbsp olive oil

1 onion, finely chopped

sea salt and freshly ground
   black pepper

2 garlic cloves, finely chopped

3 celery stalks, finely chopped

3 carrots, finely chopped

½ cup dry white wine

1 x 14oz (400g) can diced tomatoes

1 x 15½oz (440g) can chickpeas,
   drained and rinsed

⅔ cup hot vegetable stock

handful of fresh green beans,
   sliced diagonally

1 Heat the oil in a large saucepan over low heat. Add the onion and a pinch of salt and cook for about 5 minutes until soft. Stir in the garlic, celery, and carrots and cook about 5 minutes longer.

2 Increase the heat, add the wine, and let bubble until the alcohol has cooked away. Add the tomatoes, bring to a boil, and pour in the stock. Add the chickpeas, reduce the heat slightly, and simmer gently for 15 minutes.

3 Add the green beans and cook for 5–10 minutes, until tender. Season well with salt and pepper. Serve hot with crusty bread.

VARIATION

Substitute canned butter beans or lima beans for the chickpeas.

COOK'S NOTES

This dish tastes even better the next day as the flavors mature. Simply reheat in a pan.

EVERYDAY

Gnocchi with Gorgonzola and walnut sauce

SERVES 4

1 tbsp butter

1 onion, finely chopped

⅓ cup coarsely
   chopped walnuts

1 tbsp all-purpose flour

2 cups whole milk

4½oz (125g) Gorgonzola cheese

sea salt and freshly ground
   black pepper

1 package (about 18oz/500g) fresh
   or frozen gnocchi

handful of fresh basil leaves,
   to garnish (optional)

1 In a saucepan, melt the butter over low heat. Add the onion and cook gently for about 5 minutes until soft. Now add the walnuts and cook for another couple of minutes. Remove from the heat and stir in the flour, then add a little milk. Return to the heat and add the remaining milk,

stirring constantly for 4–6 minutes until the sauce thickens.

2 Remove from the heat again and stir in the Gorgonzola. Season with salt and pepper.

3 In a separate saucepan, cook the gnocchi as the package directs. Drain well. Add to the sauce, stirring gently to coat. Garnish with the basil leaves (if using), and serve immediately with a tomato and arugula salad.

Cheat...
If available, buy a carton of ready-made blue cheese pasta sauce to use, instead of making your own.

Spinach, squash, and horseradish bake

PREP 10 MINS   COOK 30 MINS

SERVES 4

2 handfuls of fresh spinach leaves, rinsed and drained

1 small to medium butternut squash, halved, seeded, peeled, and thinly sliced

2 garlic cloves, finely chopped

1½ cups heavy whipping cream

3–4 tsp cream-style white horseradish

sea salt and freshly ground black pepper

1 Preheat the oven to 400°F (200°C). Put the spinach in a saucepan with a little water (the water clinging to the freshly-rinsed leaves should be enough), and cook, stirring, for a few minutes over medium-low heat until just wilted. Drain and squeeze out the excess water. Set aside.

2 Put the squash and garlic in a saucepan, pour in the cream, and simmer over low heat for 10 minutes. Using a slotted spoon, remove the squash and layer it in an ovenproof dish with the wilted spinach.

3 Stir the horseradish into the cream remaining in the pan, then pour the mixture over the squash. Season with salt and lots of pepper. Cover with foil and bake for 20 minutes.

VARIATION
Use fresh pumpkin instead of the butternut squash.

> **COOK'S NOTES**
> Make sure you use heavy cream in this dish; it is very stable and won't separate during cooking.

Spiced bean and herb hash

PREP 10 MINS   COOK 30 MINS

SERVES 4

1 tsp olive oil, plus extra as needed

1 tbsp butter

1 red onion, coarsely chopped

sea salt and freshly ground black pepper

handful of fresh thyme sprigs, leaves picked

1lb (450g) russet (baking) potatoes, peeled and cubed

1 x 14oz (400g) can chili beans

⅔ cup hot vegetable stock

handful of flat-leaf parsley, finely chopped

1 Heat the oil and butter in a nonstick frying pan over low heat. Add the onion, a pinch of salt, and the thyme leaves, and cook for about 5 minutes until the onion is soft.

2 Add the potatoes and cook until lightly browned at the edges—you may need to add more olive oil to accomplish this.

3 When the potatoes are nearly tender—about 15 minutes—stir in the chili beans. Pour in the hot stock and simmer for 10 minutes. Stir in the parsley and season well with salt and pepper. Serve hot.

Potato and pea curry

PREP 10 MINS • COOK 30 MINS

SERVES 4

1in (2.5cm) piece of fresh ginger, finely chopped
2-3 fresh hot green chile peppers, seeded and finely chopped
1 tsp cumin seeds
1 tsp mustard seeds
small handful of dried curry leaves (optional)
6 tomatoes, peeled and chopped
1½lb (675g) all-purpose waxy potatoes, peeled and cubed
1 tsp turmeric
1¼ cups hot vegetable stock
½ cup frozen peas
sea salt and freshly ground black pepper
handful of fresh cilantro, chopped

1 Heat the oil in a large frying pan over medium heat. Add the ginger, chiles, cumin seeds, and mustard seeds, and crumble in the curry leaves. Cook for a couple of minutes until the mustard seeds start to pop. Stir in the tomatoes and cook for a few more minutes.

2 Add the potatoes and turmeric and pour in the stock. Bring to a boil, reduce the heat slightly, cover, and simmer for about 15 minutes or until the potatoes are tender.

3 Stir in the peas and cook for another 3-5 minutes. Season well with salt and pepper and stir in the cilantro. Serve hot with rice or naan bread.

Cheat...
Heat a couple of teaspoons of ready-made curry paste instead of the dried spices.

COOK'S NOTES

This is a fairly dry curry; if you want more liquid, simply add more stock.

Shepherdless pie

PREP 15 MINS • COOK 30 MINS

Special equipment • food processor

SERVES 4

1½lb (675g) russet (baking) potatoes, peeled and quartered
1 tbsp butter, plus extra for dotting on top
1 tbsp olive oil
1 onion, finely chopped
1 bay leaf
sea salt and freshly ground black pepper
3 celery stalks, finely chopped
3 carrots, finely chopped
7oz (200g) mushrooms, coarsely chopped
handful of fresh thyme sprigs, leaves picked (reserve some for garnish)
splash of soy sauce
1 x 15oz (425g) can aduki beans, drained and rinsed
⅔ cup hot vegetable stock

1 Preheat the oven to 400°F (200°C). To make the topping, boil the potatoes in a saucepan of salted water for 15-20 minutes, or until soft. Drain the potatoes, then mash. Add the butter and mash again. Set aside and keep warm.

2 Meanwhile, heat the oil in a large frying pan over low heat. Add the onion, bay leaf, and a pinch of salt, and cook for 5 minutes until the onion is soft. Add the celery and carrots and cook for another 5 minutes.

3 Pulse the mushrooms several times in a food processor—you want them finely chopped, but not mushy. Add these to the pan along with the thyme leaves and soy sauce and cook for 5-10 minutes, until the mushrooms begin to release their juices. Add the aduki beans and season well with salt and pepper. Pour in the stock, bring to a boil, reduce the heat slightly, and simmer for 5 minutes.

4 Scrape into a baking dish and top with the reserved mashed potatoes. Dot with butter and bake until the topping is crisp and golden. Serve hot.

VARIATION If you can't find aduki beans, use drained canned lentils or even red kidney beans.

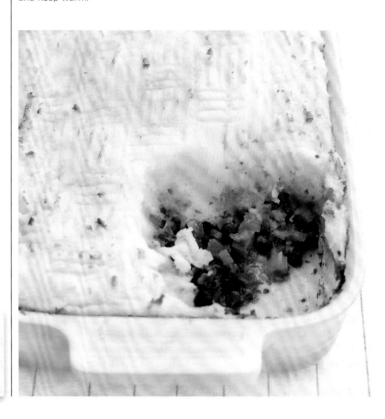

EVERYDAY

EVERYDAY

Green bean and cauliflower gratin

PREP 10 MINS · COOK 30 MINS

SERVES 4

1 tbsp butter
1 tbsp all-purpose flour
1¼ cups whole milk
pinch of paprika
sea salt and freshly ground
   black pepper
1 cup shredded sharp Cheddar cheese
2 tsp Dijon mustard
1 head cauliflower, broken into
   small florets
1 x 14oz (400g) can green beans,
   drained and rinsed

1 Preheat the oven to 400°F (200°C). To make the cheese sauce, melt the butter in a saucepan over low heat. Remove from the heat and stir in the flour until well blended. Add a little of the milk and whisk until smooth.

Return to the heat and slowly whisk in the remaining milk. Keep whisking for another 5–10 minutes until the sauce is smooth and thickened.

2 Remove from the heat, sprinkle in the paprika, and season well with salt and pepper. Stir in half of the cheese and the mustard and set aside.

3 Cook the cauliflower in boiling salted water for 5–10 minutes until tender. Drain.

4 Put the cauliflower in a baking dish with the beans and toss together. Pour in the sauce and top with the remaining cheese. Bake for 10–15 minutes until bubbly-hot. Serve hot.

Chunky ratatouille

PREP 15 MINS · COOK 30 MINS

SERVES 4

1 tbsp olive oil
1 onion, finely chopped
sea salt and freshly ground
   black pepper
1 bay leaf
2 garlic cloves, thinly sliced
1–2 tsp dried oregano
pinch of fennel seeds
1 eggplant, cut into chunks
½ cup dry red wine
⅔ cup tomato juice
2 small zucchini, cut into chunks
3 tomatoes, coarsely chopped
large handful of Swiss chard leaves
freshly chopped flat-leaf parsley
   leaves, for garnish

1 Heat the oil in a large saucepan over low heat. Add the onion, a pinch of salt, and the bay leaf, and cook for 5 minutes until the onion is soft.

2 Add the garlic, oregano, fennel seeds, eggplant, and wine. Let

bubble for a minute, then add the tomato juice. Cook for about 10 minutes or until the eggplant is soft.

3 Now add the zucchini and chopped tomatoes and cook for 5–10 minutes longer. Stir in the Swiss chard and cook until all the vegetables are tender. Taste and season if needed.

4 Garnish with the parsley and serve hot with fluffy rice or crusty bread and a salad.

VARIATION
Swap the Swiss chard for spinach or even Savoy cabbage.

COOK'S NOTES

Chop the vegetables smaller if you prefer; the ratatouille will stew down a little quicker.

Lemony dal

PREP 10 MINS   COOK 30 MINS

SERVES 4

1 tbsp olive oil
1 onion, finely chopped
sea salt and freshly ground
    black pepper
2 garlic cloves, finely grated
2in (5cm) piece of ginger, finely grated
pinch of turmeric
pinch of garam masala
1½ cups red lentils
grated zest and juice of 1 lemon
3¾ cups hot vegetable stock
2 tomatoes, peeled and chopped
handful of fresh cilantro,
    finely chopped

1 Heat the oil in a frying pan over low heat. Add the onion and a pinch of salt and cook for 5 minutes until soft. Stir in the garlic, ginger, turmeric, and garam masala, and cook for 1 minute.

2 Stir in the lentils and lemon zest, pour in the stock, and simmer for about 20 minutes until the lentils are tender.

3 Season well with salt and pepper and stir in the lemon juice, tomatoes, and cilantro. Serve hot with naan bread or chapattis.

Zucchini stuffed with raisins, red onion, and pine nuts

PREP 10 MINS   COOK 20 MINS

SERVES 4

8 zucchini
1 tbsp olive oil
1 red onion, finely chopped
pinch of sea salt
pinch of crushed red pepper flakes
handful of pine nuts, toasted
handful of golden raisins
½ cup crumbled feta cheese

1 Preheat the oven to 400°F (200°C). First, prepare the zucchini by cutting in half lengthwise. Scoop out the flesh and chop it coarsely. Set the chopped zucchini aside with the zucchini shells.

2 Heat the oil in a large frying pan over low heat. Add the onion and a pinch of sea salt. Cook for 5 minutes until soft, then stir in the chopped zucchini and pepper flakes and cook for a couple minutes longer.

3 Stir in half of the pine nuts and the raisins, then remove from the heat. Spoon the mixture into the zucchini shells and top with the feta. Place on a baking sheet and roast in the oven for about 10 minutes until the zucchini is tender and the filling is heated through.

4 Sprinkle the remaining pine nuts over the top and serve hot.

EVERYDAY

Sweet potato and butter bean stew

PREP 10 MINS   COOK 30 MINS

SERVES 4

1lb (450g) sweet potatoes, peeled and cut into thick slices
2 tbsp maple syrup
1 tbsp olive oil
1 red onion, finely chopped
1 tsp cumin seeds
sea salt and freshly ground black pepper
1 x 14oz (400g) can diced tomatoes
splash of balsamic vinegar
1 x 14oz (400g) can butter beans, drained and rinsed
handful of Swiss chard or spinach leaves
⅔ cup Greek-style yogurt
handful of fresh mint leaves, for garnish

1 Cook the sweet potatoes with the maple syrup in a saucepan of boiling salted water for 10 minutes until just barely tender. Drain well and set aside to keep warm.

2 Meanwhile, heat the oil in a large saucepan or deep frying pan over low heat. Add the onion, cumin seeds, and a pinch of salt, and cook for 5 minutes until the onion is soft. Stir in the tomatoes, including the juices, and the balsamic vinegar, and cook for about 10 minutes. Taste and season with salt and pepper.

3 Add the butter beans and simmer for 5 minutes, then stir in the Swiss chard. Cook for a couple of minutes more until the leaves just wilt.

4 Remove from the heat and top with the sweet potatoes. Spoon the yogurt over the top and sprinkle with the mint leaves.

COOK'S NOTES

Canned whole peeled plum tomatoes are often juicier and cheaper than ready-cut ones. Just snip them in the can, using a pair of kitchen scissors.

Asparagus, broccoli, ginger, and mint stir-fry

PREP 15 MINS   COOK 15 MINS

Special equipment • wok

SERVES 4

1 tbsp sesame oil or vegetable oil
2 fresh red chile peppers, seeded and finely chopped
2in (5cm) piece of fresh ginger, sliced and cut into thin strips
2 garlic cloves, finely chopped
1 bunch of scallions, cut into 2in (5cm) lengths
1 red bell pepper, seeded and sliced into thin strips
1 head broccoli, about 10oz (300g), cut into florets
1 bunch of thin asparagus, trimmed and halved crosswise
1 tbsp granulated sugar
sea salt and freshly ground black pepper
handful of fresh mint leaves

1 Heat the oil in a wok over medium-high heat and swirl to coat. Add the chiles, ginger, and garlic, and toss for a few seconds, then add the scallions. Stir-fry for 3–5 minutes until shiny.

2 Now add the bell pepper and stir-fry for a few minutes. Add the broccoli and stir-fry for a few minutes more before adding the asparagus.

Continue stir-frying for another minute or two until all the vegetables are crisp-tender.

3 Sprinkle in the sugar and season well with salt and pepper. Stir-fry for a few seconds until the sugar has dissolved. Remove from the heat and stir in the mint leaves. Serve immediately, either alone or with fluffy rice.

Cheat...

Use a bag of prepared and chopped vegetables, either frozen or fresh.

COOK'S NOTES

Stir-frys require quick work; have all ingredients prepared, chopped, or sliced before starting. You can use your own selection of vegetables— just remember to add them in the right order, with the ones that require longer cooking going in first.

Thai red vegetable curry

 PREP 15 MINS   **COOK 20 MINS**

SERVES 4

1–2 tbsp Thai red curry paste from a jar
1 x 14oz (400g) can unsweetened coconut milk
2 eggplants, cut into chunks
6 kaffir lime leaves, torn in half lengthwise (optional)
1¼ cups hot vegetable stock
1 tbsp palm sugar or brown sugar
splash of soy sauce
sea salt
1 red bell pepper, seeded and cut into strips
1 green bell pepper, seeded and cut into strips
juice of 1 lime
handful of fresh cilantro

1 Heat the curry paste in a large frying pan or wok over medium-high heat for a few seconds, stirring around the pan. Shake the can of coconut milk to blend, then open it and pour into the pan. Bring to a gentle boil, stirring to mix with the curry paste, and cook for 2–3 minutes until it releases its aroma.

2 Add the eggplant, lime leaves, stock, sugar, and soy sauce. Season with salt and return to a boil. Reduce the heat slightly and simmer for about 15 minutes, or until the eggplant is soft.

3 Now stir in the peppers and lime juice. Taste and adjust the seasoning accordingly, adding more sugar (sweetness), lemon juice (sour), or salt as needed. Stir in the cilantro and serve immediately with some jasmine or sticky rice.

COOK'S NOTES

You could add firm tofu to this curry; it's best bought from an Asian supermarket because it is often homemade and tastes far superior.

Spicy garlic green vegetable medley

 PREP 15 MINS   **COOK 15 MINS**

Special equipment • wok

SERVES 4

handful of hazelnuts
1 tbsp sesame oil or vegetable oil
3 garlic cloves, thinly sliced
2 fresh green jalapeño chile peppers, seeded and finely chopped
1 tbsp soy sauce
1 tbsp Chinese rice wine
1–2 heads bok choy, quartered lengthwise
handful of fresh spinach leaves or Swiss chard
2 handfuls of sugar snap peas or snow peas, sliced into thin strips
sea salt and freshly ground black pepper

1 Spread the hazelnuts on a baking sheet. Toast under a hot broiler until golden brown, shaking the pan frequently. Put the hazelnuts in a clean dish towel and rub off the skins. Chop coarsely and set aside.

2 Heat the oil in a wok over medium-high heat and swirl it around to coat the pan. Add the garlic and chiles and cook for 10 seconds, then add the soy sauce and Chinese rice wine and cook for a few seconds more.

3 Add the bok choy and spinach and stir-fry for 1 minute. Add the sugar snap peas and stir-fry for 1 more minute. Toss well, then season with salt and pepper. Serve immediately with the hazelnuts scattered over the top. Serve with rice.

 VARIATION Add some whole oyster mushrooms along with the green vegetables.

Cheat...
Don't be put off by ready-made stir-fry sauces; there are some great-tasting Asian-inspired ones available.

Grated zucchini and goat cheese omelet

PREP 10 MINS COOK 15 MINS

SERVES 1

3 large eggs, lightly beaten
1 small zucchini, coarsely grated
sea salt and freshly ground
    black pepper
1 tbsp butter
½ cup crumbled soft goat cheese
small handful of fresh thyme sprigs,
    leaves only, for garnish (optional)

1 Combine the egg and zucchini in a bowl. Season with salt and pepper.

2 Melt the butter in a small nonstick frying pan over medium-high heat until foaming, then pour in the egg mixture, swirling it around to the edges of the pan. Gently slide a knife or heatproof spatula around the edge of the pan to lift the edges of the omelet.

3 When the edges have begun to cook, scatter the goat cheese evenly over the entire surface. Continue cooking until the egg mixture in the center is almost set, but still soft. Remove from the heat and leave for a minute or two–the retained heat will continue to cook the egg.

4 Season with pepper and garnish with thyme leaves. Carefully fold the omelet into thirds or in half and slide it out of the pan onto a plate. Serve immediately.

VARIATION
Vary the type of cheese to suit your preference. Feta, smoked, or even cream cheese is tasty.

Lentils with mushrooms and leeks

PREP 10 MINS COOK 25 MINS

SERVES 4

1 tbsp olive oil, plus extra if needed
1 onion, finely chopped
1 bay leaf
sea salt and freshly ground
    black pepper
2 garlic cloves, finely chopped
3 leeks, sliced
2 tsp Marmite or Vegemite, or
    a splash of light soy sauce
8oz (225g) mushrooms, halved or
    quartered if large
1 x 14oz (400g) can green or Puy
    lentils, drained and rinsed
1¼ cups hot vegetable stock
handful of curly parsley, stems
    removed and finely chopped

1 Heat the oil in a large frying pan over low heat. Add the onion, bay leaf, and a pinch of salt, and cook for 5 minutes until the onion is soft.

2 Add the garlic and leeks and stir in the Marmite. Cook for 5 minutes longer, until the leeks begin to soften.

3 Now add the mushrooms and cook until they release their juices–you may need to add a little more oil. Season well with salt and pepper, then stir in the lentils and hot stock. Bring to a boil, reduce the heat slightly, and simmer gently for 15 minutes.

4 Remove from the heat and stir in the parsley. Taste and season again if needed. Serve with roasted tomatoes and fresh crusty bread.

> **COOK'S NOTES**
>
> Add vegetarian sausages to this dish for extra protein. Roast them first in a preheated 400°F (200°C) oven for 15–20 minutes, then add to the frying pan along with the lentils in step 3, and simmer gently until ready to serve.

Baked eggs with tomatoes and peppers

PREP 10 MINS COOK 20 MINS

SERVES 4

1 tbsp olive oil

1 red onion, sliced

pinch of salt

2 red bell peppers, seeded and sliced

2 yellow or orange bell peppers, seeded and sliced

2 fresh red jalapeño chile peppers, seeded and finely chopped

3 tomatoes, peeled and coarsely chopped

2 handfuls of fresh spinach leaves

pinch of paprika

4 large eggs

freshly ground black pepper

1 Preheat the oven to 400°F (200°C). Heat the oil in an ovenproof frying pan over low heat. Add the onion and a pinch of salt. Cook for 5 minutes until the onion is soft, then add the peppers and chiles. Cook for another 5 minutes, until the peppers soften.

2 Stir in the tomatoes and cook until they begin to soften. Stir in the spinach and paprika and cook for a few minutes more until the spinach just begins to wilt.

3 Use a spoon to make a small indentation in the mixture for each of the eggs, then carefully break an egg into each one. Slide the pan into the oven and cook for about 5 minutes until the eggs are just baked. Be careful not to let them overcook—the residual heat will keep cooking them after you have removed them from the oven. Sprinkle with pepper and serve immediately.

EVERYDAY

Rice and peas

PREP 5 MINS COOK 25 MINS

SERVES 4

1 tbsp olive oil

1 onion, finely chopped

2 garlic cloves, finely chopped

2–3 fresh hot chile peppers, seeded and finely chopped

2½ cups long-grain white rice, rinsed

1 x 14oz (400g) can black-eyed peas, drained and rinsed

1 x 14oz (400g) can unsweetened coconut milk

3 cups hot vegetable stock, or as needed

1 Heat the oil in a saucepan over low heat and cook the onion for 5 minutes until soft. Add the garlic and chiles and cook for a few seconds more.

2 Stir in the rice, making sure the grains are well coated, then add the peas, coconut milk, and most of the stock. Cover the pan and cook over low heat for about 20 minutes until all the liquid has been absorbed and the rice is tender; if you need to add more stock, do so.

3 Serve hot, either on its own or with vegetables.

VARIATION

Use red kidney beans instead of black-eyed peas.

COOK'S NOTES

Do rinse the rice before you use it; this will help remove some of the starch.

EVERYDAY

Pea and mint risotto

PREP 10 MINS **COOK 25 MINS**

SERVES 4

5 cups vegetable stock, plus
  more as needed
1 tbsp olive oil
1 tbsp butter
1 onion, finely chopped
sea salt and freshly ground
  black pepper
1½ cups Arborio or other
  short-grain risotto rice
¾ cup dry white wine
1 cup thawed frozen or fresh peas
½ cup freshly grated Parmesan cheese
handful of fresh mint leaves
handful of fresh basil leaves

1 First, pour the stock into a large saucepan and heat to a gentle simmer.

2 Heat the oil and butter in a large nonstick frying pan over low heat. Add the onion and a pinch of salt. Cook for about 5 minutes until soft, then stir in the rice, making sure the grains are completely coated. Increase the heat, pour in the wine, and let bubble for a couple of minutes until the smell of alcohol has evaporated.

3 Reduce the heat slightly and add the simmering stock about ½ cup at a time, stirring with a wooden spoon; when each addition of stock has been absorbed, add some more. Continue like this for about 20 minutes until the rice is tender yet still firm to the bite. Use more stock as needed—every risotto is different.

4 Stir in the peas, Parmesan, mint, and basil. Season well with salt and pepper and serve hot.

VARIATION Fresh asparagus tips also taste wonderful in a risotto.

COOK'S NOTES

For extra creaminess, stir in another tablespoon of butter at the end of the cooking time.

Squash, sage, and blue cheese risotto

PREP 15 MINS **COOK 30 MINS**

SERVES 4

1 butternut squash, halved, seeded,
  peeled, and cut into bite-sized pieces
pinch of crushed red pepper flakes
2 tbsp olive oil
5 cups vegetable stock, or more
  as needed
1 tbsp butter
1 onion, finely chopped
pinch of sea salt
2 garlic cloves, finely chopped
4 fresh sage leaves, torn (optional)
1½ cups Arborio or other
  short-grain risotto rice
¾ cup dry white wine
½ cup crumbled Gorgonzola or similar
  blue cheese
freshly ground black pepper

1 Preheat the oven to 400°F (200°C). Put the squash in a roasting pan, sprinkle with the pepper flakes, and drizzle with 1 tablespoon of the oil. Mix together using your hands. Roast in the oven for about 15 minutes until golden and beginning to soften.

2 Meanwhile, pour the stock into a large saucepan and heat to a gentle simmer. Heat the remaining oil and the butter in a large nonstick frying pan over low heat. Add the onion and a pinch of salt and cook for 5 minutes until the onions are soft. Stir in the garlic and sage leaves and cook for a few seconds more.

3 Next, stir in the rice, making sure that the grains are completely coated. Increase the heat to medium-high, pour in the wine, and let bubble for a couple of minutes until the smell of alcohol has evaporated.

4 Reduce the heat slightly and add the simmering stock about ½ cup at a time, stirring with a wooden spoon; when each addition of stock has been absorbed, add some more. Continue like this for about 20 minutes until the rice is tender yet still firm to the bite. Use more stock if needed. Stir in the roasted squash and the Gorgonzola, season with pepper, and serve hot.

VARIATION If you're not a fan of blue cheese, simply omit and stir in freshly grated Parmesan instead.

Eggplant stuffed with tomato rice

PREP 10 MINS COOK 30 MINS

SERVES 4

4 small eggplants, halved lengthwise
3–4 tbsp olive oil
1 cup long-grain white rice, rinsed
1¼ cups tomato juice
1 tsp granulated sugar
sea salt and freshly ground
    black pepper
1 onion, finely chopped
small handful of fresh dill,
    finely chopped

1 Preheat the oven to 400°F (200°C). Scoop out the flesh from the eggplants, chop into bite-sized chunks, and set aside. Place the shells in a roasting pan and brush with 1–2 tbsp oil. Cover with foil and roast in the oven for 10–15 minutes while you cook the rice.

2 Prepare the rice according to the package directions. Drain if needed, then pour in the tomato juice. Sprinkle in the sugar and season well with salt and pepper. Stir until the tomato juice is absorbed.

3 Heat 1 tablespoon of the oil in a large frying pan over low heat. Add the onion, dill, and a pinch of salt. Cook until the onion is soft, then add the reserved eggplant flesh and cook for another 5 minutes. Season with pepper and stir in the tomato rice mixture.

4 Remove the eggplant shells from the oven and carefully spoon the mixture into them. Drizzle with the remaining tablespoon of olive oil and return to the oven for another 5 minutes until heated through. Serve hot with a crisp green salad.

Veggie Pad Thai

PREP 15 MINS COOK 15 MINS

Special equipment • wok

SERVES 4

9oz (250g) wide or medium
    rice noodles
3–4 tbsp vegetable oil
8oz (225g) firm tofu, diced
2 garlic cloves, finely chopped
1 large egg, lightly beaten
⅔ cup hot vegetable stock
juice of 1 lime
1 tsp Asian fish sauce, such as
    nam pla (optional)
2 tsp tamarind paste
2 tsp demerara (raw) sugar
1 tbsp soy sauce
1 fresh hot red chile pepper, seeded
    and finely chopped
⅓ cup dry-roasted peanuts, coarsely
    chopped
1 bunch of scallions, finely chopped
1 cup fresh bean sprouts (optional)
handful of fresh cilantro

1 Soak the rice noodles in a bowl of boiling hot water for 10 minutes, then drain. Heat 1 tablespoon of the vegetable oil in a wok over medium-high heat and swirl it around the pan. Add the tofu and cook for about 10 minutes until golden—you may need to use more oil. Remove with a slotted spoon and set aside.

2 Add another tablespoon of oil to the pan. When hot, add the garlic and cook for 10 seconds, then add the egg and cook, stirring and breaking it up with a wooden spoon, until scrambled. Remove from the pan and set aside.

3 Now add another tablespoon of the oil. Again, when hot, add the drained noodles and stir gently to coat with the oil. Pour in the stock, lime juice, fish sauce (if using), tamarind paste, sugar, and soy sauce; toss to combine. Let bubble for a few minutes, then stir in the chile.

4 Add half of the peanuts, the scallions, and the bean sprouts, and stir-fry for 1 minute. Now top with the reserved scrambled egg, stir to combine, and transfer to a serving plate. To serve, scatter the remaining peanuts over the top and sprinkle with cilantro.

Cheat...
Buy a prepared Pad Thai sauce and toss with the noodles for a quick home-from-work dish.

EVERYDAY

Potato cakes

PREP 10 MINS COOK 15 MINS

SERVES 2-4
about 2 cups leftover mashed
    potatoes
1 small onion, peeled and grated
handful of fresh chives,
    finely chopped
1 cup crumbled feta cheese
1 large egg, lightly beaten
sea salt and freshly ground
    black pepper
1 tbsp olive oil, plus more as needed
flour

1 Mix the mashed potatoes with
the onion, chives, feta cheese, and egg.
Season with plenty of salt and pepper.

2 Heat about 1 tablespoon olive oil
in a nonstick frying pan over medium
heat. Using floured hands, scoop up
large balls of the mixture, roll, and
flatten slightly. Carefully add to the
hot oil and cook for 2-3 minutes on
each side until golden, adding more
oil to the pan as needed. Serve hot
with a green salad.

Potato gnocchi

PREP 20 MINS COOK 5 MINS

SERVES 4
about 2 cups leftover mashed
    potatoes
1 large egg, lightly beaten
1-2 tbsp all-purpose flour, plus extra
    for the work surface
sea salt
tomato or Gorgonzola sauce, or olive
    oil and pesto (to serve)

1 Put the leftover mashed potatoes
in a bowl. Mix in the egg. Stir in
enough flour to form a soft dough.
Transfer to a floured work surface
and knead gently for a couple of
minutes—don't overwork the dough
or it will become tough.

2 Divide the mixture into four
equal portions and roll each into
a cylinder. Cut each one into pieces

about 1¼in (3cm) long. Use the back
of a fork to make a ridged pattern
on each piece.

3 Cook in a large pot of boiling
salted water for 2-3 minutes—when
they float to the surface, they are
ready. Scoop out using a slotted
spoon and divide among 4 shallow
bowls. Serve immediately with a
tomato or Gorgonzola sauce, or a
drizzle of extra virgin olive oil and
some pesto over the top.

COOK'S NOTES

*It's important that the potatoes
aren't too wet. You could boil
them in their skins, which will
help, but remember to peel them
before mashing.*

Potato and leek soup

PREP 5 MINS COOK 30 MINS

SERVES 4

1 tbsp olive oil
1 onion, finely chopped
4 leeks, sliced
sea salt and freshly ground
    black pepper
4 cups hot vegetable stock
about 1lb (450g) leftover boiled
    potatoes, cut into bite-sized pieces
    (about 2½ cups)
leaves from a few sprigs of
    fresh thyme

1 Heat the oil in a large saucepan over low heat. Add the onion and cook for about 5 minutes until soft. Add the leeks and cook for another 5 minutes. Season well with salt and pepper. Pour in the stock and bring to a boil. Reduce the heat slightly and simmer for about 10 minutes.

2 Add the potatoes and sprinkle with the thyme leaves. Continue cooking until the potatoes are heated through, then serve hot with some fresh crusty bread and a crisp green salad.

VARIATION
Add some chopped pre-cooked bacon or ham to the soup.

EVERYDAY

Potato and horseradish mash

 PREP 15 MINS COOK 20 MINS

SERVES 4

1 tbsp olive oil
1 tbsp butter
7 bacon slices, chopped
1lb (450g) leftover boiled potatoes,
    cut into bite-sized pieces (about
    2½ cups) or 2 cups leftover
    mashed potatoes
1 tbsp cream-style white horseradish
sea salt and freshly ground
    black pepper
8oz (225g) curly-leaf kale, cooked,
    chopped, and squeezed dry

1 Heat the oil and butter in a large nonstick frying pan over medium heat. When the butter has melted, add the bacon. Cook, stirring occasionally, for 5-6 minutes or until golden and crispy. Stir in the potatoes and horseradish and season well with salt and pepper.

2 Stir in the kale until well mixed. Cook for a few minutes until lightly golden and a little crispy on the bottom. Serve hot with some cooked red cabbage on the side.

EVERYDAY CHICKEN

Grilled, poached, steamed, baked, fried—
and always easy.

EVERYDAY CHICKEN

Chicken is not only one of the most versatile foods to cook, it is also a good value. Every part of it can be used in different ways: it can be roasted whole and unadorned (see p222); cut into serving-size pieces, seasoned with exotic spices, and cooked quickly under the broiler or slowly in the oven until meltingly tender. However chicken is cooked, it's always a favorite.

Chicken doner kebab.
For recipe, see page 120.

Free-range or organic?

Buying chicken can sometimes be confusing, with labeling varying from "free-range" and "organic," to "corn-fed" and "farm-fresh."

Free-range birds have been provided access to open-air runs. "Traditional free-range" follow stricter standards—the birds are given more freedom and space. Free-range birds must have continuous daytime access to the open air, for at least 50% of their lifetime.

Organic birds have been fed on a completely organic diet, given no meat by-products, and won't have been given antibiotics. They usually have outdoor access, and are reared for up to 12 weeks, twice as long as intensively-farmed chickens. They are often the most expensive choice, but you can taste the difference in the meat. Choose chickens that have a recognized "organic" certification.

Corn-fed simply means that the birds have been fed on a diet of corn or maize, resulting in a yellow, golden skin. It doesn't mean that they are free-range or organic.

Farm-fresh is a misleading label, and can still mean that the bird has been intensively farmed.

chicken nutrition

Chicken is packed with protein and is low in saturated fat. Most of the fat is in the skin, but this can easily be avoided by removing it before or after cooking. A 3½oz (100g) piece of skinless chicken breast has around 100 calories with 2g of fat; with the skin on, it has about 200 calories with 12g of fat. It's a good low-cholesterol meat choice, and provides all the essential amino acids, along with vitamins B6 and B12, needed for a healthy diet.

Quick-cook cuts A disjointed chicken provides many
different cuts, each one suiting various quick cooking methods.

CHOOSE		USE	COOK
	**BREAST** The breast is available on the bone (the most succulent), or as a fillet. It is the leanest and most popular part of the chicken, and is quick to cook. Breasts are usually around 6-7oz (175-200g) in weight, and are the most expensive cut of chicken.	Breast meat is more delicate than leg or thigh: if overcooked, it can become very dry. It can be dry-cooked (under the broiler, or on the grill), roasted, poached, pan-fried, or added to a casserole.	**Broil or grill** 4-5 mins each side over medium-low heat **Roast** 15-20 mins at 400°F (200°C) **Poach** 15-20 mins **Steam** 20-30 mins **Pan-fry** 6-8 mins each side, over high heat
	**LEG** The leg contains the drumstick, which is the lower end of the leg. The leg can also be bought attached to the thigh—a quarter joint. As the leg does all the work, there is more muscle, which turns the meat darker and makes it more flavorful. Legs are a cheaper alternative to breast meat.	Chicken legs are easy to cook. They can be dry-cooked (under the broiler, or on the grill), oven-cooked, poached, or added to a casserole. To check they are cooked, insert a skewer into the thickest part of the leg. If the juices run clear, they are cooked through; if not, cook for longer.	**Broil or grill** 15-20 mins each side, over low heat **Roast** 35-40 mins at 400°F (200°C) **Poach** 20-25 mins **Grill** 30-40 mins over medium-low heat
	**THIGHS** They are available on or off the bone, skin on, and skinless. As with the leg, the meat is darker, but thigh meat is more tender than leg meat. They are cheaper but smaller than the breast portions, so you should allow two per person.	Thighs with the bone in are a good choice for slow cooking. Boned thighs can be stuffed with a variety of flavors, from mushrooms to nuts and spices, and then pan-fried or roasted until cooked through. The meat from boneless thighs can be skinned and chopped for casseroles or stews, or for skewering onto kebabs.	**Roast (bone in)** 35-40 mins at 400°F (200°C) **(bone out)** 25-30 mins at 400°F (200°C) **Broil or grill (bone out)** 25-30 mins, over high heat **Pan-fry (bone in)** 8-10 mins each side, over medium-high heat **(bone out)** 6-8 mins each side, over medium-high heat
	WINGS Bony wing sections have dark meat and are delicious when cooked until the skin is crispy. There is not much meat on them, so allow 4-5 per person. Wings contain around 100 calories each, so they are not a low-fat option.	To get the best from chicken wings, they need to be marinated for a few hours in something hot and spicy (such as cayenne pepper, olive oil, and garlic), or sticky and sweet (such as honey, soy sauce, and Worcestershire sauce). They need a hot, dry heat, so are best oven-roasted or grilled.	**Roast** 30-40 mins at 400°F (200°C) **Broil or grill** 30-40 mins over medium-low heat

Time-saving techniques
Six quick and simple ways to prepare and cook chicken—each technique results in a different flavor and texture. The first three are preparation techniques, and the last three are cooking techniques.

Flatten
Pounding a chicken breast so it is thin and even will speed up the cooking time.

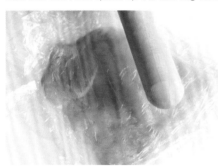

1 Place a skinless chicken breast fillet between two sheets of plastic wrap on a clean board.

2 Pound evenly with a meat mallet, or the side of a rolling pin, until it is an even thickness, about ¼in (5mm).

3 Remove the plastic wrap and season. Flattened chicken breast fillet needs only 2-3 minutes of pan-frying or grilling on each side.

Stuff
Stuffing a chicken breast adds extra flavor and keeps the chicken moist.

1 Lay a skinned chicken breast on a clean board and pound briefly with a meat mallet or the side of a rolling pin to flatten it a little.

2 Working out from the middle, slash each side with a knife, making sure you don't cut all the way through, to form a pocket for the filling.

3 Fill and pull together tightly. Wrap with pancetta or bacon, or cook cut-side down and cook in a little olive oil for 6-8 minutes each side, or until cooked through.

Skewer
Threading small pieces of chicken onto skewers will speed up the cooking time.

1 Soak wooden skewers for 30 minutes in cold water, so they don't burn. Use 2 chicken breast fillets or 2 thigh fillets for 6 skewers.

2 Cut 1 portion into bite-sized pieces, then thread onto the skewers, about 6 per stick. Cut the other portion into strips, and thread onto the skewers. Marinate (see overleaf for suggestions).

3 Sit the skewers on a hot ridged cast-iron grill pan or under a broiler and cook for 3-4 minutes each side, or until cooked through and charred.

Roast
Oven-roasting suits most cuts (see left), as well as a whole bird.

1 Preheat the oven to 400°F (200°C). Sit a 3lb (1.35kg) chicken in a roasting pan and smear with butter (using your hands).

2 Season and sprinkle with a handful of fresh thyme leaves. Stuff two lemon halves into the cavity to help it stay moist, then put in the oven.

3 Cook for 30 minutes, remove, and spoon the juices in the pan all over the bird (basting), then cook for about another hour, until golden and cooked. To test, pierce the thigh with a skewer: if the juices run clear, it's ready.

Steam
Steaming keeps the chicken moist. A healthy way to cook chicken breasts.

1 Preheat the oven to 400°F (200°C). Lay out a large piece of foil, then sit a chicken breast, plump side up, in it.

2 Season well, add in a handful of fresh herbs and a few lemon wedges, and pour in 1 tablespoon of dry white wine, then close the foil, leaving plenty of room for the chicken, sealing the edges together tightly to seal.

3 Sit on a baking sheet, and put in the oven to cook for 20-30 minutes, or until cooked through. Be careful when opening the parcel as it will be hot, and full of steam.

Poach
Cooking in liquid keeps the chicken moist. Suits breasts and legs.

1 Put 2 breasts or legs, plump side up, in a deep-sided frying pan with some lemon slices, a handful of fresh parsley (or fresh herb of your choice), a pinch of salt, and 1 teaspoon of black peppercorns.

2 Pour in enough cold water to cover, then bring to a boil. Simmer gently, sitting a lid loosely on top, and cook for 15-20 minutes for breasts, or 20-25 minutes for legs.

3 Turn off the heat and leave the chicken in the pan for about 5 minutes. Remove with a slotted spoon and serve immediately.

5 quick flavor mixes for chicken

Transform chicken from simple to special with these fresh, hot, and aromatic spice and herb combinations. Use as rubs or marinades before broiling, roasting, or barbecuing.

Thai spice
A wonderful assortment of colorful, aromatic, and pungent spices.

Mix together a couple of finely shredded **lemongrass stalks**, 6 finely chopped and seeded **red** and **green chiles**, a thumb-sized piece of grated **fresh ginger**, 1 tbsp **lime juice**, a handful of **fresh cilantro**, and 1 tbsp **dark soy sauce**. Will keep, chilled, for 3–4 days.

Use to marinate chicken pieces (preferably overnight), before pan-frying or roasting in the oven.

Caribbean spice
A diverse fusion of hot and peppery tropical spices.

Process a handful of **fresh thyme** leaves, 2–3 **Scotch Bonnet chiles**, 1 tbsp **black peppercorns**, 1 tsp **sea salt**, and 2 tsp **allspice** in a food processor, or pound in a mortar and pestle until finely ground. Will keep, chilled, for 3–4 days.

Smother the chicken portions in olive oil, add to a plastic bag with the spice mix, and shake. Let marinate, preferably overnight. Broil or grill for 30–40 minutes, turning once, until cooked through.

Indian spice
A delicious warm and fragrant mix of dry spices, fiery chiles, and cooling yogurt.

Crush 1 tsp **cardamom seeds** and 1 tsp **coriander seeds**, then seed and chop 2 **jalapeño chiles**. Measure out 3 tsp each of **garam masala** and **turmeric**. Will keep, chilled, for 3–4 days.

Put the crushed spices in a hot pan with a little oil or ghee. Cook for a minute, then add the chiles. Mix 8oz (225g) Greek yogurt with the ground spices and smother over chicken thighs. Cook for 8–10 minutes each side.

Mediterranean herbs
A classic mix: light, sweet, and woody herbs with the sharp tang of lemon.

Combine 2 tsp **dried oregano** in a bowl with 3 **crushed garlic cloves**, a few **fresh rosemary** and **thyme sprigs**, 1 tbsp **black pitted olives** (optional), and 2 **lemon wedges**. Will keep, refrigerated, for 3–4 days.

Rub chicken thighs or legs with olive oil, season, and place in a roasting pan. Smother the chicken pieces with the mix, and cook in the oven at 400°F (200°C) for 35–40 minutes.

Moroccan spice A blend of sweet and tangy flavors, scented and perfumed to add a distinctive taste and aroma.

Combine 1 tbsp each of **smoked paprika** and **harissa paste** with 2 tbsp **lemon juice**, 2 **cinnamon sticks**, and a handful of **preserved lemons**, chopped.

Cook chicken thighs in a large flameproof casserole dish with a little olive oil, then add the spice mixture, along with some tomato paste, and cook, covered, over medium heat for 30–40 minutes. At the end of cooking, stir in some chopped **fresh flat-leaf parsley**.

Storing chicken

Chill Cooked and uncooked chicken should be kept in the refrigerator at all times, and used within a couple of days of purchase (or by the use-by date on the package). Keep uncooked chicken tightly wrapped in plastic wrap at the bottom of the refrigerator, and keep it away from other foods, particularly cooked meats. Don't let it sit for long at room temperature, as this is when germs can breed.

Freeze Freeze uncooked chicken right away, and make sure it is well wrapped in plastic wrap, so it doesn't get freezer burn. It will freeze for up to 6 months. Never freeze uncooked chicken ready-stuffed. Cooked chicken is best frozen in a freezer-proof plastic container with a sealable lid. Only freeze cooked chicken if it is covered in a sauce, otherwise it will become dry and tasteless. Freeze for up to 3 months. Defrost in the refrigerator overnight.

Reheating chicken

Chicken can be reheated only once. Don't reheat it if it's still warm—it needs to be cooled quickly and completely chilled in the refrigerator. Reheat it until it is piping hot, as bacteria is killed at high heat (above 165°F/75°C, to be precise). Put your dish in the microwave, cover with a plate to retain moisture, and cook on high for 3–4 minutes.

Tools of the trade

For pan-frying, a large **heavy-bottomed frying pan** is essential. A **pair of metal tongs** are also good to have on hand for turning the chicken while it's cooking. A **heavy-duty roasting pan** and **baking sheet** are good to have, as they don't buckle under high heat. A **cast-iron ridged grill pan** is excellent for cooking chicken, and a combination of **wooden and metal skewers** is needed for kebabs.

Psst...

To save on time and money spent on store-bought spice blends, get creative. Go through your cupboards and process your own blend of herbs and spices in the food processor. Keep in a sealed jar until needed (no more than 6 months). Turmeric and cumin seeds, below, can be blended with other Indian spices.

Tools for cooking everyday chicken dishes.

Garlic and chile chicken with honey-sweet potatoes

  PREP 15 MINS **COOK 1¼ HRS**

SERVES 4

8 chicken pieces (preferably a mixture of free-range thighs and drumsticks)
sea salt and freshly ground black pepper
4 sweet potatoes, peeled and coarsely chopped
1–2 tbsp honey
2 tbsp olive oil
2 fresh red jalapeño chile peppers, seeded and sliced
a few sprigs of fresh thyme
½ garlic bulb, cloves separated, peeled, and smashed
½ cup dry white wine
1¼ cups hot chicken stock

1 Preheat the oven to 400°F (200°C). Season the chicken well with salt and pepper and coat the sweet potatoes with the honey.

2 In a large heavy flameproof casserole, heat 1 tablespoon of the oil

over medium heat. Add the sweet potatoes and cook for 5 minutes until beginning to brown, then remove from the pan and set aside.

3 Increase the heat to medium-high and heat the remaining oil in the same pan. Brown the chicken for about 5 minutes on each side until nicely golden all over. Add the chiles, thyme, and garlic. Return the sweet potatoes to the pan and season well.

4 Pour in the wine and stock, cover the pan, and transfer to the oven to cook for 1 hour. Check the casserole a few times during cooking, stirring if needed, or add a small amount of stock if it is too dry. Serve hot with thick slices of fresh crusty bread.

Substitute your favorite winter squash for the sweet potatoes.

Spanish-style chicken with pine nuts

PREP 10 MINS **COOK 1 HR**

SERVES 4

2 tbsp olive oil
8 chicken thighs (preferably free-range)
1 onion, finely chopped
sea salt and freshly ground black pepper
3 garlic cloves, finely chopped
6 ripe tomatoes, peeled and chopped
½ cup dry red wine
4 cups hot chicken stock
handful of pine nuts, toasted
handful of golden raisins (optional)

1 In a large cast iron or other flameproof casserole, heat 1 tbsp of the oil over medium-high heat. Add the chicken and cook for about 5 minutes on each side until golden all over. Remove from the pan and set aside.

2 Reduce the heat to medium. Add the remaining oil, the onion, and a pinch of salt to the same pan and cook for about 5 minutes until soft.

3 Stir in the garlic and fresh tomatoes and season with pepper. Cook for a few minutes until the tomatoes start to break down. Add the red wine, increase the heat slightly, and let bubble for a few minutes.

4 Stir in the hot stock and bring to a boil. Reduce the heat to low and return the chicken to the pan along with the pine nuts and raisins. Gently simmer for 30–40 minutes, adding a little hot water if the mixture becomes dry. Serve hot with rice or boiled new potatoes.

COOK'S NOTES

An enameled cast-iron Dutch oven is ideal for this sort of dish. It can be used on the cooktop or in the oven, and you can cook the dish as fast or slow as you wish without the food burning.

Chicken thighs stuffed with pistachios and chiles

  PREP 15 MINS **COOK 35 MINS**

Special equipment • food processor

SERVES 4

For the stuffing
1 cup shelled and skinned pistachios, ground in a food processor
handful of chopped flat-leaf parsley
2–3 fresh red jalapeño chile peppers, seeded and finely chopped
olive oil
sea salt and freshly ground black pepper

4 large skinless boneless chicken thighs (preferably free-range)
8 thin slices prosciutto
1 tbsp olive oil

1 Preheat the oven to 400°F (200°C). To make the stuffing, mix together the nuts, parsley, chiles, and a drizzle of olive oil in a bowl. Season well with salt and pepper and set aside.

2 Using a sharp knife, cut diagonal slashes across the chicken pieces, but without slicing all the way through. Carefully spoon the stuffing mixture into the gaps, dividing it evenly among the pieces. You may have some stuffing left over. (See Cook's Notes.)

3 Lay out 4 slices of the prosciutto on a flat work surface and place a chicken thigh on top of each one. Roll up each thigh in the prosciutto so that you have 4 parcels. Use the remaining prosciutto to wrap around each thigh in the opposite direction, so the chicken is completely enclosed.

4 Place the parcels in a roasting pan, drizzle with the olive oil, and roast in the oven for 30–35 minutes or until cooked through. Serve with a salad and bread.

 VARIATION
If you can't find large thigh fillets, use skinless boneless chicken breast halves instead.

COOK'S NOTES
If you have some stuffing mixture left over, sprinkle it over the wrapped chicken pieces before they go into the oven.

Chicken poached in coconut milk

  PREP 5 MINS **COOK 15 MINS**

SERVES 4

8 boneless chicken breast halves (preferably free-range), skin on, about 7oz (200g) each
2 cups hot chicken or vegetable stock
1 x 14oz (400ml) can unsweetened coconut milk, well shaken to blend
3 bay leaves
3 garlic cloves, peeled but left whole

1 To poach the chicken, put the breasts in a large pan over medium heat, then pour in the hot stock and the coconut milk. Add the bay leaves and garlic cloves. Bring to a boil, then cover the pan, reduce the heat to low, and simmer for 10–15 minutes until the chicken is cooked through. Poke a sharp knife into the flesh to check doneness—the juices should run clear.

2 Using a slotted spoon, remove the chicken from the pan and leave to cool for a minute or two. When cool enough to handle, discard the skin and either slice or shred the chicken using two forks and serve with fluffy rice.

 VARIATION
You could poach the chicken in boiling water and 2–3 tbsp soy sauce if you have no coconut milk.

COOK'S NOTES
Serve any rice you wish, but basmati is always a good choice. For maximum flavor, wait until the chicken is cooked before making the rice, then use the coconut poaching liquid instead of water for cooking it.

Chicken with cider and cream

PREP 10 MINS | COOK 1 HR

SERVES 4

about 1 tbsp olive oil
2 onions, cut into 8 wedges
sea salt and freshly ground
    black pepper
2 garlic cloves, finely chopped
8 chicken thighs (preferably free-range)
1¼ cups hard cider, apple cider, or
    unsweetened apple juice
1¼ cups heavy whipping cream
a few sprigs of fresh rosemary

1 Preheat the oven to 400°F (200°C). Heat 1 tablespoon olive oil in a large cast iron or other flameproof casserole over medium-low heat. Add the onion and a pinch of salt and cook for 5 minutes until soft. Now add the garlic and cook for 10 seconds.

2 Push the onions to one side of the casserole and increase the heat to medium-high. Add a little more oil if needed and add the chicken thighs, skin-side down. Brown for about 10 minutes, turning once, until golden.

3 Increase the heat slightly and pour in the cider. Let bubble for a few minutes, then reduce the heat to a simmer and add the cream. Add the rosemary sprigs and season well with salt and pepper.

4 Cover and transfer to the oven to cook for about 40 minutes. If it is becoming too dry, add a little hot water or stock. Serve hot with mashed potatoes and crusty bread to mop up all the juices.

Chicken with noodles and basil

PREP 5 MINS | COOK 15 MINS |

Special equipment • wok

SERVES 4

1 tbsp sesame oil
2 large skinless boneless chicken
    breast halves (preferably free-
    range), sliced
1 tbsp soy sauce
1 tbsp honey
10oz (300g) thick or medium ready-
    to-use udon noodles
handful of fresh basil leaves, torn

1 Heat the oil in a large wok or frying pan over medium-high heat. When hot, swirl it around the pan and add the chicken. Stir-fry quickly for a few minutes until beginning to turn golden. Remove from the pan and set aside to keep warm.

2 Add the soy sauce and honey to the pan and let bubble for a minute or so. Return the chicken to the pan along with the noodles and stir so that everything is well coated.

3 When ready to serve, stir in the basil. Serve immediately.

Chicken with fava beans

SERVES 4

8 chicken thighs (preferably free-range)
sea salt and freshly ground
    black pepper
2 tbsp olive oil
1 onion, finely chopped
2 celery stalks, finely chopped
2 garlic cloves, finely chopped
a few sprigs of fresh rosemary, leaves
    picked and finely chopped
¾ cup dry white wine
7–10oz (300g) package frozen fava
    beans (or fresh, if in season), or
    frozen baby lima beans
2 cups hot chicken stock

1 Preheat the oven to 400°F (200°C).

2 Season the chicken with salt and pepper. Heat 1 tbsp of the oil in a large flameproof casserole over medium-high heat. Add the chicken, skin-side down, and brown for 10–12 minutes, turning once, until golden all over. Remove from the pan and set aside.

3 Reduce the heat to low and add the remaining oil to the casserole. Add the onion and a pinch of salt and cook for 5 minutes until soft. Now add the celery, garlic, and rosemary and cook for another 5 minutes. Increase the heat, pour in the wine, and let bubble for about 5 minutes.

4 Stir in the fava beans and return the chicken to the pan, tucking the pieces in and around the beans. Pour in the stock, cover, and cook in the oven for 45 minutes to 1 hour. Check halfway through the cooking time, adding a little hot water if the mixture appears dry. Serve with oven-roasted tomatoes and fresh crusty bread.

VARIATION
You could make this dish using good-quality link sausages instead of chicken.

Cheat...
Frozen fava beans are a fantastic stand-in for fresh; always keep a bag on hand in the freezer.

Chicken with chicory and bacon

SERVES 4

1 tbsp butter
pinch of demerara (raw) sugar
3 heads chicory, halved lengthwise
1 tbsp olive oil
4 large boneless chicken breast halves
    (preferably free-range), skin on
6–12 bacon slices

1 Preheat the oven to 400°F (200°C). Put the butter and the sugar in a large frying pan over low heat. Cook until the sugar has dissolved and the butter has melted. Add the chicory, and cook, turning, for 5–8 minutes until golden, then set aside.

2 Increase the heat to medium-high and add the olive oil to the same pan. When hot, add the chicken, skin-side down, and brown for 3–5 minutes on each side until golden all over. Transfer the chicken to a roasting pan.

3 Wrap 1 or 2 slices of bacon around each reserved chicory portion to cover and tuck them into the roasting pan between the chicken pieces. (Pack everything tightly in the pan, so the dish will produce plenty of juices.) Roast in the oven for 25 minutes until golden. Serve hot with roast potatoes.

VARIATION
Use pancetta or prosciutto instead of bacon.

COOK'S NOTES
Sprinkle Parmesan or Gruyère cheese over the chicory once you have put it in the roasting tin, if you like.

EVERYDAY

Chicken stir-fried with scallions, basil, and lemongrass

PREP 10 MINS   COOK 15 MINS

Special equipment • wok

SERVES 4

2–3 skinless boneless chicken breast
   halves (preferably free-range), about
   7oz (200g) each, sliced into strips
sea salt and freshly ground
   black pepper
1 tbsp cornstarch
2 tbsp sesame oil
bunch of scallions, sliced diagonally
3 garlic cloves, sliced
1 stalk fresh lemongrass, tough outer
   leaves removed, chopped
2 fresh red mild chile peppers, seeded
   and sliced
1 tbsp Chinese rice wine
handful of fresh basil leaves

1 Season the chicken with salt and
pepper. Put the cornstarch in a bowl
and toss the chicken strips in it until
very well coated.

2 Heat 1 tablespoon of the oil in a
wok over high heat. Swirl around the
pan, then add the chicken and stir-fry
quickly, moving the chicken around the
pan for 3–5 minutes until golden and
cooked through. Remove with a slotted
spoon and set aside to keep warm.

3 Carefully wipe out the wok with
paper towels, reduce the heat to
medium-high, and add the remaining
oil. When hot, add the scallions, garlic,
lemongrass, and chiles. Stir-fry for a
couple of minutes, then increase the
heat to high once again, and add the
rice wine. Let bubble for a few minutes.

4 Return the chicken to the pan to
just heat through, stir in the basil, and
serve at once with some fluffy rice.

VARIATION

This is equally tasty
made with shrimp
instead of chicken.

COOK'S NOTES

*Tossing the chicken in cornstarch is
key; it gives it an almost batter-
like coating, and makes the chicken
light and a little crispy.*

Five-spice and honey chicken with peppered greens

PREP 10 MINS   COOK 40 MINS

SERVES 4

2 handfuls of Chinese greens, such as
   bok choy, sliced
splash of soy sauce
1in (2.5cm) piece of fresh ginger,
   finely grated
pinch of crushed red pepper flakes
sea salt and freshly ground
   black pepper
1–2 tbsp honey
juice of 2 limes
3 tbsp olive oil
2 tbsp Asian five-spice paste or 2 tsp
   five-spice powder
8 chicken pieces (a mixture of
   thighs and drumsticks, preferably
   free-range)

1 Preheat the oven to 400°F (200°C).
Put the greens in a large bowl. Add
the soy sauce, ginger, and pepper
flakes and season well with salt and
pepper. Set aside.

2 In another bowl, mix together the
honey, lime juice, 1 tablespoon of the
oil, and the five-spice paste until well
combined. Coat the chicken well and
season with salt and pepper. Leave to
marinate for at least 20 minutes if
you have time.

3 Heat 1 more tablespoon of the oil
in a large frying pan over medium-
high heat. Working in batches, add the
chicken pieces, skin-side down. Cook
for 5–8 minutes on each side until
golden and crispy, then transfer to
a roasting pan. Roast in the oven
for about 40 minutes until beginning
to char.

4 Meanwhile, wipe out the frying pan
with paper towels, reduce the heat
slightly, and add the greens. Drizzle
in the remaining 1 tablespoon oil, and
stir-fry for about 5 minutes until
beginning to wilt. Serve hot with the
crispy-skinned chicken.

EVERYDAY

Pan-fried chicken stuffed with spinach and Gruyère

 PREP 15 MINS   COOK 30 MINS

SERVES 4

8oz (225g) fresh spinach leaves
½ cup shredded Gruyère cheese
pinch of grated fresh nutmeg
sea salt and freshly ground
    black pepper
4 large skinless boneless chicken
    breast halves or thighs (preferably
    free-range), about 9oz (250g) each
1 tbsp olive oil
8–12 cherry tomatoes

1 First, prepare the spinach. Put in a saucepan with a little water (the water clinging to the freshly-rinsed leaves may be enough) and cook for a few minutes, stirring, until just wilted. Alternatively, put in a microwave-safe bowl, cover loosely, and wilt in the microwave on medium for 2 minutes. Drain and squeeze out the excess water. Mix the spinach with the Gruyère and nutmeg and season well with salt and pepper.

2 Slice each of the chicken pieces lengthwise to form a pocket—be careful not to cut all the way through.

Stuff each one with some of the mixture, then fold over to seal.

3 Heat the olive oil in a frying pan over medium-high heat. Carefully add the chicken breasts, pocket-side down, and leave to cook undisturbed for 5–7 minutes. Carefully turn over and cook the other side for about the same time until golden and cooked all the way through.

4 Meanwhile, add the tomatoes to the pan toward the end of the cooking time. Leave them to sit undisturbed for 5 minutes until they begin to split. Remove the chicken from the pan when it is cooked and set aside to keep warm. Stir the tomatoes around for a couple of minutes to break them up a little, then serve with the warm chicken.

COOK'S NOTES

For that little something extra, add a splash of good balsamic vinegar to the tomatoes while they are cooking.

Chicken stuffed with wild mushrooms and thyme

 PREP 10 MINS   COOK 25 MINS

Soaking • 30 minutes

SERVES 4

scant 1oz (25g) mixed dried
    mushrooms
4 large skinless boneless chicken
    breast halves (preferably
    free-range), about 9oz (250g) each
sea salt and freshly ground
    black pepper
handful of fresh thyme sprigs
splash of Asian hot chili oil (optional)
1 tbsp olive oil

1 Put the dried mushrooms in a small heatproof bowl. Add just enough boiling water to cover and leave to soften for 30 minutes. Drain through a fine sieve, reserving the soaking liquid. Coarsely chop the mushrooms if they are large.

2 Slice the chicken breasts lengthwise to form a pocket—be careful not to cut all the way through. Season well with salt, pepper, and half of the thyme sprigs. Put the soaked mushrooms, remaining thyme, and chili oil (if using) in a bowl, and

season well. Mix together, then stuff each chicken breast with the mixture and fold over the top to seal.

3 Heat the oil in a large frying pan over medium-high heat. Carefully add the chicken, pocket-side down. Leave to cook undisturbed for 5–7 minutes, then carefully turn over and cook the other side for about the same time until cooked through. Remove from the pan and set aside to keep warm.

4 Pour the reserved mushroom soaking liquid into the pan. Increase the heat and let bubble and reduce by half. To serve, spoon a little of the reduced mushroom stock over the chicken and serve with creamy mashed potatoes.

COOK'S NOTES

Do pass the reserved liquid from the mushrooms through a fine sieve before using, as it can be very gritty.

Chicken cooked in wine with capers

SERVES 4

4 skinless boneless chicken breast
 halves (preferably free-range),
 about 7oz (200g) each
1 tbsp all-purpose flour
1–2 tbsp olive oil
⅔ cup dry white wine
⅔ cup hot chicken stock
handful of capers, rinsed, gently
 squeezed dry, and coarsely
 chopped if large
sea salt and freshly ground
 black pepper
handful of flat-leaf parsley, finely
 chopped

1 Sandwich the chicken breasts
between 2 large sheets of plastic wrap
and pound with a meat mallet or the
side of a rolling pin until thin and an
even thickness. Lightly dust each one
with flour.

2 Heat the oil in a large heavy frying
pan over high heat. Cook the chicken
breasts two at a time for 6–8 minutes,
turning once, until golden. Remove
from the pan and set aside on a plate
to keep warm.

3 Pour the wine into the pan and
increase the heat. Let bubble for
a few minutes, scraping up any bits
from the bottom of the pan with a
wooden spoon, until the alcohol has
evaporated. Now pour in the stock
and boil for about 5 minutes until
the sauce has reduced and slightly
thickened. Add the capers, taste,
and season with salt and pepper
if needed.

4 Return the chicken to the pan,
heat through for a few seconds, then
sprinkle with the parsley. Serve
immediately with crusty bread.

Chicken flattened and breaded with lemon and sage

SERVES 4

4 large skinless boneless chicken
 breast halves, 7oz (200g) each
sea salt and freshly ground
 black pepper
1 cup toasted homemade bread crumbs
 (from 3–4 slices firm white bread)
grated zest and juice of 1 lemon
1 tbsp all-purpose flour
1 egg, lightly beaten
1 tbsp olive oil
4–6 fresh sage leaves, finely chopped

1 Sandwich the chicken breasts
between 2 sheets of plastic wrap and
pound with a meat mallet or the side of
a rolling pin until very thin and evenly
flattened. Season with salt and pepper.

2 Combine the bread crumbs and
lemon zest in a bowl and season well
with salt and pepper. Mix together,
then turn out onto a plate. Now put

the flour on another plate and the
beaten egg onto yet another. Coat the
chicken first in the flour, then the egg,
and finally in the bread crumbs.

3 Heat the oil in a heavy frying pan
over high heat. Cook the chicken two
pieces at a time for 8–10 minutes,
turning once, until golden. Add oil as
needed. Transfer to a warm platter.
Squeeze the lemon juice into the pan,
scraping up any browned bits with
a wooden spoon, and mix in the sage.
Scrape the mixture over the chicken
and serve hot, with a mixed salad.

Cheat...
*If you don't want to
make your own, you can
buy ready-made dried
bread crumbs and
store them until
required.*

Chinese-style salt and pepper chicken drumsticks

 PREP 10 MINS **COOK 25 MINS**

Special equipment • bamboo steamer

SERVES 4

8 chicken drumsticks
2 tbsp all-purpose flour
1 tbsp sea salt
1 tbsp freshly cracked black pepper
about 2 tbsp vegetable oil
3 fresh hot red chile peppers, seeded and sliced into strips lengthwise
bunch of scallions, sliced diagonally
lemon wedges, for serving

1 Lay the chicken drumsticks in a bamboo or other steamer basket (or use a colander fitted inside a large pot if you don't have a steamer basket). Place the steamer over a pan of boiling water, cover, and steam for 10–15 minutes. Remove the chicken from the pan and let cool slightly.

2 Preheat the oven to 400°F (200°C). Mix together the flour, salt, and pepper. Firmly pat the mixture all over the chicken to coat. Place the drumsticks in a roasting pan with 1 tbsp of vegetable oil and cook for 10–15 minutes until crispy and golden.

3 Meanwhile, heat the remaining 1 tablespoon of vegetable oil in a wok or frying pan over high heat. Add the chiles and scallions and cook for about 5 minutes until lightly browned at the edges. Remove with a slotted spoon and drain on paper towels. To serve, sprinkle the scallion mixture over the hot drumsticks and garnish with lemon wedges for squeezing.

 VARIATION Use chicken wings instead of drumsticks—they will need a little less cooking time for both the steaming and roasting.

Flattened chicken with tomato sauce

 PREP 10 MINS **COOK 20 MINS**

SERVES 4

4 small skinless boneless chicken breast halves (preferably free-range), about 4oz (115g) each
sea salt and freshly ground black pepper
1 tbsp all-purpose flour
2 tbsp olive oil
1 onion, very finely diced
2 garlic cloves, grated
1 x 14oz (400g) can diced tomatoes, with juices

1 Sandwich each chicken breast between 2 large sheets of plastic wrap and pound with a meat mallet or the side of a rolling pin until evenly flattened and about ¼in (6mm) thick. Season well with salt and pepper, dust with the flour, and set aside.

2 Heat 1 tablespoon of the oil in a large frying pan over low heat. Add the onion and cook for 5 minutes until

soft. Add the garlic and cook, stirring, for about 10 seconds.

3 Stir in the tomatoes and their juices and bring to a boil. Reduce the heat to a low simmer and cook for about 20 minutes, stirring occasionally. Season well with salt and pepper.

4 Meanwhile, heat the remaining oil in another frying pan over high heat. Add the chicken and cook for 10–15 minutes, turning once, until golden and cooked through. Remove from the pan and serve immediately with the rich tomato sauce spooned over the top.

COOK'S NOTES

A tablespoon of pesto stirred into the sauce really peps up the flavors; alternatively, stir in a pinch of red pepper flakes.

EVERYDAY

Hot and sour chicken

PREP 10 MINS · **COOK 20 MINS**

SERVES 4

2 cups hot vegetable or chicken stock
splash of soy sauce
2 skinless boneless chicken breast
    halves (preferably free-range),
    about 6oz (175g) each
2–4 tbsp Thai tom yum paste
1 bunch of scallions, sliced
8oz (225g) mushrooms, halved or
    quartered, if large
6 tomatoes, peeled and quartered
splash of Asian fish sauce such as
    (*nam pla*)
sea salt and freshly ground
    black pepper

1 To poach the chicken, bring the stock and soy sauce to a boil in a large pan. Add the chicken, reduce the heat, and simmer for 10–15 minutes until the chicken is cooked. Remove with a slotted spoon and set aside. Slice or shred when cool enough to handle.

2 Stir the tom yum paste into the stock until it dissolves, then add the scallions, mushrooms, and tomatoes, and simmer for 5–8 minutes. Return the chicken to the pan.

3 If the liquid has reduced too much during cooking, add more stock. Add a splash of fish sauce, taste, and season accordingly with salt and pepper—or add more fish sauce. Serve hot.

Cheat...
If you use cherry tomatoes, you don't have to peel them first.

COOK'S NOTES

Tom yum paste is available in most large supermarkets and speciality Asian food stores.

Lemon-soy skewered chicken with hot dipping sauce

PREP 15 MINS · **COOK 10 MINS**

Special equipment · 8 skewers

SERVES 4

1 stalk fresh lemongrass, tough outer
    leaves removed, finely chopped
juice of 1 lemon
1 tbsp soy sauce
1 tsp granulated sugar
sea salt and freshly ground
    black pepper
4 skinless boneless chicken breast
    halves or thighs, 7oz (200g) each
peanut or vegetable oil
4–5½oz (150g) thin rice stick noodles

For the dipping sauce
4 garlic cloves, finely grated
4 fresh hot red chile peppers, seeded
    and finely chopped
1 tbsp rice wine vinegar
pinch of granulated sugar
juice of 1 lemon

1 Combine the lemongrass, lemon juice, soy sauce, and sugar in a bowl. Season with salt and pepper. Cut each chicken fillet in half lengthwise and add to the lemongrass mixture. Let marinate while you prepare the noodles and dipping sauce.

2 Prepare the rice noodles as the package directs; drain and keep warm.

3 To make the dipping sauce, combine the garlic, chiles, vinegar, and sugar in a small saucepan. Add 2 tablespoons water and heat gently until the sugar has dissolved—do not boil. Allow to cool, then stir in the lemon juice.

4 Thread the chicken lengthwise onto 8 medium skewers, allowing two for each serving. Heat a ridged cast-iron grill pan or frying pan until hot. Brush lightly with oil and grill the chicken for 3–4 minutes on each side until cooked through and lightly charred. Serve with the dipping sauce and the rice noodles.

VARIATION
This dish is equally good made with pork instead of chicken.

EVERYDAY

Piri piri chicken

PREP 10 MINS **COOK 1 HR**

Marinating • 30 minutes
Special equipment • food processor

SERVES 4
For the piri piri
2–3 fresh red hot chiles, seeded
and finely chopped
2 garlic cloves, peeled
handful of fresh cilantro,
finely chopped
handful of flat-leaf parsley,
finely chopped
2–3 tbsp olive oil
1 tbsp tomato purée
juice of 1 lemon
sea salt and freshly ground
black pepper

1 whole chicken, about 3½lb (1.6kg),
spatchcocked (see Cook's Notes)

1 To make the piri piri, put the chiles, garlic, cilantro, and parsley in a food processor. Add a little of the oil and pulse on and off until it begins to form a paste. Add the remaining oil, tomato purée, and lemon juice, season with salt and pepper, and process to blend.

2 Put the chicken in a shallow glass or ceramic dish and season all over with salt and pepper. Rub with the piri piri paste so that the entire chicken is evenly covered. Cover with plastic wrap and leave to marinate for at least 30 minutes at room temperature, or preferably overnight in the refrigerator.

3 Preheat the oven to 400°F (200°C). Place the chicken in a shallow roasting pan and roast for 40–50 minutes in the oven until cooked through, golden, and crispy. Let rest a few minutes, then cut into quarters and serve with rice and a green salad.

COOK'S NOTES

"Spatchcocked" simply means that the chicken has been flattened and the backbone removed. It cooks far quicker this way. Buy one ready-prepared, ask the butcher to do it for you, or do it yourself (see p432).

Ground chicken with exotic mushrooms, soy, and lime

PREP 10 MINS **COOK 20 MINS**

Special equipment • food processor

SERVES 4
2 or 3 skinless boneless chicken
breast halves, about 7oz (200g)
each, coarsely chopped
1 tbsp olive oil
1 onion, finely chopped
sea salt and freshly ground
black pepper
1 garlic clove, finely chopped
1 fresh red jalapeño chile pepper,
seeded and finely chopped
12oz (350g) mixed fresh exotic or
wild mushrooms (such as oyster,
shiitake, and enoki), or cultivated
mushrooms, finely chopped
3 tbsp soy sauce
juice of 2 limes
handful of fresh cilantro,
finely chopped
handful of fresh basil leaves,
finely chopped
hot cooked rice, to serve

1 Pulse the chicken in a food processor until finely chopped. Set aside.

2 Heat the oil in a large frying pan over medium heat. Add the onion and a pinch of salt and cook for 5 minutes until soft. Stir in the garlic and chile and cook for a few seconds more.

3 Add the chicken to the pan, season well with salt and pepper, and cook, stirring occasionally, for a few minutes until the chicken is no longer pink. Stir in the mushrooms and cook for about 5 minutes longer.

4 Stir in the soy sauce and lime juice and cook for 2 minutes. Taste and season again if needed. Just before serving, stir in the cilantro and basil. Serve immediately with the hot rice, either on the side or mixed together.

VARIATION

For a lower-fat version, grind turkey breast instead of chicken.

COOK'S NOTES

A splash of Asian fish sauce (such as nam pla) adds extra zest to this dish.

Jerk chicken with roasted pineapple

PREP 10 MINS · COOK 40 MINS

Marinating • 30 minutes
Special equipment • food processor

SERVES 4
For the jerk marinade
2 fresh red hot chiles, seeded
2 fresh green hot chiles, seeded
pinch of ground cinnamon
pinch of grated fresh nutmeg
pinch of sea salt
1 tsp freshly cracked black pepper
grated zest and juice of 2 limes
3 tbsp light or dark brown sugar
2 tbsp vegetable oil
handful of flat-leaf parsley
handful of fresh cilantro leaves
a few sprigs of fresh thyme leaves

1 whole chicken, about 3½lb (1.6g),
   disjointed into 2 each of legs,
   thighs, wings, plus 1 whole breast,
   cut into four equal pieces
1 x 20oz (535g) can pineapple
   chunks, drained

1 First, make the marinade. Combine the chiles, cinnamon, nutmeg, salt, pepper, lime zest and juice, brown sugar, oil, parsley, cilantro, and thyme in a food processor. Process to a paste, adding a little more oil if needed.

2 Using the tip of a sharp knife, deeply slash each chicken piece, then put in a plastic freezer bag. Add the jerk paste, seal the bag, and knead to work the paste into the chicken until the pieces are coated. Let marinate 30 minutes at room temperature.

3 Preheat the oven to 400°F (200°C). Loosely arrange the chicken in a roasting pan and roast for 40 minutes until golden and crisp. During the last 10 minutes of cooking, scatter the pineapple between the chicken pieces to brown lightly. Serve hot with rice.

Cheat...
Feel free to use a store-bought jerk seasoning instead of making your own.

Baked chicken with onion, garlic, and tomatoes

PREP 5 MINS · COOK 1½ HRS

SERVES 4
8 chicken pieces, skin on, about
   1¾lb (800g) total
sea salt and freshly ground
   black pepper
1 tbsp flour
2 tbsp olive oil
6 bacon slices, chopped
1 onion, finely chopped
2 garlic cloves, finely chopped
3 celery stalks, finely chopped
3 carrots, finely chopped
½ cup dry white wine
1 x 14oz (400g) can diced tomatoes,
   with juices
1¼ cups hot vegetable or chicken stock

1 Preheat the oven to 400°F (200°C). Season the chicken well with salt and pepper, then dust with the flour.

2 Heat 1 tablespoon of the oil in a large cast iron or other flameproof casserole over high heat. Add the chicken pieces, skin-side down, along with the bacon and cook the chicken for 10–15 minutes, turning once, until golden. Remove the chicken and bacon from the pan with a slotted spoon and set aside.

3 Reduce the heat to low and add the remaining oil to the casserole with the onion and a pinch of sea salt. Cook for 5 minutes until soft, then add the garlic, celery, and carrots. Cook for 5–6 minutes longer, until soft.

4 Increase the heat to high once again and add the wine. Let bubble for a few minutes until the smell of alcohol evaporates. Add the tomatoes and their juices and pour in the stock. Boil gently for a few minutes more, stirring frequently. Reduce the heat to a simmer and return the chicken and bacon to the casserole. Spoon the tomato sauce over the chicken, cover, and transfer to the oven to cook for about 1 hour. Add more stock if it appears dry. Serve with creamy mashed potatoes.

Grilled chicken with satay sauce

SERVES 4

1 x 14oz (400ml) can unsweetened
   coconut milk
1 tsp Thai red curry paste
1¼ cups hot vegetable stock
2 tbsp demerara (raw) or light
   brown sugar
4 tbsp crunchy peanut butter
sea salt and freshly ground
   black pepper
juice of 1 lime, or as needed
4 skinless boneless chicken breast
   halves (preferably free-range),
   about 7oz (200g) each
splash of olive oil

To serve (optional)
cucumber, thinly sliced
white wine vinegar
granulated sugar
chopped fresh cilantro leaves

1 First, make the satay sauce. Pour the coconut milk into a heavy saucepan and bring to a gentle boil. Reduce the heat slightly and simmer until it releases its sweet fragrance. Now stir in the curry paste until blended; then stir in the stock and sugar and simmer for 5 minutes.

2 Add the peanut butter and stir until well blended. Remove from the heat and season with salt and the lime juice. Taste and adjust the seasoning as needed. Set aside to keep warm.

3 Slash each chicken breast diagonally several times, making sure that you don't slice all the way through. Rub them all over with a little olive oil and season well with salt and pepper. Heat a ridged cast-iron grill pan until hot and cook the chicken for 10–12 minutes, turning once, until cooked through and nicely charred.

4 Meanwhile, prepare the cucumber salad. Sprinkle the cucumber with vinegar and a pinch of sugar; scatter the cilantro on top. Serve the chicken breasts with the satay sauce and the cucumber salad (if desired).

Cheat...
Serve up the chicken
with some store-bought
peanut satay sauce.

Chicken scallops with chiles and parsley

SERVES 4

4 skinless boneless chicken breast
   halves (preferably free-range),
   about 7oz (200g) each
sea salt and freshly ground
   black pepper
1 tbsp all-purpose flour
1 cup toasted bread crumbs
handful of flat-leaf parsley, finely
   chopped
2 fresh red jalapeño chile peppers,
   seeded and finely chopped
1 egg, lightly beaten
1–2 tbsp olive oil
10oz (300g) fresh spinach leaves
juice of 1 lemon
a few drops of Asian hot chili oil

1 Sandwich the chicken breasts between 2 large sheets of plastic wrap. Pound with a meat mallet or the side of rolling pin until thin and evenly flattened. Season well with salt and pepper and dust with flour.

2 In a bowl, mix together the bread crumbs, parsley, and chiles. Dip the

chicken in the beaten egg, then coat with the bread crumb mixture.

3 In a large frying pan, heat the oil over high heat. Add the chicken pieces, two at a time, and cook for 6–8 minutes, turning once, until golden and cooked through. Remove from the pan and set aside to keep warm.

4 Now reduce the heat slightly and add the spinach to the same pan with a sprinkling of water. Cook, stirring, for a few minutes until just wilted. Sprinkle with some of the lemon juice and serve on warm plates, along with the chicken. Squeeze the remaining lemon juice and a few drops of chili oil over the top and serve immediately.

COOK'S NOTES

You can prepare the chicken the night before. Coat the chicken pieces with the bread crumbs as directed, cover loosely, and refrigerate until ready to cook.

EVERYDAY

EVERYDAY CHICKEN

Chicken with cayenne, lemon, and oregano

PREP 10 MINS COOK 40 MINS

SERVES 4

8 large chicken thighs (preferably free-range), about 9oz (250g) each
1–2 tbsp olive oil
1 tsp cayenne pepper
juice of 1 lemon
1 tbsp dried oregano
sea salt and freshly ground black pepper
bunch of scallions, sliced
6–8oz (200g) arugula
drizzle of good balsamic vinegar
small handful of freshly shaved Parmesan cheese, for serving (See Cook's Notes)

1 Preheat the oven to 400°F (200°C). Put the chicken, oil, cayenne, lemon juice, and oregano in a bowl. Season well with salt and pepper. Toss with your hands until the chicken is well coated. Let marinate for 30 minutes at room temperature, if you have time; otherwise, proceed with Step 2.

2 Spread the chicken in a large shallow roasting pan and roast for 30–40 minutes until slightly charred at the edges.

3 Meanwhile, mix together the scallions and arugula. When ready to serve, drizzle a little balsamic vinegar and a pinch of salt over the arugula salad. Top with the Parmesan shavings and serve alongside the chicken.

COOK'S NOTES

Make sure that you use a big enough roasting pan with lots of room. This way the chicken will roast, rather than steam—which it will do if it is too tightly packed.

Chicken breasts in cilantro yogurt

PREP 10 MINS COOK 30 MINS

SERVES 4

8oz (225g) Greek-style plain yogurt
handful of fresh cilantro leaves, finely chopped, plus extra for garnish
2 tbsp medium-hot curry powder, preferably Madras
sea salt and freshly ground black pepper
4 large skinless boneless chicken breast halves (preferably free-range), about 7oz (200g) each
8oz (225g) baby new potatoes, halved if large
1 tbsp olive oil
1 lemon, cut into wedges

1 Preheat the oven to 400°F (200°C). Combine the yogurt, cilantro, and 1 tablespoon of the curry powder in a large bowl. Season with salt and pepper and mix well. Add the chicken pieces and leave to marinate for a few minutes.

2 Arrange the coated chicken pieces in a shallow roasting pan without crowding and roast in the oven for about 30 minutes until cooked through and lightly charred.

3 Meanwhile, put the potatoes into a separate roasting pan. Drizzle with the oil and add the remaining curry powder. Mix together using your hands until the potatoes are evenly coated, then roast in the oven for 20 minutes or until golden.

4 Serve the chicken and potatoes together with a sprinkling of cilantro and the lemon wedges on the side.

Baked chicken with apricots and almonds

PREP 10 MINS | COOK 1 HR

SERVES 4

8 chicken pieces, skin on, about 1¾lb (800g) in total
sea salt and ground black pepper
2 tsp ground cinnamon
2 tbsp olive oil
1 onion, finely chopped
3 garlic cloves, finely chopped
pinch of ground ginger
1 cinnamon stick
1 x 15½oz (440g) can chickpeas, drained and rinsed
4 cups hot chicken stock
handful of whole blanched almonds
handful of dried apricots
handful of fresh cilantro, finely chopped
juice of 1 lemon
couscous, for serving
harissa, for serving

1 Preheat the oven to 400°F (200°C). Season the chicken well with salt and pepper and sprinkle with the cinnamon. Heat 1 tablespoon of the olive oil in a large flameproof casserole over medium-high heat. Working in batches if necessary, add the chicken pieces, skin-side down, and cook for about 5–10 minutes, turning once, until golden all over. Remove and set aside.

2 Reduce the heat to medium and add the remaining oil, onion, and a pinch of salt to the casserole. Cook for 5 minutes until soft. Add the garlic, ginger, and cinnamon stick, and cook for few seconds. Stir in the chickpeas.

3 Return the chicken to the casserole and pour in the stock. Bring to a boil and add the almonds and apricots. Cover and bake for about 1 hour until the chicken is cooked through and the sauce begins to thicken.

4 Stir in the cilantro and squeeze with the lemon juice. Serve hot with fluffy couscous and harissa.

VARIATION
Use turkey instead of chicken for a slightly lower-fat version.

Chicken fajitas with tomato and avocado salsa

PREP 15 MINS **COOK** 15 MINS

SERVES 4

For the salsa

1 ripe avocado
handful of cherry tomatoes, chopped
1 bunch of scallions, finely chopped
handful of fresh flat-leaf parsley, finely chopped
1 tbsp olive oil
1 tbsp white wine vinegar
sea salt and freshly ground black pepper

1 tbsp olive oil
2 onions, halved and sliced
2 red and 2 green bell peppers, seeded and cut into strips
2 fresh red jalapeño chile peppers, seeded and finely chopped
2 garlic cloves, thinly sliced
4 skinless boneless chicken breast halves (preferably free-range), about 6oz (175g) each, cut into strips
½ cup dry white wine
handful of fresh cilantro, finely chopped
8–12 corn tortillas, warmed

1 First, make the salsa. Halve, pit, peel, and chop the avocado. Put in a bowl with the tomatoes, scallions, and parsley. Drizzle in the olive oil and vinegar. Season with salt and pepper and stir to mix.

2 To make the chicken fajitas, heat the oil in a large hot frying pan over low heat. Add the onions and red and green bell peppers and sauté for 5 minutes until soft. Stir in the chiles and garlic and cook briefly.

3 Increase the heat to medium-high and add the chicken. Keep the mixture moving around the pan so that it doesn't burn and the chicken is evenly cooked. Stir-fry for 3–5 minutes until the chicken is no longer pink. Pour in the wine and cook for 5 minutes. Stir in the cilantro.

4 To serve, spoon the mixture onto the tortillas. Top with the salsa and roll into wraps. Serve any extra filling on the side.

Chicken doner kebab

PREP 15 MINS **COOK** 15 MINS

Marinating • 1 hour

SERVES 4

1 tsp cayenne pepper
1 tbsp olive oil
juice of 1 lemon
4 skinless boneless chicken breast halves, about 6oz (175g) each, cut into thin strips
4 pita breads
1 small head of crispy lettuce, such as romaine or iceberg, shredded
1 onion, thinly sliced
¼ head red cabbage, shredded
hot chili sauce
prepared garlic mayonnaise
1 ripe tomato, sliced
¼ cucumber, sliced
whole pickled jalapeños, for serving

1 In a bowl, mix together the cayenne pepper, olive oil, and a quarter of the lemon juice. Add the chicken strips and leave to marinate in the refrigerator for 1 hour.

2 Preheat the broiler. Arrange the chicken strips in a shallow baking dish and cook under the broiler for about 10 minutes, turning occasionally.

3 Lightly toast the pita breads and cut open to form a pocket.

4 Stuff each pita pocket with a handful of lettuce, onion, and red cabbage, then the chicken pieces. Dress with lemon juice, chili sauce, and garlic mayonnaise to taste. Garnish with tomato, cucumber, and a jalapeño. Serve immediately.

VARIATION

Use whole wheat pita bread for an even healthier dish.

Chicken with pancetta, peas, and mint

PREP 15 MINS · COOK 1¾ HRS

Special equipment • large flameproof casserole

SERVES 4

2 tbsp olive oil

4 large or 8 small chicken pieces such as thighs and breasts, about 1½lb (675g) total, skin on

2 onions, finely chopped

8oz (200g) pancetta, cubed

2 garlic cloves, finely chopped

1 cup dry white wine

2½ cups chicken stock

sea salt and freshly ground black pepper

8–10oz (300g) frozen peas

handful of flat-leaf parsley, finely chopped

handful of fresh mint leaves, finely chopped

1 Preheat the oven to 300°F (150°C). Heat 1 tablespoon of the oil in a large flameproof casserole over medium heat. Add the chicken pieces and cook for about 8 minutes, turning, until golden. Remove the chicken pieces from the pan, and set aside.

2 Reduce the heat to low and add the remaining oil and onions to the casserole. Cook gently for 5 minutes until soft, then add the pancetta. Increase the heat a little and cook for another 5 minutes until the pancetta is browned. Stir in the garlic, then pour in the wine. Increase the heat to high and let bubble for few minutes until the alcohol has evaporated.

3 Add the stock and bring to a boil once again. Season with salt and pepper and stir in the peas, parsley, and mint. Return the chicken pieces to the casserole, cover, and transfer to the oven to cook for 1½ hours. Check the level of liquid occasionally while cooking—it needs to be fairly dry, but if it does require more liquid to prevent sticking, just add a little hot water. Serve hot with fresh crusty bread or sautéed potatoes.

Marsala chicken with pine nuts and golden raisins

PREP 15 MINS · COOK 45 MINS

Special equipment • large cast-iron pan or flameproof casserole

SERVES 4

2 tbsp olive oil

8 chicken pieces such thighs and breasts (preferably free-range), about 1¾lb (800g) total, skin on

1 onion, finely chopped

2 carrots, finely chopped

2 celery stalks, finely chopped

1¼ cups dry Marsala wine

sea salt and freshly ground black pepper

½ cup pine nuts, toasted

½ cup golden raisins

handful of flat-leaf parsley, finely chopped

1 Heat the oil in a large cast-iron pan over medium heat. Add the chicken pieces and cook for about 8 minutes, turning, until golden. Remove from the pan and set aside.

2 Reduce the heat to low. Add the onion, carrots, and celery to the pan and cook gently for 5 minutes until soft. Pour in the Marsala, season with salt and pepper, and simmer gently for about 30 minutes, adding a bit of hot water if the chicken begins to stick to the pan. (Don't add too much water, since this dish has little sauce, and the water will dilute the flavor.)

3 Stir in the pine nuts and raisins and cook for a few more minutes. Just before serving, stir in the parsley. Serve with a lightly-dressed green salad and crusty bread.

EVERYDAY

10
WAYS WITH...

A favorite ingredient, and 10 ways to cook it.

10 WAYS WITH...
STEAK

Griddled steak with peppery crust

PREP 10 MINS **COOK** 10 MINS

Special equipment • food processor • ridged cast-iron grill pan or griddle

SERVES 2

Process 1 teaspoon each of **black peppercorns**, **red peppercorns**, **green peppercorns**, **mustard seeds**, **caraway seeds**, and **sea salt**, 2 teaspoons **brown sugar**, and 2 seeded fresh **red chiles** into a grainy mixture. Roll a 12oz (350g) piece of steak evenly in the mixture. Heat a ridged cast-iron grill pan until hot. Cook the steak, turning only once, remove from the pan, and let rest on a warm plate for 10 minutes before serving.

Steak sandwich with horseradish and watercress

PREP 5 MINS **COOK** 10 MINS

Special equipment • ridged cast-iron grill pan or griddle

SERVES 1

Cook a 5½oz (150g) **top round** steak to perfection on a hot ridged cast-iron grill pan, and let rest. Cut 2 slices of fresh crusty **bread**, or halve and lightly toast half a ciabatta. Spread one slice of the bread or a ciabatta half with a dollop of **creamed horseradish**, then top with the steak and **watercress** and some sliced fresh **tomatoes**. Season generously with sea salt and freshly ground black pepper. Place the other slice of bread or ciabatta half on top to make a sandwich and serve immediately.

Asian steak salad with bok choy

PREP 15 MINS **COOK** 5 MINS

SERVES 4

Slice 10oz (300g) **sirloin steak** into thin strips and put in a bowl. Mix together 1 tablespoon **vegetable oil**, 1 tablespoon **soy sauce**, the juice of 1 **lime**, a 1in (2.5cm) piece of minced fresh **ginger**, 2 crushed **garlic cloves**, and 1 teaspoon **granulated sugar**. Pour over the steak, and marinate while you prepare the other ingredients. Spread 7oz (200g) **bean sprouts** over a platter. Quarter 1 head **bok choy** lengthwise and sauté with a little oil in a frying pan over medium heat for 3–4 minutes. Remove from the pan and arrange on top of the bean sprouts. Add the marinated steak to the same pan, increase the heat to high, and stir-fry for a few minutes until cooked. Pour in the remaining marinade mixture along with 1 tablespoon **rice wine vinegar** and cook vigorously for 1 minute. Pour the steak strips over the bean sprouts and bok choy, gently toss, and serve immediately.

The perfect steak

PREP 2 MINS **COOK** 10 MINS

Special equipment • ridged cast-iron grill pan or griddle

SERVES 1

Season an 8oz (225g) **bottom round** or **T-bone** steak with sea salt and freshly ground black pepper and drizzle with a little olive oil. Heat a ridged cast-iron grill pan, then add the steak and cook undisturbed for 3–4 minutes on each side. Remove from the pan and let rest for 5 minutes before serving.

The perfect steak

EVERYDAY

5 Seared steak with arugula

PREP 5 MINS

Special equipment • ridged cast-iron grill pan or griddle

SERVES 4

Season two 6oz (175g) **sirloin steaks**. Heat the grill pan, and cook the steaks over very high heat, one at a time, for 1 minute on ea3ch side. Remove and rest. Arrange 7oz (200g) **arugula** on a serving plate, sprinkle with freshly shaved **Parmesan cheese** and **cherry tomatoes**, halved. Diagonally slice the steak and place on top of the salad with juices. Dress with an **olive oil** and **balsamic vinegar** dressing.

6 Breaded steak with black olives

PREP 15 MINS

SERVES 4

Sandwich four 4½oz (125g) pieces of **sirloin steak** between two pieces of plastic wrap. Pound with a meat mallet or rolling pin until thin and set aside. Blend or process 4½oz (125g) **black olives**, a handful of fresh **flat-leaf parsley**, and 6 **sun-dried tomatoes** to a coarse paste. Evenly spread three-quarters of the paste onto each steak and roll tightly. Mix the remaining paste with 4½oz (125g) seasoned and toasted **fresh bread crumbs**. Dredge the steaks in a little **flour**, coat in a beaten **egg**, and roll in the bread crumbs. Roast in a preheated 425°F (200°C) oven for 15–20 minutes until the coating is crisp. Slice the steaks diagonally and serve with garlic and chile-seasoned **spinach**.

7 Steak and oyster mushroom salad

PREP 5 MINS

Special equipment • ridged cast-iron grill pan or griddle

SERVES 4

Cook two 4½oz (125g) **sirloin steaks** to perfection on a hot grill pan. Let rest for 5 minutes, then slice into thick strips. Heat 1 tablespoon of **olive oil** in a frying pan over medium heat. Add 6oz (175g) **oyster mushrooms** and sauté for 5 minutes. Toss with the steak strips. Whisk together 3 tablespoons of olive oil, 1 tablespoon of **white wine vinegar**, and 1 teaspoon of **coarse-grain mustard**. Drizzle the dressing over the salad, then stir in a handful of chopped **curly parsley**. Season and serve with fresh crusty **bread**.

8 Steak and vegetable parcels

PREP 15 MINS

SERVES 4

In a frying pan over high heat, sear 8oz (225g) **cubed sirloin** or **bottom round** steak in a little **olive oil** for about 5 minutes. Pour in ⅔ cup hot **beef stock**, and let bubble for a few minutes, then stir in 3 peeled, cubed, and cooked **potatoes** and 3 diced and cooked **carrots**. Season with salt and pepper. Roll out 12oz (350g) **prepared pie crust** to about ¼in (5mm) thick, then cut into 4 squares. Divide the steak mixture evenly to the middle of each square. Sprinkle a handful of grated **Cheddar cheese** over each. Brush the edges of each square with a little water, then pull the corners up to the middle to make a parcel; pinch the edges of the pastry together to seal. Brush each parcel with beaten egg yolk and bake in a preheated 400°F (200°C) oven for about 20 minutes or until golden.

Steak and oyster mushroom salad

Paprika steak skewers

9

Paprika steak skewers

PREP 10 MINS   **COOK** 10 MINS

Marinating • 1 hour

Special equipment • skewers • ridged cast-iron grill pan or griddle

SERVES 4

Slice 12oz (350g) **bottom round** steak into 1in (2.5cm) cubes, and mix in a bowl with 2 teaspoons **paprika**, the juice of 1 **lemon**, a small handful of finely chopped **flat-leaf parsley**, 1 tablespoon **olive oil**, a pinch of **sea salt**, and some freshly ground **black pepper**. Skewer the steak cubes (if using wooden or bamboo skewers, soak in cold water for at least 30 minutes first), and let rest in the refrigerator for 1 hour. Heat a ridged cast-iron grill pan until hot, then cook for 1–2 minutes on each side, turning a quarter turn each time. Allow to rest for a couple of minutes before serving with a drizzle of olive oil and **mashed potatoes** with flat-leaf parsley.

10

Swedish-style steak

PREP 20 MINS   **COOK** 20 MINS

SERVES 4

Peel and boil 2¼lb (1kg) waxy **potatoes** for about 15 minutes. Drain, put in a bowl, and cover with cold water. Cut 10oz (300g) **sirloin steak** into large chunks, then sear in a hot frying pan with a little **olive oil**. Set aside. Blend 16 tablespoons of **butter** with 5 crushed **garlic cloves** and a handful of chopped fresh **flat-leaf parsley**. Season with salt and pepper. Cut the potatoes into thick slices and layer in the bottom of a baking dish. Put the steak on top, cover with the butter, and roast in a preheated 400°F (200°C) oven for 20 minutes. Serve with a **tomato salad**.

127

10 WAYS WITH...
CHEESE

EVERYDAY

1 Cheesy leeks on toast

PREP 10 MINS COOK 10 MINS

SERVES 2

Heat 1 tablespoon of **olive oil** in a saucepan over low heat. Add 1 chopped **leek** and sauté gently until soft. Remove and set aside. Put 2 tablespoons **butter**, ⅔ cup beer (preferably **brown ale**), and 6oz (175g) grated sharp **Cheddar cheese** in the same pan and cook gently, stirring, until melted and smooth. Remove from the heat and stir in 1 tablespoon of **flour** until smooth, then return to the heat, stirring continuously. Remove from the heat, stir in 2 teaspoons of **mustard**, a splash of **Worcestershire sauce**, and the reserved leeks. Season. Allow to cool, then stir in 2 **egg yolks** until combined. Toast 4 slices of **bread** on one side, turn, then arrange on a baking sheet and spread with the cheesy leeks. Broil for a few minutes, until bubbling and golden.

2 Baked Camembert

PREP 5 MINS COOK 10 MINS

SERVES 4

Take a whole **Camembert cheese** still packaged in its wooden box. Remove all plastic packaging, and return the cheese to the box. Cut a series of small crosses in the top of the Camembert and stick a small sprig of fresh **rosemary** into each one. Bake the Camembert in the box, without the lid, in a preheated 350°F (180°C) oven for about 10 minutes or until starting to bubble and melt. Serve immediately with fresh crusty **bread**, a farmhouse-style **apple chutney** (or apple preserves), and fresh **apple** slices and **celery**.

3 Seared halloumi cheese with figs

PREP 10 MINS COOK 20 MINS

SERVES 4

Take 8 large ripe **figs** and cut into quarters lengthwise. Cut 10oz (300g) **halloumi cheese** into ¼in (6mm) slices. Put the halloumi and figs in a large non-stick frying pan over medium heat and cook for 2–3 minutes on each side until starting to brown. Once cooked, add to a platter of mixed salad greens. Pour ¼ cup **red wine vinegar** into the same pan and increase the heat slightly. Add a small handful of chopped fresh **cilantro leaves**, 1 seeded and finely chopped fresh **red chile**, and 1 crushed **garlic clove**. Let bubble over medium-high heat until reduced in volume by three-quarters, and pour sparingly over the figs and cheese. Drizzle with a little olive oil and serve immediately.

4 Cheese fondue

PREP 10 MINS COOK 15 MINS

SERVES 4

Pour 1 cup of **dry white wine** into a saucepan and bring to a boil. Add 7oz (200g) grated **Swiss cheese** and stir until melted. Then add 7oz (200g) grated Gruyère cheese and stir again until melted and smooth. Once thickened, pour the sauce into a warm bowl and serve with fresh crusty **bread** on skewers for dipping into the cheesy fondue.

Seared halloumi cheese with figs

5 Feta and watermelon salad with pumpkin seeds

PREP
5
MINS

SERVES 4

Halve 1 small ripe **watermelon**, and cut the flesh into bite-sized pieces. Put in a bowl and crumble in 5½oz (150g) **feta cheese** along with ½ teaspoon ground **black pepper**, 1 tablespoon **chili oil**, and a small handful of finely **chopped mint leaves**. Toss gently to combine. In a small frying pan, toast 1¾oz (50g) **pumpkin seeds** with a little **sea salt** for a few minutes and sprinkle liberally over the top of each portion. Serve immediately.

6 Dauphinoise with Swiss cheese and pancetta

PREP
20
MINS

SERVES 4

In a frying pan over medium heat, cook 7oz (200g) cubed **pancetta** until just crisp. Remove from the pan and drain on paper towels. Simmer 3lb 3oz (1½kg) peeled and thinly sliced **potatoes** in 1¼ cups **milk** and 1¼ cups **heavy cream** for 10 minutes until potatoes start to soften, then remove the potatoes (reserving the milk mixture). Layer the potatoes, 5½oz (150g) sliced **Swiss cheese,** and the pancetta in a baking dish. Season and add more cheese. Add the milk mixture, cover with foil, and cook in a preheated 400°F (200°C) oven for about 45 minutes, removing the foil for the last 15 minutes to brown the top.

7 Easy cheese soufflé with mustard

PREP
30
MINS

Special equipment • ramekins

SERVES 4

Melt 2 tablespoons **butter** in a pan over low heat. Add 1 teaspoon of **all-purpose flour**. Cook, stirring, for a couple of minutes, then gradually add 1¼ cups **milk**, stirring constantly. Add 1¾oz (50g) grated **Gruyère cheese**, scant 1oz (25g) grated **Parmesan cheese**, and 1 teaspoon of **coarse-grain mustard**. Continue stirring until melted. Season. Once cool, beat in 4 **egg yolks**. Beat 4 **egg whites** to soft peaks. Carefully fold the whites into the cheese mixture, a little at a time, until combined. Divide the mixture among 4 ramekins, leaving space at the top, and bake in a preheated 400°F (200°C) oven for 12–15 minutes until risen. Serve immediately.

8 Tandoori paneer

PREP
20
MINS

Marinating • 30 minutes

Special equipment • blender or food processor • skewers • ridged cast-iron grill pan or barbecue

SERVES 4

In a blender or food processor, blend 3 **garlic cloves**, 2 seeded fresh **green chillies**, a 1in (2.5cm) piece of fresh **ginger**, the grated zest and juice of ½ a **lemon**, and 3 tablespoons **Greek-style yogurt** until smooth. Add 1 tablespoon **garam masala** and 1 teaspoon **ground cumin**, and blend again. Season with **sea salt** and freshly ground **black pepper**. Cut 9oz (250g) **paneer cheese** into 1in cubes, and marinate in the tandoori mixture for 30 minutes. Thread the cubes onto skewers (if using wooden or bamboo skewers, soak in cold water for at least 30 minutes first), and grill in a hot ridged cast-iron grill pan for 5–8 minutes, turning halfway through cooking, until golden. Serve hot and sizzling on a bed of shredded **lettuce**, sliced **red onions**, and sliced ripe **tomatoes**.

Easy cheese soufflé with mustard

EVERYDAY

Rice balls filled with cheese

9 Shredded red cabbage with blue cheese dressing

PREP 10 MINS

Special equipment • blender or food processor

SERVES 4

Mix together 4½oz (125g) **blue cheese** such as Danish blue or cambozola with 8oz (225g) **Greek-style yogurt**, a small handful of chopped **tarragon leaves**, and plenty of freshly ground **black pepper**. Blend or process until smooth. Finely shred 1 **red cabbage**, and mix with scant 1oz (25g) **raisins** and scant 1oz (25g) toasted **pine nuts**. Toss with the blue cheese dressing and serve with fresh crusty whole wheat or rye **bread**.

10 Rice balls filled with cheese

PREP 15 MINS **COOK 5 MINS**

SERVES 4

Generously season 8oz (225g) cold cooked **Arborio** or **other risotto rice**, then roll into 12 even-sized balls. Push a cube of **mozzarella cheese** into the center of each ball, then cover so that the cheese is enclosed. Roll each ball in some beaten **egg**, then in some toasted fresh **bread crumbs**. Cook in a little **olive oil** over medium heat for 2–5 minutes until golden. Serve hot.

131

10 WAYS WITH...

SALMON

1 Chinese salmon with black bean sauce

PREP 10 MINS — COOK 15 MINS

Marinating • 30 minutes
Special equipment • ridged cast-iron grill pan or griddle

SERVES 4

Mix 4 tablespoons **black bean sauce** with a 1in (2.5cm) piece of fresh **ginger**, grated, 3 **garlic cloves**, minced, and 1 seeded and finely chopped fresh **hot red chile**. Spread the mixture all over 4 **salmon fillets**, about 5½oz (150g) each, and season with **sea salt** and freshly ground **black pepper**. Marinate in the refrigerator for 30 minutes. Heat a ridged cast-iron grill pan until hot. Add the salmon fillets, skin-side down, and cook for 4 minutes or until opaque and lightly charred. Turn over, and cook on the other side for another 4 minutes. Serve hot with **rice** or **noodles**.

2 Salmon cakes

PREP 15 MINS — COOK 20 MINS

SERVES 4

Mix 10oz (300g) cooked **fresh salmon** and 5½oz (150g) chopped **smoked salmon** in a bowl. Add 1 finely chopped **onion**, 2 crushed **garlic cloves**, 1 seeded and finely chopped **hot red chile**, 10oz (300g) cooked **mashed potatoes**, 1 tablespoon each of chopped **tarragon** and **dill**, and 2 beaten **eggs**. Season, then use your hands to combine and mold into 2in (5cm) balls. Flatten into patties and evenly coat in toasted fresh **bread crumbs**. Place the cakes in a roasting pan coated with vegetable oil and roast in a preheated 400°F (200°C) oven for 20 minutes or until golden, turning once. Serve with a **green salad**.

3 Salmon with dill and Madeira

PREP 15 MINS — COOK 20 MINS

SERVES 4

Place four 5½oz (150g) **salmon fillets** skin-side down on a baking sheet and season. Add a sprinkle of fresh **dill**. Loosely cover with foil and bake in a preheated 400°F (200°C) oven for 15 minutes until cooked. In a shallow pan, heat 2 tablespoons **olive oil** over low heat and gently sauté 2 finely chopped **shallots** and 2 crushed **garlic cloves** for about 5 minutes. Add a drizzle of **Madeira wine**, increase the heat, and let bubble until reduced by half. Stir in a handful of chopped **dill**. Serve the salmon with boiled **potatoes** and **green beans**, with the dressing over the top.

4 Poached salmon with cilantro and lime

PREP 5 MINS — COOK 25 MINS

SERVES 4

Cut a side fillet of **salmon**, about 1lb 5oz (600g), in half lengthwise so that it opens up, but is not separated. Coarsely chop a large handful of fresh **cilantro**, mix with 2 peeled, segmented, and coarsely chopped **limes**, and season. Spread the mixture evenly on the opened salmon, season once again, then fold closed. Place the salmon on a large sheet of foil and carefully pour ¼ cup of **dry white wine** over the fish. Fold the foil over and seal. Place on a baking sheet and bake in a preheated 400°F (200°C) for 25 minutes until opaque. Serve hot with boiled new **potatoes**.

Poached salmon with cilantro and lime

5 Salmon with soy sauce and garlic

PREP 5 MINS **COOK 15 MINS**

Marinating • 1 hour

SERVES 4

Mix together 4 tablespoons **soy sauce**, 2 crushed **garlic cloves**, and the grated zest and juice of ½ a **lemon**. Pour the mixture over 4 **salmon steaks**, about 5½oz (150g) each, and allow to marinate in the refrigerator for 1 hour. Transfer the salmon to a baking sheet and liberally sprinkle with sesame seeds. Bake in a preheated 400°F (200°C) oven for 15 minutes until the salmon is opaque. Serve hot with a **spinach salad**.

6 Salmon kedgeree

PREP 10 MINS **COOK 20 MINS**

SERVES 4

Melt 4 tablespoons **butter** in a pan over low heat, add 1 finely chopped **onion**, and sauté gently for a few minutes until soft. Add 2 cups **long-grain rice** such as basmati, and stir until the grains are well coated. Gradually add enough **vegetable stock** to cover the rice and bring to a boil. Cover, reduce the heat, and simmer gently for 15–20 minutes, until all the liquid has been absorbed and the rice is cooked. Add 1lb 2oz (500g) sliced **cooked salmon**, 1 teaspoon each of **curry powder**, and **cayenne pepper**. Season and serve hot with fresh **mango** slices.

7 Salmon, horseradish, and kale bake

PREP 10 MINS **COOK 25 MINS**

SERVES 4

Put 4 skinned **salmon fillets**, about 5½oz (150g) each, in a deep skillet and cover with **milk**. Poach gently over low heat for about 10 minutes until opaque and cooked, then transfer the salmon to a casserole dish using a slotted spoon. Discard the poaching liquid. Trim the tough stalks from 2 handfuls of **kale**, and coarsely chop the leaves. Boil or steam for about 5 minutes until nearly soft, then drain and add to the salmon. Combine gently. Make a cheese sauce with the addition of 1–2 tablespoons **creamed horseradish**, pour evenly into the casserole, and bake in a 400°F (200°C) oven for about 15 minutes, until golden.

8 Salmon jungle curry

PREP 10 MINS **COOK 20 MINS**

SERVES 4

In a large frying pan or wok, heat 2 tablespoons **vegetable oil** until hot. Add 2 tablespoons **Thai green curry paste** and stir to combine. Throw in 3 crushed **garlic cloves**, a 2in (5cm) piece of fresh **ginger**, cut into fine strips, and 2 fresh **hot red chiles**, seeded and cut into fine strips. Keep stirring for 2–3 minutes, then pour in 14fl oz (400ml) **coconut milk**. Bring to a boil, then add a good splash of **fish sauce**, 7oz (200g) drained **bamboo shoots**, 2 heaping tablespoons **baby Thai eggplants** or pea eggplants (if available), and 2½oz (75g) **baby corn**, sliced lengthwise. Reduce the heat slightly and simmer for 5 minutes. Add 14oz (400g) skinless **fresh salmon**, cut into 1½in (4cm) chunks, and a small handful of fresh **Thai basil leaves**. Simmer for another 5–10 minutes, until the salmon is opaque and cooked. Season well and serve hot with sticky **Thai jasmine rice**.

Salmon jungle curry

EVERYDAY

Salmon salad with mint yogurt dressing

EVERYDAY

9 Salmon salad with mint yogurt dressing

PREP 15 MINS · COOK 25 MINS

SERVES 4

Put 2 tablespoons each of **red wine vinegar** and finely chopped **mint**, a pinch of **sea salt**, some freshly ground **black pepper**, and 4 tablespoons **Greek-style yogurt** in a bowl, and mix well. Set aside. Place a fillet of **salmon**, about 1¼lb (550g), on a large piece of foil. Sprinkle with fresh **dill**, chopped, and a few slices of **lemon**. Season and loosely seal the foil to make a parcel. Place on a baking sheet and bake in a preheated 400°F (200°C) oven for 20–25 minutes. Allow to cool. Plate the salmon, drizzle with dressing, and scatter with fresh **mint leaves**. Serve with a **cucumber salad**.

10 Sushi-style smoked salmon

PREP 20 MINS · COOK 35 MINS

SERVES 4

Prepare 10oz (300g) short-grain **sushi rice** according to package instructions. It should come out nice and sticky. Spread rice out over a baking sheet, cover with a clean dish towel, and let cool. Once the rice has cooled completely, arrange a double layer of plastic wrap in a square or rectangular shallow pan, then spoon in the rice. Smooth out evenly so that the rice is about 2in (5cm) deep. Layer pieces of **smoked salmon**, about 10oz (300g) in total, all over the rice to cover, and press it all down gently. Using a sharp knife dipped in hot water, slice into neat rectangles or squares, and serve.

10 WAYS WITH...

MEAT

EVERYDAY

1 Ground beef fruity curry

PREP 10 MINS · COOK 30 MINS · ❄

SERVES 4

Add 1 finely chopped **onion** and 1 tablespoon of **olive oil** to a large frying pan over low heat. Season. Sauté for 5 minutes until soft, then stir in 2 seeded and finely chopped fresh **medium-hot red chiles**, a 1in (2.5cm) piece of fresh **ginger**, grated, and 2 minced **garlic cloves**. Add 2 tablespoons **curry powder**. Stir again. Add 1½lb (700g) **ground beef** and cook, stirring, until the meat is no longer pink. Pour in ⅔ cup hot **vegetable stock** and bring to a boil. Reduce the heat, add 2 peeled, cored, and diced **Granny Smith apples** and a handful of **raisins**, and simmer for 10 minutes, until thickened. Adjust the seasoning and serve hot with **rice**.

2 Stuffed squash with ground beef

PREP 15 MINS · COOK 45 MINS

SERVES 4

Halve a **butternut squash** and scoop out the seeds and some flesh to make a "bowl" in each half. Place in a roasting pan, drizzle with **olive oil**, and roast in a preheated 400°F (200°C) oven for 10–15 minutes, until softened. In a large frying pan over low heat, sauté 1 finely chopped **onion** in a little olive oil for 5 minutes, until soft. Add 1½lb (700g) **ground beef** and cook, stirring, until starting to brown. Season well and stir in a handful of finely chopped **flat-leaf parsley**. Remove the squash from the oven, spoon the beef mixture into each half, cover with foil, and roast for 20–30 minutes. Remove the foil, sprinkle with 1¾oz (50g) grated **Gruyère cheese**, and return to the oven until the cheese has melted. Serve hot.

3 Nachos topped with ground beef and cheese

PREP 5 MINS · COOK 20 MINS

SERVES 4

In a large frying pan over medium-high heat, cook 1lb 2oz (500g) **ground beef** with a drizzle of **olive oil** for 10 minutes or until no longer pink. Add a splash of **hot sauce** to taste and season. Place 3 large handfuls of **tortilla chips** in a baking dish. Spoon the ground beef over the chips and top with 4½oz (125g) grated **Cheddar cheese**. Place under the broiler for a few minutes, until the cheese has melted, then serve with **guacamole**, **salsa**, and **sour cream**.

4 Greek stuffed tomatoes

PREP 10 MINS · COOK 1½ HRS

SERVES 4

Slice the tops off 4 large **beefsteak tomatoes** and scoop out the pulp. Coarsely chop the pulp and reserve the tomato shells and their "lids." Heat ½ tablespoon **olive oil** in a large frying pan over medium heat. Add 14oz (400g) **ground lamb** and cook, stirring, until no longer pink. Add the tomato pulp and a pinch each of **paprika**, **ground cumin**, and **ground cinnamon**. Cook, stirring, until the pulp starts to break down. Stir in 2 seeded and finely chopped fresh **green chiles**, 1 tablespoon each of **tomato paste** and **harissa**, and a handful of chopped **mint leaves**. Pour in ⅔ cup hot **vegetable stock** and bring to a boil. Reduce the heat and simmer for 15 minutes, until thickened. Season. Spoon the mixture into the tomato shells, put their lids on, and place in a roasting pan. Cover with foil and bake in a preheated 400°F (200°C) oven for about 1 hour. Serve with a **green salad** and a dollop of **Greek-style yogurt**.

Greek stuffed tomatoes

5 Meatballs with butternut squash

PREP 15 MINS COOK 30 MINS

SERVES 4

Combine 1lb 2oz (500g) **ground beef**, 1 finely chopped **onion**, 2 minced **garlic cloves**, and 1 **egg**. Season, form 12 even-sized balls, and chill. Peel, halve, and seed a **butternut squash** and cut into chunks. Place on a roasting pan with a little **olive oil** and sprinkle with **crushed red pepper flakes** and **sea salt**. Roast in a preheated 400°F (200°C) oven for 15-20 minutes, until golden. Meanwhile, cook the meatballs in a little olive oil over medium-high heat until browned. Transfer to the roasting pan with the squash and roast for 10 minutes. Serve with chopped **cilantro** and a spoonful of **tomato sauce**.

6 Turkish pizza with ground lamb and pine nuts

PREP 5 MINS COOK 20 MINS

SERVES 4

In a large frying pan over low heat, sauté 1 finely chopped **onion** in a little **olive oil** for 5 minutes until softened, then add 2 minced **garlic cloves** and 1lb (450g) **ground lamb**. Cook, stirring, until the meat is browned, then add a pinch of **chili powder** and the juice of 1 **lemon**. Season and spoon the beef mixture evenly onto four **flat breads**, such as pita or naan, and top with a handful of **pine nuts** and a sprinkling of **paprika**. Cook in a preheated 400°F (200°C) oven for 5-10 minutes or until lightly browned. Garnish with fresh **cilantro** and serve with **hummus**.

7 Ground beef and chickpeas cooked with orange and cinnamon

PREP 10 MINS COOK 20 MINS

SERVES 4

In a large pan over low heat, sauté 1 finely chopped **red onion** in a little **olive oil** for 5 minutes, until soft. Add 2 grated **garlic cloves**, a 1in (2.5cm) piece of fresh **ginger**, grated, and a pinch of **ground cinnamon**. Season generously, add 1½lb (675g) **ground beef**, and cook until the meat is brown. Add the zest and juice of 1 **orange**, and stir in a 14oz (400g) can of drained and rinsed **chickpeas**. Pour in ⅔ cup hot **vegetable stock** and bring to a boil. Reduce the heat and simmer, stirring, for 15 minutes. Adjust the seasoning and serve with **rice**.

8 Mediterranean burgers

PREP 10 MINS COOK 15 MINS

SERVES 4

Combine 1lb 2oz (500g) **ground beef** with 1 finely chopped **onion**, 2 minced **garlic cloves**, 1 tablespoon **dried oregano**, 2 seeded and finely diced **red bell peppers**, and a handful each of finely chopped fresh **basil leaves** and **flat-leaf parsley**. Season generously and add a splash of **red wine** to achieve a good moist texture. Using your hands, mix together until well combined. Divide the mixture evenly into 4 large balls, then flatten into burgers. Melt 1 tablespoon **butter** in a nonstick frying pan over medium-high heat and cook the burgers for 3-5 minutes on each side, or until nicely browned and cooked through. Serve in **hamburger buns** or on crusty rolls with **lettuce leaves** and **sliced tomato**.

Mediterranean burgers

Ground beef and chickpeas cooked with orange and cinnamon

EVERYDAY

9 Ground lamb and eggplant bake

PREP 10 MINS · COOK 30 MINS

SERVES 4

Heat 1 tablespoon **olive oil** in a large pan over medium-high heat. Cook 1 sliced **eggplant** until golden on both sides, adding more oil if needed. Remove from the pan and drain on paper towels. In the same pan, sauté 1 finely chopped **onion** in a little olive oil for 5 minutes, until soft. Add 2 minced **garlic cloves** and a pinch of **dried oregano**. Cook for 1 minute, then stir in a pinch each of **ground allspice** and **ground cinnamon**. Season. Add 1½lb (675g) **ground lamb**, and cook, stirring, until no longer pink. Layer the lamb and eggplant slices in an ovenproof casserole dish, starting with the lamb, and finishing with a layer of eggplant. Mix ⅔ cup **Greek-style yogurt** with 1 **egg** and season. Spoon the mixture over the eggplant and bake in a preheated 400°F (200°C) oven for 20-30 minutes, until set and golden. Serve hot.

10 Ground beef with noodles

PREP 5 MINS · COOK 20 MINS

SERVES 4

In a large frying pan over medium heat, cook 1lb 2oz (500g) **ground beef** in a little **olive oil**, stirring, until no longer pink. Add ⅓ cup **tomato juice** or sauce and simmer for 10 minutes. Stir in a handful of fresh **thyme leaves** and season. Meanwhile, melt 1 tablespoon **butter** in another frying pan over medium heat and sauté 7oz (200g) **white button mushrooms** (larger ones halved and small ones kept whole) for 5-10 minutes, until golden. Stir the mushrooms into the ground beef mixture and serve with cooked wide **egg noodles** tossed in a little butter and a grating of Cheddar or **Gruyère cheese**.

10 WAYS WITH...
SAUSAGES

EVERYDAY

Bratwurst with sweet red onions

 PREP 10 MINS **COOK 30 MINS**

SERVES 4

Peel and slice 3 **red onions** and add to a large frying pan with a drizzle of **olive oil**. Sauté over low heat for about 5 minutes until soft, then sprinkle in 1 tablespoon **demerara sugar**. Continue to cook over very low heat for about 20 minutes, stirring occasionally, until the onions begin to caramelize. Meanwhile, put 8 good-quality **bratwurst** in a roasting pan. Drizzle with a little olive oil and cook in a preheated 400°F (200°C) oven for 20-25 minutes, turning occasionally, until browned all over and the juices run clear. Serve the sweet onions and sausages in hot dog buns with a squirt of **mustard**.

Sausage rolls

 PREP 15 MINS **COOK 20 MINS**

SERVES 4

Remove the casings from 8 good-quality **pork sausages**. Crumble the peeled sausages into a bowl and add 2 peeled, cored, and chopped **Granny Smith apples** and a few chopped **sage leaves**. Mix well. Roll out 1lb 2oz (500g) prepared **puff pastry** (preferably made with butter) into an oblong shape about 12 x 6in (30 x 15cm) and ¼in (5mm) thick. Mold the sausage meat into a large sausage shape about as long as the pastry and place down the center of the pastry. Brush the edges of the pastry with a little **water**, then fold one side over so that the edges meet and cover the meat; seal using the back of a fork or by pinching together with your finger and thumb. Cut into 8 sausage rolls, brush with a little beaten **egg yolk**, and cook in a preheated 400°F (200°C) oven for about 20 minutes, until golden. Serve hot.

Toad in the hole

 PREP 15 MINS **COOK 40 MINS**

SERVES 4

Sift ¾ cup **all-purpose flour** into a bowl with a pinch of **sea salt**. Make a well in the center, crack in 2 **eggs**, pour in a little **milk** from 1¼ cups, and stir with a wooden spoon. Begin to whisk the batter, adding the remaining milk a little at a time. Season with **sea salt** and freshly ground **black pepper** and stir in a few chopped **sage leaves**. Leave the batter in the refrigerator to rest while you cook the sausages. Put 8 **spicy sausages**, halved if large, into an oven-safe baking dish that's large enough to hold them without overlapping. Drizzle with a little **olive oil** and cook in a preheated 400°F (200°C) oven for 15-20 minutes, until the sausages are browned. Remove the dish from the oven and pour the prepared batter over the sausages. Return to the oven and cook for 15 minutes more until the batter is risen and golden.

Spicy sausage, onion, and potato bake

 PREP 10 MINS **COOK 40 MINS**

SERVES 4

Place 8-12 **spicy sausages** into a roasting pan along with 9oz (250g) **baby new potatoes** and 2 **red onions**, peeled and cut into eight wedges each. Mix together 4 tablespoons **coarse-grain mustard**, 1 tablespoon **red currant jelly**, and 1 tablespoon **olive oil**. Add to the sausage mix and combine well using your hands. Sprinkle with chopped **rosemary leaves** and season with **sea salt** and freshly ground **black pepper**. Roast in a preheated 400°F (200°C) oven for 30-40 minutes until golden. Serve immediately with a leafy salad.

Toad in the hole

EVERYDAY

5 Sausages in cider with lentils

PREP 10 MINS · COOK 50 MINS

SERVES 4

In a large heavy frying pan over medium-high heat, lightly brown 8 good-quality **sausages** in a little **olive oil** for 8–10 minutes. Remove from the pan and set aside. Reduce the heat to low and, in the same pan, sauté 1 chopped **onion** in olive oil for 5 minutes until soft. Add 2 chopped **garlic cloves** and a few sprigs of **rosemary**. Season well with **sea salt** and freshly ground **black pepper**. Stir in 7oz (200g) dried **brown** or **Puy lentils**. Increase the heat and add 1¼ cups **hard cider**. Simmer for a few minutes, then pour in 2 cups hot **vegetable stock**. Return the sausages to the pan, tucking them in among the lentils, and simmer for 40 minutes, adding with hot water as needed. Season to taste and serve.

6 Sausage and chestnut stuffing

PREP 10 MINS · COOK 20 MINS

SERVES 4

In a frying pan over low heat, sauté 1 chopped **onion** in a little **olive oil** for about 5 minutes until soft. Season with **sea salt** and freshly ground **black pepper** and set aside to cool. Peel the casings from 6 good-quality **pork sausages** and add the meat to a bowl. Chop 9oz (250g) roasted **chestnuts** and add to the sausage meat along with a handful of fresh **flat-leaf parsley leaves** and the cooled onions. Mix together and season generously. Use to stuff a **turkey** or a whole **chicken**. Alternatively, roll the mixture into balls about 2in (5cm) in diameter and roast in a preheated 400°F (200°C) oven for 20 minutes or cook in a little olive oil until golden.

7 Spicy sausage and tomato skewers

PREP 15 MINS · COOK 20 MINS

Special equipment • skewers • ridged cast-iron grill pan

SERVES 4

Cut 12 spicy **sausages** into 1in (2.5cm) pieces and thread onto skewers with 12 **cherry tomatoes** and a few **bay leaves**. (If using wooden skewers, soak in cold water for at least 30 minutes.) Brush with **olive oil** and sprinkle with chopped **rosemary leaves**. Season with **sea salt** and freshly ground **black pepper**. Heat a ridged cast-iron grill pan until hot. Add the skewers and grill for 5–8 minutes on each side until the sausages are cooked through and lightly charred.

8 Sausage, zucchini, and bulgur wheat

PREP 10 MINS · COOK 25 MINS

SERVES 4

Put 4½oz (125g) **bulgur wheat** in a bowl and just cover with boiling **water**. Let stand for 10 minutes, then stir well with a fork to fluff up the grains. Season with **sea salt** and freshly ground **black pepper**. In a heavy frying pan over low heat, sauté 1 finely chopped **onion** and a pinch each of sea salt and **paprika** in a little **olive oil** for about 5 minutes until soft. Increase the heat to medium and add 8oz (225g) good-quality **sausage meat** to the pan. Cook, stirring to break up any lumps, until no longer pink. Reduce the heat slightly and add 2 grated **zucchini**. Cook slowly, stirring from time to time, for another 10–15 minutes. Remove from the heat and stir in the bulgur wheat. Sprinkle with a handful of finely chopped **flat-leaf parsley leaves** and serve immediately.

Spicy sausage and tomato skewers

Chorizo and baby onion casserole

9 Zucchini stuffed with sausage meat and red onion

PREP 15 MINS   COOK 40 MINS

SERVES 4

Halve 4 large **zucchini** lengthwise. Scoop out the flesh, coarsely chop, and set aside with the zucchini "shells." In a frying pan, sauté 1 chopped large **red onion** in a little **olive oil** over low-medium heat for a few minutes until soft. Add 2 chopped **garlic cloves** and the chopped zucchini flesh, season well with **sea salt** and freshly ground **black pepper**, and sauté for few minutes more. Next, add 8oz (225g) good-quality **sausage meat** and a pinch of ground **cinnamon**. Cook, stirring to break up any lumps, until the meat is no longer pink. Brush the zucchini shells with a little olive oil, season, and place in a roasting pan. Pack each zucchini shell with the sausage meat mixture. Any leftover mixture can be rolled into balls and cooked alongside the stuffed zucchini. Roast in a preheated 400°F (200°C) oven for 30–40 minutes until the zucchini are soft and beginning to char and the meat is cooked through. Serve hot, either whole or cut into slices, with the leftover meatballs alongside.

10 Chorizo and baby onion casserole

PREP 15 MINS   COOK 1 HR

Special equipment • flameproof casserole

SERVES 4

Cook a handful of peeled whole small **cipollini onions** or **pearl onions** in **olive oil** in a flameproof casserole until golden. Sprinkle in a pinch of **fennel seeds**, 2 chopped **garlic cloves**, and 1 seeded and finely chopped fresh **red chile**. Throw in 8oz (225g) sliced or cubed **chorizo** and cook for a couple of minutes, then pour in a 14oz (400g) can **diced tomatoes**. Fill the can with hot **water** and pour this in too. Stir and season with **sea salt** and freshly ground **black pepper**. Cook, covered, in a preheated 400°F (200°C) oven for about 40 minutes. Add some hot water as needed if seems too dry. Serve hot with creamy **mashed potatoes**.

143

10 WAYS WITH...
EGGS

1 The perfect omelet

SERVES 1

Lightly whisk 2 **eggs** with a tiny drop of **milk** and season with **salt** and **pepper**. Heat a small frying pan until hot and add 1 tablespoon **butter**. Once the butter is melted and foaming, pour in the egg mixture and pull the edges away from the side of the pan toward the center using a spatula; keep doing this so that any uncooked mixture runs to the edge. After about 30 seconds, most of the egg should be set. It will still be soft and uncooked in the middle, but residual heat will continue cooking the omelet after you have taken it out of the pan. Sprinkle a handful of grated **cheese** down the center of the omelet, then fold one half of the omelet over the top of the other. Slide onto a plate and serve immediately.

2 French toast

SERVES 1

Lightly whisk together 2 **eggs** and season with **salt**. Pour into a wide and shallow bowl and place 2 slices of day-old white **bread** in the beaten egg mixture so that they are completely covered and soak up all the liquid. Heat a nonstick frying pan over medium-high heat. Add a tablespoon of **butter** and, when hot, put the slices of bread in the pan. Cook for 2–3 minutes on each side until golden. Serve immediately.

3 Indian spiced scrambled eggs

SERVES 2

Whisk together 4 **eggs** and 4 tablespoons **milk** and season with **salt** and **pepper**. Melt 1 tablespoon **butter** in a deep-sided frying pan. Once the butter is foaming, pour in the egg mixture and stir with a wooden spoon or spatula over low heat until the eggs begin to scramble lightly. Add a pinch each of ground **turmeric** and **garam masala**, and stir. They will continue to cook after being removed from the heat, so take them off when they are still creamy. Serve immediately with hot buttered multigrain toast and smoked salmon if you wish.

4 Egg fried rice

Special equipment • wok

SERVES 4

Whisk together 2 **eggs** with some **salt** and **pepper**. Heat 1 tablespoon **sesame oil** in a wok over medium-high heat. Swirl around the pan, then add 10oz (300g) completely cold cooked **basmati rice** (use rice cooked the day before and refrigerated overnight for the best results). Stir-fry for a few minutes, then add the beaten eggs. Continue stir-frying for a few more minutes while the eggs begin to set. Stir in a handful of cooked or fresh garden **peas** and a bunch of **scallions**, finely chopped. Season with salt and pepper, and serve right away.

The perfect omelet

5 Baked eggs with tomatoes

  PREP 5 MINS

Special equipment • 4 ramekins

SERVES 4

Spoon 1 tablespoon **heavy cream** into 4 ramekins, then break an **egg** into each one, being careful not to break the yolks. Season with **salt** and **pepper**, then top each egg with another tablespoon of heavy cream and 1 tablespoon per ramekin of peeled, chopped **tomatoes**. Place the ramekins in a roasting pan and pour in enough hot **water** to come halfway up their sides. Cover the pan with foil, then carefully slide into a preheated 350°F (180°C) oven. Cook for about 15 minutes, then serve immediately with some whole wheat toast.

6 Peppered tuna with eggs

  PREP 15 MINS

SERVES 4

Place 4 **eggs** in a saucepan, cover with **water**, bring to a boil, and then simmer for 10 minutes. Meanwhile, roll a 9oz (250g) fresh **tuna loin** in some cracked **black pepper**. In a pan over medium heat, sear the tuna in a little hot **olive oil** for 3-4 minutes on each side. Remove tuna from pan, slice, and serve with a handful of pitted and sliced **black olives**, 10 **anchovies** in oil, drained, and the peeled and quartered eggs. Arrange on a plate with **arugula**, squeeze half a **lemon** over the dish, add a drizzle of extra virgin olive oil, and season to taste.

7 Egg curry with turmeric

  PREP 10 MINS

SERVES 4

Heat a little **olive oil** in a heavy frying pan over low heat. Add 1 finely chopped **onion**, 1 seeded and finely chopped fresh hot **green chile**, and a 1in (2.5cm) piece of fresh **ginger**, grated. Sauté for 5 minutes, until soft. Stir in 1-2 tablespoons ground **turmeric** and 2 tablespoons **Indian curry paste**. Pour in 1¼ cups **tomato juice** and ⅔ cup **heavy cream**. Season with **salt** and **pepper** and simmer for 15-20 minutes. Meanwhile, put 4 **eggs** in a saucepan, cover with **water**, bring to a boil, and then simmer for 10 minutes. When cool enough to handle, shell and quarter the eggs and add to the sauce to just heat through. Serve immediately.

Baked eggs with tomatoes

8 Blue cheese and herby baked omelet

 PREP 5 MINS

SERVES 4

Whisk together 8 **eggs** and ⅔ cup **heavy cream**. Season generously with **salt** and **pepper** and stir in a bunch of fresh **chives**, finely chopped, and a bunch of fresh **flat-leaf parsley**, finely chopped. In a large ovenproof nonstick frying pan over low-medium heat, sauté 2 sliced red onions in a little **olive oil** and **butter** for 5-8 minutes until soft. Season again, add the egg mixture to the frying pan, and cook for 2-3 minutes, pulling the mixture away from the edge of the pan toward the center. Sprinkle with 4½oz (125g) **blue cheese** and transfer to a 400°F (200°C) oven. Bake for 10-15 minutes until set and golden. Remove from the oven and let cool for a few minutes before removing from pan and slicing. Serve at once.

9   Cheese and herb frittata

PREP 15 MINS   COOK 15 MINS

SERVES 4

Preheat the broiler to its highest setting. Whisk together 8 **eggs** in a large bowl. Season with **salt** and **pepper**. Stir in a handful of fresh **flat-leaf parsley**, finely chopped, and a few finely chopped fresh **tarragon leaves**. Add 4½oz (125g) grated **Gruyère cheese** and stir to combine. Melt 4 tablespoons **butter** in a nonstick frying pan about 8in (20cm) in diameter. When the butter begins to foam, pour in the egg mixture and reduce the heat to low. Swirl the egg mixture around the pan so that it runs toward the edges and cook for 10-12 minutes, until the bottom is set and slightly brown; the top will still be runny. Then place the pan under the hot broiler for a couple of minutes, watching closely, and remove as soon as the top of the frittata is set. Let stand for a few minutes, then run a knife around the edge and slide the frittata onto a plate. Cut into wedges and serve.

10   Egg and fennel potato salad

PREP 10 MINS   COOK 20 MINS

SERVES 4

Put 4 **eggs** in a saucepan, cover with **water**, bring to a boil, and then simmer for 10 minutes. Cook 9oz (250g) **new potatoes** in lightly salted boiling water for 15-20 minutes until soft; drain. Drizzle **olive oil** over the potatoes while they are still hot and season with **salt** and **pepper**. Mix in a handful of fresh **flat-leaf parsley**, finely chopped, and 1 **fennel bulb**, trimmed and finely chopped. Shell and quarter the hard-boiled eggs and add to the potato salad. Serve immediately.

EVERYDAY

Egg and fennel potato salad

EVERYDAY

10 WAYS WITH...
BACON AND HAM

1 Crispy bacon and avocado wraps

  PREP 5 MINS · COOK 10 MINS

SERVES 4

Cook 8oz (225g) thick **bacon strips** over medium-high heat until golden and crispy. Use to fill 4 **flour tortillas**, along with a handful of **romaine lettuce**, shredded, and 1 ripe **avocado**, peeled, pitted, and cut into slices. Squeeze the juice of 1 **lemon** and lots of freshly ground **black pepper** into 3-4 tablespoons **mayonnaise**, stir well, and use to top the bacon mix. Roll up the tortillas and serve immediately.

2 Savory cheese and bacon muffins

  PREP 15 MINS · COOK 25 MINS

Special equipment • 4 x 5fl oz (150ml) metal pudding molds or ramekins

SERVES 4

Cook 5½oz (150g) sliced **Canadian bacon** until cooked but not too crispy, then cut into bite-sized pieces. Mix together 7oz (200g) **Cheddar cheese**, cut up into small dice, with 1¼ cups fresh **bread crumbs**, ½ bunch of **scallions**, finely chopped, 3 **eggs**, and ½ cup **milk**. Stir in the bacon and a handful of chopped fresh **chives**. Season generously with **salt** and **pepper**, then spoon into 4 buttered ramekins or metal pudding molds. Bake in the oven at 375°F (190°C) for about 25 minutes until risen and golden. Serve hot or cold.

3 Prosciutto, grape, and walnut salad

  PREP 10 MINS · COOK 2 MINS

SERVES 4

Whisk together 3 tablespoons **extra virgin olive oil** with 1 tablespoon freshly squeezed **lemon juice** and 1 teaspoon **honey**. Season with **salt** and **pepper** and set aside. Melt 1 tablespoon **butter** with a pinch of **demerara sugar** in a small frying pan over medium heat. Once the sugar has dissolved, add a handful of halved **walnuts** and stir until well coated. Remove from the pan and set aside on a plate. Put 2 handfuls of mixed salad in a large shallow serving bowl. Add a handful of seedless **black grapes**, the walnuts, and 1 ripe **avocado**, peeled, pitted, and sliced. Toss gently with a little dressing. Top with 8oz (225g) **prosciutto**. Drizzle with some more dressing and serve immediately.

4 Fish wrapped in bacon

  PREP 5 MINS · COOK 20 MINS

SERVES 4

Wrap 8oz (225g) **bacon strips** around 4 thick **haddock fillets**, about 5½oz (150g) each. Place the wrapped fish in a roasting pan, drizzle with a little **olive oil**, and throw in some sprigs of fresh **rosemary**. Cook in a preheated 400°F (200°C) oven for 15-20 minutes until the fish is cooked and the bacon is golden and crispy. Serve immediately with minted peas or lima beans.

Savory cheese and bacon muffins

Pancetta and potatoes with greens

 PREP 10 MINS COOK 15 MINS

SERVES 4

Heat a large frying pan over medium-high heat. Add 1 tablespoon **butter** and 1 tablespoon **olive oil**, pour in 3 cubed cooked **potatoes**, and sauté for 5-10 minutes until golden and crispy, adding more oil if needed. Season with **salt** and **pepper**. Push the potatoes to one side of the pan, add 6oz (175g) cubed **pancetta**, and cook until crispy. Stir in 7oz (200g) lightly cooked **shredded greens** such as kale and cook until wilted down and well combined. Season again if needed, and serve immediately with fresh crusty bread.

Bacon, pear, and blue cheese salad

 PREP 10 MINS COOK 10 MINS

SERVES 4

Whisk together 3 tablespoons **extra virgin olive oil**, 1 tablespoon **white wine vinegar**, and a pinch of **sugar**. Season with **salt** and **pepper**. Add 1¾oz (50g) crumbled **blue cheese** such as Stilton and whisk together well until the dressing thickens. Set aside. In a small frying pan, cook 8oz (225g) **bacon strips** for 5-9 minutes until crispy, then cut into small pieces. Core and slice 3 ripe **pears** and add to a shallow bowl with 2 handfuls of mixed salad greens and the bacon pieces. Crumble 1¾oz (50g) blue cheese over the salad, drizzle with the dressing, and serve immediately.

Ham with minted peas and fava beans

 PREP 10 MINS COOK 30 MINS

SERVES 4

Heat a little **olive oil** In a large frying pan over low heat. Sauté 1 chopped **onion** for about 5 minutes until soft. Add 2 finely chopped **garlic cloves** and stir in 5½oz (150g) frozen fava beans and 2½oz (75g) frozen **peas**. Pour in ⅔ cup **chicken stock** and bring to a boil. Reduce the heat slightly and simmer for another 15 minutes. Stir in a handful of fresh **mint leaves**, chopped, and 6oz (175g) cooked **ham**, cut into cubes. Serve at once with a salad on the side.

Pancetta and artichoke risotto

PREP 10 MINS COOK 30 MINS

SERVES 4

In a large frying pan over medium heat, cook 5½oz (150g) cubed **pancetta** in a little **olive oil** until crispy. Remove with a slotted spoon and set aside. Add 1 tablespoon **butter** and 1 tablespoon olive oil to the same pan, reduce the heat to low, and sauté 1 finely chopped **onion** for about 5 minutes until soft. Stir in 9oz (250g) **Arborio** or other **risotto rice** until well coated, then pour in ¾ cup **dry white wine**. Increase the heat and let bubble for a few minutes, then measure out 3 cups **vegetable stock** and pour in about ⅔ cup. Keep stirring and adding stock, a little at a time, until the rice has absorbed all the liquid and is creamy but still has a bite to it. Use more or less stock as needed. Transfer the pancetta back into the pan and stir. Add a 14oz (400ml) can drained halved **artichoke hearts** and gently stir again until heated through. Serve hot with freshly grated **Parmesan cheese** for sprinkling on top.

Ham with minted peas and fava beans

Pancetta with scallops

9 Bacon and tomato sauce with gnocchi

PREP 10 MINS · COOK 20 MINS

SERVES 4

In a heavy saucepan over medium-high heat, cook 5½oz (150g) diced **Canadian bacon** or cubed **pancetta** for 5–8 minutes until crispy, then set aside. In the same pan, bring 1¼ cups **tomato sauce** to a boil. Stir in a heaping teaspoon pre-made **red or green pesto** and return the bacon to the pan. Reduce the heat and simmer gently for about 15 minutes. In a separate large pot, cook 10oz (300g) **gnocchi** in boiling salted water according to the package instructions, then drain and serve with the sauce. Top with freshly grated **Parmesan cheese** and torn fresh **basil leaves** and serve immediately.

10 Pancetta with scallops

PREP 5 MINS · COOK 10 MINS

SERVES 4

Heat a nonstick frying pan over medium-high heat. Add 1 tablespoon **butter** and 1 tablespoon **olive oil**. Season 12 fresh **scallops** with **salt** and **pepper** and add to the pan. Sear for 2 minutes on one side (or longer, depending on thickness), then turn over and cook on the other side for a few minutes more, turning the scallop that went into the pan first and working your way to the last one. Remove from the pan with a slotted spoon and place on a serving dish covered in foil to keep warm. Add a drizzle of olive oil to the same pan, pour in 5½oz (150g) cubed **pancetta**, and cook for 5–8 minutes until crisp. When cooked, pour over the scallops, along with any juices from the pan. Serve immediately with mixed salad leaves and lemon wedges.

10 WAYS WITH...
TURKEY

1 Turkey and tarragon broth

SERVES 4

In a large pan over low heat, sauté 1 finely chopped **onion** in a little **olive oil** for about 5 minutes until soft. Add 2 finely chopped **garlic cloves** and season with **sea salt** and freshly ground **black pepper**. Add 3 peeled and sliced **carrots** and a few chopped **tarragon leaves** and cook for 10 minutes, until the carrots begin to soften. Pour in 3 cups hot **chicken stock** and bring to a boil. Reduce the heat to a simmer and add 3 cubed cooked **potatoes**, 8oz (225g) shredded or sliced cooked turkey, and a few more fresh tarragon leaves. Simmer gently until heated through and serve with fresh **bread**.

2 Turkey curry

SERVES 4

In a large frying pan over low heat, sauté 1 finely chopped **onion** in 1 tablespoon **olive oil** for 5 minutes until soft. Stir in 3 finely chopped **garlic cloves** and season with **sea salt** and **black pepper**. Add 1 teaspoon crushed **coriander seeds**, 4 **cardamom pods**, a handful of crushed **curry leaves**, a 1in (2.5cm) piece of fresh **ginger**, grated, and 2–3 seeded and finely chopped fresh medium-hot **red chiles**. Cook for few minutes, then pour in a 14oz (400g) can whole peeled **tomatoes**, chopped and including any juices. Bring to a boil, reduce the heat slightly, and simmer for 15 minutes. Add 7oz (200g) **shredded** or **sliced cooked turkey**. Stir in ⅔ cup heavy cream. Simmer gently for 10 more minutes until the turkey is hot and the sauce is creamy. Season and serve.

3 Turkey cutlets stuffed with prunes and pecans

Special equipment • cocktail sticks or skewers

SERVES 4

Put 4 skinless **turkey breast cutlets**, about 7oz (200g) each, between 2 sheets of plastic wrap. Pound with a meat mallet or the edge of a rolling pin to an even thickness of about ¼in (5mm). Slice the breasts in half so that you have 8 pieces. Chop a large handful of **pitted prunes** and mix with a handful of finely chopped roasted **pecans** and a handful of finely chopped **flat-leaf parsley**. Spoon the mixture into the middle of each pounded piece of turkey, then roll up and secure with a cocktail stick. Place the turkey rolls in a roasting pan, drizzle with **olive oil**, and roast in a preheated 400°F (200°C) oven for 20–30 minutes until cooked through.

4 Shredded turkey, mint, and pomegranate salad

SERVES 4

Arrange 2 handfuls of **arugula** on a serving plate and top with 10oz (300g) **sliced cooked turkey breast**. Scatter a bunch of **scallions**, sliced, a handful of fresh **mint leaves**, and the seeds of 1 **pomegranate** over the turkey. Whisk together 3 tablespoons **extra virgin olive oil**, 1 tablespoon freshly squeezed **lemon juice**, 1 tablespoon **pomegranate molasses**, and a pinch of ground **cinnamon**. Season with **sea salt** and freshly ground **black pepper**. Taste the dressing, adding a pinch of **sugar** if it needs sweetening. Drizzle over the salad and serve at once.

Turkey cutlets stuffed with prunes and pecans

Turkey and mixed rice salad

PREP 10 MINS

SERVES 4

Mix together 7oz (200g) cold cooked **rice** with a 14oz (400g) can drained **chickpeas**. Season with **sea salt** and **pepper**. Stir in 8oz (225g) **shredded** or **sliced cooked turkey breast**, 1¾oz (50g) dried **cranberries**, and a handful of toasted **pine nuts**. Whisk together 3 tablespoons **olive oil**, 1 tablespoon **white wine vinegar**, 1 teaspoon **coarse-grain mustard**, and 1 teaspoon **honey**, and season again. To serve, drizzle the dressing over the rice and stir in chopped **flat-leaf parsley**.

Turkey, chile, and cashew stir-fry

PREP 5 MINS **COOK 15 MINS**

Special equipment • wok

SERVES 4

In a wok over low heat, stir-fry a bunch of **scallions**, sliced, in a drizzle of **sesame oil** for 5 minutes. Slice 2 large skinless **turkey breast cutlets**–about 7oz (200g) each. Stir-fry in the oil with the scallions until no longer pink. Add 3 sliced **garlic cloves** and 2 red and 1 green seeded and shredded fresh **chiles**. Continue to stir-fry for another 10 minutes, then add a handful of raw **cashews** and a splash of **soy sauce** and toss the turkey well. Serve immediately with a splash of **sweet chile sauce** and some **fluffy rice**.

Turkey breasts with honey and roasted hazelnuts

PREP 15 MINS **COOK 40**

Special equipment • food processor

SERVES 4

Heat 2 tablespoons honey in a small pan, then brush it over 4 **turkey breasts**, skin on and about 7oz (200g) each. Season with **sea salt** and freshly ground **black pepper**. Pulse a handful of toasted **hazelnuts** in a food processor until ground, then pour onto a plate. Roll each of the turkey breasts in the ground nuts until evenly coated. Place in a roasting pan skin-side up and roast in a preheated 400°F (200°C) oven for 25–40 minutes until the turkey is cooked through. Pierce with a knife to check–the juices should run clear. Let the turkey rest for a few minutes, then slice and serve with sautéed **potatoes** and **broccoli** tossed in **lemon juice** and **chili oil**.

Marinated turkey cutlets with harissa and lemon

PREP 10 MINS **COOK 45 MINS**

Marinating • 30 minutes

SERVES 4

Mix 3 tablespoons **harissa** with the juice of 1 **lemon** and a handful of finely chopped **mint leaves**. Take 4 large **turkey breast cutlets**, skin on and about 7oz (200g) each, and slash 3 or 4 times on the diagonal, slicing through the skin and into the meat. Coat with the harissa mixture, making sure that it gets into the slashes. Season with **sea salt** and freshly ground **black pepper**. Allow to marinate in the refrigerator for at least 30 minutes, or preferably overnight. Place in a roasting pan, and roast in a preheated 400°F (200°C) oven for 30–45 minutes until the turkey is cooked through and the skin is golden and crispy. Let rest for 5 minutes, then slice and serve with some **salad greens** with a squeeze of **lemon** and a **potato salad** made with **olive oil**.

Marinated turkey cutlets with harissa and lemon

Asian turkey and noodle soup

9 Asian turkey and noodle soup

PREP 10 MINS

SERVES 4

Pour 3 cups hot **vegetable stock** into a large saucepan. Add a generous splash of **soy sauce**, 1 stalk **lemongrass**, peeled and finely chopped, a 1in (2.5cm) piece of fresh **ginger**, sliced, and 2 large skinless **turkey breast fillets**, about 7oz (200g) each. Bring to a boil, reduce the heat slightly, and simmer for 15–20 minutes, depending on size, until the turkey is fully poached and cooked through. Remove from the pan using a slotted spoon and shred when cool. Add 10oz (300g) fine **rice noodles** and 1 seeded and sliced fresh **red chile** to the poaching liquid and simmer for 5 minutes. If necessary, add boiling **water** to cover the noodles. Return the shredded turkey to the pan with a handful of fresh **cilantro** and heat through. Season with **sea salt** and freshly ground **black pepper** to taste. Serve immediately.

10 Turkey and corn meatballs

PREP 15 MINS

Special equipment • food processor

SERVES 4

In a food processor, pulse 2 skinless **turkey breast cutlets**, about 7oz (200g) each, until ground—be careful not to turn them into a paste. Add a 14oz (400g) can drained **corn kernels** and a bunch of **scallions**, chopped. Pulse until well combined. Transfer the mixture to a bowl, add a handful of fresh **flat-leaf parsley**, finely chopped, and season well with **sea salt** and freshly ground **black pepper**. Add 1 **egg** and use your hands to mix everything together until well combined. Form into balls a little larger than a walnut and roll until tightly formed; you should end up with 12 balls. Dredge each ball in **flour**. Cook a few at a time in a little **olive oil** in a large nonstick frying pan over medium-high heat for about 5–8 minutes until golden. Serve hot.

155

FASTER PASTA

Simple sauces and easy bakes, many ready in under 20 minutes.

FASTER PASTA

If there is pasta in your store cupboard, a quick and easy meal is just minutes away. Pasta can taste delicious on its own, simply seasoned and drizzled with olive oil, or it can be the vehicle for a variety of sauces. Convenient and versatile, there are dozens of shapes to choose from, and each has sauces it works best with.

Types of pasta Here are the most widely available shapes and how to use them.

dried versus fresh

This is one occasion when fresh is not always best. If making your own pasta or buying it fresh from the deli, then fresh is superior. However, if buying pasta from the supermarket, dried pasta is usually the best option, because the fresh pasta is often too wet. Choose a good brand, preferably one made in Italy, where it is made with durum wheat.

EVERYDAY

LONG	RIBBON	SHORT	TUBULAR	STUFFED

LONG

SPAGHETTI ("strings")
Long, thin, round, and rigid. Probably the most common of all shapes, and extremely versatile.

LINGUINE ("small tongues")
Similar to spaghetti in appearance, but flat rather than round. Can be used whenever a recipe calls for spaghetti.

CAPELLI D'ANGELO ("angel hair")
Very fine strands. Not sturdy enough for sauce, so best added to soups and broths.

BUCATINI (buco = "hole")
A fat, long, and hollow spaghetti.

OTHER TYPES
Fusilli lunghi (long fusilli), spaghettini (thin spaghetti)

BEST WITH...
Oil-based or tomato sauces are ideal, as each strand of pasta gets well coated. Perfect tossed with seafood, especially linguine, which is wonderful paired with clams.

RIBBON

TAGLIATELLE (to "cut")
This wide, flat pasta is the most well-known of the ribbon pastas. It is often flavored with spinach to produce a green pasta, or tomato to produce a red one.

PAPPARDELLE (pappare = "to stuff oneself")
The widest of the ribbon pastas. As a rule of thumb, big pasta needs a big sauce.

FETTUCCINI ("little ribbons")
Long and flat, similar to tagliatelle, but a little wider.

OTHER TYPES
Lasagne

BEST WITH...
A robust chunky sauce. Meat- or tomato-based sauces—such as ragù—work well, as do thick, cream-based sauces, which are heavy and cling well to the wide ribbons.

SHORT

FARFALLE ("butterflies")
Look like little butterflies, or bows, and have a ridged edge. They are quite delicate, and go well with light sauces.

FUSILLI ("little spindles")
Look like short springs. A good choice to serve in a salad, as they hold their shape well. They often come in a variety of colors.

CONCHIGLIE ("shells")
These are available in a variety of sizes, either very small (which are added to soups), or really large ones that look like sea shells.

OTHER TYPES
Orecchiette, trofie, strozzapreti, radiatore

BEST WITH...
Short pasta is fairly dense, so it can take chunky sauces, and works particularly well with rich meat sauces and oily sauces. If serving with a vegetable sauce, cut the vegetables to match the size of the pasta shapes.

TUBULAR

PENNE ("quills")
The most well-known tubular pasta. They have pointed ends, and are either smooth or ridged. A versatile pasta shape, it can be combined with numerous sauces.

RIGATONI ("ridged")
Very similar to penne, but ridged, and without the pointed "pen" ends.

MACARONI ("dumpling")
Hollow, curved pasta tubes that can be small or large. Very sturdy, they go well with a cheese sauce.

OTHER TYPES
Ziti, cavatappi, gigantoni

BEST WITH...
These shapes are ideal for trapping and holding thick and chunky rich sauces. Serve with a heavy meat ragù, or a chunky arrabbiata sauce.

STUFFED

RAVIOLI (to "wrap")
Widely known, and usually bought fresh. Delicious flat parcels of egg pasta, they can be filled with meat, cheese, vegetables, or seafood, depending on the region in which they're made.

TORTELLINI (torta = "cake")
Ring-shaped pasta, filled and pinched in the middle. They can be bought dried or fresh, and are often filled with classic combinations, such as spinach and ricotta cheese.

OTHER TYPES
Cannelloni, tortelloni

BEST WITH...
This depends on what the pasta is stuffed with. Ravioli stuffed with pumpkin and ricotta cheese is delicious with melted butter and sage, for instance. Make sure the sauce complements and doesn't drown the flavor of the filling.

How to cook pasta

Use lots of water. Pasta needs room to move around while it is cooking, otherwise it will stick together. Use a very large pan with plenty of water. As a rule, 2oz (60g)of pasta needs about 2 cups of water. Don't try to cook too much at one time.

Don't add oil to the water while it cooks. If anything, this prevents the sauce from clinging to it.

Bring the water to a rolling boil and add a pinch of salt just before adding the pasta. Keep at a rolling boil while cooking.

Watch the clock. Fresh pasta will cook much quicker than dried. Some will cook in a couple of minutes, so always have your sauce prepared.

Cook until _al dente_, meaning it still has a bit of bite to it. You can remove a piece while it's cooking to test it.

Drain and return to the pan with a little of its cooking water, which will prevent it from sticking.

Go easy on the sauce. The sauce is supposed to coat the pasta, not drench it. Remember the pasta is the main ingredient, and the correct way is to add the sauce to the pasta, not the pasta to the sauce.

Serve instantly, as pasta doesn't take kindly to being reheated.

Make your own pasta

It's far easier than you think, satisfying, and tastes wonderful. This method makes enough pasta for 4 people.

1 Make the dough Put 3½ cups of "00" flour or bread flour onto a large clean surface and make a well in the center. Add a pinch of salt, then 3 large eggs plus 2 egg yolks to the well. Using a fork, gradually stir the egg and bring the flour in from the sides so it begins to turn into a paste. Keep adding the flour a little at a time until it is all incorporated.

2 Knead Using your hands, bring the mixture together, then begin kneading the dough using the heel of your hand. Knead for about 10 minutes, or until the dough is still springy but has a smooth texture. Wrap in plastic wrap and rest in the refrigerator for about 30 minutes.

3 Roll On a floured (or semolina-sprinkled) surface, roll the pasta out to an oval shape about 1in (2.5cm) thick. Set the machine to its widest setting and feed through the dough a couple of times, turning the wheel as you go. Continue, changing the roller settings as you go so the pasta becomes thinner. As it gets longer, use your hands to guide it through. Now it is ready to cut to your preferred shape. Leave to dry in bundles for 10 minutes before cooking.

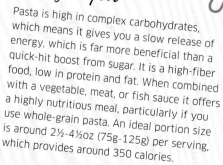

good for you

Pasta is high in complex carbohydrates, which means it gives you a slow release of energy, which is far more beneficial than a quick-hit boost from sugar. It is a high-fiber food, low in protein and fat. When combined with a vegetable, meat, or fish sauce it offers a highly nutritious meal, particularly if you use whole-grain pasta. An ideal portion size is around 2½–4½oz (75g–125g) per serving, which provides around 350 calories.

How to store

Dried A cool dark pantry, for up to 1 year. If opened, keep in a sealed jar, or in its packaging, well-wrapped with plastic wrap.

Fresh In the refrigerator for 2–3 days. Can be frozen for up to 1 month.

Cooked In the refrigerator, in a sealed container, for 2–3 days. Not suitable for freezing.

Psst...

Did you know that in Italy, pasta is always served as a first course? Traditionally this was done in order to fill you up before the more expensive main course of meat or fish was served.

3 easy lunchbox recipes

A simple way to try some of the pasta shapes in the chart opposite. Or, you can use cold leftover pasta instead.

Pasta with vegetables Cook 8oz (225g) of pasta shells until *al dente*. Drain and return to the pan with a little of the pasta water. Toss with 2 tbsp olive oil, 2 finely chopped garlic cloves, and season. Leave to cool, then add 2 chopped tomatoes, a handful of basil leaves, torn, 3 finely chopped scallions, 1 seeded and finely sliced yellow bell pepper, and ¼ cucumber, cut into chunks. Toss together.

Pasta with beans Cook 8oz (225g) of pasta bows until *al dente*. Drain and return to the pan with a little of the pasta water. Toss with 2 tbsp of olive oil and ½ a drained and rinsed can of flageolet beans. Leave to cool, then add a handful of fresh flat-leaf parsley, finely chopped, and season.

Pasta with tuna Cook 8oz (225g) of pasta twists until *al dente*. Drain and return to the pan with a little of the pasta water. Toss with 2 tbsp of olive oil, the juice of 1 lemon, 1 seeded and finely chopped red chile, and a 6oz (175g) can of drained tuna steaks. Season and leave to cool.

EVERYDAY

EVERYDAY

Pasta with zucchini and saffron

PREP 10 MINS

SERVES 4

1 tbsp olive oil
1 onion, finely chopped
3 garlic cloves, finely chopped
pinch of saffron threads
3–4 zucchini, cut in half and diced
sea salt and freshly ground
   black pepper
1 cup heavy whipping cream
pinch of crushed red pepper flakes
   (optional)
8oz (225g) dried fettuccine
handful of finely chopped flat-leaf
   parsley (optional)
½ cup freshly grated Parmesan cheese

1 Heat the oil in a large frying pan, add the onion, and cook over medium heat for 5 minutes or until soft. Add the garlic and saffron, cook for a few seconds more, then add the zucchini. Season well with salt and pepper. Stir in the cream and pepper flakes and gently simmer for about 4 minutes.

2 Meanwhile, cook the pasta as the package directs, until it is tender yet still firm to the bite. Drain, reserving a bit of the cooking water. Return the pasta to the pot and toss with the reserved cooking water.

3 Add the sauce, toss, then add the parsley, if using, and toss once more. Sprinkle with Parmesan and serve.

VARIATION Swap the zucchini for asparagus when in season.

Pasta with no-cook tomato sauce

PREP 5 MINS

SERVES 4

6 ripe tomatoes, cored and
   coarsely chopped
2 garlic cloves, finely chopped
handful of fresh basil leaves, torn
3 tbsp extra virgin olive oil
sea salt and freshly ground
   black pepper
12oz (350g) dried farfalle

1 Put the tomatoes, garlic, basil, and olive oil in a large bowl and season well with salt and pepper. Stir to combine, then leave to sit while you cook the pasta—the flavors will develop.

2 Cook the pasta as the package directs, until it is tender yet still firm to the bite. Drain well, then toss with the tomato sauce and serve.

COOK'S NOTES

A pinch of crushed red pepper flakes also works well in this dish. The longer you leave the tomato mixture to sit, the tastier it gets.

Pasta with hot pepper sauce

  PREP 10 MINS COOK 15 MINS

SERVES 4

1 tbsp olive oil
1 onion, finely chopped
sea salt and freshly ground
   black pepper
2 garlic cloves, finely chopped
2 fresh red hot chile peppers, seeded
   and finely chopped
2 red and 1 yellow bell pepper,
   seeded and coarsely chopped
12oz (350g) dried penne or medium
   pasta shells (conchiglie)
handful of fresh basil leaves, torn
¼ cup freshly grated Parmesan cheese
splash of good-quality balsamic
   vinegar (optional)

1 Heat the oil in a frying pan, add the onion, and cook over low heat for 5 minutes or until soft. Season well with salt and pepper. Add the garlic and chiles and cook for a few seconds more. Add the bell peppers and cook, stirring occasionally for 5 minutes or until soft.

2 Meanwhile, cook the pasta as the package directs, or until it is tender yet still firm to the bite. Drain, reserving a small amount of the cooking water. Return the pasta to the pot and toss together with the reserved cooking water. Add the pepper mixture and the basil and toss again. Sprinkle with Parmesan and balsamic vinegar (if using), and serve with a crisp salad on the side.

Cheat...
To speed things up, use a 12oz (350g) jar of roasted peppers and toss it with hot pasta.

Pasta with beef and mushroom sauce

   PREP 10 MINS COOK 25 MINS

Freeze • the sauce can be frozen

SERVES 4

1 tbsp olive oil
1 onion, finely chopped
sea salt and freshly ground
   black pepper
1¼lb (500g) lean ground beef
8oz (200g) mushrooms, chopped
2 garlic cloves, finely chopped
pinch of oregano
1 x 14oz (400g) can diced tomatoes
1 tsp prepared pesto
12oz (350g) dried tortiglioni or other
   tube-shaped pasta

1 Heat the oil in a large frying pan, add the onion, and cook over low heat for 5 minutes or until soft. Season well with salt and pepper, then stir in the ground beef and cook, stirring and breaking up any large chunks, until no longer pink, about 5 minutes.

2 Add the mushrooms, garlic, oregano, and tomatoes with their juices and stir well. Simmer for 10 minutes, then stir the in the pesto. Taste and season again, if needed.

3 Meanwhile, cook the pasta as the package directs, or until it is tender yet still firm to the bite. Drain, reserving a small amount of the cooking water. Return the pasta to the pot and toss together with the reserved cooking water. Add the meat sauce and toss again. Serve immediately.

Cheat...
Chop canned tomatoes while they are still in the can with a pair of scissors or a knife.

COOK'S NOTES

Tossing pasta with a little of the water it was cooked in helps the sauce cling to it better.

Pasta with sun-dried tomato pesto

PREP 10 MINS

Special equipment • food processor

SERVES 4

½ of a 10oz (300g) jar sun-dried
    tomatoes in oil, drained
handful of pine nuts
2 garlic cloves, coarsely chopped
handful of fresh basil leaves, plus
    extra for garnish
½ cup freshly grated Parmesan
    cheese, or as needed
sea salt and freshly ground
    black pepper
extra virgin olive oil
12oz (350g) dried fusilli

1 Combine the sun-dried tomatoes,
pine nuts, garlic, basil, and ½ cup
Parmesan in a food processor. Pulse
until blended. Season with salt and
pepper. Taste and add more Parmesan
and a splash of oil, as needed.

2 Meanwhile, cook the pasta as the
package directs, until it is tender yet
still firm to the bite. Drain, reserving
a small amount of the cooking water.
Return the pasta to the pot and toss
together with the reserved cooking
water. Add the pesto and toss again.
Drizzle with extra virgin olive oil,
garnish with basil leaves, and serve.

VARIATION
Use a handful of blanched
almonds instead of the pine nuts.

Cheat...
For a quick sauce,
combine the sun-dried
tomatoes with 2 tbsp of
prepared pesto.

Pasta with tomato sauce

PREP 5 MINS **COOK 25 MINS**

Freeze • the sauce can be frozen

SERVES 4

1 x 28oz (800g) can diced tomatoes,
    with juices
1 tbsp tomato purée
2 tbsp olive oil
sea salt and freshly ground
    black pepper
12oz (350g) dried penne
freshly grated Parmesan cheese,
    for serving

1 Place the tomatoes, tomato purée,
and olive oil in a saucepan, season
well with salt and pepper, and bring
to a boil. Reduce the heat to a simmer
and cook, uncovered, for 20 minutes.

2 Meanwhile, cook the pasta as the
package directs, until it is tender yet
still firm to the bite. Drain, reserving
a small amount of the cooking water.
Return the pasta to the pot and toss
together with the reserved cooking
water. Add the tomato sauce and toss
again. Sprinkle with Parmesan, season
with more black pepper, and serve.

VARIATION
Use rigatoni instead of penne.

Cheat...
Use a 12oz jar of
prepared tomato sauce for
the pasta. Drizzle with
olive oil and serve with
fresh basil.

Pasta with Pecorino and peas

PREP 10 MINS **COOK 20 MINS**

SERVES 4

1 tbsp olive oil
1 onion, finely chopped
sea salt and freshly ground
    black pepper
1 garlic clove, finely chopped
1 fresh red jalapeño chile pepper,
    seeded and finely chopped
2 tsp all-purpose flour
¼ cup dry white wine
⅔ cup whole milk
1 cup frozen peas
1 cup freshly grated Pecorino cheese,
    plus extra for serving
12oz (350g) dried farfalle

1 Heat the oil in a large frying pan, add the onion and a pinch of salt, and cook over low heat for 5 minutes or until soft. Stir in the garlic and chile and cook for a few seconds more. Stir in the flour until well blended, then add the wine and allow to bubble for a couple of minutes. Stir in the milk.

2 Stir in the peas, then add the Pecorino and cook at a low simmer—do not allow to boil—for 10 minutes or until the sauce has thickened slightly. Season well with salt and pepper.

3 Meanwhile, cook the pasta as the package directs, until it is tender yet still firm to the bite. Drain, reserving a small amount of the cooking water. Return the pasta to the pot and toss together with the reserved cooking water. Add the sauce, toss again, top with extra Pecorino, and serve.

VARIATION
Use Parmesan if you don't have Pecorino, but reduce the amount a little, as Pecorino is far milder.

EVERYDAY

Pasta with spicy sausage

PREP 15 MINS **COOK 25 MINS**

SERVES 4

1 tbsp olive oil
1 large red onion, very finely chopped
6–8 good-quality pork sausages,
    skins removed
1 fresh red jalapeño chile pepper,
    seeded and finely chopped
1 tsp cayenne pepper
½ cup dry white wine
2 garlic cloves, finely chopped
pinch of oregano
sea salt and freshly ground
    black pepper
⅔ cup hot vegetable stock or
    mushroom stock
1 cup heavy whipping cream
12oz (350g) dried penne rigate
small handful of finely chopped
    flat-leaf parsley

1 Heat the oil in a large frying pan, add the onion, and cook over low heat for 5 minutes or until soft. Chop the sausages and add to the pan, using the back of a fork to mash them. Cook until they are no longer pink, about 5 minutes, then stir in the chile and cayenne.

2 Increase the heat, add the wine, and allow to bubble for a few minutes. Add the garlic and oregano and season well with salt and pepper. Pour in the stock and cream, bring to a boil, then simmer for 10 minutes.

3 Meanwhile, cook the pasta as the package directs, until it is tender yet still firm to the bite. Drain, reserving a small amount of the cooking water. Return the pasta to the pot and toss together with the reserved cooking water. Add the sauce and toss again. Garnish with parsley and serve.

COOK'S NOTES

Make sure to break up the meat really well—it needs to have a crumbly texture.

Pasta with butternut squash, cream, and sage

PREP 15 MINS **COOK 20 MINS**

SERVES 4

1 butternut squash, peeled, cut in half, seeded, and cubed
pinch of crushed red pepper flakes
2 tbsp olive oil
1 red onion, finely chopped
2 garlic cloves, finely chopped
6 fresh sage leaves, coarsely chopped
⅔ cup heavy whipping cream
sea salt and freshly ground black pepper
12oz (350g) dried small to medium pasta shells (conchiglie)
freshly grated Parmesan cheese, for serving

1 Preheat the oven to 400°F (200°C). Place the squash in a large roasting pan, sprinkle with the pepper flakes, and drizzle with 1 tablespoon of the oil. Toss to coat, then spread in an even layer in the pan and roast for 10–15 minutes, or until the squash starts to soften.

2 Meanwhile, heat the remaining oil in a large frying pan, add the onion, and cook over low heat for 5 minutes or until soft. Stir in the almost-cooked squash, the garlic, and the sage leaves. Pour in the cream and simmer gently for 5 minutes. Season well with salt and lots of pepper.

3 Meanwhile, cook the pasta as the package directs, until it is tender yet still firm to the bite. Drain, reserving a small amount of the cooking water. Return the pasta to the pot and toss together with the reserved cooking water. Add the sauce, toss again, sprinkle with Parmesan, and serve.

Pasta with fennel and olives

PREP 10 MINS **COOK 20 MINS**

SERVES 4

2 fennel bulbs, trimmed and coarsely chopped
1 tbsp olive oil
1 red onion, finely chopped
sea salt and freshly ground black pepper
½ cup dry white wine
2 garlic cloves, finely chopped
handful of pitted black olives, such as kalamata, coarsely chopped if large
12oz (350g) dried linguine
freshly grated Parmesan cheese, for serving

1 Put the fennel in a saucepan, pour over enough boiling water to cover, and simmer for a couple of minutes until crisp-tender. Drain, reserving a little of the cooking liquid.

2 Heat the oil in a large frying pan, add the onion and a pinch of salt, and cook over low heat for 5 minutes or until soft. Increase the heat, add the wine, and simmer for 3–5 minutes. Add the garlic, fennel, and reserved cooking liquid. Add the olives and cook over low heat for 5 minutes. Season with salt and pepper.

3 Cook the pasta as the package directs. Drain, reserving a bit of the cooking water. Return the pasta to the pot and toss with the cooking water. Add the fennel and olives, toss again, sprinkle with Parmesan, and serve.

VARIATION Use dried spaghetti instead of linguine.

Pasta with pancetta and arugula

PREP 5 MINS · COOK 15 MINS

SERVES 4
1 tbsp olive oil
1 onion, finely chopped
pinch of sea salt
1 red hot chile pepper, seeded and
    finely chopped
8oz (225g) pancetta, cut into
    small dice
2 garlic cloves, finely chopped
12oz (350g) dried spaghetti
5–7oz (200g) arugula
freshly grated Parmesan cheese,
    for serving

1 Heat the oil in a large frying pan, add the onion and a pinch of salt, and cook over low heat for 5 minutes or until soft. Add the chile and cook for a few minutes more.

2 Add the pancetta and cook for 5 minutes until crisp and golden. Stir in the garlic and cook for a few seconds.

3 Meanwhile, cook the pasta as the package directs. Drain, reserving a bit of the cooking water. Return the pasta to the pot and toss with the reserved cooking water. Add the pancetta mixture and arugula and toss again. Sprinkle with Parmesan and serve.

VARIATION
Instead of Parmesan, serve with mozzarella, torn into pieces.

COOK'S NOTES
Don't add the arugula until the very last minute, or the leaves will begin to cook and lose their precious peppery flavor.

Pasta with anchovies, chiles, and lemon

PREP 10 MINS · COOK 10 MINS

SERVES 4
1 tbsp olive oil
2 red onions, finely chopped
pinch of sea salt
2 garlic cloves, grated or crushed
1 fresh red jalapeño chile pepper,
    seeded and finely chopped
1 fresh green jalapeño chile pepper,
    seeded and finely chopped
finely grated zest of 1 lemon
12oz (350g) dried linguine
    or spaghetti
12 anchovies in oil, drained
handful of finely chopped fresh
    flat-leaf parsley
juice of 1 lemon, for serving

1 Heat the oil in a frying pan, add the onions and a pinch of salt, and cook over low heat for 5 minutes or until soft. Add the garlic, chiles, and lemon zest. Cook for a few minutes, stirring so the mixture does not brown.

2 Meanwhile, cook the pasta as the package directs. Drain, reserving a small amount of the cooking water. Return the pasta to the pot and toss with the reserved cooking water.

3 Stir the anchovies into the onion mixture, then toss with the pasta, add the parsley, and toss again. Serve with a squeeze of lemon.

COOK'S NOTES
You should be able to find white anchovies in oil at the deli counter of the supermarket.

EVERYDAY

Pasta with crab and lemon

PREP 5 MINS · **COOK 10 MINS**

SERVES 4

1 tbsp olive oil
1 large onion, cut into quarters, then finely sliced
pinch of sea salt
2 garlic cloves, finely sliced
grated zest and juice of 1 lemon
handful of fresh flat-leaf parsley
7oz (200g) fresh or canned crabmeat, picked over to remove any shell
12oz (350g) linguine or spaghetti
chili oil, to serve (optional)

1 Heat the oil in a large frying pan, add the onion and a pinch of salt and cook over low heat for 5 minutes, until soft. Stir in the garlic and lemon zest and cook for a few seconds more.

2 Stir in the parsley and crabmeat, then season well with salt and lots of pepper. Add lemon juice to taste.

3 Meanwhile, cook the pasta according to package directions, until tender but still firm to the bite. Drain, reserving a small amount of the cooking water. Return the pasta to the pot and toss together with the reserved cooking water. Add the crab sauce, toss again, drizzle with chili oil, and serve.

VARIATION

Add 1 teaspoon of capers or 1 small chopped green bell pepper to the crabmeat.

COOK'S NOTES

Fresh crabmeat has a taste far superior to canned. If you are using canned crabmeat, make sure to drain it well.

Pasta with spinach and ricotta

PREP 10 MINS · **COOK 15 MINS**

SERVES 4

2 tbsp olive oil
2 garlic cloves, finely sliced
¼ cup dry white wine
9oz (250g) bag fresh spinach, rinsed
3 ripe tomatoes, diced
sea salt and freshly ground black pepper
12oz (350g) dried farfalle
1 cup whole milk ricotta cheese
extra virgin olive oil, to serve

1 Heat the oil in a large frying pan, add the garlic, and cook gently over low heat for a few seconds. Add the wine, increase the heat, and allow to bubble for a few minutes.

2 Add the spinach and cook, stirring, for 3–5 minutes, until wilted. Stir in the tomatoes, season with salt and pepper, and cook for a few seconds.

3 Meanwhile, cook the pasta according to package directions until tender but still firm to the bite. Drain, reserving a small amount of the cooking water. Return the pasta to the pot and toss together with the reserved cooking water.

4 Stir three-quarters of the ricotta into the spinach mixture, taste, and season, if needed. Add to the pasta and toss again. Serve topped with some of the remaining ricotta crumbled over and a splash of extra virgin olive oil.

COOK'S NOTES

Shop around for good ricotta cheese—the fresher the better for this dish.

Pasta with eggplant sauce

PREP 10 MINS COOK 25 MINS

SERVES 4

1 large eggplant, cut into small cubes
sea salt and freshly ground
 black pepper
2–3 tbsp olive oil
¼ cup dry red wine
1 onion, finely diced
2 garlic cloves finely chopped
1 x 14oz (400g) can diced tomatoes,
 with juices
pinch of dried oregano
1 tsp sun-dried tomato pesto
12oz (350g) dried medium pasta
 shells (conchiglie)
Parmesan cheese, grated,
 to serve (optional)

1 Place the eggplant cubes in a colander and sprinkle well with salt. Cover the eggplant directly with a plate, then place a heavy weight on top for 10 minutes to extract the bitter juices. Use your hands to squeeze out excess moisture.

2 Heat the oil in a large frying pan, add the eggplant cubes, and cook over medium heat for 4–6 minutes, until golden. Add the wine, increase the heat, and allow to bubble for a couple of minutes. Stir in the onion and garlic, cook for a few seconds, then stir in the tomatoes with their juices. Add the oregano and pesto and simmer gently for 15 minutes.

3 Meanwhile, cook the pasta according to package directions until tender but still firm to the bite. Drain, reserving a small amount of the cooking water. Return the pasta to the pot and toss together with the reserved cooking water. Taste the sauce and season with salt and pepper. Add the sauce to the pasta and toss again. Sprinkle with grated Parmesan and serve.

Pasta with mushroom sauce

PREP 10 MINS COOK 20 MINS

SERVES 4

4 tbsp olive oil
8oz (225g) button mushrooms,
 finely chopped
4½oz (125g) small whole mushrooms
4½oz (125g) wild mushrooms, sliced
½ cup dry white wine
3 garlic cloves, finely chopped
sea salt and freshly ground
 black pepper
handful of fresh flat-leaf parsley,
 finely chopped
pinch of mild paprika
1 cup heavy whipping cream
12oz (350g) pappardelle or tagliatelle

1 Gently heat the oil in a large frying pan, add all the mushrooms, and cook over low heat for 5 minutes, until they begin to release their juices. Add the wine, increase the heat, and allow to bubble for a couple of minutes. Add the garlic and lots of pepper.

2 Reduce the heat, stir in the parsley and paprika, then pour in the cream and cook, stirring occasionally, over low heat for 5 minutes.

3 Meanwhile, cook the pasta according to package directions, until tender but still firm to the bite. Drain, reserving a small amount of the cooking water. Return the pasta to the pot and toss together with the reserved cooking water. Taste the sauce and season with salt and pepper if needed, then toss with the pasta and serve.

EVERYDAY

Pasta with lamb meatballs and olives

PREP 15 MINS COOK 25 MINS

Freeze • the sauce can be frozen

SERVES 4

1 onion, very finely diced
2 garlic cloves, very finely chopped
1lb (450g) ground lamb
sea salt and freshly ground
    black pepper
1 tbsp olive oil, or as needed
1 x 14oz (400g) can diced tomatoes,
    with juices
handful of pitted black olives,
    such as Kalamata, coarsely
    chopped if large
12oz (350g) dried spaghetti
handful of finely chopped flat-leaf
    parsley
finely grated fresh Parmesan cheese,
    for serving

1 Combine the onion, garlic, and ground lamb in a bowl. Season with salt and pepper and mix with your hands until well blended. Roll the mixture into balls that are a bit larger than a walnut.

2 Heat the oil in a frying pan. Add the meatballs in batches and cook for about 5 minutes or until they begin to brown. Transfer to a plate and repeat.

3 Return the meatballs to the frying pan and add the tomatoes and olives; bring to a boil, then reduce to a simmer and cook for 20 minutes. Season to taste with salt and pepper.

4 Cook the pasta. Drain, reserving a bit of the cooking water. Return the pasta to the pot and toss with the reserved water. Stir the parsley into the sauce and spoon over the pasta. Sprinkle with Parmesan and serve.

COOK'S NOTES

Do not worry if some of the lamb meatballs fall apart during cooking—they will make the sauce even more delicious and add texture to the finished dish.

Pasta with sausage and artichokes

PREP 10 MINS COOK 20 MINS

SERVES 4

1 tbsp olive oil
1 onion, finely diced
sea salt and freshly ground
    black pepper
1 red jalapeño chile pepper, seeded
    and finely chopped
6 good-quality pork sausages, skinned
    and chopped
pinch of dried oregano
1 x 14oz (400g) can artichoke hearts,
    drained and coarsely chopped
3 ripe tomatoes, peeled and diced
handful of pitted black olives, such as
    Kalamata, coarsely chopped if large
12oz (350g) dried penne

1 Heat the oil in a frying pan, add the onion and a pinch of salt, and cook over low heat for 5 minutes, or until soft. Add the chile and cook for a few seconds, then add the sausages, breaking them up with the back of a fork until coarsely mashed. Cook until

no longer pink, about 10 minutes, stirring occasionally. Drain off any excess fat, then add the oregano and artichokes and cook for a few minutes more. Add the tomatoes and olives, then season well with salt and pepper.

2 Meanwhile, cook the pasta as the package directs. Drain, reserving a small amount of the cooking water. Return the pasta to the pot and toss with the reserved cooking water. Add the sauce, toss again, and serve.

VARIATION

Use sun-dried tomatoes and capers instead of the tomatoes and olives.

COOK'S NOTES

Using good-quality pork sausages will make all the difference in the finished dish.

Pasta with asparagus and zucchini

PREP 10 MINS · COOK 20 MINS

SERVES 4

1 tbsp olive oil

1 onion, finely chopped

pinch of sea salt

4 small zucchini, 2 diced and
    2 coarsely grated

3 garlic cloves, finely chopped

1 bunch thin asparagus, trimmed
    and stalks cut crosswise into thirds

½ cup dry white wine

1–2 tsp capers, rinsed and chopped

finely grated zest of 1 lemon

12oz (350g) dried penne

handful of finely chopped flat-leaf
    parsley

finely grated Parmesan cheese,
    for serving

1 Heat the oil in a large frying pan, add the onion and a pinch of salt, and cook over low heat for 5 minutes or until soft. Add all the zucchini and cook for 10 minutes, stirring frequently, until they have cooked down and softened. Do not allow them to brown.

2 Stir in the garlic and asparagus. Add the wine, increase the heat, and allow to bubble for 2–3 minutes. Return to a simmer. Cook for 2–3 minutes, until the asparagus is tender, then stir in the capers and lemon zest.

3 Meanwhile, cook the pasta as the package directs. Drain, reserving a small amount of the cooking water. Return the pasta to the pot and toss together with the reserved cooking water. Add the vegetable mixture and parsley, and toss again. Sprinkle with Parmesan and serve.

VARIATION

Use Pecorino instead of Parmesan.

Pasta with seafood and tomatoes

PREP 10 MINS · COOK 20 MINS

SERVES 4

1 tbsp olive oil

1 onion, finely chopped

sea salt and freshly ground
    black pepper

3 garlic cloves, finely chopped

1 x 14oz (400g) can diced tomatoes,
    with juices

12oz (350g) dried linguine or
    spaghetti

12oz (350g) assorted cooked
    seafood, such as shrimp,
    squid, and mussels

handful of finely chopped flat-leaf
    parsley

1 Heat the oil in a large frying pan, add the onion and a pinch of salt, and cook over low heat for 5 minutes or until soft. Stir in the garlic and cook for a few seconds. Add the tomatoes and their juices, bring to a boil, then simmer gently for 10 minutes.

2 Meanwhile, cook the pasta as the package directs. Drain, reserving a small amount of the cooking water. Return the pasta to the pot and toss with the reserved cooking water.

3 Add the seafood to the tomato mixture for the last few minutes of cooking, to reheat. Season with salt and pepper, add the parsley, then toss with the pasta. Serve immediately.

VARIATION

Use uncooked seafood, but add it to the sauce in plenty of time for it to cook through.

COOK'S NOTES

Use good-quality canned tomatoes —the finished dish will be all the better for them.

Pasta with flageolet beans, parsley, and lemon

PREP 10 MINS | COOK 10 MINS

SERVES 4

1 red onion, finely diced
1 x 14oz (400g) can flageolet beans, drained and rinsed
handful of coarsely chopped parsley
1 garlic clove, finely chopped
2 tbsp good-quality balsamic vinegar
finely grated zest of 1 lemon, plus the juice of ½ lemon
sea salt and freshly ground black pepper
12oz (350g) dried orecchiette or other small pasta shells

1 Combine the onion, beans, parsley, garlic, vinegar, lemon zest, and lemon juice in a large bowl and stir gently to mix. Season well with salt and pepper. Leave to sit while you cook the pasta –the flavors will develop.

2 Meanwhile, cook the pasta as the package directs, until it is tender yet still firm to the bite. Drain, reserving a small amount of the cooking water. Return the pasta to the pot and toss with the reserved cooking water. Add the sauce, toss again, and serve.

VARIATION
Add a few chopped anchovies, some torn mozzarella, or a handful of arugula to the sauce.

COOK'S NOTES

The sauce can be refrigerated for up to 24 hours. Before using, return to room temperature and stir in a little olive oil.

Pasta with broccoli and lemon

PREP 10 MINS | COOK 25 MINS

SERVES 4

1 head of broccoli, about 12oz (350g), cut into florets
1 tbsp olive oil
1 red onion, finely chopped
sea salt and freshly ground black pepper
1 red jalapeño chile pepper, seeded and finely chopped
¼ cup dry white wine
finely grated zest of 1 lemon
2 garlic cloves, finely chopped
12oz (350g) dried penne
juice of 1 lemon, to serve
freshly grated Parmesan cheese, for serving (optional)

1 Cook the broccoli in a large pan of boiling salted water for 10-15 minutes or until soft and slightly overcooked. Drain and chop coarsely. Heat the oil in a large frying pan, add the onion and a pinch of salt, and cook over low heat for 5 minutes or until soft. Stir in the chile, then add the wine. Increase the heat and bubble for a couple of minutes.

2 Lower the heat and add the lemon zest and garlic. Season well with salt and pepper, then stir in the broccoli, toss together, and set aside.

3 Meanwhile, cook the pasta as the package directs, until it is tender yet still firm to the bite. Drain, reserving a small amount of the cooking water. Return the pasta to the pot and toss together with the reserved cooking water. Add the broccoli mixture, then squeeze in the lemon juice. Toss again, sprinkle with Parmesan, and serve.

VARIATION
Add some diced pancetta while cooking the onion, or add cooked diced ham to the broccoli mixture.

Cheat...
Use frozen broccoli florets instead of the fresh broccoli.

Pasta with pork, roasted garlic, and balsamic vinegar

 PREP 10 MINS **COOK 30 MINS**

SERVES 4

1 bulb garlic, left whole with the top third sliced off
1 tbsp olive oil, plus extra for garlic
1 onion, thinly sliced
10oz (300g) pork tenderloin, cut into bite-sized cubes
1–2 tbsp balsamic vinegar
1 tbsp tomato purée
1 tbsp all-purpose flour
1¼ cups hot vegetable stock, or more as needed
sea salt and freshly ground black pepper
small handful of finely chopped flat-leaf parsley
12oz (350g) dried pappardelle

1 Preheat the oven to 400°F (200°C). Rub the cut-side of the garlic with oil, then wrap loosely in foil and bake for 20 minutes. Remove from the oven and set aside to cool. Heat the oil in a frying pan, add the onion, and cook over medium heat for 5 minutes or until lightly golden. Add the pork and cook, stirring often, until golden all over, about 5 minutes. Add the balsamic vinegar, increase the heat, and cook a few more minutes.

2 Stir in the tomato purée, followed by the flour and then the stock. Stir well to get rid of any lumps. Bring to a boil, then cook on a fairly high simmer for 10 minutes or until the sauce has thickened and reduced. Add a bit of boiling water if the sauce reduces too quickly. Season well with salt and pepper. Squeeze the cooled garlic out of its skin, chop coarsely, then stir into the sauce along with half the parsley.

3 Meanwhile, cook the pasta as the package directs. Drain, reserving a small amount of the cooking water. Return the pasta to the pot and toss with the reserved cooking water. Add the sauce, toss again, then sprinkle with the remaining parsley, and serve.

COOK'S NOTES

If you have the time once you have added the stock, let the sauce simmer over very low heat for another 20 minutes. The flavor will improve greatly. If it starts to look a little dry, add some more hot vegetable stock or water.

Pasta with black olives

 PREP 10 MINS **COOK 10 MINS**

Special equipment • food processor

SERVES 4

1 cup pitted black olives, such as Kalamata
2 garlic cloves
finely grated zest and juice of 1 lemon
2 tbsp extra virgin olive oil
sea salt and freshly ground black pepper
12oz (350g) dried linguine or spaghetti
handful of finely chopped flat-leaf parsley
handful of fresh basil leaves, torn into shreds
scant 1oz (25g) chunk of Parmesan cheese, shaved with a vegetable peeler

1 Combine the olives, garlic, lemon zest, and lemon juice in a food processor and pulse until chopped. With the motor running, add the oil until the mixture forms a smooth paste. Transfer to a bowl. Taste and season with salt and pepper.

2 Meanwhile, cook the pasta as the package directs. Drain, reserving a small amount of the cooking water. Return the pasta to the pot and toss with the reserved cooking water.

3 Add the parsley and basil and toss again. Toss the olive paste into the pasta, or spoon it over the top. Shave Parmesan over all and serve.

Cheat...
Use 1 tbsp store-bought tapenade instead of making your own olive paste.

Pasta with tuna and roasted onion

Special equipment • grill pan

SERVES 4

3 red onions, each cut into
   eight wedges
handful of ripe cherry tomatoes
a few fresh sprigs of thyme
3 tbsp olive oil
sea salt and freshly ground
   black pepper
2 x 6oz (175g) fresh tuna steaks
12oz (350g) dried penne
finely grated zest of ½ lemon
pinch of crushed hot red
   pepper flakes
drizzle of good-quality balsamic
   vinegar, for serving (optional)

1 Preheat the oven to 400°F (200°C).
Combine the onions, tomatoes, and
thyme in a large roasting pan, drizzle
with 2 tablespoons of the olive oil,
season with salt, and toss to coat.
Roast for 15 minutes or until the
onions are soft and lightly charred.

2 Heat a grill pan until hot. Rub the
tuna steaks with the remaining oil and
season with salt and pepper. Cook for
6–8 minutes, turning once, until they
reach the desired doneness. Remove
from the heat and set aside to rest.

3 Meanwhile, cook the pasta as the
package directs. Drain, reserving a
small amount of the cooking water.
Return the pasta to the pot and toss
together with the reserved cooking
water. Add the roasted onion mixture,
the lemon zest, and pepper flakes and
toss again. Cut the tuna into bite-sized
chunks, and add to the pot. Season
to taste and toss gently. Drizzle with
balsamic vinegar, and serve.

Cheat...
Use canned tuna, but
make sure it is good-
quality. Simply
add it to the
cooked pasta.

Pasta with porcini and Parmesan

SERVES 4

1 tbsp olive oil
1 red onion, finely chopped
sea salt and freshly ground
   black pepper
¼ cup dry red wine
1¾oz (50g) dried porcini mushrooms,
   soaked in 1¼ cups boiling water
   for 15 minutes
1 x 1¾oz (50g) rind from a piece of
   Parmesan cheese (or a 1¾oz chunk
   of Parmesan cheese), plus freshly
   grated Parmesan, for serving
12oz (350g) dried tagliatelle
   (fettuccine)
handful of finely chopped
   flat-leaf parsley
few sprigs of fresh thyme
   (leaves only)
2 tomatoes, peeled and diced

1 Heat the oil in a frying pan, add
the onion and a pinch of salt, and
cook over low heat for 5 minutes or
until soft. Turn up the heat, add the
wine, and allow to bubble for a couple
of minutes. Drain the mushrooms,
reserving the liquid, and coarsely
chop. Add the mushrooms and cook
for 1–2 minutes. Stir in the Parmesan.

2 Strain the reserved mushroom
liquid through a sieve, then pour into
the pan. Bring to a boil, then simmer
for 10 minutes, stirring occasionally.
Meanwhile, cook the pasta as the
package directs. Drain, reserving a
small amount of the cooking water.
Return the pasta to the pot and toss
with the reserved cooking water.

3 Remove the Parmesan from the
sauce, stir in the parsley, thyme, and
tomatoes, and season. Add the sauce
and toss again, then serve with grated
Parmesan and black pepper.

VARIATION
Use an assortment of dried
wild mushrooms instead of
the porcini.

Pasta with pesto and pine nuts

PREP 5 MINS **COOK 10 MINS**

Special equipment • food processor

SERVES 4

handful of fresh basil, leaves only
2 garlic cloves, chopped
½ cup freshly grated Parmesan cheese
2 tbsp pine nuts, plus 1 tbsp toasted
   pine nuts
¼ cup olive oil
sea salt and freshly ground
   black pepper
12oz (350g) dried spaghetti

1 Combine the basil, garlic, Parmesan, and the 2 tbsp untoasted pine nuts in a food processor. Pulse until blended. Scrape the mixture from the sides of the bowl, cover, and, with the machine running, pour in the olive oil until a coarse paste forms. Season to taste.

2 Meanwhile, cook the pasta as the package directs. Drain, reserving a small amount of the cooking water. Return the pasta to the pot and toss with the reserved cooking water. Add the pesto, toss again, then top with the toasted pine nuts and serve.

VARIATION Use small pasta shells (conchiglie) instead of spaghetti.

COOK'S NOTES

Double the pesto recipe, spoon half of it into a jar, and top with a thin layer of olive oil—it will keep in the refrigerator for up to 1 week.

Pasta carbonara with pancetta and cream

PREP 10 MINS **COOK 15 MINS**

SERVES 4

1 tbsp olive oil
5½oz (150g) pancetta or slab bacon,
   cut into small cubes
2 sage leaves, finely sliced
6 large eggs
⅔ cup heavy whipping cream
1 cup freshly grated
   Parmesan cheese
pinch of freshly grated nutmeg
sea salt and freshly ground
   black pepper
12oz (350g) dried linguine
   or spaghetti
small handful of finely chopped
   fresh flat-leaf parsley, for serving

1 Heat the oil in a large frying pan, add the pancetta and sage, and cook over medium heat for 5 minutes or until golden.

2 Combine the eggs, cream, Parmesan, and nutmeg in a bowl, season with salt and pepper, then blend with a fork. Set aside.

3 Meanwhile, cook the pasta as the package directs. Drain, reserving a small amount of the cooking water. Return the pasta to the pot and toss with the reserved cooking water.

4 Give the egg mixture one final stir, then add to the hot pasta and stir thoroughly to combine. Put the lid on the pot, leave to sit for 1 minute, then stir again. Add the pancetta and sage and toss together. Sprinkle with parsley and serve.

VARIATION Toss cooked or thawed frozen peas into the final dish.

Cheat...
Use 1 cup of store-bought carbonara sauce—but don't expect it to be as good as the real thing!

Pasta with roasted peppers and chiles

 PREP 10 MINS COOK 25 MINS

SERVES 4

6 small red bell peppers
3 tbsp olive oil
2 garlic cloves, finely chopped
1 fresh red jalapeño chile pepper, seeded and finely chopped
1 fresh green jalapeño chile pepper, seeded and finely chopped
pinch of dried oregano
few sprigs of fresh thyme (leaves only)
12oz (350g) dried penne
¼ cup finely grated Pecorino cheese
hot chili oil, for serving

1 Preheat the oven to 400°F (200°C). Generously coat the bell peppers with 2 tablespoons of the oil. Place them in a shallow roasting pan and roast, turning, for 15 minutes or until soft and charred. Remove from the oven, seal in a plastic or paper bag, and set aside to cool.

2 Place the remaining 1 tablespoon of oil in a frying pan, add the garlic and chiles, and cook for a few minutes over low heat, without browning. Stir in the oregano and thyme.

3 Remove the peppers from the bag and, using your hands, rub away the skins. Cut the peppers and discard the seeds and white membranes. Cut the flesh into strips, then add to the frying pan. Season and let stand.

4 Cook the pasta as the package directs. Drain, saving a small amount of the cooking water. Return the pasta to the pot and toss with the reserved cooking water. Scrape in the pepper mixture, add the Pecorino, and toss well. Drizzle with chili oil and serve.

 VARIATION
Use roasted pumpkin or any mix of roasted vegetables instead of the peppers.

COOK'S NOTES

Seal the roasted peppers in a bag—the steam loosens the skins, making them easier to peel.

Macaroni and cheese with red onion

 PREP 5 MINS COOK 30 MINS

SERVES 4

1 tbsp butter
1 tbsp all-purpose flour
1¼ cups whole milk
1¼ cups shredded sharp Cheddar cheese
sea salt and freshly ground black pepper
12oz (350g) dried elbow macaroni
1 small red onion, very finely diced

1 Preheat the oven to 400°F (200°C). Melt the butter in a small saucepan, then remove from the heat and stir in the flour with a wooden spoon until well blended. Return to the heat and gradually add the milk, whisking constantly, until the sauce begins to thicken. Remove from heat and stir in 1 cup of the cheese until smooth. Season with salt and pepper.

2 Meanwhile, cook the pasta as the package directs. Drain, reserving a small amount of the cooking water.

Return the pasta to the pot and toss together with the reserved cooking water. Mix in the cheese sauce, add the onion, and stir to blend well.

3 Spoon into a baking dish, top with the remaining cheese, and bake for 10–15 minutes or until bubbly-hot.

 **VARIATION**
Use penne for this dish, instead. Or add some cooked fresh or thawed frozen peas to the sauce.

Cheat...
Use an 8oz (250g) container of prepared cheese sauce. Stir in 1 tsp grainy mustard to enhance the flavor.

Pasta with clams and parsley

PREP 10 MINS COOK 15 MINS

SERVES 4

1 tbsp olive oil
1 onion, finely diced
sea salt and freshly ground
 black pepper
3 garlic cloves, finely diced
handful of finely chopped
 flat-leaf parsley
½ cup dry white wine
1lb (450g) fresh clams,
 well scrubbed
12oz (350g) linguine or spaghetti
splash of olive oil

1 Heat the oil in a large frying pan, add the onion and a pinch of salt, and cook over low heat for 5 minutes or until the onion begins to soften. Stir in the garlic and parsley, then cook for a few seconds more.

2 Add the wine, increase the heat, then stir in the clams. Allow to bubble, shaking the pan from time to time, for 5 minutes, or until the shells start to open. Turn off the heat and cover.

3 Meanwhile, cook the pasta as the package directs. Drain, reserving a small amount of the cooking water. Return the pasta to the pot and toss with the reserved cooking water. Add a splash of olive oil, season with salt and pepper, then add the clams and their juices. Toss together and serve.

COOK'S NOTES

For safety's sake, discard any clams that are open before you cook them, and discard any that are closed after you've cooked

Pasta with lamb and tomato sauce

PREP 5 MINS COOK 30 MINS

SERVES 4

1 tbsp olive oil
1 onion, finely diced
pinch of sea salt
1lb (450g) ground lamb, or very
 finely chopped lean lamb
¾ cup dry red wine
finely grated zest of 1 lemon
pinch of paprika
few sprigs of fresh thyme
 (leaves only)
3 garlic cloves, finely chopped
12oz (350g) pappardelle
freshly grated Parmesan cheese,
 for serving

1 Heat the oil in a frying pan, add the onion and a pinch of salt, and cook over low heat for 5 minutes or until soft. Add the lamb and cook, stirring, until browned, about 5 minutes. Turn up the heat, add the wine, and allow to bubble for 2 minutes.

2 Add the lemon zest, paprika, and thyme. Stir in the garlic, cook for a few seconds, then add the tomatoes and their juices. Bring to a boil, then simmer gently for about 15 minutes.

3 Meanwhile, cook the pasta as the package directs, until it is tender yet still firm to the bite. Drain, reserving a small amount of the cooking water. Return the pasta to the pot and toss together with the reserved cooking water. Add the lamb sauce, toss again, sprinkle with Parmesan, and serve.

COOK'S NOTES

If possible, let the lamb sauce simmer, covered, over very low heat for 1 hour. Or, transfer to a cast-iron flameproof casserole and bake at 400°F (200°C) for an hour.

Minestrone soup

 PREP 10 MINS COOK 40 MINS

SERVES 4

1 tbsp olive oil
1 onion, finely chopped
sea salt and freshly ground
   black pepper
1 tsp dried oregano
4 carrots, cut into small dice
3 celery stalks, cut into small dice
3 garlic cloves, finely chopped
¾ cup dry red wine
1 tbsp tomato purée
2¼ cups hot vegetable stock
1 x 14oz (400g) can diced tomatoes,
   with juices
about 8oz (225g) cold leftover
   cooked pasta, such as elbow
   macaroni or vermicelli, coarsely
   chopped if large
handful of flat-leaf parsley,
   finely chopped
freshly grated Parmesan cheese,
   for serving

1 Heat the oil in a large saucepan over low heat. Add the onion and a pinch of salt and cook gently for 5 minutes or until soft. Add the oregano, then stir in the carrots and celery. Cook, stirring occasionally, for about 10 minutes until softened. Now stir in the garlic and cook for a few seconds more. Pour in the wine, increase the heat, and let bubble for a couple of minutes until the alcohol has evaporated. Stir in the tomato purée and season well with salt and pepper.

2 Stir in the stock and the tomatoes with their juices. Bring to a boil, reduce the heat slightly, and gently simmer for about 20 minutes, adding a bit of hot water or extra stock if the minestrone gets too thick (but don't make it too thin).

3 Stir in the pasta, sprinkle with parsley, and serve hot with Parmesan cheese for sprinkling over the top and a salad of mixed greens on the side.

COOK'S NOTES

Always keep any leftover rind from Parmesan cheese—you can add it to your minestrone while it's cooking for extra flavor.

Pasta and eggplant bake

  PREP 15 MINS COOK 50 MINS

SERVES 4

2 eggplants, halved lengthwise and
   cut into ¼in (5mm) slices
sea salt and freshly ground
   black pepper
2 tbsp olive oil, or as needed
1 onion, finely chopped
2 garlic cloves, finely chopped
pinch of dried oregano
pinch of sweet paprika
1 x 28oz (750g) can ground tomatoes
   or tomato purée
about 8oz (225g) cold leftover cooked
   pasta, such as penne or farfalle
½ cup grated Parmesan cheese

1 Place the eggplant slices in a colander and sprinkle well with salt. Cover with a plate, then place a heavy weight on top for 10 minutes to extract the bitter juices. Use your hands to squeeze out excess moisture.

2 Meanwhile, preheat the oven to 400°F (200°C). Heat 1 tbsp of the oil in a large heavy saucepan over low heat. Add the onion and a pinch of salt and cook gently for 5 minutes or until soft. Stir in the garlic, oregano, and paprika, then stir in the tomatoes. Bring to a boil, reduce the heat slightly, and simmer gently for about 15 minutes. Season to taste with salt and pepper.

3 While the sauce is cooking, heat 2 tablespoons of olive oil in a large frying pan over medium heat. Working in batches, cook the eggplant slices for 3 minutes on each side until golden, adding more oil to the pan as needed. Drain on paper towels.

4 Line the bottom of a baking dish with eggplant slices, overlapping slightly. Cover with some of the tomato sauce, then add a layer of pasta. Repeat the layers, ending with a final layer of tomato sauce. Top with the cheese and bake for 20 minutes or until bubbly and golden. Serve with a crisp green salad tossed with a light vinaigrette.

Cheat...
Use a jar of store-bought tomato sauce instead of making your own.

Pasta salad

 PREP 15 MINS COOK 10 MINS

SERVES 4

8oz (225g) pasta, such as penne,
    fusilli, or farfalle
2 tbsp mayonnaise
handful of arugula
1 cup cooked fresh or thawed
    frozen peas
6 cherry tomatoes, finely chopped
sea salt and freshly ground
    black pepper

1 Cook the pasta in a large pan of boiling salted water for 10 minutes, or until it is cooked but still has a bit of bite to it. Drain, reserving a tiny amount of the cooking water, return to the pan, and toss.

2 In a large bowl, mix together the pasta, mayonnaise, arugula, peas, and tomatoes. Season with salt and pepper. Cover with plastic wrap and refrigerate until 1 hour before serving. Serve at cool room temperature.

EVERYDAY

Pasta with meat sauce

 PREP 15 MINS COOK 30 MINS

SERVES 4
1 tbsp olive oil
1 onion, finely chopped
sea salt and freshly ground
    black pepper
2 garlic cloves, finely chopped
8–10oz (300g) boneless sirloin
    beef (rump) steak, cut into bite-
    sized chunks
1 beef bouillon cube, crumbled
2 cups hot water
8oz (225g) cold leftover cooked pasta,
    such as penne, farfalle, or fusilli
handful of grated Parmesan cheese
handful of fresh flat-leaf parsley,
    finely chopped

1 Heat the oil in a large frying over low heat. Add the onion and a pinch of salt and cook gently for 5 minutes or until soft. Stir in the garlic and cook for a few seconds more. Now add the beef and cook over high heat for a few minutes until browned all over. Sprinkle with the bouillon cube, pour in the water, and bring to a boil, scraping up any browned bits from the bottom of the pan with a wooden spoon. Reduce the heat slightly and leave to simmer for 20 minutes.

2 Stir in the pasta, taste, and season well with salt and ground pepper. Cook 3–5 minutes, or until the pasta is heated through. Serve hot, with Parmesan cheese and parsley sprinkled over the top.

PIZZAS, QUESADILLAS, AND CRÊPES

Quick ways to top, stuff, or roll.

PIZZAS, QUESADILLAS, AND CRÊPES

Fast meal solutions couldn't be simpler. Top ready-made pizza dough with your favorite foods, serve up a quick quesadilla with whatever happens to be in the refrigerator, or fill a crêpe with sweet or savory treats–the variations are endless. Making pizzas, quesadillas, and crêpes is fun, and they can all be prepared ahead, ready for last-minute toppings–ideal for busy households when everyone eats at different times.

Pizzas

A meal in itself, this Italian bread crust is topped with a variety of ingredients, the most classic being simply tomato and mozzarella. The bread-base dough needs to be cooked at an extremely high heat to become firm and crisp. The traditional Italian-style pizza has a thin, crisp, and delicate base, lightly smeared with a tomato sauce, and topped with 2–3 toppings. American-style pizza has a thicker doughy base with more toppings.

Tips and tricks

A hot oven is essential. Traditionally, pizzas are made in a wood-burning oven at about 750°F (400°C), so the top melts and the base turns crispy in minutes. As conventional ovens don't get this hot, preheat the oven and a flat baking sheet or pizza stone at least 1 hour before cooking.

"00" flour This is a super-fine Italian flour, and is the best flour to use for making pizza, as it produces a soft, stretchy dough. It can be found in speciality supermarkets or good delicatessens. Alternatively, use all-purpose or bread flour.

Rising The longer the dough takes to rise, the better the flavor of the crust will be.

Kneading Do take the time to knead the dough for at least 10 minutes so the gluten develops in the dough and becomes firm when cooked.

Topping Keep it simple, and don't overcrowd the pizza. Overcrowding it with toppings will prevent it from cooking quickly. You don't need to use cheese, but if you do, use mozzarella, mild Cheddar, Parmesan cheese, or feta cheese.

reheat and eat

Pizza is best eaten fresh, but if you have leftovers and want to reheat it, place it on a plate and put it in the microwave for 1 minute on medium to warm it through (any longer and it will get soggy), then put it on a preheated baking sheet in a hot oven for a couple of minutes to crisp up the crust. Otherwise, it is good eaten cold or at room temperature.

How to freeze pizzas

Part-baked bases Roll out the dough, then bake in a hot oven for about 5 minutes, or until firm. Cool completely, then wrap in plastic wrap and freeze for up to 3 months.

Dough Double up quantities and freeze some for later, or freeze leftover dough. Prepare the dough, let it rise, then knock the air out of it. Divide into fourths and put in a plastic bag, seal, and freeze for up to 3 months.

Pizza toppings

- Crumbled sausage, artichoke, and mozzarella cheese
- Spicy tomato sauce, olives, capers, and chorizo
- Tomato sauce, mozzarella, ham, and spinach
- Tomato sauce, eggplant, olives, and mozzarella
- Tomato sauce, pine nuts, raisins, and spinach

Psst...

Uncooked pizza dough can be kept in the refrigerator. Once the dough has risen, knock out the air and leave to cool. Lightly oil a plastic bag, add the dough, seal, and keep in the refrigerator for up to 2 days before using.

Pizza bianca with prosciutto, arugula, and mozzarella. For recipe, see page 185.

Perfect pizza dough

A quick dough mixture using dried yeast—the quantities given here make 4 thin-crust Italian-style pizzas.

1 Sift 4 cups of "00" or all-purpose flour into a bowl and add a pinch of salt and a package of dried yeast. Make a well in the center of the flour, then slowly add 1¼–1½ cups of warm water. Mix with a wooden spoon or the dough beaters of a food mixer, until it comes together, then add ¼ cup of olive oil and continue to mix until it forms a soft dough.

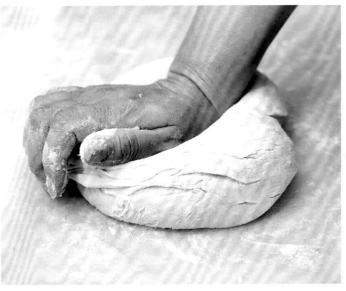

2 Place the dough on a floured surface and knead firmly, using the heel of your hand, folding the dough over as you go. Do this for about 10 minutes, until it becomes soft and spongy.

3 Put the dough in a bowl, cover with plastic wrap or a dish towel, and leave in a warm place (you can preheat the oven and leave the bowl on top of the stove above) for 30–40 minutes, or until it has doubled in size.

4 Turn the dough out onto the floured surface again, and knead with your knuckles for a couple of minutes to knock out the air (known as "knocking back"). Divide the dough into fourths and roll each piece out as thinly as you can, rolling away from you, and turning it as you go. You may have to pull and stretch the dough a little as it tends to spring back. You need it to be about 10in (25cm) in diameter, although it doesn't have to be perfectly round. Transfer to a hot, lightly oiled baking sheet and top with your favorite toppings (see previous page for some ideas).

EVERYDAY

STEP-BY-STEP

Quesadillas

The ultimate fast food snack, quesadillas are essentially a toasted sandwich, using tortillas. You can use **wheat**, **whole wheat**, or **corn** tortillas and fill them with cheese and your favorite ingredients. Corn tortillas are the wheat-free option, made with ground maize, giving them their distinctive yellow color. "Queso" means "cheese" in Spanish, so this is the one ingredient that must be added.

How to freeze quesadillas

Freeze uncooked tortillas in a sealed plastic bag for up to 3 months. Cooked and filled tortillas don't freeze well.

Quesadilla fillings

- Brie, grated apple, and chutney
- Mozzarella, cooked butternut squash, and green chile
- Gruyère cheese, grated zucchini, and ham
- Cheddar cheese, tuna, and scallions

Tips and tricks

Store Keep tortillas in plastic wrap once opened, as they go dry quickly. Keep for 1 week. Sprinkle with water to refresh, if needed.

Cheese Choose cheese that melts easily, such as mild Cheddar or mozzarella cheese.

Serve Eat right away. To keep warm, if you are making a few, wrap them in foil and put in a warm oven.

Leftovers Tear up leftover tortillas and add to soup.

Perfect quesadillas A satisfying dish that's ready in minutes.

1 Have all your ingredients ready-prepared; 2 wheat or corn tortillas and your chosen fillings. Here we're using scant 1oz (25g) Gruyère cheese, grated, and a handful of sliced jalapeño chiles from a jar.

2 Heat a small frying pan with a little olive oil (you can omit this if you prefer), then place one tortilla in the pan. Add the topping ingredients, leaving a little room around the edge so the cheese doesn't spill out.

3 Top with another tortilla and press down with a spatula. Leave it to warm through for a couple of minutes.

4 Flip it over to cook the other side for a minute or two, then transfer to a plate, slice into half or quarters, and serve.

Crêpes

Crêpes, or pancakes, are made with a light batter mix, and are cooked as thin as possible so they are almost lacy in texture. They can be served hot or cold and filled or topped with savory or sweet fillings. The ingredients are staples (flour, milk, and egg), so crêpes are a perfect spur-of-the-moment dish. American-style pancakes are thicker and smaller, made with added baking powder. They are usually served with sweet toppings of cream or maple syrup for breakfast.

How to freeze crêpes

Cooked crêpes can be frozen for up to 1 month. Layer them between sheets of parchment paper (see right). Cool, seal in a plastic bag, and freeze.

Pancake fillings

- Sautéed leeks, goat cheese, and thyme
- Mushrooms, spinach, tomatoes, and chile
- Salmon and cream cheese
- Figs, honey, and mascarpone
- Banana, toffee sauce, and toasted almonds

EVERYDAY

Perfect crêpes A simple batter mix and a good pan are all you need.

1 Sieve 4½oz (125g) all-purpose flour into a bowl with a pinch of salt. Make a well in the center and crack 1 egg into it. Gradually add 1-1¼ cups milk, stirring with a wooden spoon and incorporating the flour as you go. Continue stirring until all the milk is added, then whisk until smooth. Put in the refrigerator to rest for 30 minutes.

2 Heat a drizzle of oil in a nonstick crêpe pan or frying pan and swirl it around. Pour out any extra. Add a little of the batter, swirling it around so it coats the bottom of the pan.

3 Cook for 1-2 minutes over medium heat, until the edges start to look dry. Then, using a round-ended knife, loosen the edges and flip it using a spatula to cook the other side.

4 Check the second side, after a minute or two. When brown speckles appear, transfer to a plate to serve. Fill with your favorite fillings, or serve flat, drizzled with lemon juice and sprinkled with sugar.

EVERYDAY

Pizza bianca with rosemary and garlic

PREP 10 MINS · COOK 10 MINS

MAKES 1
1 ball pizza dough (see p181)
all-purpose flour, for dusting
semolina flour or cornmeal
handful of fresh rosemary leaves
2 garlic cloves, finely chopped
olive oil
sea salt

1 Preheat the oven to 475°F (245°C). Put a heavy baking sheet in the oven to get hot. (They both need to be really hot before cooking the pizza.)

2 Place the dough on a floured surface and use a rolling pin to roll it out as thin as you can—about 10-12in (25-30cm) in diameter. Brush the hot baking sheet with oil, sprinkle with semolina, and place the dough on top.

3 Prick the dough all over with a fork, then scatter the rosemary, garlic, and plenty of salt over the top and pat flat. Drizzle with olive oil, then bake for 10 minutes or until crispy.

VARIATION
Sprinkle with mozzarella torn into pieces, or with crumbled blue cheese.

COOK'S NOTES
If you make pizza often, invest in a pizza stone—then your crust will always be wonderfully crispy.

Pizza bianca with four cheeses

PREP 10 MINS · COOK 15 MINS

MAKES 1
1 ball pizza dough (see p181)
all-purpose flour, for dusting
semolina flour or cornmeal
1 ball (2½oz/75g) fresh mozzarella, torn into pieces, or more to taste
handful of freshly grated Parmesan cheese, or more to taste
¼ cup crumbled Gorgonzola or other blue cheese, or more to taste
¼ cup shredded Gruyère, or more to taste
pinch of oregano

1 Preheat the oven to 475°F (245°C). Put a heavy baking sheet in the oven to get hot. (They both need to be really hot before cooking the pizza.)

2 Place the dough on a floured surface and use a rolling pin to roll it out as thin as you can—about 10-12in (25-30cm) in diameter. Brush the hot baking sheet with oil, sprinkle with semolina, and carefully place the dough on top.

3 Cover each quarter segment of the pizza with a different cheese. Sprinkle with the oregano, then bake for 10-15 minutes or until the crust is crispy and the cheese is golden and bubbling.

VARIATION
Sprinkle the pizza with pine nuts and raisins just before you pop it in the oven.

COOK'S NOTES
If you are making more than one pizza, cook one at a time so the oven isn't overcrowded and remains as hot as it can be.

Pizza bianca with prosciutto, arugula, and mozzarella

 PREP 10 MINS   COOK 10 MINS

MAKES 1
1 ball pizza dough (see p181)
all-purpose flour, for dusting
semolina flour or cornmeal
8oz (200g) mozzarella,
    torn into chunks
freshly ground black pepper
4 thin slices prosciutto, whole or cut
    into strips
handful of arugula

1 Preheat the oven to 475°F (245°C). Put a heavy baking sheet in the oven to get hot. (They both need to be really hot before cooking the pizza.)

2 Place the dough on a floured surface and use a rolling pin to roll it out as thin as you can—about 10-12in (25-30cm) in diameter. Brush the hot baking sheet with oil, sprinkle with semolina, and place the dough on top.

3 Top the crust with the mozzarella, season with freshly ground black pepper, and bake for 10 minutes or until the crust is crispy and the top is bubbling. Drape the prosciutto over the top, scatter evenly with arugula, season again with pepper, and serve.

VARIATION

Add some diced tomato along with the arugula.

COOK'S NOTES

You might want to cut the prosciutto into pieces with a pair of kitchen scissors so the pizza will be easier to eat.

Pizza with tomatoes, olives, and capers

 PREP 10 MINS   COOK 15 MINS

MAKES 1
1 ball pizza dough (see p181)
all-purpose flour, for dusting
semolina flour or cornmeal
2-3 tbsp crushed tomatoes or sauce
3 tomatoes, sliced
handful of pitted black olives
1-2 tsp capers, rinsed
freshly ground black pepper

1 Preheat the oven to 475°F (245°C). Put a heavy baking sheet in the oven to get hot. (They both need to be really hot before cooking the pizza.)

2 Place the dough on a floured surface and use a rolling pin to roll it out as thin as you can—about 10-12in (25-30cm) in diameter. Brush the hot baking sheet with oil, sprinkle with semolina, and carefully place the dough on top.

3 Spread the crushed tomatoes onto the pizza crust, using the back of a spoon to smooth it out evenly. Top with the tomato slices, then scatter with the olives and capers. Bake for 10-15 minutes or until the crust is crisp and golden. Season with freshly ground black pepper and serve.

VARIATION

Use diced tomatoes instead of crushed. Process them briefly with a hand-held blender beforehand.

Cheat...

Buy a jar of tomato-based pizza topping—there are plenty of varieties available.

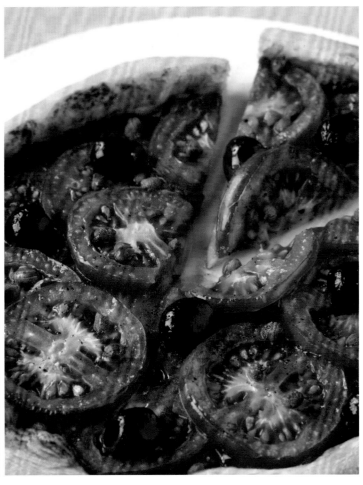

EVERYDAY

Pizza with sausage

PREP 10 MINS   COOK 20 MINS

MAKES 1
3 good-quality pork sausages, skinned
   and chopped
¼ freshly grated Parmesan cheese
   (optional)
   sea salt and freshly ground
      black pepper
1 ball pizza dough (see p181)
all-purpose flour, for dusting
semolina flour or cornmeal
3-4 tomatoes, thinly sliced

1 Preheat the oven to 475°F (245°C). Put a heavy baking sheet in the oven to get hot. (They both need to be really hot before cooking the pizza.)

2 Put the sausage in a dry frying pan and cook over medium heat for 5 minutes, or until no longer pink, breaking up any lumps with a wooden spoon. Drain off any excess fat from the pan. Stir in the Parmesan and season with salt and pepper.

3 Place the dough on a floured surface and roll it out as thin as you can—about 10-12in (25-30cm) in diameter. Brush the hot baking sheet with oil, sprinkle with semolina, and carefully place the dough on top.

4 Cover the pizza with tomato and bake for 5 minutes, then remove from the oven and spoon the sausage mixture over the top. Bake for another 5-7 minutes, or until the °crust is golden and crispy.

COOK'S NOTES

Get the children involved in the pizza-making. Or, if that sounds too messy, ask them to choose their toppings and arrange them on the pizza bases before the pizzas are cooked.

Pizza with mozzarella and mushrooms

PREP 10 MINS   COOK 15 MINS

MAKES 1
1 tbsp olive oil
4½oz (125g) mushrooms, sliced
sea salt and freshly ground
   black pepper
1 ball pizza dough (see p181)
all-purpose flour, for dusting
semolina flour or cornmeal
2-3 tbsp tomato sauce
5½oz (150g) mozzarella, torn
   into pieces
hot chili oil, to serve (optional)

1 Preheat the oven to 475°F (245°C). Put a heavy baking sheet in the oven to get hot. (They both need to be really hot before cooking the pizza.)

2 Meanwhile, heat the oil in a frying pan, add the mushrooms, and cook over low heat for 5 minutes, or until they begin to soften. Season well with salt and pepper.

3 Place the dough on a floured surface and roll it out as thin as you can—about 10-12in (25-30cm) in diameter. Brush the hot baking sheet with oil, sprinkle with semolina, and carefully place the dough on top.

4 Add the tomato sauce over the pizza and smooth it out evenly with the back of a spoon. Top with the cheese, then the mushrooms. Bake for 10 minutes, until the crust is golden and crispy and the cheese is bubbling. Drizzle with chili oil, and serve.

 VARIATION
Use wild mushrooms and buffalo mozzarella.

COOK'S NOTES

You can freeze the rolled-out part-baked untopped pizza dough (see p180).

Calzone with cheese, ham, and spinach

 PREP 15 MINS COOK 20 MINS

MAKES 1
1 ball pizza dough (see p181)
all-purpose flour, for dusting
semolina flour or cornmeal
8oz (225g) fresh spinach, wilted
    and well drained
4½oz (125g) cooked ham, chopped
4½oz (125g) mozzarella, torn
    into pieces
handful of torn basil leaves

1 Preheat the oven to 475°F (245°C). Put a heavy baking sheet in the oven to get hot. (They both need to be really hot before cooking the pizza.)

2 Place the dough on a floured surface and roll it out as thin as you can—about 10-12in (25-30cm) in diameter. Brush the hot baking sheet with oil, sprinkle with semolina, and place the dough on top.

3 Spread the spinach over half the dough, leaving a ½in (1cm) border around the edge. Top with the ham, mozzarella, and basil leaves. Moisten the edges of the dough with a little water, then fold in half and seal together with your fingers. Sprinkle the top with a little water, then bake for 15 minutes, until golden and crispy.

VARIATION
Add the cooked ingredients of your choice, but keep it simple—no more than three or four are really necessary.

COOK'S NOTES
Sprinkling the top of the calzone with a little water helps crisp up the dough.

Pizza with spinach and ricotta cheese

 PREP 15 MINS COOK 10 MINS

MAKES 1
1 ball pizza dough (see p181)
all-purpose flour, for dusting
semolina flour or cornmeal
2-3 tbsp tomato sauce
8oz (225g) spinach, wilted
    and well drained
2-3 tbsp ricotta cheese
sea salt and freshly ground
    black pepper

1 Preheat the oven to 475°F (245°C). Put a heavy baking sheet in the oven to get hot. (They both need to be really hot before cooking the pizza.)

2 Place the dough on a floured surface and use a rolling pin to roll it out as thin as you can—about 10-12in (25-30cm) in diameter. Brush the hot

baking sheet with oil, sprinkle with semolina, and place the dough on top.

3 Spoon the tomato sauce over the pizza and smooth it out evenly with the back of a spoon, then spread the spinach on top. Dot with small spoonfuls of ricotta, season with salt and pepper, then bake for 10 minutes, or until the crust is golden and crispy.

EVERYDAY

Quesadilla with spiced beef and tomato

PREP 5 MINS

COOK 20 MINS

MAKES 1

2 tbsp olive oil
4½oz (125g) lean ground beef
cayenne pepper, to taste
sea salt and freshly ground
    black pepper
small handful of very finely chopped
    flat-leaf parsley
2 wheat or corn tortillas
1 tomato, diced
½ cup shredded sharp Cheddar cheese

1 Heat 1 tablespoon of the oil in a frying pan, then add the beef and season with cayenne. Cook over medium heat for 5 minutes, stirring, breaking up any large pieces, until the meat is no longer pink. Turn down the heat and moisten with a little hot water. Season with a pinch of salt and pepper. Cook for 5-10 minutes, until the beef is cooked through. Stir in the parsley.

2 Heat the remaining oil in a nonstick frying pan and cook one tortilla for 1 minute or until lightly golden. Spoon the beef mixture over the tortilla, leaving a little border around the edge, then scatter with the tomato and cheese. Top with the other tortilla, pressing it down with the back of a spatula to sandwich the two together. Scoop up the quesadilla with the spatula, carefully turn it over, and cook the other side for another minute or until it is golden. Slice in half or in quarters and serve.

VARIATION Scatter some grated cheese, like Gruyère or Emmentaler over the beef mixture.

COOK'S NOTES

If you are only using a couple of tortillas from a package, either wrap the remaining tightly in plastic wrap and keep in the refrigerator, or wrap and freeze for up to 1 month.

Calzone with peppers, capers, and olives

PREP 15 MINS

COOK 20 MINS

MAKES 1

1 ball pizza dough (see p181)
all-purpose flour, for dusting
semolina flour or cornmeal
3-4 roasted red peppers from a jar,
    drained and chopped
handful of pitted black olives,
    coarsely chopped
1-2 tsp capers, rinsed
2-3 tbsp ricotta or fresh mozzarella,
    torn into pieces
sea salt and freshly ground
    black pepper

1 Preheat the oven to 475°F (245°C). Put a heavy baking sheet in the oven to get hot. (They both need to be really hot before cooking the pizza.)

2 Place the dough on a floured surface and use a rolling pin to roll it out as thin as you can—about 10-12in (25-30cm) in diameter. Brush the hot baking sheet with oil, sprinkle with semolina flour, and carefully place the dough on top.

3 Spoon the peppers, olives, capers, and ricotta onto half of the dough base, leaving a ½in (1cm) border around the edge. Season well with salt and pepper. Moisten the edges of the dough with a little water, then fold in half and seal together with your fingers. Sprinkle the top with a little water, then bake for 15-20 minutes or until golden and crispy.

Quesadilla with cheese and chiles

PREP 5 MINS **COOK** 5 MINS

MAKES 1

½ tbsp olive oil
2 wheat or corn tortillas
½ cup shredded sharp
 Cheddar cheese
1 mild green chile pepper, seeded and
 finely chopped
1–2 tsp pickled sliced green jalapeño
 chiles from a jar, drained
small handful of chopped cilantro
freshly ground black pepper

1 Heat the oil in a nonstick frying pan and cook one tortilla for 1 minute or until barely golden.

2 Scatter the cheese over the tortilla, then add the chile, jalapeños, cilantro, and a pinch of pepper.

3 Top with the other tortilla, pressing it down with the back of a spatula to sandwich the two together. Scoop up the quesadilla with a spatula, carefully turn it over, and cook the other side for another minute or until golden on the outside and the cheese is melted. Slice in half or in quarters and serve.

COOK'S NOTES

Leave a border when adding the filling, and don't overfill, or the cheese will ooze out.

Quesadilla with avocado, scallions, and chiles

PREP 10 MINS **COOK** 5 MINS

MAKES 1

4 scallions, finely chopped
1–2 Thai or other red hot chiles,
 seeded and finely chopped
juice of ½ lime
sea salt and freshly ground
 black pepper
1 tbsp olive oil
2 wheat or corn tortillas
½ avocado, sliced
½ cup shredded sharp Cheddar cheese

1 Place the scallions, chiles, and lime juice in a bowl, season well with salt and pepper, and mix together. Leave to sit for a couple of minutes to let the flavors develop.

2 Heat the oil in a nonstick frying pan, then cook one tortilla for 1 minute or until lightly golden. Scatter the avocado and cheese over the tortilla, leaving a little border around the edge, and spoon over the scallion mixture.

3 Top with the other tortilla, pressing it down with the back of a spatula to sandwich together. Scoop up the quesadilla with the spatula, carefully turn it over, and cook the other side for another minute or until golden. Slice in half or in quarters and serve.

Quesadilla with mushrooms and Gruyère cheese

PREP 5 MINS | COOK 10 MINS

MAKES 1
2 tbsp olive oil
4½oz (125g) cremini mushrooms, sliced
sea salt and freshly ground black pepper
pinch of crushed red pepper flakes
handful of flat-leaf parsley, chopped
2 wheat or corn tortillas
1¾oz (50g) Gruyère cheese, grated

1 Heat 1 tablespoon of the oil in a frying pan, then cook the mushrooms with a pinch of salt over low heat for 5 minutes, or until they begin to release their juices. Add the red pepper flakes and stir in the parsley.

2 Heat the remaining oil in a nonstick frying pan and cook one tortilla for 1 minute, or until golden. Using a slotted spoon to drain them, spoon the mushrooms onto the tortilla, leaving a little room around the edge. Top with the cheese and season with salt and pepper.

3 Top with the other tortilla, pressing it down with the back of a spatula to sandwich the two together. Scoop the quesadilla up, carefully turn it over, and cook the other side for another minute, or until it is golden and the cheese melted. Slice in halves or quarters and serve.

Quesadilla with feta cheese, green olives, and peppers

PREP 5 MINS | COOK 15 MINS

MAKES 1
2 tbsp olive oil
2 red bell peppers, seeded and coarsely chopped
sea salt and freshly ground black pepper
2 wheat or corn tortillas
handful of pitted green olives, sliced
4½oz (125g) feta cheese, crumbled

1 Heat 1 tablespoon of the oil in a frying pan, add the peppers, and cook over low heat for 10 minutes, or until soft. Season well with salt and pepper.

2 Heat the remaining oil in a nonstick frying pan, then cook one tortilla for 1 minute. Scatter the peppers, olives, and feta onto it, leaving a little room around the edge.

3 Top with the other tortilla, pressing it down with the back of a spatula to sandwich the two together. Scoop the quesadilla up, carefully turn it over, and cook the other side for another minute, or until golden. Slice in halves or quarters and serve.

VARIATION
Use mozzarella instead of feta.

Cheat...
Save on chopping and use 1 tablespoon of roasted red peppers from a jar.

Quesadilla with chicken and sweet onion

 PREP 5 MINS COOK 15 MINS

MAKES 1

2 tbsp olive oil
2 red onions, finely sliced
pinch of rosemary sprigs, finely chopped
sea salt and freshly ground black pepper
2 wheat or corn tortillas
4½oz (125g) pre-cooked chicken, sliced
1¾oz (50g) Cheddar cheese, grated

1 Heat 1 tablespoon of the oil in large frying pan over medium heat. Add the onions, rosemary, and a pinch of sea salt and cook for 10 minutes, or until the onions begin to soften.

2 Heat the remaining oil in a nonstick frying pan and cook one tortilla for 1 minute, or until golden. Spoon the onion mixture onto the tortilla, leaving a little room around the edge. Top with the chicken and cheese and sprinkle with black pepper.

3 Top with the other tortilla, pressing it down with the back of a spatula to sandwich the two together. Scoop the quesadilla up, carefully turn it over, and cook the other side for another minute, or until it is golden. Slice in halves or quarters and serve.

Quesadilla with ham, gherkin, and smoked cheese

 PREP 5 MINS COOK 5 MINS

MAKES 1

1 tbsp olive oil
2 wheat or corn tortillas
2½oz (75g) smoked cheese or sharp mature Cheddar cheese, grated
4½oz (125g) cooked ham, sliced
2 gherkins, sliced
sea salt and freshly ground black pepper

1 Heat the oil in a nonstick frying pan, then cook one tortilla for 1 minute, or until golden.

2 Sprinkle with the cheese, leaving a little room around the edge. Top with the ham and gherkins, then season with salt and pepper.

3 Top with the other tortilla, pressing it down with the back of a spatula to sandwich the two together. Carefully turn it over and cook the other side for another minute, until golden and the cheese melted. Slice in halves or quarters and serve.

 VARIATION Use baby gherkins instead of big ones–they are much sweeter.

EVERYDAY

Crêpes with asparagus, feta cheese, and dill

PREP 5 MINS · COOK 15 MINS

Chilling • 30 minutes
Special equipment • electric mixer

MAKES 2

For the batter
1 cup all-purpose flour
sea salt and ground black pepper
1 large egg
1¼ cups milk

For the filling
4–6 thin asparagus spears, trimmed and cut into thirds
handful of finely chopped dill
1 cup crumbled feta cheese
olive oil, for cooking

1 Sift the flour into a mixing bowl with a pinch of salt and make a well in the center. Put the egg and a little of the milk in the well. Using a wooden spoon, gradually stir the egg mixture, letting a little of the flour fall in as you go and adding the rest of the milk a little a time. When incorporated, beat with an electric mixer to remove any lumps. Transfer to the refrigerator for 30 minutes.

2 Cook the asparagus in a pan of boiling salted water for 4 minutes or until tender. Drain and refresh in cold water. Place in a bowl and mix with the dill, feta, and a pinch of pepper.

3 Heat a frying pan over medium-high heat. When hot, add a tiny amount of oil, then swirl it around the pan and pour the excess into a cup. Add 2 tablespoons of batter to the pan and swirl so it covers the bottom. Loosen the edges of the crêpe with a spatula and cook until golden. Flip the crêpe and cook the other side for 30 seconds to 1 minute, until set. Slide the crêpe onto a plate and repeat.

4 Spoon half of the feta mixture onto one half of a crêpe and roll or fold it. Fill a second crêpe in the same way.

Cheat...
Ready-made crêpes are available in the produce department of many stores; or look for a crêpe mix in the baking aisle.

COOK'S NOTES

Make a batch of pancakes ahead of time and allow to cool. Stack between sheets of wax paper, then wrap in plastic wrap and freeze.

Curried crêpes

PREP 10 MINS · COOK 20 MINS ♥

Chilling • 30 minutes
Special equipment • electric mixer

MAKES 2

For the batter
1 cup all-purpose flour
pinch of sea salt
1 large egg
1¼ cups milk

For the filling
1 tbsp olive oil, plus more as needed
handful of small uncooked shrimp, shelled and deveined
1–2 tbsp medium-hot curry paste
small handful of fresh cilantro
1 lemon, halved

1 Sift the flour into a mixing bowl with a pinch of salt and make a well in the center. Put the egg and a little of the milk in the well. Gradually stir the egg mixture, letting a little of the flour fall in as you go and adding the rest of the milk a little a time. When incorporated, beat the mixture with a balloon whisk or electric mixer to remove any lumps. Transfer to the refrigerator to rest for 30 minutes.

2 Heat 1 tbsp olive oil in a frying pan, add the shrimp, and cook over high heat for 2–4 minutes, until pink. Stir in the curry paste, add a little hot water, and simmer 10 minutes, until thickened. Add the cilantro, a squeeze of lemon juice, and a pinch of salt.

3 Heat a small frying pan over medium-high heat. When hot, add a tiny amount of oil, then swirl around the pan and pour the excess into a cup. Add 2 tablespoons of batter to the pan and swirl so it covers the bottom. Loosen the edges of the crêpe with a spatula and cook for 1 minute or until golden. Flip the crêpe and cook the other side for 30 seconds to 1 minute, until set. Slide the crêpe onto a warm plate and repeat.

4 Spoon half the shrimp mixture onto one half of a crêpe, and roll or fold into quarters. Fill a second crêpe, then serve with a squeeze of lemon.

COOK'S NOTES

The batter will keep in the refrigerator for up to 24 hours, so you could serve savory pancakes one night and sweet ones the next morning.

Moroccan-style crêpes

PREP 5 MINS **COOK 25 MINS**

Chilling • 30 minutes
Special equipment • electric mixer

MAKES 2
For the batter
1 cup all-purpose flour
**sea salt and freshly ground
    black pepper**
1 large egg
1¼ cups milk

For the filling
1 tbsp olive oil, plus more as needed
1 eggplant, cut into small dice
2 tomatoes, finely chopped
pinch of ground cinnamon
**small handful of finely chopped mint
    leaves**
lemon wedges, for serving

1 Sift the flour into a bowl with a pinch of salt and make a well in the center. Put the egg and a little of the milk in the well. Gradually stir the egg mixture, letting a little of the flour fall in as you go and adding the rest of the milk a little a time. When blended, beat with an electric mixer to remove any lumps. Rest in the refrigerator for 30 minutes.

2 Heat 1 tablespoon olive oil in a frying pan, add the eggplant, and cook over medium heat for 5–8 minutes, stirring frequently, until golden. Add the tomatoes and cook for another 5 minutes or until they start to break down a little. Season well with salt and pepper, then stir in the cinnamon and the mint.

3 Heat a small frying pan over medium-high heat. When hot, add a tiny amount of oil, then swirl it around the pan and pour the excess into a heatproof cup. Add 2 tablespoons of batter to the pan and swirl so it covers the bottom. Loosen the edges of the crêpe with a spatula or blunt knife and cook for 1 minute or until golden. Flip the crêpe and cook the other side for 30 seconds to 1 minute, until set. Slide the crêpe onto a warm plate and repeat.

4 Spoon half the eggplant mixture on top of a crêpe and roll or fold it, or simply serve the eggplant mixture on top. Prepare a second crêpe and serve with a squeeze of lemon.

Crêpes with goat cheese and chives

PREP 15 MINS **COOK 5 MINS**

Chilling • 30 minutes
Special equipment • electric mixer

MAKES 2
For the batter
1 cup all-purpose flour
**sea salt and freshly ground
    black pepper**
1 large egg
1¼ cups milk

For the filling
1 cup crumbled soft goat cheese
**small handful of finely
    chopped chives**
1 tomato, peeled
olive oil

1 Sift the flour into a bowl with a pinch of salt and make a well in the center. Put the egg and a little of the milk in the well. Gradually stir the egg mixture, letting the flour fall in as you go and adding the rest of the milk a little a time. When incorporated, beat the mixture with an electric mixer to remove lumps. Transfer to the refrigerator to rest for 30 minutes.

2 Mix the goat cheese and chives in a bowl, then season with salt and

pepper. Cut the tomato in half, scoop out the seeds, then dice the flesh and mix with the cheese mixture.

3 Heat a small frying pan over medium-high heat. When hot, add a tiny amount of oil, then swirl around the pan and pour the excess into a cup. Add 2 tablespoons of batter to the pan and swirl so it covers the bottom. Loosen the edges of the crêpe with a spatula and cook for 1 minute or until golden. Flip the crêpe and cook the other side for 30 seconds to 1 minute, until set. Slide the crêpe onto a warm plate and repeat.

4 Spoon half the cheese mixture onto one half of a crêpe and roll it up. Fill a second crêpe in the same manner.

VARIATION

 Use feta or cream cheese instead of goat cheese.

COOK'S NOTES

For ease, snip the chives with kitchen scissors, rather than chopping them with a knife.

EVERYDAY

Crêpes with blue cheese and bacon

PREP 5 MINS · COOK 10 MINS

Chilling • 30 minutes

Special equipment • electric mixer

MAKES 2

For the batter

1 cup all-purpose flour
sea salt and freshly ground
black pepper
1 large egg
1¼ cups milk

For the filling

3 bacon slices, chopped
olive oil
½ cup Gorgonzola or other blue cheese

1 Sift the flour into a bowl with a pinch of salt and make a well in the center. Put the egg and a little of the milk in the well. Stir the egg mixture, adding a little of both the flour and the milk as you go. When it's all incorporated, beat with an electric mixer to remove any lumps. Transfer to the refrigerator for 30 minutes.

2 Cook the bacon with a drizzle of olive oil in a frying pan over medium-high heat for 5 minutes or until golden. Drain on paper towels.

3 Heat a crêpe pan or small frying pan over medium-high heat. When hot, add a tiny amount of oil, then swirl it around the pan and pour the excess into a heatproof cup. Add 2 tablespoons of batter to the pan and swirl so it covers the bottom. Loosen the edges of the crêpe with a spatula or blunt knife and cook for 1 minute or until golden. Flip the crêpe and cook the other side for 30 seconds to 1 minute, until set. Slide the crêpe onto a warm plate and repeat.

4 Spoon half the bacon onto one half of a crêpe and top with half the cheese. Fold the crêpe over and cook for a minute or so, turning once, until the cheese begins to melt, then slide the crêpe onto a plate. Fill and cook a second crêpe in the same manner. Serve immediately.

Crêpes with zucchini and Emmentaler

PREP 10 MINS · COOK 15 MINS

Chilling • 30 minutes

Special equipment • electric mixer

MAKES 4

For the batter

1 cup all-purpose flour
sea salt and freshly ground
black pepper
1 large egg
1¼ cups milk

For the filling

1 tbsp olive oil, plus more as needed
2 small zucchini, coarsely grated
1 cup shredded Emmentaler or other
Swiss cheese

1 Sift the flour into a mixing bowl with a pinch of salt and make a well in the center. Put the egg and a little of the milk in the well. Gradually stir the egg mixture, letting a little of the flour fall in as you go and adding the rest of the milk a little a time. When it's all incorporated, beat the mixture with a balloon whisk or electric mixer to remove any lumps. Transfer to the refrigerator to rest for 30 minutes.

2 Heat 1 tablespoon olive oil in a frying pan, add the zucchini, and cook over medium heat for 5–8 minutes or until lightly golden. Season well with salt and pepper, then remove from the heat and stir in the cheese.

3 Heat a small frying pan over medium-high heat. When hot, add a tiny amount of oil, then swirl it around the pan and pour the excess into a cup. Add 2 tablespoons of batter to the pan and swirl so it covers the bottom. Loosen the edges of the crêpe with a spatula and cook for 1 minute, until golden. Flip and cook the other side for 30 seconds to 1 minute, until set. Slide the crêpe onto a warm plate and repeat.

4 Spoon a quarter of the zucchini mixture onto half of a crêpe, sprinkle with pepper, then roll or fold it. Fill three more crêpes in the same manner.

VARIATION

Use 4 asparagus spears per crêpe instead of zucchini.

Crêpes with garlicky mushrooms

PREP 10 MINS **COOK 15 MINS**

Chilling • 30 minutes
Special equipment • electric mixer

MAKES 2
For the batter
1 cup all-purpose flour
sea salt and freshly ground
black pepper
1 large egg
1¼ cups milk

For the filling
1 tbsp olive oil, plus more as needed
4½oz (125g) mushrooms, sliced
2 garlic cloves, finely chopped

1 Sift the flour into a mixing bowl with a pinch of salt and make a well in the center. Put the egg and a little of the milk in the well. Gradually stir the egg mixture, letting a little of the flour fall in as you go and adding the rest of the milk a little a time. When incorporated, beat the mixture with an electric mixer to remove any lumps. Transfer to the refrigerator to rest for 30 minutes.

2 Heat 1 tablespoon olive oil in a frying pan, add the mushrooms, and cook over medium heat for 5 minutes or until beginning to soften. Stir in the garlic and cook for a few minutes more, until the mushrooms have released their juices. Season well with salt and pepper.

3 Heat a small frying pan over medium-high heat. When hot, add a tiny amount of oil, then swirl it around the pan and pour the excess into a cup. Add 2 tablespoons of batter to the pan and swirl so it covers the bottom. Loosen the edges of the crêpe with a spatula and cook for 1 minute or until golden. Flip and cook the other side for 30 seconds to 1 minute, until set. Slide the crêpe onto a warm plate and repeat.

4 Spoon half the mushroom mixture onto one quarter of a crêpe, then fold it in four. Fill a second crêpe in the same manner.

Crêpes with peppers and basil

PREP 10 MINS **COOK 20 MINS**

Chilling • 30 minutes
Special equipment • electric mixer

MAKES 2
For the batter
1 cup all-purpose flour
sea salt and freshly ground
black pepper
1 large egg
1¼ cups milk

For the filling
1 tbsp olive oil, plus more as needed
2 red bell peppers, seeded and cut into strips
pinch of granulated sugar
handful of basil leaves, torn

1 Sift the flour into a mixing bowl with a pinch of salt and make a well in the center. Put the egg and a little of the milk in the well. Gradually stir the egg mixture, letting a little of the flour fall in as you go and adding the rest of the milk a little a time. When it's all incorporated, beat the mixture with a balloon whisk or electric mixer to remove any lumps. Transfer to the refrigerator to rest for 30 minutes.

2 Heat 1 tablespoon olive oil in a large frying pan, add the peppers, the sugar, and a pinch of salt, and cook over low heat for 10–15 minutes or until soft. Stir in the basil.

3 Heat a small frying pan over medium-high heat. When hot, add a tiny amount of oil, then swirl it around the pan and pour the excess into a cup. Add 2 tablespoons of batter to the pan and swirl it around so it covers the bottom. Loosen the edges of the crêpe with a spatula or blunt knife and cook for 1 minute or until golden. Flip the crêpe and cook the other side for 30 seconds to 1 minute, until set. Slide the crêpe onto a warm plate and repeat until all the batter has been used.

4 Spoon half the pepper mixture onto half of a crêpe, then fold it in two. Fill a second crêpe in the same manner.

195

EASY TARTS
AND PIES

Pastry bakes, with and without tops!

EASY TARTS AND PIES

Nothing beats a homemade tart or pie—it's real back-to-basics cooking. Whether you are making your own pastry or taking a shortcut with ready-made, home baking is time well spent in the kitchen. Tarts are open, with a pastry base, whereas pies are often deeper, and almost always topped. Both can be made with either sweet or savory fillings.

Types of pastry Choose the right pastry for the right dish.

PASTRY		USE FOR
	**SHORTCRUST** The most widely used pastry, and the easiest to make. It's a half-fat-to-flour combination, and is made by rubbing the fat into the flour with the addition of a little water. For richer pastry, egg yolk is used instead of water. This pastry is usually used for savory dishes.	Savory tart base Pie crust
	**PUFF** Has a higher fat content than shortcrust, but the end result is lighter. Making puff pastry takes a long time, so for quick-cook pastries, buy ready-made pastry, preferably made with butter.	French-style sweet pastry Savory pie topping "En croute"–savory dish encasing meat or fish
	**SWEET** This is a type of shortcrust pastry made with added sugar. The sugar is added to the flour and can be confectioners' (powdered) sugar or granulated sugar.	Sweet dessert tart or tartlet
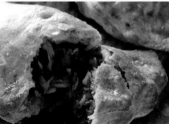	**SUET** This is made with self-rising flour instead of all-purpose, and the fat content is either a beef suet or, for vegetarians, a vegetable suet. It's a heavier pastry with a dough-like texture.	Steam pudding (sweet or savory) Pastry
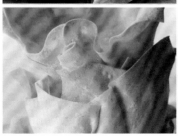	**FILO** Also known as phylo, filo pastry is a paper-thin delicate mixture of flour and oil that has been beaten and stretched. It has the lowest fat content of all the pastries. It's not easy to make at home, so buy it fresh or frozen. It can be fragile to work with, as it gets brittle when dry, so keep it covered with plastic wrap and brush thoroughly with melted butter.	Greek and Middle Eastern dishes Encasing a sweet or savory filling

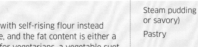

Onion Tart. For recipe, see page 198.

Dough know-how

Cool hands make good "short" and crisp pastry. Always use your fingertips, and don't overwork the pastry, otherwise it will become tough. Wash your hands in ice-cold water (then dry them) before starting to rub in the fat.

Keep all ingredients cool before starting, especially the butter. A good tip is to measure out all the ingredients and cut the butter into cubes, then sit everything in the refrigerator for 1 hour before starting.

Measure ingredients accurately, as baking is a science, and it won't work without the correct quantities.

The less liquid, the better the pastry. Be careful when adding water; do so a little at a time. Too much, and the pastry will be tough and may shrink from the edges of the pan when baked. Make sure the water is ice-cold.

Don't add too much flour when dusting the work surface or rolling pin, as it will dry out the pastry.

Chill the pastry dough, if time permits. It will make it easier to roll.

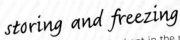

storing and freezing

Uncooked pastry can be kept in the refrigerator for 1–2 days. Wrap well in a plastic bag and seal, or wrap in plastic wrap. Although cooked pastry remains the most crisp at room temperature, leftover meat- or custard-filled pies and tarts must be refrigerated.

Uncooked pastry can be frozen for up to 3 months. Wrap well in a plastic bag or plastic wrap. Cooked pastry shells can be frozen for up to 6 months.

STEP

Make perfect shortcrust pastry Shortcrust is the most versatile pastry, suitable for both tarts and pies.

1 Sift 2 cups of all-purpose flour into a large bowl and add a pinch of salt. Cut 9 tablespoons of butter into cubes and add to the flour.

2 Rub the butter lightly into the flour using your fingertips, lifting it as you go. For light pastry, you want as much air in it as possible. Continue rubbing the mixture in until it resembles fine bread crumbs.

3 Add about 2 tablespoons of cold water and, using a blunt knife or a pastry blender, bring the pastry together.

4 Gather the pastry together into a ball using your fingertips. It should come away from the sides of the bowl easily. If it is too dry and crumbly, add a sprinkling of water until it comes together. Cover the pastry with plastic wrap, and let rest for 30 minutes in the refrigerator.

Line a tart pan Use these simple steps to line any size or shape of pan.

Psst...

To work out the amount of pastry you need to line a pan, the rule of thumb is to subtract 2 from the diameter of the tart pan in inches, and this will be the amount of pastry, in ounces, you need. So an 8in (20cm) pan would need 6oz (175g) of pastry. This is useful if you are using a different size pan than the recipe states. The filling quantity will also need adjusting.

1 Roll out the pastry (see previous page for quantities and method) on a lightly floured surface to a circle about 2in (5cm) wider than the tart pan. The pastry should be fairly thin.

2 Carefully drape the pastry over a rolling pin and gently lay it over the tart pan, so the pastry hangs over the edge.

3 Gently ease the pastry into the sides of the pan using your fingertips or knuckles, being careful not to tear it.

4 Once in place, prick the base all over with a fork, then roll a rolling pin over the top of the pan to remove the pastry that hangs over the edge. Put in the refrigerator to rest for 30 minutes.

Bake blind
Baking the pastry before filling will ensure your tart has a crisp base.

Line the uncooked pastry shell with parchment paper, then add enough pie weights or dry beans to cover the bottom. This will keep the pastry from rising up while it is cooking. The tart is now ready to bake blind in the oven at 400°F (200°C) for 15 minutes, or until the edges of the pastry are cooked.

Tools of the trade
A **selection of pie and tart pans** of varying shapes and sizes (metal pans produce crispier pastry than glass or ceramic ones); a **rolling pin**, either wooden or marble; some **pie weights** to bake the pastry blind (dry beans or rice can be used instead); **parchment paper** for lining the pastry shell; and a **pastry brush** for brushing butter or egg wash over pies and pastries, and brushing filo pastry layers.

EVERYDAY

Ready-made pastry
For convenience, ready-made pastry is a good substitute for homemade. Shortcrust and puff pastry can be bought fresh or frozen, ready-rolled or in blocks. There are low-fat versions, but all-butter pastry will taste more homemade. Blocks of pastry (that you roll out yourself) tend to produce better results than the ready-rolled, as the ready-rolled are often a little wetter in texture. The recipes in this chapter refer to the readily available types of pre-rolled pastry, unless otherwise stated.

Pastry block Ready-made pastry can be bought in a fresh or frozen block. Roll out on a floured surface as you would with homemade dough.

Ready-rolled This is ready-made pastry that has already been rolled. Available fresh or frozen, and a handy cheat when time is short.

Onion tart

PREP 15 MINS   COOK 55 MINS

Special equipment • 8in (20cm) round pie dish • pie weights or dry beans

SERVES 6
1 tbsp olive oil
4 onions, thinly sliced
1 tbsp all-purpose flour
1¼ cups whole milk
2 tsp mild paprika
sea salt and freshly ground
   black pepper
1 sheet prepared dough for an 8-9in
   (20-23cm) pie
1 egg, lightly beaten, for egg wash

1 Preheat the oven to 400°F (200°C). Heat the oil in a large nonstick frying pan over low heat. Add the onions and cook gently for about 15 minutes until quite soft, stirring constantly, to prevent browning.

2 Remove from the heat and stir in the flour with a wooden spoon. Add a little of the milk and stir until combined. Return the pan to the heat and slowly add the milk, stirring continuously as the mixture thickens. Add 1 teaspoon of the paprika and season well with salt and pepper. Remove from the heat and set aside.

3 Roll out the pastry on a floured work surface and use to line an 8in (20cm) round pie dish. Trim away any excess, line the pastry shell with parchment paper, and fill with pie weights or dry beans. Bake in the oven for 15-20 minutes until the edges of the pastry are golden. Remove the beans and paper, brush the bottom of the shell with a little of the egg wash, and return to the oven for a couple of minutes to crisp. Reduce the oven temperature to 350°F (180°C).

4 Carefully spoon the onion mixture into the pastry shell and sprinkle with the remaining paprika. Return the pie to the oven and bake for 15-20 minutes until lightly golden. Serve warm.

COOK'S NOTES
Do make sure you cook the onions very slowly over low heat—you want them to soften, but not color.

Meat and potato pie

PREP 15 MINS   COOK 1½ HRS

Special equipment • 1 qt (1.1-liter) pie dish or 4 small individual pie dishes

SERVES 4
3 all-purpose waxy potatoes, peeled
   and cut into bite-sized chunks
1½lb (675g) round, chuck, or
   Swiss steak
about 1 tbsp olive oil, plus extra
1 onion, finely chopped
1 tbsp all-purpose flour
1 tbsp Worcestershire sauce
2 cups hot beef stock
sea salt and freshly ground
   black pepper
half of a 17.3oz (425g) box frozen
   puff pastry sheets (1 sheet), thawed
   as package directs
1 egg, lightly beaten, for egg wash

1 Cook the potatoes in a pan of boiling salted water for 15 minutes until soft. Drain and set aside. Put the meat in a large frying pan with a few drops of olive oil and cook over high heat for 5-8 minutes until browned all over. Remove with a slotted spoon and set aside. Using the same pan, heat 1 tablespoon olive oil over low heat. Add the onion and a pinch of salt and cook gently for 5 minutes until soft. Stir in the flour and continue to cook for a few minutes longer.

2 Increase the heat and add the Worcestershire sauce and stock. Bring to a boil, reduce the heat slightly, and return the meat to the pan. Cover and simmer gently for 30 minutes, stirring occasionally. Stir in the potatoes and season well with salt and pepper.

3 Meanwhile, preheat the oven to 400°F (200°C). Spoon the meat filling into a 1-quart (1.1-liter) pie dish or 4 individual ones. On a floured work surface, roll out the pastry so there is a border all around, extending about 2in (5cm) beyond the pie dish. Cut out a strip of 1in (2.5cm) pastry in from the edge to make a collar. Moisten the edge of the pie dish with a little water; fit the pastry strip all the way around, and press down firmly. Brush the pastry collar with a little of the egg wash, then top with the pastry lid. Trim away the excess. Using your finger and thumb, pinch the edges together to seal.

4 Brush the top of the pie all over with the egg wash and make 2 slits in the top with a sharp knife to allow steam to escape. Bake in the oven for about 30 minutes until puffed and golden. Serve hot.

VARIATION
Use the same amount of pie dough instead of puff pastry, if you prefer.

Chicken and sweet corn pie

PREP 15 MINS **COOK** 1 HR

Special equipment • 1-quart (1.1-liter) pie dish or individual pie dishes

SERVES 4

2 tbsp olive oil
3 skinless boneless chicken breast
    halves, cut into bite-sized chunks
sea salt and freshly ground
    black pepper
1 onion, finely chopped
1 tbsp all-purpose flour,
    plus extra for dusting
⅔ cup heavy whipping cream
1¼ cups hot vegetable stock
1 x 12oz (350g) can whole kernel
    corn, drained
handful of flat-leaf parsley,
    finely chopped
half of a 17.3oz (425g) box frozen
    puff pastry sheets (1 sheet), thawed
    as package directs
1 large egg, lightly beaten, for
    egg wash

1 Preheat the oven to 400°F (200°C). Heat 1 tablespoon of the oil in a large frying pan over medium-high heat. Season the chicken with salt and pepper. Add to the pan and cook, stirring, for 7–10 minutes until golden brown all over. Remove from the pan and set aside.

2 Heat the remaining oil over low heat and add the onion and a pinch of salt. Cook gently for 5 minutes until soft. Remove from the heat and stir in the flour and a little cream. Return the pan to low heat and add the remaining cream and the stock, stirring for 5–8 minutes until the mixture thickens. Stir in the corn and parsley and season with salt and pepper.

3 Spoon the mixture into a 1-quart (1.1-liter) pie dish. On a floured work surface, roll out the pastry so there is a border all around, extending about 2in (5cm) beyond the pie dish. Cut out a strip of pastry 1in (2.5cm) in from the edge to make a collar. Moisten the edge of the pie dish with water; fit the pastry strip all the way around and press down firmly. Brush the collar with a little egg wash, then top with the pastry lid. Trim away the excess. Using your finger and thumb, pinch or press the edges together to seal.

4 Brush the top with the egg wash, cut a slit to let steam escape during cooking, and bake 30–40 minutes until the pastry is golden and puffed. Serve hot.

 VARIATION
Add sliced mushrooms to the filling at the same time you add the onion.

Sausage pie

PREP 15 MINS **COOK** 40 MINS

Special equipment • 8in (20cm) square fluted pie dish or tart pan • pie weights or dry beans

SERVES 4

1 sheet prepared dough for an 8–9in
    (20–23cm) pie
all-purpose flour
1 large egg, lightly beaten
½ tbsp olive oil
1 onion, finely chopped
sea salt and freshly ground
    black pepper
1lb (450g) good-quality pork
    sausages, skinned and crumbled
1 tsp dried oregano
4 tomatoes, sliced

1 Preheat the oven to 400°F (200°C). Roll out the pastry on a floured work surface and use to line an 8in (20cm) square baking dish or tart pan. Trim away any excess, line the pastry shell with parchment paper, and fill with pie weights or dry beans. Bake for 15–20 minutes until the edges are golden. Remove the beans and paper, brush the bottom of the pastry with a little of the beaten egg, and return to the oven for 2–3 minutes to crisp.

Remove from the oven and set aside. Reduce the oven to 350°F (180°C).

2 Meanwhile, heat the oil in a large frying pan over low heat. Add the onion and a pinch of sea salt and cook gently for about 5 minutes until soft. Add the sausage meat, breaking it up with a fork or the back of a fork. Season well with salt and pepper and sprinkle with the oregano. Cook, stirring frequently, over medium-low heat for about 10 minutes until no longer pink. Leave to cool, then mix in the remaining beaten egg.

3 Spoon the sausage mixture into the pastry shell, then layer the tomatoes over the top. Bake in the oven for 20 minutes until lightly golden. Let cool for 10 minutes, then slice and serve.

 VARIATION
You could always chop the tomatoes and combine with the sausage mixture, instead of layering them on top.

Roasted red pepper tart

PREP 15 MINS • **COOK 1 HR**

Special equipment • 9in (23cm) square loose-bottomed fluted tart pan • pie weights or dry beans • food processor

SERVES 6–8

4 large red bell peppers

1 tbsp olive oil

1 sheet prepared dough for an 8–9in (20–23cm) pie

all-purpose flour

2 large eggs, plus 1 extra yolk, lightly beaten, for egg wash

1 tbsp mascarpone cheese

handful of fresh basil leaves

salt and freshly ground black pepper

1 tsp sun-dried tomato or red pesto

1 Preheat the oven to 400°F (200°C). Put the peppers in a roasting pan. Using your hands, smear each one with olive oil. Roast in the oven for 20 minutes until lightly charred. Transfer to a plastic bag and leave until cool enough to handle. Use your fingers to rub away the skins (it's okay if some of it remains), and slice open the peppers to remove the seeds and membranes. Cut into strips or chop coarsely.

2 Meanwhile, roll out the pastry on a floured work surface and use to line a 9in (23cm) square fluted tart pan with a removable bottom. Trim away the excess, line the pastry shell with parchment paper, and fill with pie weights or dry beans. Bake in the oven for 15–20 minutes until the edges of the pastry are golden. Remove the beans and paper, brush the bottom of the shell with the extra egg yolk, and return to the oven for 2–3 minutes to crisp. Remove from the oven and set aside. Reduce the oven temperature to 350°F (180°C).

3 Put the roasted peppers, 2 eggs, mascarpone, and a handful of basil leaves in a food processor, and pulse until combined. Season well with salt and pepper. Spread the pesto evenly over the bottom of the pastry shell, then scrape in the pepper mixture. Bake for 25–35 minutes until set. Leave to cool for 10 minutes before removing the sides of the pan. Garnish with extra basil leaves, and serve with an arugula and fennel salad.

Artichoke, green olive, and feta tart

PREP 15 MINS • **COOK 1 HR**

Special equipment • 14 x 5in (35 x 12.5cm) loose-bottomed fluted tart pan • pie weights or dry beans

SERVES 6

1 sheet prepared dough for an 8–9in (20–23cm) pie

all-purpose flour

2 large eggs, plus 1 extra yolk, lightly beaten, for egg wash

1 tbsp olive oil

1 onion, finely chopped

2 garlic cloves, finely chopped

1 x 14oz (400g) can artichoke hearts, drained and chopped

12 green olives, pitted

6oz (175g) feta cheese, crumbled (about 1½ cups)

a few sprigs of fresh thyme

1 cup heavy whipping cream

salt and freshly ground black pepper

1 Preheat the oven to 400°F (200°C). Roll out the pastry on a floured work surface and use to line the tart pan. Trim away the excess, line the pastry shell with parchment paper, and fill with pie weights or dry beans. Bake for 15–20 minutes until the edges are golden. Remove the beans and paper, brush the bottom of the shell with a little egg wash, and return to the oven for 2–3 minutes to crisp. Remove from the oven and set aside. Reduce the oven temperature to 350°F (180°C).

2 Heat the oil in a saucepan over low heat. Add the onion and a pinch of salt and cook gently for about 5 minutes until soft. Add the garlic and cook for a few seconds more. Spoon the onion mixture evenly over the bottom of the tart shell. Arrange the artichokes and olives evenly over the top and sprinkle with the feta and thyme leaves.

3 Mix together the cream and the 2 eggs and season well with salt and pepper. Carefully pour over the tart filling. Bake in the oven for 25–35 minutes until set, puffed, and lightly golden. Leave to cool for about 10 minutes before removing the sides of the pan. Serve warm with an arugula and tomato salad.

Swiss chard and Gruyère cheese tart

Special equipment • 9in (23cm) loose-bottomed fluted tart pan • pie weights or dry beans

SERVES 6

1 sheet prepared dough for an 8–9in (20–23cm) pie

all-purpose flour

2 large eggs, plus 1 extra yolk, lightly beaten, for egg wash

1 tbsp olive oil

1 onion, finely chopped

sea salt and freshly ground black pepper

2 garlic cloves, finely chopped

a few sprigs of fresh rosemary, leaves picked and finely chopped

1 bunch Swiss chard, about 9oz (250g), stems trimmed, leaves coarsely chopped

1 cup shredded Gruyère cheese

1 cup cubed or crumbled feta cheese

1 cup heavy whipping cream

1 Preheat the oven to 400°F (200°C). Roll out the pastry on a floured work surface. Use to line a 9in (23cm) fluted round tart pan with a removable bottom. Trim away the excess, line the pastry shell with parchment paper, and fill with pie weights or dry beans. Bake for 15–30 minutes until the edges are golden. Remove the beans and the paper and brush the bottom of the shell with a little of the egg wash. Return to the oven for 1–2 minutes to crisp. Remove from the oven and set aside. Reduce the oven temperature to 350°F (180°C).

2 Heat the oil in a saucepan over low heat. Add the onion and a pinch of sea salt and cook gently for 5 minutes until soft. Add the garlic and rosemary, cook for a few seconds, then stir in the Swiss chard. Cook for about 5 minutes, stirring, until it wilts.

3 Spoon the onion and chard mixture into the pastry shell. Sprinkle in the Gruyère and scatter the feta overtop. Season well with salt and pepper. Mix together the cream and 2 eggs until well blended and carefully pour over the filling. Bake for 30–40 minutes until set and golden. Leave to cool for 10 minutes before removing the sides of the pan. Serve warm or at room temperature.

Instead of Swiss chard, use an equal amount of fresh spinach.

Cheese and onion pie

Special equipment • 8–9in (20–23cm) round pie pan

SERVES 4

1 tbsp olive oil

1 large onion, finely chopped

sea salt and freshly ground black pepper

2 large eggs

1 cup shredded sharp Cheddar cheese

2 sheets prepared dough for an 8–9in (20–23cm) pie

1 Preheat the oven to 400°F (200°C). Heat the oil in a saucepan over low heat. Add the onion and a pinch of salt and cook for a couple of minutes until translucent and just starting to soften. Scrape into a bowl and leave to cool completely. Lightly beat 1 of the eggs and stir into the cooled onion. Stir in the cheese and season with salt and pepper.

2 Roll out one piece of pastry on a floured work surface. Use it to line an 8–9in (20–23cm) round pie pan, folding over the edges, and fill with the cheese and onion mixture. Moisten the edge of the pastry with a little water, then top with the other circle of pastry. Trim away the excess, then pinch together with your finger and thumb to seal. Using a sharp knife, make two slits in the top of the pie to allow steam to escape.

3 Lightly beat the remaining egg to make an egg wash and brush all over the top of the pie. Bake in the oven for 25–35 minutes until cooked and golden. Serve with a green salad and boiled or steamed new potatoes.

Use a mixture of cheese for the filling if you like—half Cheddar, along with a crumbly light cheese such as Cheshire or Caerphilly is a good combination.

Olive and anchovy open tart

PREP 10 MINS   COOK 15 MINS

SERVES 6
1 x 17.3oz (425g) box frozen puff
   pastry sheets, thawed
1 egg, lightly beaten, for egg wash
¼ cup tomato purée or tomato sauce
12 flat anchovy fillets, drained
12 pitted black olives
freshly ground black pepper

1 Preheat the oven to 400°F (200°C).
On a lightly floured work surface, place
1 sheet of puff pastry on top of the
other. Roll out the pastry into a single
sheet to a thickness of ⅜in (.4cm) and
lay it on a baking sheet. Using a knife,
score a line about 2in (5cm) in from the
edge all the way around to form a
border, but do not cut all the way
through the pastry. Next, using the
edge of the knife, score the pastry all
the way around the outer edges.

2 Brush the border with the egg wash,
then smooth the tomato sauce over the
inside area, right up to the edges. Lay
the anchovies and olives evenly over
the tart so that everyone gets a taste
of each, and season with pepper.

3 Bake for 15 minutes until the
pastry is cooked and the edges are
puffed and golden. Cut into 6 squares
and serve warm with a crisp salad.

VARIATION Top with green instead
of black olives, or use
a mixture of both.

COOK'S NOTES
If feeding fussy eaters, lay the
anchovies at one end and the
olives at the other.

Spicy beef pies

PREP 20 MINS   COOK 50 MINS

SERVES 2
2 tbsp olive oil
9oz (250g) round (rump) steak
1 onion, finely chopped
pinch of sea salt
2 garlic cloves, finely chopped
1-2 fresh green jalapeño chile
   peppers, seeded and finely chopped
2in (5cm) piece of fresh ginger,
   finely chopped
1 tsp coriander seeds, crushed
4½oz (125g) mushrooms, finely
   chopped
½ tsp cayenne pepper
1 sheet prepared dough for an 8-9in
   (20-23cm) pie
all-purpose flour
1 egg, lightly beaten, for egg wash

1 Preheat the oven to 400°F (200°C).
Heat 1 tablespoon of the oil in a large
frying pan over medium-high heat.
Add the steak and cook, browning for
3 minutes on each side to seal.
Remove from the pan and set aside.

2 Heat the remaining oil over low
heat. Add the onion and a pinch of sea
salt and cook for about 5 minutes until
soft. Add the garlic, chiles, ginger, and
crushed coriander and cook, stirring,
for 2 minutes until fragrant. Add the
mushrooms, season with the cayenne,
and continue cooking over low heat for
5 minutes until the mushrooms soften
and begin to release their juices.

3 Slice the reserved steak into
strips, and return to the pan along
with 1 tablespoon of water. Cook,
stirring often, for about 2 minutes
until the mixture is thick and moist,
but not runny. Set aside to cool.

4 On a floured work surface, roll the
pastry into a rectangle and cut into
four equal squares, 6-7in (15-18cm).
Moisten each square around the
edges with a little water. Divide the
meat and onion filling into 4 equal
portions and spoon each one into the
middle of a square. Bring together the
opposite corners of each pastry square
to form a triangle, pinching the edges
together to seal. Brush all over with
the egg wash and bake in the oven for
20-30 minutes until golden. Serve hot.

VARIATION You could always fold these
into half-moon shapes to make
pastries. Roll out the pastry, cut
out 4 large circles, and fill with
the spicy beef mixture.

COOK'S NOTES
These pies can be made a day
ahead. Fill the pastry and make
into parcels, then keep in the
refrigerator until needed. Brush
with the egg wash and bake
as above.

Lamb and pea pie

PREP 15 MINS · COOK 1¼ HRS

Special equipment • 1-quart (1.1-liter) pie dish

SERVES 4
1–2 tbsp olive oil
1 onion, finely chopped
sea salt and freshly ground
    black pepper
2 garlic cloves, finely chopped
12oz (350g) lamb leg steaks, cut into
    bite-sized pieces
1 tsp ground turmeric
½ tsp ground allspice
2 tbsp all-purpose flour, plus extra for
    dusting
4 cups hot vegetable stock
2 waxy all-purpose potatoes, peeled
    and cut into small cubes
1 cup frozen peas, thawed
1 sheet prepared dough for an
    8–9in (20–23cm) pie
1 egg, lightly beaten,
    for egg wash

1 Heat 1 tablespoon of the oil in a large saucepan over low heat. Add the onion and a pinch of sea salt and cook gently for about 5 minutes until soft. Increase the heat to medium, and add a little extra oil if needed. Add the lamb and sprinkle with the turmeric and allspice. Cook, stirring occasionally, for 6-8 minutes until the lamb is browned all over.

2 Remove from the heat and stir in the flour and 1 tablespoon of the stock. Return to the heat and pour in the remaining stock. Bring to a boil, reduce the heat to low, and add the potatoes. Simmer gently, stirring occasionally so that they don't stick, for about 20 minutes until the potatoes have cooked and the sauce has thickened. Add the peas and season well with salt and pepper.

3 Meanwhile, preheat the oven to 400°F (200°C). Spoon the meat filling into a 1-quart (1-liter) pie dish. On a floured work surface, roll out the pastry so that it is about 2in (5cm) larger than the top of the pie dish. Cut out a strip of pastry about 1in (2.5cm) in from the edge to make a collar. Moisten the edge of the pie dish with a little water; fit the pastry strip all the way around, and press down firmly. Brush the pastry collar with a little of the egg wash, then top with the pastry lid. Trim away the excess pastry. Using your finger and thumb, pinch together the edges to seal.

4 Brush the top of the pie all over with the remaining egg wash. Using a sharp knife, make 2 slits in the top to allow steam to escape. Bake for 30-40 minutes until cooked and golden all over. Serve hot.

Corn and pepper filo triangles

PREP 20 MINS · COOK 20 MINS

SERVES 2
1 tbsp olive oil
1 onion, finely chopped
sea salt and freshly ground
    black pepper
3 red bell peppers, seeded and diced
1 x 12oz (350g) can whole kernel
    corn, drained
6oz (175g) feta cheese, crumbled or
    cut into small cubes (about 1½ cups)
7oz (200g) filo pastry sheets, thawed
    as package directs
melted butter, plus extra for glazing

1 Preheat the oven to 400°F (200°C). Heat the oil in a frying pan over low heat. Add the onion and a pinch of salt and cook gently for 5 minutes until soft and translucent. Stir in the peppers and continue cooking for 10 minutes until the peppers are soft. Stir in the corn and feta and season with pepper.

2 Lay out the filo sheets in four stacks of 3 or 4 layers about 12 x 4in (30 x 10cm), brushing each layer with a little melted butter. Divide the corn mixture between each stack of pastry, spooning it onto the bottom right-hand corner of each one. Fold this corner so that it forms a triangle and encloses the filling, then fold down the top right-hand corner. Repeat until you have made 5 folds in all for each one—similar to folding a flag—and end up with 4 large triangles.

3 Brush the triangles all over with a little melted butter and place on an oiled baking sheet. Bake in the oven for about 20 minutes until crisp and golden. Serve hot.

Squash, thyme, and goat cheese tart

PREP 15 MINS • COOK 50 MINS

Special equipment • 8in (20cm) round loose-bottomed fluted tart pan • pie weights or dry beans

SERVES 4–6

1 sheet prepared dough for an 8–9in (20–23cm) pie
all-purpose flour
2 large eggs, very lightly beaten
1–2 tbsp olive oil
1 onion, finely chopped
sea salt and freshly ground black pepper
2 garlic cloves, finely chopped
1 butternut squash, about 2¼lb (1kg) peeled, seeded, and chopped into small cubes
a few sprigs of fresh thyme
4½oz (125g) soft goat cheese, crumbled
1 cup heavy whipping cream

1 Preheat the oven to 400°F (200°C). Roll out the pastry on a floured work surface and use to line an 8in (20cm) fluted round tart pan with a removable bottom. Trim away the excess dough, line the pastry shell with parchment paper, and fill with pie weights or dry beans. Bake for 15–20 minutes until the edges of the pastry are golden. Remove the beans and paper, brush the bottom of the pastry shell with a little of the beaten egg, and return to the oven for 2–3 minutes to crisp. Remove from the oven and set aside. Reduce the oven temperature to 350°F (180°C).

2 Meanwhile, heat 1 tablespoon of the oil in a large frying pan over low heat. Add the onion and a pinch of salt and cook gently for 5 minutes until soft. Add the garlic, squash, and half of the thyme leaves and continue cooking over low heat for 10–15 minutes until the squash softens and begins to turn golden. You may have to add a little more olive oil.

3 Spoon the squash and onion mixture into the pastry shell, then crumble the goat cheese over the top. Mix together the cream and remaining beaten egg and season well with salt and pepper. Carefully pour the cream mixture over the tart filling and sprinkle with the remaining thyme leaves. Bake for 20–25 minutes until the tart is puffed and set. Let cool for at least 10 minutes before removing the sides of the pan. Serve warm with an arugula salad.

VARIATION

To make individual tarts, use 6 x 4in (10cm) fluted round tart pans with removable bottoms. Cut out the pastry into 6 rounds and use to line each pan.

Pea and pancetta tart

PREP 10 MINS • COOK 1¼ HRS

Special equipment • 8in (20cm) round loose-bottomed straight-sided tart pan • pie weights or dry beans

SERVES 4–6

1 sheet prepared dough for an 8–9in (20–23cm) pie
all-purpose flour
2 large eggs, plus 1 extra yolk, lightly beaten, for egg wash
1 tbsp olive oil
1 onion, finely chopped
sea salt and freshly ground black pepper
4½oz (125g) pancetta, cut into cubes
6 fresh sage leaves, coarsely chopped
1½ cups frozen peas
⅔ cup heavy whipping cream

1 Preheat the oven to 400°F (200°C). Roll out the pastry on a floured work surface and use to line the tart pan with a removable bottom. Trim away the excess, line the pastry shell with parchment paper, and fill with pie weights. Bake for 15–20 minutes until the edges of the pastry are golden. Remove the beans and paper, brush the bottom of the shell with a little of the egg wash, and return to the oven for 2–3 minutes to crisp. Remove from the oven and set aside. Reduce the oven temperature to 350°F (180°C).

2 Meanwhile, heat the oil in a large frying pan over low heat. Add the onion and a pinch of salt and cook gently for about 5 minutes until soft. Add the pancetta and sage, increase the heat a little, and cook for 6–8 minutes until the pancetta is golden and crispy. Stir in the peas and season with salt and pepper.

3 Spoon the onion and pancetta mixture into the pastry shell and level the top. Mix together the cream and the 2 eggs and season well. Carefully pour the cream mixture over the filling to cover. Bake for 20–30 minutes until set and golden. Let cool for 10 minutes before removing the sides of the pan. Serve warm with a tomato salad.

COOK'S NOTES

The tart will be much easier to slice if you leave it to cool for a while first—the residual heat means that it remains soft for a little while once you have taken it out of the oven.

Egg and ham pie

PREP 15 MINS | COOK 35 MINS | ❄

Special equipment • 10 x 6in
(25 x 15cm) rectangular tart pan

SERVES 6

2 sheets prepared dough for an 8–9in
    (20–23cm) pie
all-purpose flour
7oz (200g) cooked ham, chopped into
    bite-sized pieces
6 large eggs, plus 1 extra yolk, lightly
    beaten, for egg wash
⅓ cup heavy whipping cream
sea salt and freshly ground
    black pepper

1 Preheat the oven to 400°F (200°C).
Roll out each piece of pastry on a
floured work surface to fit a 10 x 6in
(25 x 15cm) rectangular tart pan. Use
one of the pieces to line the pan,
making sure that the pastry fits
neatly into the corners.

2 Scatter the ham evenly over the
bottom of the pastry shell. Carefully
break the 6 eggs into the shell,
positioning them evenly, leaving the
yolks whole. Drizzle cream over the
top and season well.

3 Moisten the edges of the pastry
shell with water, then cover with the
other piece of pastry to make a lid.
Trim away the excess and press the
edges of the pastry together to seal.
Brush with a little of the egg wash
and bake for 25–35 minutes until
golden brown. Leave to cool for at
least 10 minutes before slicing. Serve
warm or cold with a tomato salad.

Curried vegetable pies

PREP 15 MINS | COOK 45 MINS | ❄

Special equipment • 6in (15cm) round
biscuit cutter

SERVES 2

2 carrots, diced
2 all-purpose waxy potatoes, peeled
    and finely diced
2 sheets prepared dough for an 8–9in
    (20–23cm) pie
all-purpose flour
1 egg, lightly beaten, for egg wash
1 tbsp prepared curry paste or 1 tsp
    Madras curry powder
2 tbsp Greek-style plain yogurt
1 garlic clove, finely chopped
1in (2cm) fresh ginger, finely chopped
2 scallions, thinly sliced
handful of fresh cilantro, chopped
juice of ½ lemon
salt and freshly ground black pepper

1 Preheat the oven to 400°F (200°C).
Boil the carrots and potatoes in a pan
of salted water for about 15 minutes
until soft; drain well.

2 Roll out each sheet of pastry on
a floured work surface, then cut out
two 6in (15cm) circles from each sheet.
Put the pastry rounds on a parchment-
lined baking sheet, and brush the
edges with a little of the egg wash.

3 Put the carrots and potatoes in
a bowl and gently mix together with
the curry paste and yogurt. Add the
garlic, ginger, scallions, cilantro, and
lemon juice, and season well with salt
and pepper. Stir through gently until
well mixed.

4 Divide the vegetable mixture
evenly among the pastry circles,
spooning it into the center of each
one. Fold over the pastry to make a
half-moon shape and pinch the edges
together to seal. Using a sharp knife,
make 2 slashes in the top of each pie,
then brush all over with the remaining
egg wash. Bake for 20–30 minutes
until golden. Serve hot or cold with
a crisp green salad on the side.

Tomato and harissa tart

PREP 10 MINS COOK 15 MINS

SERVES 6

1 x 17.3oz (425g) box frozen
   puff pastry sheets, thawed as
   package directs
all-purpose flour
2 tbsp red pepper or sun-dried
   tomato pesto
6 tomatoes, halved
2–3 tbsp harissa sauce, to taste
1 tbsp olive oil
a few sprigs of fresh thyme,
   leaves picked

1 Preheat the oven to 400°F (200°C).
On a lightly floured work surface,
place 1 sheet of puff pastry on top of
the other, aligning the edges. Roll out
the pastry into a single sheet, to a
thickness of about ⅜in (.4cm), and lay
it on a baking sheet. Using a sharp

knife, score a line about 2in (5cm) in
from the edge all the way around to
form a border, but do not cut all the
way through the pastry. Next, using
the edge of the knife, score the pastry
all the way around the outer edges.
This helps it to puff when cooking.

2 Working inside the border, smother
the pastry with the pesto. Arrange the
tomatoes on top, cut-side up. Mix the
harissa with the olive oil and drizzle
over the tomatoes. Scatter the thyme
leaves over the top.

3 Bake for about 15 minutes until
the pastry is cooked and golden.
Serve hot.

Spiced pork and chicken pie

PREP 20 MINS COOK 1¼ HRS

Special equipment • 9in (23cm) round
loose-bottomed straight-sided tart pan

SERVES 6–8

2 tbsp olive oil
2 skinless boneless chicken
   breast halves
1 onion, finely chopped
pinch of crushed red pepper flakes
½ tsp ground cinnamon
½ tsp ground allspice
4 good-quality pork sausages, skinned
sea salt and freshly ground
   black pepper
2 sheets prepared dough for an 8–9in
   (20–23cm) pie
2 large eggs, plus 1 extra yolk, lightly
   beaten, for egg wash
½ tsp cayenne pepper (optional)

1 Preheat the oven to 400°F (200°C).
Heat 1 tbsp of the oil in a large frying
pan over high heat. Add the chicken
and cook for 6–8 minutes on each
side until lightly browned and cooked
through. Remove from the pan and let
cool, then shred into chunky pieces.

2 Add the remaining oil and the
onion to the same pan and reduce the
heat to low. Cook gently for 5 minutes
until soft. Stir in the pepper flakes,
cinnamon, allspice, and sausage meat,
breaking up the meat with a fork until
it is crumbly. Increase the heat
slightly and cook for 10–15 minutes

until the meat is no longer pink.
Season well with salt and plenty of
pepper. Return the shredded chicken
to the pan, stirring until evenly
coated. Remove from the heat and
leave to cool.

3 Roll out one piece of pastry on a
floured work surface to fit a 9in (23cm)
straight-sided round tart pan with a
removable bottom. Use to line the pan,
allowing the edges to hang over the
sides. Stir 2 beaten eggs into the meat
mixture to bind. Stir in the cayenne.
Spoon the mixture into the pastry
shell. Wet the edge of the pastry shell
and top with the other piece of pastry
to make a lid. Press the edges together
to seal, and trim away the excess.
Using a sharp knife, make a slit in the
top to allow steam to escape.

4 Brush the top all over with the egg
wash and bake for 35–45 minutes
until the pastry is cooked through and
golden. Leave to cool for 10 minutes
before removing the sides of the pan.
Serve hot with French fries or potato
wedges, or cold with some chutney.

COOK'S NOTES

If the pie is browning too quickly,
reduce the oven temperature to
375°F (190°C), or drape a piece of
foil over the top of the pie.

Fish and leek pie

Special equipment • 1 quart (1 liter) pie dish

SERVES 4

1 tbsp olive oil
1 onion, finely chopped
sea salt and freshly ground
   black pepper
4 leeks, thinly sliced
1 tbsp all-purpose flour
⅔ cup hard cider, apple cider, or
   unsweetened apple juice
handful of flat-leaf parsley,
   finely chopped
⅔ cup heavy whipping cream
1½lb (675g) raw skinless, boneless
   white fish, such as haddock or
   pollack, cut into chunks
half of a 17.3oz (425g) box frozen
   puff pastry sheets (1 sheet), thawed
   as package directs
all-purpose flour
1 egg, lightly beaten, for egg wash

1 Preheat the oven to 400°F (200°C). Heat the oil in a large frying pan over low heat. Add the onion and a pinch of salt and cook gently for about 5 minutes until soft. Add the leeks, and continue to cook gently for another 10 minutes until softened. Remove from the heat, stir in the flour, and add a little of the cider. Return to the heat, pour in the remaining cider, and cook for 5-8 minutes until thickened.

2 Stir in the parsley and cream and cook 1-2 minutes, then remove from the heat and stir in the fish. Spoon the mixture into a 1-quart (1.1-liter) pie or other baking dish. Season well with salt and pepper.

3 Roll out the pastry on a floured work surface so that it is about 2in (5cm) larger all around than the top of the pie dish. Cut out a strip of pastry about 1in (2.5cm) in from the edge to make a collar. Moisten the edge of the pie dish with a little water; fit the pastry strip all the way around and press down firmly. Brush the pastry collar with a little of the egg wash, then top with the pastry lid. Trim away the excess and pinch together the edges to seal. Using a sharp knife, make 2 slits in the top to allow steam to escape.

4 Brush the top of the pie all over with the egg wash and bake for 20-30 minutes until the pastry is puffed and golden. Serve hot.

Asparagus and herb tart

Special equipment • 12 x 7in (30 x 18cm) loose-bottomed fluted rectangular tart pan • pie weights or dry beans

SERVES 6-8

1 sheet prepared dough for an 8-9in
   (20-23cm) pie
all-purpose flour
2 large eggs, plus 1 extra yolk, lightly
   beaten, for egg wash
12oz (350g) bunch of fresh asparagus,
   woody ends trimmed
1 tbsp olive oil
1 bunch of scallions, finely chopped
handful of fresh mint leaves,
   finely chopped
sea salt and freshly ground
   black pepper
1 cup shredded Cheddar cheese
1 cup heavy whipping cream
pinch of freshly grated nutmeg

1 Preheat the oven to 400°F (200°C). Roll out the pastry on a floured work surface and use to line the tart pan. Trim away the excess, line the pastry shell with parchment paper, and fill with pie weights. Bake 15-20 minutes until the edges are golden. Remove the weights and paper and use a little of the egg wash to brush the bottom of the shell. Return to the oven for 2-3 minutes to crisp. Remove from the oven and set aside. Reduce the oven temperature to 350°F (180°C).

2 Meanwhile, blanch the asparagus in a large saucepan of boiling salted water for 3-4 minutes until al dente Drain and quickly refresh in very cold water; drain again and pat dry. Heat the oil in a small frying pan over low heat. Add the scallions and cook gently for a couple of minutes. Remove from the pan with a slotted spoon and scatter over the bottom of the pastry shell. Neatly arrange the asparagus on top.

3 Scatter the mint over the top and season well with salt and pepper. Sprinkle the cheese evenly over the top. Mix together the cream and the 2 eggs, then mix in the nutmeg. Pour the cream mixture over the tart filling, and bake for 30-40 minutes until set, puffed, and golden. Leave in the pan to cool for at least 10 minutes before removing the sides. Serve with a tomato salad.

COOK'S NOTES

"Al dente" means "to the tooth." It is used to describe pasta, rice, and vegetables that are tender, yet still firm to the bite. You don't want sloppy, overcooked asparagus.

EVERYDAY

Brie and bacon tart

  PREP 15 MINS | COOK 1½ HRS

Special equipment • 12 x 7in (30 x 18cm) rectangular loose-bottomed fluted tart pan • pie weights or dry beans

SERVES 6-8

1 sheet prepared dough for an 8-9in (20-23cm) pie

all-purpose flour

2 large eggs, plus 1 extra yolk, lightly beaten, for egg wash

1 tbsp olive oil

1 onion, finely chopped

sea salt and freshly ground black pepper

5 thick-cut bacon slices (125g), chopped into bite-sized pieces

8 semi-dried tomatoes, or 8 oil-packed sun-dried tomato halves, drained and coarsely chopped

4½oz (125g) Brie cheese, sliced into long strips

small handful of fresh chives, finely chopped

1 cup heavy whipping cream

2 garlic cloves, finely grated

1 Preheat the oven to 400°F (200°C). Roll out the pastry on a floured work surface and use to line the tart pan, letting the pastry hang over the edges. Trim away the excess, line the pastry shell with parchment paper, and fill with pie weights or dry beans. Bake for about 20 minutes until the edges are golden. Remove the weights or beans and paper, brush the bottom of the shell with a little egg wash, and return to the oven for 1-2 minutes to crisp. Remove from the oven and set aside. Reduce the oven temperature to 350°F (180°C).

2 Heat the oil in a large frying pan over low heat. Add the onion and a pinch of salt and cook gently for about 5 minutes until soft. Increase the heat slightly, add the bacon, and cook for 5-8 minutes until crispy and golden. Remove from the heat, drain off excess fat as needed, and stir in the tomatoes.

3 Spoon the onion and bacon mixture into the pastry shell. Top evenly with the Brie strips and sprinkle with the chives. Mix together the cream and the 2 eggs. Add the garlic and season well with salt and pepper. Carefully pour over the tart filling. Bake in the oven for 30-40 minutes until set, puffed, and lightly golden. Serve with a crisp green salad.

VARIATION Use soft goat cheese instead of Brie.

Mixed mushroom and walnut tart

   PREP 15 MINS | COOK 1 HR | ❄

Special equipment • 14 x 5in (35 x 12.5cm) rectangular loose-bottomed fluted tart pan • pie weights or dry beans

SERVES 6

1 sheet prepared dough for an 8-9in (20-23cm) pie

all-purpose flour

2 large eggs, plus 1 extra yolk, lightly beaten, for egg wash

3-4 tbsp olive oil

5oz (140g) fresh exotic or wild mushrooms (such as porcini or shiitake), coarsely chopped

7oz (200g) cultivated mushrooms, coarsely chopped

3 garlic cloves, finely chopped

½ cup walnut halves and pieces, coarsely chopped

sea salt and freshly ground black pepper

2 handfuls of fresh spinach leaves, coarsely chopped

1 cup heavy whipping cream

1 Preheat the oven to 400°F (200°C). Roll out the pastry on a floured work surface and use to line a 14 x 5in (35 x 12.5cm) fluted rectangular tart pan with a removable bottom. Trim away the excess, line the pastry shell with parchment paper, and fill with pie weights or dry beans. Bake for 15-20 minutes until the edges are golden. Remove the beans and paper, brush the bottom of the shell with a little of the egg wash, and return to the oven for 2-3 minutes to crisp. Remove from the oven and set aside. Reduce the oven temperature to 350°F (180°C).

2 Heat the oil in a large deep-sided frying pan over low heat. Add the mushrooms, garlic, and walnuts and season well with salt and pepper. Cook, stirring occasionally, for about 10 minutes until the mushrooms release their juices. Add the spinach and cook, stirring, for 5 minutes until just wilted. Spoon the mixture into the pastry shell.

3 Mix together the cream and the 2 eggs. Season well with salt and pepper. Carefully pour the cream mixture over the mushroom filling. Season with a pinch of pepper and bake for 15-20 minutes until set. Leave to cool for 10 minutes before removing the sides from the pan. Serve hot or cold.

EVERYDAY

Gruyère, potato, and thyme tartlets

PREP 20 MINS · **COOK 1 HR**

Special equipment • 4 x 4in (10cm) tart pans with removable bottoms • pie weights or dry beans

SERVES 4

1 sheet prepared dough for an 8–9in (20–23cm) pie
all-purpose flour
2 large eggs, plus 1 extra, lightly beaten, for egg wash
2 all-purpose waxy potatoes, peeled and cut into ½in (1cm) dice
2 tbsp olive oil
1 small onion, very finely diced
sea salt and freshly ground black pepper
a few sprigs of fresh thyme, leaves picked
⅔ cup shredded Gruyère cheese
1 cup heavy whipping cream

1 Preheat the oven to 400°F (200°C). Roll out the pastry on a floured surface and use to line the tart pans. Trim the excess, line the pastry shells with parchment paper, and fill with pie weights or dry beans. Bake in the oven for 15–20 minutes until the edges are golden. Remove the beans and paper, brush the bottoms with egg wash, and return to the oven for 2–3 minutes to crisp. Remove, set aside, and reduce the oven temperature to 350°F (180°C).

2 Boil the potatoes in a small pan of salted water for about 5 minutes until just starting to soften but still not tender; do not overcook. Drain.

3 Meanwhile, heat the oil in a large nonstick frying pan over low heat. Add the onion and a pinch of sea salt and cook gently for about 5 minutes until soft. Add the partially-boiled potatoes and the thyme and season with some pepper. Cook, stirring occasionally, for about 10 minutes until the potatoes begin to brown.

4 Remove from the heat and stir in the Gruyère. Taste and season some more if needed. Divide the mixture evenly among the pastry shells. Mix together the cream and the 2 eggs, then carefully pour equal amounts into each tart. Place the tarts on a baking sheet and bake in the oven for 20–30 minutes until set and golden. Serve hot.

COOK'S NOTES

Always remember to reduce the oven temperature when cooking the custard mixture; if you don't, it may curdle.

Creamy spinach tart

PREP 15 MINS · **COOK 1 HR**

Special equipment • 8in (20cm) round loose-bottomed fluted tart pan • pie weights or dry beans • food processor

SERVES 4–6

1 sheet prepared dough for an 8–9in (20–23cm) pie
all-purpose flour
2 large eggs, plus 1 extra yolk, lightly beaten, for egg wash
1 tbsp olive oil
1 onion, finely chopped
sea salt and freshly ground black pepper
2 garlic cloves, finely chopped
1lb (450g) fresh spinach leaves
7oz (200g) watercress, tough stems removed
1 cup heavy whipping cream
pinch of grated fresh nutmeg

1 Preheat the oven to 400°F (200°C). Roll out the pastry on a floured work surface and use to line the tart pan. Trim away the excess, line the pastry shell with parchment paper, and fill with pie weights or dry beans. Bake for 15–20 minutes until the edges are golden. Remove the beans and paper, brush the bottom of the shell with a little of the egg wash, and return to the oven for 2–3 minutes to crisp. Remove from the oven and set aside.

Reduce the oven temperature to 350°F (180°C).

2 Heat the oil in a large frying pan over low heat. Add the onion and a pinch of sea salt and cook gently for about 5 minutes until soft. Add the garlic and cook for a few more seconds. Spoon the mixture into the pastry shell.

3 Put the spinach and watercress in a food processor and pulse a few times until chopped but not mushy. Pour in the cream and the 2 eggs and pulse again until everything is combined. Season well with salt and pepper, then pulse once more. Carefully pour into the pastry shell, sprinkle with the nutmeg, and bake for 20–30 minutes until set. Let cool for 10 minutes before removing the sides of the pan. Serve with steamed new potatoes.

Cheat...

If time is short, buy a ready-made tart shell.

EVERYDAY

Filo pie with Swiss chard, ricotta, and tomatoes

PREP 15 MINS · COOK 30 MINS

Special equipment • 8in (20cm) round nonstick loose-bottomed cake pan

SERVES 4-6

7oz (200g) ricotta cheese

1¼lb (550g) Swiss chard, leaves and stems chopped

4-6 oil-packed sun-dried tomatoes, drained and chopped

4 fresh tomatoes, sliced

1 large egg

sea salt and freshly ground black pepper

12 sheets filo pastry

2 tbsp butter, melted

1 Preheat the oven to 350°F (180°C). In a bowl, mix together the ricotta, Swiss chard, sun-dried and fresh tomatoes, and egg. Season well with salt and pepper.

2 Lay 2 sheets of filo pastry one on top of the other in an 8in (20cm) nonstick round cake pan with a removable bottom, letting them hang over the edge on two sides. Next, lay 2 more sheets of filo at right angles to the first layer. Continue in this way until you have 8 sheets for the base of the pie.

3 Spoon the ricotta mixture into the filo shell. Fold in the edges of the pastry and top the pie with the remaining 4 sheets filo pastry, tucking them in neatly. Brush all over with the melted butter and bake in the oven for 20-30 minutes until golden and crisp. Serve hot with a crisp green salad and some sweet onion chutney.

COOK'S NOTES

Always work quickly with filo, and don't let it dry out because it becomes very brittle.

Smoked mackerel and scallion tart

PREP 15 MINS · COOK 50 MINS

Special equipment • 7in (18cm) round loose-bottomed straight-sided tart pan • pie weights or dry beans

SERVES 4

1 sheet prepared dough for an 8-9in (20-23cm) pie

all-purpose flour

2 eggs, plus 1 extra yolk, for egg wash

1 tbsp olive oil

1 bunch of scallions, finely chopped

sea salt and freshly ground black pepper

2 smoked mackerel fillets, about 3½oz (100g) each, skinned and flaked

1 cup crème fraîche

handful of flat-leaf parsley, finely chopped

1 bunch of fresh chives, finely chopped

1 Preheat the oven to 400°F (200°C). Roll out the pastry on a floured work surface and use to line the tart pan. Trim away the excess, line the pastry shell with parchment paper, and fill with pie weights or dry beans. Bake for 15-20 minutes until the edges are golden. Remove the beans and paper, brush the bottom of the shell with a little of the egg wash, and return to the oven for 2-3 minutes to crisp. Remove from the oven and set aside. Reduce the oven temperature to 350°F (180°C).

2 Meanwhile, heat the oil in a small frying pan over low heat. Add half of the scallions and a pinch of salt and cook gently for about 5 minutes. Spoon evenly over the bottom of the pastry shell, along with the remaining uncooked scallions. Scatter the mackerel over the top and season with plenty of black pepper.

3 Mix together the crème fraîche and the 2 eggs. Add the parsley and chives and season with a little salt. Stir to blend. Carefully pour over the tart filling, then bake for 20-30 minutes until set and golden. Leave to cool for 10 minutes before removing the sides of the pan. Serve with a fresh tomato and cucumber salad.

Steak, mushroom, and ale pie

 PREP 15 MINS **COOK 1¼ HRS**

Special equipment • 1-quart (1.1-liter) pie dish

SERVES 4

1 tbsp olive oil

2lb (900g) round, chuck, or Swiss steak, chopped into bite-sized pieces

a few sprigs of fresh rosemary, leaves picked and finely chopped

1 Bovril or other beef boullion cube

1 tbsp all-purpose flour, plus extra for dusting

⅔ cup pale ale

1¼ cups hot water

2 tbsp butter

7oz (200g) mushrooms, quartered

sea salt and freshly ground black pepper

half of a 17.3oz (425g) box frozen puff pastry sheets (1 sheet), thawed as package directs

1 egg, lightly beaten, for egg wash

1 Heat the oil in a frying pan over medium-high heat. Add the meat and cook, stirring, for 4–6 minutes until browned. Add the rosemary, crumble in the boullion cube, and sprinkle in the flour. Stir until well combined. Increase the heat to high and add a little of the ale, stirring all the time. Pour in the remaining ale and let bubble for a couple of minutes. Add the hot water and bubble for a few minutes more. Reduce the heat to low, cover the pan, and simmer for about 30 minutes, stirring occasionally, so that the meat doesn't stick to the pan. If the mixture dries out too much, add a little more hot water.

2 Meanwhile, preheat the oven to 400°F (200°C). Melt the butter in a medium frying pan over medium heat. Add the mushrooms and cook for 4–6 minutes until golden. Stir the mushrooms and their juices into the meat mixture. Season well with salt and pepper.

3 Spoon the meat filling into the pie dish. On a floured work surface, roll out the pastry so there is a border all around, extending about 2in (5cm) beyond the pie dish. Cut out a strip of pastry about 1in (2.5cm) in from the edge to make a collar. Moisten the edge of the pie dish with a little water; fit the pastry strip all the way around and press down firmly. Brush the pastry collar with a little of the egg wash, then top with the pastry lid. Trim away the excess. Using your finger and thumb, pinch the edges together to seal.

4 Brush the top of the pie with the egg wash and make 2 slits in the top with a sharp knife to allow steam to escape. Bake 20–30 minutes until the pastry is puffed and golden. Serve hot with creamy mashed potatoes.

Filo pie with spinach, ricotta, pine nuts, and raisins

 PREP 15 MINS **COOK 35 MINS**

Special equipment • 8in (20cm) round or square loose-bottomed cake pan

SERVES 4

1 tbsp olive oil

1 onion, finely chopped

sea salt and freshly ground black pepper

2 garlic cloves, finely chopped

1¼lb (550g) fresh spinach leaves

handful of dark raisins

⅓ cup pine nuts, toasted

7oz (200g) ricotta cheese

1 large egg, lightly beaten

12 sheets filo pastry

about 2 tbsp butter, melted

1 Preheat the oven to 350°F (180°C). Heat the oil in a frying pan over low heat. Add the onion and a pinch of salt and cook gently for 5 minutes until soft. Add the garlic and cook for a few seconds more.

2 Add the spinach, and cook, stirring, for 3 minutes until it wilts. Season well with salt and pepper. Remove from the heat, stir in the raisins and pine nuts, and leave to cool. Add the ricotta and beaten egg and stir well.

3 Lay 2 sheets of filo pastry one on top of the other in an 8in (20cm) nonstick round or square cake pan with a removable bottom, letting it hang over the edge on two sides. Next, lay 2 more sheets of filo at right angles to the first layer. Continue in this way until you have used 8 sheets for the base of the pie.

4 Spoon the spinach and ricotta mixture into the pie. Fold in the edges of the pastry and top the pie with the remaining 4 sheets filo pastry, tucking them in neatly. Brush all over with the melted butter and bake in the oven for 20–30 minutes until golden and crisp. Serve warm.

EVERYDAY

GET THE MOST FROM YOUR ROAST

Recipes for roast meat, poultry, and fish, and how to use the leftovers.

GET THE MOST FROM YOUR ROAST

Cooking one dish one day and enjoying it in different ways in the days to come is a clever way to plan your weekly meals. Not only is it economical, it is also a great time-saver. By being a little creative and resourceful in the kitchen, you'll be able to turn your leftovers into something special—from delicious roast meat sandwiches to simple salads and stir-fries.

plan ahead

If you are planning to cook once and eat for the week, a little planning is required. Buy a larger cut of meat or larger fish than you need, and make sure it is good quality. Think about all the flavors and cuisines that would work with the meat or fish, and buy a few more ingredients accordingly. Think about types of dishes and textures, as you don't want soup every day, but a risotto with leftovers one day, and a pie the next, is fine. Remember that a dish is only as good as its ingredients, so buy everything fresh and seasonal if you can.

Using leftover vegetables How to store, and ideas for what to make.

LEFTOVER

TURN INTO

ROOT VEGETABLES

Store
Put cooked root vegetables in a rigid sealable plastic container, and don't overpack, as they can get soggy. Let cool before sealing.

Refrigerator
Will keep well for 1–2 days.

Freezer
Leftover root vegetables don't freeze well unless they have been slightly undercooked. Keep for up to 1 month.

Vegetable bake
Layer vegetables in an ovenproof dish. Mix an 8oz (200g) carton of Greek yogurt with 1 egg and a handful of shredded Cheddar cheese. Season, then stir and pour over the vegetables. Bake in a preheated 400°F (200°C) oven for 30 minutes, or until golden.

Pasta sauce
Stir chopped vegetables into a simmering tomato sauce, cook until heated through, and toss with chunky pasta shapes.

Frittata
Add chopped vegetables to an omelet. Melt 1 tablespoon of butter in a small frying pan over medium heat. Pour 3–4 beaten eggs into the pan and cook for a minute or two. Add the leftover vegetables, sprinkle some Gruyère cheese over the top, and cook in a hot oven until set and golden.

Bolognese
Stir chopped leftover vegetables into a simmering pan of ground beef and tomato sauce.

See Cook's Notes in recipes to find out where you can use leftover root vegetables.

GREENS

Store
Store in a covered bowl or rigid plastic container. Let cool before covering or sealing.

Refrigerator
Will keep well for 1–2 days. Any longer and it tends to go limp and lose its fresh taste.

Freezer
Leftover greens don't freeze well.

Soup
Add leftover greens to your soup at the end of cooking, or just before puréeing.

Cheese on toast
Mix into a Gruyère or Cheddar cheese sauce, pile on top of crusty toasted bread, and cook under a broiler until melted.

Lamb or chicken casserole
Stir into a lamb or chicken casserole for the last 15 minutes of cooking.

Lasagna
Add well-drained greens to your lasagna as you layer the ingredients in the dish.

Fish cakes and vegetarian burgers
Finely chop and add to fish cakes or vegetarian burgers before frying.

Alternatively, just **reheat greens** in a little olive oil and toss in lemon juice and chili oil. Dig in with some fresh crusty bread.

See Cook's Notes in recipes to find out where you can use leftover greens.

MASHED POTATOES

Store
Spoon leftover mashed potatoes into a rigid plastic container. The more shallow it is, the quicker they will cool. When completely cool, seal and refrigerate.

Refrigerator
Will keep well for 1–2 days. They will dry out if left too long.

Freezer
Keep for up to 1 month. Will get watery if left too long.

Gnocchi
Mix 1 egg into ¾ cup mashed potatoes, then stir in enough flour to make a stiff dough. Using floured hands, roll a small portion of the dough into a narrow cylinder. Repeat with the remaining dough. Cut into 1in (2.5cm) pieces, indent with a fork, and refrigerate on a floured baking sheet for 15 minutes before boiling. Serve with a sauce.

Fish cakes
Mix mashed potatoes with flaked cooked salmon and a handful of leftover peas. Stir in 1 teaspoon of horseradish sauce and 1 teaspoon of coarse-grain mustard. Add one egg to bind, and flatten into cakes with floured hands. Cook in hot vegetable oil until golden.

Bubble and squeak
Mix mashed potatoes with leftover vegetables, such as cabbage, and cook in 4 tablespoons of hot oil or melted butter until it becomes golden and crispy. Add flavorings such as Worcestershire sauce, horseradish sauce, or mustard.

See Cook's Notes in recipes to find out where you can use leftover mashed potatoes.

Using leftover meat and fish What to do with your leftover roast, and some great dish ideas.

LEFTOVER

TURN INTO

CHICKEN
Store
Remove the meat from the carcass. Wrap the meat and carcass separately in plastic wrap, then foil. Refrigerate within 2 hours after cooking. Keep away from uncooked meats. Remove stuffing before storing (store separately in a plastic container). Store leftover gravy in a plastic container.

Refrigerator
Will keep well for 2–3 days; use leftover gravy within 2 days.

Freezer
Keep for up to 3 months.

A variety of recipes, including:

Cardamom chicken curry (see p224).

Chicken and pea filo pie (see p224).

Chicken and sweet corn soup (see p225).

Chicken salad with carrot and apple relish (see p225).

A **pasta bake** or a fragrant **pilaf**.

LAMB
Store
Remove leftover lamb from the bone in large pieces. Wrap the lamb tightly in foil and slice as needed. The bone can be used for stock, but wrap it separately in foil. Store away from uncooked meats. Refrigerate within 2 hours after it has been cooked.

Refrigerator
Will keep well for 1–3 days.

Freezer
Keep for up to 3 months.

A variety of recipes, including:

Flat breads topped with lamb and hummus (see p228).

Hot and fiery lamb masala (see p228).

Lamb, tomato, and bean casserole (see p229).

Lamb and potato pie (see p229).

A Moroccan-style **shepherd's pie**.

PORK
Store
Slice and store in a shallow rigid plastic container and seal, or put on a plate and wrap well with plastic wrap. If there is a large amount, pack in smaller quantities. Store away from uncooked meats. Refrigerate within 2 hours after cooking. Store leftover gravy in a plastic container.

Refrigerator
Will keep well for 1–3 days; use leftover gravy within 2 days.

Freezer
Keep for up to 3 months.

A variety of recipes, including:

Roast pork in pita bread (see p232).

Pork and yellow split pea soup (see p232).

Pork and spring greens (see p233).

Sweet and sour pork (see p233).

A shredded pork and lemongrass **burger**, or pork, bacon, and spinach **pie**.

FISH
Store
Store in a shallow rigid plastic container and seal, or put on a plate and wrap well with plastic wrap. Store away from uncooked meats. Refrigerate within 2 hours after cooking.

Refrigerator
Will keep well for 1–2 days.

Freezer
Keep for up to 3 months.

A variety of recipes, including:

Baked salmon with salsa verde and cucumber (see p236).

Salmon and shrimp fish pie (see p236).

Salmon and roasted tomato pasta (see p237).

Salmon with new potatoes, flageolet beans, and parsley sauce (see p237).

A green **salad** or **fish cakes**.

BEEF
Store
Store large pieces in an airtight container, as it will remain moist if left unsliced until needed. Refrigerate within 2 hours after cooking. The bone can be used for stock, but wrap it separately in foil. Leftover gravy can be stored in a plastic container, but use within 2 days.

Refrigerator
Will keep well for 2–3 days.

Freezer
Keep for up to 3 months.

A variety of recipes, including:

Beef and Stilton pie (see p240).

Thai-style beef salad (see p240).

Beef stroganoff (see p241).

Beef with beet and spinach (see p241).

Beef and mushroom **stir-fry** or sliced beef, Gorgonzola cheese, and red onion marmalade **pitas**.

TURKEY
Store
Remove meat from the carcass. Wrap the meat and carcass separately in plastic wrap, then foil. Refrigerate within 2 hours after cooking. Keep away from uncooked meats. Remove stuffing before storing (store separately in a plastic airtight container). Store leftover gravy in a plastic container.

Refrigerator
Will keep well for 2–3 days; use leftover gravy within 2 days.

Freezer
Keep for up to 3 months.

A variety of recipes, including:

Turkey, almond, and cranberry pilaf (see p244).

Turkey and noodles (see p244).

Warm turkey and chickpea salad (see p245).

Spiced turkey and greens stir-fry (see p245).

A **curry**, or turkey, ham and Gruyère cheese **quesadillas**.

EVERYDAY

Make stock Turn a carcass or meat bones into delicious stock.

Chicken A great kitchen staple to have in your refrigerator or freezer.

1 Place the cooked chicken carcass in a large pot, then add a handful of raw vegetables such as carrot chunks and tops, celery chunks, onion pieces with skin on, fresh thyme or rosemary sprigs, a bay leaf, and black peppercorns.

2 Pour in enough cold water to cover completely. You will probably need around 10 cups.

3 Bring to a boil, reduce to a gentle simmer, and cook with the lid half-on for about 1 hour, skimming off any fat that rises to the top of the pan if necessary.

4 Remove the carcass and discard, then pour the liquid through a sieve into a large storage container.

Beef Richer and darker than chicken, particularly if you roast the bones.

1 Use either leftover rib bones from a roast, or purchase a bag of beef bones from your butcher. Add the bones to a large roasting pan, add a handful of vegetables such as carrot chunks and tops, celery chunks, onion pieces with skin on, and season with salt and pepper. Roast for 30 minutes.

2 Add the roasted bones and vegetables to a large deep pot with some fresh sprigs of thyme, rosemary, or another woody herb of your choice, then pour in enough cold water to cover completely.

3 Bring to a boil, then reduce to a gentle simmer. Cook with the lid half-on for about 1 hour, skimming off any fat that comes to the top of the pan if necessary.

4 Remove the bones and discard, then pour the liquid through a sieve into a large storage container.

fish stock

When buying fresh fish, ask your fishmonger for some fish heads. Add these to a large pot, pour in enough water to cover, season well, and add some fresh thyme, chopped onion, and chopped fennel. Season, bring to a boil, and simmer for about 15 minutes, skimming off any foam that rises to the top. Pass through a fine sieve (preferably twice, in case of fine bones), refrigerate, and use within 2 days, or freeze for up to 3 months. Use white fish for stock, as oily fish such as salmon is too strong in flavor.

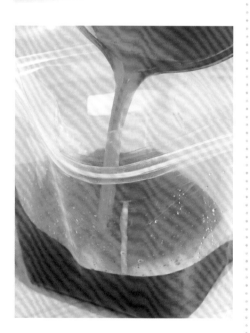

How to store stock

Leave to cool for 30 minutes, then cover and refrigerate. To freeze, pour the cool stock into 1-pint (600ml) zipper-seal plastic bags or rigid plastic containers with lids, and freeze for up to 3 months. Or, pour the stock into ice cube trays and freeze, then transfer the frozen cubes to a plastic bag.

4 ideas for leftovers
Whip up a quick 5-minute snack with your leftover chicken, pork, beef, or salmon.

Sandwiches
Ideal for picnics and packed lunches.

Coronation chicken
Mix shredded **leftover chicken** in a bowl with **mayonnaise** to coat. Add a pinch of **paprika** and a pinch of **curry powder** and mix well. Add a handful of **raisins** and season. Spoon into a sliced roll with a handful of arugula.

Roast pork and apple
Halve a bread roll and smother one half with **applesauce**, top with slices of **leftover pork**, then top with a few slices of a **sweet apple**. Season and serve with **leftover pork skin cracklings**, if desired.

Salads
Freshen up your leftovers with a citrusy dressing and crisp salad ingredients.

Beef, arugula, and radish
Put a couple of handfuls of **arugula** on a plate, then top with slices of **leftover beef**. Slice 3–4 **radishes** thinly and sprinkle these over the beef. Drizzle with a little **balsamic vinegar** and the juice of ½ an **orange**. Season and serve immediately.

Salmon and noodle
Put **cooked medium rice noodles** in a bowl. Toss with flaked **leftover salmon** and a few sliced **scallions**. Mix together 3 tablespoons of **extra virgin olive oil**, 1 tablespoon **white wine vinegar**, juice of ½ a **lime**, a pinch of **sugar**, a pinch of **crushed red pepper flakes**, and season. Drizzle over the salad and garnish with fresh basil leaves. Serve immediately.

ROAST CHICKEN

PREP 15 MINS · COOK 1 HR

SERVES 4, PLUS LEFTOVERS

3lb (1.35kg) whole chicken (preferably free-range)

4 tbsp butter, at room temperature

1 lemon, quartered

sea salt and freshly ground black pepper

⅔ cup hot vegetable stock or water

1 Preheat the oven to 400°F (200°C). Place the chicken in a flameproof roasting pan, then smear evenly all over with the butter–this ensures crisp, golden skin. Stuff the lemon quarters into the body cavity–to help keep the meat moist–and season the chicken all over with sea salt and freshly ground black pepper.

2 Roast in the oven for about 1 hour or until it is cooked through and golden, basting with the juices at intervals as it cooks (about 3 times in all). To check whether the chicken is cooked through, pierce a knife into the thickest part of the thigh. If the juices run clear, it is done; if it is at all pink or bloody, cook for a little while longer. Remove from the oven, place on a large plate, cover loosely with foil, and leave to rest in a warm place for about 15 minutes before carving.

3 To make the gravy, tilt the roasting pan at a slight angle and skim off any fat. Add the stock or water and bring to a boil, scraping up any browned bits from the bottom with a wooden spoon. Reduce the heat slightly and simmer for 10 minutes. Pass through a sieve if you wish, or serve as is with the carved chicken. Serve with roast or sautéed potatoes and seasonal vegetables.

EVERYDAY

Cardamom chicken curry

PREP 10 MINS **COOK 30 MINS**

SERVES 4

1 tbsp sunflower oil

1 onion, finely chopped

2in (5cm) piece of fresh root ginger, thinly sliced

10 green cardamom pods, lightly crushed

2 tsp onion seeds (optional)

2 fresh red hot chile peppers, seeded and finely chopped

3 garlic cloves, finely chopped

2 tsp garam masala

12oz (350g) leftover roast chicken, skin removed, coarsely shredded or sliced

sea salt and freshly ground black pepper

1 x 14oz (400g) can diced tomatoes, with juices

3 tbsp heavy whipping cream

2 handfuls of fresh spinach leaves, rinsed

1 Heat the oil in a Dutch oven or deep frying pan over low heat. Add the onion and cook gently for about 5 minutes until soft. Add the ginger, cardamom, onion seeds, and chiles, and cook for another 3 minutes, stirring occasionally.

2 Now add the garlic and garam masala and stir for a few seconds until fragrant, before adding the chicken. Season well with salt and pepper. Stir in the tomatoes and their juices, then fill the can with hot water and add this to the pan as well. Bring to a boil, then stir in the cream.

3 Reduce the heat slightly and simmer gently for 25–30 minutes; if the curry looks too thick, add a little more hot water and stir through. Add the spinach and stir well until it has wilted. Taste and season again if needed. Serve hot with some fluffy white rice and a crisp green salad on the side.

VARIATION For a healthier option, use Greek-style plain yogurt instead of cream.

Chicken and pea filo pie

PREP 20 MINS **COOK 30 MINS**

Special equipment • 8in (20cm) square pie or cake pan

SERVES 6

12 sheets filo pastry

4 tbsp butter, melted, plus extra if needed

12oz (350g) leftover roast chicken, skin removed, coarsely shredded or sliced

9oz (250g) boiled new potatoes, halved

1 cup frozen peas

1–2 tbsp mild curry powder

sea salt and freshly ground black pepper

3–4 tbsp hot vegetable stock

1 Preheat the oven to 400°F (200°C). Lightly brush 6 sheets of the filo with melted butter. Use to line the bottom of the cake pan, allowing excess to drape over the sides.

2 Toss together the chicken, potatoes, peas, and curry powder, and season well with salt and pepper. Carefully pour in a little of the stock. Use just enough to moisten the mixture and produce a little sauce; too much would ultimately make the pastry soggy.

3 Spoon the filling into the filo pastry shell. Fold the pastry edges in toward the middle and top the pie with the remaining 6 filo sheets, each brushed with a little melted butter. Tuck the edges of the pastry neatly down at the sides and make sure that the top is well glazed with melted butter. Bake for 20–30 minutes or until the pastry is crisp and golden. Serve hot with mixed greens.

Chicken and sweet corn soup

   PREP 10 MINS **COOK 30 MINS**

Special equipment • blender or food processor

SERVES 4

1 tbsp olive oil
2 tbsp butter
1 onion, finely chopped
2 x 12oz (350g) cans corn
    kernels, drained
12oz (350g) leftover roast chicken,
    skin removed, coarsely shredded
3 garlic cloves, finely chopped
sea salt and freshly ground
    black pepper
4 cups hot chicken stock
handful of flat-leaf parsley,
    finely chopped

1 Heat the olive oil and butter in a Dutch oven or large deep frying pan over low heat. Add the onion and cook gently for about 5 minutes, or until soft.

2 Add 1 can of the drained corn to a food processor and pulse on and off for a few times until the kernels are a chunky purée. Scrape this into the pan with the onion. Stir in the chicken and garlic and season with sea salt and freshly ground black pepper. Increase the heat slightly and cook for a few minutes longer to blend flavors.

3 Now add the remaining corn and the stock and bring to a boil. Reduce the heat slightly and simmer for 20 minutes. Taste and season again with salt and pepper if needed. Stir in the parsley just before serving.

Chicken salad with carrot and apple relish

  PREP 15 MINS

SERVES 3–4

For the carrot and apple relish
2 carrots
2 sweet red eating apples
2 preserved lemons, finely chopped
small handful of golden raisins
sea salt and freshly ground
    black pepper

2 handfuls of fresh spinach
    leaves, rinsed
12oz (350g) leftover roast
    chicken, sliced
½ cup pine nuts, toasted
    (see Cook's Notes)
1 tbsp olive oil
juice of ½ lemon

1 To make the carrot and apple relish, coarsely grate the carrots into a bowl. Quarter and core the apples and grate into the bowl with the carrot. Add the preserved lemons and raisins and mix together. Season with salt and pepper.

2 Lay the spinach leaves in a large shallow salad bowl and top with the chicken and pine nuts. When ready to serve, drizzle with the olive oil and lemon juice and sprinkle with a pinch of salt. Serve with the carrot and apple relish.

COOK'S NOTES

Toast the pine nuts in a small dry frying pan: heat gently for a couple of minutes, tossing frequently, until they turn golden, but watch carefully because they can quickly burn.

ROAST LEG OF LAMB

PREP 15 MINS **COOK 1¾ HRS**

SERVES 4, PLUS LEFTOVERS

4½lb (2kg) bone-in leg of lamb, trimmed

4 garlic cloves, peeled but left whole

handful of fresh rosemary sprigs, plus extra for garnish

sea salt and freshly ground black pepper

2 cups hot vegetable stock

1 tsp red currant jelly

1 Preheat the oven to 400°F (200°C). Pierce the lamb evenly all over with a sharp knife, then stuff the garlic cloves and small sprigs of rosemary into the slits. Season the lamb all over with salt and pepper.

2 Place the lamb in a flameproof roasting pan and roast in the oven for about 15 minutes just to lightly brown the outside. Reduce the oven temperature to 350°F (180°C) and continue to roast for another 1 hour for rare, basting it with its juices halfway through the cooking time; allow 1½ hours for well done. Transfer the lamb to a large plate, cover loosely with foil, and leave to rest in a warm place for 15 minutes while you make the gravy.

3 To make the gravy, tilt the roasting pan and skim off any fat. Place the pan over high heat, add the stock and jelly, and bring to a boil, scraping up any bits from the bottom of the pan with a wooden spoon. Reduce the heat slightly and simmer, stirring all the time, for 5–8 minutes. Taste and season if needed.

4 To serve, garnish with fresh rosemary and carve at the table. Serve with creamy mashed potatoes, fresh mint sauce, and seasonal vegetables.

Flat breads topped with lamb and hummus

 PREP 10 MINS   COOK 20 MINS

SERVES 2

1 tbsp olive oil, plus extra
 for drizzling
1 onion, finely chopped
3 garlic cloves, finely chopped
9oz (250g) leftover shredded
 roast lamb
pinch of ground allspice
pinch of ground cinnamon
sea salt and freshly ground
 black pepper
2 flat breads or plain naan
handful of pine nuts, toasted
handful of fresh mint leaves,
 coarsely chopped
hummus, to serve

1 Preheat the oven to 400°F (200°C).
Heat the 1 tablespoon olive oil in a
frying pan over low heat. Add the
onion and cook gently for about
5 minutes until soft.

2 Stir in the garlic and cook for a
few more seconds. Now stir in the
lamb. Sprinkle with the allspice and
cinnamon and cook for a few minutes,
stirring occasionally. Season with salt
and pepper.

3 Lay the flat breads on a baking
sheet and drizzle with a little olive oil.
Spoon on the lamb mixture and bake
for about 10 minutes until the lamb is
heated through. Scatter the pine nuts
and mint leaves over each and top
with a generous dollop of hummus.
Serve immediately.

COOK'S NOTES

*If you prefer the lamb ground,
process in a blender or food
processor until finely chopped.*

Hot and fiery lamb masala

 PREP 15 MINS   COOK 40 MINS

SERVES 4

2 tbsp ghee or 1 tbsp sunflower oil
1 onion, finely chopped
1 tsp ground cumin
1 tsp ground coriander
2 bay leaves
2 tsp whole black peppercorns,
 lightly crushed
3 tsp mild paprika
1–2 tsp hot chili powder
3 garlic cloves, finely chopped
2in (5cm) piece of fresh ginger,
 thinly sliced
1 x 26–28oz (750g) jar or can of
 crushed tomatoes or tomato purée
3 tbsp heavy whipping cream
½ cup cashews, ground
10oz (300g) leftover roast lamb,
 coarsely shredded or sliced
sea salt and freshly ground
 black pepper

1 Heat the ghee in a large deep
frying pan over low heat. Add the
onion and cook gently for about
5 minutes until soft. Now add the

cumin, coriander, bay leaves,
peppercorns, paprika, and chili
powder, stirring, and cook for a couple
of minutes longer until fragrant.

2 Add the garlic and ginger and cook
for a few more seconds, stirring, then
pour in the tomatoes, cream, and nuts.
Bring to a boil, reduce the heat
slightly, and add the lamb. Simmer
gently for 25–30 minutes. Taste and
season with salt and pepper. Serve
hot with basmati rice and a crisp
green salad on the side.

 VARIATION

Stir in some fresh spinach or
1 cup of frozen peas, thawed,
for the last 5–10 minutes
of cooking.

COOK'S NOTES

*Ghee is clarified butter that
is used in Indian cooking. You
will find it in speciality Asian
markets—it will give your masala
a touch of authenticity.*

Lamb, tomato, and bean casserole

 PREP 15 MINS COOK 25 MINS

SERVES 4

1 tbsp olive oil

1 onion, finely chopped

8 tomatoes, peeled and quartered

2 cups hot vegetable stock

sea salt and freshly ground
  black pepper

12oz (350g) leftover roast lamb, cut
  into bite-sized pieces

1 x 14oz (400g) can flageolet beans,
  drained and rinsed

handful of flat-leaf parsley,
  finely chopped

handful of fresh thyme sprigs,
  leaves picked

1 Heat the oil in a Dutch oven or large deep frying pan over low heat. Add the onion and cook gently for about 5 minutes until soft.

2 Add the tomatoes and pour in the stock. Season well with salt and pepper. Bring to a boil, then reduce the heat slightly. Stir in the lamb and beans and simmer gently for about 20 minutes, adding a little hot water if the casserole appears dry.

3 Just before serving, stir in the parsley and thyme and serve hot with fresh crusty bread or a crisp green salad.

Lamb and potato pie

PREP 20 MINS COOK 50 MINS

Special equipment • 8in (20cm) round pie pan

SERVES 4

1lb (450g) all-purpose waxy potatoes,
  peeled and quartered

1 tbsp olive oil

1 onion, finely chopped

handful of fresh rosemary sprigs,
  leaves picked and chopped

12oz (350g) leftover roast lamb,
  sliced or coarsely shredded

sea salt and freshly ground
  black pepper

1 tbsp all-purpose flour

1¼ cups hot vegetable stock

2–3 tsp mint sauce (see p423)

1 sheet prepared dough for an 8–9in
  (20–23cm) pie

1 egg, lightly beaten, for egg wash

1 Preheat the oven to 400°F (200°C). Boil the potatoes for about 15 minutes until just tender; drain and set aside. Heat the olive oil in a large saucepan over low heat. Add the onion and cook gently for about 5 minutes until soft.

Stir in the rosemary and add the lamb. Season well with salt and pepper.

2 Stir in the flour until blended, then pour in the stock. Keep stirring for about 10 minutes over medium heat until the liquid begins to thicken, then add the reserved potatoes and stir in the mint sauce. Simmer for another 10 minutes. Allow to cool slightly.

3 Divide the pastry into 2 pieces, one a little larger than the other. Roll out the larger piece into a large circle on a floured work surface. Use to line the pan, letting the pastry hang over the edges. Roll out the other piece to make a pastry lid for the top of the pie.

4 Spoon the lamb mixture into the pastry shell, then sit the pastry lid on top. Moisten the edges of the pastry with water and pinch together to seal. Trim away the excess. Brush evenly with a little egg wash and bake in the oven for 40–50 minutes until the pastry is cooked through and golden. Leave to cool in the pan for at least 15 minutes before cutting into wedges to serve.

ROAST PORK

PREP 20 MINS · COOK 1¾ HRS

SERVES 6, PLUS LEFTOVERS

4½lb (2kg) boneless pork loin, skin or exterior fat scored

4 garlic cloves, finely chopped

handful of black olives, pitted and finely chopped

pinch of dried oregano

sea salt and freshly ground black pepper

olive oil

1 Preheat the oven to 425°F (220°C). Untie the roast, if needed, and lay it fat-side down on a work surface. Mix together the garlic, olives, and oregano in a bowl, and season with salt and pepper. Rub the garlic and olive mixture in a line down the middle of the pork, then roll the pork up tightly and secure with kitchen twine. Place it in a large flameproof roasting pan. Rub all over with olive oil, then rub in sea salt to season well.

2 Roast the pork for about 20 minutes until the outside is golden and crispy. Reduce the oven temperature to 375°F (190°C), and continue to roast for another 1 hour to 1 hour 20 minutes, or until the pork is cooked through. Transfer to a large plate and leave to rest in a warm place for about 15 minutes before slicing.

3 Cut the pork into slices and serve with homemade gravy, applesauce, crispy roast potatoes, and seasonal vegetables on the side.

COOK'S NOTES

The butcher will score the skin for you if you ask. For easy carving, remove the crispy crackling in one piece, then slice the meat. Cut up the crackling to serve.

231

EVERYDAY

Roast pork in pita bread

 PREP 10 MINS **COOK 30 MINS**

SERVES 2

1 tbsp olive oil
1 tbsp butter
1 onion, finely chopped
½ cup fresh bread crumbs, made from
    about 2 slices of firm-textured
    white bread
4 fresh sage leaves, finely chopped
1 large egg, lightly beaten
sea salt and freshly ground
    black pepper
4 pita breads
8oz (225g) leftover roast pork, sliced
applesauce, store-bought
    or homemade

1 Preheat the oven to 400°F (200°C). Heat the olive oil and butter in a frying pan over low heat. Add the onion and cook gently for about 5 minutes until soft. Stir in the bread crumbs and sage and cook for a few minutes. Remove from the heat and allow to cool.

2 Stir the beaten egg into the bread crumb mixture and season well with salt and pepper. Spoon into a buttered dish and bake for about 20 minutes.

3 Warm the pita breads, then slice open the pocket and stuff with the pork, a spoonful of bread stuffing, and some applesauce. Serve immediately with a crisp salad.

Pork and yellow split pea soup

 PREP 15 MINS **COOK 45 MINS**

SERVES 4

1 tbsp olive oil
1 tbsp butter
1 onion, finely chopped
3 garlic cloves, finely chopped
sea salt and freshly ground
    black pepper
1 cup dried yellow split peas,
    picked over and rinsed
6 cups hot vegetable or
    chicken stock
12oz (350g) leftover roast pork, cut
    into bite-sized cubes
handful of curly parsley,
    finely chopped

1 Heat the olive oil and butter in a medium-sized soup pot over low heat. Add the onion and cook gently for about 5 minutes until soft. Stir in the garlic and cook for a few seconds longer until fragrant. Season with salt and pepper.

2 Stir in the split peas and pour in the stock. Bring to a boil and boil rapidly for about 10 minutes. Reduce the heat slightly, stir in the pork, and simmer gently for another 40 minutes, adding a little hot water if the soup gets too thick. Season well and stir in the parsley just before serving.

VARIATION
 Add some cubed pancetta or a few slices of chopped bacon, if you wish. Add when the onions have softened and cook until golden.

COOK'S NOTES
The split peas will count as one of your five-a-day portions. Make sure that you rinse the peas well because they can sometimes be a little gritty.

Pork and spring greens

PREP 10 MINS — COOK 15 MINS

Special equipment • wok

SERVES 4

1 tbsp olive oil
12oz (350g) leftover roast pork, coarsely shredded
4 garlic cloves, thinly sliced
2 heads of collard greens or other leafy greens, shredded
2 tsp onion seeds (optional)
sea salt and freshly ground black pepper

1 Heat the oil in a wok over medium-high heat. When the oil is hot, add the pork. Cook for about 5 minutes, stirring and tossing it in the pan.

2 Add the garlic and the greens and continue to stir-fry over medium-high heat for 1 minute, or until the greens have just wilted. Stir in the onion seeds, then season well with sea salt and ground pepper. Serve immediately with roast new potatoes as a side dish.

VARIATION

Add a splash of soy sauce at the end of cooking. Since it's salty, reduce the seasoning in step 2, if necessary.

COOK'S NOTES

Choose your greens with the seasons—use Savoy cabbage, Brussels sprouts, or kale in the winter, and the lighter delicate greens, such as spinach and chard, in the spring and summer.

Sweet and sour pork

PREP 10 MINS — COOK 30 MINS

Special equipment • wok

SERVES 4

For the sweet and sour sauce
2 tbsp tomato purée
2 tbsp soy sauce
2 tbsp pineapple juice
2 tbsp white wine vinegar
1 tbsp granulated sugar
sea salt and freshly ground black pepper
1 tbsp cornstarch
1¼ cups hot vegetable stock

1 tbsp olive oil
1 onion, peeled and cut into eighths
12oz (350g) leftover roast pork, coarsely shredded
7oz (200g) snow peas, cut in half crosswise diagonally

1 First, make the sweet and sour sauce. In a bowl, mix together the tomato purée, soy sauce, pineapple juice, vinegar, and sugar. Season with salt and pepper.

2 Heat the oil in a wok over medium heat. Add the onion and stir-fry for a few minutes until soft, moving it around the pan often so that it doesn't brown. Pour in the sauce and keep stirring.

3 Mix the cornstarch into a paste with 1 tablespoon water and add to the sauce along with the stock. Bring to a boil, stirring constantly.

4 Now add the pork, reduce the heat to low, and cook for about 15 minutes until the sauce begins to thicken. Add the snow peas for the last 5 minutes of cooking. Taste and season if needed. Serve immediately with rice or noodles.

BAKED SALMON

PREP 15 MINS **COOK 1¼ HRS**

SERVES 4, PLUS LEFTOVERS

7–8lb (3.2–3.6kg) fresh whole salmon, gutted, scaled, and cleaned

8 tablespoons cold butter, cut into pieces

sea salt and freshly ground black pepper

handful of flat-leaf parsley sprigs, plus extra, for garnish

lemon wedges, for serving

1 Preheat the oven to 350°F (180°C). Lay a large piece of heavy-duty foil on a baking sheet. (You will need enough foil to enclose the fish.) Place the salmon in the middle of the foil and scatter the butter all over the top. Season well with salt and pepper, then scatter the parsley sprigs over the fish, tucking a few inside the cavity.

2 Loosely pull together the edges of the foil to enclose the salmon and crimp together to seal. Bake for about 1 hour 10 minutes, calculating the cooking time at 10 minutes per pound (450g), or just until it is opaque throughout.

3 Unwrap the foil, remove any straggly bits of parsley, and carefully transfer the salmon to a warm serving plate and garnish with fresh parsley or watercress. Pass the lemon wedges at the table for squeezing. Serve with new potatoes and salad or blanched or grilled asparagus.

VARIATION

Salmon is delicious with flavors such as horseradish or beet, as they cut wonderfully through the richness. Serve with a spoonful of each on the side, and a watercress salad.

COOK'S NOTES

It's vital that the fish is 100% fresh when you buy it—it should never smell "fishy.'" Use wild salmon for a special treat.

EVERYDAY

Baked salmon with salsa verde and cucumber

PREP 15 MINS

SERVES 4

For the salsa verde
handful of fresh basil leaves
handful of fresh mint leaves
handful of fresh flat-leaf parsley leaves
2 tbsp white wine vinegar
2 tsp capers, rinsed, gently squeezed
   dry, and finely chopped
2 garlic cloves, finely chopped
8 anchovies in oil, drained and
   finely chopped
2 tsp coarse-grain mustard
sea salt and freshly ground
   black pepper
6 tbsp extra virgin olive oil

1 cucumber
12oz (350g) leftover baked salmon,
   sliced or flaked into chunks

1 To make the salsa verde, finely chop all the herbs and put in a bowl. Drizzle in the vinegar and stir through. Add the capers, garlic, and anchovies, and stir again. Now add the mustard and season well with salt and pepper.

Slowly stir in the olive oil. Taste and adjust the seasoning if needed, adding a little more vinegar or oil as required. Transfer to a serving bowl.

2 Peel the cucumber, slice in half lengthwise, and scoop out the seeds with a teaspoon. Dice the flesh and put in a serving bowl.

3 To serve, arrange the salmon on a platter or 4 serving plates. Spoon a little salsa verde and cucumber onto the side and serve with the bowls of salsa verde and cucumber at the table for people to help themselves.

VARIATION

Use raspberry vinegar instead of white wine vinegar–it works wonderfully with salmon.

Salmon and shrimp fish pie

PREP 15 MINS **COOK 35 MINS**

Special equipment • 1 quart (1.1 liter) ovenproof dish

SERVES 2

1½lb (700g) floury potatoes, such as
   russet, peeled and quartered
1¼ cups milk, plus 2 tbsp
sea salt and freshly ground
   black pepper
12oz (350g) leftover salmon,
   flaked into chunks
7oz (200g) peeled and deveined
   cooked shrimp
1 tbsp butter, plus extra for topping
1 tbsp all-purpose flour
1 tbsp coarse-grain mustard

1 Preheat the oven to 400°F (200°C). Cook the potatoes in a pan of boiling water for 15 minutes until tender, drain, then mash well. Add the 2 tbsp milk, season with salt and pepper, and mash again until smooth. Set aside.

2 Evenly arrange the salmon and shrimp in the baking dish, season with salt and pepper, and set aside.

3 Gently melt the butter in a saucepan over low heat. Remove from the heat and stir in the flour with a wooden spoon. Add a little milk from the 1¼ cup and beat with the spoon until smooth. Return the pan to the heat and continue adding the milk, a little at a time, stirring all the time until the sauce has thickened. Whisk well with a balloon whisk to ensure that there are no lumps, then stir in the mustard to blend.

4 Pour the sauce over the fish and shrimp and toss to mix. Cover with the mashed potatoes and dot with extra butter. Bake for 15–20 minutes or until the filling is heated through and the topping is crisp and golden.

Cheat...

Use 1 cup of pre-made white or cheese sauce and stir the mustard into it.

Salmon and roasted tomato pasta

PREP 15 MINS COOK 20 MINS

SERVES 4
12 cherry tomatoes
1 tbsp olive oil
12oz (350g) dried pasta,
    such as penne
12oz (350g) leftover baked salmon,
    flaked into chunks
sea salt and freshly ground
    black pepper
hot chili oil

1 Preheat the oven to 200°C (400°F). Put the tomatoes in a roasting pan and drizzle with the olive oil. Roast in the oven for 15–20 minutes until the tomatoes are beginning to char slightly and the skins are bursting.

2 Meanwhile, cook the pasta as the package directs, until it is tender yet still firm to the bite. Drain, reserving a small amount of the cooking water. Return the pasta to the pot and toss together with the reserved cooking water. Add the salmon and roasted tomatoes, toss gently to mix, and season with salt and pepper. Drizzle with a little chili oil and serve immediately.

VARIATION
Add some arugula or fresh basil leaves when you combine the salmon and tomatoes.

Salmon with new potatoes, flageolet beans, and parsley sauce

PREP 15 MINS COOK 30 MINS

SERVES 4
1½lb (700g) new potatoes,
    halved if large
1 tbsp butter
1 tbsp all-purpose flour
1¼ cups whole milk
⅔ cup heavy whipping cream
sea salt and freshly ground
    black pepper
handful of curly parsley,
    very finely chopped
1 x 14oz (400g) can flageolet beans,
    drained and rinsed
handful of fresh dill, finely chopped
12oz (350g) leftover baked salmon,
    sliced or flaked into chunks

1 Cook the potatoes in a pot of boiling water for 15–20 minutes until tender. Drain and set aside to keep warm.

2 Meanwhile, melt a tablespoon of butter in a saucepan over low heat. Remove from the heat and stir in the flour. Add a little of the milk and beat with a wooden spoon until smooth. Return to the heat and slowly add the milk, and then the cream, a little at a time, stirring constantly. Simmer for 5–8 minutes, then use a balloon whisk to get rid of any lumps. Remove from the heat, season well with salt and pepper, and stir in the parsley.

3 Put the beans in a saucepan and gently heat through. Season if you like, and stir in the dill. Serve the salmon on a platter or individual plates with the flageolet beans and new potatoes on the side, and the parsley sauce spooned over the salmon and beans.

ROAST RIB OF BEEF

 PREP 10 MINS **COOK 1¼ HRS**

SERVES 4, PLUS LEFTOVERS

5lb (2.3kg) beef rib roast, bone in (2 ribs)

olive oil

sea salt and freshly ground black pepper

1–2 tbsp coarse-grain mustard

1 Preheat the oven to 400°F (200°C). Rub the beef all over with olive oil and season with sea salt and ground black pepper.

2 Place the beef bones-side-down in a roasting pan and rub the mustard over the fatty area. Roast for about 15 minutes until it begins to brown, then reduce the oven temperature to 350°F (180°C). Roast for 1 hour or until the meat reaches the desired doneness (see Cook's Notes).

3 Remove the beef from the oven and leave to rest, loosely covered, in a warm place for about 20 minutes. Slice and serve with, roasted potatoes, horseradish sauce, and seasonal vegetables or a salad of your choice. Remember to save your beef bones for making stock.

 VARIATION

If cooking beef off the bone, reduce the cooking time by a couple of minutes per 1lb (450g).

COOK'S NOTES

Always preheat the oven so that it is hot and at the correct temperature before the meat goes in. For beef on the bone: for rare, cook for 10–12 minutes per pound (450g) plus 12 minutes; for medium, cook for 12–15 minutes per pound (450g) plus 12 minutes; for well-done, cook for 18–20 minutes per pound (450g) plus 18 minutes.

EVERYDAY

Beef and Stilton pie

 PREP 20 MINS  **COOK 40 MINS**

Special equipment • 1 quart (1.1 liter) pie dish

SERVES 2

1 tbsp olive oil
1 tbsp butter
2 onions, coarsely chopped
12oz (350g) leftover roast beef, sliced
⅔ cup beef stock
sea salt and freshly ground
   black pepper
4½oz (125g) blue cheese, such as
   Stilton or Gorgonzola
half of a 17.3oz (425g) box frozen
   puff pastry sheets (1 sheet),
   thawed as package directs
1 egg, lightly beaten, for egg wash

1 Preheat the oven 400°F (200°C). Heat the oil and butter in a saucepan over low heat. Add the onions and cook very gently for 5-8 minutes, or until soft.

2 Add the beef and pour in the stock. Bring to a boil, reduce the heat slightly, and simmer for about 10 minutes. Season with salt and pepper. Cool slightly, then spoon the mixture into a 1 quart (1.1 liter) pie dish and crumble the cheese over the top.

3 On a floured work surface, roll out the pastry until it is a little larger than the pie dish. Cut out a strip of pastry about 1in (2.5cm) from the edge to make a collar. Wet the edge of the pie dish with a little water; fit the pastry strip all the way around and press down firmly. Brush the collar with a little egg wash and top with the pastry lid. Trim away the excess. Using your finger and thumb, pinch together the edges to seal. Brush all over with the egg wash, make a slit in the top, and bake for 30-40 minutes until golden and puffed. Serve hot.

Thai-style beef salad

 PREP 15 MINS

SERVES 4

12oz (350g) leftover
   roast beef, sliced
2 carrots, cut into julienne strips
½ onion, cut into thin strips
4½oz (125g) bamboo shoots
handful of fresh mint leaves
handful of fresh basil leaves
handful of fresh cilantro, leaves only,
   plus extra for garnish
sea salt and freshly ground
   black pepper
juice of 1 lime
2-3 tsp granulated sugar
1 fresh Thai or other small red
   hot chile pepper, seeded and
   finely chopped
1-2 tbsp Asian fish sauce, such as
   nam pla

1 Combine the beef, carrots, onion, bamboo shoots, mint, basil, and cilantro in a large bowl, and toss gently to mix. Season with sea salt and black pepper.

2 To make the dressing, in a small bowl, mix together the lime juice, sugar, chile, and fish sauce. Taste and adjust seasoning if needed. Pour the dressing over the salad, then garnish with extra cilantro. Serve with roasted baby new potatoes on the side, if desired.

> **COOK'S NOTES**
>
> *Raw onion can be strong—if you prefer a milder flavor, soak the strips of onion in cold water for 10 minutes before using, or use finely sliced scallions instead.*

Beef stroganoff

  PREP 15 MINS **COOK 30 MINS**

Soaking • 30 minutes

SERVES 4

scant 1oz (25g) dried porcini
   mushrooms
1 tbsp olive oil
1 onion, finely chopped
sea salt and freshly ground
   black pepper
12oz (350g) leftover roast beef,
   sliced into strips
⅔–1¼ cups hot vegetable or beef
   stock, as needed
1¼ cups heavy whipping cream
pinch of crushed red pepper flakes

1 Soak the porcini mushrooms in
1¼ cups boiling water for 30 minutes.

2 Heat the olive oil in a large frying
pan over low heat. Add the onion and
sweat gently for 5 minutes until soft.
Season with salt and pepper.

3 Drain the mushrooms (reserve
the liquid) and add to the onion,
along with the beef. Pour the
mushroom soaking liquid through
a fine nylon sieve and add to the
pan with about half of the stock.
Bring to a boil, then reduce the heat
to a simmer. Add the cream and red
pepper flakes and simmer gently for
about 20 minutes, adding more of
the stock as needed.

4 Taste and adjust the seasoning
as needed, and serve hot with some
fluffy white rice or noodles.

Beef with beets and spinach

PREP 15 MINS

SERVES 4

12oz (350g) leftover roast beef, sliced
10oz (300g) fresh spinach leaves
1lb (450g) cooked whole beets,
   quartered
3 tbsp extra virgin olive oil
1 tbsp balsamic vinegar
juice of ½ clementine or tangerine
sea salt and freshly ground
   black pepper
handful of fresh thyme, leaves picked

1 In a large bowl, gently toss
together the beef, spinach, and beets.
In a small bowl, whisk together the
extra virgin olive oil, balsamic vinegar,
and citrus juice. Season well with salt
and pepper.

2 When ready to serve, drizzle
the salad with the dressing and
scatter the thyme leaves over the
top. Serve at once.

 VARIATION

Use freshly squeezed
orange juice if you can't find
clementines or tangerines.

Cheat...

For speed, drizzle with
balsamic vinegar and
leave out the other
dressing ingredients.

ROAST TURKEY

PREP 15 MINS COOK 3¼ HRS

SERVES 6, PLUS LEFTOVERS

16 tbsp butter, at room temperature

3 onions (1 finely chopped, 2 peeled and quartered)

4¼oz (125g) fresh bread crumbs

handful of flat-leaf parsley, finely chopped

sea salt and freshly ground black pepper

9lb (4kg) whole turkey

1 First, make the stuffing. Melt half of the butter in a medium frying pan over low heat, add the chopped onion, and cook for about 5 minutes until soft. Remove from the heat and stir in the bread crumbs and parsley. Season well with salt and pepper. Set aside to cool.

2 Preheat the oven to 400°F (200°C). Place the turkey in a roasting pan and season inside and out. Smear with the remaining butter. Stuff the quartered onions inside the cavity and the stuffing into the neck end. Roast for about 20 minutes until the skin begins to turn golden, then reduce the oven temperature to 375°F (190°C).

3 Loosely cover the turkey with foil and roast for 20 minutes per pound. Baste every hour with the juices from the pan and check to see if the turkey is cooked about 20 minutes before the end of the cooking time. Pierce a meaty part of the bird with a skewer. If the juices run clear, it is done; if not, cook for a little longer. Remove the foil for the last 10–15 minutes.

4 Remove the turkey from the pan and transfer to a warmed platter. Cover loosely with foil and let rest in a warm place for 15 minutes. Serve slices of turkey with gravy, roasted potatoes, and cranberry sauce.

Turkey, almond, and cranberry pilaf

 PREP 15 MINS **COOK** 40 MINS

SERVES 4
1 tbsp olive oil
1 onion, finely chopped
3 garlic cloves, finely chopped
1¼ cups basmati rice
3 cups hot vegetable or
    chicken stock
12oz (350g) leftover roast turkey,
    sliced or shredded, skin removed
sea salt and freshly ground
    black pepper
1 cup sliced almonds, toasted
1½ cups dried cranberries
handful of fresh thyme sprigs,
    leaves picked

1 Heat the oil in a flameproof casserole over low heat. Add the onion and cook gently for about 5 minutes until soft. Add the garlic and cook, stirring, for a few seconds. Stir in the rice to coat well.

2 Pour in the stock and bring to a boil. Reduce the heat slightly and stir in the turkey. Simmer gently, covered, adding more hot stock or water, if needed, for 20–25 minutes or until the stock has been absorbed and the rice is tender. Season with salt and pepper.

3 Just before serving, add in the cranberries, almonds, and thyme and gently stir through. Serve hot, with a crisp salad and fresh crusty bread on the side.

Turkey and noodles

PREP 15 MINS **COOK** 15 MINS

Special equipment • wok

SERVES 4
1 tbsp sunflower oil
1lb (450g) wok-ready medium
    rice noodles
1 bunch scallions, finely chopped
2 garlic cloves, finely chopped
12oz (350g) leftover roast turkey,
    sliced or coarsely shredded,
    skin removed
2 tbsp Asian oyster sauce
2 tbsp Asian fish sauce, such as
    nam pla
1 fresh hot chile pepper, seeded
    and finely chopped
1 tsp granulated sugar
7oz (200g) bean sprouts
sea salt and freshly ground
    black pepper

1 Heat the oil in a wok over medium-high heat. Add the noodles and stir-fry for a couple of minutes. Toss in the scallions. Now add the garlic and stir-fry for a few seconds more. Remove the mixture from the wok and set aside.

2 Add the turkey to the wok and stir-fry over medium heat for a minute or so, then add the oyster sauce, fish sauce, chile, and sugar. Cook, stirring and tossing, for about 1–2 minutes just to heat through.

3 Return the noodle mixture to the wok and stir in the bean sprouts, tossing to coat with the sauce. Taste and season well with salt and pepper. Serve immediately.

Warm turkey and chickpea salad

  PREP 15 MINS COOK 10 MINS

SERVES 4

1 x 14oz (400g) can chickpeas,
    drained and rinsed
1 tbsp olive oil
pinch of mild paprika
juice of 1 lemon
sea salt and freshly ground
    black pepper
12oz (350g) leftover roast turkey,
    sliced or coarsely shredded,
    skin removed
handful of fresh dill, finely chopped

1 Combine the chickpeas and olive oil in a saucepan. Add the paprika and lemon juice and season well with salt and black pepper. Simmer very gently over low heat for about 5–8 minutes, or until the chickpeas have softened slightly and are warmed through.

2 To serve, toss the chickpeas with the leftover turkey, taste, and season again if needed. Scatter the fresh dill over the top and serve warm with a fresh green salad or some wilted spinach.

VARIATION

You could use canned white beans instead of chickpeas: try cannellini or butter beans.

Spiced turkey and greens stir-fry

 PREP 10 MINS COOK 25 MINS

Special equipment • food processor • wok

SERVES 4

12oz (350g) leftover roast turkey,
    coarsely chopped, skin removed
2 heads of Asian greens
    such as bok choy, trimmed
    and coarsely chopped
1 tbsp sunflower oil
1 onion, finely chopped
2in (5cm) piece of fresh ginger, thinly
    sliced and then cut into thin strips
3 garlic cloves, finely chopped
2 fresh green chile peppers, seeded
    and finely chopped
1 tbsp soy sauce
1 tbsp mirin (Japanese rice wine)
handful of fresh basil leaves, torn
sea salt and freshly ground
    black pepper

1 Put the turkey in a food processor and process, pulsing the machine on and off, until very finely chopped; be careful not to turn it into a paste. Cook the greens in a pot of boiling salted water for 3– 5 minutes or until just wilted. Drain, refresh with cold water, and drain again. Set aside.

2 Heat the oil in a wok or large frying pan over low heat. Add the onion and cook gently for about 5 minutes until soft. Add the ginger, garlic, and chiles, and cook for another 5 minutes, stirring and tossing constantly.

3 Stir in the turkey. Add the soy sauce and mirin and stir-fry for 5–8 minutes until the turkey is warmed through. Stir in the reserved greens and the basil and season with salt and pepper. Serve immediately.

BATCH AND FREEZE

Some to eat now, and some for the freezer.

BATCH AND FREEZE

Make-ahead dishes for the freezer save you time and effort, meaning you can shop less, cook less, and have meals ready for the oven or microwave—a lifesaver for the busy cook. Batch cooking can simply mean doubling up on your cooking one night and freezing half, or dedicating a day to cooking several quantities for the freezer.

Psst...

Slow defrosting overnight in the refrigerator is not only the safest way to defrost, it is also the best way to retain the food's original flavor and texture. Once food is thawed, warm it through as soon as possible.

Foods you can freeze and what to freeze them in.

EVERYDAY

FOOD		PACKAGING	STORAGE LIFE	DEFROST AND REHEAT
	SOUPS AND STOCKS These are ideal for freezing. Once cooked, leave to cool completely, then pack into portions as needed. Don't freeze in over-large portions, as defrosting will take too long.	Pack in sealable freezer bags. The liquid will expand a little, so leave room for this, or spoon stock into ice cube trays or rigid sealable plastic containers and freeze. Once frozen, remove from the tray, transfer to a freezer bag, seal, and label.	Soups for up to **3 months** Stocks for up to **6 months**	Thaw overnight in the refrigerator, then reheat in a pan until piping hot, or heat in the microwave on high for a few minutes.
	SAUCES AND GRAVIES These are great for freezing and take up little space. If sauces call for the addition of egg yolk or cream, omit and add later. Cool completely before freezing.	Freeze in sealable freezer bags or ice cube trays. If using ice cube trays, once frozen, remove from the tray, transfer to a freezer bag, and seal. For thicker sauces, flatten in the bag so storage space is minimal. Leave air space for expansion. Label.	Up to **3 months**	Thaw overnight in the refrigerator, then reheat in a pan until piping hot, or heat in the microwave on high for a few minutes.
	STEWS AND CASSEROLES These freeze well and are ideal for batch cooking. Foods with a very high fat content will go rancid after a couple of months in the freezer, so choose lean cuts of meat. When doubling up recipes, be careful with the seasoning. As a rule, you will only need to add 1½ times the seasoning. Cool completely before freezing.	Freeze in sealable freezer bags or foil containers, or ladle into rigid sealable plastic containers. Make sure meat is well covered with liquid, otherwise it will dry out. Label.	Up to **3 months**	Thaw overnight in the refrigerator, then reheat in a pan until piping hot, or heat in the microwave on high for a few minutes. Make sure that the meat is really hot and do not reheat more than once.
	PIES AND PASTRIES Baking is the ideal time to batch cook. You can freeze pastry cooked or uncooked. Cool completely before freezing.	**Uncooked** Freeze blocks of pastry layered with wax paper, then wrapped in plastic wrap. Label. **Cooked** Freeze pastry shells and pies wrapped in a double layer of plastic wrap. Label.	**Uncooked** pies and pastry for up to **3 months** **Cooked** pies and pastry cases for up to **6 months**	**Uncooked** tart shells and pastries can be cooked from frozen in the oven at 400°F (200°C) for 15 minutes. **Cooked** pies and pastry shells should thaw overnight in the refrigerator, then reheat in the oven at 350°F (180°C), for about 30 minutes, or until piping hot.

Portion sizes

Planning If you plan to make more than double or triple batches at a time, think ahead a little, as soups and stews only freeze for up to 3 months, and you don't want too much of one dish.

Amounts When batch-cooking soups, allow about 1 cup per person. Don't freeze portion sizes any larger than 2 cup portions.

Sizes It's advisable to freeze sauces in different portion sizes to suit your requirements, and don't forget to freeze plenty of portions-for-one, for when you are home alone and don't want to cook.

foods that don't freeze well

Cream cheese or **cottage cheese** will separate or become watery, as will **cream**, unless it has been lightly whipped first. **Mayonnaise** and **hollandaise** sauce will also separate when they are defrosted. **Fatty foods** become fattier, and eventually turn rancid, and salad ingredients such as **cucumber**, **lettuce**, **celery**, and **tomatoes** turn to water once defrosted. If you are unsure whether something will freeze, test a small amount first to avoid any waste.

5 tips for freezing
Follow these guidelines and there will be no loss of quality, texture, taste, color, or nutrients.

If freezing large amounts of different foods, use different colored bags or boxes, use labels, and adopt a color coding system for yourself so you know what is what.

The coldest part of the freezer is the bottom, so foods will freeze quicker if stored here. Keep this in mind if you want to save on solid containers, and are using an ice cube tray or cookware to freeze food before re-packing into foil, double-wrapped plastic wrap, or bags.

When putting containers of food in the freezer, leave plenty of room around them so they can freeze quicker. Once frozen, they can be removed from the container and packed tightly in foil, plastic wrap, or resealable freezer bags.

Always be aware that the fresher the food is when it goes in the freezer, the better it will be when it comes out.

Remember to rotate things in the freezer so everything gets used in time. It's first in, first out!

Frozen pre-prepared vegetables stay fresh in space-saving freezer-proof plastic bags.

Freezer packaging
The right packaging will protect the food so it keeps for longer.

PLASTIC CONTAINERS
Rigid plastic containers can be used to freeze all foods. Use ones that are durable so they don't become brittle and crack at low temperatures. They are available in all shapes and sizes and are easy to label and reuse.

FOIL
Foil can be used to create your own dish, especially if you have a limited collection of ovenware. Double-line an ovenproof dish with foil, then fill with the food for cooking. Cook as per the recipe, leave to cool completely, then put in the freezer. Once frozen, lift out the foil dish and either wrap well in plastic wrap, or cover with a large freezer bag, seal, and return to the freezer. You could also fill the foil-lined dish and freeze the uncooked dish.

ICE CUBE TRAYS
Ideal for freezing small amounts of sauce or stock. Carefully fill with the liquid and freeze when completely cool. Once frozen, transfer the cubes to plastic freezer bags or plastic containers and seal (otherwise the food will get freezer burn). Use this method to freeze leftover red wine, which you can then add to gravies or sauces.

BAGS FOR LIQUID
Line a plastic container with a freezer-proof bag, then fill with stock, soup, or sauce and seal well, leaving some room for the contents to expand. Freeze until solid, then remove the container and stack the solid bag (labeled).

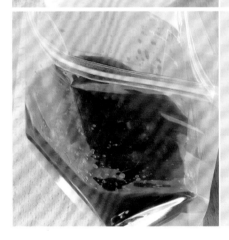

PLASTIC FREEZER BAGS
Most foods can be stored in plastic freezer bags. They need to be strong, leakproof, and resistant to moisture. Bags with a built-in seals are ideal for all sauces and stews and blanched vegetables.

FOIL DISHES
A good choice if freezing foods for a few months. Use heavy-duty aluminum ones. You can cook, freeze, and reheat them in the oven. The foil trays can be recycled, but not the lids, if they are cardboard.

Labeling
Always label and date your food, using a permanent pen, so it won't rub off. Write directly onto the packaging or use labels designed for the freezer (they won't get damp and peel away). If leaving it for other people to reheat, write instructions on the bag or label.

Contents: *Chicken Casserole*

Weight/Portions: *1lb (for 4)*

Packed on: *09/23/08*

Expires on: *11/23/08*

Reheating directions: *350° F* for *45* minutes or until done

Psst...
Never re-freeze anything that's already been frozen. There is an increased risk of bacteria multiplying in the thawing process before re-freezing, and the quality of the food will be severely impaired.

3 quick sauces
Batch-freeze these for when you're short on time. You'll be able to make lasagna, curries, and pasta dishes in minutes.

Curry sauce
Use with chicken, shrimp, or vegetables. Makes enough sauce for 6–8 servings.

Make

Heat 2 tablespoons of **olive oil** in a large deep-sided frying pan and add 2 finely chopped **onions**. Cook over low heat for about 8 minutes, or until soft and translucent. Stir in 2 teaspoons of **ground cumin**, 3 chopped **garlic cloves**, 3 seeded and finely chopped **medium-hot red chiles**, a grated 2in (5cm) piece of **fresh ginger**, and cook for a few seconds, then stir in 2 teaspoons each of **garam masala** and **turmeric**, 2 tablespoons of **tomato purée**, and 3 x 14oz (400g) cans of **diced tomatoes**. Season well, bring to a boil, and simmer for about 20 minutes. Process until smooth with an immersion blender, or in a food processor.

Freeze

Leave to cool completely, then transfer to sealable freezer bags in the required portion sizes, label, and freeze.

Reheat

To use, defrost overnight in the refrigerator, then reheat in a pan for 15–20 minutes over medium-high heat, or in a microwave on high for a few minutes, adding some heavy cream or yogurt, if you wish.

Cheese sauce
Use with vegetables, bakes, or pasta. Makes enough sauce for 6–8 servings.

Make

Melt 11 tablespoons of **butter** in a large pan, then remove from the heat and stir in 2 tablespoons of **all-purpose flour** to form a roux. Pour in a little milk, taken from 4 cups of **milk**, then put it back on the heat and slowly add the milk, stirring all the time. When all the milk has been added, switch to a balloon whisk and whisk until smooth, over low heat, for about 5 minutes. Remove from the heat and add 1½ cups of grated **Cheddar cheese** and 2 teaspoons of **Dijon mustard** and season well with sea salt and freshly ground black pepper.

Freeze

Leave to cool completely, then transfer to sealable freezer bags in the required portion sizes, label, and freeze.

Reheat

To use, defrost overnight in the refrigerator, then reheat in a pan for 10–15 minutes, over low-medium heat, or in a microwave on high for a few minutes.

Red pepper sauce
Use with pasta, vegetables, or chicken. Makes enough sauce for 6–8 servings.

Make

Roast 6 **red bell peppers** in the oven at 400°F (200°C) for 15–20 minutes, or until charred and blistered. Leave to cool in a plastic bag (see p59), then peel and chop. Heat 2 tablespoons of **olive oil** in a large deep-sided frying pan and add 2 finely chopped **onions**. Cook over low heat for about 8 minutes, or until soft and translucent, then add 3 chopped **garlic cloves** and cook for a few seconds. Add the roasted peppers and stir, then pour in about 3 cups of **vegetable stock** and bring to a boil. Simmer for about 15 minutes, then process with an immersion blender. Stir in 1 tablespoon of **red pesto**, season well, then process again.

Freeze

Leave to cool completely, then transfer to sealable freezer bags in the required portion sizes, label, and freeze.

Reheat

To use, defrost overnight in the refrigerator, then reheat in a pan for 15–20 minutes, over medium-high heat, or in a microwave on high for a few minutes. Check for seasoning, and add some fresh herbs, if you wish.

EVERYDAY

Chestnut and bacon soup

PREP 15 MINS

Special equipment • blender or food processor

SERVES 8

2 tbsp olive oil
2 onions, finely chopped
9oz (250g) bacon or pancetta, chopped into
    bite-sized pieces
4 garlic cloves, finely chopped
1 tbsp rosemary leaves, finely chopped
sea salt and freshly ground black pepper
3 x 7oz (200g) packs roasted chestnuts, chopped
4 cups hot chicken stock

1 Heat the oil in a large pan, add the onions, and cook over low heat for 5–8 minutes or until soft. Add the bacon or pancetta and cook for 5 minutes or until crispy. Stir in the garlic and rosemary, then season with salt and freshly ground black pepper.

2 Stir in the chestnuts, pour in the stock, and bring to a boil. Lower the heat and simmer for 15–20 minutes. Using a slotted spoon, remove a few spoonfuls of the bacon and set aside. Purée the rest of the soup in a food processor or blender. Season again with salt and pepper if needed, then add the reserved bacon pieces.

3 Let cool completely, then transfer to a freezer-proof container. Make sure the bacon pieces are covered, seal, and freeze for up to 3 months.

4 To serve, defrost overnight in the refrigerator, transfer to a saucepan, and heat until piping hot. Add a little hot water if the soup is too thick. Serve with a drizzle of extra virgin olive oil and some fresh crusty bread.

Bean and rosemary soup

PREP 15 MINS

SERVES 8

2 tbsp olive oil, plus a little extra (according
    to taste)
2 onions, finely chopped
sea salt and freshly ground black pepper
1 tbsp finely chopped rosemary leaves
a few sage leaves, finely chopped
4 celery stalks, finely chopped
3 garlic cloves, finely chopped
2 tbsp tomato purée or tomato paste
2 x 14oz (400g) cans cannellini beans
4 cups hot chicken stock
2lb (2.5kg) potatoes, cut into ½in (1cm) cubes

1 Heat the oil in a large saucepan, add the onions, and cook over low heat for 6–8 minutes or until soft. Season well with salt and pepper, then stir in the rosemary, sage, celery, and garlic and cook over very low heat, stirring occasionally, for 10 minutes.

2 Stir through the tomato purée and beans, add a little more olive oil if you wish, and cook gently for 5 minutes. Pour in the stock, bring to a boil, then add the potatoes and simmer gently for 15 minutes or until cooked. Taste and season again with salt and pepper if needed. Cool.

3 Transfer to a freezer-proof container. Seal and freeze for up to 3 months.

4 To serve, defrost in the refrigerator overnight, then transfer to a saucepan and simmer until piping hot. Add a little hot stock if the soup is too thick.

Sweet corn chowder

PREP 15 MINS

SERVES 8

2 tbsp olive oil
2 onions, finely chopped
sea salt and freshly ground black pepper
6–8 medium potatoes, cut into bite-sized chunks
2 x 12oz (350g) cans corn, drained
5 cups hot vegetable stock
handful of fresh flat-leaf parsley, finely chopped
4 tbsp heavy cream (optional), to serve

1 Heat the oil in a large saucepan, add the onions, and cook over low heat for 6–8 minutes or until soft. Season with sea salt and freshly ground black pepper, then stir in the potatoes and cook over low heat for 5 minutes.

2 Mash the corn a little with the back of a fork, then add to the pan. Pour in the stock, bring to a boil, then reduce to a simmer and cook for 15 minutes or until the potatoes are soft. Stir in the parsley and season again with salt and pepper if needed.

3 Let cool completely, then transfer to a freezer-proof container and seal. Freeze for up to 3 months.

4 To serve, defrost overnight in the refrigerator and transfer to a saucepan and heat until piping hot. Stir in the cream, if using, and serve with fresh crusty bread.

Red lentil and tomato soup

PREP 15 MINS

Special equipment • blender or food processor

SERVES 8

2 tbsp olive oil
2 onions, finely chopped
4 garlic cloves, grated or finely chopped
pinch of crushed red pepper flakes
4 carrots, finely chopped
sea salt and freshly ground black pepper
1lb (450g) red lentils
3 x 14oz (400g) cans whole tomatoes, chopped in the can
1½ quarts (1.4 liters) hot vegetable stock

1 Heat the oil in a large soup pot, add the onions, and cook over low heat for 6–8 minutes, or until soft and translucent. Stir in the garlic, red pepper flakes, and carrots, season with salt and pepper, and cook for 2 minutes.

2 Add the lentils, stir, then add the tomatoes and stock. Bring to a boil, then simmer over very low heat for 35–40 minutes, or until the lentils are soft. Transfer to a blender or food processor and process until blended and smooth. Taste and season with salt and pepper if needed.

3 Leave to cool completely, then transfer to a freezerproof container, seal, and freeze for up to 3 months. To serve, defrost in the refrigerator overnight, then transfer to a pan and heat until piping hot.

Cauliflower soup

PREP 15 MINS

Special equipment • blender or food processor

SERVES 8

2 tbsp olive oil
2 onions, finely chopped
sea salt and freshly ground black pepper
3 garlic cloves, finely chopped
4 celery stalks, finely chopped
2 bay leaves
1½lb (675g) potatoes, cut into bite-sized cubes
15 cups hot vegetable stock
2 heads of cauliflower, trimmed and cut into florets
drizzle of heavy cream (optional), to serve

1 Heat the oil in large pan, add the onions, and cook over low heat for 6–8 minutes or until soft. Season with salt and pepper, then add the garlic, celery, and bay leaves and cook for 5 minutes or until the celery begins to soften. Stir in the potatoes and cook for 5 minutes, then pour in the stock, bring to a boil, and cook for 15 minutes or until the potatoes are nearly soft.

2 Add the cauliflower and cook for 10 minutes or until it is soft but not watery. Remove the bay leaves and discard, then transfer the soup to a food processor or blender and blend until smooth. Add a little more hot stock if it seems too thick. Taste and season with salt and pepper as needed.

3 Let cool completely, then transfer to a freezer-proof container, seal, and freeze for up to 3 months.

4 To serve, defrost in the refrigerator overnight, transfer to a pan, and heat until piping hot. Add the heavy cream, if using, and serve with crusty bread.

Leek and potato soup

PREP 15 MINS

Special equipment • blender or food processor

SERVES 8

2 tbsp olive oil
2 onions, finely chopped
sea salt and freshly ground black pepper
3 garlic cloves, finely chopped
6 sage leaves, finely chopped
2lb (900g) leeks, cleaned and finely sliced
5 cups hot vegetable stock
2lb (900g) potatoes, coarsely chopped
⅔ cup heavy cream, to serve

1 Heat the oil in a large pan, add the onions, and cook over low heat for 6–8 minutes or until soft. Season with salt and pepper, then stir in the garlic and sage. Add the leeks and stir well, then cook over low heat for 10 minutes or until the leeks are starting to soften.

2 Pour in the stock, bring to a boil, then add the potatoes and simmer for 20 minutes or until soft. Transfer to a food processor or blender and process until blended and smooth. Taste and season if needed.

3 Let cool completely, then transfer to a freezer-proof container, seal, and freeze for up to 3 months.

4 To serve, defrost in the refrigerator overnight, then transfer to a pan, stir in the cream, and heat until piping hot.

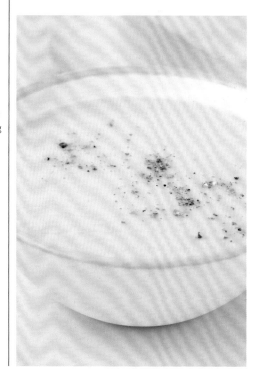

EVERYDAY

EVERYDAY

Black bean and coconut soup

PREP 15 MINS · COOK 30 MINS ·

Special equipment • blender or food processor

SERVES 8

2 tbsp olive oil
2 red onions, finely chopped
2 bay leaves
sea salt and freshly ground black pepper
4 garlic cloves, finely chopped
2 tsp ground cumin
2 tsp ground coriander
1 tsp chili powder
2 x 14oz (400g) cans drained black beans
4 cups hot vegetable stock
1 x 14oz (400ml) can coconut milk
flour tortillas, to serve

1 Heat the oil in a saucepan, add the onions and bay leaves, and cook over low heat for 6–8 minutes until the onions soften. Season with salt and pepper. Stir in the garlic, cumin, coriander, and chili powder and cook for a few seconds.

2 Stir in the black beans, then pour in the stock and coconut milk. Bring to a boil, then reduce to a simmer and cook for 15–20 minutes. Remove the bay leaves and discard, then transfer the soup to a food processor or blender and pulse a couple of times so some of the beans are puréed and some remain whole. Add a little more stock if it is too thick. Season again with salt and pepper.

3 Let cool completely, then transfer to a freezer-proof container, seal, and freeze for up to 3 months.

4 To serve, defrost in the refrigerator overnight, then transfer to a pan and heat until piping hot. Serve with tortilla triangles.

Ribollita

PREP 20 MINS ·

SERVES 8

2 tbsp olive oil
2 onions, finely chopped
sea salt and freshly ground black pepper
4 garlic cloves, finely chopped
4 carrots, finely chopped
8 tomatoes, peeled and coarsely chopped
2 x 14oz (400g) cans drained cannellini beans
1lb (450g) potatoes, cut into bite-sized pieces
12oz (350g) calvo nero or kale, chopped
5 cups hot vegetable stock
1 tbsp rosemary leaves, finely chopped
½ ciabatta, cut into cubes, to serve
drizzle of olive oil, plus extra to serve
freshly grated Parmesan, to serve

1 Heat the oil in a saucepan, add the onions, and cook over low heat for 6–8 minutes or until soft. Season with salt and pepper, then stir in the garlic and carrots and cook for 5 minutes.

2 Stir in the tomatoes, beans, potatoes, and calvo nero and cook for 5 minutes. Pour in the stock, add the rosemary, and simmer over low heat for 15–20 minutes or until the potatoes are soft. Taste and season again with salt and pepper.

3 Let cool completely, then transfer to a freezer-proof container, making sure everything is covered with liquid. Seal and freeze for up to 3 months.

4 To serve, defrost overnight in the fridge. Preheat the oven to 400°F (200°C). Place the ciabatta cubes on a baking sheet, drizzle with olive oil, and bake in the oven for 10 minutes or until golden. Meanwhile, transfer the soup to a saucepan and heat until hot. Serve topped with the ciabatta, a drizzle of olive oil, and a sprinkling of Parmesan.

Scotch broth

PREP 20 MINS · COOK 1¾ HRS ·

SERVES 8

1lb (450g) lamb neck
sea salt and freshly ground black pepper
2 tbsp olive oil
1 onion, finely chopped
4 carrots, finely chopped
4 celery stalks, finely chopped
2 cups hot chicken stock, or more as needed
8oz (225g) pearl barley
handful of curly parsley, finely chopped

1 Put the lamb in a large saucepan, cover with cold water, and season with salt and pepper. Bring to a boil, then simmer for 30 minutes or until cooked. Remove with a slotted spoon, let cool slightly, then shred and set aside. Reserve the cooking liquid.

2 Heat the oil in a large saucepan, add the onion, and cook over low heat for 5 minutes or until soft. Add the carrots and celery and cook over very low heat for 10 minutes. Strain the reserved liquid, then add to the pan and pour in the stock. Season with salt and pepper, then add the pearl barley and lamb. Bring to a boil, then reduce to a simmer and cook over really low heat for 1 hour or until the pearl barley is cooked. Add some hot water if it begins to dry out too much. Stir in the parsley, then taste and season again with salt and pepper if needed.

3 Let cool completely, then transfer to a freezer-proof container, making sure the lamb is covered with liquid (add a little chicken stock if it isn't). Seal and freeze for up to 3 months.

4 To serve, defrost in the refrigerator overnight, then transfer to a pan and heat until piping hot. Serve with crusty bread.

Spiced butternut squash soup

Special equipment • blender or food processor

SERVES 8

2 tbsp olive oil
2 onions, finely chopped
sea salt and freshly ground black pepper
3 garlic cloves, finely chopped
4 sage leaves, finely chopped
2 red chiles, seeded and finely chopped
pinch of freshly grated nutmeg
1 large butternut squash or 2 small ones, halved,
    peeled, seeded, and chopped into small pieces
2 potatoes, cut into small pieces
5 cups hot vegetable stock
chili oil and grated Gruyère cheese, to serve

1 Heat the oil in a large soup pot, add the onions, and cook over low heat for 6–8 minutes or until soft. Season with sea salt and freshly ground black pepper, then add the garlic, sage, chiles, and nutmeg and cook for a few seconds.

2 Stir in the squash, then add the potatoes and stock. Bring to a boil, reduce to a simmer, and cook for 20–30 minutes or until the squash and potatoes are soft. Transfer to a food processor or blender and process until blended and smooth. Season again with sea salt and freshly ground black pepper.

3 Let cool completely, then transfer to a freezer-proof container, seal, and freeze for up to 3 months.

4 To serve, defrost in the refrigerator overnight, transfer to a pan, and heat until piping hot. Serve with a drizzle of chili oil and a sprinkling of Gruyère.

Chunky minestrone soup

SERVES 8

2 tbsp olive oil
2 onions, finely chopped
3 garlic cloves, finely chopped
4 celery stalks, finely chopped
4 carrots, finely chopped
9oz (250g) pancetta, cut into small cubes
handful of flat-leaf parsley, finely chopped
handful of fresh sage leaves, finely chopped
2 tbsp tomato paste or purée
1 x 28oz (800g) can chopped tomatoes
2 x 14oz (400g) cans borlotti beans, drained, rinsed,
    and drained again
sea salt and freshly ground black pepper
2 cups hot chicken stock, or more as needed
8oz (225g) fresh or frozen peas
10oz (300g) green beans, cut into thirds
10oz (300g) small pasta shapes such as ditalini
grated Parmesan, to serve

1 Heat the oil in a heavy-bottomed pan, add the onions, and cook over low heat for 6–8 minutes or until soft. Add the garlic, celery, and carrots and cook, stirring, for 10 minutes, until soft. Stir in the pancetta and cook for 5 minutes or until browned.

2 Add the herbs, tomato paste, tomatoes, and beans and stir to combine. Season with salt and pepper, then pour in the stock. Bring to a boil, then cover with a lid and simmer for 40 minutes. Add the peas and beans for the last 5 minutes of cooking. Taste and season with salt and pepper.

3 Let cool completely, then transfer to a freezer-proof container, seal, and freeze for up to 3 months.

4 To serve, defrost overnight in the refrigerator, then transfer to a large saucepan. Add the pasta and simmer until the soup is piping hot and the pasta is *al dente*. Season, top with the Parmesan, and serve.

Thick vegetable soup

SERVES 8

2 tbsp olive oil
2 onions, finely chopped
sea salt and freshly ground black pepper
4 garlic cloves, finely chopped
1 tbsp finely chopped rosemary leaves
4 celery stalks, finely chopped
4 carrots, finely chopped
4 zucchini, finely chopped
1 x 28oz (800g) can whole tomatoes, chopped
4 cups hot vegetable stock
handful of flat-leaf parsley, finely chopped

1 Heat the oil in a large pan, add the onions, and cook over low heat for 6–8 minutes or until soft. Season with sea salt and freshly ground black pepper, then add the garlic, rosemary, celery, and carrots and cook over low heat, stirring occasionally, for 10 minutes.

2 Add the zucchini and cook for 5 minutes, then stir in the tomatoes and squash with the back of a fork. Add the stock, bring to a boil, then reduce to a simmer and cook for 20 minutes. Season with salt and pepper, then stir in the parsley.

3 Let cool completely, then transfer to a freezer-proof container, seal, and freeze for up to 3 months.

4 To serve, defrost in the refrigerator overnight, then transfer to a pan and heat until piping hot. Serve with crusty bread.

EVERYDAY

Roasted red pepper soup

PREP 15 MINS

Cooling • 15 minutes

Special equipment • blender or food processor

SERVES 8

10 red bell peppers
3 tbsp olive oil
2 onions, finely chopped
3 garlic cloves, finely chopped
pinch of crushed red pepper flakes
sea salt and freshly ground black pepper
8 cups hot vegetable stock
large handful of fresh basil leaves, torn, to serve
drizzle of extra virgin olive oil, to serve

1 Preheat the oven to 400°F (200°C). Place the peppers in a roasting pan and coat with 1 tablespoon of the oil, using your hands. Roast for 40 minutes or until soft. Transfer to plastic bags, knot, and allow to cool for 15 minutes. Remove the skins and seeds and discard, then coarsely chop the peppers, saving any juices.

2 Heat the remaining oil in a large heavy-bottomed soup pot, add the onions, and cook over low heat for 5 minutes or until beginning to soften. Stir in the garlic and red pepper flakes and season with salt and pepper. Add the roasted peppers and their juices, pour in the stock, and bring to a boil. Reduce to a simmer and cook for 15 minutes. Transfer to a food processor or blender and process until blended and smooth. Season to taste again with salt and pepper.

3 Let cool completely, then transfer to a freezer-proof container, seal, and freeze for up to 3 months.

4 To serve, defrost overnight in the refrigerator, then transfer to a soup pot and heat until piping hot. Stir in the basil, drizzle with oil, and serve with some crusty bread.

Tomato and chorizo soup

PREP 20 MINS

SERVES 8

2 tbsp olive oil
9oz (250g) chorizo, cut into small cubes
2 red onions, finely chopped
4 celery stalks, finely diced
4 carrots, finely diced
3 garlic cloves, finely chopped
sea salt and freshly ground black pepper
1 x 28oz (800g) can diced tomatoes
4 cups hot vegetable stock
2 x 14oz (400g) cans chickpeas, drained
handful of fresh cilantro, finely chopped, to serve

1 Heat half the oil in a large heavy-bottomed saucepan, add the chorizo, and cook over medium heat, stirring occasionally, for 5 minutes or until beginning to crisp. Remove and set aside.

2 Heat the remaining oil in the pan, add the onions, and cook over low heat for 6–8 minutes or until soft. Stir in the celery, carrots, and garlic, season with salt and pepper, then cook over low heat, stirring occasionally, for 8 minutes or until tender. Add the diced tomatoes, stock, and chickpeas and simmer for 15 minutes. Return the chorizo to the pan, then taste and season again with salt and pepper if needed.

3 Let cool completely, then transfer to a freezer-proof container, seal, and freeze for up to 3 months.

4 To serve, defrost overnight in the refrigerator, then transfer to a pan and heat until piping hot. Stir in the cilantro and serve.

Tomato soup

PREP 15 MINS

Special equipment • blender or food processor

SERVES 8

3 tbsp olive oil
3 onions, finely chopped
4 garlic cloves, finely chopped
3lb (1.35kg) tomatoes, quartered
sea salt and freshly ground black pepper
2 tsp superfine sugar
1 tbsp tomato paste or purée
2½ cups hot vegetable stock
⅔ cup heavy cream (optional), to serve

1 Heat the oil in a large, heavy soup pot, add the onions, and cook over low heat for 10 minutes, stirring so the onions don't burn. Stir in the garlic and tomatoes and season with salt and pepper. Add the sugar and tomato paste or purée, stir, and then cook over very low heat for 30 minutes.

2 Pour in the stock, bring to a boil, then lower the heat and simmer for 10 minutes. Transfer to a food processor or blender and process until blended and smooth. Taste and season again with salt and pepper if needed.

3 Let cool completely, then transfer to a freezer-proof container, seal, and freeze for up to 3 months.

4 To reheat, defrost overnight in the refrigerator, then transfer to a pan and heat until piping hot. Stir in the cream, if using, and serve with crusty bread.

Chili beef and bean soup

PREP 20 MINS · COOK 2 HRS

SERVES 8

2 tbsp olive oil
2 onions, finely chopped
sea salt and freshly ground black pepper
2 red bell peppers, seeded and finely chopped
2–3 red chiles, seeded and finely chopped
1¼lb (550g) beef stew meat, cut into
    1in (2.5cm) cubes
1 tbsp all-purpose flour
4 pints (2.3 liters) hot beef stock
2 x 14oz (400g) cans kidney beans, drained
handful of flat-leaf parsley, finely chopped,
    to serve

1 Heat the oil in a large heavy-bottomed saucepan, add the onions, and cook over low heat for about 6–8 minutes or until soft. Season with salt and pepper, then stir in the peppers and chiles and cook for 5 minutes. Add the meat and cook, stirring frequently, for 5–10 minutes or until beginning to brown all over.

2 Sprinkle in the flour, stir well, then cook for 2 minutes. Add the stock, bring to a boil, then cover with a lid and reduce to a simmer. Cook for 1½ hours or until the meat is tender. Add the kidney beans and cook for 10 minutes more, then season to taste with salt and pepper.

3 Let cool completely, then transfer to a freezer-proof container, making sure the meat is covered (add a little more stock if it isn't). Seal and freeze for up to 3 months.

4 To serve, defrost the soup overnight in the refrigerator, then transfer to a pan and heat until piping hot. Stir in the parsley and serve.

Split pea and bacon soup

PREP 15 MINS · COOK 2¼ HRS

Special equipment • blender or food processor

SERVES 8

2 tbsp olive oil
15oz (425g) bacon or pancetta, chopped into
    bite-sized pieces
2 onions, finely chopped
sea salt and freshly ground black pepper
4 celery stalks, finely chopped
4 carrots, finely chopped
1¼lb (550g) yellow split peas
6 cups hot vegetable stock

1 Heat half the oil in a large heavy-bottomed saucepan, add the bacon, and cook over medium heat, stirring occasionally, for 5 minutes or until crispy. Remove with a slotted spoon and set aside. Heat the remaining oil in the pan, add the onions, and cook over low heat for 6–8 minutes or until soft. Season with salt and pepper, then add the celery and carrots and cook over low heat for 5 minutes.

2 Add the peas and stock and bring slowly to a boil. Cover with a lid, reduce to a simmer, and cook for 2 hours or until the peas are tender. Check occasionally and add hot water if the soup begins to look too thick. Transfer to a food processor or blender and process until smooth and blended. Return the bacon to the pan, then season with salt and pepper.

3 Let cool completely, then transfer to a freezer-proof container, seal, and freeze for up to 3 months.

4 To serve, defrost overnight in the refrigerator, transfer to a saucepan, and heat until piping hot. Serve with crusty bread.

Beef ragù

PREP 20 MINS · COOK 45 MINS

SERVES 8

4 tbsp olive oil
2 large onions, finely diced
1½lb (675g) lean beef, cut into ½in (1cm) dice
8 garlic cloves, finely diced
1¼ cups red wine
2 x 28oz (800g) cans chopped tomatoes
4 bay leaves
1 tsp fresh thyme leaves, finely chopped
sea salt and freshly ground black pepper

1 Heat the oil in a large heavy-bottomed saucepan, add the onions, and cook over medium heat, stirring frequently, for 5 minutes or until soft. Add the beef and cook, stirring frequently, for another 5 minutes or until no longer pink. Add the garlic and cook for another minute, then pour in the wine and allow to simmer and reduce for 5 minutes.

2 Add the tomatoes, bay leaves, and thyme, bring to a boil, then reduce the heat and simmer for 30 minutes, stirring occasionally. Taste and season with salt and pepper.

3 Let cool completely, then remove and discard the bay leaves. Divide the ragù evenly among 4 freezer bags (2 portions per bag), seal, and freeze for up to 6 months.

4 To serve, defrost in the refrigerator overnight, then transfer to a saucepan and heat until piping hot. Serve with pasta or creamy mashed potatoes.

EVERYDAY

EVERYDAY

Lamb and eggplant ragù

PREP 20 MINS · COOK 35 MINS

SERVES 8
½ cup olive oil
2 onions, finely diced
2 medium eggplants, cut into ½in (1cm) dice
1lb (450g) lean lamb, cut into ½in (1cm) dice
6 garlic cloves, finely chopped
3 x 14oz (400g) cans chopped tomatoes
3 bay leaves
1 tbsp dried oregano
handful of flat-leaf parsley, chopped
sea salt and freshly ground black pepper

1 Heat the oil in a large heavy-bottomed saucepan, add the onions, and cook over medium heat, stirring, for 3 minutes. Add the eggplants and cook, stirring frequently, for 5 minutes or until starting to brown. Add the lamb, combine well, and cook, stirring frequently, for 5 minutes or until no longer pink.

2 Stir in the garlic and cook for 1 minute. Add the tomatoes, bay leaves, oregano, and parsley, bring to a boil, then reduce the heat and simmer for 20 minutes, stirring occasionally. Taste and season with salt and pepper.

3 Let cool completely, then remove the bay leaves and discard. Divide the ragù evenly among 4 freezer bags, seal, and freeze for up to 3 months.

4 To serve, defrost overnight in the refrigerator, then transfer to a saucepan and heat until piping hot. Serve with pasta or rice.

Rich tomato sauce

PREP 10 MINS · COOK 30 MINS

SERVES 8
4 tbsp olive oil
4 garlic cloves, finely sliced
2 x 28oz (800g) cans whole tomatoes, chopped
2 tbsp tomato paste or purée
2 tsp dried oregano
2 bay leaves
sea salt and freshly ground black pepper
2 heaping tsp pesto

1 Heat the oil in a large heavy-bottomed saucepan, add the garlic, and cook over low heat for a few seconds. Add the tomatoes and tomato paste or purée, bring to a boil, then add the oregano and bay leaves and simmer for 25 minutes, stirring occasionally.

2 Season with salt and pepper, cook for 2 minutes, then stir in the pesto and remove from heat.

3 Let cool completely, then remove the bay leaves and discard. Divide the sauce evenly among 4 freezer bags (2 portions per bag), seal, and freeze for up to 6 months.

4 To serve, defrost overnight in the refrigerator or at room temperature for 6 hours, transfer to a saucepan, and heat until warmed through. Serve with pasta or use to make a lasagna or moussaka.

Spinach sauce

PREP 15 MINS · COOK 20 MINS

SERVES 8
4 tbsp olive oil
2 large onions, finely diced
4 garlic cloves, finely sliced
2 red chiles, seeded and finely chopped
1¼lb (550g) baby spinach leaves, rinsed and coarsely chopped
1¼ cups dry white wine
2 tbsp all-purpose flour
3 cups milk
sea salt and freshly ground black pepper

1 Heat the oil in a large heavy-bottomed pan, add the onions, and cook over medium heat, stirring frequently, for 5 minutes or until soft. Stir in the garlic and chiles and cook for 2 minutes. Add the spinach and cook for 3 minutes or until wilted.

2 Add the wine and allow to simmer for 5 minutes or until reduced by half. Add the flour and combine well. Pour in half the milk and stir well to combine. Add the rest of the milk a little at a time, stirring constantly, and cook for 5 minutes or until you have a creamy sauce. Season well with salt and pepper.

3 Leave to cool completely, then divide among 4 freezer bags (2 portions per bag). Seal and freeze for up to 3 months.

4 To serve, defrost overnight in the refrigerator, transfer to a saucepan with a little milk and warm through gently but do not overcook. Use as a sauce for chicken, fish, or new potatoes or stir in some grated Cheddar cheese and serve with pasta.

Beef with prunes and pine nuts

SERVES 8

2½lb (1.1kg) lean beef, cut into
  ¾in (2cm) cubes
1 tsp freshly ground black pepper
1 tsp cayenne pepper
6 tbsp olive oil
2 large onions, sliced
sea salt
6 garlic cloves, chopped
4½oz (125g) pine nuts
5½oz (150g) prunes, pitted
⅔ cup dry sherry
2 tbsp fresh thyme leaves
2 bay leaves
1 tbsp all-purpose flour
2 cups hot beef stock

1 Put the beef in a mixing bowl, add the pepper and cayenne, and mix well. Heat the oil in a large heavy-bottomed saucepan over medium heat, add the beef, and cook, stirring frequently, for 5 minutes or until browned all over. Remove beef with a slotted spoon and set aside. Add the onions, season with sea salt, and cook for 5 minutes or until soft.

2 Return the meat to the pan, add the garlic, pine nuts, and prunes, and cook for 1 minute. Add the sherry, thyme, and bay leaves, and allow to bubble for 5 minutes while the alcohol evaporates. Stir in the flour and add the stock. Combine well, then bring to a boil and simmer for 10 minutes.

3 Let cool completely, then transfer to a freezer-proof container or 4 freezer bags (2 portions per bag), seal, and freeze for up to 3 months.

4 To serve, defrost overnight in the refrigerator, then transfer to a pan and set over medium heat for 15–20 minutes or until piping hot.

Beef stew with orange and bay leaves

Special equipment • large cast-iron pan or flameproof casserole

SERVES 8

3 tbsp olive oil
3lb (1.35kg) beef stew meat, cut into
  bite-sized pieces
sea salt and freshly ground
  black pepper
1½ cups dry white wine
3 bay leaves
6 cups hot vegetable stock
2 cinnamon sticks
pinch of freshly grated nutmeg
2 x 14oz (400g) cans chickpeas,
  drained, rinsed, and drained again
2 oranges, peeled and sliced into rings
handful of fresh cilantro, finely
  chopped, to serve

1 Preheat the oven to 350°F (180°C). Heat the oil in a large cast-iron casserole, add the meat, season with salt and pepper, and cook over medium heat, stirring occasionally, for 10 minutes or until brown on all sides. Carefully add the wine, then stir the meat around the pan and allow the liquid to bubble for a couple of minutes while the alcohol evaporates.

2 Add the bay leaves, then pour in the stock. Add the cinnamon and nutmeg and season again with salt and pepper. Bring to a boil, add the chickpeas, then cover with a lid and put in the oven to cook for 1 hour. Add the oranges and cook for 30 minutes.

3 Let cool completely, then transfer to a freezer-proof container, making sure the meat is well-covered. Seal and freeze for up to 3 months.

4 To serve, defrost overnight in the refrigerator, then transfer to a large pan and heat for 15 minutes or until piping hot. Stir in the cilantro and serve with crusty bread.

EVERYDAY

Beef and parsnip stew

 PREP 30 MINS COOK 1¾ HRS

Special equipment • large cast-iron or flameproof casserole

SERVES 8

3 tbsp olive oil
2 onions, finely chopped
handful of fresh thyme leaves
4 garlic cloves, finely chopped
sea salt and freshly ground black pepper
2½lb (1.1kg) beef round steak, cut into
    bite-sized pieces
4 large carrots, coarsely chopped
5 parsnips, coarsely chopped
3 cups hot beef stock
1 tbsp butter
14oz (400g) button mushrooms, any large
    ones halved
hot vegetable stock, as needed

1 Preheat the oven to 350°F (180°C). Heat the oil in large cast-iron casserole, add the onions, and cook over low heat for 6–8 minutes or until soft. Stir in the thyme and garlic and season with salt and pepper. Add the steak and cook, stirring often, for 10 minutes or until browned. Add the carrots and parsnips, then pour in the stock. Bring to a boil, then reduce to a simmer, cover with a lid, and put in the oven to cook for 1 hour.

2 Just before the hour is up, melt the butter in a small frying pan, add the mushrooms, and cook, stirring often, for 5–8 minutes or until golden. Add to the pot and cook for another 30 minutes. Add hot vegetable stock if the stew is beginning to look dry.

3 Let cool completely, then transfer to a freezer-proof container, seal, and freeze for up to 3 months.

4 To serve, defrost overnight in the refrigerator, then transfer to a large casserole and reheat in an oven preheated to 350°F (180°C) for 30–40 minutes or until piping hot.

Beef stew with olives

 PREP 15 MINS COOK

Special equipment • large cast-iron or flameproof casserole

SERVES 8

3 tbsp olive oil
3½lb (1.6kg) beef stew meat, cut into
    bite-sized cubes
4 garlic cloves, finely chopped
2 tsp cumin
1½ cups dry white wine
2 tbsp white wine vinegar
a few sprigs of rosemary
6oz (175g) black olives, pitted
16 small cipollini onions or pearl onions, peeled
sea salt and freshly ground black pepper
5 cups hot vegetable stock

1 Preheat the oven to 400°F (200°C). Heat the oil in a cast-iron casserole, add the meat, and cook over medium heat, stirring frequently, for 10 minutes or until browned all over. Lower the heat and stir in the garlic and cumin. Add the wine and wine vinegar, increase the heat, and let bubble and reduce for a few minutes while the alcohol evaporates.

2 Add the rosemary, olives, and onions, stir, and season with salt and pepper. Pour in the stock, bring to a boil, then reduce to a simmer. Cover with a lid and cook in the oven for 1½ hours or until the meat is tender.

3 Let cool completely, then transfer to a freezer-proof container, seal, and freeze for up to 3 months.

4 To serve, defrost overnight in the refrigerator, then transfer to a large saucepan and heat gently until piping hot. Alternatively, place in a covered ovenproof dish and heat in an oven preheated to 350°F (180°C) for 30 minutes. Serve with rice.

Beef shank with Marsala

 PREP 45 MINS COOK 1½ HRS

Special equipment • large cast-iron or flameproof casserole

SERVES 8

3½lb (1.6kg) beef shank, cut into bite-sized pieces
all-purpose flour, to dust
sea salt and freshly ground black pepper
3 tbsp olive oil
2 red onions, coarsely chopped
4 carrots, coarsely chopped
1¼ cups Marsala
7oz (200g) Puy lentils, rinsed and picked over
5 cups hot vegetable stock
2 bay leaves

1 Preheat the oven to 350°F (180°C). Dust the meat with a little flour, then season with salt and black pepper. Heat half the oil in a large cast-iron casserole, add the meat, and cook over medium heat, stirring often, for 10 minutes or until browned on all sides. Remove with a slotted spoon and set aside.

2 Heat the remaining oil in the casserole, add the onions, and cook over low heat for 6–8 minutes or until soft. Stir in the carrots and cook for 5 minutes. Return the meat to the pan, pour in the Marsala, and let it bubble for a few minutes while the alcohol evaporates. Stir in the lentils, add the stock, and bring to a boil. Season with salt and pepper, then add the bay leaves. Cover with a lid and put in the oven to cook for 1½ hours. Check occasionally and add a little hot water if it looks dry.

3 Let cool completely, then transfer to a freezer-proof container, making sure the meat is submerged in the stock. Seal and freeze for up to 3 months.

4 To serve, defrost overnight in the refrigerator, then transfer to a large pot and cover with a little hot water. Heat very gently for 15–20 minutes or until piping hot. Serve with crusty bread.

Lamb daube

PREP 50 MINS · **COOK 2½ HRS**

Marinating • 30 minutes

Special equipment • large cast-iron pot or flameproof casserole

SERVES 8

3lb (1.35kg) lamb shoulder or leg of lamb, cut into bite-sized pieces

1¼ cups red wine

1 star anise

zest of 1 orange, grated

sea salt and freshly ground black pepper

3 tbsp olive oil

2 onions, finely chopped

14oz (400g) bacon or pancetta, cut into bite-sized pieces

4 celery stalks, finely chopped

4 carrots, finely chopped

4 leeks, cleaned and coarsely chopped

4 cups hot vegetable stock

2 handfuls of pitted green olives

1 Put the lamb, wine, star anise, and orange zest in a bowl, season with sea salt and freshly ground black pepper, cover, and marinate for 30 minutes (or overnight in the fridge).

2 Preheat the oven to 400°F (200°C). Heat half the oil in a large cast-iron pot. Remove the meat with a slotted spoon (reserve the marinade) and add to the pot. Cook over medium heat, stirring often, for 10 minutes or until browned all over. Remove with a slotted spoon and set aside. Heat the remaining oil in the pot, add the onions, and cook over low heat for 6–8 minutes or until soft. Stir in the bacon or pancetta and cook for 6–10 minutes or until crispy. Add the celery and carrots and cook over low heat, adding more oil if needed, for 5 minutes or until they begin to soften.

3 Stir in the leeks and cook for a few minutes, then return the meat to the pot and pour in the marinade and stock. Stir in the olives, bring to a boil, then season with salt and pepper. Cover with a lid and cook in the oven for 30 minutes. Turn the oven down to 300°F (150°C) and cook for another 1½–2 hours. Check occasionally and add a little hot water if the daube looks dry. Let cool completely, then transfer to a freezer-proof container, making sure the meat is submerged in the stock. Seal and freeze for up to 3 months.

4 To serve, defrost overnight in the refrigerator, then transfer to a pan and heat slowly for 15–20 minutes or until piping hot. Alternatively, place in a casserole dish, cover with a lid, and reheat in an oven preheated to 350°F (180°C) for 30–40 minutes or until piping hot. Serve with sautéed potatoes and crusty bread.

Caribbean stew with allspice and ginger

PREP 30 MINS · **COOK 30 MINS**

Marinating • 30 minutes

Special equipment • blender or food processor • large cast-iron pot or flameproof casserole

SERVES 8

1–2 Scotch Bonnet chiles, seeded

2 tsp allspice

handful of fresh thyme leaves

2 tsp tamarind paste

2in (5cm) fresh ginger, peeled and coarsely chopped

sea salt and freshly ground black pepper

3 tbsp olive oil

4 large skinless chicken breasts, cut into bite-sized pieces

1 tbsp all-purpose flour

5 cups hot chicken stock

4 bell peppers (a mix of colors), seeded and coarsely chopped

5 tomatoes, peeled and coarsely chopped

1 Put the chiles, allspice, thyme, tamarind, ginger, and some salt and pepper in a food processor and pulse, turning the machine on and off, until it turns into a paste. Add a little of the oil and process again. Pour into a plastic bag, add the chicken, and squish together. Allow to marinate for 30 minutes (or overnight in the fridge).

2 Heat the remaining oil in a large cast-iron pot, add the chicken and paste, and cook, stirring often, over medium heat for 10 minutes or until the chicken is evenly browned. Stir in the flour, then add a little of the stock and stir to scrape up any crispy bits that are stuck to bottom of the pot. Pour in the rest of the stock and keep stirring until the flour has dissolved.

3 Stir in the peppers and tomatoes and season well with salt and pepper. Bring to a boil, then reduce to a simmer and cook over low heat for 30 minutes or until the sauce has begun to thicken slightly. Taste and season again if needed. Let cool completely, then transfer to a large freezer-proof container, making sure the chicken is well-covered with sauce. Seal and freeze for up to 3 months.

4 To serve, defrost overnight in the refrigerator, then transfer to a large saucepan or casserole and heat gently for 15–20 minutes or until piping hot. Alternatively, cover and reheat in an oven preheated to 350°F (180°C) for 30–40 minutes or until piping hot. Serve with baked or mashed sweet potatoes.

Chili con carne

SERVES 8

6 tbsp olive oil

3 large onions, diced

2½lb (1.1kg) lean ground beef

⅔ cup dry sherry

8 garlic cloves, chopped

4 green bird's-eye chiles, finely chopped

1 tsp cayenne pepper

1 tsp paprika

2 x 14oz (400g) cans kidney beans, drained and rinsed

4 bay leaves

3 x 14oz (400g) cans chopped tomatoes

2 tsp dried oregano

sea salt and freshly ground black pepper

1 Heat the oil in a large heavy-bottomed pan, add the onions, and cook for 5 minutes, or until starting to soften. Add the meat and cook over medium heat, stirring, until no longer pink. Stir in the sherry and garlic and cook for 1 minute, then add the chiles, cayenne, and paprika and cook for 5 minutes.

2 Add the kidney beans and bay leaves, cook for 2 minutes, then add the tomatoes and oregano. Bring to a boil, season, then simmer over low heat for 40 minutes, stirring occasionally.

3 Let cool completely, then transfer to a freezer-proof container (or 4 freezer bags), seal, and freeze for up to 3 months.

4 To serve, defrost in the refrigerator overnight, then heat in a saucepan, stirring frequently, for 5 minutes or until piping hot.

Pork and bean casserole

SERVES 8

6 tbsp olive oil

3 large onions, diced

6 celery stalks, diced

2½lb (1.1kg) lean pork, cut into ¾in (2cm) cubes

2 tsp paprika

14oz (400g) can cannellini beans, drained and rinsed

14oz (400g) can flageolet beans, drained and rinsed

14oz (400g) can lima beans, drained and rinsed

8 garlic cloves, finely chopped

⅔ cup dry white wine

1¼ cups hot vegetable stock, or more as needed

juice of 1 lemon

handful of fresh flat-leaf parsley, chopped

sea salt and freshly ground black pepper

1 Heat the oil in a large heavy-bottomed pot over medium heat, add the onions and celery, and cook, stirring, for 5 minutes, or until soft. Add the pork and cook, stirring occasionally, until no longer pink. Stir in the paprika, then add the beans and garlic and cook for 1 minute.

2 Stir in the wine and let bubble for 3 minutes while the alcohol evaporates. Add the stock, lemon juice, and parsley, season, bring to a boil, lower the heat, and simmer for 20 minutes.

3 Let cool completely, then transfer to a freezer-proof container (or 4 freezer bags—2 portions per bag), seal, and freeze for up to 3 months.

4 To serve, defrost in the refrigerator overnight, then transfer to a saucepan and heat for 15–20 minutes, until piping hot. Alternatively, microwave for 3 minutes on high, stir, and microwave for another 2 minutes, or until piping hot.

Braised turkey with vegetables

SERVES 8

2 tbsp olive oil

1 tbsp butter

4 turkey breast fillets (skin on)

sea salt and freshly ground black pepper

2 onions, sliced

2 carrots, sliced

1 fennel bulb, sliced

a few fresh tarragon leaves, coarsely chopped

2 cups hot chicken stock, or more as needed

handful of fresh flat-leaf parsley, finely chopped, to serve

zest of 1 lemon, grated, to serve

1 Preheat the oven to 350°F (180°C). Heat the oil and butter in a large frying pan, season the turkey with salt and pepper, then cook over medium heat, stirring occasionally, for 10 minutes, or until lightly browned all over. Transfer to a shallow casserole dish.

2 Add the vegetables and tarragon and season again. Pour stock almost to the top of the dish, but not enough to cover the ingredients. Cover with a lid and cook in the oven for 40 minutes, or until the turkey and vegetables are tender.

3 Let cool completely, then remove the turkey with a slotted spoon, discard the skin, and slice the meat. Transfer to a freezer-proof container, add the sauce and vegetables, and make sure the turkey is well-covered in the sauce—pour in a little cooled stock if it isn't. Seal and freeze for up to 3 months.

4 To serve, defrost overnight in the refrigerator, then transfer to a large pan and heat gently for 15–20 minutes, or until piping hot. Top with the parsley and lemon zest and serve with a pinch of freshly ground black pepper.

Lamb, spinach, and chickpea hotpot

PREP 25 MINS | COOK 20 MINS

SERVES 8

1½lb (675g) lean lamb, cut into
 ¾in (2cm) dice
2 tbsp all-purpose flour
1 tsp paprika
6 tbsp olive oil
2 large red onions, diced
6 garlic cloves, chopped
2 x 14oz (400g) cans chickpeas,
 drained and rinsed
¾ cup dry white wine
2 x 14oz (400g) cans diced tomatoes
sea salt and freshly ground
 black pepper
1¼lb (550g) baby leaf spinach

1 Put the lamb, flour, and paprika in a mixing bowl and combine well. Heat the oil in a large heavy-bottomed pot over medium heat, add the onions, and cook, stirring frequently, for 5 minutes, or until soft. Add the lamb and cook, stirring occasionally, for 5 minutes, or until evenly browned. Stir in the garlic and chickpeas and cook for 1 minute.

2 Pour in the wine and simmer for about 3 minutes while the alcohol evaporates. Add the tomatoes, bring to a boil, reduce the heat, and simmer for 15 minutes. Season with salt and pepper, stir in the spinach, and cook for 3 minutes.

3 Let cool completely, then transfer to a freezer-proof container (or 2 large freezer bags—4 portions per bag), seal, and freeze for up to 3 months.

4 To serve, defrost overnight in the refrigerator, transfer to a deep baking dish, cover, and put in a 350°F (180°C) preheated oven for 15 minutes. Or, microwave on high for 3 minutes, stir, and microwave for 3 minutes more, or until piping hot.

Game stew

PREP 45 MINS | COOK 1 HR

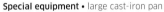

Special equipment • large cast-iron pan

SERVES 8

3lb (1.35kg) (boned weight) mixed
 game, such as pheasant, venison,
 and duck, cut into bite-sized pieces
all-purpose flour, to dust
sea salt and freshly ground
 black pepper
2 tbsp olive oil
2 tbsp brandy
2 onions, finely chopped
4 garlic cloves, finely chopped
4 celery stalks, finely diced
4 carrots, finely diced
1 bouquet garni
1¼lb (550g) cremini
 mushrooms, quartered
1½ cups dry white wine
1 tbsp red currant jelly
5 cups hot chicken stock

1 Preheat the oven to 350°F (180°C). Dust the meat lightly with flour, then season with salt and pepper. Heat half the oil in a large cast-iron pot, add the meat, and cook over medium heat, stirring, for 6–8 minutes, or until browned on all sides. Remove with a slotted spoon and set aside.

2 Add the brandy to the pot and stir to deglaze; add the rest of the oil and onions and cook over low heat for 6 minutes, or until soft. Stir in the garlic, celery, carrots, and bouquet garni, and cook over low heat, stirring often, for 8 minutes, or until tender.

3 Stir in the mushrooms, raise the heat, add the wine, and allow to bubble for 2 minutes while the alcohol evaporates. Stir in the red currant jelly, then pour in the stock. Cover with a lid and put in the oven for 1 hour, or until the meat is tender. Let cool completely, then transfer to a freezer-proof container, making sure the meat is submerged in the stock. Seal and freeze for up to 3 months.

4 To serve, defrost in the refrigerator overnight, then transfer to a large saucepan and heat gently for 15–20 minutes, or until piping hot. Serve with creamy mashed potatoes.

Beef and celery root casserole with stout and anchovies

PREP 30 MINS | COOK 1½ HRS | ❄

Special equipment • large cast-iron pan or flameproof casserole

SERVES 8

3 tbsp olive oil
2½lb (1.1kg) beef stew meat or pot roast, cut into bite-sized pieces
2 onions, finely chopped
handful of fresh thyme leaves
8 salted anchovies
1 large celery root, peeled and cut into bite-sized pieces
1 pint (600ml) bottle stout
4 cups hot vegetable stock
sea salt and freshly ground black pepper
5 medium potatoes, cut into chunky pieces

1 Preheat the oven to 350°F (180°C). Heat half the oil in a large cast-iron pot, add the meat, and cook over medium heat, stirring occasionally, for 10 minutes or until evenly browned. Remove with a slotted spoon and set aside. Heat the remaining oil in the pan, add the onions and thyme, and cook over low heat for 6-8 minutes or until soft.

2 Stir in the anchovies, then stir in the celery root and cook for 5-8 minutes. Add a little of the stout and stir to scrape up any bits that are stuck to the bottom of the pan. Add the remaining stout and the stock, season with salt and pepper, then return the meat to the pot, cover with a lid, and put in the oven for 1 hour.

3 Add the potatoes with a little hot water if the casserole looks dry. Cook for 30 minutes or until the potatoes are cooked and the beef is tender. Let cool completely, then transfer to a freezer-proof container, making sure the meat is covered in liquid. Seal and freeze for up to 3 months.

4 To serve, defrost in the refrigerator overnight, then transfer to a saucepan and heat very gently for 15-20 minutes or until piping hot. Alternatively, put in a casserole dish and reheat in an oven preheated to 350°F (180°C) for 30-40 minutes or until piping hot.

VARIATION Use 4 carrots, coarsely chopped, instead of–or as well as–the celery root.

Pork with fennel and mustard

PREP 20 MINS | COOK 20 MINS | ❄

SERVES 8

6 tbsp olive oil
2 large onions, sliced
3 fennel bulbs, sliced
2½lb (1.1kg) lean pork, cut into ¾in (2cm) cubes
8 garlic cloves, chopped
⅔ cup dry white wine
2 tbsp whole- or coarse-grain mustard
1 tsp paprika
large handful of flat-leaf parsley, coarsely chopped
1 tbsp chopped fresh sage leaves
1 tbsp chopped fresh rosemary leaves
2 tbsp all-purpose flour
3 cups milk
sea salt and freshly ground black pepper

1 Heat the oil in a large heavy-bottomed pot, add the onions and fennel, and cook for 5 minutes or until beginning to soften. Add the pork and cook, stirring occasionally, for 5 minutes or until no longer pink. Add the garlic and cook for 1 minute, then stir in the wine and mustard, increase the heat a little, and allow to bubble for 3 minutes while the alcohol evaporates.

2 Stir in the paprika, parsley, sage, and rosemary, then add the flour and mix well. Add a little of the milk, mix to an even paste, then stir in the rest of it. Season with salt and black pepper and cook for 5 minutes, adding a little more milk if it looks dry.

3 Let cool completely, then transfer to a freezer-proof container (or 4 freezer bags–2 portions per bag), seal, and freeze for up to 3 months.

4 To serve, defrost overnight in the refrigerator, then microwave for 2 minutes on high. Stir, then microwave for another 2 minutes or until piping hot.

Shepherd's pie

PREP 30 MINS · COOK 20 MINS

SERVES 8
2½lb (1.1kg) potatoes
2 tbsp butter
sea salt and freshly ground
    black pepper
6 tbsp olive oil
3 large onions, diced
4 large carrots, diced
2½lb (1.1kg) ground lamb
6 garlic cloves, chopped
2 tsp dried oregano
3 x 14oz (400g) cans diced tomatoes
9oz (250g) frozen peas

1 Put the potatoes in a pot of boiling water and cook for 15 minutes, until soft. Drain, then mash well. Add the butter and mash again until creamy. Season with salt and pepper, then set aside.

2 Meanwhile, heat the oil in a large heavy-bottomed saucepan over medium heat, add the onions and carrots, and cook for 5 minutes or until the onions are starting to soften. Add the lamb and cook, stirring constantly, for 10 minutes or until no longer pink. Add the garlic and oregano, cook for 1 minute, then stir in the tomatoes and bring to a boil.

3 Add the peas, season with salt and pepper, then return to a boil and lower the heat. Simmer for 20 minutes, stirring occasionally. Pour a 1½in (3.5cm) layer of lamb sauce into 2 large tin-foil dishes (4 portions per dish) and top with the mashed potatoes.

4 Let cool completely, then cover with lids, seal, and freeze for up to 6 months. To serve, remove the lids and bake from frozen in an oven preheated to 350°F (180°C) for 25 minutes or until brown on top and piping hot inside.

EVERYDAY

Coq au vin

PREP 15 MINS · COOK 40 MINS

SERVES 8
3 tbsp butter
3 tbsp olive oil
2 large onions, diced
10 garlic cloves, chopped
10oz (300g) side pork, chopped
2 tbsp fresh thyme leaves
1lb 10oz (750g) button mushrooms
4 cups good red wine
4 cups hot chicken stock
2½lb (1.1kg) skinless chicken pieces
sea salt and freshly ground
    black pepper

1 Heat the butter and oil in a large heavy-bottomed pot over medium heat, add the onions, and cook for 5 minutes or until starting to soften. Add the garlic and side pork (or bacon) and cook for 5 minutes, stirring frequently. Add the thyme and mushrooms and cook for 2 minutes.

2 Pour in the wine, increase the heat, and allow to bubble for 5 minutes while the alcohol evaporates. Pour in the stock, bring to a boil, then add the chicken pieces and season with salt and pepper. Combine well, bring to a boil again, then lower the heat and simmer for 25 minutes.

3 Let cool completely, then transfer to a freezer-proof container (or 2 large freezer bags–4 portions per bag), seal, and freeze for up to 3 months.

4 To serve, defrost overnight in the refrigerator, then transfer to a casserole dish, cover, and cook in an oven preheated to 350°F (180°C) for 25 minutes or until piping hot.

Beef and tomato lasagna

PREP 30 MINS COOK 20 MINS

SERVES 8

6 tbsp olive oil
3 large onions, finely diced
1½lb (675g) lean ground beef
8 garlic cloves, chopped
3 tbsp tomato paste or purée
3 x 14oz (400g) cans diced tomatoes
2 tsp dried oregano
4 bay leaves
sea salt and freshly ground pepper
3 tsp pesto
3 tbsp butter
3 heaping tbsp all-purpose flour
3½ cups milk
10oz (300g) mozzarella, grated
1lb (450g) oven-ready lasagna
    noodles

1 Heat the oil in a large heavy-bottomed saucepan over medium heat, add the onions, and cook, stirring occasionally, for 5 minutes or until starting to soften. Add the beef and cook, stirring constantly, for 5 minutes, or until no longer pink. Add the garlic, cook for 1 minute, then stir in the tomato paste. Add the tomatoes, oregano, and bay leaves, bring to a boil, then reduce the heat and simmer for 20 minutes. Season with salt and pepper, remove from the heat, then stir in the pesto and set aside.

2 Melt the butter in a saucepan over low heat, add the flour, and stir well. Add a little of the milk, mix well, then add ⅔ cup more milk, stirring vigorously until smooth. Add the rest of the milk, combine well, then bring to a boil, stirring constantly. Reduce the heat and simmer for 2 minutes to ensure the flour is cooked. Remove from heat, stir in the mozzarella, then season with salt and pepper.

3 Pour ½in (1cm) of the beef sauce in the bottom of a large freezer-proof baking pan (or 2 medium-sized ones). Cover with a layer of lasagna noodles, then add ½in (1cm) more beef sauce, followed by a small amount of the cheese sauce and another layer of lasagna. Repeat until all the meat sauce has been used up. Make sure you have enough cheese sauce for an even ¼in (5mm) layer on the top. Let cool completely, then double-wrap in plastic wrap and freeze for up to 3 months.

4 To serve, remove the plastic wrap and place the dish straight from the freezer to an oven preheated to 350°F (180°C) for 35–40 minutes or until browned on top and piping hot inside.

Chicken and cornmeal cobbler

PREP 20 MINS COOK 1¾ HRS

Special equipment • large shallow cast-iron pan or flameproof casserole
• 1½in (4cm) cutter

SERVES 8

2 tbsp olive oil
6 skinless boneless chicken breasts,
    cut into bite-sized pieces
sea salt and freshly ground pepper
2 red onions, finely sliced
4 celery stalks, coarsely chopped
2 cups red wine
5 carrots, coarsely chopped
1½ pints (900ml) hot vegetable stock
1 cup + 2 tbsp all-purpose flour, plus a
    little extra to dust
1¼ cups cornmeal
4 tbsp butter
handful of fresh flat-leaf parsley,
    finely chopped
splash of milk
1 egg yolk, lightly beaten

1 Heat half the oil in a large shallow cast-iron pan or flameproof casserole, season the chicken with salt and pepper, then cook over medium heat, turning occasionally, for 10 minutes, or until lightly golden all over. Remove with a slotted spoon and set aside.

2 Preheat the oven to 350°F (180°C). Heat the remaining oil in the pan, then add the onions and cook over low heat for 6–8 minutes, or until soft. Add the celery and cook for 5 minutes, or until soft. Pour in the wine, increase the heat, and allow to boil for a couple of minutes while the alcohol evaporates. Add the carrots, return the chicken to the pan, then season well with salt and pepper. Pour in the stock and cook, uncovered, over low heat, stirring occasionally, for 1 hour, or until all the ingredients are tender. Top with a little hot water if it begins to look dry.

3 Meanwhile, put the flour, cornmeal, and a pinch of salt in a large mixing bowl. Add the butter and rub it in with your fingertips until you have a bread crumb texture. Stir in the parsley, then add the milk a little at a time until the dough comes together. Form into a ball and put in the refrigerator to rest for 20 minutes. Flatten out the chilled dough on a floured surface, then roll it out with a rolling pin. Cut out about 18 rounds using the cutter, then add to the casserole, brushing them with the egg yolk before you move the pot into the oven to cook for another 30 minutes.

4 Leave to cool completely, then double-wrap the pan in plastic wrap, making sure the meat is all covered, and freeze for up to 3 months. To serve, defrost overnight in the refrigerator. Preheat the oven to 350°F (180°C) and cook for 30–40 minutes until piping hot.

VARIATION Add 2 teaspoons of creamed horseradish to the cornmeal topping, or the same amount of wholegrain mustard.

Eggplant parmesan

PREP 20 MINS · COOK 20 MINS

Special equipment • large ovenproof freezer-proof dish

SERVES 8

6 tbsp olive oil
8 garlic cloves, finely sliced
2 x 28oz (800g) cans diced tomatoes
2 tbsp tomato paste or purée
2 tsp dried oregano
1 tsp fresh thyme leaves
sea salt and freshly ground
   black pepper
3 eggplants, cut into ½in (1cm) slices
10oz (300g) Parmesan, grated
14oz (400g) mozzarella, torn
   into pieces

1 Heat 4 tbsp of the oil in a large heavy-bottomed saucepan over low heat, add the garlic, and cook for 30 seconds. Add the chopped tomatoes, tomato paste, oregano, and thyme and bring gently to a boil. Season with salt and pepper, then remove from the heat.

2 Put the eggplant slices in a bowl and brush with the rest of the oil. Heat a nonstick frying pan over medium heat, then cook in batches for 3 minutes on each side until golden brown. When each piece is done, remove with a slotted spoon and set aside.

3 Pour a ½in (1cm) layer of tomato sauce in the bottom of a large freezer-proof baking pan (or 2 medium-sized ones) and cover with eggplant slices. Sprinkle with a handful of Parmesan, then repeat the process until all of the ingredients are used up (you should get 3-4 layers), making sure there is a ½in (1cm) layer of tomato sauce on top. Cover with the mozzarella.

4 Let cool completely, then double-wrap with plastic wrap and freeze for up to 3 months. To serve, defrost overnight in the refrigerator, then reheat in an oven preheated to 350°F (180°C) for 25 minutes or until browned on top and piping hot in the center. Serve with a crisp green salad.

VARIATION Put an extra layer of torn mozzarella pieces in the middle of each baking pan.

Vegetarian leek and mushroom lasagna

PREP 25 MINS · COOK 20 MINS

Special equipment • large ovenproof freezer-proof dish

SERVES 8

½ cup olive oil
4 leeks, cut into ¼in (5mm) slices
1¼lb (550g) cremini mushrooms,
   sliced and 9oz (250g) cremini
   mushrooms, grated
2-3 red chiles, seeded and finely
   chopped
6 garlic cloves, chopped
⅔ cup dry white wine
small handful of fresh thyme leaves
2 tbsp all-purpose flour
3 cups milk
12oz (350g) medium-sharp Cheddar
   cheese, grated
6 tomatoes, coarsely chopped
sea salt and freshly ground
   black pepper
1lb (450g) oven-ready lasagna noodles
2 tomatoes, sliced

1 Heat the oil in a large heavy-bottomed saucepan, add the leeks, and sauté over low heat for 5 minutes or until starting to soften. Stir in the mushrooms and cook, stirring frequently, for 5 minutes or until they release their juices. Add the chiles and garlic and cook for 1 minute. Pour in the wine, increase the heat, and allow to bubble for 3 minutes while the alcohol evaporates.

2 Stir in the thyme, then add the flour and mix well. Add a little of the milk, mix well, then add the rest of the milk and cook for 5 minutes, stirring frequently. Add almost all the cheese (reserve some for the topping), remove from the heat, and combine well. Add the coarsely chopped tomatoes and season with salt and pepper.

3 Put a ½in (1cm) layer of the mixture in the bottom of a large freezer-proof baking dish, then cover evenly with a layer of the lasagna noodles. Pour in another layer of sauce and cover with lasagna noodles. Repeat the process until all the sauce is used up—you need to finish with a layer of sauce. Top with the remaining cheese and the sliced tomatoes.

4 Let cool completely, then double-wrap the dish in plastic wrap and freeze for up to 3 months. To serve, remove the plastic wrap and place the dish straight from the freezer to an oven preheated to 350°F (180°C) for 30-40 minutes or until browned on top and piping hot inside.

STORE CUPBOARD

Meal solutions using dried, canned, bottled, and frozen foods.

STORE CUPBOARD

All you need is a well-stocked pantry to form the basis of a good meal. It's the bones of your cooking and will transform any dish. With a few added fresh ingredients, meal-times shouldn't be a chore. And when you don't have time to go shopping, it means there is always something in the cupboard to make a quick supper with.

Store cupboard essentials A list of dry and preserved goods to always have on hand for last-minute meals.

| HERBS, SPICES | PASTA, RICE, NOODLES | PULSES, GRAINS, NUTS, FRUITS | OILS, CONDIMENTS, SAUCES | JARS, CANS, AND POWDERS |

HERBS, SPICES

PAPRIKA
Best for pork and chicken dishes.
Store for 6 months.

DRIED HERBS
Oregano, thyme, mixed dried herbs, bay leaves.
Best for chicken, lamb, and fish dishes, stews, and casseroles.
Store for 6 months.

GROUND CORIANDER AND SEEDS
Best for curries.
Store for 6 months.

CRUSHED RED PEPPER FLAKES
Best for adding spice and heat to Indian, Thai, and Mediterranean dishes.
Store for 6 months.

GROUND CUMIN AND SEEDS
Best for adding to a lamb stew or marinade.
Store for 6 months.

GROUND CINNAMON AND STICKS
Best for chicken and lamb stews.
Store for 6 months.

CURRY POWDER
Best for chicken, lamb, and beef.
Store for 6 months.

CAYENNE PEPPER
Best for chicken and meat dishes.
Store for 6 months.

PASTA, RICE, NOODLES

PASTA
For a variety of shapes and sizes, and sauce pairings, see p158.
Best for sauces and bakes.
Store for 1 year.

RICE
Basmati, brown, long grain, risotto (arborio or carnaroli), paella.
Best for pilaf, kedgeree, salads, and serving as an accompaniment to meat and fish.
Store for 6 months.

NOODLES
Rice and egg noodles, available in a selection of types and thicknesses. You can buy straight-to-wok noodles that require no cooking, just heating through.
Best for Asian-style dishes, soups, salads, or stir-fries.
Store for 6 months.

PULSES, GRAINS, NUTS, FRUITS

PULSES
Canned and dried Puy lentils, red lentils, green lentils, and yellow split peas. A selection of canned and dried chickpeas, flageolet beans, kidney beans, lima beans, and cannellini beans.
Best for stews, salads, bakes, casseroles, dips, and soups.
Store for 1 year.

GRAINS
Farro, pearl barley, couscous, bulgur wheat, and polenta.
Best for salads and hotpots.
Store for 1 year.

NUTS AND SEEDS
A selection of whole peanuts, walnuts, and cashews, chopped and ground almonds, pine nuts, and dried whole chestnuts. Sesame seeds, sunflower seeds, and pumpkin seeds.
Best for toppings, and in salads and stir-frys.
Store for 6 months.

DRIED FRUIT
A selection of raisins and golden raisins, dates, figs, and apricots.
Best for salads and stews.
Store for 6 months.

OILS, CONDIMENTS, SAUCES

OILS
Olive, extra virgin olive, sunflower, peanut, and sesame oil.
Best for salads, dressings, marinades, stir-frys, pan frying, and baking.
Store for 6 months.

VINEGARS
Red wine, white wine, rice wine, balsamic, and sherry vinegar.
Best for salads, dressings, and marinades.
Store for 1 year.

MUSTARDS
English, Dijon, and coarse-grain.
Best for cooking and dressing.
Store for 1 year.

PESTO AND PASTES
Harissa, tomato paste, and Thai curry paste.
Best for curries, stirring into casseroles, or pesto for adding to pasta.
Store for 6 months.

SAUCES
Soy sauce, Worcestershire sauce, fish, and oyster sauce.
Best for stir-fries, stews, and casseroles.
Store for 1 year.

SALT AND PEPPER
Sea salt and whole peppercorns. For the best flavor, grind black peppercorns in a peppermill rather than buying them ground.
Best for seasoning hot and cold food.
Store for 1 year.

JARS, CANS, AND POWDERS

OLIVES AND CAPERS
Black and green olives, and small jarred salted capers.
Best for pasta, salads, and dips.
Store for 1 year.

TOMATOES
Canned whole, and chopped. Jarred sun-dried tomatoes.
Best for stews, casseroles, and pasta sauces.
Store for 1 year.

SWEET CORN
Best for soups or stews.
Store for 1 year.

TUNA AND SALMON
Tuna and salmon, canned, in oil or brine.
Best for pasta, salads, fish cakes, and bakes.
Store for 1 year.

ANCHOVIES
Jarred or canned in olive oil or salt.
Best for pasta, salads, casseroles, and stews.
Store for 1 year.

COCONUT MILK
Best for Thai curries.
Store for 1 year.

STOCK CUBES (BOUILLON)
Chicken, beef, or vegetable.
Best for gravies, sauces, soups, and stews.
Store for 1 year.

Refrigerator and freezer staples

Keep both well-stocked with these must-haves.

REFRIGERATOR

FREEZER

BUTTER AND HARD CHEESE

Butter enriches all hot dishes, but you can use olive oil for a healthy alternative. Cheese adds instant protein to a quick dish.
Best for sauces, bakes, baking, and sandwiches.
Store for 1 month (or until its use-by date), or freeze for up to 3 months.

MILK

1% low fat is the most popular, as it contains less than half the fat content of whole.
Best for sauces, batters, and puddings.
Store for 7 days (or until its use-by date), or freeze for 1 month.

EGGS

Keep them in the refrigerator, unless you plan to use them within a couple of days of purchase.
Best for omelets, salads, and sandwiches.
Store for 3 weeks (or until their use-by date).

VEGETABLES

You can buy quite a few vegetables pre-frozen, but peas and fava beans are the only vegetables that withstand the process without it impairing their flavor. They make a great standby.
Best for instant soups, adding to fish or meat pies, casseroles, or as a meal accompaninent.
Store for 6 months.

MEAT

Beef, and lamb or pork sausages.
Best for chilli and ragù, hot dogs, sausages, or sandwiches.
Store for 6 months.

FISH AND SEAFOOD

Fish fillets (such as haddock, pollack, and salmon) and prawns or shrimp (shell on or off).
Best for fish pie and barbecues.
Store for 3 months.

5 easy store cupboard meals
Use store cupboard staples to make a complete meal if fresh foods are not available, or if you have not had time to shop.

1 Tuna and rice salad

Mix 5½oz (150g) of cooked and cooled **basmati rice** with a 7oz (200g) **can of tuna**, drained, and a 14oz (400g) **can cannellini beans**, drained. Add 1 tablespoon of **olive oil** and 1 tablespoon of **white wine vinegar** and toss together with a pinch of **crushed red pepper flakes**. Season and serve on its own, or as part of a salad.

2 Sicilian-style spaghetti

Process a handful of **sun-dried tomatoes** in a food processor with a little **olive oil** and a handful of **pine nuts** until chopped. Heat 1 tablespoon of olive oil in a pan, add the tomato mixture, and cook for a few seconds, then stir in 6 **salted anchovies**, and cook until they begin to disintegrate. Stir in a handful of **golden raisins** and 1 tablespoon of **capers**. Toss with 6oz (175g) of hot cooked **spaghetti**.

3 Salmon stir-fry

Heat 1 tablespoon of **sesame oil** in a frying pan or wok and add 6oz (175g) straight-to-wok **medium rice noodles**. Toss, then add a splash of **soy sauce** and **Asian fish sauce**, and a **can of salmon**, drained and flaked, and cook for few minutes. Season, add a handful of chopped **roasted peanuts**, and serve.

4 Lentil stew

Cook 4½oz (125g) of **puy lentils** in 3 cups of hot **chicken stock** and a pinch of **ground cumin** for about 30 minutes or until cooked and softened. Add a 14oz (400g) **can of chickpeas**, drained, and season with **sea salt** and **pepper**. Simmer gently for 10 minutes, and add a splash of **chili oil** to taste.

5 Couscous salad

Put 5½oz (150g) of **couscous** into a bowl and add just enough hot **vegetable stock** to cover the couscous. Set aside for 5 minutes, then season and fluff up with a fork. Combine 2 tablespoons of **extra virgin olive oil** with 1 tablespoon of **Dijon mustard** and a pinch of **paprika**, and add to the couscous. Stir in a handful of **sun-dried tomatoes**, chopped, 1 teaspoon of **capers**, and a handful of **mixed pitted olives**, halved. Serve with salad and hot pita bread.

EVERYDAY

Wild rice with sun-dried tomatoes and cashews.
For recipe, see page 276.

store cupboard versus fresh

Frozen food can sometimes be more nutritious than fresh, particularly when fresh vegetables are out of season and have clocked up hundreds of air miles to reach your supermarket. Vegetables for the freezer are frozen soon after being picked, so the nutrient loss is minimal (provided you don't cook them for too long).

Canned foods are without doubt the ultimate in convenience food, and are an economical source of nutrients, needing no preparation at all. They are, however, often canned with lots of added sugar or salt, so check the label before you buy.

Noodle broth with dried mushrooms

Soaking • 20 minutes

SERVES 4

scant 1oz (25g) package mixed dried
    mushrooms (shiitake, oyster,
    porcini), rinsed
1 tbsp sesame oil or sunflower oil
2in (5cm) piece of fresh ginger, thinly
    sliced and cut into thin strips
2 x 5½oz (150g) packets of fresh thick
    or medium udon noodles
4 cups hot vegetable stock
2 tbsp soy sauce
2 tbsp Asian fish sauce, such as *nam pla*
salt and freshly ground black pepper
splash of hot chili oil, to taste

1 Put the dried mushrooms in a
heatproof bowl and cover with about
1¼ cups boiling water. Leave to soak
for 20-30 minutes.

2 Heat the oil in a large sauté pan
over low heat. Add the ginger and
cook for 2-3 minutes until fragrant.
Add the noodles and stir for a couple
of minutes more to break them up.

3 Pour in the hot stock, soy sauce,
and fish sauce, and bring to a boil.

4 Meanwhile, strain the mushrooms
through a fine sieve, reserving the
liquid. Add the mushrooms to the pan
and reduce the heat to low. Strain the
reserved soaking liquid through a fine
sieve again to remove any grit and
pour the strained liquid into the pan.
Simmer gently for 20-30 minutes.
Taste and season with salt and pepper.
Add a splash of chili oil
to taste and serve hot.

VARIATION
Sprinkle in a teaspoon of toasted
sesame seeds, if you like.

COOK'S NOTES

The flavors of this soup develop
more if it is made a few hours
ahead, then simply reheated
to serve.

Lebanese-flavored lentils

mushy. Keep an eye on the pan and
add more hot water if the lentils
appear dry.

SERVES 4

1 tbsp olive oil
1 onion, finely chopped
1 tsp cumin seeds
1 tsp ground cinnamon
1 tsp ground allspice
sea salt and freshly ground
    black pepper
1½ cups dried Puy lentils, picked over
    and rinsed well
4 cups hot vegetable stock
½ cup pine nuts
½ cup dried apricots, coarsely chopped

1 Heat the oil in a large deep frying
pan over low heat. Add the onion and
cook gently for about 5 minutes until
soft and translucent. Stir in the cumin
seeds, cinnamon, and allspice, and
season well with salt and pepper.

2 Stir in the lentils until thoroughly
mixed. Pour in the hot stock. Bring
to a boil, then reduce the heat to low.
Simmer gently for 30-40 minutes
until the lentils are tender but not

3 Meanwhile, toast the pine nuts in
a small dry frying pan over low heat
for about 5 minutes until they begin
to turn golden; watch carefully, as
they can burn very quickly. Stir the
pine nuts into the lentils along with
the apricots. Taste and season again
if needed. Serve hot.

VARIATION
Use pistachios or almonds
instead of the pine nuts.

COOK'S NOTES

Always rinse dried lentils
thoroughly before using. They
can be muddy and gritty.

Pearl barley and borlotti bean one-pot

1 tbsp olive oil
1 onion, finely chopped
sea salt and freshly ground black
 pepper
½ cup dry red wine
1½ cups pearl barley
1 x 15oz (425g) can borlotti
 beans, drained and rinsed
1 x 14oz (400g) can diced tomatoes,
 with juices
4 cups hot vegetable stock
hot chili oil, to serve (optional)

1 Heat the oil in a large heavy saucepan over low heat. Add the onion and a pinch of salt and cook gently for 5 minutes until soft. Increase the heat, pour in the wine, and bubble for about 5 minutes.

2 Reduce the heat to low, add the pearl barley, and stir well until it has absorbed all the liquid. Stir in the beans, tomatoes, and hot stock. Return to a boil and continue boiling for 5 minutes.

3 Reduce the heat to low once again, season well with salt and pepper, and gently simmer for 25–40 minutes until the pearl barley is cooked and all the stock has been absorbed. If the mixture starts to dry out, add a little hot water.

4 Drizzle with a splash of chili oil and serve hot, either on its own or with some fresh crusty bread.

VARIATION
This is delicious cooked with farro instead of pearl barley. You can find farro in health food stores, Italian delis, or in some supermarkets.

EVERYDAY

Thai green curry

SERVES 4
1 tbsp sunflower or vegetable oil
1 onion, finely diced
1–2 tbsp bottled Thai green curry
 paste (depending on taste)
1 x 14oz (400g) can unsweetened
 coconut milk, well shaken
2 tbsp Asian fish sauce, such
 as *nam pla*
1–2 tsp palm sugar, demerara (raw)
 sugar, or brown sugar
2–3 kaffir lime leaves (optional)
salt and freshly ground black pepper
1 x 8oz (225g) can bamboo shoots,
 rinsed and drained
1 x 8oz (225g) small bay shrimp,
 rinsed and drained, if canned

1 Heat the oil in a wok or large deep frying pan over medium-low heat. Add the onion and cook for about 5 minutes until soft and translucent. Stir in the curry paste and cook for another 2–3 minutes until fragrant.

2 Pour in the coconut milk, then fill the empty can with water and add this to the wok. Bring to a boil, reduce the heat slightly, and add the fish sauce, sugar, and lime leaves (if using). Season with salt and pepper.

3 Simmer over low heat for about 15 minutes, then stir in the bamboo shoots and shrimp and cook until warmed through. Taste and adjust the seasonings if needed. Serve hot.

VARIATION
Use chicken or tofu instead of shrimp.

COOK'S NOTES

A good Thai curry requires a good curry paste as its base. Unless you are going to make your own, try to buy a good-quality one that has been made in Thailand.

Aduki bean stew

PREP 10 MINS · COOK 30 MINS

SERVES 4

1 tbsp olive oil
1 onion, finely chopped
sea salt and freshly ground
    black pepper
2 garlic cloves, finely chopped
½–1 tsp cayenne pepper (depending
    on how hot you like it)
1 x 15oz (425g) can aduki beans,
    drained and rinsed
1 x 14oz (400g) can diced tomatoes,
    with juices
2 cups hot vegetable stock
about 12 black olives, such as
    Kalamata, pitted

1 Heat the olive oil in a saucepan over low heat. Add the onion and a pinch of sea salt and cook gently for 5 minutes until soft. Stir in the garlic and cayenne.

2 Add the beans and tomatoes, including any juices, then pour in the stock. Bring to a boil, then reduce the heat to low. Simmer for 15–20 minutes, stirring in the olives during the last 5 minutes of cooking. If the stew dries out, add a little hot water.

3 Serve with a crisp salad, new potatoes, or rice.

VARIATION
This is delicious with a couple of chopped preserved lemons stirred in along with the olives. Halve the lemons, scoop out and discard the flesh, and then chop the remainder.

Mixed bean medley

PREP 10 MINS · COOK 40 MINS

SERVES 4

1 tbsp olive oil
1 onion, finely chopped
sea salt and freshly ground
    black pepper
2 garlic cloves, finely chopped
4 thick bacon slices, cut crosswise into
    ¼in (.6cm) strips, or 4½oz (125g)
    pancetta, cut into small cubes
pinch of crushed red pepper flakes
2 tsp dried oregano
1 x 15oz (425g) can mixed beans,
    drained and rinsed
1¾ cups pale ale
3¾ cups hot vegetable stock

1 Heat the oil in a large deep-sided frying pan over low heat. Add the onion and a pinch of salt and cook gently for about 5 minutes. Stir in the garlic, and cook for about 30 seconds.

2 Increase the heat slightly, and add the bacon or pancetta. Cook for about 5 minutes until it begins to turn golden. Drain off excess fat, if needed. Sprinkle in the pepper flakes and oregano and stir in the beans.

3 Pour in the ale, bring to a boil, and cook over high heat for 5 minutes. Add the stock, reduce the heat slightly, and simmer gently for 20–25 minutes, stirring occasionally, until the mixture thickens. Serve hot with crusty bread to mop up the flavorful gravy.

VARIATION
Use any combination of your favorite cooked beans or lentils.

COOK'S NOTES
If the mixture begins to dry out a little, add some water—but don't add too much, because it will dilute the flavor.

Hot and sour coconut broth

PREP 10 MINS · COOK 30 MINS

SERVES 4

5 cups hot chicken stock

1 x 14oz (400g) can unsweetened
   coconut milk, well shaken

4 tbsp Asian fish sauce, such as *nam pla*

1 tbsp soy sauce

2–3 tsp Asian tom yum paste

2 tsp palm sugar, demerara (raw)
   sugar, or brown sugar

2 kaffir lime leaves (optional)

scant 1oz (25g) mixed dried mushrooms
   (such as shiitake, oyster, and porcini),
   rinsed well, coarsely chopped

sea salt

1 Bring the chicken stock to a boil in
a large saucepan. Stir in the coconut
milk and continue boiling for about
5 minutes.

2 Reduce the heat to a simmer, then
add the fish sauce, soy sauce, tom
yum paste, sugar, lime leaves, and
mushrooms. Continue to simmer
gently over low heat for about
20 minutes until the mushrooms
are tender.

3 Taste and season with salt if
needed, or add a little more sugar,
fish sauce, or soy sauce. Serve hot
in small bowls.

Curried sweet corn fritters

PREP 10 MINS · COOK 30 MINS · ❄

SERVES 4

1 cup all-purpose flour

sea salt and freshly ground
   black pepper

2 large eggs

1¼ cups whole milk

2 tsp curry powder,
   preferably Madras

¼ cup semolina flour

1 x 15oz (425g) can corn kernels,
   drained

¼ to ⅓ cup vegetable oil for frying

1 Sift the flour into a bowl with
a pinch of salt. Make a well in the
center, break the eggs into it, then
pour in a little of the milk. Using
a wooden spoon, stir the egg,
incorporating the flour little by
little and adding the remaining
milk as you go.

2 Switch to a whisk and beat until
there are no lumps. Add the curry
powder, semolina, and corn, and
season well with salt and pepper.
Stir to blend well.

3 To cook the fritters, heat ½–1 tbsp
vegetable oil in a nonstick frying pan
over medium heat. Carefully drop in
1 large tablespoon of the batter. Make
two fritters at a time if the pan is big
enough, but do not overcrowd. Fry for
about 2 minutes until the bottom is
golden and crisp. Flip over using a
spatula and cook the other side for
2 minutes. You will need to stir the
batter each time before using, and
add more oil to the pan as you go.

4 Drain the fritters briefly on paper
towels and serve piping hot from
the pan, either on their own or with
a green salad on the side.

 VARIATION
Substitute ground cumin for
the curry powder, or use
cayenne pepper or paprika.

COOK'S NOTES

The batter for these is best used
right away, and the fritters are
best eaten instantly!

Wild rice with sun-dried tomatoes and cashews

PREP 10 MINS | COOK 30 MINS

Soaking • 15 minutes

SERVES 4–6

12 dry-packed sun-dried tomatoes
1 tbsp olive oil
1 onion, finely chopped
sea salt and freshly ground
   black pepper
1⅔ cups long-grain and
   wild rice blend
1 tsp turmeric
4 cups hot vegetable stock
1 cup raw cashews

1 Put the sun-dried tomatoes in a heatproof bowl. Add just enough hot water to cover and leave to soak for about 15 minutes. Drain, chop coarsely, and set aside

2 Meanwhile, heat the oil in a large heavy sauté pan·over low heat. Add the onion and a pinch of salt and cook gently for about 5 minutes until soft. Stir in the rice and turmeric until the grains are well coated.

3 Pour in the stock and increase the heat a little. Season with salt and pepper. Cook for about 5 minutes, allowing the mixture to come to a boil, then stir. Reduce the heat slightly, cover, and simmer gently for 20–30 minutes until all the stock has been absorbed and the rice is cooked. If the rice is drying out too much while cooking, add a little more hot vegetable stock or hot water.

4 Stir in the sun-dried tomatoes, then toast the cashews in a dry frying pan over low heat for 5 minutes until lightly golden. Add to the rice mixture, and stir through. Taste and season if needed. Serve hot.

VARIATION

Vary the type of nuts to your preference and, if you use sun-dried tomatoes packed in oil, add a little of the oil for extra flavor.

Chickpea curry with cardamom

PREP 10 MINS | COOK 30 MINS

SERVES 4

1 tbsp vegetable oil
1 onion, finely chopped
sea salt and freshly ground
   black pepper
1 tsp cumin seeds
1 tsp turmeric
1 tsp ground coriander
6 green cardamom pods,
   lightly crushed
1 x 15½oz (440g) can chickpeas,
   drained and rinsed
1 x 14oz (400g) can diced tomatoes,
   with juices
1–2 tsp garam masala
1 tsp hot chili powder, or more to taste

1 Heat the oil in a large heavy saucepan over low heat. Add the onion and a pinch of salt and cook gently for about 5 minutes until soft. Stir in the cumin seeds, turmeric, coriander, and cardamom, and continue cooking for about 5 minutes until fragrant.

2 Add the chickpeas to the pan and stir well, crushing them very slightly with the back of a wooden spoon. Stir in the tomatoes, including any juices, then fill the empty can with water and add this also. Sprinkle in the garam masala and chili powder and bring to a boil. Reduce the heat to low and simmer gently for about 20 minutes until the sauce begins to thicken. Season with salt and pepper.

3 Serve hot with naan bread and basmati rice.

Tuna and white beans with olives

PREP 10 MINS

SERVES 4

1 x 14oz (400g) can butter
    beans, drained
1 x 14oz (400g) can cannellini or
    other white beans, drained
2 x 7oz (200g) cans tuna in olive
    oil, drained
2 tbsp white wine vinegar
sea salt and freshly ground
    black pepper
1 tsp whole-grain mustard
½ tsp mild paprika
about 12 black olives, such as
    Kalamata, pitted and halved
2 tsp capers, drained

1 Combine all the beans and the tuna
in a large bowl. Add the vinegar, taste,
and season well with salt and pepper.

2 Stir in the mustard, paprika, olives,
and capers. Taste and season again
if needed. Serve immediately, or
refrigerate for a couple of hours until
needed. If making ahead, return to
room temperature before serving.

VARIATION

Use flageolet beans instead
of cannellini if you prefer—
these have a much softer
texture.

Tomato bulgur wheat with capers and olives

PREP 15 MINS · **COOK 15 MINS**

SERVES 4

2 cups bulgur wheat
sea salt and freshly ground
    black pepper
⅔–1¼ cups tomato juice
1 tbsp capers, drained
12 black olives, such as kalamata,
    pitted and halved
12 green olives, pitted and halved

1 Pour the bulgur wheat into a large
heatproof bowl, then pour in just
enough boiling water to cover—about
1¼ cups. Let stand for 15 minutes.

2 Season generously with salt and
pepper and stir well with a fork to
fluff up the grains. Add the tomato
juice, a little at a time, until the bulgur
has absorbed all the juice. Let stand
for a few minutes between each
addition—the bulgur will absorb
quite a lot of moisture.

3 Now add the capers and olives,
taste, and season again if needed.
Serve with a crisp green salad and
some warm pita bread.

COOK'S NOTES

*Capers are an invaluable pantry
ingredient because they perk
up so many dishes. Once you
have opened a jar, however,
make sure that you keep it in
the refrigerator.*

EVERYDAY

EVERYDAY

Couscous stuffing with harissa and walnuts

PREP 15 MINS COOK 15 MINS

SERVES 4

1½ cups couscous
1½ cups hot vegetable stock
sea salt and freshly ground
    black pepper
2 tsp harissa sauce (Middle Eastern
    chili paste)
handful of dark raisins
½ cup walnut halves and pieces
4 preserved lemons

1 Pour the couscous into a heatproof bowl, pour in the stock, and leave to stand for 10 minutes. Stir with a fork to fluff up the grains.

2 Season well with salt and pepper, then stir in the harissa, raisins, and walnuts. Halve the preserved lemons, scoop out and discard the flesh, and chop the remainder. Stir into the couscous.

COOK'S NOTES

Use as a stuffing for turkey, chicken, or oily fish, such as mackerel. Harissa is fairly hot; if you don't want any heat, substitute with the same quantity of tomato purée.

Vegetarian moussaka

PREP 15 MINS COOK 30 MINS

SERVES 4

1 tbsp olive oil
1 onion, finely chopped
sea salt and freshly ground
    black pepper
1 tsp dried mint leaves
3 tsp dried oregano
1 x 15oz (425g) can aduki beans,
    drained and rinsed
1 x 28oz (800g) can crushed tomatoes
    or tomato purée
¾ cup pine nuts
freshly ground black pepper
9oz (250g) Greek-style plain yogurt
1 large egg

1 Preheat the oven to 400°F (200°C). Heat the oil in a saucepan over low heat. Add the onion and a pinch of sea salt and cook gently for about 5 minutes until soft. Stir in the mint and 1 teaspoon of the dried oregano.

2 Add the beans, tomatoes, and pine nuts, and bring to a boil. Reduce the heat to low and simmer gently for 15–20 minutes until thickened. Season well with salt and pepper.

3 Spoon the bean mixture into a baking dish. Mix together the yogurt, egg, and remaining oregano. Spoon evenly over the top of the bean mixture. Bake for 15–20 minutes until the top is golden, puffed, and set. Serve hot with a crisp green salad.

Fried polenta with tomato sauce

PREP 10 MINS **COOK** 25 MINS

SERVES 2

3–4 tbsp olive oil
1 onion, finely chopped
sea salt and freshly ground
 black pepper
1 tsp dried oregano
1 tsp crushed red pepper flakes
1 x 14oz (400g) can diced tomatoes,
 with juices
half of a 35oz (975g) package
 precooked Italian-style polenta,
 cut into rounds ¼in (.6cm) thick

1 Heat 1 tablespoon of the oil in a large deep-sided frying pan over low heat. Add the onion and a pinch of salt and cook gently for 5 minutes until soft.

2 Sprinkle in the oregano and pepper flakes, stir in the tomatoes, including any juices, and simmer gently for about 20 minutes. Season with salt and pepper.

3 Meanwhile, heat 1 tablespoon of oil at a time in a large nonstick frying pan over high heat. Working in batches, cook the polenta slices for 5 minutes on each side until crisp and golden. Remove from the pan with a spatula, drain on paper towels, and keep warm. Repeat until all the polenta has been cooked.

4 To serve, divide the crispy polenta rounds between 2 warm serving plates and top with the spicy tomato sauce. Serve an arugula salad on the side with balsamic vinaigrette.

COOK'S NOTES

This dish also works well as a starter for 4 people. Make the sauce ahead, to save time.

Store cupboard pasta

PREP 10 MINS **COOK** 15 MINS

SERVES 4

12oz (350g) dried penne or pasta of
 your choice
1 tbsp olive oil
3 tsp capers, rinsed and gently
 squeezed dry
handful of black olives, pitted
6 sun-dried tomatoes in oil, drained
 and chopped (reserve a little of the
 oil, optional)
sea salt and freshly ground
 black pepper

1 Cook the pasta as the package directs, until it is tender yet still firm to the bite. Drain, reserving a small amount of the cooking water. Return the pasta to the pot and toss together with the reserved cooking water.

2 Meanwhile, in another pan, heat the olive oil over low heat. Add the capers, olives, and sun-dried tomatoes, and cook gently for about 5 minutes, mashing them slightly with the back of a fork.

3 Scrape the mixture into the cooked pasta, and toss until evenly mixed. Add a little of the reserved oil from the sun-dried tomatoes. Season well with salt and pepper, and serve at once.

Bean burgers

PREP 15 MINS · COOK 10 MINS

Special equipment · food processor

SERVES 4–6

1 x 15oz (425g) can aduki beans, drained and rinsed
1 x 15½oz (440g) can chickpeas, drained and rinsed
1 onion, coarsely chopped
6 anchovies in olive oil, drained
1 tbsp coarse-grain mustard
sea salt and freshly ground black pepper
2 large eggs, lightly beaten
2–3 tbsp all-purpose flour, plus extra for dusting
2–3 tbsp vegetable or sunflower oil

1 Put the drained beans in a food processor and pulse the machine on and off several times until coarsely chopped. Add the onion, anchovies, and mustard, and season well with salt and pepper. Pulse a few times more. You want the mixture to be well combined, but not puréed. Now add the eggs and pulse again until blended. Add 2–3 tablespoons flour to bind the burgers and pulse until incorporated.

2 Heat 1 tablespoon of the oil in a large nonstick frying pan over medium heat. Once the oil is hot, spoon out a portion of the bean mixture (there is enough to make 6 burgers) and, using well-floured hands, form into a patty just before adding to the pan. Working in batches, cook 2 or 3 patties at a time for 4–6 minutes, turning only once, until firm and golden. Add more oil to the pan as needed. Set aside and keep the burgers warm as you cook the remaining patties.

3 Serve each burger inside a bun with crisp lettuce and tomato ketchup.

COOK'S NOTES

Do use the pulse button on the food processor—this gives you more control in achieving the consistency you want. Although the mixture is fairly wet to work with, you will need the 2 eggs for binding. If you prefer more texture, just don't blend the beans as much.

Pasta in brodo

PREP 5 MINS · COOK 15 MINS

SERVES 4

6 cups good-quality chicken stock
2 x 9oz (250g) packages of dried stuffed tortellini (with the filling of your choice)
sea salt and freshly ground black pepper

1 Pour the stock into a soup pot or large saucepan and bring to a vigorous boil. Reduce the heat slightly to a rolling boil and add the pasta.

2 Cook for about 10 minutes or as the package directs, just until tender. Turn off the heat, taste the stock, and season with sea salt and pepper, if needed.

3 To serve, ladle the broth into 4 warm bowls, dividing the tortellini evenly among them, and serve with fresh crusty bread.

VARIATION

Sprinkle with freshly chopped flat-leaf parsley if you have some, or a herb of your choice.

COOK'S NOTES

If using fresh pasta in this dish, just follow the cooking guidelines on the package, again cooking in the stock instead of water. You'll find dried filled pasta in large supermarkets, warehouse stores, or Italian delicatessens.

Lentil dumplings with hot pepper and cumin

PREP 15 MINS COOK 20 MINS

Special equipment • blender or food processor

SERVES 2

4½oz (125g) dried red lentils, rinsed and picked over to remove any grit
sea salt and freshly ground black pepper
1 onion, coarsely chopped
1in (2.5cm) piece of fresh ginger, coarsely chopped
pinch of ground cumin
pinch of crushed red pepper flakes
2 tbsp all-purpose flour, plus extra for dusting
2 tbsp vegetable or sunflower oil

To serve
½ cup Greek-style yogurt
2 tsp mint sauce (see p423)

1 Put the lentils in a saucepan. Add 2 cups water and a pinch of salt. Gently cook over low heat for about 10–15 minutes until the lentils are tender but not mushy. Pour the lentils into a sieve to drain. Put the onion and ginger in a food processor and process until finely chopped. Spoon in the cooked lentils, add the cumin and pepper flakes, and season with salt and pepper. Pulse a few times until the mixture begins to form a paste. Sprinkle in the 2 tablespoons flour and continue to pulse until the mixture just comes together.

2 Spread some extra flour onto a plate. Scoop up 1 tablespoon of the lentil mixture and, with floured hands, lightly form into a ball and gently roll in the flour until well coated. Repeat until all the mixture has been used.

3 Heat enough vegetable oil for shallow-frying in a large nonstick frying pan over medium heat. Carefully add the dumplings, cooking a few at a time if the pan is not large enough. Cook for 1–2 minutes on each side until golden. Remove from the pan with a slotted spoon and drain on paper towels.

4 To serve, mix together the yogurt and mint sauce in a small bowl. Serve alongside the warm dumplings with a crisp green and tomato salad.

Biryani with cardamom and cinnamon

PREP 15 MINS COOK 25 MINS

SERVES 4

1 tbsp vegetable oil
1 onion, finely chopped
sea salt and freshly ground black pepper
6 green cardamom pods, crushed
2 dried bay leaves
1 cinnamon stick, broken in half
1 tsp whole black peppercorns, lightly crushed under a heavy pot
½–1 tsp chili powder
a few saffron threads
4¾ cups hot vegetable stock
2½ cups white basmati rice
½ cup sliced almonds
handful of dark raisins

1 Heat the oil in a large deep-sided frying pan over low heat. Add the onion and a pinch of salt and cook gently for about 5 minutes until soft.

Stir in the cardamom, bay leaves, cinnamon, crushed peppercorns, and chili powder, and cook for another 5 minutes or until fragrant.

2 Stir the saffron into the stock. Rinse the rice in cold water several times, until the water is no longer cloudy. Add the rice to the onion mixture, stirring to coat. Pour in the saffron-stock and bring to a boil. Reduce the heat, cover, and simmer for about 15 minutes, stirring occasionally and adding a little hot water if needed.

3 Lightly toast the almonds in a small, dry nonstick frying pan over low heat for a couple of minutes, stirring frequently, until starting to turn golden. Stir the almonds and raisins into the biryani, taste, and season well with salt and pepper. Serve hot either on its own, or topped with cooked chicken or shrimp.

FOOD FOR FRIENDS

MENU PLANNERS

Themed menu ideas, each with a "countdown" plan of action, designed for effortless entertaining, will take you through every step– from prep to plate.

15-MINUTE DINNER

Fish is the perfect choice for speedy cooking, as it requires very little done to it, and can sit in a warm oven until required, leaving little last-minute cooking. The throw-together fruit dessert uses a "cheat" store-bought tart base, and can be assembled just before serving.

Mushrooms in garlic sauce p340

Lemon sole with herbs p78

Mixed berry cake p472

COUNTDOWN

15 MINUTES

- **Main course** Put the fish in the oven to cook (step 2).
- **Dessert** Prepare the fruit for the dessert and chill.

10 MINUTES

- **Starter** Prepare the garlic mushrooms and keep warm.

5 MINUTES

- **Main course** Make the dressing for the fish and put to one side.

SERVE

- Serve the mushrooms.
- Keep the fish warm (in the turned-off oven).
- Remove the fruit from the refrigerator. Add the fruit to the cake base with ice cream just before serving.

DINNER IN 30 MINUTES
INDULGENT MEAL FOR TWO

A quick and easy, colorful menu, using a few indulgent ingredients, such as scallops and ripe, juicy figs. All dishes are simple, letting the quality of the ingredients speak for themselves. A perfect menu if cooking for two: just remember to halve the quantities, as the original recipes serve 4 people.

FOOD FOR FRIENDS

Scallops with sweet chile sauce p347

Seared duck with five-spice and noodles p70

Fresh figs with cassis cream p469

COUNTDOWN

30 MINUTES

- **Dessert** Prepare the figs and the cassis cream, cover, and put in the refrigerator.

20 MINUTES

- **Main course** Rub the duck breasts with the five-spice paste and start cooking them.

10 MINUTES

- **Starter** Cook the scallops and arrange on warmed serving plates with the lettuce garnish.

SERVE

- Serve the scallops.
- Remove the figs from the refrigerator.
- Combine the noodles and duck and keep warm.

LOW-FAT

A super-quick, fresh menu that is low in fat and calories, but high in flavor. Both the starter and dessert can be prepared ahead of time and kept in the refrigerator, and you can use ready-cooked salmon for the main dish if you are short on time.

Chilled tomato and red pepper soup p41

Baked salmon with salsa verde and cucumber p236

Asian fruit salad p472

COUNTDOWN

30 MINUTES

- **Dessert** Prepare the fruit salad, cover, and put in the refrigerator.
- **Starter** Prepare the soup, ladle into serving bowls, and put in the refrigerator to chill.

20 MINUTES

- **Main course** Prepare the salsa verde and cucumber and put in the refrigerator.
- **Main course** Arrange the cooked salmon on plates. Or, cook salmon fillets wrapped in foil in a medium oven for 20 minutes.

10 MINUTES

- **Main course** Remove the salsa verde and cucumber from the refrigerator and spoon over the plates of salmon. Cover until ready to serve.
- **Starter** Prepare the garnish for the soup.

SERVE

- Garnish and serve the soup.
- Remove the fruit salad from the refrigerator.

FOOD FOR FRIENDS

DINNER IN 30 MINUTES continued
VEGETARIAN

This menu can be prepared in a flash. The starter requires no cooking, and can be prepared ahead and left to chill. The main course is a quick and healthy stir-fry. Meat can easily be served with the stir-fry, if you are also cooking for non-vegetarians.

Fresh tomatoes stuffed with fruity couscous p46

Asparagus, broccoli, ginger, and mint stir-fry p92

Apricots with Amaretti cookies and mascarpone p471

COUNTDOWN

30 MINUTES

- **Starter** Prepare the tomatoes, cover, and put to one side.

20 MINUTES

- **Dessert** Make the dessert and put in the refrigerator to chill.
- **Main course** Prepare the vegetables for the stir-fry.
- **Main course** Start cooking the rice to go with the stir-fry (if required).

10 MINUTES

- **Starter** Plate up the tomatoes for the starter, and garnish if required.

SERVE

- Serve the tomatoes.
- Stir-fry the vegetables.
- Remove the dessert from the refrigerator.

FISH

Fish can be served twice within a menu. This is easy and quick—the starter is a no-cook salad, the main course can be left in the oven while you prepare the rest of the meal, and the dessert can be prepared ahead and placed in the refrigerator to chill.

Smoked fish, fennel, and mango salad p52

Butterflied sardines stuffed with tomatoes and capers p73

Boozy berries with mint and elderflower cream p464

COUNTDOWN

30 MINUTES

- **Dessert** Prepare the dessert and put in the refrigerator to chill.

20 MINUTES

- **Main course** Prepare the sardines and put in the oven to bake.

10 MINUTES

- **Starter** Prepare the smoked fish salad; slice the fennel and prepare the mango.
- **Main course** Prepare a crisp green salad to accompany the main course.

SERVE

- Serve the fish salad.
- Turn off the oven, but leave the sardines inside to keep warm.
- Remove the dessert from the refrigerator.

FOOD FOR FRIENDS

DINNER IN 60 MINUTES

HEALTHY

A healthy menu for entertaining that's both delicious and quick—it's perfectly acceptable for fish to appear twice on the menu. Not only is it ready to eat in an instant, it is also low in fat and good for you. The exotic dessert can be prepared ahead of time, leaving you free to keep your guests company.

Smoked trout with beet, apple, and dill relish p40

Baby zucchini with fish and couscous p387

Middle Eastern oranges with honey p466

FOOD FOR FRIENDS

COUNTDOWN

60 MINUTES

- **Starter** Prepare step 1 and step 3 of the starter, leaving out the apple. Cover and put in the refrigerator.
- **Dessert** Separate the oranges into segments for the dessert and put to one side.

45 MINUTES

- Preheat the oven.
- **Main course** Slice the zucchini for the main course (step 1).
- **Dessert** Prepare the dessert, arrange on a platter, and put in the refrigerator to chill.

30 MINUTES

- **Main course** Prepare the fish couscous, cover with foil, and put in the oven.

15 MINUTES

- **Starter** Remove the starter ingredients from the refrigerator and add the apple to the beet.
- **Main course** Prepare a crisp green salad to serve with the main course, if desired.

SERVE

- Check on the couscous. If cooked, turn off the oven.
- Serve the starter.
- Remove the dessert from the refrigerator.

DECADENT

This is a deceptively easy menu for entertaining. It requires no tricky techniques, but will still impress your guests. The dessert can be prepared ahead, and the goat cheese starter takes little time and effort to assemble.

Grilled goat cheese with honey p335

Pork fillet stuffed with olives and jalapeño peppers, wrapped in bacon p67

Caramel banana tart p494

COUNTDOWN

60 MINUTES
- **Dessert** Prepare the tart up to the end of step 2.
- **Main course** Prepare the pork fillet (step 1), and put in the oven.

45 MINUTES
- **Starter** Prepare the starter up to the end of step 1.

30 MINUTES
- **Main course** Check on the pork in the oven and prepare the serving suggestion: a spinach and tomato salad.

15 MINUTES
- **Starter** Place the cheese for the starter on the toast and complete the recipe. Put to one side.

SERVE
- Put the tart in the oven.
- Serve the starter.
- Remove the pork from the oven and allow it to rest before slicing and serving.

FOOD FOR FRIENDS

291

DINNER IN 60 MINUTES continued

SPICY

A simple menu with lots of authentic Thai flavors. The easy and refreshing no-cook dessert is perfect to round off the meal, and the bite-sized starter can be made ahead, leaving you time to concentrate on the main course.

FOOD FOR FRIENDS

Thai fish cakes p361

Pad Thai p381

Lychees with ginger and star anise p473

COUNTDOWN

60 MINUTES

- **Dessert** Prepare the lychee dessert, cover, and chill.

45 MINUTES

- **Starter** Make the mixture for the fish cakes and shape into patties. Put in the refrigerator to firm up (step 1).

30 MINUTES

- **Main course** Prepare the ingredients for the Pad Thai and put to one side.
- **Starter** Cook the fish cakes and keep warm, covered, in a warm oven.

15 MINUTES

- **Main course** Soak the noodles for the Pad Thai and complete steps 2 and 3. Transfer to serving bowls and keep warm.

SERVE

- Garnish the fish cakes and serve.
- Remove the dessert from the refrigerator to bring to room temperature.

MEDITERRANEAN-STYLE

This is packed with a mix of cuisines from the Mediterranean that compliment each other. The main course is easy to execute, and quick to cook, as the meat is pounded thin. The traditional, indulgent dessert is the perfect treat to round off the meal.

Shrimp with garlic and hot pepper p334

Beef scallops with anchovies, capers, and olives p64

Orange and chocolate tiramisu p462

COUNTDOWN

60 MINUTES

- **Dessert** Prepare the tiramisu, cover, and chill.
- **Starter** Marinate the shrimp in the chile and garlic mixture, cover, and put in the refrigerator to chill.

45 MINUTES

- **Main course** Pound the steaks for the scallops, mix the anchovy paste and smother over the meat, cover, and put to one side.

30 MINUTES

- **Main course** Prepare the arugula salad for the main course.

15 MINUTES

- **Starter** Cook the shrimp for the starter.

SERVE

- Serve the shrimp.
- Start cooking the scallops.
- When ready to serve, remove the tiramisu from the refrigerator.

GET AHEAD
SPRING

A delicious menu, with all the flavors of spring: lamb is at its best, and the asparagus season has just started. The frittata can be made ahead and served cold, as can the lemon tart. The tart is perfect for serving after the rich lamb, which will sit in the oven, needing little attention.

FOOD FOR FRIENDS

Asparagus frittata on crostini p321

Roast leg of lamb p226

Lemon tart with almond pastry p492

COUNTDOWN

DAY BEFORE

- **Starter** Prepare the frittata, cool, cover, and chill.
- **Dessert** Make the lemon tart, cover, and chill.

2 HOURS

- **Main course** Spike the lamb with the rosemary and garlic and put it in the hot oven (step 2).

1 HOUR

- **Starter** Toast the crostini for the starter and put to one side.
- **Dessert** Remove the tart from the refrigerator.
- **Main course** Cook spring greens or carrots and new potatoes as accompaniments and keep warm.

SERVE

- Cut the frittata and assemble the crostini.
- Remove the lamb from the oven and let it rest while you serve the starter.

SUMMER

This is an easy menu, ideal for serving four or more people al fresco. All three dishes can be made the day before. The main dish is much lighter than most meat dishes, and can be served alongside a fresh green salad.

Eggplant and Taleggio arancini p354

Sausage and tomato pie p203

Dark chocolate and lemon mousse p473

COUNTDOWN

DAY BEFORE

- **Starter** Prepare the arancini, cover, and chill.
- **Dessert** Make the mousses, cover, and chill.
- **Main course** Make the pastry for the pie and chill (step 1).

2 HOURS

- **Main course** Roll the pastry out and line the pan. Chill. Make up the sausage meat mixture (step 2).

1 HOUR

- **Main course** Assemble the pie and put in the oven to bake (step 3).
- **Main course** Prepare a salad to accompany the pie.

SERVE

- Arrange the arancini on serving plates and garnish.
- Check on the tart.

AUTUMN

This simple, seasonal menu is perfect for making ahead, as the flavors develop on reheating. Using ingredients that are in season means you get the best quality produce, at the best prices, and a better flavor to your finished dish.

FOOD FOR FRIENDS

Leek and potato soup p253

Beef, fennel, and mushroom hotpot p381

Sticky pecan tart p489

COUNTDOWN

DAY BEFORE

- **Main course** Make the hotpot. Cool, cover, and chill.
- **Dessert** Make the pastry shell for the dessert (step 1) and chill.
- **Starter** Make the soup. Chill.

2 HOURS

- **Dessert** Prepare the pecan mixture for the tart.

1 HOUR

- **Main course** Put the hotpot in the oven to warm through. Add hot water if too dry.
- **Dessert** Fill the pastry shell with the pecan mixture and bake in the oven.

SERVE

- Reheat the soup until piping hot and serve with bread.
- Check on the hotpot.
- Check on the tart.

WINTER

Ribollita just gets better the longer ahead it's made, so it's perfect for a comforting winter menu. The dessert can be assembled in advance, and the casserole can sit simmering in the oven while you entertain your guests.

Ribollita p254

Pork and bean casserole p262

Apple streusel cake p514

COUNTDOWN

DAY BEFORE

- **Starter** Make the ribollita and chill.
- **Dessert** While the ribollita is simmering, prepare the filling for the cake (step 1). Chill.

2 HOURS

- **Dessert** Assemble the cake (first half of step 2), wrap in plastic wrap, and chill.
- **Main course** Prepare the casserole and put in the oven to cook.

1 HOUR

- **Starter** Remove the ribollita from the refrigerator and bring it to a gentle simmer.

SERVE

- Put the cake in the oven to cook while you serve the starter and main course.

FOOD FOR FRIENDS

297

PARTY FOOD
CANAPÉS

For a cocktail party, a generous selection of meat and vegetarian food is needed, and it should be easy to eat with your hands, presented in bite-sized portions, or on sticks. This menu meets both criteria. Lots of the dishes can conveniently be made ahead of time.

FOOD FOR FRIENDS

Roast pumpkin and ricotta crostini p314

Roasted sweet potato and pepper tortilla p345

COUNTDOWN

4 HOURS
- Make the **shrimp and chicken empanadas**, leave to cool, and put in a sealable container.

3 HOURS
- Make the **tortilla**, chill, and cut up into bite-sized pieces. Cover and put to one side.
- Toast the bread, ready for the **crostini**.

1 HOUR
- Roast the pumpkin and prepare the ricotta mixture for the **crostini**. Assemble, plate, and cover.
- Cook the **lamb**, then skewer it and keep warm until needed.
- Make the **smoked chicken with basil mayonnaise**.

30 MINUTES
- Cook the **scallops**, then skewer with the prosciutto and plate.
- Make the **cucumber rounds** and top with the mayonnaise. Plate.

SERVE
- Garnish all the dishes, if you like.
- Put some aioli or mayonnaise in a small dish to accompany the empanadas.
- Uncover dishes and serve.

Scallops skewered with prosciutto p327

Shrimp and chicken empañadas p347

Smoked chicken with basil mayonnaise on cucumber rounds p320

Skewered lemon, rosemary, and dukkah lamb p357

BUFFET

This buffet menu is colorful and has a wide range of flavors and textures. You should serve around six different dishes for variety. Most of them can be prepared ahead, relieving last-minute pressure, and they won't spoil if left out on the table for a while.

FOOD FOR FRIENDS

Halloumi with garlic, chili, and cilantro p341

Sliced beef and arugula salad with green olive and raisin salsa p41

COUNTDOWN

4 HOURS

- Make the pastry for the **tartlets** (if making your own); chill in the refrigerator. Line the pastry shells and chill.
- Cook the potato for the **tartlets** (step 2) and chill.
- Make the **dip**, cover, and chill.

3 HOURS

- Bake the pastry shells blind, then fill and bake (step 3–4).
- Make the dried fruit chutney for the **chorizo**.

1 HOUR

- Make the **bulgur wheat** dish, cover, and chill.

30 MINUTES

- Make the salsa for the **beef and arugula salad**, cover, and chill.
- Cook the **halloumi** with the garlic, chili, and cilantro and arrange on plates.
- Prepare the **chorizo** and plate up with the chutney.

SERVE

- Plate the **beef and arugula salad** with the salsa, remove the **dip** from the refrigerator, and place all other dishes in serving bowls or plates. Garnish.

Baba ghanoush p323

Chorizo with dried fruit chutney p342

Tomato bulgur wheat with capers and olives p277

Gruyère cheese, potato, and thyme tartlets p213

AL FRESCO
PICNIC

A tasty mix of traditional foods—pork pie makes for a delicious picnic food, and it can be packed whole or pre-sliced, as can the panini. Sweet muffins are an easy sweet dish to pack and eat. Half of the food can be prepared the day before and kept chilled.

FOOD FOR FRIENDS

Spiced pork and chicken pie p210

Crayfish and crisp lettuce panini with herbed mayonnaise p319

COUNTDOWN

DAY BEFORE

- Make the **spiced pork and chicken pie**, leave to cool, then pack in a sealed container.
- Bake the **blueberry muffins**, leave to cool, and pack in a sealed container.

2 HOURS

- Prepare the **hummus**, cover, and leave in the refrigerator.

1 HOUR

- Make the **chicken with aduki beans and parsley**, put in a sealable container, and leave in the refrigerator.

30 MINUTES

- Prepare the **crayfish paninis**, wrap individually in parchment paper, and tie with string.
- Prepare the **Chicken Caesar salad** and pack loosely in a sealable container (so you don't crush the lettuce leaves).

PACKING

- Remove the chicken with aduki beans from the refrigerator and transfer the hummus to a sealable container.
- Pack forks, knives, napkins, and beverages.

Hummus p323

Chicken Caesar salad p47

Chicken with aduki beans and parsley p53

Blueberry muffins p520

AL FRESCO continued
VEGETARIAN PICNIC

This picnic has plenty of food that can be made ahead for convenience. The dishes are all easy to pack and won't spoil in hot weather. Even though it is vegetarian, it won't disappoint the meat eaters, as there is a hearty pie and some meaty lentils.

Lebanese-flavored lentils p272

Tomato, red onion, and mozzarella salad p48

COUNTDOWN

DAY BEFORE

- Make the **cheese and onion pie**, leave to cool, and put in a sealable container.
- Make the **banana, date, and walnut loaf**, leave to cool, and put in a sealable container.

2 HOURS

- Prepare the **potato and paprika omelet**, leave to cool, slice into portions, and put into a sealable container.

1 HOUR

- Prepare the **lentils**, cover, and leave to sit in a bowl while you prepare the **chickpeas**. Cover both dishes and leave to sit so the flavors have time to develop.

30 MINUTES

- Stir the **lentils** and the **chickpeas** and pack in sealable containers.

PACKING

- Make the **tomato, red onion, and mozzarella salad** last and pack in a sealable container.
- Pre-slice the **pie** and **loaf** if desired, or pack a knife. Pack plenty of napkins and beverages.

Potato and paprika omelet p332

Chickpeas in olive oil and lemon p342

Cheese and onion pie p205

Banana, date, and walnut loaf p518

AL FRESCO continued
BARBECUE

This selection of dishes combines the bold and gutsy flavors of spicy meat with two delicately flavored seafood dishes. The potato dish can be prepared ahead and will be a delicious complement to the other flavors. The lamb koftas can be prepared ahead and are easy to serve and eat.

Wasabi beef and bok choy p443

Marinated sweet and hot tuna steaks p448

COUNTDOWN

60 MINUTES

- Light the grill. Prepare the **patatas bravas**, then put in the oven.
- Mix up the lamb mixture for the **lamb koftas**, cover, and chill.
- Prepare the **beef** (step 1). If using wooden skewers, soak them in cold water.

45 MINUTES

- Marinate the **tuna steaks** (step 1) and **pork tenderloin** (step 1), and put both in the refrigerator.
- Make the dressing for the **squid with arugula salad**, and put to one side.
- Make up the **lamb koftas**.

30 MINUTES

- Put the marinated **beef** and **pork** on the grill along with the **lamb koftas**. Cook until ready and keep warm on a wire rack above the grill.
- Check on the **patatas bravas**. Remove and cover, if ready, or turn the oven off and keep warm.

15 MINUTES

- Put the **tuna** and the **squid** on the barbecue, along with the bok choy for the beef dish, and cook until charred.

SERVE

- Toss the arugula with the dressing and add the squid.
- Warm some pita bread on the grill for serving with the koftas. Plate all the meat and fish along with the potatoes.

Chargrilled squid with arugula salad p434

Chile-slashed pork tenderloin p444

Lamb koftas p448

Patatas bravas p332

FOOD FOR FRIENDS

307

AL FRESCO continued

VEGETARIAN BARBECUE

Lots of exciting flavors and textures are needed for a no-meat barbecue: crunchy salads and meaty vegetables, such as eggplant and mushrooms, create a satisfying and healthy al freso meal. Pop some sweet corn and vegetable skewers on the grill, too, if you like (see p433).

Potato and leek croquettes p358

Zucchini stuffed with raisins, red onion, and pine nuts p91

COUNTDOWN

60 MINUTES

- Light the grill. Make the **potato croquettes** and put in the refrigerator to firm up.
- Prepare the **lentil, fava bean, and feta salad** and put to one side, covered, to let the flavors develop.

45 MINUTES

- Prepare the **mushrooms with croutons, cherry tomatoes, and feta**, cover, and put to one side.

30 MINUTES

- Cook the **potato croquettes**, then sit on a wire rack above the grill to keep warm.
- Prepare the **carrot salad with cabbage and peanuts**, cover, and put to one side.

15 MINUTES

- Put the prepared **eggplant** on the grill and cook until charred.
- Put the **zucchini** on the grill and cook until charred, or cook in the oven (step 3).

SERVE

- Plate up all the salads in dishes or bowls.
- Plate the zucchini, eggplant, and croquettes onto platters.

Carrot salad with cabbage and peanuts p50

Lentil, fava bean, and feta salad p40

Grilled eggplant with spiced tomato sauce p454

Grilled mushrooms with croutons, cherry tomatoes, and feta p455

FOOD FOR FRIENDS

309

NO-FUSS FINGER FOOD AND DIPS

Easy food for casual gatherings—no forks required.

NO-FUSS FINGER FOOD AND DIPS

A little planning is the key to an effortless party, along with great food, plenty of drinks, and happy guests. Individual bites that can be eaten without plates and cutlery are ideal party food, and can be served with drinks at an informal party, or before the main meal at a more formal sit down dinner. Decide what type of party you are having, and you're halfway there.

FOOD FOR FRIENDS

5 instant store cupboard nibbles
Perfect for unexpected guests.

BREADSTICKS
Let guests help themselves to plain, cheese, or sesame-coated sticks. Fill up decorative glasses with them and offer a selection of ready-bought dips. Or, wrap them with prosciutto and serve with a plate of mozzarella drizzled with a fruity extra virgin olive oil.

TORTILLA CHIPS
These are great for dipping or topping. Serve a variety of plain and spicy chips. Top with pieces of chicken and sliced peppers from a jar, or with a spoonful of finely chopped tomatoes and capers and a dollop of sour cream.

MELBA TOAST
Top these crisp bites with a simple ready-made pâté and a caper berry, or a meat pâté and a teaspoon of fruity chutney. For a sweeter bite, cover with cream cheese and top with a slice of exotic fruit such as kiwi, mango, or papaya.

NUTS AND SEEDS
A bowl of mixed nuts is a good standby accompaniment for drinks. Better still, pan-fry a selection of nuts with a little sugar and sprinkle with toasted sesame seeds; or, toast some sunflower and pumpkin seeds with a sprinkling of soy sauce or tamarind.

RICE PAPER
Soak in water for 20 seconds, drain, and fill with scallions and other vegetables cut into matchstick-sized pieces, or cooked shrimp and fresh ginger, and roll into cones. Tie the cones with fresh chives for a polished finish.

Fuss-free entertaining

Keep it simple. It will make life easier if food loosely falls into some sort of theme—Middle Eastern or Mediterranean, for example. It can simplify shopping and will prevent too many competing flavors.

Budget. Have a rough idea of how much you want to spend, and write a shopping list. The more choices you offer, the more costly it will be.

Seasons. In summer, all items can be served cold, but in winter it is preferable to have at least 2 or 3 hot items on the menu.

Variety. Choose a good variety of ingredients, from meat and fish to vegetables and herbs. Always include 3–4 vegetarian dishes.

Prepare. Make up as much as you can the day before (dips, for instance) and keep in the refrigerator, or even earlier, and freeze. Assemble at the last minute.

Skewer it
Flavorful little bites on sticks are the perfect easy-to-eat finger food. The combinations are endless—here are some ideas to get you started.

Sausage and squash A great combination that can be made ahead, and served hot or cold. Roast a pan of chipolata or other spicy Italian-style sausages, halved, with a peeled, seeded, and cubed butternut squash. Toss with olive oil, freshly ground black pepper, and a sprinkling of hot red pepper flakes (if you wish) and cook in the oven at 400°F (200°C) for about 30 minutes, until cooked through. Thread onto skewers.

Watermelon and feta cheese An updated version of the classic cheese and pineapple combination. Chop watermelon flesh into small bite-sized pieces and skewer with small cubes of good-quality feta cheese cubes.

Spiced shrimp Toss a handful of shelled raw shrimp with olive oil, sea salt and ground black pepper, and a pinch of cayenne pepper. Pan-fry in a little hot oil until pink, then skewer onto lemon grass stalks or wooden skewers.

Seared tuna and lime Cut a raw tuna steak into bite-sized pieces and toss with olive oil and freshly ground black pepper. Sear briefly on a hot ridged cast-iron grill pan for 1 minute, then skewer with segmented pieces of lime.

Skewered bites of Sausage and squash, Watermelon and feta, Spiced shrimp, and Seared tuna and lime.

4 instant bases Use vegetables for a no-effort quick canapé.

Belgian endive

These bitter leaves are fabulous scoops for homemade dips, or can be filled with a **store-bought dip** or **hummus** for convenience. Red endive is also available, so mix and match for plenty of color. These bases won't wilt quickly, and so can be prepared a few hours ahead.

Cucumber

Slices of cucumber make the simplest of bases, and can be used for a variety of toppings, such as **store-bought tzatziki** and a **mint leaf** for garnish. Slice a few hours ahead and top at the last minute.

Radicchio

These bitter leaves make excellent cups to fill and serve as substantial finger food. Fill with a mixture of **couscous**, **raisins**, and **toasted pine nuts** or try filling with strong-flavored **blue cheese** tossed with **diced apple** and **walnuts**. If filling with a food that isn't too wet, they can be prepared a couple of hours ahead.

Baby peppers

These are sweet peppers, great halved and filled with a **strong cheese**, crumbled **feta cheese**, or a **store-bought dip** sprinkled with black pepper. They stay crisp for a long time, so prepare the night before, keep in a plastic bag in the refrigerator, then fill at the last minute.

servings per person

Most recipes in this chapter serve **8** people. If you want to increase the recipe yield, simply double the quantities, although do watch the herbs and spices, as these only need to be increased by half.

If serving finger foods and dips as a substitute for a main course, allow **8–12** pieces per person.

If serving finger foods and dips as appetizers only, allow **4–6** pieces per person, per hour. So the longer the party, the more appetizers needed.

It's always better to have too much than too little. Many appetizers will keep for the next day.

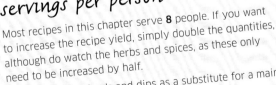

Mayonnaise It's easier than you think, and a great base for dips. Eggs should be at room temperature before you start.

1 Add 2 egg yolks to a glass bowl with a pinch of sea salt, 1 teaspoon of dijon mustard, and 2 teaspoons of white wine vinegar. In a cup, measure out ¾ cup of light olive oil. Using a balloon whisk, whisk the egg yolk, slowly adding drops of olive oil. Continue adding the oil, a drop at a time, whisking constantly.

2 The mixture will begin to thicken and emulsify. Continue adding the oil, a little more quickly now, whisking until all the oil has been added. Don't add the oil too quickly, as the mixture will curdle. (If this does happen, add an egg yolk to a clean bowl, then add the curdled mixture slowly and whisk until it emulsifies again.)

3 When the mayonnaise has thickened and all the oil has been incorporated, taste and add a little more vinegar and sea salt and black pepper, if needed. If it is too thick, dilute with a little warm water. Serve with cold cooked meats, fish, or eggs.

Roast pumpkin and ricotta crostini

PREP 20 MINS · **COOK 50 MINS**

SERVES 16

For the crostini
about 2 tbsp olive oil
16 slices crusty baguette
sea salt and freshly ground
    black pepper
1 garlic clove, peeled
    but left whole

about 1lb (450g) kabocha squash
    (Japanese pumpkin), peeled, seeded
    and cut into chunks
2 tbsp olive oil
2 garlic cloves, crushed
grated zest and juice of 1 lemon
2 sprigs of fresh rosemary, leaves
    picked and chopped
7oz (200g) ricotta cheese
4 sprigs of fresh lemon-scented
    thyme, leaves picked

1 Preheat the oven to 400°F (200°C).
To make the crostini, pour 2 tbsp olive
oil over a baking sheet, then gently
press the bread into the oil on both
sides. Season with salt and pepper.
Bake for 10–15 minutes until golden
brown. Remove from the oven and
lightly rub each slice with the garlic
clove. Set aside on a wire rack to cool.

2 Put the pumpkin on a baking sheet
and toss with the olive oil, garlic,
lemon zest, and rosemary. Season
with salt and pepper, then roast for
about 35 minutes until tender and
golden. Leave to cool slightly.

3 To serve, in a bowl, combine the
ricotta, thyme, and a little lemon juice.
Spoon a little of the ricotta mixture
onto each of the crostini and top with
a chunk of roasted pumpkin, squeezing
it a little with your fingers before
putting it in place. Arrange on a large
serving dish or platter and serve.

VARIATION For a sweet and sour flavor,
sprinkle a little good-quality
balsamic vinegar over the
pumpkin just before roasting.

COOK'S NOTES

Use ordinary fresh thyme
leaves if you can't find the
lemon-scented variety.

Cannellini and dill crostini

PREP 20 MINS · **COOK 15 MINS**

Special equipment · blender or
food processor

SERVES 16

For the crostini
about 2 tbsp olive oil
16 slices crusty baguette
sea salt and freshly ground
    black pepper
1 garlic clove, peeled but left whole

1 x 14oz (400g) can cannellini beans,
    rinsed and drained
1 tbsp chopped fresh dill
3 anchovy fillets in olive oil, drained
2 small fresh red jalapeño chile
    peppers, seeded and finely chopped
2 scallions, thinly sliced
2 tbsp olive oil, for drizzling
⅓ cup black olives, pitted and
    finely chopped

1 Preheat the oven to 400°F (200°C).
To make the crostini, pour 2 tbsp olive
oil over a baking sheet, then gently
press the bread into the oil on both
sides. Season with salt and pepper.

Bake for 10–15 minutes until golden
brown. Remove from the oven and
lightly rub each slice with the garlic
clove. Set aside on a wire rack to cool.

2 Combine the cannellini beans, dill,
anchovies, chiles, and scallions in a
blender or food processor and purée
until smooth. Season with salt and
pepper and transfer to a bowl. Spoon
the bean mixture over the crostini,
drizzle with the olive oil, and sprinkle
with the chopped black olives. Serve.

VARIATION Serve the cannellini topping
with your favorite grilled
fish and roasted vine-
ripened cherry tomatoes.

COOK'S NOTES

Canned cannellini beans make a
great store-cupboard standby. It
takes no effort at all to turn them
into a topping for crostini or a dip
for crudités or an antipasto platter.

Roasted eggplant dip with pine nuts

PREP 15 MINS • **COOK 45 MINS**

Special equipment • blender or food processor • outdoor grill or a ridged cast-iron grill pan

SERVES 4

2 large eggplants

4 garlic cloves, crushed

small handful of fresh oregano, leaves picked (optional)

finely grated zest and juice of 1 lemon

⅓ cup olive oil

1 cup pine nuts, toasted and coarsely chopped

½ cup Greek-style yogurt

sea salt and freshly ground black pepper

1 Heat an outdoor grill or grill pan until very hot. Pierce each eggplant several times with a knife. Place the whole eggplants on the grill and cook, turning occasionally, for 30–45 minutes until the skin is charred and blistered; it will become quite black. Remove from the heat and let cool before peeling the skin and chopping the flesh.

2 Put the eggplant, garlic, oregano (if using), lemon zest and juice, and oil in a food processor and process, pulsing the machine on and off, to a chunky spread. Transfer to a bowl and stir in the pine nuts and yogurt. Season with salt and pepper and mix well.

3 Serve with torn chunks of sourdough bread or toasted baguette slices.

> ### COOK'S NOTES
> You could always roast the eggplants in the oven at 400°F (200°C) for about 30 minutes.

Oysters with chile and lime mayo

PREP 15 MINS

Special equipment • oyster knife

SERVES 6–8

For the chile and lime mayo

2 fresh Thai or other small red hot chile peppers, seeded if you prefer

1 garlic clove, finely chopped

sea salt and freshly ground black pepper

1 large egg yolk

¾ cup olive oil

juice of 1 lime

24 live oysters in the shell

1 tbsp chopped fresh dill

2 scallions, thinly sliced on the diagonal

rock salt, for serving

1 To make the mayo, using a mortar and pestle, pound together the chiles, garlic, and a good pinch of sea salt to form a paste. Spoon it into a large bowl, then add the egg yolk. Stir thoroughly with a whisk until smooth.

2 Gradually add the oil, drop by drop, whisking continuously and ensuring that it is absorbed completely before making the next addition. Once the mixture starts to thicken, add the oil in a slow, thin drizzle. When a third of the oil has been blended in, start adding the lime juice a little at a time. Continue adding the lime juice and whisking until everything is well incorporated. Season with pepper, cover with plastic wrap, and refrigerate until needed.

3 To prepare the oysters, discard any that have opened or do not close tightly when tapped on the work surface. Use an oyster knife and hold the oysters over a bowl as you open them. Carefully shuck the oysters one by one, catching any liquid in the bowl, and transferring the opened oysters in their shells to the refrigerator as you work. Refrigerate the bowl of accumulated oyster juices.

4 Put a layer of rock salt on a platter—this is to keep the oysters level. Arrange the open oyster shells on top of the salt and spoon the chilled oyster liquid over each oyster. Sprinkle with the dill and scallions, then dab a little chile and lime mayonnaise over the top of each oyster and serve immediately.

Artichoke and fennel dip

PREP 20 MINS

Special equipment • blender or food processor

SERVES 8

1 x 14oz (400g) can artichoke hearts, drained
1 x 14oz (400g) fennel bulb, trimmed and chopped
2 tbsp tahini (see Cook's Notes)
juice of 1 lemon
1 garlic clove, chopped
1 tbsp olive oil
sea salt and freshly ground black pepper

1 Combine the artichokes, fennel, tahini, lemon juice, garlic, and oil in a food processor. Process until smooth and creamy. Season with salt and pepper to taste.

2 Serve with grilled Turkish flat bread, pita bread, or over a fresh tomato and parsley salad.

COOK'S NOTES

Tahini is a ground sesame seed paste—you'll find it in large supermarkets or health food stores. It has a rich, nutty flavor, and is used throughout the Middle East.

Mushroom and mascarpone dip

PREP 15 MINS **COOK 45 MINS**

Special equipment • blender or food processor

SERVES 8

2¼lb (1kg) small-to-medium mushrooms, quartered
4 tbsp olive oil
1 garlic clove, crushed whole with the flat side of a knife
finely grated zest and juice of 1 lemon
2 anchovies in oil, drained and finely chopped
sea salt and freshly ground black pepper
small handful of flat-leaf parsley leaves, plus extra for garnish
8oz (250ml) mascarpone cheese or sour cream
drizzle of extra virgin olive oil (optional)
pinch of paprika

1 Preheat the oven to 400°F (200°C). Spread the mushrooms on a baking sheet lined with parchment paper and toss with the olive oil, garlic, lemon zest and juice, and anchovies. Season with salt and pepper. Roast for 35–45 minutes until golden. Set aside to cool.

2 Transfer the cooled mushroom mixture to a food processor. Add the handful of parsley leaves and process, turning the machine on and off, to a chunky purée.

3 Put the mushroom purée in a serving bowl with the sour cream and stir through gently. Season well, stir again, and sprinkle with extra parsley leaves. Drizzle with a little extra virgin olive oil, if desired, and sprinkle with the paprika. Serve with chunks of grilled or toasted ciabatta or other country-style bread.

COOK'S NOTES

This makes a great topping for bruschetta. Simply toast some slices of ciabatta, rub with garlic, and top with the dip. Drizzle with a little extra virgin olive oil and serve with an arugula and shaved Parmesan salad.

Dill and fava bean dip

PREP 30 MINS · **COOK 25 MINS**

Special equipment • blender or food processor

SERVES 8

1½lb (750g) fresh fava beans
3 tbsp olive oil
1 small onion, finely chopped
sea salt and freshly ground
  black pepper
1 x 14oz (400g) can cannellini beans,
  rinsed and drained
1 tbsp chopped fresh dill
2 scallions, thinly sliced diagonally

1 Remove the fava beans from their pods and slip off the skins. Set aside.

2 Heat the oil in a saucepan over low heat. Add the onion and cook gently for about 5 minutes until soft.

3 Add the fava beans and cook for 10–15 minutes, stirring occasionally. Add 2 cups water, season with salt and pepper, and partially-cover the pan with a lid. Bring to a gentle simmer and continue cooking for 25 minutes, mashing the beans a bit as you cook. Drain and allow to cool.

4 Add the cooled fava bean mixture to a food processor. Add the drained cannellini beans, dill, and scallions, and process to a chunky purée. Season with salt and pepper. Transfer to a serving bowl and serve with fresh crusty bread.

Cheat...
Use frozen fava beans instead of fresh. Leave them to defrost first, then slip off their skins, if needed.

COOK'S NOTES
This is good picnic food, served on bruschetta or rustic bread with hard-boiled eggs.

Arugula, ricotta, and black olive dip

PREP 15 MINS

Special equipment • blender or food processor

SERVES 4

about 1 cup arugula
2 garlic cloves, crushed through
  a press
⅓ cup black olives, pitted
finely grated zest and juice of 1 lemon
⅓ cup olive oil
9oz (250g) ricotta cheese
freshly ground black pepper

1 Combine the arugula, garlic, olives, lemon zest and juice, and oil in a food processor and process until smooth.

2 Transfer to a medium bowl, then stir in the ricotta and season with pepper. Mix well.

3 Serve with torn chunks of crusty sourdough bread or with toasted baguette slices.

 VARIATION
This makes a great pasta sauce—simply toss with hot drained pasta.

COOK'S NOTES
Use good-quality dry black olives with plenty of flavor, and make sure the arugula is very fresh. Buy it loose if possible, as bagged leaves go rotten much quicker.

Chile, ginger, and roasted pumpkin dip

PREP 20 MINS · COOK 45 MINS

Special equipment • blender or food processor

SERVES 8

2¼lb (1kg) kabocha squash (Japanese pumpkin), peeled and cut into chunks
¼ cup olive oil
4 garlic cloves
1 tbsp grated or chopped fresh ginger
sea salt and freshly ground black pepper
1 fresh red jalapeño chile pepper, seeded and thinly sliced
4 sprigs of flat-leaf parsley, leaves only, plus extra for garnish
grated zest and juice of 1 lemon
⅔ cup Greek-style yogurt
drizzle of extra virgin olive oil (optional)
pinch of paprika

For serving

slices of toasted sourdough bread
cooked pancetta or prosciutto, crumbled

1 Preheat the oven to 400°F (200°C). Place the squash on a baking sheet and toss with the olive oil, garlic, and ginger. Season with salt and pepper. Roast for about 30 minutes until tender and golden. Set aside to cool.

2 Transfer the cooled squash to a blender or food processor and add the chile, parsley, and lemon zest and juice. Pulse the machine on and off until a chunky purée is formed. Season with salt and pepper.

3 Scrape the purée into a mixing bowl and stir in the yogurt to blend. Season with salt and pepper, then spoon into a serving bowl. Top with a drizzle of extra virgin olive oil. Garnish with the reserved parsley and a sprinkle of paprika and serve on grilled sourdough bread, with browned bits of pancetta or prosciutto scattered over the top.

COOK'S NOTES

This dip is good with grilled or roasted meat. To make it extra hot, simply add another chile pepper.

Red pepper and walnut dip

PREP 20 MINS · COOK 30 MINS

Special equipment • blender or food processor

SERVES 8

⅓ cup olive oil
1 onion, thinly sliced
sea salt
4 red bell peppers, seeded and cut into strips
2 garlic cloves, crushed
1 cup toasted walnuts, chopped
grated zest and juice of 1 lemon

1 Heat the oil in a heavy frying pan over low heat. Add the onion and a pinch of salt and gently cook for about 5 minutes until soft.

2 Stir in the peppers and cook for about 30 minutes until very soft, stirring frequently. Stir in the garlic and cook 30 seconds. Let cool slightly.

3 Scrape the pepper mixture into a blender. Add the walnuts and lemon zest and juice and blend to a chunky purée. Serve at room temperature with warm pita bread or carrot and cucumber sticks for dipping.

VARIATION

Use macadamia nuts instead of walnuts. You may also like to add about ½ cup Greek-style yogurt and chopped cilantro, stirring into the mixture at the end.

COOK'S NOTES

To toast the walnuts, spread the nuts in a single layer on a baking sheet. Toast in a preheated 350°F (180°C) oven for 8–10 minutes, stirring once or twice to make sure they do not burn.

Shrimp, avocado, and watercress sandwich

PREP 30 MINS **COOK 5 MINS**

SERVES 4

1 tbsp olive oil
24 raw shrimp, peeled and deveined
1 tbsp finely chopped fresh ginger
1 fresh red Thai chile pepper,
    finely chopped
1 garlic clove, chopped
1 ripe avocado
1 small cucumber, preferably Persian,
    thinly sliced diagonally
a few sprigs of fresh mint, leaves
    picked and coarsely torn
1 tbsp finely chopped dill
1 tbsp chopped rinsed and drained
    capers
½ small red onion, finely chopped
1 cup sour cream
juice of 1 lime
salt and freshly ground black pepper
8 thick slices crusty bread
4 handfuls of watercress

1 Heat the oil in a frying pan over medium-high heat and cook the shrimp, ginger, and chile for 3–5 minutes, stirring, until the shrimp turn pink and opaque. Stir in the garlic and cook for 30 seconds. Set aside to cool, then chop coarsely.

2 Halve, pit, and peel the avocado. Dice the flesh and put it in a bowl. Add the cucumber, mint, dill, capers, onion, sour cream, and lime juice. Scrape in the chopped shrimp mixture and toss gently to mix, being careful not to mash the avocado. Season with salt and pepper.

3 Spread the mixture evenly over 4 slices of the bread. Arrange the watercress on top so that it will come out over the sides of the sandwich. Cover with the other bread slices to make 4 sandwiches and serve.

Crayfish and crisp lettuce panini with herbed mayonnaise

PREP 15 MINS

SERVES 4

2¼lb (1kg) cooked
    crayfish tails
½ cup mayonnaise
juice of 1 lime
small handful of chopped mixed
    fresh herbs such as cilantro,
    Vietnamese mint or basil,
    and chives
1 anchovy fillet in olive oil,
    drained and minced
freshly ground black pepper
4 Italian-style crusty bread rolls
1 head oakleaf or other butter lettuce,
    leaves separated
2 fresh peaches, pitted and sliced

1 Remove all the meat from the crayfish tails, leaving it in large chunks, if possible. Divide into 4 equal portions and set aside.

2 To make the herbed mayonnaise, combine the mayonnaise, lime juice, herbs, and anchovy in a bowl. Season with pepper and stir to blend well.

3 Slice the rolls in half, but without cutting all the way through. Open them up and spread with the herbed mayonnaise. Arrange some of the lettuce leaves over the rolls, then put the crayfish on top. Arrange peach slices between the crayfish, then spoon a little more of the mayonnaise over the top. Close up the rolls and serve immediately.

VARIATION Use peeled and deveined cooked shrimp in place of the crayfish.

COOK'S NOTES

Instead of sandwiching this combination in bread rolls, serve as a salad with chopped scallions or red onion over the top. Or add avocado slices and orange segments. For a more savory twist, add steamed asparagus and halved cherry tomatoes.

Smoked trout, fennel, and mascarpone crostini

 PREP 25 MINS **COOK 15 MINS**

SERVES 4

2 tbsp olive oil
4 thick slices crusty sourdough bread
sea salt and freshly ground
    black pepper
1 garlic clove, peeled but left whole
2 smoked trout, 10oz (300g) each
1 x 5½oz (150g) fennel bulb, trimmed,
    halved, and thinly sliced
½ cup mascarpone cheese
¼ cup sliced almonds, toasted
juice of ½ lemon
sprigs of fresh chervil, to garnish
4 lemon wedges for serving

1 Preheat the oven to 400°F (200°C). Pour the olive oil onto a baking sheet, then gently press the bread into the oil on both sides. Season with salt and pepper. Bake for 10–15 minutes until golden brown. Remove from the oven and lightly rub each slice with the garlic clove. Set aside on a wire rack to keep the crostini crisp.

2 Meanwhile, remove the skin from the smoked trout and gently remove the flesh from the bones, trying to keep it in big chunks.

3 Put the trout, fennel, mascarpone, sliced almonds, and lemon juice in a bowl. Season with pepper and gently stir to mix.

4 To serve, arrange the trout mixture over the crostini, season with some more pepper, and garnish with the chervil. Serve with lemon wedges for squeezing over.

COOK'S NOTES

To toast the almonds, spread them out in a small dry frying pan. Toast over medium heat for a few minutes until golden, stirring frequently to prevent them from burning.

Smoked chicken with basil mayonnaise on cucumber rounds

 PREP 20 MINS

SERVES 6–8

1 smoked chicken breast, about
    9oz (250g)
3 tbsp mayonnaise
1 tbsp prepared pesto
freshly ground black pepper
2 small cucumbers, preferably
    Lebanese or Persian, cut crosswise
    into slices ¼in (5mm) thick

1 Remove the skin from the chicken. Slice across the breast into thin slices and then finely chop into small cubes. In a bowl, combine the smoked chicken, mayonnaise, and pesto. Season with pepper and mix well.

2 Spoon a generous teaspoon of the smoked chicken mixture onto a slice of cucumber and arrange on platters.

Salt cod and red pepper dip

PREP 25 MINS · COOK 1 HR

Special equipment • blender or food processor

SERVES 12

2 red bell peppers
2 garlic cloves, peeled
1 small red onion, finely chopped
4 tbsp olive oil
sea salt and freshly ground
    black pepper
1 x 14oz (400g) can crushed
    peeled tomatoes
about 1lb (450g) salt cod
2 tbsp finely chopped fresh marjoram
2 tbsp finely chopped fresh dill
good handful of fresh basil leaves,
    finely chopped
good handful of flat-leaf parsley,
    finely chopped
juice of 1 lemon

1 Preheat the oven to 400°F (200°C). Slice the tops off the peppers and remove the seeds and membrane. Put a garlic clove and half of the chopped onion in the cavity of each pepper. Place the peppers on a baking sheet lined with parchment paper. Drizzle with 1 tablespoon of the olive oil and season with salt and pepper. Roast in the oven for about 1 hour. Remove from the oven and set aside to cool.

2 Heat the remaining 3 tablespoons olive oil in a heavy frying pan over low heat. Add the remaining onion and cook for about 5 minutes until soft. Add the can of crushed tomatoes, including the juices, and cook for another 10 minutes, stirring from time to time. Season with salt and pepper.

3 Meanwhile, slice the skin off the salt cod and flake the flesh into chunks. Add to the tomato sauce after the 10 minutes' cooking time and cook gently for another 10 minutes. Set aside to cool.

4 Put the cooled peppers (with garlic and onion) in a food processor with the cooled tomato and cod mixture. Working in batches if necessary, purée until smooth. Transfer to a serving bowl and season with salt and pepper. Stir in the marjoram, dill, basil, parsley, and lemon juice, to blend well. Serve with crostini, broken pieces of toasted bread, or grilled Turkish flat bread.

Asparagus frittata on crostini

PREP 20 MINS · COOK 20 MINS

SERVES 4

4 tbsp olive oil
4 thick slices crusty sourdough bread
sea salt and freshly ground
    black pepper
1 garlic clove, peeled but left whole
8 fresh asparagus spears, trimmed
2 tbsp finely chopped onion
4 eggs
½ cup heavy whipping cream
½ cup freshly grated Parmesan cheese
1 small bunch of flat-leaf parsley,
    to garnish

1 Preheat the oven to 400°F (200°C). Pour 2 tablespoons of the oil onto a baking sheet, then gently press the bread into the oil on both sides. Season with salt and pepper. Bake for 10–15 minutes until golden brown. Remove from the oven and lightly rub each slice of bread with the garlic clove. Set aside on a wire rack to keep crisp.

2 Meanwhile, cook the asparagus in lightly salted boiling water for 1–3 minutes, just until bright green. Drain, refresh in cold water, and drain again. On a cutting board, slice each asparagus in half lengthwise. Heat the remaining oil in a heavy frying pan over low heat and cook the onion for about 5 minutes until soft. Add the halved asparagus spears and cook for 1–2 minutes.

3 Preheat the oven broiler to its highest setting. In a bowl, whisk together the eggs, cream, and Parmesan. Season with salt and pepper and pour over the asparagus and onion mixture in the pan. As the bottom is cooking, tilt the pan a little, allowing some of the uncooked egg mixture from the top to spill over and under the frittata. Continue cooking for 3–5 minutes until almost set. To finish, place the pan under the broiler and cook until the top of the frittata is golden brown and there is no evidence of uncooked egg.

4 To serve, tear the frittata into 4 rough pieces and place on top of the crostini. Scatter the parsley over the top and serve immediately.

Beef mini-burgers on pizza bases with chile and beet salad

  PREP 30 MINS · COOK 15 MINS

SERVES 8

1 x 13.8oz (391g) can refrigerated classic pizza crust
all-purpose flour
1 x 14oz (400g) jar good-quality tomato sauce

For the burgers
1lb (450g) lean ground beef
1 cup freshly grated Parmesan cheese
½ cup fresh bread crumbs (from about 2 slices of firm white bread)
3 tbsp olive oil
1 garlic clove, crushed through a press
2 tbsp finely chopped red onion
¼ teaspoon pimentón (Spanish smoked paprika)
2 large eggs, lightly beaten
2 tbsp chopped flat-leaf parsley
4 sprigs of fresh thyme, leaves picked
sea salt and freshly ground black pepper

For the chile and beet salad
12oz (350g) raw beets, peeled and coarsely grated
1 small fresh red chile pepper, seeded and finely chopped
1 tbsp olive oil
juice of ½ lemon

1 Combine the ground beef, Parmesan, bread crumbs, oil, garlic, onion, paprika, eggs, parsley, and thyme in a bowl and season with salt and pepper. Mix together well by hand. With damp hands, form the mixture into 36–40 balls about the size of small walnuts. Place about 2in (5cm) apart on a large baking sheet lined with parchment paper and press down with your thumb to flatten a little. Chill to firm while you prepare the dough.

2 Preheat the oven to 400°F (200°C). On a lightly floured surface, roll or press the dough to about ¼in (5mm) thick. Using a biscuit cutter, cut into 1¾–2in (4–5cm) discs and place on another large baking sheet lined with parchment paper.

3 Place the sheet of pizza crusts on a rack in the lower third of the oven and the sheet of meatballs in the upper third. Bake for 10–15 minutes until the crusts are golden and the burgers are cooked through. Meanwhile, warm the tomato sauce in the microwave or in a small saucepan over medium heat.

4 To make the salad, combine all the ingredients in a bowl and toss to mix. Spoon a little of the tomato sauce onto each pizza crust, then top with a burger. Garnish each burger with a dab of beet salad and serve immediately.

Chicken mini-burgers with tomato and chile sauce

  PREP 30 MINS · COOK 30 MINS

Chilling • 1 hour
Special equipment • food processor

SERVES 12

1¾lb (800g) skinless boneless chicken breasts, cut into chunks
1 tbsp finely chopped flat-leaf parsley
1 tsp thinly sliced sage leaves
1 garlic clove, finely chopped
1 cup dates, finely chopped
½ cup toasted hazelnuts, skinned and chopped
2 tsp dukkah (Egyptian spice blend)
2 large eggs, lightly beaten
2 tbsp olive oil, plus extra
¾ cup fresh bread crumbs (from about 3 slices of firm white bread)
salt and freshly ground black pepper
1 x 14oz (400g) jar tomato sauce
2 small fresh red chile peppers, seeded and finely chopped
6 fresh basil leaves, torn

To serve
12 thick baguette slices
1 garlic clove, peeled but left whole
2 yellow bell peppers, broiled, skinned, seeded, and sliced
2 red bell peppers, broiled, skinned, seeded, and sliced

1 Pulse the chicken in a food processor until finely ground; be careful not to process it into a paste. Transfer to a bowl and add the herbs, garlic, dates, hazelnuts, dukkah, eggs, oil, and bread crumbs. Mix together thoroughly and season with salt and pepper. Cover with plastic wrap and chill for 1 hour.

2 To cook the burgers, position the top rack of the oven about 8in (20cm) from the broiler and preheat the broiler to medium-hot. Form the mixture into 12 burger-style portions, then brush with a little extra oil. Broil for 6–8 minutes on each side until cooked through, brushing lightly with oil while cooking. Set aside for 15 minutes in a warm place.

3 Warm the tomato sauce in a small saucepan over medium heat, adding the fresh chile and basil. Brush the baguette slices with olive oil and toast on both sides under the broiler. Rub each slice with the garlic clove.
To serve, arrange the bread slices on a platter, top each with a small mound of the bell pepper slices, and then a chicken burger. Spoon a little tomato sauce over each burger and serve.

Hummus

PREP 10 MINS

Special equipment • blender or food processor

SERVES 8-10

1 x 15½oz (440g) can chickpeas, drained and rinsed
2 garlic cloves, crushed
juice of 1 lemon, plus extra if needed
2-3 tbsp tahini
pinch of paprika
2-3 tbsp olive oil
sea salt

1 Combine the chickpeas, garlic, lemon juice, tahini, and paprika in a blender or food processor. Blend to a smooth purée.

2 With the motor running, gradually add the oil, a little at a time, until the hummus reaches a dipping consistency. Taste and season with salt, adding some extra lemon juice if you like. Blend again.

3 Serve as a dip with pita bread.

Baba ghanoush

PREP 15 MINS **COOK 40 MINS**

Special equipment • blender or food processor

SERVES 8-10

1 large eggplant
1 tbsp olive oil
2-3 tbsp tahini
2 garlic cloves, grated or crushed through a press
juice of 1 lemon, plus extra if needed
pinch of ground cumin
sea salt and freshly ground black pepper

1 Preheat the oven to 400°F (200°C). Pierce the eggplant a few times all over with a knife. Next, using your hands, rub the eggplant with the olive oil. Roast in the oven for 30-40 minutes until softened and beginning to char.

2 When the eggplant is cool enough to handle, peel off the skin and put the roasted flesh in a blender or food processor. Add the tahini, garlic, lemon juice, and cumin and blend to a purée.

3 Taste and season with salt and pepper, adding more lemon juice if needed. Blend again briefly. Spoon into a bowl or serving dish and serve with pita bread for dipping.

COOK'S NOTES

Make this dip ahead and leave it in the refrigerator overnight. Remember to allow enough time for it to return to room temperature before serving.

Bruschetta with tomato and basil

 PREP 10 MINS

MAKES 8
6 ripe tomatoes, coarsely diced
handful of fresh basil leaves, torn
4 tbsp extra virgin olive oil
sea salt and freshly ground
    black pepper
1 loaf ciabatta
3 garlic cloves, peeled but left whole

1 Put the tomatoes, basil, and olive oil in a bowl. Season really well with salt and pepper. Set aside to allow the flavors to develop.

2 Preheat the broiler to its highest setting. Slice the ciabatta in half horizontally, then cut each piece into quarters so you have a total of 8 pieces of bread. Watching carefully, toast under the broiler, turning once, until both sides are golden.

3 Immediately rub the cut side of each piece of toast with the garlic. Spoon on the tomato and basil mixture and serve immediately.

COOK'S NOTES

The longer you can leave the tomatoes sitting in the oil and basil, the better. Peel and seed the tomatoes, if you wish.

Mini-chicken tikka tortillas with yogurt, cucumber, and mint dip

 PREP 20 MINS

SERVES 10–12
For the yogurt, cucumber, and mint dip
⅔ cup Greek-style yogurt
½ cucumber, peeled, halved,
    seeded, and diced
1 bunch fresh mint leaves
sea salt and freshly ground
    black pepper

half of an 8oz (225g) bag plain tortilla
    chips (about 40 chips)
½ to 1 cup prepared mango chutney
12oz (350g) ready-cooked chicken
    tikka or other boneless cubes of
    Indian-spiced chicken
fresh cilantro, for garnish

1 To make the dip, combine the yogurt, cucumber, and mint. Season well with salt and pepper. Taste and season more if needed.

2 Spread the tortilla chips out in a single layer on a plate. Add 1 teaspoon of mango chutney and some diced chicken to each one.

3 Now spoon on about 1 teaspoon of the yogurt, cucumber, and mint dip and garnish with a cilantro leaf. Serve at once.

Quail eggs with celery salt

 PREP 10 MINS   **COOK** 15 MINS

Special equipment • food processor

SERVES 4

2 celery stalks, finely chopped
sea salt
12 quail eggs, hard-boiled and peeled
   (or buy ready-prepared ones)

1 Preheat the oven to 400°F (200°C). Place the chopped celery on a baking sheet, sprinkle with a couple of pinches of salt, and toss to coat. Spread the celery into an even layer, then roast in the oven for 5–8 minutes until crisp and dry. Transfer the celery to a food processor and process until fine—this is your celery salt.

2 To boil fresh quail eggs, place them in a pan of gently boiling water, then simmer for 2½ minutes. Drain and rinse in cold water until cool. Carefully peel away the egg shells. Place the quail eggs on a serving plate and sprinkle lightly with a little sea salt. Transfer the remaining celery salt to a small bowl and serve alongside the eggs for dipping.

Cheat...
You can buy ready-made celery salt, but it's fun to make your own and it tastes so much fresher.

COOK'S NOTES
Serve a bowl of mayonnaise alongside the eggs as well, with some fresh crusty bread.

FOOD FOR FRIENDS

Garlic and chile shrimp and squid skewers

  PREP 20 MINS **COOK** 10 MINS

Marinating • 30 minutes

Special equipment • cocktail sticks or mini-wooden skewers

SERVES 6

12 large raw shrimp, peeled
   and deveined
6 baby squid, cleaned and
   halved lengthwise
2 fresh red jalapeño chile peppers,
   seeded and finely sliced
3 garlic cloves, finely chopped
1 tbsp olive oil
small handful of flat-leaf
   parsley leaves
1in (2.5cm) piece of fresh ginger,
   finely grated
sea salt and freshly ground
   black pepper

1 Combine the shrimp, squid, chiles, garlic, oil, parsley, and ginger in a bowl and season with salt and pepper. Leave to marinate in the refrigerator for at least 30 minutes or overnight.

2 Soak 6 cocktail-size bamboo skewers in cold water for 30 minutes and preheat the oven broiler to its highest setting.

3 Thread 1 shrimp, 1 piece of squid, then a second shrimp and another piece of squid onto each of the skewers. Place the skewers on a baking sheet without crowding and broil each side for 1–2 minutes until just cooked through. Serve hot with Yogurt, cucumber, and mint dip (p324).

Cheat...
You could use the leftovers in a salad, or a fish pie.

COOK'S NOTES
Use some of the spicy marinade to brush over the shrimp while they are cooking.

Sesame shrimp toasts

  PREP 15 MINS COOK 10 MINS

Special equipment • blender or food processor

SERVES 4

10oz (300g) peeled and deveined
   cooked shrimp
2 garlic cloves, peeled but left whole
small handful of fresh cilantro
1 red chile, seeded and finely chopped
juice of 1 lime
sea salt and freshly ground
   black pepper
4 slices white bread
4½oz (125g) sesame seeds

1 Preheat the broiler to its highest setting. Blend or process the shrimp, garlic, cilantro, chile, and lime juice to a paste. Season well with salt and pepper and blend again briefly.

2 Lightly toast the bread, then spoon the shrimp mixture evenly over one side of each of the toasts. Spread to cover completely, pressing the mixture down firmly.

3 Lightly oil a baking sheet and pour in the sesame seeds in an even layer. Place the toasts, shrimp-side down, on the seeds, and press so that the seeds stick and coat the mixture. Carefully flip the toasts over and cut them into triangles.

4 Slide the baking sheet under the hot broiler and cook the toasts for a few minutes until the sesame seeds begin to turn golden. Keep a careful eye on them, as they can burn very quickly. Serve immediately.

Potato skins with spicy tomato sauce

  PREP 10 MINS COOK 25 MINS

SERVES 8-10

4 large baking potatoes
1-2 tbsp olive oil
sea salt and freshly ground
   black pepper
6 ripe tomatoes, coarsely chopped
pinch of cayenne pepper
small handful of fresh flat-leaf
   parsley, finely chopped
⅔ cup sour cream

1 Put the potatoes in the microwave and cook on full power for 3-4 minutes until softened. (Alternatively, rub the potatoes with a little olive oil and bake in a preheated 400°F/200°C oven for about 1 hour until soft when pierced with a knife.) Set aside until cool.

2 Preheat the oven to 400°F (200°C). Once the potatoes are cool, quarter each one and scoop out the flesh, leaving a thin layer of flesh in the skin to make a shell. Put the skins hollow-side up on a baking sheet and drizzle with the olive oil. Sprinkle with a pinch of sea salt.

3 Mix together the tomatoes, cayenne, and parsley and season with sea salt and black pepper. Spoon a little of the mixture into each potato skin. Bake in the oven for 15-20 minutes, until the skins are golden and crispy. Top each of the potato skins with some sour cream and serve on a large plate.

COOK'S NOTES

To sour your own cream, add a squeeze of lemon juice to some light cream and set aside for 10 minutes before using.

Scallops skewered with prosciutto

PREP 10 MINS
COOK 8 MINS

Special equipment • skewers

SERVES 8

8 fresh scallops, halved
1 tbsp olive oil
juice of 1 lemon
sea salt and freshly ground
    black pepper
8 slices prosciutto, halved

1 If using wooden skewers, soak them in cold water for 30 minutes. Preheat the oven to 375°F (190°C). Mix the scallops with the oil and lemon juice and season with salt and pepper.

2 Wrap each scallop half in a piece of prosciutto, then thread onto metal or wooden skewers. Carefully put two scallop halves on each skewer, or fewer depending on their size.

3 Lay the skewers on a baking sheet and roast in the oven for 5–8 minutes, until the prosciutto starts to crisp. Serve hot with an arugula garnish.

COOK'S NOTES

If serving non-meat eaters, omit the prosciutto and cook the scallops for a few minutes less.

Beet-topped mini-rye breads

PREP 15 MINS

SERVES 8–10

8 thin slices rye bread
    or pumpernickel
4½oz (125g) Gorgonzola, cubed
10oz (300g) package ready-cooked
    beets (not in vinegar),
    finely diced
2–3 tbsp creamed horseradish

1 Cut the rye bread into small squares—about 6 squares per slice, depending on how big the slices are.

2 Top each bread square with a cube of Gorgonzola, a teaspoonful of diced beets, and a tiny topping of creamed horseradish. Arrange on platters and serve.

VARIATION

For a quick alternative, replace the Gorgonzola with hummus.

TAPAS-STYLE

Spanish-inspired food for sharing,
plate after plate.

TAPAS-STYLE

Tapas are a style of eating rather than a particular dish. It's a way of life in Spain, where appetizing hot or cold bites are eaten with drinks. There are robust rustic dishes, such as grilled chorizo, and simple platters of jamon (Spanish ham), olives, and cheese. The most typical of all is the delicious Spanish omelet, the tortilla, which nearly always makes an appearance when tapas are served.

FOOD FOR FRIENDS

What are tapas?

Tapas derives from the word *tapar*, which means "to cover." Traditionally, small bites of food, such as a piece of toasted bread with a slice of ham on top, would be balanced on top of a glass of wine or sherry. Simple, traditional tapas such as olives, cheeses, and meats are still served all over Spain in bars to accompany an apéritif before lunch or dinner. There are no standard tapas to serve together, just plenty of small bowls, with a good range of fresh flavors. When making tapas for a group, serve them all on one platter, along with a choice of two dishes of meat, fish, vegetables, and egg and cheese.

A selection of tapas in traditional Spanish-style clay bowls.

The Spanish platter A selection of good meats, cheeses, and pickles makes for perfect tapas.

COOKED MEATS

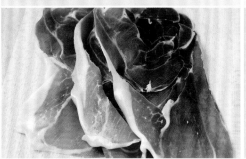

JAMON SERRANO (SPANISH HAM) is a delicious, sweet dry-cured ham that is served raw and sliced paper-thin. It has a deep, rich texture due to the traditional curing methods.

JAMON IBERICO is another cured ham, highly prized and expensive. It comes from the Iberico pig that is native to Spain.

CHORIZO There are lots of varieties of chorizo, the spicy pork sausage of Spain. It can be smoked, unsmoked, fresh, or cured. Its unique taste is spiced with aromatic flavors, and usually features garlic and paprika. Cured chorizo can be served raw, sliced alongside cheese and olives. Fresh chorizo is often cubed and cooked.

CHEESE

MANCHEGO is the most widely known and widely available Spanish cheese. This salty cheese is made from milk from the Manchego sheep and can be soft or hard, depending on how long it has had to ripen. There are two types: the artisanal (farmhouse) type which is made with unpasteurized milk, and the commercial type made with pasteurized milk. They are both available either semi-cured or cured. Manchego is perfect served alone with a chunk of bread, with a glass of fino or manzanilla sherry, or with quince paste or honey.

You can serve **Parmesan cheese** as an alternative to Manchego, but keep in mind it's stronger and saltier, so you'll need less of it.

OLIVES AND PICKLES

MANZANILLA OLIVES are the most popular choice for tapas. They are large, green, sweet Spanish olives that are often stuffed with anchovies or flavored with lemon, thyme, or oregano. They are the simplest tapas dish. Place them in a small bowl with cocktail sticks for serving.

PICKLED CAPERS Jars of pickled capers and whole caper berries with their stalks on are a popular tapas accompaniment.

PICKLED ANCHOVIES White anchovies are often served in little bowls, either marinated in a dash of white wine vinegar and a sprinkling of freshly chopped parsley, or teamed with strips of roasted red pepper and served with cocktail sticks, or on top of sliced bread or toast, sprinkled with paprika.

The ultimate Spanish omelet A simple tortilla made

with potatoes, onions, and eggs.

1 Peel and slice 5 medium potatoes, about ¼in (5mm) thick. Put about 1¼ cups of olive oil in a deep-sided ovenproof frying pan (preferably nonstick), then add the potatoes and cook at a gentle simmer for about 15 minutes, or until the potatoes are soft when you poke them with a sharp knife. Remove the potatoes with a slotted spoon and put them in a large bowl to cool.

2 Halve, peel, and quarter 3 medium onions and slice to make crescent moon shapes. Pour most of the oil out of the pan (you can sieve and re-use) and add the onions and a pinch of salt. Cook over low heat until soft and beginning to caramelize. Add to the potatoes and leave to cool.

3 Whisk 5 eggs with a fork, then pour into the cooled potato and onion mixture, season with sea salt and freshly ground black pepper, and combine gently so all the potatoes get coated, trying not to break them up too much. Preheat the oven to 400°F (200°C). Heat 1 tablespoon of the olive oil in the frying pan until hot, then carefully slide the mixture in, spreading it evenly so it covers the base of the pan. Reduce the heat to medium-low and cook for 6–10 minutes, or until almost set.

4 Cook in the oven for another 10 minutes, or until set and golden. Alternatively, cook one side, then invert onto a plate and add back to the pan to cook the other side. Remove from the pan, leave to cool and completely set, then slice into wedges. Serve warm or cold.

The Spanish kitchen

The essentials

Olive oil is a staple in the Spanish kitchen, and is used liberally in cooking, or used to drizzle over tapas dishes such as roasted peppers or marinated artichokes. It can be served in a bowl with rustic bread for dipping.

Garlic is essential in Spanish cooking and is added in generous quantities to many dishes. Use for aioli (garlic mayonnaise), or for garlic shrimp.

Onions are used extensively in Spanish cooking. Choose the mild, sweet, yellow-skinned ones to make the Spanish omelet (see left).

The spice rack

Paprika (pimento) is the best-known spice of Spanish cooking. The highest-quality paprika comes from the western La Vera region, and is oak-smoked to give it its distinctive smoked flavor. It is made from ground chile peppers, and comes as hot (*picante*) or sweet (*dulce*) paprika. It imparts a wonderful color and depth of flavor to a variety of dishes, particularly pork and chicken, and is used in many tapas recipes, or simply added as garnish.

Saffron is a sweet, yellow, expensive spice, and should be used sparingly—not only because of its cost, but because it can have an overpowering taste if overused. Its strands are traditionally used in paella, chicken dishes, and can also be added to zucchini salads.

Cinnamon is used throughout Spain to flavor meat and vegetable dishes. It comes as a bark, or ground to a deeply aromatic powder. Add the bark to rice dishes while cooking, or add the powder to chicken dishes.

Nutmeg is another aromatic spice often used in Spanish cooking. Use it sparingly and freshly ground into potato dishes, meat stews, or sweet dishes such as custards.

Paprika is a key ingredient in Spanish cooking.

Patatas bravas

PREP 15 MINS COOK 30 MINS

SERVES 4

6 tbsp olive oil

1½lb (675g) all-purpose waxy
potatoes, peeled and cut into
¾in (2cm) dice

2 onions, finely chopped

1 tsp crushed red pepper flakes

2 tbsp dry sherry

finely grated zest of 1 lemon

4 garlic cloves, finely chopped

half of a 14oz (400g) can diced
tomatoes, with juices

handful of flat-leaf parsley, chopped

sea salt and freshly ground
black pepper

1 Preheat the oven to 400°F (200°C).
Heat half the oil in a nonstick frying
pan, add the potatoes, and cook,
turning frequently, over medium-low
heat for 20 minutes or until starting
to brown. Add the onions and cook for
another 5 minutes.

2 Add the pepper flakes, sherry,
lemon zest, and garlic and cook for
2 minutes before adding the tomatoes
and parsley. Season with salt and
pepper and cook over medium heat
for 10 minutes, stirring occasionally.

3 Stir in the remaining oil and
transfer to a shallow baking dish.
Bake for 30 minutes until heated
through. Serve hot, with a crisp
green salad, if desired.

Cheat...
You can leave out the
oven cooking and cook
them on the stove
instead. The oven
cooking intensifies
the flavor.

Potato and paprika omelet

PREP 10 MINS COOK 55 MINS

Cooling • 15 minutes

SERVES 4

1 cup olive oil

1lb (450g) all-purpose waxy potatoes,
peeled and cut into slices ½in
(1cm) thick

3 onions, thinly sliced

2 tsp paprika

6 large eggs

sea salt and freshly ground
black pepper

1 Heat the oil in a nonstick frying
pan 10in (25cm) wide and 2in (5cm)
deep. Add the potatoes and cook over
low heat for 15–20 minutes or until
beginning to soften but not brown.
Carefully remove from the oil with
a slotted spoon and place in a bowl.

2 Add the onions to the pan and cook
slowly for 10–15 minutes or until
beginning to soften but not brown.
Remove from the oil with a slotted
spoon and add to the potatoes with the
paprika. Allow to cool for 15 minutes.
Discard all but 3 tbsp of the oil and
return the pan to the heat until hot.

3 Meanwhile, break the eggs into
a mixing bowl and beat with a fork.
Season well with salt and pepper and
add to the potatoes and onion
mixture, stirring gently to mix. Scrape
the mixture into the frying pan and
cook over low heat for 15–20 minutes
or until set, then place under a hot
broiler until the top turns golden.
Leave to rest for 5 minutes, then
carefully transfer to a serving plate.
Slice and serve hot or cold.

COOK'S NOTES

*To remove the omelet from the
pan, first be sure it's not stuck to
the sides or the bottom; then place
a large plate over the top and hold
it firmly in place while quickly
inverting the pan.*

Mini pork meatballs in spiced tomato sauce

PREP 30 MINS | COOK 20 MINS

SERVES 4

10oz (300g) ground pork
1 small onion, finely chopped
1 tsp capers, drained and
    finely chopped
2 tsp black olives, finely chopped
1 tbsp all-purpose flour
1 large egg, lightly beaten
sea salt and freshly ground
    black pepper
4 tbsp olive oil
1 x 14oz (400g) can diced tomatoes,
    with juices
2 garlic cloves, finely chopped
1 tsp paprika

1 Preheat the oven to 400°F (200°C). Combine the pork, onion, capers, olives, and flour in a bowl, add the egg, and season with salt and pepper. Using your hands, mix thoroughly, then form into 12–15 ¾in (2cm) balls.

2 Heat the oil in a frying pan and cook the meatballs for 8–10 minutes until golden brown. Drain, transfer to a baking dish, and set aside.

3 Combine the tomatoes, garlic, and paprika in a saucepan, season with salt and pepper, then cook over medium heat for 10 minutes, stirring occasionally. Pour the tomato sauce over the meatballs and bake for 20 minutes until bubbly-hot. Serve hot.

Stuffed mushrooms

PREP 20 MINS | COOK 15 MINS

SERVES 4

12 medium mushrooms, stems removed
4 tbsp olive oil
3 tbsp fresh bread crumbs (from a
    slice of firm-textured white bread)
1 onion, finely chopped
2 garlic cloves, crushed
1 small fresh red jalapeño chile
    pepper, seeded and finely chopped
handful of flat-leaf parsley, chopped
5½oz (150g) ground pork
1 tomato, finely chopped
sea salt and freshly ground
    black pepper

1 Brush the mushroom caps all over with a little of the oil. Put the remaining oil in a bowl with the bread crumbs, onion, garlic, chile, parsley, pork, tomato, salt, and pepper. Mix with your hands to form a paste. Arrange the caps, stem-side up, on a parchment-lined baking sheet and mound the filling into each cavity.

2 Place the baking sheet on a rack, 8in (20cm) from the heating element, and broil for 12–15 minutes or until cooked through and golden brown. Serve with a drizzle of olive oil.

Marinated anchovies, salted almonds, and olives

PREP 15 MINS

Marinating • 1 hour

SERVES 4

For the olives

9oz (250g) assorted green and black olives (not pitted)

2 garlic cloves, thinly sliced

finely grated zest of 1 orange

2 fresh red chile peppers, seeded and very finely chopped

1 tsp whole black peppercorns, coarsely crushed

3 tbsp extra virgin olive oil

For the anchovies

2–3 x 2oz (56.7g) cans of flat anchovies packed in olive oil

2 garlic cloves, finely sliced

small handful of dill, finely chopped

1 tsp white wine vinegar

freshly ground black pepper

For the almonds

1 cup whole natural almonds (skins on)

1 tsp sea salt

1 Put the olives in a small bowl with the garlic, orange zest, chiles, and peppercorns. Drizzle with the oil, stir, then leave to marinate for at least 1 hour at room temperature, or longer in the refrigerator.

2 Meanwhile, put the anchovies and their oil in a small serving bowl. Add the garlic, dill, and vinegar, season with black pepper, and stir gently. Leave to marinate for at least 30 minutes.

3 While the olives and anchovies are marinating, put the whole almonds in a dry medium frying pan and heat gently over low heat. Sprinkle them with the salt, toss to coat, then cook, stirring frequently so they don't burn, for 5 minutes or until lightly toasted.

4 Transfer the almonds, olives, and anchovies to serving bowls, or make individual mounds of each on a serving dish. Serve at room temperature.

Shrimp with garlic and hot pepper

PREP 5 MINS **COOK 10 MINS**

SERVES 4

4 tbsp olive oil

6 garlic cloves, thinly sliced

1 tsp crushed red pepper flakes

1 tbsp dry sherry

8–9oz (250g) raw shrimp, shelled and deveined

salt and freshly ground black pepper

1 Heat the oil in a frying pan over medium-low heat. Add the garlic and pepper flakes and cook gently, stirring, for about 1 minute.

2 Add the sherry and shrimp, turn up the heat, and cook, stirring occasionally, for 5 minutes or until the juices have reduced by half. Season with salt and pepper and serve with crusty bread and a crisp salad.

> **COOK'S NOTES**
>
> You can use shell-on shrimp if you prefer for this dish—provide a finger bowl and napkins, though!

Grilled goat cheese with honey

PREP 10 MINS COOK 5 MINS

SERVES 4
2 tbsp honey
2 tbsp dry sherry
1 x 10oz (300g) log of goat cheese,
    cut into ½in (1cm) thick slices
1 baguette, cut into 12 slices, each
    about ½in (1cm) thick, toasted
2 tbsp dried oregano

1 Put the honey and sherry in a small pan and cook over low heat, stirring, until the honey has dissolved.

2 Place a round of cheese on each piece of toast and pour a little of the honey mixture on top. Sprinkle with the oregano and broil about 8in (20cm) from the heat source for 3-5 minutes or until just starting to brown. Serve immediately with a crisp salad.

COOK'S NOTES

Drizzle with a little more honey to serve, if you wish. There are numerous varieties of honeys available—try heather or orange blossom honey.

Chorizo with peppers

PREP 10 MINS COOK 10 MINS

SERVES 4
2 tbsp olive oil
2 red bell peppers, seeded and cut
    into ¾in (2cm) squares
2 green bell peppers, seeded and cut
    into ¾in (2cm) squares
3 garlic cloves, crushed
9-10oz (300g) chorizo, cut into
    ¾in (2cm) cubes
2 tbsp dry sherry
1 tsp dried oregano
sea salt and freshly ground
    black pepper

1 Heat the oil in a frying pan, add the peppers, and cook over medium heat, stirring occasionally, for 5 minutes. Add the garlic, chorizo, and sherry and cook for 5 minutes more.

2 Sprinkle the oregano over the top, season with salt and pepper, and serve.

COOK'S NOTES
This is delicious served alongside— or on top of—toasted ciabatta or another country-style crusty bread, grilled or toasted if you prefer.

335

Feta-stuffed peppers

 PREP 15 MINS

SERVES 4

5½oz (150g) feta cheese
3 garlic cloves, crushed through
   a press
1 tbsp finely chopped flat-leaf parsley
1 tsp freshly ground black pepper
12 fresh piquillo peppers (see
   Cook's Notes)
4 tbsp olive oil

1 Preheat the oven to 400°F (200°C). Combine the feta, garlic, parsley, and pepper in a bowl and mash together with a fork to form a smooth paste.

2 Cut the stem end off the peppers. Using a melon baller, remove the seeds and membranes from inside the peppers, then stuff with the feta mixture. Brush with oil, then pack tightly into a small baking dish. Spoon the remaining oil over the top and bake for 20 minutes, until the peppers are tender. Serve hot.

COOK'S NOTES

If you can't get fresh piquillo peppers, use some from a jar and drain well before using.

Mushrooms on toast with Manchego cheese

 PREP 10 MINS

SERVES 4

2 tbsp olive oil
7oz (200g) mushrooms, coarsely
   chopped
sea salt and freshly ground black
   pepper
3 garlic cloves, finely chopped
1 tsp paprika
3 tbsp dry sherry
handful of flat-leaf parsley, finely
   chopped
8 slices country-style bread, toasted
3½oz (100g) Manchego cheese, shaved
   into strips with a vegetable peeler

1 Preheat the oven to 400°F (200°C). Heat the oil in a frying pan, add the mushrooms and salt, and cook over medium heat for 5 minutes, until the mushrooms start to release juices.

2 Add the garlic and paprika and cook for 1 minute. Add the sherry and 1 teaspoon of pepper, then increase the heat and allow to bubble until the liquid has reduced by three-quarters. Stir in the parsley and remove from the heat. Set aside.

3 Lay the toast out on a baking sheet, then carefully spoon the mushroom mixture on top. Sprinkle liberally with the Manchego shavings and bake in the oven for 2 minutes or until the cheese has melted. Serve hot with a crisp salad, if desired.

Ham with pears

Cooling • 30 minutes

SERVES 4

½ cup fino sherry
1 cup water
½ cup granulated sugar
3 firm but ripe Bosc pears, peeled and
    quartered
5½oz (150g) thinly sliced Serrano
    ham or prosciutto, cut into pieces
hot chili oil or yogurt and mint,
    for serving

1 Combine the sherry, water, and sugar in a saucepan and bring to a boil. Add the pears, return to a boil, and simmer for 10–15 minutes until they are just tender. Turn off the heat and allow to cool for 30 minutes.

2 Wrap each pear cube in a piece of ham. Drizzle with chili oil, or serve with plain yogurt and fresh mint.

Grilled sardines on toast

Marinating • 20 minutes

SERVES 4

8 fresh sardines, cleaned, gutted,
    and filleted
4 tbsp olive oil
3 garlic cloves, thinly sliced
1 fresh green chile pepper, seeded
    and finely chopped
juice of 1 lemon
1 tsp fennel seeds, crushed
2 tbsp finely chopped flat-leaf parsley
sea salt and freshly ground
    black pepper
ciabatta, sliced and toasted,
    for serving

1 Brush the sardines with a little of the oil and cook under a medium-hot broiler for 3 minutes on each side. Remove and allow to cool.

2 Meanwhile, mix together the remaining oil, garlic, chile, lemon juice, fennel, salt, and pepper in a large bowl. Add the sardines, tossing to coat well, then marinate for 20 minutes. Serve on slices of toasted ciabatta.

Spinach, pine nuts, and raisins

PREP 5 MINS

SERVES 4

1 tbsp olive oil
3 tbsp dark raisins
3 tbsp pine nuts
3 tbsp dry sherry
7oz (200g) spinach, rinsed, drained, and coarsely chopped, but not completely dried
1 tsp paprika
sea salt and freshly ground black pepper

1 Combine the oil, raisins, and pine nuts in a frying pan over medium heat. When they start to sizzle, cook for 1–2 minutes, stirring constantly, until lightly browned. Add the sherry and cook until reduced by half.

2 Add the spinach and paprika and stir constantly for 5 minutes or until the spinach has wilted. Season with salt and pepper and serve hot or cold.

VARIATION Replace the sherry with dessert wine or white wine, or a splash of white wine vinegar for sharpness. Use broccoli instead of spinach.

Battered fish with lemon mayonnaise

PREP 20 MINS

Special equipment • food processor

SERVES 4

1 whole large egg, plus 1 egg yolk
juice and finely grated zest of 1 lemon
1 cup olive oil
sea salt and freshly ground black pepper
1¼ cups all-purpose flour
1 tsp baking soda
1 tsp paprika
⅔ cup cold sparkling soda water
1 cup olive oil, for frying
10oz (300g) skinless boneless white fish, such as haddock, cut into ½in (1cm) strips

1 To make the mayonnaise, combine the egg, egg yolk, lemon juice, and zest in a food processor and mix until pale yellow. Add the oil a few drops at a time and blend, then add the remaining oil in a steady stream until it forms a smooth emulsion. Season with salt and pepper, transfer to a serving bowl, cover, and refrigerate.

2 Whisk together the flour, baking soda, paprika, and soda water. Season with salt and pepper, then whisk until smooth. Meanwhile, heat the oil in a deep-sided frying pan and place over medium-high heat until it reaches 400°F (200°C) on a deep-fry thermometer. Adjust as needed; the oil should be very hot but not smoking.

3 Put the fish in the batter one piece at a time and coat well. Carefully place the fish in the hot oil. Cook the fish in batches for 2–3 minutes, turning, until rich golden brown. Remove with a slotted spoon and place on paper towels to drain. Sprinkle with a little salt and serve hot, with the lemon mayonnaise.

VARIATION Use beer instead of soda water in the batter. It will give a crisp, rich dark batter.

Cheat...
Mix the juice of 1 lemon with 2 large tablespoons ready-made mayonnaise, instead of making your own.

FOOD FOR FRIENDS

Sweet corn fritters

PREP 10 MINS **COOK** 15 MINS

Chilling • 15 minutes

SERVES 4

1¼ cups all-purpose flour
2 tbsp cold sparkling soda water
1 tsp baking powder
1 x 11–12oz (340g) can corn
   kernels, drained
1 tsp cayenne pepper
sea salt and freshly ground
   black pepper
3 tbsp olive oil

1 Combine the flour, soda water, and baking powder in a bowl and whisk together to form a smooth batter. Stir in the corn and cayenne and season with salt and pepper. Refrigerate for 15 minutes until chilled.

2 Heat the oil in a shallow frying pan over medium-high heat. Stir the batter, then carefully drop a spoonful into the pan—it should spread out to be 3–4in (7.5–10cm) across. Stir the batter again and add 2–3 more spoonfuls, depending on the size of your pan, and, working in batches, cook for 4–6 minutes, turning once, until golden brown. Remove with a slotted spoon or spatula and place on paper towels to drain. Serve with aioli (garlic mayonnaise) and a crisp salad.

COOK'S NOTES

The fritters will be crisper if the mixture is cold when it goes into the hot pan. Use fresh corn, sliced off the cob, if you can.

Baby Gem lettuce with blue cheese and beets

PREP 15 MINS

Special equipment • food processor

SERVES 4

5½oz (150g) Roquefort or Gorgonzola,
   crumbled (about 1½ cups)
1 tsp paprika
3 tbsp plain yogurt
1 tbsp chopped fresh mint
sea salt and freshly ground
   black pepper
1 head Little Gem (baby
   romaine) lettuce
3 small beets, sliced

1 Pulse half of the cheese, the paprika, yogurt, and mint in a food processor to make a paste. Move to a bowl, add the remaining cheese, and season with salt and pepper.

2 Separate the lettuce leaves to create 8 "boats," then fill each with beet slices and the cheese mixture. Serve with bread and chorizo.

VARIATION

Instead of Baby Gem, use endive (chicory) or raddiccio—it is bitter, but works well with blue cheese.

Mushrooms in garlic sauce

PREP 10 MINS **COOK 15 MINS**

SERVES 4

4 tbsp olive oil
1lb (450g) mushrooms, halved
4 garlic cloves, finely sliced
2 fresh red chiles, seeded and
    finely sliced
4 tbsp dry sherry
1 chicken bouillon cube
freshly ground black pepper

1 Heat the oil in a large frying pan, add the mushrooms, garlic, and chiles, and cook for 2 minutes over low heat. Add the sherry, crumble in the bouillon cube, and season with pepper. Increase the heat to medium and cook for 10 minutes, stirring occasionally, or until the mushrooms have released their juices.

2 Cook for 3 minutes more, or until the juices have reduced by half. Serve warm, with crusty bread.

Fried calamari

PREP 15 MINS **COOK 10 MINS**

SERVES 4

2 large eggs
2 tbsp cold sparkling soda water
1½ cups all-purpose flour
1 tsp crushed red pepper flakes
1 tsp sea salt
1lb 2oz (500g) small squid,
    gutted, cleaned, and cut into
    ½in (1cm) rings
1 cup vegetable oil or sunflower oil
lemon wedges, to serve

1 Break the eggs into a bowl, add the soda water, and beat well with a whisk. Mix the flour, pepper flakes, and salt in a shallow bowl. Dip each piece of squid into the egg mixture, then coat evenly with flour.

2 Meanwhile, heat the oil in a deep frying pan over medium-high heat until hot. Carefully add the squid one piece at a time, working in small batches. Cook each batch for 2-3 minutes or until golden brown all over. Remove with a slotted spoon and drain on paper towels. Serve hot, with a squeeze of lemon.

COOK'S NOTES

Do use small squid, as it tends to be much more tender than the larger ones, and buy it fresh.

Tomato, bean, and zucchini stew

 PREP 10 MINS **COOK 20 MINS**

SERVES 4

3 tbsp olive oil
1 large onion, finely chopped
2 zucchini, cut into bite-sized chunks
3 garlic cloves, finely sliced
1 x 14oz (400g) can borlotti beans, drained and rinsed
3 fresh tomatoes, diced
1 tsp paprika
1 tsp dried oregano
sea salt and freshly ground black pepper
hot chili oil, to serve (optional)

1 Heat the oil in a deep-sided frying pan, add the onion, and cook over medium heat for 3 minutes. Add the zucchini and cook for another 5 minutes, stirring frequently.

2 Add the garlic and beans, cook for 1 minute, then stir in the tomatoes, paprika, and oregano. Cook for 10 minutes, stirring occasionally, then season with salt and pepper. Drizzle with chili oil, if desired, and serve with crusty bread.

Halloumi with garlic, chili, and cilantro

 PREP 10 MINS **COOK 15 MINS**

SERVES 4

3 tbsp olive oil
2 fresh red chiles, seeded and finely sliced
4 garlic cloves, finely sliced
9oz (250g) halloumi cheese, cut into slices ¼in (5mm) thick
handful of fresh cilantro, chopped
sea salt and freshly ground black pepper

1 Heat the oil in a shallow frying pan, add the chiles, and cook over medium heat for 2 minutes. Add the garlic, cook for 1 minute, then remove from the heat. Using a slotted spoon, transfer the garlic and chiles to a plate and set aside. Reserve the oil left in the pan.

2 Return the pan with the oil to the heat and carefully add the halloumi. Cook for 3 minutes on each side, until golden. Add the cilantro and the chile-garlic mixture, then season well. Toss together and cook for 2 minutes to blend the flavors. Serve with crusty bread or a tomato salad.

COOK'S NOTES

Because halloumi cheese doesn't melt, it is great for cooking on a grill or cast-iron grill pan.

Chickpeas in olive oil and lemon

SERVES 4

3 tbsp olive oil

2 garlic cloves, finely sliced

1 x 14oz (400g) can chickpeas,
    drained and rinsed

juice of ½ lemon

zest of 1 lemon

handful of fresh flat-leaf
    parsley, chopped

sea salt and freshly ground
    black pepper

extra virgin olive oil or hot chili oil

1 Heat the oil in a frying pan, add
the garlic and chickpeas, and cook for
2 minutes. Stir in the lemon juice, zest,
and parsley, then cook over medium
heat for an additional 2 minutes.

2 Remove from the heat and season
well with salt and pepper. Serve hot
or cold with a generous splash of
extra virgin olive oil or chili oil.

VARIATION

Use dried chickpeas if
time permits. Soak them
the night before, then
drain and simmer for
1–1½ hours, until soft.

Chorizo with dried fruit chutney

SERVES 4

¾ cup dried apricots, chopped

½ cup dark raisins

1 tbsp olive oil

1 onion, finely chopped

10oz (300g) chorizo, cut into
    bite-sized chunks

3 tbsp dry sherry

½ cup chopped toasted walnuts

freshly ground black pepper

1 Preheat the oven to 400°F (200°C).
Put the apricots and raisins in a bowl,
cover with a little hot water, and leave
to soften for 10 minutes. Meanwhile,
heat the oil in a frying pan, add the
onion, and cook over medium heat for
5 minutes, until soft. Add the chorizo
and cook for 5 minutes more, stirring
occasionally. Drain off any excess fat.

2 Drain the fruit, add it to the pan,
then add the sherry and walnuts.
Increase the heat and cook for
2 minutes, scraping up any brown bits
from the pan with a wooden spoon.
Season with pepper, then transfer to
a small baking dish. Cover with foil,
then bake for 15 minutes. Serve with
crusty bread and salad.

Marinated squid salad

 PREP 15 MINS COOK

Marinating • 30 minutes

SERVES 4

10oz (300g) small squid, gutted
and cleaned
7 tbsp olive oil
sea salt and freshly ground
black pepper
2 tbsp white wine vinegar
3 garlic cloves, crushed
1 tsp paprika
handful of fresh flat-leaf parsley,
finely chopped

1 Cut the squid into pieces–a mixture of strips and rings–and brush with a little of the oil and season well.

2 Heat 1 tablespoon of the oil in a frying pan, add the squid, and cook over a medium heat, stirring constantly, for 2–3 minutes, or until the squid is cooked. Remove from the heat and transfer to a serving bowl.

3 Mix the remaining oil with the vinegar, garlic, paprika, and parsley, then season. Pour over the squid, toss gently, and leave to marinate for at least 30 minutes. Serve with crusty bread and a green salad.

FOOD FOR FRIENDS

Sweet balsamic onions

 PREP 10 MINS COOK 35 MINS ♡

SERVES 4
3 tbsp olive oil
1lb (450g) whole baby onions, peeled
3 garlic cloves, finely sliced
3 tbsp balsamic vinegar
sea salt and freshly ground
black pepper
olive oil or hot chili oil, to serve

1 Preheat the oven to 350°F (180°C). Heat the oil in a deep-sided frying pan, then add the onions and cook over low heat, stirring frequently, until browned, about 15 minutes.

2 Transfer the onions to a small baking dish, packing them in tightly. Sprinkle with the garlic and spoon the balsamic vinegar over the top. Season well with salt and pepper, then bake, stirring every 5 minutes, until tender and glazed, about 20 minutes. Serve hot or cold with a good drizzle of olive oil or chili oil, and some crusty bread and cheese.

 VARIATION
Sprinkle in some fresh thyme leaves and finely chopped rosemary instead of the garlic.

COOK'S NOTES

The onions can be prepared well in advance and will keep under oil for weeks in the refrigerator.

Skewered swordfish with capers

 PREP 15 MINS COOK 10 MINS

Special equipment • skewers or cocktail sticks

SERVES 4

1lb (450g) swordfish steaks, cut into ¾in (2cm) cubes
sea salt and freshly ground black pepper
3 tbsp olive oil
1 tbsp white wine vinegar
2 tbsp capers, rinsed and drained
2 garlic cloves, thinly sliced
hot chili oil

1 Preheat the oven to 400°F (200°C). Thread three pieces of swordfish onto each of 12–15 six-inch bamboo or other short skewers. (Be sure to soak for 30 minutes to prevent burning.) Place in a baking dish and season well with salt and pepper.

2 Mix the oil, vinegar, capers, and garlic in a small bowl, crushing half the capers with the back of a fork or knife. Pour evenly over the swordfish and bake in the oven for 10 minutes. Serve with a splash of chili oil and some crusty bread.

Lamb with lemon and olives

PREP 25 MINS COOK 20 MINS

SERVES 4

3 tbsp olive oil
1 onion, finely chopped
1lb 2oz (500g) lean lamb, such as the leg, cut into ¾in (2cm) cubes
6 garlic cloves, thinly sliced
1 lemon, cut into eighths, seeds removed
1 tsp chopped fresh rosemary
handful of flat-leaf parsley, chopped
1 tsp paprika
3 tbsp pitted green olives

1 Preheat the oven to 400°F (200°C). Heat the oil in a frying pan, add the onion, and cook over medium heat for 5 minutes or until it is beginning to soften. Add the lamb and cook, stirring occasionally, for 5 minutes or until no longer pink on the outside. Add the garlic and lemon and cook for 1 minute, then add the rosemary, parsley, paprika, and olives and cook for 2 minutes, stirring well.

2 Transfer the mixture to a small baking dish, packing it in tightly. Add 2 tablespoons water and bake for 20 minutes.

3 Remove from the oven and allow to rest for 10 minutes before serving with crusty bread and a crisp green salad with a citrus vinaigrette.

Roasted sweet potato and pepper tortilla

PREP 15 MINS   COOK 45 MINS

SERVES 4-6

1¼lb (550g) sweet potatoes, peeled
    and cut into ¾in (2cm) cubes
1 tsp crushed red pepper flakes
5 tbsp olive oil
2 small onions, finely chopped
6 large eggs
sea salt and freshly ground
    black pepper

1 Preheat the oven to 400°F (200°C). Put the sweet potatoes on a nonstick baking sheet, add the pepper flakes and 2 tbsp of the oil, and mix well. Roast for 30 minutes, turning occasionally, until just tender.

2 Meanwhile, heat the remaining oil in a frying pan with an ovenproof handle. Add the onions and cook over medium heat, stirring, for 5 minutes or until soft. Stir in the sweet potatoes.

3 Break the eggs into a mixing bowl, season with salt and pepper, and beat well with a fork. Pour into the sweet potato mixture and cook over low heat for 10 minutes or until set. Transfer the pan to the oven to brown the top of the tortilla. Loosen the edges with a blunt knife or spatula and invert onto a plate. Serve with a mixed green salad.

COOK'S NOTES

If your frying-pan handle is plastic or wooden, wrap it with a double layer of foil before putting it in the oven. To turn out the tortilla, make sure it is not stuck to the sides and bottom of the pan, place a plate over the frying pan, and carefully and quickly turn it over.

Chicken with cinnamon and peppers

PREP 25 MINS   COOK 20 MINS   ♥

SERVES 4

1lb (450g) skinless boneless chicken
    breast halves (preferably free-
    range), cut into 1½in (4cm) cubes
1 tsp ground cinnamon
1 tsp paprika
4 tbsp olive oil
1 red bell pepper, seeded and
    cut into strips
1 green bell pepper, seeded and
    cut into strips
1 onion, sliced
3 garlic cloves, thinly sliced
⅔ cup hot chicken stock
generous splash of chili oil, to serve

1 Preheat the oven to 400°F (200°C). Put the chicken in a mixing bowl and rub all over with the cinnamon and paprika, then set aside.

2 Meanwhile, heat the oil in a frying pan, add the peppers and onion, and cook over medium heat, stirring occasionally, for 5 minutes or until they start to soften. Add the chicken and cook, stirring constantly, for 5 minutes or until no longer pink. Add the garlic and cook for 1 minute, then stir in the chicken stock.

3 Transfer to a baking dish and bake for 20 minutes. Serve with a generous drizzle of chili oil over the top and mixed salad greens on the side.

Mini pork kebabs

PREP 15 MINS | **COOK 10 MINS**

Marinating • 30 minutes
Special equipment • skewers

SERVES 4

1¼lb (550g) lean pork, cut into
    ¾in (2cm) cubes
6 garlic cloves, crushed
1 tsp crushed red pepper flakes
1 tsp ground fennel seeds
1 tsp paprika
juice and zest of 1 lemon
3 tbsp fresh flat-leaf parsley,
    finely chopped
1 tbsp dry sherry
2 tbsp olive oil
salt and freshly ground black pepper

1 If using wooden skewers, soak them in cold water for 30 minutes before using. Put all the ingredients in a mixing bowl, combine well, then leave to marinate for at least 30 minutes.

2 Thread the pork onto the small skewers or cocktail sticks and cook in a hot frying pan or griddle pan for 10 minutes, turning frequently. Leave to rest for 10 minutes, then serve with a mixed salad.

Chicken wings with garlic

PREP 20 MINS | **COOK 30 MINS**

Marinating • 20 minutes

SERVES 4

12 chicken wings
2 tbsp fresh lemon juice
2 tsp paprika
3 tbsp olive oil
6 garlic cloves, thinly sliced
4 tbsp dry (fino) sherry
sea salt and freshly ground
    black pepper

1 Pierce the chicken wings all over with the tip of a sharp knife, then put them in a mixing bowl with the lemon juice and paprika and leave to marinate for 20 minutes at room temperature.

2 Heat the oil in a deep-sided nonstick frying pan, add the chicken wings, and cook over medium heat, turning frequently, for 10 minutes or until brown all over.

3 Reduce the heat, add the garlic and sherry, then season well with salt and pepper. Combine well and cook for 5 minutes, then cover and cook over low heat for 15 minutes, turning occasionally. Serve with a crisp green salad.

Shrimp and chicken empañadas

PREP 35 MINS

COOK 5 MINS

Special equipment • food processor • 4in (10cm) round biscuit cutter

MAKES 10–12

7 tbsp butter

juice of I lemon

2 cups all-purpose flour

sea salt and freshly ground
   black pepper

1 small skinless boneless chicken
   breast half, about 4¼oz (125g),
   coarsely chopped

4¼oz (125g) cooked, peeled, and
   deveined shrimp

2 tbsp olive oil

1 onion, finely chopped

3 tbsp dry (fino) sherry

3 garlic cloves, crushed

1 tbsp tomato purée

1 tsp cayenne pepper

1 tbsp finely chopped
   flat-leaf parsley

1 cup sunflower or vegetable oil

1 Melt the butter in a small pan, then add the lemon juice and ⅓ cup water. Add the flour and a pinch of salt and stir well to make a paste. Knead well on a floured work surface, wrap in plastic wrap, and refrigerate.

2 Meanwhile, process the chicken and the shrimp separately in a food processor, pulsing the machine on and off until very finely chopped. Heat the oil in a frying pan, add the onion, and cook over medium heat for 5 minutes. Add the chicken and cook for another 5 minutes, stirring occasionally, until white throughout. Add the sherry, garlic, processed shrimp, tomato purée, cayenne, and parsley and season well with salt and pepper. Mix well and cook for 10 minutes, then allow to cool for at least 5 minutes.

3 Meanwhile, on a floured work surface, roll out the pastry to ¼in (5mm) thick. Using the biscuit cutter, cut out 10–12 circles of pastry. Place 1 tablespoon of the chicken and shrimp mixture in the middle of each, and fold in half. Wet the edges a little with some cold water, then crimp together with your fingers to seal.

4 Heat the oil in a deep-sided frying pan until hot. Working in batches, cook the empañadas over medium heat, turning occasionally, for 3–5 minutes or until golden brown. Drain on paper towels. Serve with aioli and a salad.

Scallops with sweet chile sauce

PREP 10 MINS

COOK 5 MINS

Marinating • 30 minutes

SERVES 4

4 garlic cloves, finely grated

3 fresh red chile peppers, seeded and
   finely chopped

3 tbsp dry (fino) sherry

1 tsp granulated sugar

2 tbsp olive oil, plus extra for cooking

12 large sea scallops

1 Combine the garlic, chiles, sherry, and sugar in a bowl and mix well until the sugar dissolves. Add the oil and scallops, toss gently to coat, then let marinate for at least 30 minutes at room temperature or longer in the refrigerator.

2 Transfer the scallops to a plate using a slotted spoon and reserve the marinade. Heat a little olive oil in a nonstick frying pan and cook the scallops over high heat for 1 minute on each side, until nicely browned on the outside yet barely cooked through inside. Remove from the pan and set aside to keep warm. Pour the marinade into the pan and cook over high heat for 3 minutes, then pour over the scallops. Serve with a crisp green salad.

SIMPLE STARTERS

Little bites with big flavor—
ready in almost an instant!

SIMPLE STARTERS

For some, the starter is the best part of the meal, and it's not uncommon to choose a selection of starters for a whole meal rather than the traditional three courses, as they are often a lot lighter. Starters are served to stimulate the taste buds, but they should also be visually appealing and delicious. Often, the occasion will determine the choice of starter, whether it's dinner for friends, or a romantic night in. Either way, preparation is fundamental to a relaxed meal.

Menu planning Choose the right starter for the main course.

Choosing the main course first will make it easier to decide on a suitable starter. Remember, the starter is simply to whet the appetite in preparation for the rest of the meal.

The starter shouldn't be too heavy, and should balance and complement the main course.

Consider using not only different ingredients for the starter and main course, but also different cooking methods, as you don't want, for example, pan-fried food twice. Think about color and texture; serve a crisp and fresh starter if the main course is rich and creamy.

Don't mix up cuisines when menu planning. For example, if serving a Mediterranean-style main course, don't opt for a highly-spiced starter.

If time is of the essence, choose a starter that can be made ahead.

3 five-minute starters Incredibly quick and easy starters to suit any occasion.

Mediterranean salad A simple dish that relies on good-quality ingredients.

Greek mezze A tapas-style combination of textures and flavors.

Trout pâté Look for freshly smoked, rather than vacuum-packed, trout.

Place a handful of **arugula** on a serving dish and top with **sun-dried tomatoes**. Coat some **asparagus** with **olive oil** and cook on a hot ridged cast-iron grill pan until charred. Add to the tomatoes and arugula. Sit slices of **prosciutto** on an oiled baking sheet and cook in a hot oven for a few minutes until they begin to curl and crisp. Halve an **avocado**, pit, peel, and fan out on the dish. Top with the crispy prosciutto, then drizzle with a mix of olive oil, **lemon juice**, **hot red pepper flakes** and season with **salt** and **pepper**.

Serve 2 ready-made **stuffed vine leaves** with a generous spoonful of ready-made **hummus**, sprinkled with paprika. Warm 1 **pita bread** on a hot ridged cast-iron grill pan, slice, and add to the plate. Grate a couple of **carrots** and mix with a handful of **raisins** and a handful of **fresh mint leaves**. Stir in a drizzle of **extra virgin olive oil** and a drizzle of **white wine vinegar**. Serve with the vine leaves, hummus, and warm pita bread.

Process a couple of **smoked trout fillets** with some **Greek yogurt** and a spoonful of **cream cheese**, taste, then add a little **lemon juice**, a teaspoon of **creamed horseradish**, and a handful of **fresh dill** and process again. Add plenty of **freshly ground black pepper** and spoon into individual ramekins. Top with a sprig of fresh dill and serve with store-bought **Melba toast**.

Simple bruschetta toppings
All of these toppings can be prepared ahead—so all you need to do is toast the bread and serve.

Zucchini and saffron
The saffron brings a Spanish flavor to the dish.

Dice a **zucchini** into even pieces then add to a frying pan with a little **olive oil**. Cook for a couple of minutes, then add a pinch of **saffron threads** and a squeeze of **lemon juice**. Cook until the zucchini begins to turn golden. Season with **salt** and **pepper** and use to top sliced and toasted ciabatta. Garnish with **fresh basil leaves**.

Chicken liver pâté
A rich and delicious French-style pâté.

Cook 3 pieces of **chicken liver** in a pan with 1 tbsp of melted **butter**. Cook until sealed, being careful not to overcook or the liver will turn grey. Add 2 finely chopped **garlic cloves** and cook for about 30 seconds more. Pierce the liver with a knife and if there is no trace of blood, it is cooked. Add to a food processor along with a handful of small **capers**, rinsed, and process until chopped to your liking—either smooth or coarse. Slice and toast some ciabatta then top with some pâté and serve.

Roasted mixed pepper
Rub garlic over the bruschetta, if you have time.

Seed a couple of **red** and **yellow bell peppers**, slice into strips, then add to a frying pan with a little **olive oil**. Season and cook until the peppers begin to soften. Increase the heat, add a drop of **balsamic vinegar**, and cook for a few more minutes. Use to top sliced and toasted ciabatta. Garnish with **fresh basil leaves**.

Olive and pepper flakes
A rustic version of tapenade.

Finely chop a handful of **black** and **green pitted olives**. Add them to a frying pan with a little **olive oil**. Cook for a couple of minutes, then add a pinch of **crushed red pepper flakes** and season. Stir to combine and cook for a few minutes more, then use to top sliced and toasted ciabatta. Garnish with **arugula**.

Simple garnish ideas

Fried sage leaves These look and taste wonderful. Choose large fresh sage leaves, and try to leave a little stalk intact. Wash, dry well with paper towels, and dip into a bowl of seasoned beaten egg until covered. Fry in a drizzle of hot olive oil on both sides, until golden. Use to garnish salads, pâtés, or soups.

Diced tomato To peel a tomato, mark it with a little cross at its base. Sit in boiling water for 10 seconds then transfer to cold. Peel away the skin, then halve and scoop out the seeds. Chop the flesh into neat pieces. Use to garnish soups, both hot and cold, or sprinkle over fish or shrimp.

Citrus fruits Use lemons, limes, oranges, or grapefruits. Always use a sharp knife and wash the fruit first. Slice into wedges or wheels, then twist, or zest using a fine grater, or cut into spirals by pulling the zester all the way around the citrus fruit. Keep in ice water until needed. Use to garnish fish dishes, salads, or pâtés.

Psst...

Lots of starters lend themselves to upsizing to a main course. Double the quantities of the starter, such as the Seared tuna with black sesame seed crust (p354), or Anchovy, olive, and basil tarts (p359), and serve with a salad, or downsize and serve as canapés with drinks.

Seared tuna with a black sesame seed crust.
For recipe, see p354.

Marinated beef with red pepper aioli

 PREP 20 MINS

Marinating • 1 hour
Special equipment • grill pan
• food processor or blender

SERVES 4-6

about 12oz (350g) boneless beef
    ribeye steak (Scotch beef fillet),
    trimmed of excess fat and cut
    diagonally into 12 slices
3 tbsp coarse-grain mustard
1 garlic clove, finely chopped
2 fresh Thai or other small red chile
    peppers, seeded and finely chopped
4 tbsp olive oil
3 sprigs of fresh rosemary

For the red pepper aioli
1 cup mayonnaise
1 red bell pepper, roasted, peeled,
    seeded, and coarsely chopped
2 garlic cloves, crushed
2 sprigs of fresh oregano
juice of 1 lime
sea salt and freshly ground
    black pepper

1 Lay the beef slices in a shallow
glass or ceramic dish. Mix together the
mustard, garlic, chiles, olive oil, and
rosemary in a small bowl and brush
all over the meat. Cover with plastic

wrap and leave to marinate in the
refrigerator for at least 1 hour or
preferably overnight.

2 Heat a ridged cast-iron grill pan
or other grill until hot. Chargrill the
steaks for 1-2 minutes on each side
or until the meat reaches the desired
doneness, brushing lightly with the
marinade as it cooks. Set aside in
a warm place to rest for 10 minutes.

3 To make the red pepper aioli,
combine the mayonnaise, red pepper,
garlic, oregano, and lime juice in
a food processor and process until
smooth. Season with salt and pepper.

4 Serve the beef slices surrounding
a bowl of aioli in the center of the
table for people to help themselves.

COOK'S NOTES

*For finger food, slice the beef into
24 strips and thread the meat
onto skewers. Remember to soak
wooden or bamboo skewers in cold
water for at least 30 minutes
before using, so that they don't
burn while cooking.*

Chickpea fritters with bocconcini salsa

 PREP 25 MINS **COOK 15 MINS**

SERVES 4

1 x 15½oz (439g) can chickpeas,
    drained and rinsed
1 cup all-purpose flour
2 tbsp chopped flat-leaf parsley
1 tbsp chopped fresh mint leaves
1 garlic clove, crushed
¼ onion, finely chopped
2 carrots, coarsely grated
3 large eggs
1 tsp dukkah (see Cook's Notes)
finely grated zest of 1 small lemon
sea salt and freshly ground
    black pepper
2 cups olive oil, for frying
½ bunch of watercress, for garnish

For the cherry tomato and bocconcini salsa
10 cherry tomatoes, halved
4 balls bocconcini (baby mozzarella)
    cheese, torn into pieces
1 tbsp olive oil
juice of ½ lemon
small handful of fresh chives, cut into
    ¾in (2cm) lengths

1 To make the fritters, put the
chickpeas, flour, parsley, mint, garlic,
onion, carrot, eggs, dukkah, and lemon
zest in a bowl. Season with salt and
pepper. Stir until the batter is mixed.

2 Pour the oil into a heavy wide
frying pan over medium-high heat.

Carefully spoon in the chickpea batter
to make 4 large fritters. Be careful not
to overcrowd the pan, and cook in
batches if necessary. Fry the fritters
for 4-5 minutes on each side until
golden. Remove from the pan and
drain on paper towels.

3 To serve, combine the cherry
tomatoes in a bowl with the
bocconcini, the 1 tablespoon olive oil,
lemon juice, and chives. Toss gently to
mix. Arrange a chickpea fritter in the
center of each of 4 serving plates and
spoon the salsa over the top. Garnish
each serving with watercress.

VARIATION

Make the fritters smaller by
dropping a tablespoon of
batter at a time into the oil
and serve as finger food with
hummus for dipping.

COOK'S NOTES

*Dukkah is an Egyptian spice
mixture made of ground toasted
nuts and seeds, and usually
includes sesame, coriander,
and cumin seeds, as well as
hazelnuts. Look for it at Middle
Eastern supermarkets and gourmet
food shops.*

Eggplant rolls with ricotta and salsa

PREP 20 MINS · **COOK 20**

Special equipment • cocktail sticks

SERVES 4

12–14oz (400g) eggplant
sea salt and freshly ground
    black pepper
about 1 cup toasted bread crumbs
1 tbsp chopped flat-leaf parsley
1 garlic clove, crushed through a press
2 tbsp grated Parmesan cheese
2 large eggs, lightly beaten
1½ cups all-purpose flour
⅔ cup olive oil
9oz (250g) ricotta cheese
1 tbsp prepared pesto, store-bought
    or homemade

For the tomato salsa
3 tomatoes, thinly sliced
small handful flat-leaf parsley leaves
1 tbsp olive oil

1 Cut the eggplant lengthwise 8 even slices about ¼in (5mm) thick. Lightly salt them and sandwich between paper towels for about 10 minutes. Put the eggplant slices in a colander, rinse well, and drain. Pat dry with paper towels. Put the bread crumbs, parsley, garlic, and Parmesan cheese in a large flat dish. Mix until well combined. Put the lightly beaten eggs in another flat dish and the flour in a third. Dip the eggplant first in the flour, then in the egg, and finally in the bread crumbs, ensuring they are evenly coated.

2 Heat the olive oil in 2 heavy frying pans over medium heat, using half of the oil in each one. Divide the slices among the 2 pans and cook for 2–4 minutes on each side until golden. Alternatively, cook in 2 batches. Drain on a baking sheet lined with paper towels and keep warm.

3 Meanwhile, put the ricotta and pesto in a bowl and mix together with a fork. To make the tomato salsa, combine the tomato slices, parsley, and olive oil in another bowl. Season with salt and pepper and stir gently to mix.

4 To serve, put 1 tablespoon of the ricotta mixture toward the end of each of the eggplant slices. Roll each into a cylinder and secure with a heavy toothpick. Place 2 rolls in the center of each of 4 serving plates and pile the tomato salsa over the top. Alternatively, arrange the eggplant rolls in a single row on a long narrow serving dish and serve at the table with the salsa in a bowl, for your guests to help themselves.

Shrimp and zucchini balls with caper cream

PREP 30 MINS · **COOK 20 MINS**

Marinating • 1 hour

SERVES 6–8

1¼lb (550g) raw shrimp, shelled,
    deveined, and finely chopped
9oz (250g) zucchini, coarsely grated
1 garlic clove, crushed through a press
2 tbsp finely chopped flat-leaf parsley
grated zest and juice of 1 small lemon
2 large eggs, lightly beaten
sea salt and freshly ground
    black pepper
9fl oz (250ml) sour cream
1 tbsp capers, rinsed, gently squeezed
    dry, and chopped
1 tbsp finely chopped dill
2 cups olive oil, for frying

1 In a bowl, combine the shrimp, zucchini, garlic, parsley, lemon zest and juice, and eggs. Season with salt and pepper. Mix well by hand until blended. Cover with plastic wrap and refrigerate for 1 hour.

2 Meanwhile, combine the sour cream, capers, and dill in a small bowl and season with black pepper. Stir until just blended, cover with plastic wrap, and refrigerate until needed.

3 Pour the oil into a heavy wide frying pan over medium-high heat. Spoon 1 heaping tablespoon of the shrimp mixture into the palm of your hand and roll into a ball about the size of a walnut. Continue until all the mixture has been used. When the oil is hot, gently drop the balls into the oil using a slotted spoon. Fry for 4–5 minutes on each side until golden brown all over, turning gently as you go. Do not overcrowd the pan—cook in batches if necessary. Remove from the pan using the slotted spoon and drain on paper towels.

4 To serve, arrange the shrimp and zucchini balls on a serving platter with a small bowl of the caper cream and let your guests help themselves.

COOK'S NOTES

To prepare the zucchini, grate on the large holes of a cheese grater.

Eggplant and Taleggio arancini

PREP 45 MINS **COOK** 25 MINS

SERVES 6–8

⅓ cup olive oil, plus extra olive or
    vegetable oil for deep-frying
1 eggplant, cut into very small dice
sea salt and freshly ground
    black pepper
4 cups chicken or vegetable stock
5 tbsp butter, plus extra
1 onion, finely chopped
1 carrot, finely chopped
1 celery stalk, finely chopped
2 garlic cloves, finely chopped
1½ cups Arborio rice
handful of flat-leaf parsley,
    finely chopped
1 tbsp fresh thyme leaves, chopped
finely grated zest and juice of
    1 small lemon
1 cup freshly grated Grana
    Padano cheese
about 10oz (300g) Taleggio cheese,
    chilled and cut into small dice
½ cup all-purpose flour
2 large eggs, lightly beaten
1 cup fine dry bread crumbs

1 Heat 2 tablespoons of oil in a pan over medium heat. Cook the eggplant in batches, stirring, until golden brown. Season with salt and set aside.

2 Pour the stock into a saucepan and bring to a simmer. Heat the remaining olive oil and the butter in another saucepan over medium heat. Add the onion, carrot, celery, and a pinch of salt and cook until the onion is soft. Add the garlic and cook for 30 seconds. Add the rice and stir for 2 minutes. Add ½ cup of the simmering stock and stir until absorbed. Continue adding gradually for 20 minutes, until the rice is tender.

3 Remove from the heat and add the parsley, thyme, lemon, and Grana Padano. Season with salt and pepper. Spread over a baking sheet to cool. Once cooled, roll a small amount of rice into a ball, then push a piece of Taleggio and fried eggplant into the center. Cover with rice and repeat.

4 Spread the flour in a pan. Add the rice balls, shaking the pan to coat. Dip each ball into the beaten egg, and then roll in the bread crumbs to coat. Heat oil in a wok over medium-high heat. Deep-fry the rice balls in batches until golden brown all over. Drain on paper towels and serve hot.

Seared tuna with a black sesame seed crust

PREP 10 MINS **COOK** 40 SECS

Marinating • 1 hour

SERVES 4

4 tbsp olive oil, plus extra for searing
1 garlic clove, finely chopped
1 fresh red Thai chile pepper,
    finely chopped
2 tbsp black sesame seeds, plus extra
    for garnish (optional)
sea salt
2 best-quality ahi tuna steaks,
    about 10oz (300g) each, halved
    lengthwise
2 radishes
juice of 1 lemon
½ bunch of fresh chives, chopped into
    1in (5cm) lengths

1 Put the oil, garlic, chile, sesame seeds, and a good pinch of sea salt on a large flat dish or baking sheet. Mix well to combine.

2 Pat the fish dry with paper towels. Press each piece into the sesame seed mixture, pressing and turning to coat all over. Leave to marinate in the refrigerator for at least 1 hour.

3 Meanwhile, cut the radishes into thin matchsticks and put them in a bowl with half of the lemon juice. Heat a little extra oil in a frying pan over high heat. When the oil is hot, sear each tuna steak for about 20 seconds on each side. Remove and leave to rest for 5 minutes.

4 To serve, put a seared tuna steak on each of 4 serving plates and drizzle with the remaining lemon juice. Drain the radish matchsticks and scatter over the top. Sprinkle with the chives and a few extra sesame seeds and serve immediately.

COOK'S NOTES

You could double the ingredients and serve this as a main course with a salad of fresh orange segments, thinly sliced cucumber, and fresh dill or mint sprigs, as well as the radish.

Spicy chicken balls with chile and ginger sauce

PREP 45 MINS **COOK 25 MINS**

Special equipment • food processor

SERVES 8
⅓ cup dried apricots
1 tbsp honey
3 tbsp brandy
1¾lb (800g) skinless boneless chicken breasts, coarsely chopped
½ cup macadamia nuts, chopped
½ cup cooked long-grain rice
2 garlic cloves, finely chopped
2 tbsp finely chopped fresh sage leaves
1 tbsp finely chopped fresh basil leaves
1 tbsp finely chopped fresh flat-leaf parsley
2 fresh red Thai chile peppers, seeded and chopped
1 large egg
sea salt and freshly ground black pepper
olive oil or vegetable oil

For the chile and ginger sauce
juice of 4 limes
2 tbsp olive oil
2 fresh red Thai chile peppers, seeded and chopped
1 tbsp finely chopped fresh ginger
1 scallion, thinly sliced diagonally, for garnish

1 small bunch watercress, broken into small sprigs, for garnish

1 Combine the apricots, honey, and brandy in a saucepan over medium-low heat. Bring to a boil, reduce the heat slightly, cover, and simmer for 5–10 minutes until the liquid has been absorbed. Leave to cool a bit, cut the apricots into small dice, and set aside.

2 Pulse the chopped chicken in a food processor for 15–20 seconds until the meat is ground (be careful not to turn it into a paste). Transfer to a bowl and add the apricots, nuts, rice, garlic, herbs, chiles, and egg. Season with salt and pepper. Mix well and shape into walnut-size balls.

3 Heat oil in a wok or pan. Working in batches, deep-fry the balls for 5–10 minutes, until golden brown. Drain and set aside to keep warm. To make the sauce, combine the lime juice, oil, chiles, and ginger in a jar. Seal and shake until well mixed. When ready to serve, put all the spicy chicken balls on a warm serving platter, drizzle the sauce over the top, sprinkle with the scallion, and garnish with the cress. Serve immediately.

Skewered lemon and herb chicken

PREP 10 MINS **COOK 15 MINS** ♥

Marinating • 1 hour
Special equipment • 12 skewers • charcoal grill or barbecue

SERVES 4
1–1¼lb (500g) skinless boneless chicken breast
1 garlic clove, finely chopped
1 tbsp finely chopped fresh ginger
1 fresh red Thai chile pepper, finely chopped
1 tsp finely chopped rosemary, plus extra for garnish
4 fresh sage leaves, finely chopped, plus extra for garnish
4 sprigs of fresh thyme leaves finely chopped, plus extra for garnish
handful of flat-leaf parsley, chopped, plus extra for garnish
finely grated zest and juice of 1 lemon
¼ cup olive oil
sea salt and freshly ground black pepper
2 large firm ripe mangoes
juice of 1 lime

1 Soak 12 wooden skewers in cold water for 1 hour.

2 Cut chicken into bite-sized chunks. Combine the chicken, garlic, ginger, chile, chopped rosemary, sage, thyme, parsley, lemon, and oil. Season with salt and pepper and stir to coat. Marinate at room temperature for an hour, or refrigerate for up to 4 hours. Meanwhile, peel the mangoes and cut in half. Cut each half lengthwise into thin slices. Put in a bowl, add the lime juice, and season with pepper. Stir gently to mix well and set aside.

3 Heat your grill until medium-hot and brush with oil. Thread the chicken onto the skewers. Grill, turning occasionally, for 10–15 minutes, and brush lightly with the marinade. Set the skewers aside for 15 minutes and keep warm. To serve, divide the skewers among 4 plates, add the mango slices, and sprinkle with herbs.

COOK'S NOTES

If you have a rosemary bush, break off 12 long, thin stems or branches, strip them of most of the leaves, and use as skewers.

Chicken, leek, and mushroom mini pies

PREP 55 MINS

Special equipment • biscuit cutter

SERVES 4

2 tbsp olive oil

4 tbsp butter

1 small onion, finely chopped

1 small carrot, finely chopped

1 celery stalk, finely chopped

1 leek, finely chopped

1 garlic clove, finely chopped

8oz (225g) mushrooms, coarsely chopped

1–1¼lb (500g) skinless boneless chicken breasts, diced

1 tbsp chopped thyme leaves

finely grated zest of 1 lemon

¼ cup dry white wine

1 cup heavy whipping cream

sea salt and freshly ground black pepper

3 sheets ready-rolled puff pastry

2 large eggs, lightly beaten

mixed green leaves and herbs, for serving

tomato relish, for serving

1 Preheat the oven to 400°F (200°C). Brush two 12-cup mini muffin pans with olive oil. Heat the oil and butter in a saucepan over low heat. Add the onion, carrot, and celery and cook for 5 minutes. Add the leek and cook until wilted. Add the garlic and cook for 30 seconds. Add the mushrooms and cook for another 5 minutes.

2 Increase the heat to medium. Stir in the diced chicken, thyme, lemon zest, and wine. Cook for 15–20 minutes, until cooked through. Add the cream and season with salt and pepper. Continue to cook for 5 minutes, ntil the mixture starts to thicken.

3 Cut 24 x 2½in (6cm) circles from the puff pastry. Line each mini muffin cup with a pastry circle and spoon in the chicken mixture. Top each cup with a 2in (5cm) circle cut from the remaining puff pastry. Brush the tops with the egg and slit with a knife. Bake for 15–20 minutes. Invert the pans onto a wire rack. To serve, divide the pies evenly among 8 warm serving plates. Scatter some mixed leaves and herbs over the top and place a spoonful of tomato relish on the side. Serve immediately.

Grilled asparagus and pancetta

PREP 15 MINS

Special equipment • grill pan

SERVES 4

12 fresh asparagus spears, trimmed

sea salt and freshly ground black pepper

24 thin slices pancetta

1 small radicchio, torn into bite-sized pieces

1 head butter lettuce, torn into bite-sized pieces

4 cups loosely-packed arugula

7oz (200g) cherry tomatoes

1 cup freshly shaved Parmesan cheese

For the dressing

1 garlic clove, crushed

4 tbsp olive oil

1 tbsp balsamic vinegar

1 tbsp freshly squeezed orange juice

1 tsp Dijon mustard

1 Blanch the asparagus in a large saucepan of boiling salted water for 2–3 minutes or until crisp-tender. Drain and immediately refresh the asparagus in a bowl of ice water. When cool, drain again.

2 Heat a ridged cast-iron grill pan or griddle until hot. Wrap 2 slices of the pancetta around each asparagus spear. Grill the asparagus spears, turning once, for 3–4 minutes or until the pancetta is golden and beginning to char. Set aside.

3 To make the dressing, whisk together the garlic, oil, vinegar, orange juice, and mustard in a small bowl. Season with salt and pepper and whisk again.

4 Toss together the salad leaves, tomatoes, and dressing in a bowl and divide evenly among 4 shallow bowls or plates. Top each with 3 of the asparagus wraps and sprinkle the Parmesan shavings over the top. Serve immediately.

Skewered lemon, rosemary, and dukkah lamb

PREP 10 MINS · **COOK 15 MINS**

Marinating • 1 hour

Special equipment • 12 wooden skewers • charcoal grill, barbecue, or grill pan

SERVES 4

2¼lb (1kg) boneless lamb loin or leg, trimmed of all fat and cut into bite-sized cubes

1 garlic clove, finely chopped

1 tsp finely chopped rosemary leaves, plus extra for garnish

1 tbsp dukkah, plus extra for garnish (see Cook's Notes)

finely grated zest and juice of 1 lemon

4 tbsp olive oil

sea salt and freshly ground black pepper

7oz (200g) cherry tomatoes, halved

½ cup pitted Kalamata olives

about 1 cup flat-leaf parsley leaves

1 cup crumbled soft feta cheese

extra virgin olive oil for drizzling

4 lemon wedges, for serving

1 Soak 12 wooden skewers or woody rosemary sprigs (see page 355) in cold water for 1 hour.

2 Combine the lamb, garlic, rosemary, dukkah, lemon zest and juice, and olive oil in a bowl. Stir to coat and season with salt and pepper. Leave to marinate 1 hour at room temperature, or overnight in the refrigerator.

3 Heat the grill pan or an outdoor grill until medium-hot. Brush the grill lightly with a little oil. Thread the lamb onto the skewers. Grill, turning occasionally, for 10–15 minutes or until browned all over and cooked to the desired doneness. Brush lightly with the marinade while the meat is cooking. Set aside in a warm place for 15 minutes to rest.

4 Toss together the tomatoes, olives, and parsley, and divide among 4 serving plates. Top each tomato salad with 3 lamb skewers, top with the feta, and drizzle with extra virgin olive oil. Sprinkle extra dukkah over the top and serve with lemon wedges.

COOK'S NOTES

Dukkah is an Egyptian spice blend, available at Middle Eastern markets. This dish looks terrific on one large platter, for your guests to help themselves.

Pork and fennel sausages with fresh tomato salsa

PREP 10 MINS · **COOK 15 MINS**

Marinating • 1 hour

SERVES 4

4 fresh pork and fennel Italian-style sausages

3 tbsp olive oil

2 garlic cloves, finely chopped

4 sprigs of fresh dill

sea salt and freshly ground black pepper

4 ripe tomatoes, seeded and diced

½ cup Kalamata olives, pitted and coarsely chopped

large handful of fresh basil leaves

2 tbsp extra virgin olive oil

4 thick slices crusty Italian-style sourdough bread

1 Put the sausages in a shallow glass or ceramic dish. Add the 3 tablespoons olive oil, the garlic, and dill, and season with a little salt and pepper. Stir the sausages around so that they are well coated. Cover with plastic wrap and leave to marinate in the refrigerator for at least 1 hour.

2 Meanwhile, to make the salsa, combine the tomatoes, olives, basil, and extra virgin olive oil in a bowl and mix well. Season with salt and pepper to taste.

3 Heat a ridged cast-iron stovetop grill or outdoor grill until hot. Grill the sausages for 10–15 minutes until cooked through, turning halfway during cooking to brown both sides.

4 To serve, divide the sausages between 4 serving plates and serve on a piece of toasted sourdough with the tomato salsa spooned over the top. Serve immediately.

VARIATION

Try fresh sausages made from chicken and chives instead of pork and fennel.

COOK'S NOTES

For a more casual option, twist breakfast-style link sausages in the middle to create smaller sausages, marinate, and grill as above (they will take slightly less time to cook). Pile onto a platter with the salsa in a bowl on the side. Alternatively, pile the links and salsa onto bruschetta drizzled with olive oil and freshly ground pepper and top with arugula.

Croque Monsieur with prosciutto and Gorgonzola

PREP 10 MINS • COOK 15 MINS

SERVES 4

8 slices sourdough white bread
about 2 tbsp unsalted butter, at room temperature
8 thin slices prosciutto
7oz (200g) Gorgonzola cheese, thinly sliced
2 tbsp olive oil
4 large eggs

1 Butter each of the bread slices on one side. Place 4 of the bread slices buttered-side down on the work surface and divide the prosciutto and cheese evenly among them, arranging neatly on top of each slice. Cover with the remaining bread slices, buttered-side up, to make a sandwich.

2 Heat a large, heavy, lightly oiled frying pan over medium heat. When hot, carefully arrange the sandwiches in the pan without crowding. Cook for 5 minutes on each side until the bread is a golden brown and the cheese has melted. Remove from the heat.

3 Wipe out the pan and heat the olive oil until medium-hot. Break each egg into the pan separately and fry the eggs until done to your preference. Slide a fried egg on top of each toasted sandwich and serve immediately.

VARIATION

Use ham and Gruyère or a similar soft melting cheese such as Emmentaler.

COOK'S NOTES

For a lighter version, toast the sandwiches using a dry panini or sandwich press and poach the eggs instead of frying them.

Potato and leek croquettes

PREP 20 MINS • COOK 30 MINS

Chilling • 1 hour

SERVES 4

1 tbsp olive oil
1 leek, white part only, finely chopped
1 garlic clove, finely chopped
1lb (450g) baking potatoes, peeled and cut into chunks
1 large egg, plus 2 large eggs, lightly beaten
½ cup freshly grated Parmesan cheese
2 tbsp finely chopped flat-leaf parsley leaves
sea salt and freshly ground black pepper
½ cup all-purpose flour
⅔ cup fine dry bread crumbs
olive oil or vegetable oil

1 Heat the 1 tablespoon of olive oil in a saucepan over low heat. Add the leek and cook for a few minutes until it wilts. Add the garlic and cook for 30 seconds. Set aside to cool.

2 In a large saucepan of salted water, add the potatoes and bring to a boil. Boil for 15–20 minutes or until tender. Drain, return to the pan, and mash until very smooth. Add the leek and garlic mixture, the 1 egg, the Parmesan, and parsley, and season with salt and pepper. Stir and chill in the refrigerator for at least 1 hour until cool and firm.

3 To make the croquettes, take a bit of the potato mixture and place in the palm of your hand, forming into an oval shape. Continue until all the mixture has been used.

4 Spread the flour on a baking sheet. Place the croquettes on top and gently shake the pan to coat. Dip each croquette into the beaten eggs and coat with bread crumbs. Heat the oil in a heavy pan over medium-high heat, then deep-fry the croquettes, cooking in batches, for 10–15 minutes or until golden brown. Serve hot.

COOK'S NOTES

Be careful how you handle the croquettes, because they can be fragile. The colder they are when you form them, the better.

Zucchini and pea mini tortillas

PREP 20 MINS · COOK 50 MINS

SERVES 10

3 zucchini, about 1lb (450g), coarsely grated
2 cups baby spinach leaves
finely grated zest and juice of 1 lemon
2 cups frozen peas, thawed
½ cup toasted pine nuts
sea salt and freshly ground black pepper
10 x 7in (18cm) flour tortillas, halved
reduced-fat mayonnaise
snow peas, pea sprouts, and pea shoots, for serving

1 In a large bowl, mix together the zucchini, spinach, lemon zest and juice, peas, and pine nuts. Season well with salt and pepper.

2 Heat a dry frying pan over high heat. Add the tortilla halves, 2 at a time, and toast for about 15 seconds on each side. As you cook, place the tortillas under a clean dish towel, to keep them warm.

3 Lay one of the tortilla halves flat on a cutting board and brush lightly with the mayonnaise. Place some of the filling in the center and arrange some of the snow peas, pea sprouts, and pea shoots on top, so that they peek out from one end, then gently roll up the tortilla, forming a cone shape to enclose the filling. Repeat this process until you have made 20 cones.

4 To serve, arrange the cones seam-side down on individual serving plates, allowing 2 per person.

COOK'S NOTES

Fill the tortillas with prosciutto or roasted pumpkin instead of the zucchini and peas and serve with a little sour cream or Greek-style yogurt mixed with chopped fresh mint and a little freshly squeezed orange juice.

Anchovy, olive, and basil tarts

PREP 15 MINS · COOK 25 MINS

Chilling • 1 hour
Special equipment • 4-cup muffin tin

SERVES 4

1 sheet ready-rolled puff pastry (preferably made with butter)
2 large eggs
¾ cup heavy whipping cream
2 tbsp freshly grated Parmesan cheese
sea salt and freshly ground black pepper
4 anchovy fillets, drained
4 anchovy fillets in olive oil, drained
4 balls bocconcini (bite-sized balls of fresh mozzarella cheese), torn
8 pitted Kalamata olives
8 cherry tomatoes, halved
8 fresh basil leaves or small sprigs

1 Preheat the oven to 400°F (200°C). Lightly brush or spray four 4oz (125ml) ramekins or muffin cups.

2 On a lightly floured work surface, cut the pastry into 4 squares large enough to line the ramekins. Ease in the pastry, so it lines the bottom and sides of the cups. Refrigerate for 1 hour until well chilled. Combine the eggs, cream, and Parmesan in a bowl and season with salt and pepper. Mix well.

3 Place an anchovy in each of the prepared pastry cases, along with 1 torn bocconcini, 2 olives, and 4 cherry tomato halves. Spoon the egg and cream mixture into the cases and top each one with a basil leaf or sprig. Grind a little pepper over the top.

4 Bake the tarts for 25–30 minutes, until puffed and golden on top. Invert the ramekins onto a wire rack and serve warm, garnished with basil.

Smoked salmon and cream cheese roulades

**PREP
10
MINS**

SERVES 4

7oz (200g) cream cheese, at room
temperature
2 tbsp cream-style white horseradish
juice of 1 lemon
sea salt and freshly ground
black pepper
10oz (300g) smoked salmon, cut into
12in (30cm) wide rectangular slices

To serve

thinly sliced rye bread
handful of salad leaves
lemon wedges

1 Mix together the cream cheese,
horseradish, and lemon juice, then
season well with a pinch of salt and
plenty of pepper.

2 Lay out the salmon slices on
parchment paper. Spoon the cream
cheese mixture onto the salmon and
spread evenly all over the surface.

3 Starting from a short end, tightly
roll up the salmon jellyroll fashion.

Next, roll the parchment paper around
it, twisting the edges tightly so that
you have a sausage shape. Repeat
until all the salmon has been used.
Chill for 15–30 minutes to firm.

4 To serve, cut the bread into small
squares and slice the salmon roulade
crosswise into pinwheels. Place a
pinwheel on top of each square of
bread and serve with lemon wedges.

VARIATION
Add some finely chopped
fresh chives to the cream
cheese mixture.

COOK'S NOTES

*You could make the salmon
roulade ahead and freeze for
up to 1 month. When ready to
use, defrost for about 1 hour at
room temperature before slicing
and serving.*

Crab salad with grapefruit and cilantro

**PREP
10
MINS**

SERVES 4

For the dressing

3 tbsp olive oil
1 tbsp white wine vinegar
pinch of sugar
sea salt and freshly ground
black pepper

12oz (350g) cooked fresh, thawed
frozen, or canned white crabmeat
handful of baby salad leaves
handful of fresh cilantro
2 pink grapefruits, segmented

1 In a small bowl, whisk together the
oil, vinegar, and sugar for the dressing.
Season with salt and pepper.

2 In a bowl, combine the crabmeat
with a drizzle of the dressing. Divide
the salad leaves and half of the cilantro
leaves among 4 serving plates and
scatter the grapefruit over the top.

3 Drizzle the remaining dressing over
the salads. Divide the crabmeat among
the plates, spooning it neatly on top of
the leaves. Sprinkle with the remaining
cilantro and serve at once.

VARIATION
Add a pinch of crushed red
pepper flakes or a seeded
and chopped fresh chile
pepper to the dressing.

COOK'S NOTES

*Try to use fresh crabmeat,
but drained canned crabmeat
will also do. For a professional
look, tightly pack the crabmeat
for each serving in a small
straight-sided pastry or biscuit
cutter, then carefully slide it out
onto the salad leaves.*

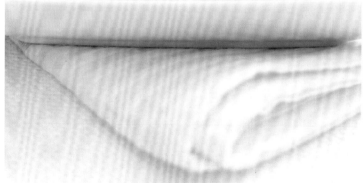

Chicken satay

PREP 15 MINS · **COOK 10 MINS**

Special equipment • 8 wooden skewers

SERVES 4

10oz (300g) skinless boneless chicken breast or thigh fillet, sliced into strips
1 tbsp peanut oil
1 tbsp soy sauce
1 tsp Asian fish sauce, such as *nam pla*
3 garlic cloves, crushed
1 tsp hot red chili paste
juice of 1 lemon
sea salt and freshly ground black pepper

For the satay sauce

3 tbsp crunchy peanut butter
juice of 1 lime
half of a well-shaken 14oz (400g) can unsweetened coconut milk (about 7oz/200g)
½ tsp medium-hot chili powder
splash of Asian fish sauce, such as *nam pla*

1 Soak 8 small wooden or bamboo skewers in cold water for 30 minutes.

2 Combine the chicken, oil, soy sauce, fish sauce, garlic, chili paste, and lemon juice in a bowl. Season with salt and pepper and mix well. Set aside to marinate while you make the satay sauce.

3 Combine the peanut butter, lime juice, coconut milk, and chili powder in a heavy saucepan over low heat. Simmer gently, stirring occasionally, for about 10 minutes until the sauce begins to thicken and the coconut milk releases its fragrance. Add a little more water if it is too thick. Remove from the heat and keep warm until needed.

4 Preheat the broiler to high. Thread the chicken strips onto the soaked skewers. Broil for 3–5 minutes on each side or until cooked through and lightly charred at the edges. Serve hot with a little crispy lettuce and a bowl of the satay sauce for dipping.

Cheat... Instead of making your own, use a ready-made bottled satay sauce as a dip.

COOK'S NOTES

When you are using wooden or bamboo skewers, always remember to soak them for 30 minutes in cold water first, so that they do not burn when cooking.

Thai fish cakes

PREP 15 MINS · **COOK 15 MINS**

Special equipment • food processor

SERVES 4

10oz (300g) peeled and deveined cooked shrimp, coarsely chopped
3 garlic cloves, peeled but left whole
small handful of fresh cilantro
2 fresh red Thai or other hot chile peppers, seeded
generous splash of Asian fish sauce, such as *nam pla*
generous splash of soy sauce
small handful of fresh basil leaves
juice of 2 limes
1 large egg, lightly beaten
salt and freshly ground black pepper
3–4 tbsp vegetable or sunflower oil
sweet chili sauce (to serve)
arugula (to serve)

1 Combine the shrimp, garlic, cilantro, chiles, fish sauce, soy sauce, basil, and lime juice in a food processor and process into a coarse paste. Add the egg and plenty of salt and pepper and process again.

2 Heat a little oil in a frying pan over medium-high heat. Scoop 1 tablespoon of the mixture, then carefully slide it into the pan and flatten slightly; it should be about ¾in (2cm) thick. Repeat until all the mixture has been used. Cook for a minute or two on each side until golden. You may need to cook in batches, adding more oil as needed. Drain the fish cakes on a plate lined with paper towels.

3 Serve hot with a drizzle of sweet chili sauce and some arugula.

COOK'S NOTES

Use Thai basil, which has a spicy, delicate flavor, instead of regular basil, if you can find it. It also has a sweeter taste than regular basil.

Vegetable tempura with chile dipping sauce

  PREP 15 MINS COOK 15 MINS

Special equipment • wok

SERVES 4

For the chile dipping sauce

2 tbsp rice wine vinegar

2 tbsp soy sauce

1 tbsp olive oil

1 tbsp granulated sugar

1 garlic clove, finely grated

2 fresh Thai or other red hot chile peppers, seeded and finely chopped

sea salt and freshly ground black pepper

2 eggplants, sliced into thin rounds

2–3 zucchini, cut into sticks 2½in (6cm) long and ½in (1cm) wide

2 red bell peppers, seeded and coarsely chopped

about 2 cups vegetable or sunflower oil for frying

¾ cup all-purpose flour

1 tbsp cornstarch

¾ –1 cup ice water

1 First, make the dipping sauce. Whisk together the vinegar, soy sauce, oil, sugar, garlic, and chiles and season with salt and pepper.

2 Once you have prepared all the vegetables, pour the oil into a wok and heat until very hot but not smoking.

3 Meanwhile, make the batter. Whisk together the flour, cornstarch, and ¾-1 cup ice water. Don't over-mix; it doesn't matter if the batter is a little lumpy.

4 Drop a little of the batter into the oil, to test whether the oil is hot enough–it should sizzle right away and become crisp. Dip the vegetable pieces one by one into the batter and shake away the excess batter. Carefully add to the oil, a few at a time, and fry for 2–3 minutes until golden and crispy. Remove with a slotted spoon and keep warm on a baking sheet lined with paper towels until all the vegetables are cooked. Serve immediately with the chile dipping sauce.

COOK'S NOTES

For a perfectly crisp tempura coating, the oil needs to be very hot and the batter light, so don't overwhisk the batter or crowd the wok.

Salt and pepper shrimp

PREP 10 MINS COOK 10 MINS

SERVES 4

2 tbsp cornstarch

1 tbsp fine sea salt

1 tbsp freshly cracked black pepper

16 raw jumbo shrimp, peeled and deveined (or more shrimp, for large appetites)

4 tbsp vegetable oil

3 fresh Thai or other red hot chile peppers, seeded and cut into strips

1 garlic clove, finely chopped

6 scallions, cut into 2in (5cm) pieces, then halved lengthwise

soy sauce, for serving

1 Mix together the cornstarch, salt, and pepper. Add the shrimp and toss until well coated. Set aside.

2 Heat 1 tablespoon of the oil in a medium frying pan over medium heat. Add the chiles, garlic, and scallions and cook for 1–2 minutes, stirring, until fragrant. Remove from the heat and cover with a lid to keep warm while you cook the shrimp.

3 Heat the remaining oil in a wok or separate frying pan over high heat. Add the shrimp and cook for 3–5 minutes, tossing them gently until they are pink and beginning to curl.

4 Remove the shrimp from the pan with a slotted spoon and divide among 4 serving plates. Top with the chile and scallion mixture and serve at once with a splash of soy sauce.

Crab balls

PREP 10 MINS
COOK 15 MINS

Special equipment • food processor

SERVES 4

12oz (350g) cooked fresh, thawed frozen, or canned white crabmeat
1 red jalapeño chile pepper, seeded
2 garlic cloves, peeled
handful of fresh cilantro
finely grated zest and juice of 1 lemon
1 tsp Asian fish sauce, such as *nam pla*
2 eggs, lightly beaten
sea salt and freshly ground black pepper
1 cup fine fresh bread crumbs
3 tbsp vegetable oil, or as needed
soy sauce and sweet chili sauce, to serve

1 Combine the crabmeat, chile, garlic, cilantro, lemon zest and juice, and fish sauce in a food processor. Process until a coarse paste forms, then add the eggs and plenty of salt and pepper. Process again.

2 Scoop the mixture up using your hands and roll into 1in (2.5cm) balls. Spread the bread crumbs onto a plate and roll the crab balls in them until well covered all over.

3 Heat a little of the oil in a frying over medium heat. Working in batches, cook a few balls at a time for about 5 minutes, turning frequently and adding more oil to the pan as needed, until nicely browned all over. Drain on paper towels.

4 Serve hot with soy sauce and sweet chili sauce for dipping.

Smoked mackerel pâté

PREP 5 MINS

Special equipment • blender or food processor

SERVES 4

3–4 smoked mackerel fillets, about 10oz (300g), skinned
10oz (300g) cream cheese, at room temperature
juice of 1–2 lemons
freshly ground black pepper
1–2 tbsp Greek-style yogurt

To serve
toasted rye bread, sliced thin
1 lemon, cut into wedges

1 Break up the mackerel into chunks and add to a food processor. Process, pulsing the machine on and off, until evenly chopped.

2 Spoon in the cream cheese and process again until a smooth paste forms. Add the lemon juice, a little at a time, processing between each addition. Taste as you go, adding more lemon as required. Season with plenty of pepper and process again.

3 Add the yogurt and blend again until completely smooth. Spoon into a flat-sided serving dish and smooth the top. Serve with toast and the lemon wedges for squeezing.

 VARIATION
Add a pinch of cayenne pepper to give the pâté a lift.

> ### COOK'S NOTES
> Make a day ahead and keep in the refrigerator. Let stand 30 mins at room temperature before serving. You don't have to add the yogurt, but it dilutes the richness a bit and makes the pâté creamy.

Asparagus with lemony dressing

PREP 10 MINS

SERVES 4

For the lemony dressing

6 tbsp olive oil

2–3 tbsp freshly squeezed lemon juice

pinch of granulated sugar

1 tsp mayonnaise

sea salt and freshly ground
   black pepper

1 bunch of fresh asparagus, about
   12oz (350g), tough ends trimmed

handful of arugula

1 First, make the dressing. Put the olive oil and lemon juice in a small bowl and whisk until blended. Whisk in the sugar and mayonnaise and season with salt and pepper.

2 Cook the asparagus in boiling salted water for 2–3 minutes, or until tender.

3 To serve, place the asparagus on the arugula and dress liberally with the dressing. Serve at once.

COOK'S NOTES

You will need to give the dressing a final whisk just before serving. For a lower-fat version, omit the mayonnaise.

Curried deviled eggs

PREP 5 MINS

SERVES 4

6 large eggs

2 tbsp mayonnaise

1–2 tsp medium-hot curry powder

¼–½ tsp cayenne pepper, to taste

sea salt and freshly ground
   black pepper

1 Cook the eggs in a pan of boiling water for about 6 minutes for hard-boiled. Remove from the pan and let cool, then peel away the shell.

2 Halve the eggs lengthwise and carefully remove the yolk using a teaspoon. Put the egg yolks in a bowl and mix together with the mayonnaise, curry powder, and cayenne. Season well with salt and pepper.

3 Now spoon the deviled egg mixture back into each egg white, dividing the mixture evenly among the halves.

4 Serve with some crispy lettuce leaves, prosciutto, and another pinch of cayenne pepper, if you wish.

Cheat...
This recipe IS a cheat— it's an emergency last-minute starter!

COOK'S NOTES

Do not overcook the eggs, otherwise the outside of the yolks will be gray instead of yellow, resulting in a less attractive finished dish.

Smoked salmon with mustard and dill dressing

PREP 5 MINS

SERVES 4
12oz (350g) good-quality
    smoked salmon
1 lemon, halved
½ cucumber, finely chopped
crusty rye or brown bread, to serve

For the mustard and dill dressing
⅓ cup extra virgin olive oil
3 tbsp white wine vinegar
1 tsp coarse-grain mustard
1 tsp honey
sea salt and freshly ground
    black pepper
handful of fresh dill, finely chopped

1 Divide the salmon among 4 serving plates and squeeze a little lemon juice over the top.

2 To make the dressing, combine the olive oil, vinegar, mustard, and honey in a small bowl. Whisk together until well combined, then season with salt and pepper. Sprinkle in half of the dill and whisk again. Taste and adjust the seasonings as needed.

3 Toss the cucumber with the remaining dill, then spoon the cucumber onto the plates. When ready to serve, drizzle with the dressing and serve with the sliced bread.

Avocado with roasted cherry tomatoes and paprika dressing

PREP 5 MINS

SERVES 4
12oz (350g) cherry tomatoes
1 tbsp olive oil
handful of fresh thyme sprigs
sea salt and freshly ground
    black pepper
2 firm but ripe avocados
handful of arugula

For the paprika dressing
⅓ cup olive oil
3 tbsp white wine or cider vinegar
1 tsp paprika
pinch of granulated sugar
½ tsp mayonnaise

1 Preheat the oven to 400°F (200°C). Put the cherry tomatoes in a roasting pan and toss with the olive oil.

Sprinkle with thyme and season with salt and pepper. Roast in the oven for 12–15 minutes, or until the tomatoes begin to burst and char slightly.

2 Whisk together the oil, vinegar, paprika, sugar, and mayonnaise and season well with salt and pepper.

3 Just before serving, halve the avocados. Carefully remove the pits, then peel away the skin. Slice each of the avocado halves lengthwise without cutting all the way through, then fan them out on individual salad plates.

4 Divide the arugula and roasted tomatoes equally among the plates and spoon the dressing over all. Serve immediately.

Butterflied mackerel with sweet potato and beet relish

PREP 15 MINS **COOK 15 MINS**

SERVES 4

2 sweet potatoes, peeled and diced
4 mackerel, about 3½oz (100g) each, butterflied (see Cook's Notes)
2 small sweet potatoes, peeled and diced
4 medium-large cooked beets, diced
1 small onion, finely chopped
1–2 tsp onion seeds, or a small handful of onion sprouts
juice of 1 orange (about ⅓ cup)

1 Cook the sweet potato in a pot of boiling salted water for 3–5 minutes until just beginning to soften; do not overcook. Drain and allow to cool.

2 Preheat the broiler to high. Place the mackerel on an oiled baking sheet and broil for 2–4 minutes on each side until cooked through.

3 Meanwhile, to make the relish, gently mix together the sweet potatoes and beets, then stir in the onion and onion seeds. Squeeze in the orange juice and toss gently to coat well.

4 Serve the mackerel hot, either with a little of the relish on the side, or served separately in a bowl for everyone to help themselves.

COOK'S NOTES

Butterflied mackerel has been flattened and had the backbone removed. Ask your fishmonger to do this, and try to keep the tail on—it looks impressive when serving.

Smoked trout with chile and lime dressing

PREP 10 MINS

SERVES 4
For the chile and lime dressing
2 tbsp rice wine vinegar
2 tsp soy sauce
splash of Asian sesame oil
½–1 tsp granulated sugar
2 fresh red jalapeño chile peppers, seeded and finely chopped
juice of 1–2 limes

12oz (350g) smoked trout
large handful of salad leaves
1 bunch of scallions, thinly sliced
4 radishes, thinly sliced

1 To make the dressing, whisk together the rice vinegar, soy sauce, sesame oil, sugar, and jalapeño. Taste and add all of the lime juice if needed, or use less if the dressing is becoming too sour.

2 Divide the smoked trout among 4 plates, then toss together the salad leaves, scallions, and radishes.

3 When ready to serve, lightly toss the salad with the some of the dressing and drizzle the remainder over the trout. Serve immediately.

COOK'S NOTES

Prepare the dressing a day ahead and leave in the refrigerator in a screw-top jar until needed. You could sprinkle over a pinch of toasted sesame seeds for extra texture, if you wish.

Mushroom and ricotta pies with red pepper pesto

 PREP 25 MINS COOK 45 MINS

Special equipment • blender or food processor

SERVES 4
½ cup olive oil
1 onion, sliced
sea salt and freshly ground
   black pepper
2 red bell peppers, sliced
2 garlic cloves, crushed
finely grated zest and juice of 1 lemon
10oz (300g) small mushrooms, halved
1 leek, white part only, thinly sliced
2 sheets pre-rolled puff pastry
   (preferably made with butter),
   thawed if frozen; or 1 x 17.3oz
   (425g) box frozen puff pastry
   sheets, thawed as package directs
7oz (200g) ricotta cheese
1 large egg yolk, lightly beaten

1 Preheat the oven to 400°F (200°C) and line a baking sheet with parchment paper. To make the red pepper pesto, heat 3 tablespoons of the oil in a heavy frying pan over low heat. Add the onion and a pinch of salt and cook gently for 5 minutes until soft. Add the peppers and cook, stirring frequently, for 10–15 minutes until tender.

2 Transfer the onion mixture to a food processor. Add the garlic and lemon zest and juice and pulse, turning the machine on and off, until the mixture

becomes a chunky purée. Season with salt and pepper. Set aside. Heat another 3 tablespoons of the oil in a clean large heavy frying pan over medium heat. Add the mushrooms and leeks and cook, stirring, for 5 minutes until the mushrooms have lightly browned. Set aside.

3 Cut each pastry sheet into 4 squares. Divide the ricotta equally among 4 of the squares, leaving a ½in (1cm) border all around the edges. Spoon the mushroom and leek mixture evenly over the ricotta. Using a sharp knife, cut diagonal slashes across the surface of the remaining 4 pastry squares, being careful not to slice all the way through, then lay one evenly over the top of each square that has the ricotta-mushroom filling. Pinch and twist together the corners of the pies to seal and brush the tops with the egg yolk to glaze.

4 Place the pies on the baking sheet and bake for 25 minutes until golden brown. Serve with the red pepper pesto and a leafy green salad.

COOK'S NOTES
The pies are slightly open on the edges, which allows steam to escape so that they don't become soggy.

Crisp sweet potato cake with shaved zucchini and chive mascarpone

 PREP 15 MINS COOK 25 MINS

SERVES 4
1¼lb (550g) sweet potatoes, peeled
   and sliced into 8 even discs, about
   ¾in (1.9cm) thick
2 tbsp olive oil, plus extra for drizzling
sea salt and freshly ground
   black pepper
1 zucchini, about 5½oz (150g)
juice of ½ lemon
⅔ cup mascarpone cheese
1 tbsp finely chopped chives, plus
   8 whole chives

1 Preheat the oven to 400°F (200°C). Put the sweet potatoes in a bowl. Add the 2 tablespoons olive oil, season with salt and pepper, and toss gently to coat. Transfer to a baking sheet and roast for 25 minutes until golden brown and tender when pierced with the tip of a sharp knife. Set aside to cool.

2 Trim off both ends from the zucchini, then shave into thin slices with a vegetable peeler. Put in a bowl with the lemon juice and season with salt and pepper. Toss gently to coat thoroughly.

3 Put the mascarpone in a separate bowl and stir in the chopped chives.

4 To serve, place a sweet potato disc in the center of each of 4 serving plates. Divide the zucchini mixture into 4 equal portions and mound over each sweet potato disc. Place another disc on top, then spoon over the chive mascarpone. Arrange 2 whole chives on top of each serving and drizzle with a little olive oil. Serve immediately.

COOK'S NOTES
This could be served as a small starter or finger food by using one potato disc for each serving instead of two. Top each piece with the shaved zucchini and chive mascarpone.

FOOD FOR FRIENDS

BIG-POT GATHERINGS

Fabulous food in one pot for effortless entertaining.

BIG-POT GATHERINGS

Cooking for larger numbers than usual can sometimes be daunting, but if you keep the food to one pot, it makes life (and the dish-washing) a lot easier. This informal way of entertaining lends itself to informal eating, when standing up and digging in with a fork is just as acceptable as everyone sitting and being served straight from the pot.

Psst...

Buy mixed stew packs from the butcher and freeze until needed, or—if freezer space permits—think about buying half a lamb or pig, cut into serving portions.

One-pot cooking pots Choose the best pot for the job.

POT		BEST FOR
	**TAGINE** A tagine is a North African cooking pot, and the type of dish it produces goes by the same name. It is a shallow dish with a conical top and is used in Moroccan cooking. Made of terracotta, tagines can be used in the oven or on the stovetop (with a heat diffuser). The cone-shaped lid collects the steam, so the food stays very moist. The bottom doubles as a serving dish.	Meat, vegetable, and fish curries, and slow-cooked stews.
	**PAELLA PAN** This is a thin, flat frying pan, about 1½in (4cm) deep, with two loop handles. It is traditionally made from carbon steel, which responds quickly to heat, but needs to be well-cared for, as it can easily turn rusty after use if not dried properly. The size of a paella pan can vary from 18in (46cm) wide, if cooking for about 8, up to as large as 52in (132cm), if cooking for a couple of hundred.	The traditional Spanish rice dish, "Paella," where a thin layer of rice is cooked with added herbs and spices, such as saffron, and a mixture of seafood and meat (chicken and rabbit). Paella is traditionally cooked outdoors for large crowds of people.
	**CASSEROLE** This is a large, heavy, deep pan, used in the oven or on the stove. A cast-iron pan with a tight-fitting lid is the best choice, as it will distribute heat evenly. Casserole pans keep food moist, and are perfect for slow cooking.	Meat or vegetable casseroles and stews that have plenty of liquid (usually stock). They are ideal for oven-to-table cooking and perfect for cooking for large numbers, as once in the oven they can be left, and casseroles don't often require accompaniments.
	**WOK** These pans are used in Asian cooking and are designed for quick, high-heat cooking. They are often made from carbon steel, which needs to be looked after to last. They are bowl-shaped, with sloping sides: this creates a hot spot at the base, where all the cooking is done. Food can sit at the sides and be brought down to the base to be cooked super-fast. Wok cooking requires food to be constantly moved around.	Stir-fries and Asian curries, using tender slices of meat, seafood, or vegetables. If all ingredients are prepped beforehand, wok cooking is ideal for large numbers, as it can be pan-to-plate in an instant.

Get ahead

When cooking for large numbers, prep needs to be kept to a minimum. Many big-pot recipes require lots of onions: use a food processor and the pulse button to chop them, then store them in a sealed plastic container in the refrigerator for a couple of days until needed. You can do the same with garlic.

freeze it

Stews and casseroles freeze exceptionally well. There are just a few rules to remember:

Cool completely before transferring to a rigid plastic container or freezer bag.

Freeze as soon as possible after cooling.

Make sure meat is well covered with sauce or gravy, so it remains tender and doesn't suffer freezer burn (see pp248–251).

The best meat cuts for big-pot cooking
These undervalued and good-value cuts of meat are perfect for long, slow cooking.

MEAT		BEST FOR

STEW MEAT
This is the generic term for tougher cuts of meat that require stewing or slow cooking. The best kind of stew meat is chuck steak, which has the most flavor and is the most tender. Shin is often served as stewing steak. For more flavor, the meat can be marinated first, or browned and sealed before liquid is added.

Stews and casseroles, or meat curries that require a long, slow cooking time. Add plenty of complementing spices and herbs, such as mustards and horseradish, or fresh rosemary and bay leaves. The quality of the finished dish will depend on the quality of the meat.

PORK BELLY
This is an extremely cheap but succulent cut of meat, which makes it ideal if you're catering for large numbers. It's full of flavor because it's full of fat (which can easily be removed after cooking). Buy in a flat slab, allowing about 5½oz (150g) per person, with or without the bones, or buy in ready-cut slices. The skin that covers the belly can be scored and rubbed with salt to produce crackling: cook high until crisp, then slow and long until the meat is meltingly tender.

Stews and casseroles, slow-roasting flat, or stuffing and rolling to roast. Add lots of flavor, such as garlic and fennel, or apples. Asian flavors, such as star anise and soy sauce, also work well.

LAMB NECK
The neck is composed of three different parts, the best end, the middle end, and the scrag end. The best end is, as the name suggests, the most tender and expensive part and can be used for roasting as it is near the shoulder and fairly lean. The middle end is a lot fattier and extremely tasty when slow-cooked. The scrag end (the piece nearest to the head) is the cheapest cut and tends to be bony, but is delicious slow cooked.

Stews, casseroles, and tagines, especially if feeding large numbers. It needs to be cooked long and slow and needs good punchy flavors to cut through the fat, such as fresh hot green chiles, harissa, or red currant jelly. Team it with fresh green vegetables such as cabbage or beans.

GROUND BEEF
Like stew meat, this is a generic term used for beef that has been ground or minced and could be a variety of cuts, so it's best to ask your butcher. Some ground beef comes from the neck, which can be fatty but is inexpensive, otherwise it is often chuck steak or sirloin, which is leaner. Fattier blends of ground beef will go a long way, but are best simmered in a sauce, such as a ragù, to tenderize the meat. Ground chuck is good for frying and for making foods like burgers and meatballs.

Casseroles and pies. Ground beef is such a versatile meat and because of its cost, it is an ideal choice for big-pot gatherings. As well as being cheap, tasty, and easy to cook with, it takes on other flavors well, such as Mexican, Italian, or Middle Eastern.

reheat and eat
Stews and casseroles are perfect for reheating; in fact they often taste better when left to sit, or served up the next day. They are ideal if family eating is staggered: the pot can sit in the oven for a few hours, happily stewing away, then be served when required. They can also be reheated for 2–3 minutes in the microwave on high.

Choosing big-pot fish

• **Monkfish** is firm and has no bones, so is ideal for big-pot dishes. Try a Provençal fish stew of tomatoes, olives, and oregano, adding pieces of monkfish for the last 15–20 minutes of cooking.

• **Shrimp** are better served without their shells when cooking large quantities. Add them to the pan —to a jambalaya, for instance—at the end of the cooking time, so they are juicy and flavorful.

• **White fish** such as haddock or cod, or cheaper alternatives such as pollack or coley, need very little cooking. Large chunky pieces can be added to the pan at the final stage of cooking, or wrapped in bacon and baked or steamed on top of spiced rice and spinach.

• **Salmon** is an easy option for big-pot cooking. It can be added to Thai-style curry, or baked with soy sauce and lemon and piled high with spiced chunky noodles.

Chicken and shrimp paella.
For recipe, see p375.

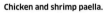

FOOD FOR FRIENDS

Chicken, eggplant, and tomato tagine

PREP 30 MINS

SERVES 8

3–4 tbsp olive oil
8 chicken pieces (thighs and breasts)
sea salt and freshly ground
   black pepper
2 eggplants, cut into bite-sized cubes
1 tsp ground cinnamon
2 onions, finely grated
3 fresh hot red chiles, seeded
   and finely chopped
2 tsp ground cumin
2 bay leaves

4lb (1.8kg) tomatoes
1 tbsp tomato paste or purée
4 preserved lemons, halved
   and pith discarded
handful of fresh cilantro,
   finely chopped

1 Heat 1 tablespoon of the oil in a large, heavy pot. Season the chicken with salt and pepper and add to the pot. Cook for 8 minutes, or until lightly golden on both sides, stirring occasionally, then remove from pot and set aside. Toss the eggplants in the cinnamon and add to the pot with

1 tablespoon oil. Cook over medium heat, stirring occasionally, for 10 minutes, until golden. Add more oil if needed. Remove and set aside.

2 Add 1 tablespoon oil, then add the onions, chiles, cumin, and bay leaves. Season with salt and pepper and cook over low heat for 5 minutes. Return the chicken and eggplant to the pan along with the tomatoes and tomato paste or purée. Cover and simmer over low heat for 25 minutes, adding hot water if the mixture starts to look too dry.

3 Stir in the preserved lemons and cilantro and serve with plenty of fluffy couscous and some harissa on the side.

Beef and orange daube

PREP 45 MINS · COOK 2 HRS

Special equipment • large cast-iron pan

SERVES 8

4 tbsp olive oil
2½lb (1.1kg) stew meat, such as chuck steak or bottom round roast, cut into bite-sized pieces
1 tbsp all-purpose flour
sea salt and freshly ground black pepper
1 bay leaf
4 tbsp butter
3 large onions, sliced
zest and juice of 2 oranges
12 salted anchovies, finely chopped
1¼ cups red wine
1¼lb (550g) cremini mushrooms, quartered
3½ cups hot vegetable stock
handful of thyme, finely chopped

1 Preheat the oven to 300°F (150°C). Put 2 tablespoons of the oil in a large cast-iron casserole over medium-high heat. Toss the meat in the flour, season with salt and pepper, then add the meat and the bay leaf to the hot oil. Cook, stirring occasionally, for 8–10 minutes, or until the meat is no longer pink. Add the butter and cook for 5 minutes, or until the meat has browned. Remove with a slotted spoon and set aside.

2 Add the remaining oil to the casserole, then cook the onions over low heat for 6–8 minutes, or until soft. Add the orange zest, increase the heat a little, then add the orange juice and scrape off any brown bits from the bottom of the pan.

3 Stir in the anchovies, then add the wine and simmer over high heat for 2 minutes. Stir in the mushrooms, add the stock and thyme, and season. Return the meat to the casserole, cover with a lid, then put in the oven to cook for 2 hours, or until the meat is meltingly tender.

Shrimp makhani

PREP 20 MINS · COOK 40 MINS

Special equipment • food processor

SERVES 8

1lb 9oz (700g) shelled, uncooked shrimp
sea salt and freshly ground black pepper
6 garlic cloves, finely chopped
6in (15cm) piece of fresh ginger, peeled and finely chopped or grated
3 tbsp vegetable oil
1 cup plain yogurt
2–3 tsp chili powder
2 cinnamon sticks, broken into pieces
4 fresh red chiles, seeded and finely chopped
6 cardamom pods, crushed
1lb 9oz (700g) tomatoes
4½oz (125g) cashews, ground, plus a handful, coarsely chopped, to garnish
2–3 tsp ground fenugreek
1 cup heavy cream

1 Season the shrimp with salt and pepper and toss with half the garlic and ginger, 1 teaspoon of the oil, the yogurt, and chili powder. Heat a large, deep frying pan, then add the shrimp, coating them with as much of the yogurt as you can. Cook over high heat, tossing frequently, for 2 minutes, or just until they turn pink. Remove and set aside.

2 Heat the remaining oil in the pan, add the rest of the ginger and garlic, cinnamon, chiles, and cardamom pods, and cook over low heat, stirring occasionally, for 2 minutes. Add the tomatoes and cook for 10 minutes, or until they start to reduce. Add a little hot water and simmer for another 10 minutes.

3 Put the tomato mixture into a food processor and blend until smooth. Pass through a sieve into the pan, then stir through the ground cashews and fenugreek and simmer for 10 minutes, adding a little hot water if the sauce becomes too thick. Add the shrimp and the cream, stir, taste, and season, if needed. Cook for 5 minutes more, then garnish with the chopped cashews and serve with rice.

COOK'S NOTES

Fenugreek is the key spice in a makhani. If you can find dried fenugreek leaves, use a handful of these, crushed, instead of the ground fenugreek.

373

Gado gado

PREP 30 MINS · COOK 20 MINS

Special equipment • food processor

SERVES 8

4 ears of corn
sea salt and freshly ground
    black pepper
12oz (350g) green beans, trimmed
1¼lb (550g) potatoes, unpeeled
1lb (450g) roasted peanuts
4 garlic cloves
3 fresh red chiles, seeded
2 tsp demerara (raw) sugar
juice of 1 lime
4 carrots, finely sliced
7oz (200g) bean sprouts
half a cucumber, chopped into
    bite-sized pieces
6 eggs, hard-boiled, shelled,
    and quartered
handful of fresh cilantro, chopped

1 Cook the corn in a large pot of salted boiling water for about 15-20 minutes until soft. Add the green beans for the last 5 minutes of cooking. Drain, slice the ears of corn into rings, and place in a shallow serving bowl. Meanwhile, cook the potatoes in a pot of salted boiling water for 15 minutes, or until just beginning to soften. Drain and set aside. When the potatoes cool, slice and add to the corn and beans.

2 Pulse the peanuts, garlic, and chiles in a food processor until finely ground. Season with salt and pepper. Add a little water and process again into paste. Add the sugar and lime juice and pulse again, adding more water if needed. The paste should be smooth but not runny.

3 Add the carrots, bean sprouts, and cucumber to the cooked vegetables, then pour in the sauce and toss to combine. Top with the hard-boiled eggs and cilantro and serve.

Pork goulash

PREP 25 MINS · COOK 1 HR · ❄

Special equipment • large cast-iron pan

SERVES 8

2½lb (1.1kg) pork shoulder, cut into
    bite-sized pieces
1 tbsp all-purpose flour
2 tsp paprika
2 tsp caraway seeds, crushed
sea salt and freshly ground
    black pepper
2 tbsp olive oil
1 tbsp cider vinegar
2 tbsp tomato paste or purée
4 cups hot vegetable stock
6 tomatoes, peeled and
    coarsely chopped
1 onion, sliced into rings
handful of curly parsley,
    finely chopped

1 Toss the meat with the flour, paprika, and caraway seeds, and season with salt and pepper. Heat the oil in a large cast-iron casserole, then add the meat and cook over high heat, stirring occasionally, for 8-10 minutes, or until the pork begins to brown. Add the vinegar and stir for a couple of minutes, scraping up any brown bits that are stuck to the bottom of the pan.

2 Add the tomato paste, followed by the stock, and bring to a boil. Reduce to a simmer, cover, and cook over low heat for 1 hour. Check occasionally and add a little boiling water if the goulash begins to dry out too much— it should remain fairly thick, though.

3 Stir in the tomatoes, season to taste if needed, then top with the onion rings and parsley and serve.

Chicken and shrimp paella

PREP
15
MINS

COOK
50
MINS

SERVES 8

8 skinless chicken thighs

6 cups hot vegetable stock

2 tbsp olive oil

4 red bell peppers, seeded
   and cut into strips

1lb 9oz (700g) uncooked
   shelled shrimp

sea salt and freshly ground
   black pepper

1 x 28oz (800g) can diced tomatoes

2¼ cups paella rice or basmati rice

14oz (400g) green beans, trimmed

a few strands of saffron

pinch of cayenne pepper

pinch of paprika

handful of flat-leaf parsley, chopped

1 Put the chicken thighs in a large saucepan, add 2 cups of the stock, cover, and cook over medium-low heat for 15–20 minutes, or until the chicken is nearly cooked. Remove the chicken with a slotted spoon and reserve the stock.

2 Meanwhile, heat the oil in a paella pan or large flat frying pan, add the peppers, and cook for 2 minutes. Add the shrimp, season with salt and ground black pepper, then cook over medium heat, stirring occasionally, for 2 more minutes, or until the shrimp are cooked and pink. Remove the shrimp and peppers with a slotted spoon and set aside.

3 Add the tomatoes, then the rice and the reserved cooking stock and stir. Season again, then add another 2 cups of the stock and the chicken. Simmer gently for 20–30 minutes, or until the rice is cooked, adding the remaining stock as needed. Add the beans for the last 10 minutes of cooking along with the saffron, cayenne, and paprika. Return the peppers and shrimp to the pan, heat through, then sprinkle with parsley and serve.

Cheat...
You can buy ready-mixed paella spices. Add with the rice in place of the saffron, cayenne, and paprika.

COOK'S NOTES

It's tradition in Spain to mix meat and fish. If you're not a fan, choose one to cook with and increase the quantities.

FOOD FOR FRIENDS

Mixed fish stew with toasted baguette

PREP
30
MINS

SERVES 8

5lb (2.25kg) mixed fish and shellfish,
  such as haddock, monkfish, flounder,
  and shelled uncooked shrimp
3 tbsp olive oil
4 garlic cloves, finely chopped
2 tbsp tomato paste or purée
1 onion, finely chopped
8 small, ripe tomatoes, peeled
  and chopped
1 tsp fennel seeds
a few strands of saffron

pinch of paprika
4 cups fish stock
sea salt and freshly ground
  black pepper
1 baguette
4½oz (125g) Gruyère cheese, grated
handful of fresh flat-leaf parsley,
  finely chopped, to garnish

1 Wash the fish, cut into bite-sized pieces, and set aside. Put the oil in a large pan, add the garlic, tomato paste, and onion, and cook over very low heat for 5–8 minutes, until the onion begins to soften.

2 Add the tomatoes, fennel seeds, saffron, and paprika, pour in the stock, and season with salt and pepper. Bring to a boil, reduce to a simmer, and cook for 10 minutes. Add the fish and shellfish and simmer for another 10 minutes, or until the fish is cooked.

3 Slice the baguette diagonally and toast. Sprinkle the soup with the cheese, garnish with the parsley, and serve with the toasted bread.

COOK'S NOTES

A rouille (spicy garlicky mayonnaise sauce) is often served with fish soups and stews. You can buy it ready-made in jars. Spread it on the toasted baguette, sprinkle with the Gruyère cheese, and add to the top of the stew.

Spiced sausage cassoulet

Special equipment • large heavy-bottomed pan

SERVES 8

4 tbsp olive oil

2 large onions, sliced

4 celery stalks, chopped

2 large potatoes, cut into ¾in (2cm) dice

16 sweet pork sausages

7oz (200g) slab bacon, cut into thin strips or lardons

6 garlic cloves, chopped

2 x 14oz (400g) cans haricot beans, drained and rinsed

1 tbsp tomato paste or purée

3 tsp paprika

2 tsp dried thyme

2 tsp dried oregano

1 tsp freshly ground black pepper

1¼ cups dry white wine

2 cups hot vegetable stock

4½oz (125g) fresh bread crumbs

handful flat-leaf parsley, chopped

3 tbsp butter

1 Preheat the oven to 300°F (150°C). Heat the oil in a large heavy-bottomed casserole, add the onions, celery, and potatoes, and cook for 5 minutes, or until starting to soften. Add the sausages and bacon and cook for 5 minutes, until starting to brown.

2 Add the garlic and cook for 1 minute, then add the haricot verts, tomato paste, paprika, thyme, oregano, and pepper. Combine well, then add the wine. Bring to a boil and simmer for 2 minutes, then add the stock and 1¼ cups hot water. Bring to a boil, simmer for 10 minutes, then remove from heat.

3 Mix the bread crumbs with the parsley and cover the top of the dish liberally. Dot with pats of butter, cover, and bake for 1½ hours. Uncover and cook for another 30 minutes. Serve with a crisp green salad.

FOOD FOR FRIENDS

Mushroom risotto

SERVES 8

6 tbsp olive oil

2 onions, finely chopped

3 tbsp butter

1lb 2oz (500g) cremini mushrooms, coarsely chopped

6 garlic cloves, finely chopped

3 red chiles, seeded and finely sliced

2¾ cups Arborio rice

2½ cups hot mushroom or chicken stock

2 tsp ground black pepper

large handful of fresh flat-leaf parsley, finely chopped

4½oz (125g) Parmesan cheese, grated

1 Heat the oil in a large cast-iron casserole, add the onions, and cook over medium heat for 5 minutes, or until soft. Stir in the butter, mushrooms, garlic, and chiles and cook for 5 minutes more, stirring.

2 Add the rice, stir well, then add 1¼ cups stock and cook over low heat, stirring occasionally, until the rice absorbs the stock. Add more stock, ⅔ cup at a time, allowing each addition to be absorbed before adding the next, until the rice is cooked.

3 Add the pepper, parsley, and half the cheese, stir, and serve with more Parmesan sprinkled on top.

VARIATION

Omit the mushrooms and add 6 sliced zucchini or 1½ bunches of chopped asparagus with the onion.

FOOD FOR FRIENDS

Seafood risotto

PREP
20
MINS

SERVES 8

2–3 tbsp olive oil

1lb (450g) shelled uncooked shrimp

salt and freshly ground black pepper

1lb (450g) mixed white fish, such as monkfish, sea bass, and haddock, cut into bite-sized pieces

16 scallops, cleaned

2 tbsp of butter

2 onions, finely chopped

4 garlic cloves, finely chopped

7 cups hot vegetable stock or light fish stock

3¼ cups risotto rice

2 cups white wine

6 tomatoes, peeled and finely chopped

large handful of flat-leaf parsley, finely chopped

handful of fresh dill, finely chopped

lemon wedges, to serve

1 Heat 1 tablespoon of the oil in a large, deep skillet, add the shrimp and a pinch of salt and pepper, and cook over medium-high heat for a couple of minutes or until they turn pink. Remove and set aside. Add the fish and a little more oil if needed and cook over medium heat for a couple of minutes or until the fish is opaque and cooked. Remove and set aside.

2 Season the scallops with salt and pepper, add to the pan with a little more oil if needed, and cook for 2 minutes on each side or until opaque. Remove and set aside. Add 1 tablespoon of butter to the pan, followed by the onions, and cook over low heat for 5–8 minutes or until soft. Add the garlic and cook for a few seconds. Meanwhile, put the hot stock in a large saucepan and bring to a low simmer.

3 Add the rice to the skillet and stir well so it soaks up all the buttery juices. Season with salt and pepper, then pour in the wine and increase the heat a little. Allow to bubble for a few seconds while the alcohol evaporates. Start adding the stock a ladleful at a time, stirring until it has all been absorbed before adding more. Continue like this until the rice is cooked but still has a bite to it, about 20 minutes. You may have some stock left over or you may need to add a little bit more near the end.

4 Stir in the tomatoes, return the shrimp, fish, and scallops to the pan, then stir in the herbs and remaining butter. Taste and season with salt and freshly ground pepper if needed, then serve with lemon wedges.

COOK'S NOTES

Adding a little butter at the end promises a really creamy risotto, but you can leave it out if you're counting calories.

Provençal lamb

PREP 25 MINS | COOK 2½ HRS

Special equipment • large cast-iron pan

SERVES 8
4 tbsp olive oil
4 onions, cut into eighths
2½lb (1.1kg) leg of lamb, cut into bite-sized chunks
2 tsp paprika
6 garlic cloves, chopped
6 tbsp black olives
2 tbsp capers
4 tsp dried oregano
2 tsp dried thyme
6 tbsp dry (fino) sherry
sea salt and freshly ground black pepper
1 x 28oz (800g) can diced tomatoes

1 Preheat the oven to 300°F (150°C). Heat the oil in a large cast-iron casserole over medium heat, add the onions, and cook for 5 minutes or until starting to soften. Add the lamb and paprika and cook, turning frequently, for 8–10 minutes or until the lamb is no longer pink.

2 Add the garlic, olives, capers, oregano, thyme, and sherry and cook for 3 minutes. Season with salt and pepper, add the tomatoes, stir well, and bring to a boil. Cover the pan with a well-fitting lid and transfer to the oven for 2½ hours. Serve with herbed mashed potatoes and olive oil.

Malaysian-style chicken with noodles

PREP 15 MINS | COOK 1 HR

Special equipment • food processor

SERVES 8
8 large chicken pieces (breasts, legs, and thighs), about 2½lb (1.1kg) in weight, or 1 large chicken, cut up
sea salt and freshly ground black pepper
5 red chiles, seeded
2 tbsp curry powder
2 tsp turmeric
2 tsp ground cumin
6 garlic cloves, finely chopped
8 shallots, finely chopped
3 tbsp vegetable oil or sunflower oil
2 x 14oz (400g) cans coconut milk
2 tsp sugar
6 tomatoes, peeled and chopped
1 red onion, finely chopped
handful of fresh cilantro, chopped, plus extra to garnish
2 cups chicken stock
1lb (450g) thick egg noodles
1 tbsp oil, for frying

1 Season the chicken with salt and pepper and set aside. Put the chiles, curry powder, turmeric, cumin, garlic, shallots, and oil in a food processor and blend to a smooth paste.

2 Heat a large pan, add the paste, and cook over medium heat for 5 minutes, stirring frequently. Add the chicken skin-side down and cook for 10 minutes or until evenly browned. Turn halfway through cooking.

3 Shake the cans of coconut milk and add to the pan along with the sugar. Season with salt and pepper, bring to a boil, then reduce the heat and allow to simmer for 20 minutes until the mixture has reduced. Add the tomatoes and onion and cook for 10 minutes more, then stir in the cilantro. Cover and leave to stand.

4 Put the stock in a pan of hot water and bring to a boil. Add the noodles and cook for 8 minutes or until almost cooked but not too soft. Drain well. Heat the oil in a wok or deep frying pan, add the noodles, and cook for 3 minutes. Season with salt and pepper, then toss well and transfer to a platter. Spoon the chicken over the noodles, garnish with the remaining cilantro, and serve.

Pork belly with onions and potatoes

PREP 25 MINS **COOK** 1½ HRS

SERVES 6–8

2¼lb (1kg) piece of pork belly
1 tsp sea salt
6 tbsp olive oil
3 large onions, cut into eighths
4 large potatoes, cut into wedges
9oz (250g) button mushrooms, halved
1¼ cups white wine
4 garlic cloves, chopped
1 heaping tbsp fresh thyme
2 cups vegetable stock
1 tsp freshly ground black pepper

1 Preheat the oven to 425°F (220°C). Deeply score the skin of the pork belly, then rub the salt and 2 tablespoons of the oil into it. Transfer to a baking pan and place in the oven for 20 minutes, or until the skin has become crackling. Remove from the oven and reduce the temperature to 300°F (150°C).

2 Heat the remaining oil in a large frying pan, add the onions and potatoes, and cook for 10 minutes, stirring constantly. Add the mushrooms and cook for 5 minutes. Add the wine and cook for 2 minutes. Transfer the mixture to a large baking dish, add the garlic, thyme, stock, and pepper, and combine. Nestle the pork into the mixture, ensuring the crackling isn't covered, and roast in the oven for 1½ hours.

3 Allow to rest for 10 minutes, then cut the pork with scissors and serve with steamed broccoli.

FOOD FOR FRIENDS

Pad Thai

PREP 15 MINS · COOK 15 MINS

Special equipment • wok

SERVES 8

1¼lb (550g) medium or thick
   rice noodles
3 tbsp sunflower oil
4 eggs, lightly beaten
1 tsp shrimp paste
4 red chiles, seeded and
   finely chopped
6 boneless, skinless chicken breasts,
   cut into ¼in (5mm) slices
2 bunches scallions,
   finely chopped
splash of Asian fish sauce (*nam pla*)
juice of 2 limes
2 tbsp demerara (raw) sugar
sea salt and freshly ground
   black pepper
10oz (300g) unsalted peanuts
handful of fresh cilantro,
   finely chopped
lime wedges, to serve

1 Put the noodles in a large bowl, cover with boiling water, and leave for 8 minutes, or until soft. Drain and set aside. Put 1 tablespoon of the oil in a large wok over high heat and swirl around the pan. Add the beaten eggs and whisk them around the wok for about a minute, or until they begin to set. Before the eggs set completely, spoon them out and set aside.

2 Add the remaining oil to the wok, then add the shrimp paste and chiles and stir. With the heat still high, add the chicken and stir constantly for 5 minutes, or until it is no longer pink. Stir in the scallions, fish sauce, lime juice, and sugar and toss to combine. Cook for a few minutes, or until the sugar has dissolved, then season with salt and pepper. Return the eggs to the wok.

3 Add the noodles to the wok and toss to coat with the sauce, then add half the peanuts and half the cilantro and toss again. Transfer to a large shallow serving bowl and sprinkle with the rest of the peanuts and cilantro. Serve with the lime wedges.

Beef, fennel, and mushroom hotpot

PREP 40 MINS · COOK 1¾ HRS · ❄

Special equipment • large cast-iron pan

SERVES 8

2½lb (1.1kg) beef stew meat, cut into
   bite-sized pieces
sea salt and freshly ground
   black pepper
1 tbsp all-purpose flour
2 tsp mild paprika
3 tbsp olive oil
2 onions, finely sliced
3 fennel bulbs, trimmed and
   cut into eighths
⅔ cup dry white wine
4 cups hot beef stock
   or vegetable stock
1 tbsp butter
1lb (450g) cremini
   mushrooms, quartered
pinch of dried oregano

1 Preheat the oven to 350°F (180°C). Season the meat well with salt and pepper, then place in a mixing bowl and toss with the flour and paprika until the pieces are evenly coated.

2 Heat half the olive oil in a large cast-iron casserole, add the meat, and cook over medium heat, stirring frequently, for 8–10 minutes, or until evenly browned. Remove with a slotted spoon and set aside.

3 Heat the remaining oil in the casserole, add the onion, and sauté for 6–8 minutes, or until soft. Season. Add the fennel and cook, stirring occasionally, for 6 minutes, or until beginning to soften slightly. Add the wine, increase the heat, and simmer for a couple of minutes until the alcohol evaporates. Return the meat to the casserole, pour in the stock, then bring to a boil. Cover and place in the oven for 1 hour.

4 After 1 hour, melt the butter in a frying pan, add the mushrooms and oregano, and sauté, stirring often, for 5 minutes, or until soft. Stir into the beef and fennel and return to the oven for another 30 minutes. Serve with boiled potatoes.

Baked turkey rolls filled with chestnuts and mushrooms

PREP 20 MINS

Special equipment • food processor

SERVES 6-8

2½lb (1.1kg) turkey breast, cut into 3in (7.5cm) strips
sea salt and freshly ground black pepper
7oz (200g) ready-cooked chestnuts
8 garlic cloves, finely chopped
large handful of flat-leaf parsley, finely chopped
4½oz (125g) dried apricots
1¼lb (550g) cremini mushrooms
1 tsp dried thyme
6 tbsp olive oil

1 Preheat the oven to 350°F (180°C). Season the turkey strips with a little salt and pepper and set aside. Meanwhile, put the chestnuts, garlic, and parsley in a food processor and blend for 10 seconds. Add the apricots and mushrooms and pulse for another 5 seconds. Add the thyme and 3 tablespoons of the oil and process for 5 seconds, or until you have a chunky paste. Season with salt and pepper.

2 Place 1 tablespoon of the mixture on each turkey strip and carefully roll it up. Place the rolls in a baking dish with the seams facing down, making sure they are tightly packed. Drizzle with the remaining olive oil, cover with foil, and bake for 30 minutes. Remove the foil and cook for another 10 minutes, or until brown. Serve with a crisp green salad.

Pork with rice and tomatoes

PREP 30 MINS

SERVES 6-8

6 tbsp olive oil
3 onions, diced
2½lb (1.1kg) lean pork, cut into 2in (5cm) chunks
6 garlic cloves, finely chopped
handful of flat-leaf parsley, chopped
1 tbsp fresh thyme
1 tbsp chopped fresh sage leaves
2 tsp paprika
⅔ cup dry white wine
2¾ cups long-grain rice
2 x 28oz (800g) cans diced tomatoes
sea salt and freshly ground black pepper

1 Preheat the oven to 300°F (150°C). Heat the oil in a large, heavy-bottomed, oven-safe pot, add the onions, and cook over medium heat for 5 minutes, or until starting to soften. Add the pork and cook for 5 minutes, or until no longer pink. Stir in the garlic, parsley, thyme, sage, and paprika, then add the wine and cook for 5 minutes. Add the rice and tomatoes, stir to combine, then season well with salt and pepper.

2 Cover and cook in the oven for 1 hour. Stir occasionally and add a little hot water if it starts to dry out. Remove from the oven and allow to stand for 10 minutes with the lid on before serving.

Lancashire hotpot

PREP
25
MINS

COOK
2
HRS

SERVES 8

2 tbsp olive oil

8 large lamb chops, each about
   7oz (200g) in weight

2lb (900g) potatoes, cut into
   ¼in (5mm) slices

sea salt and freshly ground
   black pepper

4 onions, sliced

8 anchovies, finely chopped

2 cups hot vegetable stock

1 tbsp butter

1 Preheat the oven to 350°F (180°C). Heat a drizzle of the oil in a large frying pan, add the lamb chops, and cook over medium heat for 2 minutes on each side, until lightly browned. If the pan is overcrowded, cook the chops in two batches.

2 Layer the potatoes in the bottom of a 4-pint (2.3-liter) flameproof dish, lay the chops on top, and season well with salt and pepper. Heat the remaining oil in the frying pan, add the onions, and cook over low heat, stirring frequently for 10 minutes, or until beginning to soften. Stir in the anchovies. Spoon a layer of the onion mixture on top of the chops, then add the rest of the potatoes and onion mixture in layers, finishing with a potato layer.

3 Pour in enough of the stock to come nearly up to the top of the potatoes. Dot the potatoes with butter, cover the dish tightly with foil, then bake for 2 hours, or until the potatoes are meltingly soft and the stock has been absorbed. Remove the foil for the last 20 minutes of cooking. Serve with pickled red cabbage.

VARIATION

Cook 4 lamb's kidneys with the chops and add to the dish.

COOK'S NOTES

The anchovies add richness. Don't worry if you're not a fan—they'll melt away during cooking and you won't be able to taste them.

Tomatoes stuffed with okra and rice

PREP 30 MINS | COOK 1 HR

SERVES 6-8

8 large ripe (but not too ripe)
   beefsteak tomatoes
6 tbsp olive oil
2 large onions, finely chopped
1¼lb (550g) okra, chopped
6 garlic cloves, finely chopped
4 tbsp tomato paste or purée
juice of 2 lemons
1¾oz (50g) pine nuts
9oz (250g) long-grain rice
1 tsp freshly ground
   black pepper
1¼ cups hot vegetable stock
large handful of flat-leaf parsley,
   finely chopped
1 tbsp fresh thyme
1 tsp caraway seeds (optional)

1 Carefully cut around the top of each tomato to make a hole 2in (5cm) in diameter. Using a teaspoon, remove the insides, ensuring you leave a wall at least ½in (1cm) thick. Discard the flesh and set the tomato shells aside.

2 Heat 3 tablespoons of the oil in a large frying pan, add the onions, and cook over medium heat for 5 minutes, or until starting to soften. Add the okra and cook for 3 minutes, stirring frequently. Stir in the garlic, tomato paste, lemon juice, and pine nuts. Add the rice, season with the pepper, then stir to combine and add the stock.

3 Cook for 10 minutes, or until the liquid is absorbed. Stir in the parsley and thyme and remove from the heat. Preheat the oven to 300°F (150°C).

4 Stuff the tomatoes evenly with the rice mixture. Place them in a deep baking dish, packing them in fairly tightly. Drizzle with the rest of the olive oil, sprinkle with the caraway seeds, if using, and cover with foil. Bake for 1 hour. Serve with crusty bread and a green salad.

Pork meatballs with tomatoes

PREP 30 MINS | COOK 1 HR

Chilling • 20 minutes

SERVES 6-8

3 large onions, finely diced
2¼lb (1kg) lean ground pork
handful of flat-leaf parsley,
   finely chopped
2 tsp cayenne pepper
2 tsp dried thyme
2 eggs
3 tbsp all-purpose flour
sea salt and freshly ground
   black pepper
12 large beefsteak tomatoes
6 tbsp olive oil
2 tbsp dried oregano

1 Put the onions, ground pork, parsley, cayenne, thyme, eggs, and flour in a mixing bowl, season well with salt and pepper, then mix together with your hands for 5 minutes, or until you have a chunky paste. Chill in the refrigerator for 20 minutes to firm the mixture a little. Meanwhile, preheat the oven to 350°F (180°C).

2 Take handfuls of the mixture and roll into balls about 2in (5cm) in diameter, making approximately 24 balls. Place them in a large non-stick baking pan. Cut the tomatoes in half and place them skin-side down with the meatballs, so each meatball is in between tomatoes. Drizzle with the oil, sprinkle with the oregano, then cover the sheet with foil.

3 Bake for 30 minutes, then remove the foil and cook for another 30 minutes, or until nicely browned. Serve with crusty bread and salad.

Zucchini, herb, and lemon tagine

PREP 25 MINS COOK 40 MINS

SERVES 8

2 tbsp olive oil
2 red onions, finely chopped
sea salt and freshly ground
    black pepper
4 garlic cloves, finely chopped
pinch of fennel seeds
pinch of ground cinnamon
2–3 tsp harissa (or to taste)
4 preserved lemons, halved, pith
    removed and halved again
1 x 28oz (800g) can whole
    tomatoes, chopped

1 head broccoli, broken
    into florets
6 zucchini, sliced
juice of 1 lemon
handful of fresh dill, finely chopped
14oz (400g) couscous
handful of flat-leaf parsley,
    finely chopped
harissa and lemon wedges,
    to serve

1 Heat half the oil in a large
heavy-bottomed pan, add the
onions, and cook over low heat for
5 minutes, or until soft. Season with
salt and pepper. Stir in the garlic,
fennel seeds, cinnamon, harissa,
and lemons.

2 Add the tomatoes and stir well,
crushing them with the back of a
wooden spoon. Bring to a boil, then
reduce to a simmer and cook over low
heat for 30–40 minutes, or until the
fennel is soft. If the sauce starts to
dry out, add a little hot water.

3 Meanwhile, cook the broccoli
in a pan of boiling salted water for
3–5 minutes or until tender, then
drain and refresh in cold water. Drain
again and set aside. Heat the rest of
the oil in the frying pan, add the
zucchini, and season with salt and
pepper. Cook over low heat, stirring
frequently, for 5 minutes, or until the
zucchini starts to color a little. Add a
squeeze of lemon and stir in the dill.

4 Meanwhile, put the couscous in
a large bowl and pour in just enough
boiling water to cover it. Set aside for
10 minutes, then fluff with a fork and
season with salt and pepper. Add the
broccoli and zucchini to the sauce and
stir in the parsley. Serve with the
couscous, lemon wedges, and harissa.

Spicy lamb with baby potatoes

PREP
25
MINS

SERVES 6–8

1½lb (675g) lean lamb, cut into
   ¾in (2cm) cubes
3 tsp paprika
1 tsp cayenne pepper
finely grated zest of 2 lemons
10 tbsp olive oil
3 onions, finely diced
2½lb (1.1kg) small creamer or
   new potatoes

large handful flat-leaf parsley,
   finely chopped
6 garlic cloves, finely chopped
2 tbsp finely chopped fresh thyme
1 tbsp chopped fresh rosemary
   leaves
6 preserved lemons, quartered
   and pith removed
sea salt and freshly ground
   black pepper

1 Preheat the oven to 300°F (150°C).
Put the lamb, paprika, cayenne, and
lemon zest in a mixing bowl, combine
well, then set aside. Heat 4 tablespoons
of the oil in a large, heavy-bottomed
nonstick pan, add the onions, and
cook over medium heat for 3 minutes.
Add the lamb and cook, stirring
frequently, for 5 minutes or until
no longer pink.

2 Add the potatoes and cook for
2 minutes, then add the parsley,
garlic, thyme, rosemary, preserved
lemons, and the rest of the olive oil.

Combine and toss together, season
with salt and pepper, and cover with
a lid. Place the pan in the oven and
cook, stirring frequently, for 1½ hours.
Serve warm.

Baby zucchini with fish and couscous

PREP 20 MINS · **COOK 20 MINS**

Special equipment • ridged cast-iron grill pan

SERVES 6–8
½ cup olive oil
1lb 5oz (600g) baby zucchini, halved lengthwise
juice and finely grated zest of 2 limes
3 tbsp tomato paste or purée
1 tsp Asian five-spice powder
1 tsp cayenne pepper
2 tsp paprika
1 tsp freshly ground black pepper
large handful of flat-leaf parsley, finely chopped
4 garlic cloves, finely chopped
1¼lb (550g) white fish, such as haddock, cut into bite-sized pieces
2 cups hot vegetable stock
1lb (450g) couscous

1 Preheat the oven to 300°F (150°C). Put 2 tablespoons of the oil in a bowl, add the zucchini, and mix until evenly coated. Cook in a hot grill pan for 2 minutes on each side, then set aside. You may need to do this in batches.

2 Add the rest of the oil to the bowl and mix with the lime juice and zest, tomato paste or purée, five-spice powder, cayenne, paprika, black pepper, parsley, and garlic. Then add the fish, stock, couscous, and zucchini and combine carefully.

3 Transfer to a baking pan and cover with foil. Cook in the oven for 20 minutes, then stir and serve.

Beef and leek couscous

PREP 25 MINS · **COOK 15 MINS**

SERVES 6–8
½ cup olive oil
6 leeks, cleaned and finely sliced
1½lb (675g) ground beef
2 red chiles, seeded and finely chopped
2 tsp paprika
6 garlic cloves, sliced
⅔ cup dry white wine
2 cups hot beef stock
handful of flat-leaf parsley, finely chopped
1lb (450g) couscous

1 Preheat the oven to 300°F (150°C). Heat the oil in a large casserole, add the leeks, and cook over medium heat for 5 minutes. Add the ground beef and cook, stirring occasionally, for 10 minutes or until no longer pink.

2 Stir in the chiles, paprika, and garlic and cook for 2 minutes. Pour in the wine and cook for 3 minutes, then add the stock and parsley and combine well. Stir in the couscous, then cover with a lid and cook in the oven for 15 minutes. Stir and serve.

Bulgur wheat with shrimp, okra, and dill

PREP 30 MINS COOK 20 MINS

SERVES 8

14oz (400g) bulgur
½ cup olive oil
2 large onions, finely diced
14oz (400g) okra, trimmed
6 garlic cloves,
   finely chopped
1½lb (675g) shelled,
   uncooked shrimp
½ cup white wine
large handful of fresh
   dill, chopped
sea salt and freshly ground
   black pepper

1 Preheat the oven to 300°F (150°C). Put the bulgur in an ovenproof bowl, add 1 cup boiling water, and stir well. Cover the dish with a dish towel and set aside, stirring occasionally.

2 Meanwhile, heat the oil in a large heavy-bottomed pan, add the onions, and cook over medium heat for 5 minutes or until starting to soften. Add the okra and cook for 2 minutes, then add the garlic and shrimp and cook, stirring frequently, for 5 minutes or until the shrimp have turned pink.

3 Stir in the wine and dill and cook for 5 minutes. Add the mixture to the bulgur, stir well, then season with salt and pepper. Cover with foil and cook in the oven for 20 minutes, stirring occasionally. Serve with a mixed salad.

Spicy pork with chickpeas and tomatoes

PREP 30 MINS COOK 15 MINS

SERVES 6–8

½ cup olive oil
2 large onions, finely sliced
1½lb (675g) ground pork
6 garlic cloves, finely sliced
juice of 2 lemons
2 tsp cayenne pepper
2 x 14oz (400g) cans chickpeas,
   drained, rinsed, and drained again
large handful of flat-leaf parsley,
   finely chopped
6 large tomatoes, chopped

1 Heat the oil in a large heavy-bottomed pan, add the onions, and cook over medium heat for 5 minutes or until starting to soften. Add the pork and cook, stirring frequently, for 5 minutes or until no longer pink.

2 Stir in the garlic, lemon juice, and cayenne and cook for 1 minute. Add the chickpeas and parsley, stir, then cook for 5 minutes. Add the tomatoes, stir to combine, then simmer for 15 minutes, stirring occasionally. Serve with a green salad and some crusty bread, if desired.

Venison, shallot, and chestnut pot

PREP 40 MINS · COOK 2 HRS

Special equipment • large cast-iron pan

SERVES 8

1 tbsp all-purpose flour
handful of fresh thyme leaves
sea salt and freshly ground
    black pepper
2½lb (1.1kg) boned leg or shoulder of
    venison, cut into bite-sized pieces
1 tbsp butter
3 tbsp olive oil
9oz (250g) bacon lardons or
    pancetta, cubed
9oz (250g) shallots, peeled and
    left whole
2 cups red wine

1¾oz (50g) dried mushrooms, such
    as shiitake, oyster, or porcini,
    soaked in 1¼ cups warm water
    for 20 minutes
9oz (250g) roasted chestnuts
3½ cups hot vegetable stock
3 fresh rosemary sprigs

1 Preheat the oven to 300°F (150°C).
Put the flour, thyme, and some salt
and pepper in a mixing bowl, add the
venison, and toss to coat. Heat the
butter with 2 tablespoons of the oil in
a large cast-iron casserole, add the
venison, and cook over medium heat,
stirring frequently, for 6–8 minutes or
until it is beginning to brown a little.
Remove with a slotted spoon and set

aside. Add the lardons or pancetta to
the pot and stir for 5 minutes or until
brown and crispy. Remove with a
slotted spoon and set aside.

2 Add the remaining oil, then add the
shallots and cook over medium-low
heat for 8 minutes or until they start
turning golden. Return all the meat to
the pot, season with black pepper,
then add the wine and allow to
bubble for a few minutes while
you scrape up any bits of food stuck
to the bottom of the pot.

3 Drain the mushrooms (reserving
the liquid) and stir into the pot.
Strain the liquid and add to the pot.

Stir in the chestnuts, pour in the
stock, then add the rosemary.
Cover with a lid and put in the
oven to cook for 2 hours or until
the meat is tender.

VARIATION

Use beef stew meat instead
of venison.

COOK'S NOTES

Venison is lower in fat than
any other red meat. Buy it
in the winter months when
it's in season.

FOOD FOR FRIENDS

Special fried rice with shrimp and chicken

PREP 15 MINS

Cooling • 30 minutes–1 hour, or overnight
Special equipment • wok

SERVES 8

2lb (900g) basmati rice
sea salt and freshly ground
   black pepper
5 tbsp sunflower oil
1lb (450g) uncooked shelled shrimp
   or prawns, chopped
4 large boneless, skinless chicken
   fillets, cut into 1in (2.5cm) strips
15oz (425g) pancetta, cubed
8oz (225g) white mushrooms, diced
3in (7.5cm) piece of fresh ginger,
   peeled and finely sliced
8oz (225g) frozen peas, defrosted
4 eggs, lightly beaten

2 tbsp dark soy sauce
2 tbsp mirin
bunch of scallions, finely sliced
small handful of flat-leaf parsley,
   finely chopped

1 Rinse the rice well, then place in a large saucepan. Pour boiling water over the rice and add a pinch of salt. Cover, bring to a boil, and cook for 15–20 minutes, or until done. Drain well and set aside to cool completely for 30 minutes–1 hour.

2 Heat 1 tablespoon of the oil in a wok over high heat, add the shrimp, season with salt and pepper, and cook for 10 minutes or until pink. Remove with a slotted spoon and set aside. Heat another tablespoon of the oil

in the wok, add the chicken, season, and stir-fry for 10 minutes, or until cooked and no longer pink. Remove with a slotted spoon and set aside.

3 Heat another tablespoon of the oil in the wok, add the pancetta, and cook over medium-high heat for 6–8 minutes, or until crispy and golden. Remove with a slotted spoon and set aside. Wipe the wok out with paper towels, then heat another tablespoon of the oil in it. Add the mushrooms and ginger and stir-fry for 5 minutes, or until the mushrooms start to soften. Add the peas for the last minute or two. Remove with a slotted spoon and set aside.

4 Heat the remaining oil in the wok, then pour in the eggs and cook gently, stirring them around the pan, for 1 minute. Take care not to overcook them. Add the rice, stir well, then stir in the shrimp, chicken, pancetta, mushrooms, and peas. Add the soy sauce and mirin and cook for 5 minutes, stirring all the time. Transfer to a large shallow serving dish, top with the scallions and parsley, and serve.

COOK'S NOTES

The rice needs to be completely cold before you add it to the wok. Ideally, cook it the day before and chill in the refrigerator until required.

Spicy pork with caraway seeds and cabbage

PREP 25 MINS · COOK 2½ HRS

Special equipment • food processor

SERVES 8

handful of fresh thyme leaves
4 garlic cloves, finely chopped
2 tbsp olive oil
2 tsp crushed red pepper flakes
5lb (2.25kg) piece pork belly,
    skin scored
pinch of sea salt
2 cups hard cider
Savoy cabbage, halved, cored,
    and shredded
1 tbsp butter
1 tsp caraway seeds
freshly ground black pepper

1 Preheat the oven to 425°F (220°C). Put the thyme, garlic, oil, and crushed red pepper flakes in a food processor and pulse to a paste, then rub it all over the pork. Place the pork in a roasting pan, skin-side up, and rub with the sea salt, getting it into all the cracks. Bake for 30 minutes, or until the skin is golden This is how you accomplish the wonderful crackling.

2 Lower the oven temperature to 325°F (160°C). Pour the cider around the pork, then cover with foil, carefully securing it around the edges of the pan and cook for 2 hours.

3 Just before the 2 hours are up, put the cabbage in a pan of salted boiling water and cook for 4–6 minutes, or until soft. Drain, then toss with the butter, caraway seeds, and a pinch of freshly ground black pepper. Transfer to a large shallow serving bowl.

4 Slice the pork into bite-sized pieces and arrange on top of the cabbage along with the juices. Serve with a spoonful of chili jelly on the side and some fresh crusty bread.

Hot and spicy lamb with fava beans

PREP 40 MINS · COOK 2 HRS

Marinating • 30 minutes
Special equipment • large cast-iron pan

SERVES 8

2½lb (1.1kg) leg of lamb,
    cut into bite-sized pieces
2 tbsp olive oil
4 garlic cloves, finely chopped
1–2 tbsp harissa (or to taste)
1 tbsp finely chopped fresh
    rosemary leaves
6 anchovy fillets,
    finely chopped
3 tbsp Worcestershire sauce
1 tbsp finely chopped fresh
    thyme leaves, plus a few
    extra to garnish
juice of 1 lemon
sea salt and freshly ground
    black pepper
2 onions, finely chopped
1lb (450g) shelled fava beans
1½lb (675g) potatoes, peeled and cut
    into bite-sized pieces
4 cups hot vegetable stock

1 Put the lamb in a mixing bowl, add the oil, garlic, harissa, rosemary, anchovies, Worcestershire sauce, thyme, and lemon juice and mix well. Season with salt and pepper, then transfer to a plastic bag and mix together. Leave to marinate for at least 30 minutes (or overnight in the fridge).

2 Preheat the oven to 400°F (200°C). Transfer the mixture to a large cast-iron casserole and cook over medium-high heat, turning occasionally, for 10 minutes, or until the lamb is brown on all sides. Add the onions and cook for 5 minutes.

3 Stir in the fava beans and potatoes, pour in the stock, and bring to a boil. Cover and bake for 2 hours, or until the lamb is tender. If it starts to look dry, add some hot water. Season with salt and pepper and serve garnished with a few thyme leaves.

Creole-style beef and barley

PREP 40 MINS · COOK 2 HRS

Special equipment • large cast-iron pan or flameproof casserole

SERVES 8

2½lb (1.1kg) chuck steak, cut into bite-sized pieces
1 tbsp all-purpose flour
sea salt and freshly ground black pepper
3 tbsp olive oil
2 onions, finely chopped
6 celery stalks, trimmed and finely chopped
3 green bell peppers, seeded and finely chopped
2 tbsp red wine
2 tsp cayenne pepper
2 tsp ground coriander
2 tsp ground cumin
9oz (250g) pearl barley
4 cups hot vegetable stock

1 Preheat the oven to 300°F (150°C). Toss the meat in the flour and season well with salt and pepper. Heat 2 tablespoons of the oil in a large heavy-bottomed pot, add the meat, and cook over medium heat, stirring frequently, for 8 minutes, or until lightly browned all over. Remove with a slotted spoon and set aside.

2 Heat the remaining oil in the pan, add the onions, celery, and peppers, and cook over low heat for 10 minutes, or until completely soft and almost mushy. Add the wine, increase the heat, and allow to bubble for a few minutes while the alcohol evaporates.

3 Stir in the spices, then season well with salt and pepper. Return the meat to the pan and add the pearl barley. Pour in the stock, bring to a boil, then cover and bake for 2 hours. Give it a stir halfway through cooking and add a little hot water if it starts to look dry. Stir in the parsley and serve with crusty bread.

 VARIATION Add a cup of cooked fresh corn, scraped from the cob at the end of cooking.

Cheat... Use 2 tablespoons ready-mixed Creole spices in place of the cayenne, coriander, and cumin.

Pork Normandy

PREP 45 MINS · COOK 1 HR

Special equipment • large cast-iron pan

SERVES 8

2 tbsp olive oil
1 tbsp butter
3lb (1.35kg) lean pork, cut into bite-sized pieces
2 onions, finely chopped
2 tbsp Dijon mustard
4 garlic cloves, finely chopped
6 celery stalks, finely chopped
6 carrots, finely chopped
1 tbsp finely chopped fresh rosemary leaves
3 Granny Smith apples, peeled and coarsely chopped
1¼ cups hard cider
2 cups heavy cream
1¼ cups chicken stock
1 tsp peppercorns

1 Preheat the oven to 350°F (180°C). Heat the oil and butter in a large cast-iron pot, add the pork, and toss in the butter and oil over medium heat for 8 minutes, or until golden brown on all sides. Remove with a slotted spoon and set aside.

2 Add the onions and cook over low heat for 5 minutes, or until starting to soften. Stir in the mustard, add the garlic, celery, carrots, and rosemary, and cook over low heat, stirring often, for 10 minutes, or until tender. Add the apples and cook for 5 minutes.

3 Pour in the cider, then increase the heat and boil for a few minutes while the alcohol evaporates. Return the pork to the pot and pour in the cream and stock. Stir in the peppercorns, bring to a boil, then cover and bake for 1 hour, or until the sauce has reduced and the pork is tender. Serve with fluffy rice or mashed potatoes.

FOOD FOR FRIENDS

Singapore noodles with shrimp and pork

PREP 15 MINS · **COOK** 30 MINS

Marinating • 30 minutes
Special equipment • wok

SERVES 8

2 x 1lb (450g) pork tenderloin,
  cut into 1in (2.5cm) strips
6 tbsp fish sauce
1 tbsp dark soy sauce
1 tbsp rice wine vinegar
2 tsp Asian five-spice powder
1lb (450g) thin rice vermicelli
3 tbsp vegetable oil or sunflower oil
3 garlic cloves finely chopped
1 tsp ground coriander
1lb 2oz (500g) mixed gourmet
  mushrooms, such as porcini,
  enoki, and oyster mushrooms,
  coarsely chopped, or cremini
  mushrooms, sliced
15oz (425g) shelled shrimp or
  prawns, chopped
3 onions, finely chopped
4 red chiles, seeded and finely sliced
sea salt and freshly ground
  black pepper
10oz (300g) bean sprouts
bunch of scallions, chopped
handful of fresh cilantro, chopped

1 Put the pork in a mixing bowl, add the fish sauce, soy sauce, rice wine vinegar, and five-spice powder and leave to marinate for 30 minutes (or overnight in the fridge). Meanwhile, put the vermicelli in a bowl, cover with boiling water, and leave for 6 minutes, or until soft. Drain, rinse, then drain again and set aside.

2 Heat 1 tablespoon of the oil in a wok, swirling it around well to coat the pan, then add the pork and brown over high heat for 6–8 minutes, or until beginning to turn golden and crisp. Remove with a slotted spoon and set aside. Heat another tablespoon of the oil in the wok, then add the garlic and ground coriander and stir. Add the mushrooms and cook for a couple of minutes, then add the shrimp and stir-fry over high heat for 5–8 minutes, or until pink. Remove with a slotted spoon and set aside.

3 Heat the remaining oil in the pan, then add the onions and chiles and stir-fry for 1 minute. Add the vermicelli, season with salt and pepper, then stir in the bean sprouts. Return the pork and the shrimp to the wok and stir well. Remove from the heat, top with the scallions and cilantro, and serve.

COOK'S NOTES

When cooking food in a wok, have all the ingredients prepared in advance, so you can work quickly.

FOOD FOR FRIENDS

Fish with tomatoes, potatoes, and onions

PREP 30 MINS · COOK 15 MINS

SERVES 8

3 tbsp olive oil
5 large potatoes, cut into
  bite-sized pieces
sea salt and freshly ground
  black pepper
4 garlic cloves, finely chopped
small handful of fresh parsley leaves,
  finely chopped
1¼lb (550g) cherry tomatoes, halved
1½ cups dry white wine
1½lb (675g) mixed firm fish, such as
  red mullet, haddock, and sea bass,
  cut into bite-sized pieces
16 anchovy fillets in oil, drained

1 Heat the oil in a large shallow heavy-bottomed pan, add the potatoes, and season with salt and pepper. Cook over medium heat, stirring frequently, for 10–15 minutes or until beginning to turn golden brown. Lower the heat, then stir in the garlic and parsley and cook for a few seconds before adding the tomatoes.

2 Cook for a few minutes, until the tomatoes begin to split, then increase the heat, add the wine, and allow to bubble for a couple of minutes while the alcohol evaporates. Decrease the heat to low, add the fish and the anchovies, cover, and cook for 10–15 minutes, or until the fish is cooked. Transfer to a large shallow serving dish and serve with a crisp dressed salad and some crusty bread.

Chinese-style pork belly

PREP 30 MINS · COOK 2¾ HRS

Special equipment • large cast-iron pan

SERVES 8

1–2 tbsp olive oil
4lb (1.8kg) pork belly, cut into strips
2 onions, finely chopped
sea salt and freshly ground
  black pepper
1 cup dry sherry
splash of rice wine vinegar
juice of 2 oranges
3 star anise
4in (10cm) piece fresh ginger,
  peeled and finely sliced
pinch of Asian five-spice powder
4 cups hot vegetable stock
  or chicken stock
splash of dark soy sauce
1lb (450g) thick egg noodles
1 tbsp of butter
handful of flat-leaf parsley,
  finely chopped

1 Heat 1 tablespoon of the oil in a large cast-iron pot, add the pork, and cook over high heat for 3–5 minutes on each side, or until browned. Remove and set aside. You may need to do this in batches.

2 Heat the remaining oil in the pan (if needed), add the onions, and cook over low heat for 5–8 minutes, or until soft. Season with salt and pepper. Increase the heat, add the sherry and rice wine vinegar, and allow to bubble for 5 minutes while the alcohol evaporates.

3 Add the orange juice, star anise, ginger, five-spice powder, stock, and soy sauce and stir well. Return the meat to the pot, bring to a boil, then cover with a lid and put in the oven to cook for 2½ hours. Check occasionally and add a little hot water if it is looking dry.

4 Remove the meat from the pot with a slotted spoon and cut off any excess fat. Chop into bite-sized cubes and return to the pot. Cover and set aside while you cook the noodles. Add the noodles to a pan of salted boiling water and cook for 8 minutes, or until soft. Drain well, then transfer to a shallow serving bowl. Dot with the butter, sprinkle with the parsley, and serve with the pork belly.

Pork and clam cataplana

PREP 20 MINS

COOK 30 MINS

Marinating • 30 minutes

SERVES 8

2lb (900g) lean pork
    (leg or tenderloin), cut into
    bite-sized pieces
¾ cup dry sherry
4 garlic cloves, finely chopped
2 tsp paprika
2 tsp crushed red pepper flakes
sea salt and freshly ground
    black pepper
4 tbsp olive oil
10oz (300g) chorizo, diced
2 tbsp tomato paste or purée
3 garlic cloves, grated
2 onions, grated

2 bay leaves
1½ cups dry white wine
4½lb (2kg) clams, cleaned and
    any open ones discarded
handful of flat-leaf parsley,
    finely chopped

1 Put the pork in a mixing bowl with the sherry, chopped garlic, paprika, and pepper flakes. Season with salt and pepper and set aside to marinate for 30 minutes (or overnight in the refrigerator).

2 Heat 1 tablespoon of the oil in a large saucepan, add the chorizo, and cook over medium heat, stirring often, for 5 minutes, or until starting to crisp. Remove with a slotted spoon

and set aside. Heat another tablespoon of the oil in the pan, add the pork with its marinade, and cook for 8–10 minutes, or until the meat is browned on all sides. Remove with a slotted spoon and set aside.

3 Heat the remaining oil in the pan, add the tomato paste, grated garlic, onions, and bay leaves, and stir well. Leave to simmer over very low heat for 10 minutes, or until the onion is soft. Season with salt and pepper.

4 Add the wine, increase the heat, and allow to bubble for a few minutes while the alcohol evaporates. Add the clams and cook until the shells open, about 4–5 minutes. Discard any that

don't. Return the pork and chorizo to the pan, warm through, then transfer to a large shallow serving dish. Sprinkle with the parsley and serve.

COOK'S NOTES

Don't eat any clams that haven't opened during cooking. They are inedible.

FOOD FOR FRIENDS

Turkey and mushroom stew with dumplings

 PREP 20 MINS **COOK 1 HR**

Soaking • 30 minutes
Special equipment • large cast-iron pan

SERVES 8

1¾oz (50g) dried porcini mushrooms
1 tbsp butter
2 tbsp olive oil
3lb (1.35kg) turkey breast, cut into
  bite-sized pieces
2 onions, finely chopped
4 garlic cloves, finely chopped
2 bay leaves
a few sprigs of rosemary,
  leaves coarsely chopped
sea salt and freshly ground
  black pepper
6 carrots, cut into chunky pieces
6 celery stalks, coarsely chopped
2 tbsp all-purpose flour
1 cup dry sherry
4 cups hot chicken stock
handful of flat-leaf parsley, chopped

For the dumplings
2 cups self-rising flour, sifted
2oz (60g) shredded suet or shortening
1 tbsp dried oregano

1 Put the porcini mushrooms in a bowl, cover with 1¼ cups hot water, then set aside for 30 minutes to rehydrate. Preheat the oven to 400°F (200°C). Heat the butter and half the oil in a large cast-iron pan, add the turkey, and cook over medium heat, turning the pieces frequently, for 5–8 minutes, or until browned all over. Remove with a slotted spoon and set aside.

2 Heat the remaining oil, add the onions, and cook for 6 minutes, or until soft. Stir in the garlic, bay leaves, and rosemary, season with salt and pepper, then add the carrots and celery and cook for 5 minutes. Stir in the flour and cook for another

2 minutes, or until well combined with the vegetables.

3 Increase the heat, add the sherry, and allow to boil for a few minutes, stirring continually while the alcohol evaporates, then pour in the stock. Drain the mushrooms (reserving the liquid) and add to the pan. Strain the soaking liquid, then add to the pan. Return the turkey to the pan, cover, and put in the oven to cook for 1 hour.

4 Meanwhile, make the dumplings. Put the self-rising flour, suet, and oregano in a bowl with a pinch of salt, then gradually add cold water (about ⅔ cup) until the mixture comes together and forms a dough. Flour your hands and form 16 dumplings. Add these to the pot for the last 30 minutes of cooking. To serve, sprinkle with the parsley.

Cheat...
You can prepare the dumpling mix a few hours ahead of time and keep it in the refrigerator until ready to cook.

COOK'S NOTES

You can use any kind of poultry for this dish—try chicken thighs, on the bone, chicken legs, or pork. Remember to remove the bay leaves before serving.

Crispy beef and vegetables

PREP 15 MINS · **COOK** 30 MINS

Special equipment • wok

SERVES 8

3 tbsp cornmeal

3 eggs

sea salt and freshly ground
   black pepper

3-4 tbsp vegetable oil

2½lb (1.1kg) beef bottom round, cut
   into thin strips

bunch of scallions, sliced
   in fourths lengthwise

3 red chiles, finely shredded

3 garlic cloves, finely sliced

14oz (400g) sugar snap
   peas, finely sliced

4 bok choy

3 tbsp soy sauce

3 tbsp Chinese cooking wine

4 tsp sugar

1 Put the cornmeal and eggs in a bowl, season with salt and pepper, and mix together. Heat 1 tbsp of the oil in a wok, dip the beef into the cornmeal mixture, coat evenly, then add to the wok a few pieces at a time. Add more oil if needed. Cook for 2 minutes, or until crispy and golden. Remove with a slotted spoon and set aside.

2 Wipe the wok clean with a paper towel and heat 1 tablespoon of the oil in it. Add the scallions, chiles, and garlic and cook for a few seconds, stirring constantly. Add the peas and bok choy and stir-fry for 2-3 minutes. Add the soy sauce, cooking wine, and sugar and cook until the sugar has dissolved and the wine has evaporated. Return the meat to the wok, toss together until hot, then serve with rice.

VARIATION Use uncooked shelled shrimp instead of the beef. Cook them in exactly the same way.

COOK'S NOTES

You can omit the sugar, if you like. It's not essential, and the dish will still taste great.

Lebanese meatballs

PREP 50 MINS · **COOK** 1 HR · ❄

Special equipment • large cast-iron pan or flameproof casserole

SERVES 8

1½lb (675g) ground lamb

2 onions, coarsely chopped

4 garlic cloves, finely chopped

handful of fresh cilantro,
   finely chopped

handful of flat-leaf parsley,
   finely chopped

2 tsp paprika

juice and zest of 1 lemon

2 tbsp tomato paste or purée

4 tbsp pine nuts

3 eggs

6 tbsp all-purpose flour

sea salt and freshly ground
   black pepper

8 tbsp olive oil

6 medium potatoes, cut into
   ¾in (2cm) pieces

2 red and 2 yellow bell peppers,
   seeded and sliced

3 x 14oz (400g) cans diced tomatoes

2 tsp fennel seeds, crushed

1 Preheat the oven to 300°F (150°C). Put the lamb, onions, garlic, cilantro, parsley, paprika, lemon juice and zest, tomato paste, pine nuts, eggs, and flour in a mixing bowl and season with salt and pepper. Mix well with your hands to form a chunky paste.

2 Shape a spoonful of the mixture into a ball. Repeat with the rest of the mixture to make 32 meatballs in all. Heat 3 tablespoons of the oil in a large heavy-bottomed pan. Cook the meatballs in batches for 10 minutes each, turning the meatballs several times during cooking to ensure they brown all over. As each batch is cooked, remove with a slotted spoon and set aside.

3 When all the meatballs are cooked, add the potatoes and peppers to the pan and cook over high heat, turning frequently, for 10 minutes, or until starting to brown. Add the tomatoes and fennel seeds, stir well to combine, then season with plenty of salt and pepper. Return the meatballs to the pan and stir well to coat with the sauce. Add the remaining oil, cover, and put in the oven for 1 hour. Serve hot from the pan with crusty bread and a green salad.

FOOD FOR FRIENDS

Shrimp dhansak

PREP 15 MINS

SERVES 8

12oz (350g) red lentils
sea salt and freshly ground
  black pepper
2 tbsp vegetable oil or 1 tbsp ghee
6 cardamom pods, crushed
3 tsp mustard seeds
2 tsp chili powder
2 tsp turmeric
2 tsp cinnamon
2 onions, finely chopped
4in (10cm) piece fresh ginger, peeled
  and finely chopped
4 garlic cloves, finely chopped
3–4 green chiles, seeded and
  finely sliced

1½lb (675g) shelled, uncooked
  colossal shrimp
1 fresh pineapple, peeled and cut
  into bite-sized chunks
8 tomatoes, peeled and
  coarsely chopped
handful of fresh cilantro,
  finely chopped

1 Put the lentils in a large heavy-bottomed pot, season well with salt and pepper, then pour in enough cold water to cover. Bring to a boil, then reduce to a simmer and cook for 20 minutes or until soft. Add hot water if the lentils begin to dry out. Drain and set aside.

2 Meanwhile, heat 1 tablespoon of the oil or ½ tablespoon of the ghee in a large heavy-bottomed frying pan, add the dried spices, and cook, stirring constantly, for 2 minutes or until the seeds pop. Stir in the onions, ginger, garlic, and chiles and cook for 5 minutes until soft and fragrant.

3 Add the remaining oil to the pan, then add the shrimp. Increase the heat and cook, stirring occasionally, for 6–8 minutes or until pink and cooked. Stir in the pineapple, add the lentils and tomatoes and a little hot water so the mixture is slightly soupy, and simmer for 5 minutes. Season again

with salt and pepper, stir in the cilantro, and serve.

COOK'S NOTES

Increase the number of chiles according to how hot you want it to be. The four green chiles here give you a moderately hot dhansak.

Shrimp saganaki

PREP 10 MINS · COOK 45 MINS

SERVES 8

3 tbsp olive oil
2 onions, finely chopped
4 garlic cloves, finely chopped
3 x 14oz (400g) cans whole tomatoes, chopped, with their juices
2 cups dry white wine
1 tsp sugar
sea salt and freshly ground black pepper
1½lb (675g) shelled uncooked shrimp
9oz (250g) feta cheese
handful of fresh thyme leaves

1 Heat half the oil in a large frying saucepan, add the onions, and cook over low heat for 8 minutes or until soft. Stir in the garlic and cook for a few seconds more, then add the tomatoes and their juices, the wine, and sugar and season with salt and pepper. Bring to a boil, squashing the tomatoes with the back of fork, then reduce to a simmer. Cook gently over low heat, stirring occasionally, for 30 minutes or until the sauce has thickened.

2 Meanwhile, heat the remaining oil in a large frying pan, add the shrimp, season with salt and pepper, and cook, stirring occasionally, for 5–10 minutes or until pink. Remove with a slotted spoon and set aside. Preheat the broiler to high.

3 Stir the shrimp into the sauce, remove from the pan, and sprinkle with the feta. Place under the broiler until the feta melts and turns golden brown, then sprinkle with the thyme leaves. Serve with a crisp salad and some crusty bread.

Paneer and sweet pepper curry

PREP 15 MINS · COOK 40 MINS

SERVES 8

4 tbsp ghee or vegetable oil
2 x 9oz (250g) packs paneer, cubed
4in (10cm) piece fresh ginger, peeled and sliced
3 red chiles, seeded and chopped
2 tbsp dried curry leaves, crushed
2 tsp cumin seeds
4 tsp garam masala
2 tsp turmeric
8 red bell peppers, seeded and sliced
8 tomatoes, peeled and coarsely chopped
sea salt and freshly ground black pepper
bunch of cilantro, finely chopped

1 Heat half the ghee or oil in a large wide pan, add the paneer, and cook over medium-high heat for 5–8 minutes or until golden all over. Keep turning the pieces so they don't get too brown. Remove with a slotted spoon and set aside.

2 Heat the remaining ghee in the pan, add the ginger, chiles, curry leaves, cumin, garam masala, and turmeric, stir well to coat with the oil, then add the peppers and cook over low heat for 10 minutes or until beginning to soften.

3 Add the tomatoes and cook for 10 minutes. Return the paneer to the pan, season with salt and pepper, then simmer gently for 10–15 minutes. Stir in the cilantro and serve with rice, chapati, or naan bread.

ALL-IN-ONE ROASTS

All your meat and vegetables in one pan.

ALL-IN-ONE ROASTS

Having a whole meal in one roasting pan couldn't be easier. Put the meat or fish of your choice in the pan, add your favorite vegetables, roast, and you have a whole meal for the family. It's a great way of cooking mid-week, when you don't want to use lots of cookware, and makes for minimum-effort Sunday suppers.

FOOD FOR FRIENDS

Easy meat roasts
These meats are simple to prepare and simple to cook.

Easy fish roasts
Meaty fish is simple to cook, delicious, and healthy.

CHOOSE	USE	CHOOSE	USE
 **BEEF** **Fillet**, also known as **tenderloin**, is a delicious cut that has little visible fat. The muscle tissue does little work, so the meat is very tender. Choose beef that has a good bright color.	Sear before roasting and stuff with a fruity stuffing, such as prunes, or wrap in bacon, if liked. Team with quick-cook vegetables, such as cherry tomatoes, onions, red bell peppers, or squash. Try adding a splash of Worcestershire sauce, or rubbing cracked black pepper into the skin before cooking.	 **SALMON** Salmon is easy and versatile, and perfect for an all-in-one roast, as its firm texture can stand up to fast roasting. Choose either the popular **fillet**, making sure it is quite thick, or the **steak**, which is cut across the main body of the fish, leaving the back bone intact.	It will happily take on a variety of strong flavors, such as lime, lemongrass, sesame oil, ginger, chile, and soy, or mustards, garlic, or honey. Or it can be cooked simply, sitting on top of spring vegetables, with fresh herbs such as parsley and tarragon.
 **PORK** Pork chops are delicious used in an all-in-one roast. Choose **thick chops** with the bone attached for the juiciest meat and a layer of fat around the edge. Snip this with a pair of scissors to produce some crackling. Don't overcook: the flesh should be golden and firm, but springy to the touch.	Rub with olive oil before roasting and season well. Roast with chopped apples, red onions, apricots, sage leaves, maple syrup, or cider. Or try flavors such as fennel, rosemary, garlic, or celery root. Sit the chops on top of mixed root vegetables for a really easy roast.	 **MONKFISH** Monkfish has a meaty texture and delicious sweet taste, and its lack of bones makes roasting the perfect cooking method. Only the tail is eaten (although you can sometimes buy the cheeks from the fishmonger) and these come in **fillets**. Before using, remove the transparent membrane that covers the fish.	Because of its non-intrusive flavor, it can take on quite strong flavors such as Indian and Thai spices, or salty foods such as bacon, pancetta, or chorizo. Or, team with garlic and lemon, rosemary or thyme, saffron, or fennel seeds.
 **LAMB** Lamb **chops** are great for all-in-one roasts, as they are tender enough to cook fast and have lots of flavor. Buy them with a layer of fat, as it will provide extra juices and flavor. **Loin chops** are cheaper than **rib chops**, which are meatier.	Add to a pan of butternut squash or sweet potato. Mix with fresh thyme, rosemary, or bay leaves, or splash with soy or Worcestershire sauce. They are good with mustard or red currant jelly, and delicious with cumin, coriander, cinnamon, allspice, or paprika.	 **MACKEREL** **Whole** roasted mackerel is easy to cook and handle. No turning is required once they are in the pan—they just need scoring and seasoning. You get a lot for your money with mackerel, and they make such an easy supper dish. Allow 1 or 2 per person, depending on the size of the fish, and cook as soon as you can after buying.	As it is an oily fish, team it with flavors that will cut through the fattiness, such as flavored vinegars, sherry, oranges, or lemons. Or, cook it with aromatic spices such as coriander seeds, sweet or smoked paprika, and cayenne pepper.
 **POULTRY** Chicken is incredibly versatile. Use the **breast** or **thigh**, both with bone in, for all-in-one roasts. As with duck, buy a whole one, and ask for it to be cut up. Roast with the skin on, otherwise it will dry out. It can always be removed afterward. Sear first if preferred, or add straight to the roasting pan. Don't overcook chicken, or it will become dry.	It can cope with many different flavors, from hot chiles to simply lemon and thyme. Be more adventurous with spices such as saffron, nutmeg, or cinnamon, or try it with coconut, lemongrass, and ginger.	 **HALIBUT** Halibut is a really meaty white fish that is mild flavored and extremely versatile. It is usually bought as **steaks**, either bone in or out, or as **fillets**, which are large and must be cut up into portions. It can be quick-roasted in a hot oven and lends itself to lots of quick cooking accompaniments, such as tomatoes, green beans, zucchini, or bell peppers.	It has a clean, delicate taste, so doesn't need complicating with too many flavors. Fresh herbs such as parsley, tarragon, or dill, or a little olive oil and lemon juice, will bring out its natural flavor. For a little more punch, try an anchovy or caper dressing, or tomato salsa.

4 store cupboard glazes
Grab something from the store cupboard that will add instant flavor to your roast.

Cranberry
Cranberry sauce can be brushed on a variety of meats before roasting. Great with turkey, ham, beef, and chicken.

Mix with bruised **rosemary leaves** and **port** to glaze beef. Mix with a splash of **soy sauce** and crushed **juniper berries** to glaze venison. Mix with **brown sugar** and **allspice** to glaze ham. Mix with **orange juice** and grated **fresh ginger** to glaze chicken legs.

Honey
Sweet honey has a natural affinity with pork, but is also tasty with chicken and duck.

Mix with **apricot jam** to glaze pork chops or ribs. Mix with **mustard**, grated **nutmeg**, **allspice** and crushed **cloves** to glaze ham. Mix with **soy sauce** and grated **fresh ginger** to glaze chicken legs. Add a splash of **rum** for Jamaican flavor. Add a squeeze of **lime** and grated **fresh ginger** to glaze duck legs. Mix with **pineapple juice** and **crushed red pepper flakes** to glaze chicken wings.

Mustard
Coarse-grain mustards aren't as hot as other mustards and go well with lots of meats.

Mix with **soy sauce** to glaze duck or spare ribs. Mix with **cranberry sauce** to glaze chicken. Mix with a splash of **balsamic vinegar** to glaze beef. Mix with a splash of **whiskey** to glaze pork. Mix with **orange juice** to glaze ham.

Chili sauce
Chili sauce or sweet chili sauce adds sweet and tangy kick to meat and oily fish.

Use to glaze chicken, pork, lamb, beef, duck, mackerel, and salmon. Mix with a pinch of **cayenne pepper** or **paprika** to glaze pork ribs. Mix with a squeeze of **lemon** or **lime** to glaze chicken and mackerel. Mix with **balsamic vinegar** to glaze lamb. Mix with **honey** and grated **fresh ginger** to glaze pork ribs.

Psst...
Use a heavy stainless steel roasting pan, as it conducts the heat well and won't buckle. Non-stick ones are easy to clean, but you might miss out on some of the caramelized meat juices that make great sauces and gravies.

A simple sausage supper
Sausages are an inexpensive alternative to using cuts of meat, but can make a succulent and delicious roast, especially now that they are available in so many varieties, from simple pork to rich venison, or even wild boar. Experiment with flavored and spiced ones, such as tomato and rosemary, or even vegetarian versions. Brush them with any of the glazes and add easy-cook vegetables to the roasting pan, such as bell peppers, zucchini, new potatoes, red onions, or squash.

Prepare tricky vegetables Master how to peel, slice, or clean vegetables for roasting.

Shallots Peeling shallots, part of the onion family, can be awkward and hard on the eyes.

First, **blanch** the shallots in boiling water, just for a few seconds (as you don't want them to cook), **drain** and **rinse** in cold water, then **drain** again. The skins should now **peel** away effortlessly and without tears.

Butternut squash These can be extremely large and quite tough to deal with.

A large knife is required to **cut the squash in half** lengthwise. Do this on a sturdy cutting board. Then, **trim the top and base** and **scoop out the seeds**. Using a vegetable peeler, **peel** away the skin, then either **slice** into thick half-moon shapes or **cut up** into large cubes.

Leeks Leeks need washing before using, as the leaves often contain a lot of grit and soil.

Trim the leek by slicing off both ends, then **remove** any thick outer leaves. Make a **slit lengthwise** down the leek, being careful not to go right through, then, holding the leaves apart, **rinse** under cold water.

Fennel A bulbous vegetable, with a sweet anise flavor that pairs well with fish and pork.

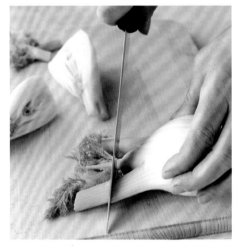

Cut the stalks away from the top of the bulb (**keep the fronds** for garnish, though, and the stalks for stock). **Trim the base** and **remove any tough outer leaves**. **Slice** as required, **quarter** lengthwise for roasting, or **finely shred** if serving raw.

Celery root This ugly root looks tough, but its velvety flesh is worth the effort.

Celery root requires a large knife, as it can be quite tough. **Slice off** the top and the base, then work your way around, **slicing away the rough outer skin**. Try to **use it immediately**, as the flesh will quickly go brown. To prevent this, rub with a lemon as you go. Cut in half, then half again, then **chop into cubes**.

more veg prep tips

Whether you are slicing, dicing, or chopping, use the right tools for the job. A sharp chef's knife and a vegetable peeler are essential.

Do lots of vegetable prep in one go, then bag it up for the refrigerator if using the next day, or freeze it.

The food processor can always be used for shredding; it's ideal for zucchini or carrots.

Salting eggplants before using reduces their bitterness.

Always wash Swiss chard and spinach thoroughly, as the leaves tend to be gritty, which can spoil a dish.

When preparing cauliflower, cut up the florets, but don't discard the green leaves, as these are extremely tasty.

When cooking fava beans, remove them from their pods and cook them very briefly, for about 30 seconds, then drain and peel away the thicker outer skin. The bright green bean inside is delicious and soft.

Make the perfect gravy
A delicious sauce for roast meat, made straight from the roasting pan.

1 Once the meat has been removed from the pan, tilt the pan and spoon away most of the fat, leaving a small amount with the remaining cooking juices.

2 Place the roasting pan over medium heat, then add ¾ cup of dry white wine and stir to loosen and scrape up all the bits from the bottom of the pan.

3 Pour in 2 cups of hot stock, still stirring and scraping the bottom of the pan. It will begin to come clean.

4 Let the gravy bubble and reduce for a few minutes, allowing the alcohol to evaporate and the sauce to thicken, then season with sea salt and freshly ground black pepper.

5 Place a conical sieve in a large heatproof container, then strain the gravy through the sieve. You can repeat this step, if you wish.

Psst...

Save all vegetable trimmings and peelings and add them to the pan while making the sauce, then strain. Or, save them for the stockpot. They will add flavor.

4 gravies
More easy sauces to accompany your meat.

White wine gravy

Melt 1 tablespoon of **butter** in a pan over low heat, remove from the heat, and stir in 1 tablespoon of **flour**. Mix to a roux, then return to the heat and slowly pour in a little **hot chicken stock**, taken from 1 cup hot stock, then add ¾ cup of **dry white wine** and simmer for a few minutes. Add the rest of the stock and 2 tablespoons of **heavy cream** and cook for a few more minutes. Season with **salt** and **pepper** and add a squeeze of **lemon juice** or chopped **fresh tarragon**. Serve with chicken.

Red wine gravy

After cooking roast beef, remove the meat then skim away most of the fat, leaving a small amount for flavor. Place pan over medium heat. Add 1 tablespoon of **flour** and stir, then add ¾ cup of **red wine** and throw in a sprig of **fresh rosemary**. Keep stirring, scraping up the bits from the bottom of the pan, then add a little **hot vegetable** or **chicken stock** and continue stirring and adding, until it thickens, allowing it to boil a little to reduce. Season well and serve as it is, or strain first.

Beef gravy

Melt 1 tablespoon of **butter** in a pan, then add a few pieces of **bacon** and cook until golden brown. Stir in a teaspoon of **tomato purée**, then remove from the heat and add 1 tablespoon of **flour**. Add a little **hot beef stock**, taken from 2 cups, then put back over the heat and continue stirring and adding until it reaches the required consistency. Cook for a few minutes to thicken and add a little **port** at the end of cooking, if you wish. Season, strain, and serve with beef.

Chicken gravy

After cooking roast chicken, remove the meat from the pan, then skim away most of the fat, leaving a small amount for flavor. Place the pan over medium heat, then add 2 cups of **hot chicken stock**, stirring to loosen bits from the bottom of the pan. Add a few **fresh thyme** sprigs and season. Allow it to cook for a few minutes, then strain and serve with chicken.

Lamb cutlets with butternut squash, beans, and mint

PREP 15 MINS
COOK 30 MINS

SERVES 4

2 tbsp olive oil
pinch of Asian five-spice powder
pinch of cayenne pepper
salt and freshly ground black pepper
8 lamb cutlets (from the sirloin),
   trimmed of excess fat
1 butternut squash, peeled, halved,
   seeded, and coarsely chopped
10 cherry tomatoes
4½oz (125g) green beans, trimmed
handful of fresh mint leaves,
   coarsely chopped

1 Preheat the oven to 400°F (200°C). In a bowl, combine 1 tablespoon of the oil with the five-spice powder and cayenne, then season with salt and pepper. Brush half of the oil mixture over the lamb cutlets and place in a roasting pan. Add the squash, drizzle with the remaining oil mixture, and toss to coat. Place in the oven to roast for 20–30 minutes or until the lamb is cooked to your liking and the squash is tender and golden. (If needed, remove the lamb and keep warm while the squash continues to cook.)

2 Meanwhile, put the tomatoes and green beans in a bowl and toss with the remaining 1 tablespoon olive oil. Add to the roasting pan for the last 10 minutes of cooking. They should char just slightly. Sprinkle with the chopped mint leaves and serve.

VARIATION

If you're on a budget, use lamb chops instead. Trim away any fat before cooking.

Duck with apple and rosemary potatoes

SERVES 4

4 large duck legs
sea salt and freshly ground
    black pepper
1¼lb (550g) baby new potatoes,
    halved if large
3 red-skinned apples, halved, cored,
    and coarsely chopped
few sprigs of fresh rosemary
drizzle of olive oil
1 Savoy cabbage, halved, cored, and
    leaves coarsely chopped
pinch of crushed red pepper flakes
    (optional)

1 Prick the skin on the duck several times with a fork but do not puncture the meat. Rub the duck generously with salt and pepper. Set aside for 30 minutes, if you have the time, to help crisp the skin. Preheat the oven to 400°F (200°C).

2 Heat a large frying pan, add the duck, and cook for 8–10 minutes or until it has rendered some of its fat and is golden all over. With a spoon, transfer the duck to a roasting pan. Add the potatoes and apples, sprinkle in the rosemary, drizzle with the oil, season with salt and pepper, and toss well. Cook, stirring once or twice, until the duck is crispy and the potatoes are golden, about 40 minutes–1 hour.

3 Put the cabbage in a pan of boiling salted water and cook for 4–5 minutes until tender. Drain and keep warm. Add to the roasting pan during the last 10 minutes of cooking and sprinkle with the pepper flakes. Transfer to a serving dish and pass red currant jelly at the table.

Use some chunky par-boiled leeks if you're not a fan of cabbage.

COOK'S NOTES

Duck legs respond well to slow cooking, but if you prefer to use duck breasts (they are sometimes more readily available, and are leaner), score the skin before cooking so it becomes crispy and reduce the roasting time by half.

Chicken with lemon and olives

Marinating • 30 minutes

SERVES 4

4 large chicken thighs with skin on
sea salt and freshly ground black
    pepper
juice of 1 lemon
drizzle of olive oil
leaves from a few sprigs fresh thyme
1 large fennel bulb, coarsely chopped
handful of green olives, pitted
¾ cup dry white wine

1 Season the chicken thighs generously with salt and pepper. Drizzle with the lemon juice and olive oil, then pat on the thyme leaves. Transfer to a large bowl or heavy-duty zipper-seal plastic bag and leave to marinate for 30 minutes. Preheat the oven to 400°F (200°C).

2 Using a slotted spoon, transfer the chicken to a small roasting pan and add the fennel—everything should fit snugly. Season well, then put in the oven for 20 minutes.

3 Add the olives and wine, being careful that it doesn't spatter. Return the pan to the oven and cook for another 20 minutes, then reduce the oven temperature to 350°F (180°C), cover the pan with foil, and cook for another 20 minutes so the alcohol cooks away but the chicken remains moist. Check doneness by piercing one of the plumpest thighs with the tip of a sharp knife—if the juices run clear, it's cooked. Serve with creamy mashed potatoes, if desired.

Cheat...
Smear the chicken with 3–4 tsp store-bought tapenade before roasting and omit the olives.

FOOD FOR FRIENDS

Rosemary and pepper sausages with new potatoes

PREP 15 MINS **COOK 40 MINS**

SERVES 4

8-12 good-quality pork sausages, each pricked once or twice with a fork

2 red onions, peeled and cut into eighths

pinch of crushed red pepper flakes

leaves from a handful of rosemary sprigs

2½lb (1.1kg) new potatoes, large ones halved

sea salt and freshly ground black pepper

1 tbsp olive oil

1 Preheat the oven to 400°F (200°C). Put the sausages in a roasting pan along with the onion, sprinkle with the pepper flakes and rosemary, then add the new potatoes. Season well with salt and pepper, then drizzle with the oil and toss well to coat.

2 Cook in the oven for 30-40 minutes, turning once or twice, until the sausages are golden all over and cooked through.

VARIATION
Add 1 tbsp coarse-grain mustard before cooking.

COOK'S NOTES

Use good-quality sausages that have a high percentage of meat and a low percentage of fat.

Pork chops with apple and baby onions

PREP 15 MINS **COOK 35 MINS**

Special equipment • food processor

SERVES 4

2 slices firm white bread, torn into pieces

handful of sage leaves

1 small onion, coarsely chopped

sea salt and freshly ground black pepper

4 pork loin chops, ¾in (2cm) thick and 4½oz (125g) in weight

12 baby onions or shallots, peeled, large ones halved

3 cooking apples, such as Granny Smith, peeled, cored, and coarsely chopped

2 tbsp demerara (raw) sugar, or granulated sugar

drizzle of olive oil

handful of rosemary sprigs

1 Preheat the oven to 400°F (200°C). Combine the bread, sage, and onion in a food processor and pulse on and off, until coarse crumbs form. Spread on a baking sheet and bake for 5 minutes or until golden. Return to the food processor and pulse again until finely chopped. Season well with salt and pepper.

2 Place the chops in a roasting pan and add the onions. Add the apples, sprinkle with sugar, then drizzle with olive oil. Add the rosemary, then season with a pinch of salt, pepper, and the golden bread crumb mixture.

3 Roast for 30-35 minutes, turning once, until the meat is cooked through. Serve with new potatoes or mashed potatoes.

VARIATION
Add some new potatoes to the pan with the apple and onions. Just make sure the pan is large enough so it roasts rather than steams.

COOK'S NOTES

If the pork is ready before everything else, take it out and keep warm—you don't want it to overcook or it will become dry.

Poussins glazed with honey and wrapped in bacon

PREP 20 MINS · **COOK 1 HR**

SERVES 4

4 poussins or small Cornish
   Game hens
2 onions, peeled and
   coarsely chopped
2 tbsp honey
12 slices bacon or pancetta
6 leeks, trimmed, rinsed, and
   chopped into 2in (5cm) chunks
1 tbsp olive oil
sea salt and freshly ground
   black pepper

1 Preheat the oven to 400°F (200°C). Wipe the poussins thoroughly with paper towels, then stuff with the onions. Brush with the honey, then cover the breast of each poussin with 3 slices of bacon. Place breast-side up in a large flameproof roasting pan.

2 Toss the leeks with the oil, then add to the pan, tucking them in around the birds. Season with salt and pepper, then put in the oven to roast for 45 minutes–1 hour or until the poussins are cooked. To test, pierce them with the tip of a sharp knife—if the juices run clear, they're ready. If the bacon begins to darken too much, loosely cover the poussins with foil.

3 Remove the birds from the pan and keep warm. Using a slotted spoon, transfer the leeks to a serving dish and keep warm. On a work surface, tilt the roasting pan to one side and skim away any fat. Place the roasting pan over 1 or 2 burners on the cooktop, add a little hot water to the pan, and turn on the heat to high. Bring to a boil, scraping up any crispy bits from the bottom of the pan, then simmer for a few minutes to thicken slightly. Pour into a gravy boat and serve with the poussins, leeks, and some creamy mashed potatoes, if desired.

FOOD FOR FRIENDS

Peppered beef with roasted beets and balsamic vinegar

PREP 15 MINS   COOK 55 MINS

SERVES 4

2½lb (1.1kg) beef tenderloin

1–2 tbsp freshly cracked
    black pepper

2–3 tbsp olive oil

1lb 2oz (500g) cooked whole beets,
    halved if large

1 tbsp good-quality balsamic vinegar

6 small sweet potatoes, peeled
    and quartered

pinch of sea salt

handful of fresh thyme sprigs

1 Preheat the oven to 375°F (190°C). Roll the beef in the pepper, gently pressing it onto the surface to cover well. Put 1 tablespoon of the oil in a roasting pan set over high heat. When very hot, add the beef and cook for 5–6 minutes, turning, until it is lightly browned on all sides.

2 Toss the beets with the balsamic vinegar and add to the pan. Toss the sweet potatoes with the remaining oil and add to the pan. Season with a pinch of salt, sprinkle with the thyme, and put in the oven to cook for about

20 minutes if you like your beef rare, 40 minutes for medium, and 50 minutes for well-done.

3 Remove the beef and keep warm while it rests. If the potatoes aren't ready, continue cooking until they are golden and beginning to char at the edges. Slice the beef and serve with the beets, sweet potatoes, and a little cream-style horseradish on the side.

VARIATION Use dried green peppercorns, if you can find them. They taste just as spicy but with a subtly different flavor.

COOK'S NOTES

To freshly crack peppercorns, crush them with a mortar and pestle, or use a rolling pin.

Roast lamb with cherry tomatoes and thyme

PREP 15 MINS **COOK 1¼ HRS**

SERVES 4

1 tbsp olive oil
2lb (900g) boneless leg of lamb, trimmed of excess fat and butterflied
2½lb (1.1kg) baby new potatoes
sea salt and freshly ground black pepper
handful of fresh thyme sprigs
12–16 cherry tomatoes on the vine
1–2 tsp red currant jelly, plus extra for serving, if desired

1 Preheat the oven to 375°F (190°C). Pour half the oil into a large flameproof roasting pan and set it over high heat. When very hot, add the lamb and cook for 8–12 minutes, turning once, until browned all over.

2 Toss the new potatoes with the remaining oil and add to the pan. Season with salt and pepper, add the thyme, and cook in the oven for 45 minutes if you like your lamb rare, 1 hour for medium, and 1 hour 15 minutes for well-done. Add the tomatoes for the last 15 minutes of cooking. Remove the lamb and keep warm while it rests.

3 Place the potatoes and tomatoes aside and keep warm. Move the pan to a work surface. Skim away any fat, add the jelly, and set over high heat. Stir well, adding boiling water until the gravy reaches the desired consistency. Allow to bubble, then reduce to a simmer and cook for a few minutes. Slice the lamb and serve with potatoes, tomatoes, gravy, and mint sauce or red currant jelly on the side.

VARIATION

Add some green beans to the pan along with the tomatoes. Blanch them beforehand in boiling water for 3 minutes.

Roast pork with bacon and endive

PREP 10 MINS **COOK 2 HRS**

SERVES 4

4lb (1.8kg) loin of pork or boneless rolled shoulder
½ tbsp olive oil
1 tbsp sea salt
1lb (450g) shallots, peeled and halved, if large
4 heads curly endive (chicory), trimmed
⅔ cup hard cider, apple cider, or unsweetened apple juice
12 slices bacon

1 Preheat the oven to 475°F (240°C). Rub the pork with the oil, then pat on the salt. Cook in the oven for 15–20 minutes or until crispy at the edges. Remove from the oven and reduce the temperature to 350°F (180°C).

2 Lift up the pork in the roasting pan, place the shallots underneath, then lower the pork on top. Drizzle with the cider and return to the oven to cook for 1 hour 40 minutes (see Cook's Notes). Meanwhile, wrap the bacon evenly around each head of endive (chicory) and add to the pan for the last 40 minutes of cooking.

3 Remove the pork and keep warm while it rests for at least 20 minutes. Carve the roast and serve with the endive (chicory), potatoes of your choice, and applesauce on the side.

COOK'S NOTES

To calculate the exact cooking time for the pork, allow 25 minutes per pound (450g), plus an extra 20 minutes. That's 2 hours in all for a 4lb (1.8kg) roast.

Fish with zucchini, eggplant, and tomatoes

PREP 15 MINS | COOK 35 MINS

SERVES 4

1½lb (675g) boneless white fish, skinned and cut into chunks
2 tbsp olive oil
1 tsp fennel seeds, crushed
finely grated zest of 1 lemon
sea salt and freshly ground black pepper
4 small to medium zucchini, cut into thick slices or chunks
2 small eggplants, cut into bite-sized chunks
12 cherry tomatoes
handful of fresh dill, finely chopped
lemon wedges, for serving

1 Preheat the oven to 400°F (200°C). Toss the fish with half the oil, half the fennel seeds, and half the lemon zest. Season well with salt and pepper, then cover and set aside.

2 Meanwhile, put the zucchini and eggplants in a roasting pan with the remaining oil, fennel seeds, and lemon zest and toss together well. Season with salt and pepper, then put in the oven to roast for 20 minutes, until the vegetables are beginning to soften.

3 Add the fish and the tomatoes and cook for 15 minutes or until the fish is cooked through. Sprinkle with the dill and serve with the lemon wedges and some crusty bread, if desired.

Roast monkfish with peppers

PREP 15 MINS | COOK 30 MINS

SERVES 4

1½lb (675g) monkfish (one or two pieces), membrane removed
4 red bell peppers, halved, seeded, and sliced into strips
1 tbsp olive oil
½ tsp mild paprika
12 slices bacon or pancetta

1 Preheat the oven to 400°F (200°C). Toss the monkfish and peppers with the olive oil, then sprinkle in the paprika. Wrap with the bacon or pancetta, covering entirely, then place in a roasting pan with the peppers.

2 Cook for 20–30 minutes or until the bacon is crispy and the fish is cooked through. Remove from the oven and keep warm while the fish rests for 10 minutes. Slice the fish and serve with the peppers and an arugula salad.

VARIATION

Add a handful of cherry tomatoes to the roasting pan along with the peppers.

Cheat...
Use 3–4 roasted red bell peppers from a jar. Simply slice and serve with the cooked fish and salad.

Marmalade-glazed ham with potatoes and endive

PREP 15 MINS COOK 1¾ HRS

SERVES 6-8

4lb (1.8kg) boneless leg of pork (unsmoked ham)

1¼ cups hard cider, apple cider, or unsweetened apple juice

2 bay leaves

3 tbsp orange marmalade

1 tbsp light or dark brown sugar

2½lb (1.1kg) new potatoes, halved if large

1 tbsp olive oil

finely grated zest of 1 orange

sea salt and freshly ground black pepper

4 heads curly endive (chicory), trimmed and quartered lengthwise

1 Place the pork in a large pot, add the cider and bay leaves, then pour in enough hot water to cover the pork. Cover, bring to a boil, then reduce to a simmer and cook for 40 minutes. Preheat the oven to 350°F (180°C).

2 Remove the pork from the pot and peel away the outer skin, leaving a layer of fat. Put the marmalade in a saucepan and heat gently over low heat until liquid. Brush the pork liberally with the marmalade, then sprinkle with the sugar.

3 Place the pork in a roasting pan. Toss the potatoes with the oil and orange zest, season well with salt and pepper, then add to the pan. Roast in the oven for 50 minutes–1 hour (see Cook's Notes). Add the endive (chicory) for the last 20 minutes of cooking, tossing it in some of the cooking juices to coat.

4 Remove the pork from the pan and keep warm while it rests for at least 15 minutes. Slice and serve with the potatoes and endive (chicory).

VARIATION

Use maple syrup instead of marmalade.

COOK'S NOTES

To calculate the cooking time for the ham, allow 20 minutes per 1lb (450g), plus 20 minutes. That's 1 hour 40 minutes in all for a 4lb (1.8kg) roast. To double check, pierce it with a knife a few minutes before the end of cooking—if it goes in easily, the ham is done.

Mackerel roasted with harissa and lime

SERVES 4

4 mackerel (or 8, if small), cleaned
3-4 tsp harissa paste (Middle
  Eastern chile sauce)
1½ tbsp olive oil
2 limes, quartered
2½lb (1.1kg) baby new potatoes,
  halved if large
handful of fresh cilantro,
  finely chopped

1 Preheat the oven to 400°F (200°C). Lay the mackerel in a roasting pan, then mix the harissa and half the oil together and drizzle over the fish, inside and out. Add the limes to the pan, then toss the potatoes with the remaining oil and add to the pan also.

2 Roast for 20-30 minutes or until the potatoes are cooked through—the fish will be cooked by then as well. Scatter with the cilantro and serve with a crisp green salad.

FOOD FOR FRIENDS

Salmon with mushrooms and bok choy

SERVES 4

1 tbsp olive oil

1 tbsp dark soy sauce

½ tbsp mirin

2in (5cm) piece of fresh ginger, peeled and finely chopped

2 garlic cloves, finely chopped

sea salt and freshly ground black pepper

4 salmon fillets, each about 5½oz (150g)

2 bok choy, quartered lengthwise

7oz (200g) mushrooms, halved if large

1 Preheat the oven to 400°F (200°C). Combine the olive oil, soy sauce, mirin, ginger, and garlic in a small bowl and mix together well. Season with salt and pepper.

2 Put the salmon, bok choy, and mushrooms in a roasting pan, then drizzle with the oil mixture and coat well. Put into the oven to roast for 20–25 minutes or until the salmon is cooked through. Serve with rice.

COOK'S NOTES

If you can't find any mirin (Japanese rice wine), use dry sherry or omit altogether.

Jamaican-style fish with sweet potatoes

SERVES 4

1 tsp ground allspice

1 tsp paprika

2in (5cm) piece of fresh ginger, peeled and thinly sliced

2 red hot chile peppers, seeded and finely chopped

1 tbsp olive oil

sea salt and freshly ground black pepper

4 white fish fillets, such as haddock or sustainable cod, each about 7oz (200g)

4 sweet potatoes, peeled and cut into bite-sized pieces

handful of fresh cilantro, finely chopped

1 Preheat the oven to 375°F (190°C). Mix the allspice, paprika, ginger, and chiles with the olive oil. Add a pinch of salt and lots of pepper. Coat the fish with most of the spice mixture. Toss the sweet potatoes with the remaining spice mixture and place in a roasting pan. Put in the oven to roast for 15 minutes.

2 Add the fish to the pan and roast for 15 minutes or until the potatoes are cooked—the fish will by cooked by then as well. Sprinkle with the cilantro and serve warm.

Lamb with roasted peppers

PREP 15 MINS **COOK 30 MINS**

SERVES 4

4 large lamb shoulder chops
   or 8 small ones
2 red bell peppers, seeded
   and coarsely chopped
2 green bell peppers, seeded
   and coarsely chopped
1 tbsp olive oil
sea salt and freshly ground
   black pepper
1 tbsp butter
1 onion, finely chopped
4½oz (125g) mushrooms,
   finely chopped
small handful of flat-leaf parsley,
   finely chopped

1 Preheat the oven to 400°F (200°C). Place the chops in a roasting pan and cut a pocket in each one. Toss the peppers with the oil, season well with salt and pepper, then add to the pan.

2 Melt the butter in a saucepan over low heat, add the onion, and cook for 5 minutes or until soft. Add the mushrooms and cook for 5 minutes or until soft. Stir in the parsley and season with salt and pepper. Remove from the heat and set aside to cool.

3 Spoon the mushroom mixture into the pocket of each lamb chop and place in the roasting pan. If there's any of the mixture left over, scatter it over the top of the chops.

4 Put in the oven to cook for 20–30 minutes, or longer if you like your meat well-done. Toss with the peppers and serve with small cubed roasted potatoes and a spoonful of hot pepper jelly or mint jelly.

Pork tenderloin roasted with cider and lentils

PREP 15 MINS **COOK 2 HRS**

SERVES 4

4 onions, peeled and cut into eighths
4 garlic cloves, finely chopped
1 cup lentils de Puy or other dried
   lentils, well-rinsed
2 cups hard cider, apple cider, or
   unsweetened apple juice
handful of flat-leaf parsley,
   finely chopped
sea salt and freshly ground
   black pepper
1lb (450g) pork tenderloin
drizzle of hot chili oil (optional)

1 Preheat the oven to 350°F (180°C). Combine the onions and garlic in a roasting pan and stir in the lentils, half of the cider, and the parsley and season with salt and pepper.

2 With the tip of a sharp knife, make 4 shallow diagonal slash marks over the top of the tenderloin. Season with salt and pepper, then place on top of the lentils. Drizzle with the chili oil (if using) and bake for 1 hour, then add the remaining cider and bake for 45 minutes more. If the meat is browning too much, cover with foil. If the lentils look dry, add a little hot water.

3 Remove the meat from the pan and keep warm. Return the pan to the oven and cook for 15 more minutes, Slice the pork and serve.

COOK'S NOTES

If you want to speed up the cooking, use a 14oz (400g) can of brown lentils instead of the dried lentils. Drain them well and use only half the quantity of cider. The time in the oven should be reduced to 45 minutes, or until the pork is cooked through.

Beef stuffed with prunes and cashews

PREP 20 MINS • **COOK 2 HRS**

Special equipment • food processor

SERVES 6

1 cup cashews

½ cup pitted prunes, coarsely chopped

handful of flat-leaf parsley

3 garlic cloves, coarsely chopped

sea salt and freshly ground black pepper

3lb (1.35kg) top round (silverside of beef)

hot chili oil or olive oil

12–14oz (400g) shallots, peeled

1 Preheat the oven to 425°F (220°C). Combine the cashews, prunes, parsley, and garlic in a food processor and pulse until well chopped. Do not over-process. Season with salt and pepper and pulse again.

2 Place the beef on a work surface and make a cut about ¾in (2cm) in from the right side. Slice downward, stopping about ¾in (2cm) from the bottom. Then slice into the beef horizontally, stopping just before you reach the end. Then slice upward, almost to the top, and finally across, almost to the opposite end. "Unfold" the meat so it resembles an open book. Spread the prune mixture over the cut surface. Now, carefully roll up the beef to enclose the filling, place it seam-side down on a work surface, and tie securely with string. Transfer to a roasting pan and season.

3 Drizzle with the oil and add the shallots to the pan. Put in the oven to roast for 15–20 minutes or until browned, then turn down the oven to 350°F (180°C) and roast for 1 hour if you prefer your beef rare, 1 hour 20 minutes for medium, or 1 hour 40 minutes for well-done. To test if the meat is cooked to your liking, pierce it with the tip of a sharp knife—if it's still bloody, it's rare. If the juices run clear, it's medium to well-done.

4 Remove from oven and keep warm while it rests for 15 minutes. Carve, then serve with vegetables.

COOK'S NOTES

If you prefer, ask your butcher to cut the beef for you. Also ask for some butchers' twine to tie up the roast; otherwise, just use ordinary white cotton string. There should be enough roast beef left over for sandwiches the next day.

Lamb with red onions

PREP 20 MINS

COOK 2 HRS

SERVES 4

8 red onions, peeled and quartered

3 tbsp olive oil

2lb (900g) potatoes, peeled and quartered

salt and freshly ground black pepper

2 tbsp mint sauce (see p423)

2lb (900g) lamb fillet

1 tbsp balsamic vinegar

1 Preheat the oven to 350°F (180°C). Put the onions in a large roasting pan and toss with 1 tablespoon of the oil. Add the potatoes, toss with the onions, then season well with salt and black pepper.

2 Mix the remaining oil with the mint sauce and use to coat the lamb. Add the fillet to the roasting pan, drizzle with the balsamic vinegar, and put in the oven to roast for 1½–2 hours.

3 Remove the lamb and keep warm while it rests for 15 minutes. Slice and serve with the red onion and potato mixture.

VARIATION

Look out for flavored balsamic vinegars. An apple balsamic vinegar would go well with the lamb, but always use a good-quality thick one.

Chicken with garlic and spiced celery root

PREP 25 MINS

COOK 45 MINS

SERVES 4

8 chicken thighs on the bone, skin on

sea salt and freshly ground black pepper

2 tbsp olive oil

4 whole heads of garlic, skin on, top ⅓ of each sliced off

4 large all-purpose waxy potatoes, peeled and cut into bite-sized chunks

1 large celery root (celeriac) or 2 small ones, peeled and cut into bite-sized chunks

1–2 tsp mild curry powder

1 Preheat the oven to 400°F (200°C). Season the chicken well with salt and pepper. Pour 1 tablespoon of the oil in a flameproof roasting pan and place over high heat. When very hot, add the chicken pieces skin-side down and cook, turning occasionally, for 5–8 minutes or until browned all over.

2 Remove the pan from the heat and add the garlic heads, turning to coat with the fat. In a large bowl, toss the remaining 1 tablespoon of oil, the potatoes, celery root, and the curry powder, to taste. Season with salt and pepper and add to the pan.

3 Roast in the oven for about 45 minutes, stirring the vegetables once or twice, until the chicken is white throughout and the potatoes are golden, but still tender. If the exposed garlic tops get too dark during cooking, slice them off before serving. Serve with wilted spinach.

COOK'S NOTES

Stir the potatoes and celery root halfway through the cooking time, then continue checking occasionally so they don't burn.

Pork with potatoes and mushrooms in wine

PREP 20 MINS COOK 1¾ HRS

SERVES 6

3lb (1.35kg) boneless pork shoulder
   roast, skin scored with the
   tip of a sharp knife
sea salt
2¼lb all-purpose waxy potatoes,
   peeled and halved or
   quartered, if large
1 tbsp olive oil
a few sprigs of fresh rosemary
1½ cups dry white wine
9oz (250g) mushrooms, trimmed
   and halved if large
1¼ cups hot vegetable stock

1 Preheat the oven to 425°F (220°C). Place the pork in a large roasting pan and rub thoroughly with the salt, getting it into all the score marks. Toss the potatoes with the oil, season with salt, then add to the pan along with the rosemary sprigs. Roast in the oven for 20 minutes, until the skin is browned and crispy.

2 Meanwhile, heat the wine in a saucepan over low heat until warm, then spoon it over the meat. Add the mushrooms, pour in the stock, then reduce the oven temperature to 350°F (180°C) and cook for 1 hour.

3 Reduce the oven temperature once again, this time to 300°F (150°C), and cook for another 30 minutes, until the potatoes are meltingly tender and the stock has almost disappeared. Remove from the oven and keep warm while the pork rests for 15 minutes. Slice the pork and serve with the potatoes, mushrooms, and some crusty bread.

COOK'S NOTES

It's easiest to ask the butcher to score the pork for you. However, if you decide to do it yourself, use a sharp knife to make cuts about ¼in (5mm) apart. Make sure your cuts go with the grain so the pork will be easier to slice.

FOOD FOR FRIENDS

Rack of lamb with flageolet beans and herbs

  PREP 15 MINS COOK 40 MINS

SERVES 4

8-bone rack of lamb, trimmed

½ tbsp olive oil

a few rosemary sprigs, leaves finely chopped

sea salt and freshly ground black pepper

⅔ cup hot vegetable stock

1 tsp red currant jelly

1 x 14oz (400g) can flageolet beans, drained and rinsed

handful of fresh mint leaves, finely chopped

1 Preheat the oven to 400°F (200°C). Rub the rack of lamb all over with the oil, sprinkle with the rosemary, and season well with salt and pepper. Place the rack in a roasting pan and roast for 30–40 minutes, or until it reaches the desired doneness.

2 Remove the lamb and keep warm while you prepare the beans. Place the roasting pan over medium to high heat, add the stock, and bring to a boil. Reduce to a simmer, stir in the jelly until dissolved, then add the beans and simmer gently, stirring, for 5 minutes. Remove from the heat and stir in the mint leaves.

3 Slice the rack into 8 rib chops and serve with the beans and some sliced crusty bread.

 **VARIATION**
Use cannellini beans or fava beans instead of the flageolet, if you like.

Glazed fillet of beef roasted with potatoes and olives

PREP 15 MINS   COOK 1½ HRS

SERVES 6

8 large all-purpose waxy potatoes, peeled and cut into bite-sized cubes
2 tbsp olive oil
sea salt and freshly ground black pepper
2 tbsp red currant jelly
4lb (1.8kg) fillet of beef
handful of black olives, pitted

1 Preheat the oven to 400°F (200°C). Put the potatoes in a large roasting pan with 1 tablespoon of the oil, toss to coat, then season well with salt and pepper. Place in the oven while you prepare the beef.

2 Put the red currant jelly in a saucepan over low heat for 5 minutes, until liquified, then brush all over the beef and season well with salt and pepper. Heat a large frying pan over high heat, add the remaining oil, and sear the beef, turning, until browned all over.

3 Turn the oven down to 350°F (180°C). Add the meat to the roasting pan and cook for 50 minutes to 1 hour for rare, 1¼ to 1½ hours for medium, or longer for well-done. Add the olives to the pan for the last 10 minutes of cooking, stirring them into the potatoes.

4 Remove the beef and keep warm while it rests for at least 15 minutes. Leave the potatoes in a little longer if they are not yet browned and tender inside. Slice the beef and serve with the potatoes and some fresh watercress.

Perfect creamy mash

PREP 15 MINS · COOK 25 MINS

SERVES 4

2lb (900g) floury potatoes, such as russet or Maris Piper, peeled and halved or, if large, quartered
sea salt and freshly ground black pepper
2–3 tbsp warm whole milk (more if needed)
2 tbsp butter

1 Put the potatoes in a large pot of salted water, bring to a boil, and cook uncovered over medium heat until tender when pierced with the tip of a sharp knife, about 20 minutes. Drain well, then return to the pan and leave to stand in a warm place, covered, for 5 minutes to allow them to dry out a little.

2 Mash well until there are no lumps, then add the milk and mash again. If the potatoes are still a little dry, add some more milk and mash once more.

3 Beat in the butter with a wooden spoon and season well with salt and pepper. Do not overbeat the potatoes, or they will become gluey. You want them fluffy and lump-free.

 VARIATION

Jazz up your mashed potato with some finely chopped herbs such as parsley or thyme, a teaspoon of coarse-grain mustard, or a handful of grated Cheddar cheese.

Perfect Yorkshire puddings

PREP 20 MINS COOK 30 MINS

Resting • 30 minutes
Special equipment • deep six-hole bun pan

SERVES 6

1¼ cups all-purpose flour
 sea salt
2 large eggs
1¼ cups whole milk
1–2 tbsp sunflower oil or corn oil

1 Preheat the oven to 425°F (220°C). Sift the flour into a mixing bowl, add a pinch of salt, and combine. Make a well in the center, then place the eggs and a little of the milk inside. Using a wooden spoon, stir the egg mixture, incorporating the flour a little at a time, gradually adding about half of the milk. When all the flour has been mixed in, add the remaining milk and mix with a balloon whisk to ensure there are no lumps. Transfer to a large liquid measuring cup, pitcher, or bowl and refrigerate to rest for 30 minutes.

2 Five minutes before the batter is ready to use, add a little of the oil to each cup in the 6-hole pan and put it in the oven for 5–8 minutes or until smoking hot. Remove the pan, give the batter a final stir, then divide the batter evenly among the 6 cups. Bake for 20–30 minutes or until puffed and golden.

COOK'S NOTES

Make sure the oil is really hot when you add the batter—this will ensure the puddings rise.

Crispy roast potatoes

PREP 25 MINS COOK 40 MINS

SERVES 4

2lb (900g) floury potatoes, such as Maris Piper, peeled and quartered
sea salt
1 tbsp all-purpose flour
4 tbsp olive oil

1 Preheat the oven to 425°F (220°C). Put the potatoes in a pot of salted water, bring to a boil, then cook uncovered over medium heat for 15 minutes or until the potatoes are just barely tender. Drain well, then return to the pan.

2 Cover the pot and place it in a warm spot for 5 minutes to allow the potatoes to dry out. Sprinkle in the flour, cover, and shake the pan up and down a few times to distribute the flour evenly.

3 Put the oil in a large roasting pan and place it in the oven until very hot. Remove the pan from the oven and carefully add the potatoes one by one, turning each potato in the hot oil to coat. Season with salt and return to the oven to roast for 30–40 minutes, turning once, until the potatoes are tender and golden and crispy on the outside.

 VARIATION

Use goose or duck fat instead of olive oil or, for a healthy option, canola oil.

Applesauce

SERVES 4

1lb (450g) cooking apples, such as Granny Smith, peeled, cored, and quartered

2–3 tbsp sugar (depending on the tartness of the apples)

1 Put the apples in a saucepan, sprinkle with 1 tablespoon water, then add the sugar. Cover and cook over low heat for 10 minutes, or until the apples have begun to lose their shape.

2 Uncover and continue cooking, stirring constantly with a wooden spoon, until the mixture reaches the desired consistency. Taste and add more sugar, if needed. Serve warm or cold with roast pork.

COOK'S NOTES

When cool, transfer to a plastic freezerproof container and freeze for up to 1 month. Defrost thoroughly before use.

Cranberry sauce

SERVES 6

12oz (350g) fresh cranberries or frozen cranberries, thawed

6 tbsp port or red wine

⅔ cup sugar

1 Put the cranberries in a heavy saucepan and add the port. Bring to a boil, cover, then simmer gently for 10–15 minutes, or until they start to soften and pop. Remove from the heat and mash with the back of a spoon to the desired consistency.

2 Stir in the sugar a little at a time, tasting as you go, until it has all dissolved and the sauce is sweet but still tart. Serve with roast turkey or chicken.

 VARIATION

Use water or fresh orange juice instead of the alcohol.

Mint sauce

SERVES 4

handful of fresh mint leaves, finely chopped

1–2 tsp granulated sugar

1 tbsp white wine vinegar

1 Put the mint in a serving bowl and add the sugar and vinegar. Set aside to infuse for 10 minutes.

2 Stir well to make sure the sugar has dissolved, then taste and adjust, adding more sugar or vinegar, if needed. Serve with lamb.

 VARIATION

Use raspberry vinegar instead of white wine vinegar.

FOOD FOR FRIENDS

423

Chunky potato wedges

  PREP 10 MINS · COOK 40 MINS

SERVES 4-6

2lb (900g) floury baking potatoes, such as russet or Maris Piper, skins on, well-scrubbed, quartered lengthwise and, if large, each quarter again sliced lengthwise
2 tbsp olive oil
sea salt

1 Preheat the oven to 400°F (200°C). Put the potatoes in a large shallow roasting pan, add the olive oil, and toss well with your hands to coat.

2 Sprinkle with plenty of salt, then roast in the oven for 40 minutes or until they are crispy and golden on the outside and tender inside.

VARIATION

Add a pinch of hot paprika to the potatoes when you toss them with the oil.

Dauphinois potatoes

  PREP 20 MINS · COOK 1¾ HRS

SERVES 4

2lb (900g) all-purpose waxy potatoes, peeled and cut into slices ⅛in (3mm) thick
1¼ cups heavy whipping cream
1¼ cups whole milk
sea salt and freshly ground black pepper
3 garlic cloves, finely chopped

1 Preheat the oven to 350°F (180°C). Combine the potatoes, cream, and milk in a large pot and season with salt and pepper. Bring to a boil, then cover and reduce the heat. Simmer for 10–15 minutes or until the potatoes are beginning to soften.

2 Transfer the potatoes to a shallow 2-quart (2.3-liter) baking dish. Sprinkle the garlic over the potatoes and season with salt and pepper. Strain the cream mixture through a fine sieve, then pour over the potatoes. Cover the dish with foil and bake for 1 hour. Remove the foil and bake 30 minutes more, or until the potatoes are hot and the top is golden.

COOK'S NOTES

Bake the casserole on a sheet pan, to catch any spills, or line the bottom of your oven with foil. This dish can easily spill when it starts boiling.

Potatoes boulangère

  PREP 25 MINS · COOK 50 MINS

SERVES 4-6

4 tbsp butter
6 onions, sliced
2lb (900g) floury baking potatoes, such as russet or Maris Piper, peeled and cut into slices ¼in (5mm) thick
3 garlic cloves, thinly sliced
3 cups vegetable or chicken stock
sea salt and freshly ground black pepper

1 Preheat the oven to 400°F (200°C). Melt the butter in a Dutch oven or large deep frying pan, add the onions, and cook, stirring often, for 10 minutes or until soft. Add the potatoes, garlic, and stock, season with salt and pepper, stir well, then cover and simmer for 5–6 minutes or until the potatoes are starting to soften but still firm to the bite.

2 Transfer the mixture to a shallow 2-quart (2.3-liter) baking dish and bake for 40–50 minutes or until the potatoes are tender and most of the chicken stock has been absorbed. Serve with roast beef.

Sweet and sour cabbage

PREP 15 MINS · COOK 1¼ HRS

SERVES 4

1 tbsp olive oil
1 large red cabbage, outer
   leaves removed, halved,
   and finely shredded
2 red-skinned eating apples,
   cut into bite-sized pieces
2in (5cm) piece of fresh ginger,
   peeled and finely sliced
⅔ cup balsamic vinegar
2 tbsp dark brown sugar
sea salt and freshly ground black pepper

1 Put the oil in a large heavy-bottomed saucepan, add the cabbage, apple, and ginger, and cook over low heat for 10 minutes or until they have begun to soften and reduce down.

2 Add the balsamic vinegar and sugar, bring to a boil, then cover and simmer for 40 minutes–1 hour or until the cabbage is soft. Stir occasionally so it doesn't stick. Season with salt and pepper and serve with roast pork or pork chops.

VARIATION

Add a handful of golden raisins to the cabbage along with the balsamic vinegar.

Quick and easy gravy

PREP 5 MINS · COOK 15 MINS

SERVES 4

2 cups chicken, beef, or vegetable stock
1 tbsp all-purpose flour
sea salt and freshly ground black pepper

1 Start with a flameproof roasting pan from which you've just removed the roasted meat. On a work surface, tilt the pan so the fat settles on top of the meat juices. Spoon out and discard almost all the fat, then add the stock and place the pan over high heat. Bring to a boil, using a wooden spoon to stir and scrape up the browned bits stuck to the bottom of the pan, then reduce the heat to a simmer.

2 Mix together the flour and a small amount of water to make a smooth paste, then stir it into the pan, using a whisk to prevent any lumps. Cook gently, stirring constantly, for 5 minutes, then taste and season with salt and pepper, if needed. Strain through a fine sieve and serve in a gravy boat.

Fruity sausage stuffing

PREP 20 MINS · COOK 40 MINS

SERVES 4

8 good-quality link sausages
2 tbsp butter
1 onion, finely chopped
sea salt and freshly ground black pepper
handful of flat-leaf parsley, finely chopped
4½oz (125g) pitted dried fruit, such as apricots,
   prunes, or cranberries, finely chopped (about 1 cup)
1 large egg, lightly beaten

1 Preheat the oven to 400°F (200°C). Use the tip of a sharp knife to make 2 shallow cuts down the length of each sausage. Pull off the skins with your fingers and discard. Put the sausage in a bowl and break it up with the back of a fork, then set aside.

2 Meanwhile, melt 1 tablespoon of the butter in a saucepan, add the onion, and cook over low heat for 5 minutes or until soft. Allow to cool for a few minutes, then add to the sausage and season well with salt and pepper. Stir in the parsley and dried fruit, then add the egg and mix well to blend.

3 Spoon into a roasting pan, dot with the remaining butter, and roast for 30–40 minutes or until the sausage mixture is lightly browned and no longer pink inside. If it is browning too quickly, cover with foil. Serve alongside your favorite meat.

Marrow squash and gratin

PREP 20 MINS **COOK 50 MINS**

SERVES 4

2 tbsp olive oil

1 onion, finely chopped

1 large marrow squash or zucchini,
about 2lb (900g), peeled, seeded, and
cut into cubes

1lb (450g) ripe tomatoes, finely chopped

3 garlic cloves, finely chopped

handful of flat-leaf parsley, finely chopped

sea salt and freshly ground black pepper

3 tbsp fresh bread crumbs (from 1–2 slices
firm-textured white bread)

½ cup freshly grated Parmesan cheese

1 Preheat the oven to 400°F (200°C). Heat the oil
in a large saucepan, add the onion, and cook over
low heat for 5 minutes or until soft. Stir in the
squash and cook for another 5 minutes, then add
the tomatoes and garlic and cook over low heat
for 10 minutes or until the tomatoes start to lose
their shape. Stir in the parsley and season well
with salt and pepper.

2 Spoon the mixture into a large gratin dish or
four small ones. Sprinkle the bread crumbs and
Parmesan over the top and bake for 20–30 minutes
or until bubbly-hot and crisp and golden on top.
Serve with chicken.

Peas and pancetta

PREP 10 MINS **COOK 30 MINS**

SERVES 4

1 tbsp olive oil

1 onion, finely chopped

8oz (225g) pancetta, cut into small cubes

2 garlic cloves, finely chopped

few rosemary sprigs, leaves finely chopped

½ cup dry white wine

2 cups frozen peas

sea salt and freshly ground black pepper

1 Heat the oil in a large frying pan, add the onion,
and cook over low heat for 5 minutes or until soft.
Increase the heat, add the pancetta, and cook for
another 5–8 minutes or until the pancetta is lightly
browned. Turn down the heat, add the garlic and
rosemary, and stir for a few seconds.

2 Increase the heat again, add the wine, and
let bubble for 5 minutes. Stir in the peas and
simmer, stirring occasionally, for 5–10 minutes.
Taste and season well with salt and pepper.
Serve with lamb.

VARIATION

Stir in a handful of finely
chopped fresh mint leaves
just before serving.

Roasted squash with sage and onion

PREP 15 MINS **COOK 40 MINS**

SERVES 4

1 butternut squash, peeled, halved lengthwise,
seeds removed, and cut into wedges

2 red onions, peeled and cut into eighths

handful of fresh sage leaves, finely chopped

pinch of crushed red pepper flakes,
or to taste (optional)

sea salt and freshly ground black pepper

1–2 tbsp olive oil

1 Preheat the oven to 400°F (200°C). Combine
the squash, onions, sage, and pepper flakes in
a large roasting pan and season well with salt
and pepper. Add the oil and combine all the
ingredients well with your hands

2 Put in the oven to roast for 30–40 minutes
or until the squash is tender inside and golden
on the outside. Serve with roast chicken or pork
and a mixed green salad on the side.

COOK'S NOTES

*You can prepare the squash
a day ahead of time. Place it
in a sealed plastic bag in the
refrigerator until ready to roast.*

Caramelized carrots

  PREP 10 MINS | COOK 25 MINS

SERVES 4

2½lb (1.1kg) carrots, scrubbed or peeled, trimmed, and cut first lengthwise and then in half, to make chunky sticks
4 tbsp butter
sprinkling of demerara (raw) or brown sugar
handful of flat-leaf parsley, finely chopped
sea salt and freshly ground black pepper

1 Put the carrots in a pot of water and boil for 5–10 minutes or until barely tender, then drain well.

2 Return to the pan with the butter, sugar, and parsley and cook over medium heat, stirring occasionally, for 10 minutes or until the carrots start to brown at the edges. Season with salt and pepper, to taste. Serve warm.

Chestnuts with squash and cranberries

   PREP 15 MINS | COOK 35 MINS

SERVES 4

1–2 tbsp olive oil
1 tbsp butter
pinch of ground allspice
pinch of ground cinnamon
1 butternut squash, peeled, halved, seeded, and cut into bite-sized cubes
sea salt and freshly ground black pepper
7oz (200g) vacuum-sealed jar or package of ready-cooked unsweetened whole peeled chestnuts, halved if large
¼ cup fresh or thawed frozen cranberries
granulated sugar, if needed

1 Preheat the oven to 400°F (200°C). Heat the oil and butter in a large frying pan, add the allspice, cinnamon, and squash, season well with salt and pepper, and cook over medium-low heat, stirring occasionally, for 15 minutes or until the squash begins to soften. Add more oil, if needed.

2 Add the chestnuts and stir to coat. Cook over low heat for 5–10 minutes, then add the cranberries and cook for 5 minutes more.

3 Taste and season again, if needed, adding a little sugar if the cranberries are too tart (and then cook until the sugar is dissolved). Serve with roast chicken or turkey.

Green beans with toasted hazelnuts

   PREP 5 MINS | COOK 5 MINS

SERVES 4

9oz (250g) tender young green beans, trimmed
sea salt
2 tbsp butter, cut into pieces
½ cup coarsely chopped toasted hazelnuts

1 Put the beans in a pan of salted water and boil for 4–6 minutes, or until they are crisp-tender (cooked but still with a bit of bite to them). Drain, then refresh under cold water so they stop cooking and retain their color.

2 Transfer to a serving dish, top with the butter and toasted hazelnuts, and serve with roast chicken or lamb.

> **COOK'S NOTES**
>
> To toast the hazelnuts, place them in a frying pan (without any fat) and cook over medium heat for 5 minutes, stirring frequently, until evenly toasted. Alternatively, place on a baking sheet and roast for 8–10 minutes in an oven preheated to 350°F (180°C).

FOOD FOR FRIENDS

BARBECUE

Fuss-free sizzling food for outdoor eating.

BARBECUE

The smoky scent of barbecued food is a pleasure we all enjoy. All you need is good food, a fierce grill, and sunshine. Choose your barbecue to suit your needs; coals can take time to heat up, whereas gas barbecues can be used in an instant. Preparing ahead is essential, so you have time to be attentive at the grill and avoid food spoilage in the heat. Above all, it's about enjoying simply cooked food.

Best meat to barbecue
Crowd-pleasing meats that contain enough fat to withstand fierce heat.

MEAT		COOKING TIME
	**BEEF STEAKS** Choose tender portions, such as rib-eye or T-bone, which have a layer of fat and marbling for good flavor. The steaks should be even thickness, about 1in (2.5cm). Add a little marinade of oil and lemon juice for extra flavor, then season with sea salt and freshly ground black pepper just before you cook them.	Cook over high heat—about 8 minutes in total for rare, about 12 minutes for medium, and about 16 minutes for well done. Always rest the meat before serving.
	**LAMB CHOPS** They benefit from quick cooking and high heat. Lamb is a relatively fatty meat, so it's perfect for the barbecue. Trim away excess fat, as it may make the fire flame. Chops should be about 1in (2.5cm) thick. Marinate with olive oil, garlic, rosemary, sea salt, and freshly ground black pepper before cooking.	Cook over medium-high heat—about 5 minutes on each side for medium rare, or longer if your prefer (but don't overcook).
	**PORK CHOPS** Choose thick pork loin chops and marinate in a flavored oil for at least 30 minutes before cooking. Sear the chops first for about one minute on each side. **Pork ribs** are also excellent for the barbecue, either cooked as a whole rack, or individually. Cook in the oven first for about 30 minutes, to be sure they're cooked through.	Cook over medium heat for 4–5 minutes on each side after searing. Cook ribs over high heat for about 15 minutes after cooking in the oven.
	**CHICKEN** Poultry requires a little patience on the barbecue and can be a tricky meat to get right. Never cook high and fast, as the skin will appear charred and cooked, but the inside won't be. Choice cuts are **wings**, **legs**, and **thighs** with bone in. Marinate in a flavored oil and roast in the oven first for 20 minutes, slash the flesh, then add to the barbecue.	Cook over medium heat for 5–10 minutes. Move to the edges of the grill to cook through over gentler heat for 15–20 minutes, turning frequently.
	**SAUSAGES** These were made for the barbecue and, when cooked correctly, can be succulent and juicy. The key is to cook low and slow; otherwise, as with chicken, the skin will burn and appear cooked, but the inside won't be. Choose sausages with high meat content and cook to a uniform color throughout.	Cook over low heat for 15–20 minutes in total, turning frequently.

Best fish and seafood to barbecue
These have meaty flesh and are ideal for grilling.

FISH AND SEAFOOD		COOKING TIME
	**SARDINES** This oily fish is perfect for the barbecue. Make sure it is very fresh (the smaller ones have more flavor). They can be gutted or left whole. Rub with oil and sprinkle with sea salt. You can also skewer sardines, from mouth to tail. Cook until the skin turns golden brown. Serve with a squeeze of lemon.	Cook over high heat for 2–3 minutes each side, depending on size.
	**MONKFISH** A superb meaty fish for the barbecue. Either cook the tail fillets whole, or cut into equal chunks and skewer. Marinate in olive oil, lemon, sea salt, and freshly ground black pepper.	Cook over medium-high heat for 8–10 minutes. Turn and baste frequently.
	**SHRIMP** Choose large uncooked shrimp with the shell on, otherwise they will turn rubbery. You can still marinate them, as some flavor will penetrate the shell. Try olive oil, lemon, chiles, sea salt, and freshly ground black pepper. Sit them on the barbecue, or skewer them for easy turning.	Cook over high heat for about 2 minutes on each side.
	**SQUID** Responds well to quick cooking and high heat. Baby squid is more tender than large squid: buy it prepared, flatten the body, score, and keep the tentacles whole. Mix with olive oil, lemon, sea salt, and freshly ground black pepper. Grill until it begins to curl up.	Cook over high heat for about 5 minutes total.
	**SALMON** If cooking fillets or steaks, make sure they are firm and chunky, so they hold together. Rub with olive oil, salt, and freshly ground black pepper and add straight to the barbecue, or cube and skewer for kebabs. If cooking whole, drizzle with oil, season, wrap in foil, and put on the barbecue.	Whole: Cook over high heat for 10–15 minutes total. Fillet and steak: Cook for about 3 minutes on each side.
	**TUNA** Use good-quality and very fresh tuna pieces about 1in (2.5cm) thick. Coat with a mixture of olive oil, sea salt, and freshly ground black pepper, then add to the barbecue. This lean fish dries out quickly if overcooked, becoming chewy and tasteless, so it's best served quite rare, or just seared.	Cook over high heat for 3–4 minutes each side. To sear, cook over a very high heat for 1–2 minutes each side.

Best vegetables to barbecue

A selection that needs minimum preparation.

VEGETABLE		COOKING TIME
 **BELL PEPPERS** Cook whole or cut into chunks: red, yellow, or orange are the sweetest, but green teams well with meats such as lamb. Rub in a little olive oil, sea salt, and freshly ground black pepper and cook until lightly charred. If cooking whole, remove, put in a plastic bag to loosen skin for removal, and seed. If cooking chunks, seed first.		Cook whole peppers over high heat for 10–15 minutes, turning every 5 minutes. Cook pieces alone, or skewered with other ingredients, for about 5 minutes, turning halfway.
CORN Barbecued whole corn, or corn on the cob, is deliciously sweet and succulent. For a nutty caramelized flavor, husk, coat in olive oil, season with sea salt and freshly ground black pepper, and grill whole or broken into chunks. Serve with butter. Or, cook whole in the husk: this will keep the kernals from charring and steam it.		Cook over high heat for about 20 minutes.
 **EGGPLANT** Slice lengthwise into slices about ½in (1cm) thick, or slice into 1in (2.5cm) rounds. Either way, coat liberally with olive oil, season well with sea salt and freshly ground black pepper, and grill until charred and crispy, with the flesh soft.		Cook egglant rounds over high heat for about 5 minutes on each side and slices about 5 minutes total.
 **ZUCCHINI** They become sweet and flavorsome on the barbecue. Slice lengthwise into slices about ¼in (5mm) thick, coat in olive oil, lemon, garlic, sea salt, and freshly ground black pepper. Add to the barbecue and cook until golden and tender. Alternatively, slice into chunks and thread onto skewers.		Cook over medium–high heat for about 5 minutes in total, turning once. They will release themselves from the barbecue rack when they're ready.
 **FENNEL** Once trimmed (keeping the fronds to cook with fish), quarter the fennel and remove the core. Coat in olive oil, lemon, sea salt and freshly ground black pepper and add to the barbecue. If you have time beforehand, soften the fennel by cooking it for 2 minutes in boiling salted water.		Cook over medium–high heat for about 10 minutes in total. Turn regularly.

3 quick marinades to add flavor and tenderize.

For meat: Szechuan pepper

This will give meat a deep spicy flavor. Mix together 2 tablespoons of **dark soy sauce**, 1 tablespoon of **Worcestershire sauce**, a splash of **mirin**, 1-2 teaspoons of **Szechuan peppercorns**, and a pinch each of grated **fresh ginger** and grated **garlic**. Loosen with some **olive oil**, then use to coat beef or chicken. Leave to marinate overnight, then add some **sea salt** and **freshly ground black pepper** before grilling.

For fish: Lime and cilantro

This fresh and zesty marinade is ideal for oily or non-oily fish. Mix together the juice of 2 **limes**, 3 tablespoons of **olive oil**, 2 chopped **limes**, and a bunch of fresh **cilantro**, finely chopped. Season well with **sea salt** and **freshly ground black pepper**. Coat the fish, then add to the barbecue. Don't marinate for too long, or the lime juice will start to cook the fish.

For vegetables: Chile baand lemon

This will give vegetables a hot and zingy flavor. Mix together 4 tablespoons of **olive oil**, the juice of 2-3 **lemons**, and add 2-3 sliced **fresh hot red chiles**, a pinch of **sugar**, and some **sea salt** and **freshly ground black pepper**. Coat the vegetables with the marinade before adding to the barbecue.

Barbecue preparation techniques
These two preparation methods, perfect for meat and fish, help flavors to penetrate, and speed up the cooking process.

Spatchcock
Flattening the bird ensures even cooking.

1 Lay a whole chicken, or other small poultry, on a large cutting board, breast-side down and legs away from you. Using a knife or poultry shears, cut down either side of the backbone from tail to head.

2 Turn the chicken over and press it firmly with the heel of your hand to crush the breastbone. Once flattened, use a sharp knife to cut slits into the legs and thighs to ensure even cooking.

Scoring
This helps the marinade and seasoning penetrate the meat.

1 Make shallow incisions in one direction across the meat, about ½in (1cm) apart, using a sharp knife.

2 Cut shallow incisions in the other direction to form a criss-cross pattern. This helps ensure even cooking. Rub in your chosen marinade or flavorings and leave to marinate for 1 hour, or overnight.

Skewer it
An ideal way to cook on the barbecue. Try vegetable skewers, too (see "The vegetarian barbecue" opposite). If using wooden skewers, always soak them in water for 30 minutes before cooking, or they will burn.

Meat kebab
This is a good way to make meat go a long way.

All meats can be threaded onto a skewer. Cut the meat into equal-sized pieces, so it cooks evenly, and thread tightly. Marinate meat before threading and skewer just the meat (such as lamb in a lemon and cumin marinade, beef in a wasabi marinade or chicken in a piri piri marinade), or mix meat with vegetables, making sure they are cut the same size as the meat. Good combinations: lamb and eggplant; pork and pineapple.

Fish kebab
Fish cooks through quickly on the grill, so these are super-speedy.

Choose firm, meaty fish, such as monkfish, as it will hold together better while it's cooking. Cut into equal-sized pieces and marinate before threading. Choose one fish and cook with a quick-cooking vegetable such as cherry tomatoes, red onion, or zucchini, or make a mixed fish kebab, choosing fish that will cook through at the same time, such as swordfish and tuna. Shrimp (with or without shell on) and scallops also skewer well.

Fruit kebab
A refreshing alternative to fruit salad. Try using lemongrass as skewers.

Choose firm, chunky fruit that will hold together. Fruits such as pineapple, apple, and banana work well, and can be brushed with a mix of fruit juice, rum, and brown sugar so they caramelize on the grill. They don't need much cooking and are best cooked on a clean barbecue, so they don't pick up meat or fish flavors or bits. They can always be cooked first and kept warm in the oven.

3 prepare-ahead salads

Barbecues always need salads to accompany the meat and fish and refresh the palate. These can be prepared ahead and left in the refrigerator for a couple of hours until ready to serve.

Tomato pasta salad
Simple, fresh, and super-quick if you have leftover pasta.

Cook 9oz (250g) **farfalle** in a pan of boiling salted water until *al dente*. Drain and return to the pan. Make a cross at the bottom of 5 **tomatoes**, sit them in a bowl of boiling water for 30 seconds, transfer to a bowl of cold water, and remove the skin. Coarsely chop and add to the pasta with a handful of **fresh flat-leaf parsley**, finely chopped, a handful of **fresh basil leaves**, and 2 grated **garlic cloves**. Season with **sea salt** and **freshly ground black pepper** and toss with some **extra virgin olive oil**.

Moroccan couscous salad
An ideal partner for kebabs, chicken, and lamb.

Put 9oz (250g) **couscous** in a large bowl with enough **hot vegetable stock** to just cover. Leave for 5 minutes, then fluff up with a fork. Cook 2 chopped **zucchini** in a little **olive oil** until golden, then add to the **couscous** with a good pinch of **paprika**, the juice of 2 **lemons**, a handful of **fresh flat-leaf parsley**, finely chopped, and a handful of chopped **olives**. Season well with **sea salt** and **freshly ground black pepper**, and stir to combine.

Curried rice salad
Perfect with barbecued lamb, and fish kebabs.

Put 6oz (175g) **cold cooked rice** in a large bowl with ½ a **red cabbage**, shredded, 1 teaspoon of **medium curry powder**, ½ teaspoon of **cayenne pepper**, 3 tablespoons of **mixed dried fruit**, a handful of **radishes**, chopped, the juice of ½ a **lemon**, 4 tablespoons of **extra virgin olive oil**, and a handful of **fresh flat-leaf parsley**, finely chopped. Season well with **sea salt** and **freshly ground black pepper** and combine.

The vegetarian barbecue
Delicious ideas for non-meat eaters.

Make vegetable skewers using a combination of vegetables (see p431 and the method opposite), adding a non-melting cheese such as **halloumi** or **paneer**. If you want to be more adventurous, coat them with yogurt and tikka paste and add some ripe figs.

Marinate vegetables with punchy flavors: mix with fresh herbs such as mint, dill, cilantro, basil, or thyme, with extra virgin olive oil, lemon juice and zest, lime, or orange. Experiment with flavors: try squash with lime and cinnamon, or zucchini with lemon and allspice.

Cook sweet potatoes in foil, then top with spicy tomato and avocado salsa and sour cream, or slice squash (skin on) into rounds and cook coated in a chili oil.

Large mushrooms are ideal for the barbecue. Remove the stem and coat with a spicy teriyaki marinade. Cook until golden, then serve sliced with hot grilled pita bread and a dollop of hummus.

Make spicy chile mushroom burgers, or cheesy vegetarian sausages and serve in rolls with homemade coleslaw.

Grill feta cheese parcels and cubes of squash and serve with balsamic grilled tomatoes and shallots.

A selection of vegetables on the grill: broccoli, eggplant, red bell peppers, and onions make a tasty accompaniment, dressed with oil and vinegar and seasoned.

Grilled swordfish with fennel, tomato, and herb salad

  PREP 20 MINS **COOK 6 MINS**

Marinating • 1 hour

SERVES 4

1 small fresh hot red chile, seeded and finely chopped
1 tbsp capers, rinsed, gently squeezed dry, and chopped
2 tbsp olive oil, plus extra for brushing the grill
juice of 1 lemon, plus extra lemon wedges, to serve
4 swordfish steaks, 9oz (250g) each
sea salt and freshly ground black pepper

For the fennel, tomato, and herb salad
1 fennel bulb, thinly sliced
9oz (250g) cherry tomatoes, halved
2 small fresh red chiles, seeded and thinly sliced lengthwise
½ bunch of fresh chives, cut into 1¼in (3cm) pieces
handful of fresh flat-leaf parsley leaves
4 sprigs of fresh dill, chopped
2 tbsp olive oil
juice of ½ lemon
1 garlic clove, crushed

1 Mix together the chile, capers, olive oil, and lemon juice in a wide shallow bowl. Add the swordfish steaks and season with salt and pepper. Rub the mixture over the steaks and allow to marinate in the refrigerator for about 1 hour.

2 Heat a barbecue or charcoal grill until hot and brush lightly with oil. Cook the fish for 2–3 minutes on each side, turning gently. Brush the cooked sides with the excess marinade. Remove from heat and divide among 4 warm serving plates.

3 Put the salad ingredients in a serving bowl, toss gently, and serve with the fish for people to help themselves. Serve with lemon wedges for squeezing over the top.

VARIATION
Omit the capers from the marinade and scatter some warmed black olives over the fish just before serving.

Grilled squid and arugula salad

   PREP 15 MINS **COOK 25 MINS**

SERVES 4

1lb 5oz (600g) whole squid (choose small young squid, rather than one large one)
4 tbsp olive oil
2 small fresh red chiles, finely chopped
1 garlic clove, crushed
grated zest and juice of 1 lemon, plus extra lemon wedges, to serve
sea salt and freshly ground black pepper

For the arugula salad
3½oz (100g) arugula
handful of fresh flat-leaf parsley leaves
2 tbsp olive oil
juice of ½ lemon

1 Clean the squid by grabbing the head and tentacles together in one hand and pulling them out of the body. Cut the head from the tentacles and discard, making sure that the tentacles remain attached as one. Cut or pull out the small beak from inside the tentacles. Pull out and discard the strip of transparent cartilage from inside the body and rinse the body (the thin outer skin should peel away) and tentacles thoroughly. Pat dry with paper towels.

2 Put the calamari tentacles and bodies (tubes and wings attached) in a bowl with the olive oil, chile, garlic, and lemon zest and juice. Season with salt and pepper.

3 Heat the grill of a barbecue or charcoal grill until hot. Grill the calamari bodies and tentacles over high heat for 1–2 minutes, turning halfway through cooking, until lightly charred on all sides. Transfer to a cutting board. Cut the tentacle clusters in half crosswise and put in a bowl. Slice the tubes into ⅛in (3mm) rings, cutting through the wings as you go, and place in the bowl with the tentacles.

4 Add the salad ingredients to the bowl and toss gently with the squid. Serve at once with lemon wedges.

VARIATION

This is also delicious with an Asian-style dressing and herbs. Add bean shoots and chopped fresh ginger, and a little more seeded and chopped fresh chile.

Stuffed sardines with crushed potatoes

PREP 15 MINS | COOK 25 MINS

SERVES 4
1lb 5oz (600g) new potatoes
4 tbsp extra virgin olive oil
sea salt and ground black pepper
2 tbsp finely chopped fresh
   flat-leaf parsley leaves
16 fresh sardine fillets

For the hazelnut stuffing
3 tbsp olive oil
1 garlic clove, crushed
1¾oz (50g) hazelnuts, finely chopped
1oz (30g) fresh white bread crumbs
2 tbsp finely chopped fresh
   flat-leaf parsley leaves

1 To make the crushed potatoes, put the potatoes in a large saucepan and cover with cold water. Bring to a boil and cook for 15–20 minutes until tender; drain. Arrange the potatoes on a flat tray and, with the flat side of a potato masher, crush slightly. Drizzle with the extra virgin olive oil and season with salt and pepper. Sprinkle with the parsley. Cover and set aside.

2 To prepare the stuffing, heat the oil in a pan over low heat. Add the garlic and cook for 30 seconds or until the garlic turns white. Add the hazelnuts, bread crumbs, and parsley and cook for 5 minutes until bread crumbs are golden brown. Season again to taste.

3 Heat the barbecue or charcoal grill until hot. Rinse the sardine fillets and pat dry with paper towels. Season with salt and pepper. Brush the grill with a little oil and arrange half of the fillets skin-side down on top. (It is best to cook the sardines in 2 batches because they cook very quickly.) Grill over high heat for about 1 minute on each side. By the time you have placed the last fillet on the grill, the first one should be ready to turn. Transfer to a plate and keep warm while you grill the remaining fillets.

4 To serve, divide half of the sardine fillets among 4 serving plates. Spoon a little of the hazelnut stuffing on top of each fillet and cover with the remaining fillets. Put the potatoes into a serving bowl for your guests to help themselves. Serve immediately with a crisp, fresh salad.

VARIATION
Use walnuts or pine nuts instead of hazelnuts.

Grilled chicken with tarragon mayonnaise

PREP 20 MINS

Marinating • 1 hour

SERVES 4
4 large chicken breasts, skin on
4 tbsp olive oil
grated zest and juice of 1 lemon
sea salt and ground black pepper

For the tarragon mayonnaise
large handful of fresh tarragon,
   leaves picked and chopped
1 garlic clove, sliced
1 egg yolk
¾ cup light olive oil
juice of ½ lemon

1 Put the chicken breasts, olive oil, and lemon zest and juice in a bowl. Season with salt and pepper and rub the marinade into the meat. Allow to marinate in the refrigerator for about 1 hour.

2 To make the mayonnaise, using a mortar and pestle, pound the tarragon, garlic, and a good pinch of sea salt into a paste. Transfer to a larger bowl, add the egg yolk, and stir thoroughly with a wooden spoon or wire whisk until smooth. Keep whisking and add the oil, a drop at a time, making sure that it is absorbed completely. Once the mixture starts to thicken, add the oil in a slow, thin drizzle. When a third of the oil has been used, start adding the lemon juice, a little at a time. Continue adding the remaining oil, whisking, until well incorporated. Season with black pepper and set aside.

3 Preheat the oven to 400°F (200°C). Heat the grill of a barbecue or charcoal grill until hot. Grill the chicken over medium heat for about 10 minutes, until charred on both sides. Transfer to a baking pan and roast in the oven for 15–20 minutes, or until cooked through. Set aside to cool.

4 Discard the skin from the cooled chicken and use your fingers to shred the meat lengthwise. Put in a bowl, add the tarragon mayonnaise, and mix well. Transfer to a serving dish and serve with torn romaine lettuce drizzled with a little lemon juice and extra virgin olive oil.

COOK'S NOTES

Any leftover chicken can be used in sandwiches with sliced avocado and mixed salad leaves.

FOOD FOR FRIENDS

Chicken and chile burgers

Chilling • 30 minutes

Special equipment • food processor

SERVES 4

1 onion, peeled and quartered
4 boneless skinless chicken breasts
2 garlic cloves, peeled and halved
2 fresh hot red chiles, seeded
handful of fresh cilantro, chopped
sea salt and freshly ground
    black pepper
1 tbsp all-purpose flour
1 egg

1 Put the onion, chicken, garlic, chiles, and cilantro in a food processor. Season with sea salt and pepper and pulse until combined—be careful not to turn it into a paste. Pour the mixture out into a bowl and mix in the flour and egg.

2 Using your hands, roll ¼ of the mixture into a ball, then flatten into a burger. Repeat until all the mixture has been used. Chill for 30 minutes, or until firm.

3 Heat the barbecue or charcoal grill until hot. Grill the burgers over medium heat for 8–10 minutes on each side, until golden and cooked through. Serve with lemon mayonnaise and fresh tomato slices.

COOK'S NOTES

To freeze, layer the burgers between sheets of parchment paper, wrap in a plastic freezer bag, and seal. Freeze for up to 3 months.

Mixed fish kebabs

Special equipment • wooden skewers

SERVES 4

5½oz (150g) monkfish fillets, cubed
5½oz (150g) salmon steaks or
    fillets, cubed
5½oz (150g) tuna steaks, cubed
grated zest and juice and 1 lime
2 garlic cloves, finely chopped
handful of fresh cilantro,
    finely chopped
2in (5cm) piece of fresh ginger,
    finely chopped
splash of olive oil
sea salt and freshly ground
    black pepper

1 If using wooden or bamboo skewers, soak in cold water for at least 30 minutes first. Put all the ingredients in a large bowl and season with salt and pepper. Using your hands, carefully combine everything until well mixed. Keep in the refrigerator until needed.

2 Heat the barbecue or charcoal grill until hot. Thread the fish cubes onto the skewers, alternating the 3 types of fish. Grill over high heat for about 3 minutes on each side, turning only once during cooking. Serve hot.

Grilled Sicilian sausages with lentil salad

 PREP 15 MINS **COOK 35 MINS**

Marinating • 1 hour
Special equipment • metal skewers

SERVES 8

16 Sicilian pork and fennel sausages
(left in one continuous length)
4 tbsp olive oil
large handful of fresh flat-leaf
parsley, finely chopped
large handful of fresh mint leaves,
finely sliced
6 fresh basil leaves, finely sliced
3 sprigs of fresh rosemary,
leaves picked

For the lentil salad
2 tbsp olive oil, plus 3 extra
for dressing
1 small onion, finely chopped
10oz (300g) brown lentils, picked
over, rinsed, and soaked in cold
water overnight

¾ cup chicken stock or water
1 carrot, finely diced
2 celery stalks, trimmed and
finely diced
1 scallion, finely
sliced diagonally
2 small fresh hot red chiles, seeded
and finely chopped
large handful of fresh flat-leaf
parsley, leaves picked
handful of fresh chervil leaves
juice of ½ lemon
sea salt and freshly ground
black pepper

1 Form the sausages into one continuous round. Pierce 2 metal skewers at right angles through the sausage coil to hold into place. Brush both sides with the oil, then place in a large shallow dish. Sprinkle with all the herbs, covering the sausage on both sides. Allow to marinate in the refrigerator for about 1 hour.

2 To prepare the lentil salad, heat the 2 tablespoons olive oil in a heavy saucepan over low heat. Add the onion and sauté gently for a few minutes, until soft. Drain and rinse the lentils and add back to the pan. Gently cook, stirring, for 2 minutes. Pour in the stock and bring to a boil. Reduce the heat slightly and gently simmer for about 35 minutes, until the liquid has been absorbed. Allow to cool.

3 Meanwhile, heat the barbecue or charcoal grill until hot. Grill the sausage coil over medium heat for 30–35 minutes, turning once during cooking and lightly brushing with the herb and oil marinade. Transfer to a plate and keep warm. Put the cooled lentils in a shallow serving dish and add the carrot, celery, scallion, chiles, parsley, and chervil. In a small bowl, whisk together the 3 tablespoons olive oil and the lemon juice to make

a dressing. Season with salt and pepper. Pour over the lentil salad and stir thoroughly.

4 To serve, put the sausage coil on a large round platter, remove the skewers, and separate the links with kitchen scissors or a sharp knife. Serve at the table with the lentil salad, so that everyone can help themselves.

COOK'S NOTES

You can find Sicilian-style pork and fennel sausages at any good Italian delicatessen.

Crispy duck char sui

PREP 15 MINS **COOK 45 MINS**

SERVES 4

4 duck thighs and legs,
   scored all over
3 garlic cloves, finely chopped
3 tbsp light soy sauce
3 tbsp rice wine
1 tbsp hoisin sauce
2 tbsp honey
2 tsp Asian five-spice powder
sea salt and freshly ground
   black pepper

1 Preheat the oven to 400°F (200°C). Place all the ingredients in a large bowl and season with salt and pepper. Mix together so that the duck is well coated. Wrap the coated duck pieces in foil and roast in the oven for 30 minutes.

2 Preheat the barbecue or charcoal grill until hot. Unwrap the duck and place it on the hot barbecue skin-side down. Grill over high heat, turning frequently, for 10–15 minutes, until golden and crisp. Transfer to a plate and leave to rest for 10 minutes.

3 Cut the duck into slices and serve with a crisp green salad.

Macadamia-stuffed chicken drumsticks

PREP 20 MINS **COOK 40 MINS**

Marinating • 1 hour

SERVES 4

For the stuffing
2 tbsp olive oil
1 small onion, finely chopped
1 garlic clove, crushed
1 tsp dukkah
6 dates, seeded and chopped
2 thick bacon strips, finely chopped
4½oz (125g) macadamia nuts,
   chopped
2 tbsp finely sliced fresh
   flat-leaf parsley

12 chicken drumsticks
4 tbsp olive oil
1 tsp dukkah (see p357), plus extra,
   to serve
3 sprigs of fresh rosemary, leaves
   picked, plus extra, to serve
sea salt and freshly ground
   black pepper
lemon wedges, to serve

1 To make the stuffing, heat the olive oil in a frying pan over low heat. Add the onion and gently sauté for a few minutes, until soft and translucent. Add the garlic, dukkah, dates, and bacon and cook for 2 minutes more. Add the chopped nuts and cook, stirring constantly, for an additional 2 minutes. Remove from the heat and stir in the parsley. Set aside to cool.

2 To stuff the chicken, rinse the drumsticks and pat dry with paper towels. Carefully loosen and pull back the skin from each drumstick. Make a cut lengthwise into the meaty part of each one and spoon a little of the stuffing into the pocket. Press the side of the pocket together and pull the skin back firmly over the cut. Place the drumsticks in a shallow dish.

3 Mix together the olive oil, 1 teaspoon dukkah, and the leaves of rosemary. Season with salt and pepper. Pour the mixture over the drumsticks, turning them to coat well. Allow to marinate in the refrigerator for 1 hour.

4 Heat the barbecue or charcoal grill until hot. Grill the drumsticks over medium heat, turning occasionally, for about 30 minutes, until cooked through. Baste with the marinade while cooking. Serve piled high on a serving dish, sprinkled with extra dukkah and rosemary leaves, and lemon wedges for squeezing over.

> **COOK'S NOTES**
>
> If you think the drumsticks need more cooking, transfer to a baking sheet and roast in a preheated 350°F (180°C) oven until cooked through. You could also stuff chicken breasts in this way.

Lamb fillet with tomato and basil salad

 PREP 15 MINS   **COOK** 20 MINS

Marinating • 1 hour

SERVES 8

4½lb (2kg) lamb loin roast

½ cup olive oil

3 garlic cloves, finely chopped

4 tbsp chopped flat-leaf parsley

3 fresh rosemary sprigs, leaves picked

pinch of crushed red pepper flakes

sea salt and freshly ground black pepper

handful of fresh flat-leaf parsley leaves, to garnish

extra virgin olive oil, for drizzling

For the tomato and basil salad

4 ripe plum tomatoes, cut into quarters lengthwise

1lb 2oz (500g) cherry tomatoes on the vine, separated but still with their stems

9oz (250g) yellow bell or cherry tomatoes, halved

1 bunch of fresh basil leaves, about 1oz (30g)

1 garlic clove, crushed

1 small red onion, thinly sliced into rounds

3 tbsp extra virgin olive oil

1 Trim the lamb of any fat and cut in half crosswise. Mix together the olive oil, garlic, parsley, rosemary, and pepper flakes in a large bowl, and season with salt and pepper. Add the lamb, massaging the marinade into the meat. Allow to marinate in the refrigerator for at least 1 hour.

2 Heat the barbecue or charcoal grill until hot. Grill the lamb over medium heat for 8–10 minutes on each side for medium-rare, or until cooked to your liking. Transfer to a plate, cover with foil, and leave to rest in a warm place for 20 minutes.

3 To make the salad, put all the ingredients in a bowl, season with salt and pepper, and toss gently. When ready to serve, slice the lamb diagonally and arrange on a serving platter. Scatter with the parsley leaves and a drizzle of extra virgin olive oil and serve accompanied by the salad.

VARIATION

Add some pesto to the tomato and basil salad, mix through, and serve with a little creamy fresh ricotta cheese spooned over the top and freshly grated Parmesan cheese.

COOK'S NOTES

The lamb could sit marinating in the refrigerator overnight, and the salad can be made ahead, too.

Grilled lamb cutlets and eggplant with red cabbage slaw

PREP 15 MINS · COOK 10 MINS

SERVES 4

1 eggplant, about 10oz (300g), thinly sliced lengthwise
sea salt and freshly ground black pepper
12 lamb cutlets, trimmed of any fat
2 tbsp olive oil

For the red cabbage slaw
½ small red cabbage
3½oz (100g) green beans, trimmed, blanched, and thinly sliced diagonally
1 small cucumber, thinly sliced lengthwise
1 scallion, thinly sliced diagonally
1 small red onion, thinly sliced into rounds
2 celery stalks, peeled and thinly sliced diagonally
2oz (60g) hazelnuts, chopped
2 tbsp extra virgin olive oil
1 tsp balsamic vinegar

1 Put the eggplant slices in a colander and sprinkle with salt. Allow to drain for 20 minutes, rinse, and pat dry with paper towels.

2 Heat the barbecue or charcoal grill until hot. Brush the lamb cutlets with olive oil and season with salt and pepper. Grill the lamb over medium heat for 3–5 minutes on each side, or until cooked to your liking. Transfer to a plate, cover with foil, and leave to rest in a warm place for 10 minutes. Meanwhile, grill the eggplant over high heat for 3 minutes on each side, until golden. Transfer to a plate and keep warm.

3 To make the slaw, finely slice or shred the red cabbage. Put the cabbage in a bowl and add the remaining salad ingredients. Season with salt and pepper, toss gently, and serve with the lamb cutlets and grilled eggplant.

Use pine nuts instead of hazelnuts in the slaw.

Pepper steak with parsley and almond pesto

PREP 10 MINS · COOK 6 MINS

Marinating • 1 hour
Special equipment • blender or food processor

SERVES 6

2¼lb (1kg) rib-eye steak, cut into 12 thin slices
1 tbsp black peppercorns
1 tbsp green peppercorns
1 tbsp pink peppercorns
sea salt
3 tbsp olive oil
1 tbsp coarse-grain mustard

For the parsley and almond pesto
4½oz (125g) blanched almonds, toasted
1 garlic clove, chopped
2 large handfuls of fresh flat-leaf parsley leaves
2 large handfuls of baby spinach leaves
grated zest and juice of 1 lemon
freshly ground black pepper
½ cup olive oil

1 Put the rib-eye slices in a large shallow dish. Using a mortar and pestle, grind the black, green, and pink peppercorns with a little salt until coarsely ground. Transfer to a bowl, add the olive oil and mustard, and mix together. Brush the marinade all over the meat and allow to marinate in the refrigerator for 1 hour.

2 Meanwhile, to make the parsley and almond pesto, put the almonds, garlic, parsley, spinach, lemon zest and juice in a blender or food processor and season with salt and pepper. Process briefly. Keep the motor running and gradually add the oil, little by little, until thick and smooth—if you like a thicker pesto, you may not need to use all the oil. Set aside in a bowl, resting a sheet of plastic wrap on top of the pesto.

3 Heat the barbecue or charcoal grill until hot. Grill the steaks over high heat for 2 minutes on each side, or until cooked to your liking, brushing lightly with the marinade while cooking. Transfer to a plate, cover with foil, and leave to rest in a warm place for 10 minutes.

4 To serve, put the steaks on individual plates and top with a spoonful of the parsley and almond pesto. Serve with thick slices of lightly oiled, grilled sourdough bread.

FOOD FOR FRIENDS

Filet mignon with horseradish cream

PREP 10 MINS · COOK 10 MINS

SERVES 4

4 filet mignon or rib-eye steaks,
   about 10oz (300g) each
2 tbsp olive oil
1 garlic clove, crushed
sea salt and freshly ground
   black pepper

For the horseradish cream
1 cup mascarpone cheese
1 tbsp freshly grated horseradish
juice of ½ lemon
1 tsp good-quality balsamic vinegar

1 Put the steaks in a large shallow dish. Add the oil and garlic and season with salt and pepper. Coat the steaks well.

2 Heat the barbecue or charcoal grill until hot. Grill the steaks over high heat for 5 minutes on each side or until cooked to your liking, brushing lightly with the oil mixture while cooking. Transfer to a plate, cover with foil, and leave to rest in a warm place for 10 minutes.

3 To make the horseradish cream, put the mascarpone in a bowl and stir in the horseradish, lemon juice, and balsamic vinegar. Season with a little black pepper. Divide the steaks among 4 warmed serving plates and serve with a dollop of the horseradish cream.

Pork kebabs with chile-mango salad

PREP 20 MINS · COOK 10 MINS

Marinating • 1 hour
Special equipment • 12 wooden skewers

SERVES 4

2 pork tenderloins, 9oz (250g) each
1 garlic clove, crushed
2 small fresh hot red chiles, seeded
   and finely chopped
1 tbsp finely chopped fresh ginger
4 tbsp olive oil
sea salt and freshly ground
   black pepper

For the chile-mango salad
2 large mangoes (see Cook's Notes)
grated zest and juice of 1 lime
1 small fresh hot red chile,
   finely sliced

1 Soak 12 wooden or bamboo skewers in cold water for 1 hour. Using a sharp knife, trim any excess fat from the pork. Cut each tenderloin in half lengthwise, then cut each half across the grain into bite-sized pieces.

2 To make the marinade, mix together the garlic, chiles, ginger, and olive oil in a shallow dish. Add the pork and turn to coat in the marinade. Season with salt and pepper and allow to marinate in the refrigerator for 1 hour.

3 Heat the barbecue or charcoal grill until hot. Thread the pieces of pork evenly onto the soaked skewers and brush the grill with a little oil. Grill the pork kebabs over low heat for about 10 minutes, or until cooked to your liking, brushing lightly with a little of the marinade while they are cooking. Transfer the kebabs to a plate, cover with foil, and leave to rest in a warm place for 15 minutes.

4 To make the chile-mango salad, peel the mangoes and cut in half (as close as possible to the pit as you can). Cut each half lengthwise into thin slices. Put the mango slices in a bowl, add the lime zest and juice and the chile, and season with black pepper. Stir gently to mix. Arrange 3 kebabs in the center of each of 4 serving plates, on top of the chile mango salad, or with the salad spooned beside them.

COOK'S NOTES

Look for mangoes that are not too ripe (preferably on the green side) for this salad. They should be firm and slightly tart.

Wasabi beef and bok choy

PREP 10 MINS   COOK 10 MINS

SERVES 4

2 tbsp olive oil

2 tsp wasabi paste

4 sirloin steaks, about
   7oz (200g) each

7oz (200g) bok choy, cut
   lengthwise into 8 pieces

5 garlic cloves, finely chopped

1 tbsp soy sauce

sea salt and freshly ground
   black pepper

1 Heat the barbecue or charcoal grill until it is hot and any flames have subsided. Mix together 1 tbsp of the olive oil and the wasabi paste. Use the mixture to coat the sirloin steaks thinly and evenly.

2 Put the steaks on the barbecue and grill over high heat for about 3 minutes on each side. Transfer to a plate and leave to rest in a warm place for 5 minutes.

3 Meanwhile, toss the bok choy in the remaining olive oil with the garlic and soy sauce. Grill on the barbecue for 2-3 minutes until charred and just wilted.

4 To serve, cut the steak into ½in (1cm) slices, season with salt and pepper, and serve with the bok choy.

Chile-slashed pork tenderloin

  PREP 10 MINS COOK 20 MINS

SERVES 4

1 pork tenderloin, about 1lb (450g)

1 red chile, seeded and finely chopped

3 garlic cloves, finely chopped

2in (5cm) piece of fresh ginger, finely chopped

5 scallions, finely sliced

2 tbsp olive oil

4 tbsp soy sauce

4 tbsp rice vinegar

1 tbsp honey

sea salt and freshly ground black pepper

1 Heat the barbecue or charcoal grill until it is hot and any flames have died down.

2 Make diagonal slashes halfway through the pork tenderloin at 1¼in (3cm) intervals. Mix together the remaining ingredients and season with salt and pepper. Spread liberally over the pork, ensuring that some of the mixture gets into the slashed openings.

3 Place the whole pork tenderloin on the barbecue and grill over medium heat for 20 minutes, turning carefully and frequently. Transfer to a plate and leave to rest in a warm place for 10 minutes.

4 To serve, cut the tenderloin on the opposite diagonal to the slashes into ½in (1cm) slices. Serve with a refreshing coleslaw.

Marinated pork tenderloin in soy and rice vinegar

  PREP 40 MINS COOK 20 MINS

Marinating • 30 minutes

SERVES 4

1 pork tenderloin, about 1lb (450g)

3 garlic cloves, finely chopped

2in (5cm) piece of fresh ginger, finely chopped

5 scallions, finely sliced

2 tbsp olive oil

4 tbsp soy sauce

4 tbsp rice vinegar

1 tbsp honey

sea salt and freshly ground black pepper

1 Score the pork tenderloin all over in a crisscross pattern about ½in (1cm) deep and place in a bowl or ceramic dish. Mix together the remaining ingredients and season with salt and pepper. Spread the mixture liberally over the pork and allow to marinate in the refrigerator for about 30 minutes.

2 Heat the barbecue until it is hot and any flames have died down. Place the whole tenderloin on the barbecue and grill over medium heat for 20 minutes, turning frequently. Transfer to a plate and leave to rest in a warm place for 10 minutes.

3 To serve, cut the tenderloin into ¼in (5mm) slices and serve with an Asian-style salad.

Lamb tenderloin basted in anchovy paste

PREP
15
MINS

COOK
40
MINS

Marinating • 30 minutes

SERVES 4

1 whole lamb tenderloin, about 1½lb (675g)
1 onion, peeled and quartered
1 x 5½oz (150g) jar salted anchovies in oil, drained
2 tbsp capers, drained
3 tbsp olive oil

1 Score the lamb fillet in a crisscross pattern about ½in (1cm) deep. Put the remaining ingredients in a blender or food processor and blend to a fine paste. Liberally rub the paste all over the lamb, making sure that it makes its way into the scores. Allow to marinate in the refrigerator for about 30 minutes.

2 Heat the barbecue or charcoal grill until it is hot and any flames have died down. Place the lamb fillet on the barbecue and grill over low heat for 40 minutes, turning frequently. Transfer to a plate and let rest in a warm place for 10 minutes.

3 To serve, cut into ½in (1cm) slices and serve with warm pita bread and hummus.

COOK'S NOTES

Use rack of lamb—you will find this cut at your butchers. To halve the cooking time, butterfly the fillet by cutting it in half (but not all the way through) and opening it out before marinating.

FOOD FOR FRIENDS

Stuffed sirloin steak with chile and parsley butter

PREP 20 MINS · COOK 6 MINS

Chilling • 30 minutes

SERVES 4
For the chile and parsley butter
5 tbsp salted butter
1 tsp crushed red pepper flakes
2 tbsp finely chopped flat-leaf parsley leaves

4 sirloin steaks, about 8oz (225g) each, cut to a minimum 1in (2.5cm) thick
sea salt and black pepper

4½oz (125g) cream cheese
1 tbsp olive oil

1 To make the chile and parsley butter, mix together all the ingredients in a bowl until well combined. Form into a sausage shape and place on a piece of parchment paper. Roll up into a tube, twist each end of the paper, and chill for 30 minutes.

2 Heat the barbecue until hot. Season each fillet steak with salt and pepper and, using a thin pointed knife, pierce the side and move the knife from side to side to create a cavity, trying not to increase the size of the opening too much. Place a portion of the cream cheese into each opening. Do not overstuff.

3 Grill the steaks on the barbecue over high heat for 3 minutes on each side, turning once. Transfer to a plate and let rest for 5 minutes.

4 Serve on a bed of baby spinach leaves with a dollop of the chile and parsley butter on top.

Texan rack of ribs

PREP 15 MINS **COOK 1¼ HRS**

Marinating • 1 hour

SERVES 4–6

4 racks of pork ribs, about 10in (25cm) long
2 lemons, sliced
2 onions, chopped
4 tbsp olive oil
4 tbsp tomato ketchup
4 tbsp Worcestershire sauce
1 tbsp ground mustard
1 tsp chili powder
1 tbsp honey
2 tbsp fresh thyme leaves
1 tsp salt
2 tsp freshly ground black pepper

1 Put the ribs in a large saucepan of salted water with the lemon slices. Bring to a boil, reduce the heat to low, and simmer gently for 40 minutes to tenderize the meat.

2 Meanwhile, put the remaining ingredients in a blender or food processor and blend well to make a smooth sauce. When the ribs are cooked, remove from the pan with a slotted spoon and drain thoroughly in a colander. Place the ribs in a bowl, coat with the sauce, and leave to cool. Marinate in the refrigerator for at least 1 hour.

3 Heat the barbecue until hot. Place the whole rib racks on the barbecue and grill over medium heat for 30 minutes, turning frequently and basting with any leftover sauce. Transfer to a plate and allow to rest in a warm place for 5 minutes.

4 To serve, slice the racks into ribs and serve warm and sticky with a crunchy salad and plenty of napkins.

Hot beef and chile burgers

PREP 20 MINS **COOK 10 MINS**

SERVES 4

14oz (400g) lean ground beef
2 onions, diced
2 garlic cloves, chopped
2 fresh hot red chiles, seeded and finely chopped
½ tsp salt
½ tsp cayenne pepper
½ tsp freshly ground black pepper
handful of fresh flat-leaf parsley, finely chopped

1 Put all the ingredients in a bowl. Using your hands, mix together really well until the texture is thick and paste-like. Form into 8 patties about ¾in (2cm) and chill until needed.

2 Heat the barbecue until hot. Cook the beef patties over medium heat for 5 minutes on each side until nicely browned and cooked through, turning only once during cooking.

3 Serve hot, sandwiched in burger buns, with fresh tomato slices and crispy lettuce.

 VARIATION Try using ground lamb instead of ground beef and add finely chopped fresh mint leaves when you add the parsley.

COOK'S NOTES

This is a great mixture to prepare ahead. Prepare the meat paste in a bowl, cover, and leave in the refrigerator for up to 2 days.

FOOD FOR FRIENDS

Lamb koftas

Chilling • 1 hour

Special equipment • blender or food processor • stainless-steel or wooden skewers

SERVES 4–6

1 red onion, peeled and quartered
2 garlic cloves, finely chopped
1 fresh red chile seeded and chopped
1 tsp finely chopped flat-leaf parsley leaves
1 tsp finely chopped cilantro
1 tsp finely chopped mint leaves
1 tsp mild paprika
finely grated zest of 1 lemon
sea salt and freshly ground black pepper
1½lb (675g) lean ground lamb

1 Put the onion, garlic, chile, parsley, cilantro, mint, paprika, and lemon zest in a blender or food processor. Season with salt and pepper and blend to a paste. Add the ground lamb and pulse until a coarse paste forms. Transfer the mixture to a bowl and chill for 1 hour or until firm, if time permits.

2 Shape the mixture into 12 sausages and carefully push each long sausage of meat onto a stainless-steel skewer to form the koftas. Return to the refrigerator until firm.

3 Meanwhile, heat the barbecue until hot. Put the skewers on the barbecue and grill over medium heat for 15 minutes, turning occasionally, until evenly browned and cooked through.

4 Serve hot with a crispy salad and hummus, if desired.

Marinated sweet and hot tuna steaks

Marinating • 30 minutes

SERVES 4

For the marinade

2 tbsp dark soy sauce
2 tbsp olive oil
juice of 2 limes
2 garlic cloves, finely chopped
1in (2.5cm) piece of fresh ginger, finely chopped
2 tbsp dark brown sugar
1 tsp cayenne pepper
sea salt and freshly ground black pepper

4 fresh tuna steaks, about 7oz (200g) each

1 Put all of the marinade ingredients in a bowl. Season with salt and pepper and mix together well. Put the tuna steaks in a plastic freezer bag, pour in the marinade, and seal, making sure that the tuna is well coated. Marinate in the refrigerator for 30 minutes if time permits.

2 Heat the barbecue until hot. Grill the tuna steaks over high heat for 2 minutes on each side, turning only once during cooking. Transfer to a plate and leave to rest in a warm place for 2 minutes.

3 Serve with a fresh green salad.

Butterflied chicken with lemon, oregano, and paprika

PREP 20 MINS · COOK 50 MINS

Marinating • 1 hour

SERVES 4–6

3 tsp olive oil

finely grated zest of 1 lemon, plus juice of 2

1 tsp paprika

½ tsp sea salt

1 tsp freshly ground black pepper

1 whole butterflied chicken, preferably free-range (you can ask your butcher to do this)

1 tbsp dried oregano

1 Combine the oil, lemon zest and juice, paprika, sea salt, and black pepper in a bowl and mix well. Add the chicken, making sure it is coated in the marinade. Allow to marinate in the refrigerator for 1 hour. (Put the chicken and its marinade in a plastic bag for better coverage, if you like.)

2 Heat the barbecue until hot. Sprinkle the chicken liberally all over with the oregano and grill over low heat for 40–50 minutes until golden and cooked through, turning frequently. Transfer to a plate and leave to rest for 15 minutes.

Cheat...
Cook over high heat on the barbecue for 15 minutes, then finish in a preheated 400°F (200°C) oven for 20 minutes.

COOK'S NOTES

To butterfly a chicken yourself, place the chicken breast-side down on a clean work surface. Using poultry shears or a good pair of kitchen scissors, cut along either side of the backbone, from thigh to wing on each side, and remove the backbone, from tail to neck. Open up the chicken and flatten by pushing down on the breastbone. Secure this position by inserting metal skewers from thigh to opposite wing.

Sausage and herb balls

PREP 15 MINS

COOK 15 MINS

Chilling • 30 minutes

Special equipment • blender or food processor

SERVES 4

1 onion, quartered

small handful of fresh mint leaves

handful of fresh flat-leaf parsley

handful of fresh basil

1 tsp dried oregano

sea salt and freshly ground black pepper

14oz (400g) good-quality sausage meat or fresh pork sausages, skinned

flour, to dust

1 Put the onion, mint, parsley, basil, and oregano in a food processor and blend into a coarse paste. Season well with sea salt and black pepper.

2 Add the sausage meat and pulse until combined. Roll the mixture into 12 balls, each about 1½in (4cm) across. Dust with a little flour to prevent them from sticking. Chill for 30 minutes or until firm.

3 Heat the barbecue until hot. Grill the sausage and herb balls over medium heat, turning occasionally, for 12–15 minutes until evenly browned and cooked through. Serve hot with a spicy or garlicky mayonnaise.

Cheat...
Use mildly-spiced sausages and omit the herbs.

COOK'S NOTES

Pour out lots of flour for dusting before rolling the sausage meat out, so you don't have to put your hands back in the bag!

Pork loin chop marinated in mustard and herbs

PREP 10 MINS **COOK 12 MINS**

Marinating • 2 hours

SERVES 4

For the marinade
- ¼ cup apple cider
- 4 tsp olive oil
- 4 tsp whole-grain or coarse-grain mustard
- 1 tbsp tomato paste or purée
- 2 tsp ground mustard
- 2 tbsp fresh thyme leaves
- 1 tbsp chopped sage leaves
- 2 tbsp finely chopped mint leaves
- 1 tbsp dried oregano
- ½ tsp sea salt
- 1 tsp freshly ground black pepper

- 4 large pork loin chops, trimmed of fat

1 Put all the ingredients for the marinade in a small bowl and mix together well.

2 Using a sharp knife, deeply score the pork chops. Put in a plastic freezer bag and pour in the marinade. Combine well, being careful not to pierce the bag. Seal and allow to marinate in the refrigerator for at least 2 hours.

3 Heat the barbecue until hot. Grill the pork chops over high heat for 10–12 minutes, turning occasionally and basting with any leftover marinade. Transfer to a plate and leave to rest in a warm place for 5 minutes. Serve with a new potato salad, if desired.

Jerk fish fillets

PREP 10 MINS **COOK 5 MINS** ♡

Marinating • 2 hours

Special equipment • blender or food processor

SERVES 4

For the jerk seasoning
- 6 garlic cloves
- 4 fresh Scotch Bonnet chiles
- 2 small onions, peeled and quartered
- 2 tbsp fresh thyme leaves
- 3 tbsp dark brown sugar
- 2 tsp ground allspice
- 1 tsp ground cinnamon
- ½ tsp ground nutmeg
- ½ tsp sea salt
- 1 tsp freshly ground black pepper

- 1½lb (675g) meaty white fish fillets such as monkfish or grouper
- lime wedges, to serve

1 Blend or process all the ingredients for the jerk seasoning to a smooth, wet paste. Put the fish in a plastic freezer bag, pour in the jerk seasoning, and seal, making sure that the fish is well coated. Allow to marinate in the refrigerator for at least 2 hours or preferably overnight.

2 Heat the barbecue until hot. Grill the fish over low heat for 3–5 minutes on each side until nicely browned and just cooked through. Be careful not to overcook; the residual heat will continue cooking the fish after it has been taken off the barbecue.

3 Cut the fish fillets into chunky slices and serve immediately with lime wedges for squeezing over, fresh crusty bread, and a crunchy salad.

Beef satay

PREP
10
MINS

Marinating • 1 hour

Special equipment • food processor or blender • metal skewers

SERVES 4
For the marinade
1 onion, quartered
2in (5cm) piece of fresh ginger
3 garlic cloves, coarsely chopped
2 fresh hot red chiles, seeded
2 tbsp ketchup
2 tbsp soy sauce
1 tbsp peanut oil
juice of 2 limes
3 tbsp brown sugar

2lb (900g) whole beef tenderloin filet, cut into 1in (2.5cm) cubes
3 tbsp crunchy peanut butter

1 Put all the ingredients for the marinade in a blender or a food processor and blend until smooth. Put the beef pieces in a plastic freezer bag and pour in the marinade, mix together, and seal. Allow to marinate in the refrigerator for at least 1 hour.

2 Thread the beef onto metal skewers, allowing about 5 pieces on each skewer and reserving the marinade. Set aside while you make the peanut sauce.

3 Pour the marinade into a small saucepan and bring to a boil. Add the peanut butter and continue cooking over medium-high heat, stirring constantly, until the mixture thickens into a sauce. Keep warm.

4 Heat the barbecue or charcoal grill until hot. Grill the beef skewers for 5 minutes, turning frequently. Leave to rest for a few minutes, then serve with the warm peanut sauce on the side for dipping.

Teriyaki chicken

PREP
15
MINS

COOK
20
MINS

Marinating • 20 minutes

SERVES 4
For the marinade
3 tbsp rice wine vinegar
5 tbsp soy sauce
5 tsp mirin or dry sherry
3 tbsp sugar
2in (5cm) piece of fresh ginger, grated

4 chicken breast fillets, skin on

1 To make the marinade, mix together all the ingredients in a bowl until the sugar has dissolved.

2 Using a sharp pointed knife or skewer, poke the chicken all over. Add to the bowl with the marinade, ensuring that the chicken is well-coated. Marinate in the refrigerator for 20 minutes.

3 Heat the barbecue or charcoal grill until hot. Remove the chicken from the marinade (reserving the marinade) and grill, skin-side up for 15–20 minutes over medium heat, turning from time to time, until browned all over. Transfer to a plate and leave to rest in a warm place for a few minutes while preparing the teriyaki sauce.

4 Put the reserved marinade in a small heavy saucepan. Bring to a boil and continue boiling until it thickens. Cut the chicken breasts into slices and serve with the hot teriyaki sauce poured over them.

Piadine with roasted pumpkin, arugula, and dill ricotta

PREP 20 MINS COOK 50 MINS

SERVES 8

2 x ¼oz (7g) packages active dry yeast
1 tsp salt
4½ cups all-purpose flour
2 tbsp olive oil, plus extra for brushing

For the filling
2¼lb (1kg) pumpkin, peeled, seeded, and cut into 1in cubes
⅓ cup olive oil
4 garlic cloves, peeled and crushed
4 fresh sage leaves, finely sliced
sea salt and freshly ground black pepper
1lb 2oz (500g) ricotta cheese
2 tbsp finely chopped Spanish onion
2 sprigs of fresh dill, finely chopped
2 handfuls of arugula

1 For the piadine, combine 2 cups of water with the yeast and salt in a bowl and stir until dissolved. Put the flour in a large bowl, make a well in the center, and add the yeast mixture and oil. Mix well. Knead the dough on a floured work surface for about 10 minutes, until smooth and elastic. Form a ball, place in a clean oiled bowl, and cover with a towel. Leave in a warm place to double in size, about 1 hour.

2 Meanwhile, preheat the oven to 400°F (200°C). Put the pumpkin on a baking sheet and toss with the olive oil, garlic, and sage. Season with salt and pepper and roast in the oven for about 40 minutes until tender and golden. Set aside to cool slightly. In a bowl, combine the ricotta, onion, and dill, and season with a little sea salt and black pepper. Set aside.

3 Heat the barbecue or charcoal grill until hot. Remove the dough from the bowl, form into a thick sausage-shape on a floured work surface, and cut into 8 portions. Form the dough into oval shapes, then flatten with the palm of your hand. Roll into long oval shapes about ¼in (5mm) thick. Brush both sides of the piadine with a little olive oil and grill over high heat for 1–2 minutes on each side until cooked. They cook quickly, so keep an eye on them.

4 As the piadine come off the grill, spread a little of the ricotta mixture evenly over the top of each one. Put some roasted pumpkin and arugula on one half of each piadina, fold the other half over the top, and serve immediately.

Grilled pepper and leek couscous

PREP 15 MINS COOK 15 MINS

SERVES 4

7oz (200g) couscous
1 tbsp soft butter
4 red bell peppers, tops removed, halved lengthwise, and seeded
5 tbsp olive oil
sea salt and freshly ground black pepper
1 leek, white part only, sliced into ¼in (5mm) discs
2 garlic cloves, crushed
grated zest and juice of 1 lemon
4 tbsp chopped flat-leaf parsley
2 tbsp chopped mint leaves

1 Put the couscous in a large bowl. Add 1 cup boiling water and the butter and stir to combine. Cover the bowl with plastic wrap and set aside for 5–10 minutes. Use a fork to separate and fluff up the grains. Set aside.

2 Heat a barbecue or charcoal grill until hot. Put the peppers in a shallow dish, add 3 tablespoons of the oil, and season with salt and pepper. Mix until the peppers are coated in the oil. Grill the peppers for about 10 minutes, until they are charred all over and softened. Allow to cool a little. Peel off the skin and reserve the pepper halves.

3 Heat the remaining 2 tablespoons olive oil in a frying pan over low heat. Add the leeks and sauté gently, stirring occasionally, for 5 minutes. Add the garlic and cook for another 30 seconds. Remove from the heat.

4 To finish, cut or tear the pepper halves into strips and put in the bowl with the couscous. Add the leek and garlic mixture, lemon zest and juice, parsley, and mint. Stir until combined and serve.

COOK'S NOTES

This dish would make a great partner with either grilled chicken or grilled fish.

Grilled asparagus and Gorgonzola

PREP 20 MINS **COOK 10 MINS**

SERVES 4

16 fresh asparagus spears,
  ends trimmed
salt and freshly ground black pepper
4 tbsp extra virgin olive oil
5½oz (150g) Gorgonzola cheese

1 Heat the barbecue or charcoal grill until hot. Cook the asparagus in boiling salted water for 2–3 minutes. Drain and immediately place on the barbecue or grill. Grill over medium heat for about 5 minutes or so, brushing the spears with a little of the oil as they are cooking and turning them as they char.

2 To serve, divide the asparagus among 4 serving plates. Gently slice or crumble the Gorgonzola over the asparagus. Sprinkle with ground black pepper and drizzle with the remaining extra virgin olive oil. Serve immediately.

VARIATION
Add some grilled prosciutto or pancetta. These are both very quick to char, so watch them closely. You could also add fresh baby spinach leaves or some thinly sliced fresh pear.

Grilled eggplant with spiced tomato sauce

PREP 15 MINS **COOK 20 MINS**

SERVES 4

2 large eggplants, cut into slices
  ½in (1cm) thick
sea salt and freshly ground
  black pepper
4 tbsp olive oil
2 garlic cloves, sliced
½ tsp paprika
1 x 14oz (400g) can diced tomatoes

1 Preheat the barbecue or ridged cast-iron grill pan until hot. Put the eggplants in a colander, sprinkle with salt, and weigh down with a plate. Leave to drain for 15 minutes, rinse, and pat dry with paper towels.

2 Meanwhile, heat 1 tablespoon of the olive oil in a pan over very low heat. Add the garlic and paprika and cook gently for a few seconds. Season with salt and pepper. Stir in the tomatoes and bring to a boil. Reduce the heat slightly and simmer gently for 15 minutes.

3 Brush the eggplant slices with the remaining oil, then grill on the barbecue or grill pan for 3 minutes on each side until golden. Drizzle with the sauce and serve immediately.

Grilled vegetables and spinach salad

PREP 30 MINS COOK 15 MINS

SERVES 4

1 medium-sized eggplant, about 12oz (350g)
sea salt and freshly ground black pepper
⅔ cup olive oil
2 yellow bell peppers, halved and seeded
2 red bell peppers, halved and seeded
2 sprigs of oregano, leaves picked
1 zucchini, about 10oz (300g), cut into diagonal slices ½in (5mm) thick
6 fresh asparagus spears, trimmed
4 canned artichoke hearts, cut into wedges
4 handfuls of baby spinach leaves
12 black olives
1 small red onion, sliced into thin rounds

For the dressing
3 tbsp olive oil
1 tbsp freshly squeezed lemon juice
1 tbsp chopped dill
2 scallions, thinly sliced

1 Heat the barbecue or charcoal grill until hot. Cut the eggplant into slices ½in (1cm) thick. Put in a colander, sprinkle with sea salt, and leave to drain for 15 minutes. Rinse and pat dry with paper towels.

2 Meanwhile, put the peppers in a shallow dish and add 4 tablespoons of the oil and the oregano. Season with salt and pepper and mix until the peppers are coated in the oil. Grill over high heat for about 10 minutes, until they are charred. Allow to cool a little, peel off the charred skin, and slice the pepper halves into strips. Set aside. Brush the eggplant and zucchini slices with a little oil and grill on both sides over high heat for 2–3 minutes on each side, until they are just tender and starting to char. Set aside.

3 Cook the asparagus in boiling salted water for 2–3 minutes. Drain and immediately place on the barbecue or grill. Grill over medium heat for about 5 minutes, brushing the spears with a little of the oil as they are cooking and turning them as they char. Brush the grill with a little oil and grill the artichoke hearts at the same time, allowing 2–3 minutes for each side. Allow to cool slightly.

4 Put all the grilled vegetables in a bowl and add the spinach, olives, and red onion. To make the dressing, in a small bowl, whisk together all the dressing ingredients and season with salt and pepper. Pour over the salad and toss gently. Serve with grilled chicken or beef.

Grilled mushrooms with croutons, cherry tomatoes, and feta

PREP 15 MINS COOK 30 MINS

SERVES 4

1lb 2oz (500g) small to medium cremini mushrooms
grated zest and juice of 1 lemon
⅔ cup olive oil
sea salt and freshly ground black pepper
½ loaf ciabatta
2 garlic cloves, crushed
2 anchovies in oil, drained and chopped
1 tbsp fresh thyme leaves
1 tsp finely chopped rosemary leaves
9oz (250g) cherry tomatoes, halved
3½oz (100g) feta cheese, crumbled
flat-leaf parsley leaves, to garnish
extra virgin olive oil, to drizzle

1 Preheat the oven to 400°F (200°C) and heat the barbecue or charcoal grill until hot. Trim the stems off the mushrooms and discard. Put the mushrooms, lemon zest and juice, and half of the olive oil in a bowl, and stir to combine. Season with salt and pepper. Grill the mushrooms on both sides over high heat for 10–15 minutes. Set aside.

2 To make the croutons, tear the bread into bite-sized pieces and put on a baking sheet. Toss with the garlic, anchovies, thyme, rosemary, remaining olive oil, and lots of black pepper. Spread out over the sheet and bake for about 15 minutes until the bread is golden and crisp on the outside.

3 To serve, mix together the mushrooms and broken bread in a bowl and divide among 4 serving plates. Arrange the tomatoes over and around the bread and mushrooms. Top with the feta, garnish with the parsley leaves, and drizzle with a little extra virgin olive oil. Serve with grilled fish or lamb.

NO-COOK DESSERTS

Simple prep-and-serve desserts for instant glamour.

NO-COOK DESSERTS

Cooking desserts often causes last-minute panic, because you run out of time, or don't have space in the oven. No-cook desserts provide an instant solution, even more so during the summer when heat isn't desired in the kitchen or on the menu.

Best fruit for no-cook desserts
Use fruit at its freshest, and when it's in season.

fresh, canned, or frozen?

Rub cut **fresh fruit**, such as apples and pears, with lime or lemon juice (fresh or bottled) before using it in desserts. The acid will prevent decay and stop the cut surfaces from turning brown. Toss a little juice in a fruit salad, too, to stop any discoloration.

Surprisingly, **canned fruit** contains almost the same nutrients as fresh, so it is a good substitute. Taste is the deciding factor, as nothing compares to eating fresh seasonal fruit. But canned, with its long shelf life and year-round availability, is a useful standby. Make sure it is packed in its own juices and has no added sugar.

Frozen fruit offers little difference from fresh, nutritionally, as they are often frozen within hours of picking, but the flavor won't be as good. Summer berries are a good fruit to freeze, as their season is short. Freezing allows you to enjoy them all year.

CHOOSE		USE	CHOOSE		USE
	**BERRIES** Choose plump and fragrant fruit with fresh green leaves. Available in the summer.	Don't pile or overcrowd when storing, as they soon turn moldy. Delicious with balsamic vinegar, mint, chocolate, or lavender.		**MANGO** Fresh mango is sweet and tangy. Choose heavy ones with tight, unblemished skin. Available year round.	Purée the flesh, mix it with Greek yogurt, then freeze for an easy frozen dessert.
	**APPLE** There are hundreds of varieties to choose from. Press them lightly–they should be firm. At their best in the autumn.	Apples add a crisp texture to fruit salads and team well with cinnamon and vanilla.		**PASSION FRUIT** This crinkled-skin fruit has a colorful and scented flesh once opened (see opposite). Available year round.	You can eat the flesh and the seeds. Toss with an exotic fruit salad, or use the juice as a sauce for ice cream, or to make a jelly with a splash of champagne.
	**ORANGE** Choose heavy ones, as these will contain the most juice. Available year round.	Sweet varieties, such as the Valencia, navel, and blood orange (perfect for a granita), team well with cinnamon, cardamom, mint, and basil.		**GRAPES** Buy grapes that are still firmly attached to the stem. Available year round.	Try freezing them individually and eating them straight from the freezer. Steep in dessert wine and serve with ice cream or mascarpone.
	**PINEAPPLE** A ripe pineapple should smell sweet, and a leaf near the top should come away easily if pulled. Available year round.	Pair with tropical fruits in a fruit salad. It has a natural affinity to coconut and mint.		**BANANA** Bananas have a high sugar content compared to other fruits. Available year round.	They are best eaten when the yellow skin is covered in faint brown speckles. Slice or mash and serve with grated chocolate.
	STONE FRUIT Peaches may require peeling, but the skin of apricots and nectarines is more palatable. Choose plump fruit, with a smooth skin. Available in the summer and autumn.	Halve and remove the pit and serve sprinkled with toasted nuts, or soak in a little liqueur and serve with ice cream. The flesh can also be puréed.		**PEAR** Choose ripe juicy dessert pears, such as Bosc, for eating raw. At their best in the autumn.	Serve with chocolate, or spices such as star anise and cinnamon. Rub with lemon juice once cut to prevent discoloration.
	POMEGRANATE Choose heavy fruit. Available in the autumn.	The jewel-like seeds look impressive sprinkled over fruits, ice creams, and sorbets. Mix juice and seeds with Middle Eastern flavors, such as cinnamon, nutmeg, and mint.		**MELON** Watermelon, honeydew, and cantaloupe are the most popular varieties. Available in the summer.	Halve and chop, and serve on its own, or as part of a mixed fruit salad. Once cut, they should be eaten as soon as possible.

STEP

Prepare fruit How to prepare tricky fruits.

Orange This technique is the quickest, easiest way to segment an orange, leaving the flesh pith-free.

1 With a sharp knife, slice away the top and bottom of the orange, then work around the fruit, slicing away the skin and pith.

2 Slice between each segment, leaving the thin layer of membrane behind until you have cut out all the segments.

Pineapple Be careful when handling the sharp outer skin, and use the sharpest knife you can find as the inner core is tough.

1 Slice off both ends of the pineapple. Stand it on its base and slice the skin from the top down, all the way around the fruit.

2 Cut it in half lengthwise, then slice away the fibrous core that runs through the center of the fruit.

Peach Removing the skin from peaches and other stone fruit, such as nectarines and plums, is necessary for many desserts and sauces.

1 Starting at the base, make a cut crosswise around the middle, just through the skin. Then repeat the cut in the other direction.

2 Place the fruit in a heatproof bowl and pour in boiling water. Remove with a slotted spoon, and when cool, pull off the skin.

Pomegranate This delicious Middle Eastern fruit has a tough skin and requires patience when preparing, but it's worth the effort.

1 Slice off the top of the pomegranate with a sharp knife. Slice into quarters.

2 The seeds are in clusters divided by a thin membrane. Pick out the seeds from each quarter.

Mango Cutting halves alongside the fibrous pit and "hedge-hogging" the mango is the cleanest way to remove the flesh.

1 Standing the mango on its side, cut down each side of the mango, from stem to base, as close to the pit as you can.

2 Cut a crisscross pattern into the flesh of both pieces, but don't go all the way through. Invert the skin so the mango cubes pop up, then remove with a knife.

Passion fruit They may look impenetrable, but the pulp, juice, and seeds of this exotic fruit are surprisingly easy to extract.

1 With a sharp knife, cut the fruit in half, across the center.

2 Using a spoon, scrape around the edge of the passion fruit to release the seeds from the membrane. Scoop out the pulp.

Fruit fool You can use any soft fruit to whip up this quick and easy dessert.

1 Put 1lb 2oz (500g) of hulled strawberries (reserving a few for garnish) in a food processor and process until puréed. Sieve in a little confectioner's sugar to taste (depending on how sweet you like it).

2 Whip 2 cups of heavy cream by hand or by using an electric mixer. Be careful not to over-beat, as it will spoil in seconds. It should form soft peaks when lifted from the bowl.

3 Sieve the puréed strawberries if you don't like the seeds, then add half the strawberry mixture to the cream, folding in gently until combined. Taste and add a little more sugar if it is too tart.

4 Spoon some of the strawberry mixture into individual dishes, or one large glass dessert dish, then layer with the strawberry cream (fool) mixture, and continue layering until both mixtures have been used up. Instead of cream, you could use mascarpone or fromage frais.

4 store cupboard essentials With these ingredients on standby, you can jazz up a dessert in an instant.

CHOCOLATE
Any kind of chocolate is a must for the store cupboard, but dark is best. It can be grated, chopped, or curled over so many desserts. Try it sprinkled over a cardamom and chocolate mousse, or stir chunks through vanilla or coffee ice cream.

DRIED FRUITS
The ultimate standby. Choose sweet ready-to-eat fruits such as apricots, plump raisins, prunes, or sour cherries. They taste great soaked in alcohol, or chopped and mixed into ice cream with a splash of rum. Serve with mascarpone, fromage frais, or Greek yogurt for an instant dessert.

NUTS
Buy roasted nuts, such as hazelnuts, pre-chopped or whole. Mix a variety of nuts, if you like, or buy them pre-mixed. Scatter over ice cream desserts, sundaes, or fruit, or mix into Greek yogurt with some honey.

SPICES
Cinnamon, nutmeg, and star anise all add an exotic touch to fruit salads, or sprinkled over ice cream. Soak in orange juice and use in trifles or chocolate mousses.

Cheesecake Add your own fruit and flavors to this simple basic recipe.

1 To make the crust, put 9oz (250g) of graham crackers in a food processor and process until crumbled, or place in a plastic bag and crush with a rolling pin. Melt 10 tbsp of butter and stir in the crumbs. Spoon into an 8in (20cm) round springform pan and spread the mixture evenly and firmly into the base.

2 Put 3 teaspoons of powdered gelatin into a glass bowl with the juice of 3–4 lemons, depending on how citrusy you like your cheesecake. Stir in 1 teaspoon of water and place the bowl over a pan of simmering water. Stir until the gelatin dissolves. Add ¼ cup of sugar and continue stirring until the sugar dissolves.

3 Make the topping by lightly whisking 1¾ cups of heavy cream, then adding 8oz (225g) of mascarpone and 9oz (250g) of cream cheese. Add a couple of drops of vanilla extract, then pour in the gelatin mixture. Stir well to combine.

4 Carefully pour the mixture over the base and smooth the top. Put in the refrigerator and leave to set for about 2 hours, or overnight if you prefer. Make sure it is completely set before releasing it from the pan. Put on a serving plate or cake stand and decorate with berries of your choice. Dust with powdered sugar to serve.

Fridge and freezer essentials

Frozen yogurts make a healthy alternative to ice cream. Serve store-bought, or make your own by blending fresh or frozen berries with Greek yogurt and putting in the freezer until frozen.

Mascarpone and cream cheese are known as the principle ingredients of cheesecake, but can be used for all types of instant no-cook desserts. Combine with fresh sliced fruit and honey, or a selection of store cupboard ingredients from p460.

Greek yogurt and fromage frais can be served as low fat alternatives to cream. Freshen with a few drops of elderflower cordial or fruit purée, or use instead of cream in the fool recipe on p460.

Orange and chocolate tiramisu

PREP
20
MINS

Chilling • 4 hours
Special equipment • electric mixer

SERVES 8
20–24 soft ladyfingers
1 cup orange juice
2 tbsp Grand Marnier or Cointreau
2 large eggs, separated
¼ cup confectioners' (powdered) sugar, sifted
1lb (450g) mascarpone cheese
finely grated zest of 1 orange
3oz (85g) orange-flavored chocolate, finely grated

1 Lay the ladyfingers flat in a shallow 2-quart (2-liter) serving dish. Drizzle with the orange juice and Grand Marnier and set aside.

2 Combine the egg yolks and confectioners' sugar in a large bowl and beat with a wooden spoon until smooth and creamy. Beat in the mascarpone until smooth.

3 Put the egg whites in a large mixing bowl and beat with an electric mixer until soft peaks form. Fold into the mascarpone mixture along with the orange zest. Pour the mixture over the ladyfingers and smooth the top. Cover and chill for at least 4 hours or overnight. To serve, garnish with grated chocolate.

VARIATION
For a more traditional version of tiramisu, use coffee and brandy instead of the orange juice and Grand Marnier.

Cheat...
Dust with cocoa
powder instead
of grating
the chocolate.

Meringue and mango mess

PREP
15
MINS

Chilling • 1 hour
Special equipment • electric mixer

SERVES 4
1 cup heavy whipping cream
1 cup Greek-style yogurt
2 tbsp confectioners' (powdered) sugar, or to taste, sifted
4 bakery-bought meringue nests, crushed
1 medium mango, peeled and sliced or chopped
2 passion fruit
mint leaves, for garnish (optional)

1 Place the cream in a large bowl and beat with an electric mixer until soft peaks form. Fold in the Greek yogurt and confectioners' sugar, then the meringues and mango. Divide the mixture between four glasses.

2 Scoop out the flesh and seeds from the passion fruit and drizzle over each serving, then cover and refrigerate for 1 hour. Garnish with mint leaves, if you'd like, and serve.

VARIATION
Use 1 cup summer berries, such as raspberries, blackberries, and strawberries, instead of the mango and passion fruit.

COOK'S NOTES
The longer you chill the desserts the softer the meringue will become; so don't refrigerate them for more than one hour if you prefer some crunch.

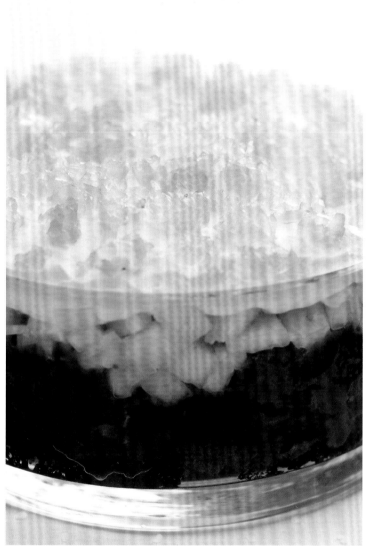

Berry gelatin cups with vanilla cream

PREP
15
MINS

Chilling • 4 hours
Special equipment • electric mixer

SERVES 4

1 package (4-serving size) instant gelatin, berry flavored
½ cup crème de cassis
½ cup heavy whipping cream
¼ tsp vanilla extract
2 tbsp confectioners' (powdered) sugar, sifted

1 Make the gelatin according to package directions in a 1-quart (1.1-liter) heatproof bowl. Pour in ⅔ cup boiling water and stir until the gelatin has dissolved. Pour in the cassis, then add up to 1 cup cold water, stirring until dissolved. Divide between 4 small wine glasses and chill for 4 hours or overnight until set.

2 Just before serving, combine the cream, vanilla, and confectioners' sugar in a bowl and beat with an electric mixer until soft peaks form. Spoon the cream over the jellies, garnish with a mint leaf or two and some berries, and serve.

VARIATION To make a non-alcoholic version, omit the crème de cassis and add water instead.

Cheat... Top with ice cream instead of the vanilla whipped cream.

Tropical trifle

PREP
15
MINS

Chilling • 30 minutes
Special equipment • electric mixer

SERVES 6

8–10oz (300g) store-bought or homemade ginger cake or gingerbread, sliced
½ cup pineapple juice
1 cup finely chopped pineapple
1¼ cups heavy whipping cream
2–3 tbsp syrup from a jar of stem ginger
2 pieces of stem ginger in syrup, finely chopped

1 Line the bottom of a serving bowl with the ginger cake slices, then drizzle with the pineapple juice and scatter the pineapple evenly over the top of the cake.

2 Combine the cream and ginger syrup in a large mixing bowl and beat with an electric mixer until soft peaks form. Spoon the mixture over the pineapple, then scatter the chopped stem ginger over the top. Refrigerate for 30 minutes, then serve.

VARIATION Use mango or banana instead of the pineapple, or a mixture of all three.

463

Strawberry and raspberry granita

PREP 10 MINS

Freeze • 4 hours
Special equipment • food processor

SERVES 6
1 cup confectioners' (powdered) sugar
1 tbsp fresh lemon juice
1½ cups fresh or frozen
   unsweetened raspberries
1½ cups fresh strawberries, hulled, or
   frozen unsweetened strawberries

1 In a food processor, combine the confectioners' sugar, lemon juice, and ⅔ cup boiling water. Pulse until the sugar dissolves. Add the raspberries and strawberries and purée.

2 Transfer the mixture to a shallow freezer-safe plastic container, cover, and freeze for 2 hours. Remove from the freezer and scrape the surface with a fork, breaking the ice into small pieces until slushy. Freeze for another 2 hours and then repeat the process every 2 hours—once or twice more—until the mixture is completely broken into tiny snow-like ice particles. Leave in the freezer until ready to serve. Although granita is best served the same day it is made, it will keep for up to 1 month in the freezer. Serve frozen scoops plain, or with a dollop of whipped cream.

COOK'S NOTES
If you prefer, strain the berry purée through a sieve to remove the seeds.

Boozy berries with mint and elderflower cream

PREP 10 MINS

Chilling • 30 minutes
Special equipment • electric mixer

SERVES 4-6
1lb (450g) mixed summer berries,
   such as strawberries (halved, if
   large), blackberries, raspberries,
   and red currants, stemmed
⅔ cup crème de cassis
1 cup heavy whipping cream
1 tbsp finely chopped mint leaves
1-2 tbsp elderflower cordial, to taste

1 Put the berries in a shallow serving bowl and drizzle the cassis over the top. Cover and refrigerate for at least 30 minutes or overnight, tossing gently once or twice to mix.

2 Put the cream in a mixing bowl and beat with an electric mixer until soft peaks form. Fold in the mint and elderflower cordial and serve with the mixed berries.

Lemon and lime syllabub

PREP 15 MINS

Chilling • 30 minutes

SERVES 4
juice of 1 lemon
juice of ½ lime
1 tbsp gin or vodka
4–5 tbsp granulated sugar
1¼ cups heavy whipping cream
finely grated lemon zest and lime
    zest, for garnish (optional)

1 Mix the lemon juice and lime juice in a bowl, add the gin or vodka and sugar, and stir until the sugar dissolves. Pour in the cream and beat with a balloon whisk until the mixture forms soft peaks.

2 Spoon into 4 serving glasses, then refrigerate for 30 minutes. Decorate with lemon zest and lime zest, if using, and serve with small, thin cookies or little shortbread rounds.

FOOD FOR FRIENDS

Lime cheesecakes

 PREP 10 MINS

Chilling • 4 hours
Special equipment • electric mixer

SERVES 4
4 British digestive biscuits or plain
    cookies, such as vanilla wafers or
    graham crackers
1 cup cream cheese, at
    room temperature
1 cup sweetened condensed milk
finely grated zest and juice of 2 limes
extra lime zest, for garnish (optional)

1 Line the bottom of each of four 6oz (175ml) ramekins with a biscuit. Put the cream cheese in a mixing bowl and beat with an electric mixer until

smooth, then beat in the condensed milk until well blended.

2 Add the lime zest and lime juice and beat until the mixture becomes thick and glossy. Divide among the ramekins and smooth the tops. Cover and refrigerate for at least 4 hours or overnight. Just before serving, garnish with the extra lime zest and serve.

COOK'S NOTES

The biscuit base does soften as it chills, but if you prefer a softer base, crumble the biscuit and mix it with a little butter melted in the microwave.

Easy banoffee pie

PREP
15
MINS

Special equipment • electric mixer

SERVES 8

8in (20cm) baked pie or tart shell
1 cup ready-made thick caramel sauce
 or dulce de leche
2–3 ripe bananas
1¼ cups heavy whipping cream
scant 1oz (25g) semisweet chocolate

1 Place the pie shell on a serving plate. Spoon in the caramel sauce and spread evenly over the bottom. Slice the bananas and scatter over the top.

2 Put the cream in a bowl and beat with an electric mixer until soft peaks form, then spoon over the bananas. Grate the chocolate, sprinkle evenly over the top, and serve.

Middle Eastern oranges with honey

PREP
15
MINS

SERVES 4

4 oranges, preferably seedless
1–2 tbsp honey
1–2 tbsp rose flower water, to taste
good pinch of ground cinnamon
seeds from 1 pomegranate
small handful of chopped, shelled, and
 skinned pistachios (optional)
handful of small mint leaves,
 for garnish

1 Slice off the top and bottom from each orange and place them on a cutting board. Carefully slice off the skin and pith, leaving as much flesh as possible, and following the curve of the orange so you maintain their shape. Thinly slice the oranges crosswise, discarding any seeds. Arrange the slices on a serving plate and drizzle with any juices from the cutting board.

2 Next, drizzle the orange slices with the honey and rose-water and sprinkle with the cinnamon. Scatter the pomegranate seeds and pistachios over the top, then garnish with the mint leaves and serve.

Cheat...
Use a 4oz (115g) package
of fresh pomegranate
seeds instead of seeding
a fresh pomegranate.

Melon with vodka, orange, and mint

 PREP 15 MINS

Marinating • 15 minutes

SERVES 6-8

1 honeydew melon, quartered
 lengthwise, seeds removed,
 and flesh sliced

1 small watermelon, preferably
 seedless, cut in half, seeds removed
 if needed, and flesh sliced

1-2 tbsp good-quality vodka

1-2 tbsp fresh orange juice
 without pulp

handful of coarsely torn fresh
 mint leaves

1 Arrange all the melon slices in a serving bowl or platter, drizzle with the vodka and orange juice, then leave to sit for 15 minutes.

2 Sprinkle with the mint and serve.

 VARIATION You can use any kind of melon, but always try to include watermelon, which will absorb the vodka.

COOK'S NOTES

Use melons that are firm yet ripe—they'll still have a bit of bite to them.

Knickerbocker glory

PREP 15 MINS

Special equipment • food processor
• immersion blender

SERVES 2

half of a 1-pint (400g) basket of
 strawberries, stems removed

drizzle of strawberry liqueur or other
 liqueur of choice

⅔ cup heavy whipping cream

2 slices plain sponge cake
 or pound cake, cut into
 pieces if needed

1 pint vanilla ice cream

¼ cup blanched almonds, toasted and
 coarsely chopped

1 Coarsely slice the strawberries, reserving two whole ones. Put the sliced berries in a bowl, drizzle with the liqueur, then purée with an immersion blender. (Alternatively, pulse in a food processor.) Whip the cream with a whisk or electric mixer until soft peaks form.

2 Place 1 piece of cake in the bottom of each of two tall glasses, then spoon in 1 tablespoon of strawberry sauce. Add a scoop of ice cream, then of whipped cream. Add another drizzle of strawberry sauce, then continue layering, ending with ice cream at the top. Sprinkle with the nuts and top with the reserved whole berries.

 VARIATION Drizzle with chocolate sauce, if you like.

COOK'S NOTES

Be extra careful not to overwhip the cream, or it will become grainy and will slightly separate.

Marinated prunes and apricots

 PREP 10 MINS

Marinating • several hours

 VARIATION
Use the dried fruit of your choice—cherries are particularly good.

SERVES 4
1 cup soft pitted prunes
1 cup soft dried apricots
2 tbsp sweet dessert wine or
   sweet Marsala
6 tbsp ricotta cheese, or as needed,
   for serving
finely grated zest of 1 orange

1 Chop the dried fruits, place in a bowl, then drizzle with the dessert wine. Cover and marinate, stirring occasionally, for several hours so the fruit softens and absorbs the alcohol.

2 Top each serving of fruit with a dollop of ricotta cheese and garnish with the orange zest.

> **COOK'S NOTES**
> Don't use fruit that is old and no longer moist—it won't absorb the alcohol.

Vanilla ice cream with coffee drizzle

PREP 10 MINS

 VARIATION
For an instant mocha dessert, use chocolate ice cream.

SERVES 2
6 scoops premium vanilla ice cream
2 freshly brewed single or double
   espressos, or strong coffee
pinch of demerara sugar (optional)

1 Remove the ice cream from the freezer and let it soften for 5-10 minutes until easy enough to scoop.

2 Place 3 scoops of ice cream in two bowls. Sweeten the coffee with sugar, if you wish, then pour the coffee over the ice cream and serve immediately.

> **COOK'S NOTES**
> If you're serving the dessert in a glass dish or in smaller glass bowls, be sure they can withstand the heat of the coffee.

Grapes marinated in port

PREP 10 MINS

Marinating • several hours

SERVES 4

1 bunch of seedless red grapes
1 bunch of seedless green grapes
drizzle of good-quality port
vanilla ice cream, for serving

1 Prick each grape with the tip of a sharp knife, then place them in a large serving dish and drizzle with port. Cover and marinate in the refrigerator for several hours or overnight.

2 To serve, allow the grapes to come to room temperature, then spoon into glass dishes and top with a scoop of vanilla ice cream.

VARIATION

For a lighter dessert, use a drizzle of white port instead.

Fresh figs with cassis cream

PREP 15 MINS

SERVES 4

12 plump fresh figs, stems removed
generous drizzle of crème de cassis
7oz (200g) mascarpone cheese

1 Cut a cross on the stem-end of each fig, cutting down about ¾ of the length, then squeeze gently to open. Place three figs in each of four dishes and drizzle with crème de cassis.

2 Mix the mascarpone with a drizzle of cassis and stir gently until lightly marbled. Add a spoonful of the mascarpone mixture and serve.

VARIATION

This dessert can also be served warm. Place the figs in a baking dish and drizzle with cassis. Cover with foil and bake in a preheated 375°F (190°C) oven for 10–15 minutes or until the figs are soft and oozing. Serve with a dollop of the cassis cream.

COOK'S NOTES

Cassis is a delicious blackcurrant liqueur that will jazz up many desserts. Keep a bottle in your pantry. Serve this dessert when figs are in season and at their best.

Peaches with meringue and raspberry sauce

PREP 15 MINS

Special equipment • stick blender

SERVES 4

1 cup fresh raspberries
4 meringue shells
4 ripe peaches, pitted and coarsely
    chopped or sliced
finely grated zest of 1 lime
whipped cream for serving (optional)

1 Put the raspberries in a bowl, then purée with a stick blender. Pass the purée through a nylon sieve to remove the seeds.

2 Break up the meringues with your hands, then scatter the pieces in one large shallow serving dish, or four individual ones. Top with the peaches, then spoon the raspberry purée over the top and garnish with lime zest. Serve with a dollop of whipped cream.

VARIATION
Garnish with lemon zest instead of lime.

Cheat...
Use 2 tablespoons of store-bought raspberry purée. It's a great standby that can jazz up desserts in an instant.

COOK'S NOTES

You can make the raspberry purée up to 1 day ahead. Keep it in the refrigerator until required.

Dark chocolate and white chocolate mousse

PREP 15 MINS

Setting • 3 hours
Special equipment • electric mixer

SERVES 4

4½oz (125g) good-quality
    semi-sweet chocolate
4½oz (125g) good-quality
    white chocolate
4 large eggs

1 Break the dark chocolate and the white chocolate into pieces and place in separate microwave-safe bowls. Microwave the chocolates, one bowl at a time, on medium for 1–2 minutes, or until just melted. Stir gently until smooth. Set aside to cool slightly.

2 Separate the eggs, adding 2 yolks to each bowl of chocolate and stirring to blend. Whisk the egg whites with an electric mixer until fluffy peaks form. Fold half of the whipped whites into the dark chocolate, stirring for a couple of minutes until the mixture is well-combined. Fold the other half of the whites into the white chocolate in the same manner.

3 Divide the chocolate mixtures among four individual glass dishes, spooning them in layers, and finishing with a dark chocolate top. Cover and refrigerate until set, at least 3 hours or, ideally, overnight.

COOK'S NOTES

Chocolate is sensitive to heating, especially white chocolate, and can burn or go grainy—in which case, you've lost it. Check the microwave frequently after about 30 seconds, then keep a constant eye on it. Use large eggs. If you only have small ones, increase the quantity to 6.

Apricots with Amaretti cookies and mascarpone

PREP
15
MINS

SERVES 4
8 Amaretti cookies
7oz (200g) mascarpone cheese
16 ripe apricots, halved and pitted
handful of blanched almonds, halved

1 Lightly crush the Amaretti with a rolling pin, then divide among 4 individual glass dishes. Lightly whip the mascarpone with a wooden spoon until smooth and thick.

2 Layer the apricots and mascarpone on top of the Amaretti, finishing with a layer of mascarpone. Sprinkle with the almonds and serve.

VARIATION
Use peaches instead of apricots.

Cheat...
Buy toasted chopped nuts and scatter over the apricots to serve.

Chocolate truffles

PREP
15
MINS

Cooling • 30 minutes
Setting • 30 minutes

MAKES 12–14
4½oz (125g) good-quality semi-sweet chocolate, plus scant 1oz (25g), finely grated
drizzle of Baileys® Irish Cream liqueur or brandy
¼ cup shelled and skinned Brazil nuts, finely chopped
¼ cup dried cherries, chopped

1 Break the chocolate into small pieces and place in a microwave-safe bowl. Microwave on medium for 1–2 minutes or until just melted, then stir until smooth. Stir in the liqueur to blend, then stir in the nuts and cherries.

2 Leave to cool for 30 minutes, then scoop up a generous teaspoonful and form into a ball. Roll in the grated chocolate to coat, then place in a parchment-lined pan. Repeat with the remaining chocolate mixture. Refrigerate the truffles for 30 minutes or until set. Serve as a sweet treat with coffee or espresso.

VARIATION
Roll the chocolates in finely chopped toasted almonds or grated white chocolate instead.

Asian fruit salad

PREP 15 MINS

SERVES 4

1 mango, peeled and sliced
1 pineapple, ends and skin removed, sliced
1 kiwi fruit, peeled and sliced
juice of 1 orange
juice of 1 lime
1 passion fruit, halved
small handful of fresh mint leaves, finely chopped

1 Arrange the mango, pineapple, and kiwi fruit in a shallow serving bowl or platter. Pour the orange juice and lime juice over the fruit.

2 Scoop out the flesh and seeds from the passion fruit and spoon over the fruit. Sprinkle with mint leaves and serve.

Mixed berry cake

PREP 10 MINS

SERVES 6

3–4 scoops soft chocolate ice cream
3–4 scoops soft vanilla ice cream
8in (20cm) round plain sponge cake
1lb 2oz (500g) mixed summer berries, such as raspberries, blackberries, strawberries, and red currants
drizzle of crème de cassis or other liqueur of your choice (optional)

1 Spoon the ice cream on to the sponge cake, then pile on the fruit.

2 Drizzle over the crème de cassis or other liqueur (if using), and serve.

VARIATION

Use a chocolate sponge cake instead of the plain one.

Dark chocolate and lemon mousse

PREP 15 MINS

Setting • 3 hours
Special equipment • electric hand whisk

SERVES 4
4½oz (125g) good-quality
   dark chocolate
3 tbsp Limoncello liqueur
2 large or 3 small eggs

1 Break the chocolate into pieces and place in a microwave-safe bowl. Microwave on medium for 1–2 minutes, or until melted, then stir until glossy and smooth. Stir in the Limoncello.

2 Separate the eggs, then place the egg whites in a bowl and whisk with an electric hand mixer until soft peaks form. Add the egg yolks to the chocolate mixture and stir to combine. Fold in the egg whites and beat for a couple of minutes until smooth. Allow to cool.

3 Spoon into 4 glass serving dishes or ramekins and put in the refrigerator to set for at least 3 hours or overnight.

VARIATION
Use brandy instead of Limoncello.

> **COOK'S NOTES**
> This contains raw eggs, so is best avoided by children and the elderly.

Lychees with ginger and star anise

PREP 10 MINS

Marinating • 30 minutes

SERVES 4
1 x 14oz (400ml) can lychees, drained
   (2 tsp juice reserved)
1 star anise
2 balls stem ginger plus 2 tbsp
   ginger syrup
Greek-style yogurt, to serve

1 Arrange the lychees and star anise in a glass serving dish. Finely dice the balls of ginger and scatter over the lychees. Mix the ginger syrup with the reserved lychee juice and drizzle over.

2 Place in the refrigerator for 30 minutes, or longer if you have the time, for the flavors to develop. Serve with dollops of Greek yogurt.

> **COOK'S NOTES**
> Star anise has a subtle and fragrant aniseed flavor that goes well with ginger.

FREEZE-AHEAD DESSERTS

Tarts, ice creams, cakes, and treats to make well before the party.

FREEZE-AHEAD DESSERTS

Making use of the freezer is an economical way of cooking. It saves on time and money, and nothing beats having ready-made desserts on hand for family dinners or unexpected guests. Not only is it convenient, but when you bake cakes and other desserts yourself, you can also be assured of the contents, avoiding any hidden ingredients so often found in store-bought ones.

Psst...

For batch cooking to be efficient, you need to plan ahead. Put a few hours aside to make a selection of cakes and other desserts for the freezer. Use seasonal fruits when they are in abundance to make desserts, ice creams, pies, and crumbles. Or simply freeze fruit for later use (see p477).

Desserts and puddings Bake, store in the freezer, and defrost when ready to use.

STORE	DEFROST	STORE	DEFROST
CAKES **Sponge cake** Freeze unfilled. Double-wrap in plastic wrap, then foil. Freeze for up to **3 months**. **Iced sponge cake** Butter icing freezes well. Freeze uncovered, wrap in foil, and double-wrap in plastic wrap. Freeze up to **2 months**. **Fruitcake** Wrap in plastic wrap and foil. Freeze for up to **3 months**. **Iced fruitcake** Double-wrap in plastic wrap and foil. Freeze for up to **3 months**.	**Sponge cake** Leave in wrapping. **Iced sponge cake** Unwrap before defrosting. Thaw both at room temperature. **Fruitcake** Thaw in the refrigerator. **Iced fruitcake** Unwrap before defrosting. Thaw at room temperature.	**STEAMED PUDDINGS** Wrap in foil, then double-wrap in plastic wrap. Freeze for up to **3 months**.	Remove plastic wrap, top with a piece of wax paper, and steam from frozen for about 2 hours, or until heated through.
CHOCOLATE DESSERTS Prepare chocolate desserts in freezer-proof containers. Double-wrap in plastic wrap. Freeze for up to **2 months**.	Thaw in the refrigerator overnight.	**MERINGUES** Freeze in sealable plastic bags, unfilled. Meringues do toughen slightly when frozen. You can freeze egg whites. Freeze for up to **1 month**.	Thaw at room temperature.
PASTRIES, TARTS, AND PIES **Cooked pastries, tarts, and pies** Custard fillings don't freeze well, but fruit fillings do. Double-wrap in plastic wrap then foil. Freeze for up to **3 months**. **Uncooked pastries, tarts, and pies** Double-wrap your lined pan/rolled out pastry (filled or unfilled) in plastic wrap then foil. Freeze for **1–2 months**.	**Cooked pastries, tarts, and pies** Thaw at room temperature. **Uncooked pastries, tarts, and pies** Thaw unfilled in refrigerator overnight. Cook filled from frozen at 350°F (180°C) for 20–30 minutes.	**BAKED COOKIES** **Baked cookies** Freeze in sealable freezer bags. Freeze for up to **1 month**. **Uncooked dough** Freeze in a ball, or balls, or pre-shape. Double-wrap in plastic wrap. Freeze for up to **1 month**.	**Baked cookies** Thaw and warm in the oven at 375°F (190°C) for about 5 minutes, to crispen up. **Uncooked dough** Thaw, shape, and bake. Bake ready-shaped from frozen at 375°F (190°C), for 5 minutes longer than recipe.
CRUMBLES Use a freezer-proof and oven-proof dish. Prepare fruit and top with crumble mixture. Let cool, then double-wrap in plastic wrap and foil. Freeze for up to **2 months**.	Cook from frozen at 400°F (200°C), for 30–40 minutes, until golden and cooked through.	**CHEESECAKE** **Uncooked** Freeze, uncovered, then double-wrap in plastic wrap. Don't freeze cooked cheesecake. Freeze for up to **2 months**.	Thaw in the refrigerator overnight.

Freeze fruit

Choose

Freeze fruits at their peak, preferably when they're in season.

If fruit or berries are past their best, put them in the blender and process until smooth. Sieve, if needed, then pack in plastic sealable containers and freeze, or freeze in ice-cube trays and when frozen, transfer to a plastic bag and use as required. Use as a sauce or pie filling.

Watermelons don't freeze well unless they're puréed for use in frozen drinks.

Bananas can be peeled and frozen if they have become too overripe for eating. They are excellent to use in puddings and cakes.

Prepare

Always pick through fruit first, discarding any that are bruised, then wash in ice cold water, drain well, and dry thoroughly. Don't leave fruit to soak in water, or it will lose its flavor. Apples, pears, peaches, apricots, and nectarines discolor once sliced, and tend to turn brown while they thaw. To prevent discoloration, here are a few tips:

Freeze in a sugar syrup This is just a mix of water and sugar, brought to a boil then left to cool. Slice the fruit into wedges or other desired size, pack into sealable plastic bags or boxes, then pour over the mixture to cover completely, seal, and freeze. Allow about 1¼ cups of water for every 1lb (450g) of fruit. Apples and pears may need to be soaked in lemon juice first; see below.

Freeze in fruit juice For ease, cut fruit can be soaked and packed in fruit juice, such as apple juice, then frozen.

Soak in lemon juice Before freezing cut apples and pears, soak in a mixture of water and lemon juice before packing in sugar syrup or fruit juice. Allow 3 tablespoons of lemon juice for every ¾ cup of water.

Steam Steaming the fruit for a few minutes before packing will prevent the fruit from turning brown.

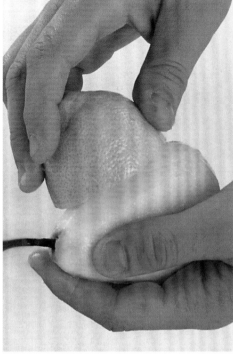

Rubbing cut or peeled fruit with half a lemon prevents the surface turning brown.

 STEP

Freeze soft fruit
Freeze fruit when it is at its best, and unblemished.

1 Spread the fruit on a tray covered in wax paper and put in the freezer, uncovered, until frozen.

2 Once frozen, pack into sealable freezer bags (the fruit will now stay separate and not stick together) and put back in the freezer. Freeze for up to 1 year.

freezing tips

A full freezer uses less energy than a half-full or empty one. If you plan to use your freezer a lot, a chest freezer is more efficient than an upright one.

Check the temperature of your freezer: it should be 0°F (-17°C) or lower.

Smaller portions will thaw quicker so don't over-pack batches of cakes.

Never put warm foods into the freezer. Allow to cool completely first.

Defrost puddings and desserts overnight in the refrigerator, when possible.

Use natural flavorings in desserts rather than artificial ones, so the flavor will be retained.

Easy ice cream without a machine

A creamy vanilla ice cream that doesn't require churning.

1 Split two vanilla beans and scrape out the seeds, reserving them for later. Add the beans to a pot with 2 cups heavy cream and bring to a boil. Add ⅓ cup of sugar and stir until dissolved.

2 In a bowl, whisk 4 egg yolks until well combined, then strain the warm cream mixture into the eggs, stirring all the time. Add the reserved vanilla seeds and stir.

3 Pour the ice-cream mixture into a metal loaf pan or plastic container. Let cool completely.

4 Once cool, put into the freezer. When frozen, double-wrap with plastic wrap and freeze for up to 3 months.

Ice cream flavors

Ginger and honey A heavenly combination of soothing flavors, perfect served with a slice of sticky walnut or pecan pie.

Mocha For chocoholics and coffee lovers. Stir chunky or chopped dark chocolate through the ice cream to add texture.

Cherry and Amaretto Sophisticated flavors for the grown-ups. Ideal for entertaining.

Strawberry and elderflower The very essence of summer. Simply process the strawberries with a drizzle of elderflower juice and serve on a hot day.

Rum and raisin The classic flavors are always a favorite. Enjoy it scooped into a cone or serve alongside a piece of home-baked cake.

Mint A simple but refreshing ice cream that requires just a few drops of natural mint extract. Add some chocolate chunks also if you wish.

The ice cream should be a smooth consistency, with no ice crystals. Take it out of the freezer for 10 minutes to soften before serving.

Fruit sorbet

Lighter than ice cream: a perfect palate cleanser. You can use any berries.

Sorbet flavors

Blood orange and Campari An impressive palate cleanser, ideal for entertaining.

Strawberry and balsamic An unusual combination–balsamic vinegar really brings out the intense flavor of the fruit.

Raspberry Use fresh or frozen raspberries for this colorful sorbet and remove the seeds with a sieve before freezing, if you like.

Lemon and lime Tart and refreshing: perfect for a hot summer day.

Mango This fruit will create smooth-textured sorbet. Serve with other tropical fruit, diced.

Passion fruit You will need at least a dozen passion fruit to make enough sorbet to serve 4. Remove the seeds before freezing.

Serve fruit sorbets on their own, or alongside a freeze-ahead tart made with the same fruit.

1 Combine ⅓ cup of sugar in a pan with ¼ cup of water. Simmer gently for 5–10 minutes, until the sugar has dissolved and the mixture has thickened.

2 Put 2¼lb (1kg) of strawberries in a food processor and process until puréed. (You can pass it through a sieve to remove the seeds, if you wish.) Pour the syrup mixture into the puréed strawberries and stir.

3 Pour the mixture into a freezer-proof container, the shallower the better (it will freeze more quickly). Let cool completely, then put into the freezer.

4 When frozen, remove and stir well to break up any ice crystals, then put back into the freezer. Sorbet is best eaten within a few days, as the fresh fruit taste starts to fade after a while.

Mocha pots

PREP 30 MINS

Special equipment • electric mixer

MAKES 6-8

5½oz (150g) semisweet chocolate, broken into pieces, plus a little extra, shaved with a vegetable peeler, for garnish (optional)

2 tbsp butter, cut into pieces

4 large eggs, at room temperature, separated

pinch of sea salt

⅓ cup granulated sugar

3 tbsp brewed espresso or strong coffee, at room temperature

⅔ cup heavy whipping cream

unsweetened cocoa powder, for dusting

1 In a bowl set over a saucepan of barely simmering water, melt the chocolate with the butter, stirring occasionally until smooth. Remove the bowl from the pan, set aside, and leave to cool to room temperature. Meanwhile, combine the egg whites and salt in a bowl and beat with an electric mixer until stiff peaks form. Gradually beat in the sugar until the mixture is stiff and shiny.

2 Stir the egg yolks into the cooled chocolate mixture, adding them one at a time. Gradually fold the beaten egg whites into the chocolate mixture, then stir in the espresso. Spoon the mixture evenly into six ⅔ cup or eight ½ cup freezer-safe ramekins or custard cups, leaving room on top for whipped cream. Place the cream in a bowl and beat with an electric mixer until stiff peaks form. Spoon the cream over the top of each mocha pot, then freeze until solid. Wrap in foil and return to the freezer.

3 To serve, defrost overnight in the refrigerator or for a few hours at room temperature. Dust with cocoa powder and garnish with shaved chocolate, if you like.

Cheat...
Omit the espresso and use coffee-flavored chocolate instead of plain semisweet chocolate.

Pear and mincemeat pie

PREP 15 MINS | **COOL 40 MINS**

SERVES 8-10

1½ cups prepared mincemeat

1 tbsp brandy

finely grated zest of 1 orange

1 x 17.3oz (425g) box frozen puff pastry sheets, thawed as package directs

¼ cup ground almonds

1 ripe pear, preferably Bosc, peeled, cored, and thinly sliced

1 egg, beaten

1 In a bowl, mix together the mincemeat, brandy, and orange zest. Roll each pastry sheet into an 11 x 8in (28 x 20cm) rectangle and reserve the scraps for another use. Lay one rectangle on a parchment-lined baking sheet, then sprinkle evenly with the ground almonds, leaving a ¾in (2cm) border around the edges. Spoon the mincemeat over the almonds, spreading evenly. Top with the pear and brush the border with beaten egg. Place the second sheet of pastry on top and press the edges together, pinching the sides with your finger and thumb. Use a sharp knife to make 2-3 slits in the top crust, for steam to escape. Freeze, uncovered, on the baking sheet until firm, then wrap in a double layer of foil and freeze.

2 To serve, defrost overnight in the refrigerator. Preheat the oven to 400°F (200°C). Carefully transfer the "pie" to a lightly greased baking sheet. Brush the pastry with the beaten egg and bake for 30-40 minutes or until golden brown and heated through.

VARIATION Use lemon zest instead of orange.

Almond and peach tart

PREP 20 MINS · COOK 30 MINS

Special equipment • electric mixer

SERVES 8

1 sheet prepared dough for
   an 8-9in (20-23cm) pie
7 tbsp butter, at room temperature
½ cup granulated sugar
2 large eggs, lightly beaten
1 cup ground almonds
¼ cup all-purpose flour, plus extra
   for dusting
4 peaches, halved and pitted
confectioners' (powdered) sugar,
   for dusting

1 Preheat the oven to 400°F
(200°C). Place a baking sheet
in the oven to warm. On a lightly
floured surface, roll the dough into
a rectangle large enough to line
the inside of a 13¾ x 4½in
(35 x 11cm) tart pan. Trim off
the excess pastry with a knife
and refrigerate the tart shell while
you make the filling.

2 Combine the butter and sugar in
bowl and beat with an electric mixer
until creamy, then beat in the eggs.
Mix in the ground almonds and flour
until blended, then spread evenly
in the tart shell. Press the peach
halves cut-side down into the almond
mixture. Carefully place the tart pan
on the hot baking sheet, then bake
for 30 minutes or until the almond
mixture is golden brown and cooked
through. Leave to cool completely,
then wrap the pan in foil and freeze.

3 To serve, defrost in the refrigerator
overnight. Carefully remove the tart
ring and serve cold, or reheat in
a preheated 350°F (180°C) oven for
20 minutes or until warmed through.
Just before serving, dust with
confectioners' sugar.

VARIATION

Instead of pears, use fresh
berries or ripe stone fruit
such as plums, nectarines,
or apricots.

FOOD FOR FRIENDS

Apricot meringue roulade

PREP 30 MINS · COOK 20 MINS

Special equipment • electric mixer

SERVES 8

4 large egg whites
pinch of sea salt
1 cup plus 2 tbsp granulated sugar
¼ cup sliced almonds
confectioners' (powdered) sugar,
   for dusting
1¼ cups heavy whipping cream
1 x 12-14oz (400g) can
   apricot halves, drained
   and coarsely chopped
seeds and pulp from 2 passion fruits

1 Preheat the oven to 375°F (190°C).
Line a 13 x 9in (33 x 23cm) jellyroll
pan with parchment paper. Combine
the egg whites and salt in a bowl
and beat with an electric mixer
until soft peaks form. Beat in the
granulated sugar 1 tbsp at a time
until the mixture is stiff and shiny.
Use a spatula to spread it evenly in
the pan. Scatter the almonds over the
top, then bake for 15-20 minutes or

until barely golden and just firm to
the touch. Invert the meringue onto a
sheet of parchment paper dusted with
confectioners' sugar. Set aside to cool.

2 Place the cream in a bowl and beat
with an electric mixer until soft peaks
form. Spread the whipped cream
over the meringue, then scatter the
apricots and passion fruit seeds over
the top. With the short side facing
you, roll the cake into a cylinder.
Wrap tightly in the parchment paper,
cover with foil, and freeze.

3 When ready to use, unwrap the
roulade on a plate, seam-side down.
Cover and defrost overnight in the
fridge, or for a few hours at room
temperature. To serve, dust with more
confectioners' sugar and cut into slices.

VARIATION

Substitute 1½ cups of raspberries
or blueberries for the apricots.

Sticky toffee puddings

PREP 20 MINS COOK 25 MINS

Special equipment • blender
• electric mixer

MAKES 8

7oz (200g) pitted dates, preferably Medjool
1 tsp baking soda
2 cups self-rising flour
8 tbsp butter, at room temperature
1 cup packed dark or light brown sugar
3 large eggs

For the toffee sauce
1 cup packed dark or light brown sugar
5 tbsp butter, cut into pieces
⅔ cup heavy whipping cream
sea salt
half-and-half or light cream, to serve

1 Preheat the oven to 375°F (190°C). Butter eight 1-cup pudding basins or ramekins. In a small pan, combine the dates with the baking soda and 1 cup of water. Simmer over medium-low heat for 5 minutes or until softened. Let cool slightly, then purée with the cooking liquid in a blender.

2 Sift the flour into a bowl, add the butter, brown sugar, and eggs, and beat with an electric mixer until well blended, then mix in the date purée. Pour the mixture into the pudding basins, then place them on a baking

sheet. Bake for 20–25 minutes or until firm to the touch. Meanwhile, make the toffee sauce. Melt the brown sugar, butter, and cream together in a pan, stirring until smooth. Stir in a pinch of salt and allow to simmer for a few minutes. Leave the sauce and puddings to cool.

3 Carefully remove the puddings from their molds, using a knife to ease them away from the sides. Transfer the puddings to a large plastic food storage bag and freeze. Pour the sauce into a small plastic container, cover, and freeze.

4 To serve, defrost the sauce and puddings overnight in the refrigerator. Place the puddings on a baking sheet and reheat in a preheated 350°F (180°C) oven for 15–20 minutes. Warm the sauce in a pan until gently bubbling. Serve the warm puddings with the hot toffee sauce and a drizzle of half-and-half, if desired.

Mini summer puddings

PREP 30 MINS COOK 10 MINS

MAKES 6

about 9 slices firm white bread, crusts removed
1½lb (675g) mixed summer berries and currants
⅓ cup granulated sugar, or to taste
confectioners' (powdered) sugar, for dusting

1 Line six 1-cup pudding basins or ramekins with the bread. You will probably find you need two halves to line the sides, a quarter to fit the base, and—once you have added the fruit—another quarter or two to cover the top. Make sure the basins are well lined—you don't want any gaps or the puddings could collapse when you turn them out.

2 Put the fruit in a saucepan with the sugar and 1 cup water. Bring to a boil, stirring until the sugar dissolves. Simmer gently for 5 minutes or until the berries start to soften and release their juices. Test for sweetness and add a little more sugar if needed. Spoon some of the juices into the basins to moisten the bread. Divide the berries evenly among the basins, pushing them down to pack in as many as possible and letting the bread absorb the juice—you do not

want any white bread showing when you turn out the puddings. Cover the tops of the berries with the remaining bread, then spoon over the remaining juices until no white bread is visible. Leave to cool. Cover each basin tightly with plastic wrap and freeze.

3 To serve, defrost overnight in the refrigerator or for a few hours at room temperature. Invert onto serving plates. Just before serving, dust with confectioners' sugar.

VARIATION
For richer puddings, use brioche instead of plain white bread.

COOK'S NOTES
The amount of fruit needed will depend upon the size of the berries you use and how juicy they are. Just remember to pack in as many berries as you can so the puddings do not collapse later. Enjoy leftover berries with some Greek yogurt as the cook's perk.

Cheat...
Use a store-bought toffee sauce, warming it just before serving.

FOOD FOR FRIENDS

Blackberry and apple cake

PREP 20 MINS   COOK 45 MINS

Special equipment • electric mixer

SERVES 6

- 8 tbsp butter, at room temperature
- ⅔ cup plus 2 tbsp granulated sugar
- 2 large eggs
- 1½ cups self-rising flour, sifted
- 2 Bramley or Granny Smith apples, peeled, cored, and coarsely chopped
- 9oz (250g) blackberries
- confectioners' (powdered) sugar, for dusting

1 Preheat the oven to 350°F (180°C). In a bowl, combine the butter and ⅔ cup sugar. Beat with an electric mixer until pale and creamy. Beat in the eggs one at a time, adding 1 tablespoon of the flour after each egg. Mix in the remaining flour and set aside. Put the apples and blackberries in a 1-quart (1.2-liter) baking dish, then stir in the remaining 2 tablespoons sugar and 2 tablespoons cold water. Spoon the mixture over the top of the fruit and smooth.

2 Bake for 45 minutes or until golden brown and firm to the touch—a skewer inserted into the center should come out clean, or with only moist fruit. Leave to cool completely, then wrap in foil and freeze.

3 To serve, defrost in the refrigerator overnight, then warm through in a preheated 350°F (180°C) oven for about 30 minutes or until hot. Dust with confectioners' sugar.

VARIATION

Replace ¼ cup of the flour with unsweetened cocoa powder and use canned pears as your fruit.

Apple tart

PREP 10 MINS   COOK 30 MINS

SERVES 6

- 1 sheet prepared dough for an 8–9in (20–23cm) pie
- flour, for dusting
- 4 Bramley or Granny Smith apples, peeled, cored, and thinly sliced
- 2–3 tbsp granulated sugar
- 1 tbsp butter, cut into bits

1 Preheat the oven to 425°F (220°C). On a lightly floured surface, roll out the dough as thinly as possible. Use the dough to line an 8in (20cm) round tart pan with a removable bottom, folding in the edges to create a double-thickness of dough around the tart, then trimming off any excess neatly. Prick the base all over with a fork. Line the tart shell with parchment paper and pie weights or dry beans, then bake for 10 minutes or until lightly colored. Remove the weights and parchment and allow the tart shell to cool. Leave the oven on.

2 Arrange the apple slices in the tart shell in a neat, overlapping design. Sprinkle with the sugar and dot with the butter. Bake for 12–15 minutes or until the apples begin to caramelize and the pastry is golden. Leave to cool. Wrap the tart in plastic wrap and then in foil, and freeze.

3 To serve, defrost overnight in the fridge. Remove the tart ring and serve at room temperature.

COOK'S NOTES

To serve the tart warm, defrost as directed above, then heat in a preheated 375°F (190°C) oven for 15–20 minutes.

Bread and butter pudding

PREP 10 MINS · COOK 35 MINS

SERVES 4-6

2 tbsp butter, at room temperature
4 thick slices firm-textured white
    bread, challah, or brioche
4 tbsp thick-cut Seville orange
    marmalade, chopped if pieces
    are large
1 large egg
1¼ cups whole milk
2 tbsp granulated sugar
1 tsp ground ginger

1 Spread the butter evenly over each slice of bread, then spread with the marmalade. Cut each slice into 4 triangles. Arrange in a lightly buttered 1-quart (1.2-liter) dish. In a bowl, lightly beat the egg into the milk, then beat in the sugar and ginger. Pour the mixture over the bread and let stand for 30 minutes.

2 Preheat the oven to 350°F (180°C). Bake for 35 minutes or until the custard is set and the top is golden brown. Leave to cool completely, then wrap in foil and freeze.

3 To serve, defrost in the refrigerator overnight. Bake uncovered in a preheated 350°F (180°C) oven for 30 minutes, until heated through.

VARIATION
For a more traditional bread pudding, omit the marmalade and ginger.

Cherry crumble

PREP 15 MINS · COOK 35 MINS

SERVES 6

8 tbsp butter, cut into
    ½in (1cm) cubes
1¼ cups all-purpose flour
1 cup ground almonds
¼ cup granulated sugar

For the filling
1¼lb (550g) ripe cherries, pitted
2 tbsp granulated sugar
2 tbsp apple juice

1 Preheat the oven to 350°F (180°C). In a bowl, rub the butter into the flour and ground almonds with your fingertips until the mixture resembles coarse bread crumbs. Stir in the sugar. Place the cherries in a 1½-quart (2-liter) dish and sprinkle with the sugar and apple juice. Scatter the crumble mixture over the top. Bake for 30-35 minutes or until golden brown. Allow the crumble to cool completely, then wrap in foil and freeze.

2 To serve, defrost in the refrigerator overnight. Reheat uncovered in a preheated 350°F (180°C) oven for 25 minutes or until bubbly-hot.

VARIATION
Instead of cherries, use the same quantity of chopped apples, soft stone fruit, or berries.

Cheat...
Use three 15oz (425g) cans of cherries, or 1lb frozen pitted cherries, thawed.

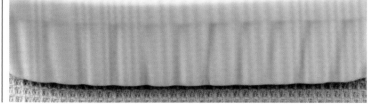

Chocolate orange profiteroles

 PREP 20 MINS   COOK 40 MINS   ❄

Special equipment • electric mixer

SERVES 6

4 tbsp butter, plus extra for greasing
1 cup all-purpose flour
2 large eggs, lightly beaten

For the chocolate sauce

5½oz (150g) semisweet chocolate,
   broken into small pieces
1¼ cups half-and-half
2 tbsp Lyle's Golden Syrup or
   light corn syrup
1 tbsp Grand Marnier or
   orange liqueur

For the filling

2 cups heavy whipping cream
finely grated zest of 1 large orange
2 tbsp Grand Marnier or
   orange liqueur

1 Preheat the oven to 425°F (220°C). Lightly grease two baking sheets with butter. In a saucepan, melt the butter in 1⅓ cups water, then bring to a boil. As soon as the mixture comes to a boil, remove from the heat and add all of the flour at once. Beat vigorously with a wooden spoon until the mixture is thick and glossy. Gradually beat in the eggs a little at a time until the mixture is smooth, thick, and shiny.

2 Spoon the mixture into 12 equal balls, spacing them well apart on the baking sheets. Bake for 10–15 minutes or until puffed, then, without opening the oven door, reduce the heat to 375°F (190°C) and bake for another 20 minutes or until crisp and golden brown. Remove from the oven. Use a knife to make a slit in the side of each puff to allow steam to escape. Return puffs to the oven for 2–3 minutes so the centers dry. Transfer to a wire rack to cool completely.

3 To make the chocolate sauce, combine the chocolate, half-and-half, syrup, and Grand Marnier in a small saucepan. Cook over low heat, stirring to blend, until the chocolate is melted and smooth. Leave to cool, then transfer to a plastic container, cover, and freeze. To make the filling, combine the cream, orange zest, and Grand Marnier in a large bowl. Beat with an electric mixer just until stiff peaks form. To fill the puffs with whipped cream, use a pastry bag fitted with a plain tip; insert the tip through the slit made in Step 2. Wrap the puffs in foil and freeze. To serve, defrost the puffs and sauce overnight in the refrigerator. Warm the sauce over low heat, then spoon the sauce over the cold profiteroles.

Pineapple upside-down cake

 PREP 10 MINS   COOK 50 MINS   ❄

Special equipment • electric mixer

SERVES 4–6

2–3 tbsp Lyle's Golden Syrup or light
   corn syrup
1 x 14oz (400ml) can pineapple rings
   in juice, drained
10 tbsp butter, at room temperature
⅔ cup granulated sugar
2 large eggs
1½ cups self-rising flour, sifted
3–4 tbsp whole milk

1 Preheat the oven to 350°F (180°C). Grease a round shallow 1-quart (1.2-liter) baking dish. Drizzle syrup to cover the bottom, then top with a layer of pineapple rings and set aside.

2 Place the butter and sugar in a bowl, then beat with an electric mixer until pale and creamy. Mix in the eggs one at a time, adding a little of the flour after each one. Fold in the remaining flour, then add the milk a little at a time until the mixture drops easily off the spatula. Pour evenly over the pineapple slices and bake for 25–30 minutes, or until the top is golden brown. Leave to cool completely in the dish, wrap in plastic wrap and then foil, and freeze.

3 To serve, defrost overnight in the refrigerator. Reheat in a 350°F (180°C) oven for 20 minutes. Cool for 10–15 minutes, then invert on a plate.

 VARIATION Replace the syrup with brown sugar and add a candied cherry to the center of each pineapple ring.

Classic treacle tart

PREP 20 MINS · COOK 35 MINS · ❄

SERVES 6

1¾ cups all-purpose flour,
   plus extra for dusting
5 tbsp cold butter, cut into
   ½in (1cm) dice
sea salt

For the filling
2 tbsp butter
3–4 slices firm white bread, made
   into coarse bread crumbs
3–4 tbsp Lyle's Golden Syrup
   or light corn syrup

1 Preheat the oven to 400°F (200°C). Make the pastry by placing the flour and butter in a bowl with a pinch of salt. Using your fingertips, rub the flour into the butter until the mixture resembles coarse crumbs. Add a few drops of iced water, then pull the pastry together until it comes away from the edge of the bowl. Transfer to a lightly floured surface and roll into a ball. Flatten slightly, wrap in plastic, and refrigerate for 20 minutes.

2 Roll the pastry into a thin circle large enough to line an 8in (20cm) round tart pan with a removable bottom. Trim off any excess dough with a knife and prick the base all over with a fork. Line the pastry shell with parchment paper, then fill with pie weights or dry beans. Bake in the oven for 15 minutes, until very lightly golden. Remove the weights and the parchment, then put the tart shell back into the oven for a few minutes to lightly brown the base. Set aside while you make the filling. Reduce the oven temperature to 375°F (190°C).

3 Combine the butter and bread crumbs in a bowl and mix with a fork until well blended. Add the syrup and stir until the mixture is smooth but still quite stiff. Spoon into the pastry shell and level the top. Bake in the oven for 10–15 minutes or until golden and set. Do not overcook or the filling will become brittle. Leave to cool, then wrap in parchment paper followed by plastic wrap and freeze.

4 To serve, defrost overnight in the refrigerator. Serve at room temperature or reheat in a preheated to 350°F (180°C) for 15–25 minutes, or until warmed through.

VARIATION
Give the tart some extra tang by adding the finely grated zest of 1 lemon.

Lemony pudding cake

PREP 15 MINS · COOK 25 MINS · ❄

Special equipment • electric mixer

SERVES 4

5 tbsp butter, at room temperature
1 cup granulated sugar
finely grated zest of 2 lemons
finely grated zest of 1 orange
3 large eggs, separated
¾ cup all-purpose flour
1 cup whole milk
juice of 2 lemons
2 tbsp prepared lemon curd

1 Preheat the oven to 350°F (180°C). Combine the butter and sugar in a bowl and beat with an electric mixer until light and creamy. Beat in the lemon zest, orange zest, and egg yolks to blend well. On low speed, beat in half of the flour and half of the milk until blended, then beat in the remaining flour and milk. Stir in lemon juice and set aside.

2 In another bowl, use the mixer fitted with clean beaters to beat the egg whites until soft peaks form, then fold into the batter. Spread the lemon curd over the bottom of a buttered 1-quart (1.2-liter) ovenproof, freezer-safe dish, then pour in the batter. Place the dish in a pan and add warm water to fill halfway up the sides. Bake for 25 minutes or until golden. Remove from the pan and let cool. Wrap in plastic wrap and then foil and freeze.

3 To serve, defrost overnight in the refrigerator. Bake uncovered in a preheated 325°F (160°C) oven for 25 minutes or until warmed through. Serve slightly warm.

VARIATION
For a zesty twist, use orange curd instead of lemon curd.

COOK'S NOTES
If the top starts to brown before the cake is warmed through, cover loosely with foil. To test if the cake is ready to serve, insert a metal skewer into the center, then remove and check if it feels hot.

Chocolate steamed pudding

PREP 15 MINS · **COOK 6 MINS** · ❄

Special equipment • electric mixer

SERVES 4

8 tbsp butter
⅔ cup granulated sugar
3 large eggs
¾ cup all-purpose flour
2 tbsp unsweetened cocoa powder
2 tsp baking powder
¼ cup ground almonds

For the chocolate sauce

4 tbsp butter
4½oz (125g) semisweet chocolate, broken into pieces
2–3 tbsp heavy whipping cream

1 Melt the butter in a microwave-safe container or in a saucepan and set aside to cool slightly. Combine the sugar and eggs in a bowl and beat with an electric mixer until pale and creamy. Sift in the flour, cocoa powder, and baking powder, then add the almonds and melted butter. Beat well until light and fluffy.

2 Scrape the mixture into a 1-quart (1.2-liter) microwave-safe, freezer-safe pudding basin or bowl. Cover and microwave on high for 5–6 minutes.

Leave the pudding to cool, then double-wrap with plastic and freeze.

3 Make the chocolate sauce by melting the butter and chocolate together in a saucepan over low heat. Stir in the cream to thicken. Leave to cool, then transfer to an airtight container and freeze.

4 To serve, defrost the pudding and sauce in the refrigerator overnight. Reheat the pudding in the microwave on high for 5–6 minutes or until piping hot. Reheat the sauce in the microwave, stirring every 30 seconds, until melted and smooth, then pour over the pudding and serve.

Cheat...
Use a store-bought chocolate sauce and warm it thoroughly just before serving.

Chocolate biscuit cake

PREP 10 MINS · ❄

SERVES 6

12 tbsp butter, cut into pieces
9oz (250g) semisweet chocolate, broken into pieces
2 tbsp Lyle's Golden Syrup or light corn syrup
1lb (450g) digestive or sweetmeal biscuits, coarsely crushed
handful of plump golden raisins
handful of natural almonds, coarsely chopped

1 Lightly grease an 8in (20cm) square baking pan. In a large saucepan, combine the butter, chocolate, and syrup. Cook over low heat, stirring, for 5–10 minutes, or until melted and smooth. Remove from the heat and stir in the biscuits, raisins, and almonds. Mix well, then press the mixture into the pan with the back of a spoon. Refrigerate to cool completely, then wrap in plastic wrap and freeze.

VARIATION

Vary the fruit and nuts to your taste—a handful of chopped cherries and hazelnuts works well, for instance.

COOK'S NOTES

To crush the digestive biscuits, put them in a plastic bag and bash with a rolling pin. Don't break them up too finely, though—you want the cake to have plenty of texture.

Classic apple crumble

 PREP 15 MINS   COOK 30 MINS ❄

SERVES 4

3 large Granny Smith or Bramley apples, peeled, cored, and coarsely chopped

4–6 tbsp granulated sugar, depending upon the tartness of the apples

For the crumble topping

4 tbsp cold butter, cut into small cubes

1¼ cups all-purpose flour

⅔ cup light brown sugar (packed) or granulated sugar

1 Preheat the oven to 375°F (190°C). Place the apples in a saucepan with the granulated sugar and 2–3 tbsp of water. Cook over low heat, stirring frequently, until the apples are tender but still hold their shape. Spoon the mixture into a 1-quart (1.2-liter) ovenproof, freezer-safe dish.

2 To make the topping, combine the butter and flour in a bowl. Using your fingertips, rub the flour into the butter until the mixture resembles coarse bread crumbs. Rub in the sugar in the same manner. Sprinkle over the apple

mixture, then bake for 30 minutes, or until the topping is barely golden. Leave to cool completely, wrap in plastic wrap and then foil, and freeze.

3 To serve, defrost in the refrigerator overnight. Uncover and bake in a preheated 350°F (180°C) oven for 30 minutes, or until the top is golden brown and the filling is bubbly-hot.

 VARIATION
Add a few blackberries or blueberries to the apples toward the end of the cooking time in Step 1.

Cheat...
A 12–14oz (400g) can of prepared apple pie filling can be your secret ingredient for an easy version of this dessert.

Apple and blackberry brown betty

PREP 15 MINS COOK 30 MINS ❄

SERVES 4

1½ cups fine dry bread crumbs

2 tbsp butter, at room temperature

finely grated zest of 1 lemon

3 Granny Smith or Bramley apples, peeled, cored, and sliced

1 cup blackberries

⅔ cup fresh orange juice

2–3 tbsp granulated sugar (depending on the tartness of the fruit)

1 Preheat the oven to 375°F (190°C). In a bowl, mix the bread crumbs with the butter and lemon zest and set aside. Place the apples in a greased 1-quart (1.2-liter) ovenproof, freezer-safe dish, then stir in the blackberries, orange juice, and enough of the sugar to sweeten as needed. Sprinkle the bread crumbs on top and bake for 30 minutes or until lightly golden. Allow to cool completely. Cover with plastic wrap and then foil and freeze.

2 To serve, defrost overnight in the refrigerator. Bake uncovered in a preheated 350°F (180°C) oven for 30 minutes, or until golden brown on top and bubbling hot.

Sticky pecan tart

PREP 15 MINS · COOK 1 HR

SERVES 6

1 sheet prepared dough for an 8–9in (20–23cm) pie
8 tbsp butter
2 tbsp Lyle's Golden Syrup or light corn syrup
⅓ cup light brown sugar (packed)
⅓ cup dark brown sugar (packed)
2½ cups pecan halves and pieces
2 large eggs, lightly beaten

1 Preheat the oven to 400°F (200°C). Line an 8in (20cm) round tart pan with a removable bottom with the dough, trimming off any excess with a knife. Transfer to the refrigerator to rest for 10 minutes. Prick the base all over with a fork. Line the tart shell with parchment paper and pie weights or dry beans and bake for 15 minutes, until barely golden. Remove the pie weights and parchment and return the tart shell to the oven for 5 minutes to lightly bake the bottom.

2 Reduce the oven temperature to 325°F (160°C). Melt the butter and syrup in a saucepan, then remove from the heat and stir in the brown sugars and pecans and allow to cool. Stir in the eggs. Scrape the mixture into the tart shell. Bake for 30–40 minutes or until the shell is crisp and golden and the filling is set. Cool, then double-wrap in plastic and freeze.

3 To serve, defrost overnight in the refrigerator. Remove the tart ring and serve at room temperature, or reheat in a preheated 325°F (160°C) oven for 20 minutes. Let cool 5–10 minutes.

VARIATION Substitute walnuts or coarsely chopped Brazil nuts for the pecans.

Cheat...
Replace the butter, syrup, and brown sugars with a 12oz (350g) jar of caramel. Shorten your baking time to 20–30 minutes.

Pear and cinnamon strudel

PREP 10 MINS · COOK 40 MINS

SERVES 4

4 firm but ripe pears, peeled, cored, and sliced
1 tsp ground cinnamon
handful of dark raisins
1–2 tbsp granulated sugar
15 sheets of filo pastry dough
1–2 tbsp butter, melted

1 Line a baking sheet with parchment paper. Combine the pears, cinnamon, raisins, and sugar in a bowl, mix well, then set aside. Brushing the sheets of filo with a little melted butter as you work, layer 3 pastry sheets onto the baking sheet, then layer another 3 next to them, overlapping slightly.

2 Place another buttered layer of 3 sheets on top of them, with the long edges facing opposite, to form a cross. Repeat with another buttered layer of 3, overlapping slightly. The horizontal sheets should still show at the edges. Spoon the filling down the center, then fold in the edges. Top with a final layer of 3 buttered filo sheets and brush butter over all. Double-wrap in plastic wrap and freeze.

3 To serve, defrost in the refrigerator overnight. Brush with more melted butter and bake in a preheated 375°F (190°C) oven for 30–40 minutes.

VARIATION Use apples instead of pears.

COOK'S NOTES
Check the strudel halfway through cooking; if the filo has begun to brown too quickly, cover with foil.

FOOD FOR FRIENDS

INDULGENT DESSERTS

Quick, but still rich and delicious.

Chocolate Amaretti roulade

PREP 30 MINS **COOK 20 MINS**

Cooling • 30 minutes

Special equipment • electric mixer • 13 x 9in (33 x 23cm) jelly roll pan

SERVES 8

6 large eggs, separated
¾ cup granulated sugar
½ cup unsweetened cocoa powder
confectioners' (powdered) sugar,
    for dusting
1 cup heavy whipping cream
2–3 tbsp Amaretto or brandy
20 Amaretti cookies, crushed,
    plus 2 extra
1¾oz (50g) semisweet chocolate

1 Preheat the oven to 350°F (180°C). Line a 13 x 9in (33 x 23cm) jelly roll pan with parchment paper. Combine the egg yolks and sugar in a large heatproof bowl set over a pan of simmering water and beat with an electric mixer until pale, thick, and creamy, about 10 minutes. Remove from the heat. Put the egg whites in a mixing bowl and beat with an electric mixer until soft peaks form.

2 Sift the cocoa powder into the egg yolk mixture and gently fold in along with the egg whites. Scrape the batter into the pan. Bake for 20 minutes or

until just firm to the touch. Loosen the edges with a knife and invert onto a sheet of parchment paper dusted with confectioners' sugar. Remove the pan, leaving the top parchment in place. Cool for 30 minutes.

3 Put the cream in a bowl and beat with an electric mixer until soft peaks form. Peel off the top parchment from the cake and trim away any ragged edges. Drizzle the Amaretto or brandy over the surface of the cake, then spread with the cream, sprinkle with the crushed Amaretti cookies, and grate most of the chocolate over the top.

4 Starting from one of the short sides, roll the cake into a long cylinder, using the parchment to help keep it tightly together. Discard the parchment and place the roulade seam-side down on a plate. Crumble the extra cookies over the top, grate the remaining chocolate over them, and dust with confectioners' sugar.

VARIATION Mix the cream with 2–3 tablespoons of sweetened chestnut purée instead of the amaretti cookies.

Lemon tart with almond pastry

PREP 20 MINS **COOK 55 MINS**

Chilling • 30 minutes

Special equipment • electric mixer • 8in (20cm) tart pan • pie weights or dry beans

SERVES 8

9 tbsp cold butter, cut into small cubes
1½ cups all-purpose flour
½ cup ground almonds
finely grated zest of 2 lemons
⅓ cup fresh lemon juice (from
    2–3 lemons)
6 tbsp granulated sugar
3 large eggs
¾ cup heavy whipping cream

1 Combine the butter and flour in a bowl and rub together with your fingertips until the mixture resembles coarse bread crumbs. Alternatively, pulse on and off in a food processor. Add the almonds, then stir in just enough ice water to form a dough. Roll out the pastry on a floured work surface and use to line an 8in (20cm) tart pan with a removable bottom. Trim off any excess around the edges, then chill for at least 30 minutes.

2 Preheat the oven to 400°F (200°C). Line the pastry shell with parchment paper and fill with pie weights or dry beans. Bake for 15 minutes, remove the paper and beans, and return to the oven for another 5 minutes or until the pastry is cooked through. Set aside and turn the oven down to 300°F (150°C).

3 Combine the lemon juice and sugar in a bowl and stir until the sugar has dissolved. Mix in the eggs and lemon zest. Stir in the cream until well blended, then pour into the tart shell. Bake for 35 minutes or until just set– the tart should wobble in the middle slightly when you shake the pan. Cool, then refrigerate until ready to serve. Serve plain or with whipped cream.

Cheat...
Use an 8in (20cm) store-bought tart shell or pie crust instead of making the almond pastry.

Baked chocolate mousse

PREP 20 MINS | **COOK 1 HR**

Special equipment • electric mixer • 9in (23cm) springform pan with a removable bottom

SERVES 8–12

18 tbsp unsalted butter, cubed

12oz (350g) bittersweet or semisweet chocolate, broken into pieces

1½ cups light brown sugar (packed)

5 large eggs, separated

pinch of salt

unsweetened cocoa powder or confectioners' (powdered) sugar

1 Preheat the oven to 350°F (180°C). Line a 9in (23cm) springform pan with a removable bottom with parchment paper. In a heatproof bowl set over a pan of simmering water, combine the butter and chocolate. Warm over low heat, stirring, until melted and smooth. Remove the bowl from the pan and allow to cool slightly; then stir in the sugar, followed by the egg yolks, one at a time, until blended.

2 Put the egg whites in a mixing bowl with a pinch of salt and beat with an electric mixer until soft peaks form. Gradually fold into the chocolate mixture, then pour into the prepared cake pan. Bake for 45 minutes to 1 hour, or until the edges appear set but the center still wobbles slightly. Leave to cool completely, then loosen the edges with a knife and release the springform. Dust with cocoa powder or confectioners' sugar before serving.

COOK'S NOTES

Be careful not to overcook the mousse. If the center is still wobbly when you take it out of the oven, it will be deliciously gooey in the middle.

Espresso crème brûlée

PREP 15 MINS | **COOK 1 HR**

Chilling • overnight

Special equipment • electric mixer

SERVES 6

5 large egg yolks

9 tbsp granulated sugar

2 cups heavy whipping cream

½ cup whole milk

3 tbsp brewed espresso or strong coffee

1 vanilla bean, split lengthwise and seeds scraped out, or 1 tsp vanilla extract

1 Preheat the oven to 325°F (160°C). Put the egg yolks in a bowl with 3 tablespoons of the sugar and beat with an electric mixer until light. Combine the cream, milk, espresso, and the vanilla bean and seeds in a saucepan. Cook over medium heat just until bubbles appear around the edges; do not boil. Gradually whisk the hot cream mixture into the egg yolk mixture in a steady stream.

Strain through a fine sieve and divide among six 6oz (175ml) ramekins.

2 Place them in a pan and add hot water to come halfway up their sides. Cover loosely with parchment paper and aluminum foil. Bake for 50 minutes– 1 hour, until just set. Remove from the water bath, cool, then cover and refrigerate overnight. A few hours before serving, pat the top of each custard with a paper towel to absorb moisture. Sprinkle 1 tbsp of the sugar over each custard, then place under the broiler, or use a cook's blowtorch until the sugar caramelizes and turns golden. Let stand until the sugar is hardened, 3–5 minutes. Serve at once.

VARIATION

For a more traditional flavor, omit the espresso and use 2 vanilla beans.

Blueberry-ripple cheesecake

PREP 20 MINS · **COOK 40 MINS**

Special equipment • 8in (20cm) deep loose-bottomed cake pan • food processor

SERVES 8
4½oz (125g) British HobNobs, digestive biscuits, or sweetmeal biscuits
4 tbsp butter
1 cup blueberries
¾ cup granulated sugar, plus 3 tbsp
12oz (350g) cream cheese, cut into pieces
1 cup mascarpone cheese
2 large eggs, plus 1 large egg yolk
½ tsp vanilla extract
2 tbsp all-purpose flour

1 Preheat the oven to 350°F (180°C). Grease the cake pan. Put the biscuits in a plastic bag and crush with a rolling pin. Melt the butter in a saucepan, then add the biscuit crumbs and stir until moistened. Press an even layer of crumbs in the bottom of the pan.

2 Combine the blueberries and the 3 tbsp sugar in a food processor and process until smooth, then push the mixture through a fine sieve into a

small saucepan. Bring to a boil, then allow to bubble for 3-5 minutes or until thickened and jam-like. Set aside. Rinse the bowl of the food processor.

3 Combine the ¾ cup sugar, cream cheese, mascarpone, eggs and extra yolk, vanilla, and flour in the food processor and blend well. Pour the mixture on to the crumb crust and smooth the top. With a teaspoon, carefully drizzle the blueberry mixture over the cream cheese mixture, swirling to make a decorative pattern. Bake for 40 minutes or until it has set but still has a slight wobble in the middle when you shake the pan. Leave to cool in the oven for 1 hour, then cool completely in the refrigerator and serve.

Cheat...
Instead of making the blueberry topping, spoon a blueberry compote over each serving.

Caramel banana tart

PREP 15 MINS · **COOK 35 MINS**

Special equipment • 8in (20cm) tart dish or pan (not loose-bottomed)

SERVES 6
5 tbsp butter, cut into pieces
⅔ cup light corn syrup
4 firm-but-ripe medium bananas
all-purpose flour for dusting
half of a 17.3oz (425g) box frozen puff pastry sheets (1 sheet), thawed as package directs

1 Preheat the oven to 400°F (200°C). Combine the butter and syrup in a small, heavy saucepan. Cook over medium-low heat until the butter has melted and the mixture is smooth, then allow to bubble for 1 minute. Pour into an 8in (20cm) round ceramic tart dish or pan (not loose-bottomed), turning the dish to coat the bottom evenly. Peel the bananas and cut into slices ½in (1cm) thick, then arrange them neatly on top of the syrup mixture— this will be the top of the tart when it's

turned out. Place the dish on a baking sheet and bake for 10 minutes.

2 Meanwhile, on a lightly floured work surface, roll the pastry into a circle about 9in (23cm) in diameter and ¼in (5mm) thick. Trim off any excess pastry.

3 Carefully remove the tart from the oven and place the pastry circle on top. Use the handle of a knife to tuck the edge down into the pan. Bake the tart for another 20-25 minutes or until the pastry is golden brown. Let stand for 5-10 minutes, then place a serving plate on top and invert the tart onto the plate. Cut into wedges and serve with vanilla ice cream.

COOK'S NOTES
The caramel gets very hot. Take great care not to touch it when you're topping the bananas with the pastry or inverting the tart.

Melting-middle chocolate fudge puddings

PREP 15 MINS • COOK 12 MINS

Special equipment • 4 x 8oz (200ml) ramekins

SERVES 4

3½oz (100g) semisweet chocolate, chopped
8 tbsp butter, cut into pieces
¾ cup light brown sugar
3 large eggs
½ tsp vanilla extract
½ cup all-purpose flour
whipped cream, for serving

1 Preheat the oven to 400°F (200°C). Butter four 8oz (200ml) ramekins well and place on a baking sheet. Combine the chocolate and butter in a large heatproof bowl set over a pan of very hot water and stir until smooth, then set aside to cool for 15 minutes.

2 Mix in the sugar, then the eggs, one at a time, followed by the vanilla extract, and finally the flour. Divide the mixture evenly among the ramekins. Bake for 10–12 minutes or until the edges are set and the tops are firm to the touch, but the middles are still soft. Carefully run a knife around the edge of each pudding, then invert onto individual serving plates and serve with whipped cream.

Cheat...
Assemble these the day before, cover, and refrigerate until ready to bake.

COOK'S NOTES
Don't overcook the puddings or the middles will be cakey rather than gooey.

Pavlovas with spiced berries

PREP 30 MINS • COOK 1½ HRS

Special equipment • electric mixer

SERVES 6

3 large egg whites
pinch of sea salt
1 cup granulated sugar
¾ cup confectioners' sugar
1½ tsp ground cinnamon
1lb (450g) package frozen mixed berries, thawed
3 tbsp port wine
½ tsp pumpkin pie spice blend
finely grated zest of 1 orange
1 cup heavy whipping cream

1 Preheat the oven to 250°F (130°C). Line a baking sheet with parchment paper. Put the egg whites in a bowl with a pinch of salt and whisk with an electric mixer until stiff peaks form. Beat in ½ cup of granulated sugar, 1 tbsp at a time, and continue beating until the mixture is stiff and shiny.

2 Sift in the confectioners' sugar and 1 tsp of the cinnamon, and fold them in with a large metal spoon. Spoon the mixture onto the baking sheet in 6 heaps, spreading each one out to make a round about 4in (10cm) in diameter. Use the back of a spoon to make a small hollow in the center of each one. Bake for 1½ hours or until crisp and easy to peel away from the parchment paper. Remove from the oven and leave to cool on a wire rack for 30 minutes.

3 Meanwhile, put half the berries and any juices from them in a pan with the port, the remaining ½ cup sugar, the pumpkin pie spice, orange zest, and ½ tsp cinnamon. Cook until the sugar has dissolved and the mixture comes to a boil. Reduce the heat and simmer gently for 5 minutes, then stir in the remaining berries, remove from the heat, and leave to cool completely.

4 Put the cream in a mixing bowl and beat with an electric mixer until soft peaks form. Place the pavlovas on individual serving plates and divide the cream among them. Spoon the spiced berries over each and serve.

VARIATION If preparing this in the summer months, use seasonal fresh berries.

Honeycomb parfait

PREP 20 MINS · **COOK 10 MINS** · ❄

Special equipment • electric hand mixer • 8in (20cm) square cake pan

SERVES 12–16

vegetable oil

2 tbsp Lyle's Golden Syrup or light corn syrup

5 tbsp granulated sugar

1 tsp baking soda

2 cups heavy whipping cream

1 x 14oz (400g) can sweetened condensed milk

1 To make the honeycomb, grease a baking sheet with vegetable oil. Combine the syrup and sugar in a saucepan and heat until melted and smooth, then let bubble until it is a deep caramel color. Remove from the heat and stir in the baking soda (it will puff up). Scrape the fluffy mixture onto the baking sheet in one mound–do not deflate it by spreading. Let sit for 30 minutes or until cool. When cold, break up into bite-sized chunks.

2 Put the cream in a mixing bowl and beat with an electric mixer until soft peaks form. Beat in the condensed milk until well blended. Stir in the honeycomb chunks, then pour into the cake pan lined with plastic wrap, smoothing the mixture into the corners. Cover with plastic wrap and freeze overnight until firm.

3 Remove the parfait from the freezer 15 minutes before serving to allow it to soften. To serve, scoop into parfait glasses or wine goblets.

VARIATION

The basic cream mixture is a good base for all sorts of flavorings. Try it with chopped praline, a fruit coulis, or even chocolate chips.

Cheat...
Instead of making honeycomb, mix in 2 chocolate honeycomb bars, broken into bite-sized pieces.

Prune and brandy tart

PREP 15 MINS · ■

Special equipment • 8in (20cm) deep loose-bottomed tart pan • pie weights or dry beans

SERVES 8

3 tbsp brandy

1 cup pitted prunes

1 sheet prepared dough (preferably all-butter) for an 8in (20cm) pie

all-purpose flour, for dusting

5 large egg yolks

¼ cup granulated sugar

1 cup heavy whipping cream

½ tsp vanilla extract

generous grating of fresh nutmeg

confectioners' sugar, for dusting

1 Preheat the oven to 400°F (200°C). In a small bowl, sprinkle the brandy over the prunes and set aside. Roll the pastry out on a lightly floured work surface and use to line the tart pan. Trim off any excess around the edges, then line the pastry with parchment paper and pie weights or dry beans. Bake for 20 minutes, then remove the parchment and beans and return to the oven for 5 minutes to crisp. Set aside while you make the filling. Reduce the oven temperature to 300°F (150°C).

2 Put the egg yolks and sugar in a mixing bowl and whisk together until well blended. Heat the cream, vanilla extract, and nutmeg in a pan until almost boiling, then very gradually whisk into the egg yolk mixture. Strain through a fine sieve into the pastry case and scatter the prunes over the top. Bake for 40–45 minutes or until just set–the tart should wobble slightly in the center when you shake the pan. Remove from the oven and leave to cool, then chill until ready to serve. Dust with confectioners' sugar just before serving.

VARIATION

For a simple baked custard tart, omit the prunes.

Lemon and lime tart

PREP 1 HR • **COOK** 45 MINS

Special equipment • electric mixer • 8in (20cm) straight-sided round loose-bottomed tart pan • pie weights

SERVES 6

1 cup all-purpose flour, plus extra for dusting
½ cup confectioners' sugar
sea salt
6 tbsp cold butter, cut into small cubes
¼ cup unsweetened cocoa powder
3 large eggs
⅔ cup granulated sugar
1 cup heavy whipping cream
zest and juice of 1 lemon
zest and juice of 1 lime

1 Sift the flour and confectioners' sugar into a bowl with a pinch of salt. Add the butter and cocoa powder and rub together with your fingertips until the mixture resembles fine bread crumbs. Add 1–2 tbsp iced water, a little at a time, and gather the mixture together until it comes away from the sides of the bowl. Wrap in plastic wrap and refrigerate for 30 minutes.

2 Preheat the oven to 400°F (200°C). Roll out the pastry on a lightly floured work surface and use to line the tart pan. Trim away any excess. Line with parchment paper, then fill with pie weights. Bake for 15 minutes, then remove the weights and paper and set to one side. Reduce the oven temperature to 325°F (170°C).

3 Put the eggs and sugar in a mixing bowl and beat with an electric mixer until pale and creamy. Add the cream, the zest and juice of the lemon and the lime, and beat briefly to combine. Pour the mixture into the tart shell and smooth the top. Bake for 30–35 minutes or until set. Allow to cool to room temperature, then serve.

Chilled black cherry cheesecake

PREP 30 MINS

Special equipment • 8in (20cm) round springform cake pan • electric mixer

SERVES 6

6 tbsp butter
1 x 7oz (200g) package digestive or sweetmeal biscuits, crushed
1lb (450g) whole milk ricotta cheese
6 tbsp granulated sugar
grated zest and juice of 4 lemons
⅔ cup heavy whipping cream
3½ tsp unflavored gelatin
1 x 12–14oz (400g) can pitted dark sweet Bing cherries in syrup, or pitted dark tart cherries in light syrup

1 Grease and line the cake pan with parchment paper. Melt the butter in a saucepan, add the biscuits, and stir until moistened. Transfer the mixture to the pan, pressing it down with the back of a spoon so it's level.

2 Mix the ricotta, sugar, and lemon zest together in a bowl. Put the cream in a bowl and beat lightly with an electric mixer until soft peaks form. Add to the ricotta mixture and beat with a wooden spoon until well-combined.

3 Combine the lemon juice and gelatin in a small heatproof bowl, then place the bowl over a pan of simmering water and stir until the gelatin dissolves. Add to the ricotta mixture and fold in well. Pour the mixture on top of the crust, spreading it out evenly. Refrigerate for 2 hours or until set and firm.

4 Meanwhile, make the sauce. Drain the cherries, pouring the juice into a saucepan. Bring it to a boil, then allow to bubble for 10 minutes or until the juices have reduced by three-quarters. Leave to cool. Pile the cherries on top of the cheesecake, spoon on the sauce, and serve.

COOK'S NOTES

To crush the biscuits, put them in a plastic bag and smash with a rolling pin.

Mini-chocolate éclairs

Special equipment • electric mixer
• piping bag

MAKES 30

6 tbsp butter, cut into pieces
1½ cups all-purpose flour
3 large eggs, lightly beaten
2 cups heavy whipping cream
7oz (200g) semisweet chocolate

1 Preheat the oven to 400°F (200°C). Melt the butter in a saucepan with 2 cups cold water, then bring to a boil. As soon as the mixture reaches a boil, remove from the heat and add all the flour at once. Beat well with a wooden spoon until thick and glossy and comes away from the sides of the pan.

2 Using a wooden spoon, lightly beat in the eggs a little at a time, beating constantly until the mixture is smooth, thick, and shiny. Let cool for a few minutes, then transfer to a piping bag.

3 Pipe 2in (5cm) lengths of the mixture onto 2 baking sheets lined with parchment paper. You should have around 30 in all. Bake for 20 minutes or until golden brown, then remove from the oven and make a slit down the side in each one. Return to the oven for 5 minutes for the insides to cook through. Then remove and leave to cool.

4 Put the cream in a mixing bowl and beat with an electric mixer until soft peaks form. Spoon or pipe the whipped cream into each éclair. Break the chocolate into small pieces and place in a heatproof bowl. Place the bowl over a pan of simmering water and stir until the chocolate is just melted and smooth. Spoon over the éclairs and serve.

COOK'S NOTES

You can make these ahead of time. At the end of step 3, place the éclairs in an airtight container and store for up to 2 days, or freeze.

Raspberry crème brûlée

Setting • 2 hours
Special equipment • 6 ramekins
• electric mixer

MAKES 6

1 cup fresh raspberries
4 large egg yolks
8 tbsp granulated sugar
2¼ cups heavy whipping cream
1 tsp vanilla extract

1 Divide the raspberries among 6 ramekins. Put the egg yolks and 2 tablespoons of the sugar in a large bowl and beat with an electric mixer until the mixture begins to thicken and becomes pale and creamy.

2 Heat the cream gently in a saucepan for 5 minutes. Do not let it boil. Remove from the heat, stir in the vanilla, and let cool for 5 minutes.

3 Slowly add the warm cream to the egg mixture, beating constantly. When it's all incorporated, pour the mixture back into the pan, and cook over low heat for a couple of minutes, stirring all the time with a wooden spoon until thick. Do not let it boil. Strain the custard through a sieve and pour into the ramekins and let cool. Cover loosely and transfer to the refrigerator to set for 2–3 hours or overnight.

4 When ready to serve, use a paper towel to blot any excess moisture from the tops of the custards. Sprinkle the tops evenly with the remaining sugar and place under a hot broiler, watching carefully, until the sugar bubbles and turns golden brown. Allow the topping to harden for 20 minutes before serving.

VARIATION

Use ripe peaches or sweet cherries instead of the raspberries.

COOK'S NOTES

Add the cream to the eggs very slowly, otherwise it could curdle and become unusable.

White chocolate and raspberry trifle

PREP
25
MINS

Chilling • 30 minutes

SERVES 6-8
8-10oz (300g) plain sponge cake
1½lb (675g) fresh or frozen
   raspberries, thawed
1lb (450g) mascarpone cheese
1 cup heavy whipping cream
7oz (200g) white chocolate

1 Slice the cake into ¾in (2cm) slices and use to line the bottom and sides of one large glass serving bowl or 6-8 individual glass dishes. If using fresh raspberries, mash them lightly so they release some of their juices, then spoon half over the sponge cake. If using frozen, drain the fruit (reserving the juice), then spoon half over the cake together with 2 tablespoons of the juice. Place in the refrigerator for at least 15 minutes while the cake soaks up the juices.

2 Meanwhile, combine the mascarpone and cream in a mixing bowl and beat with a wooden spoon until well blended. Break three-quarters of the chocolate into small pieces and place in a small heatproof bowl. Place the bowl over a pan of simmering water and stir until the chocolate is just melted and smooth. Spoon half over the raspberries and mix half with the mascarpone and cream.

3 Add the rest of the cream mixture and the remaining raspberries to the trifle(s) in layers, ending with the cream topping. Grate the remaining chocolate over the top. Refrigerate for 15-30 minutes, then serve.

VARIATION
Use 2 cans of black cherries in syrup. Drain the fruit, reserving the syrup. Spoon 2 tablespoons of it over the cake.

COOK'S NOTES
Be careful when melting the white chocolate—don't let any hot water splash on it or it will separate and become unusable.

Crêpes with caramelized apples and chocolate

PREP
15
MINS
COOK
20
MINS

Special equipment • electric hand mixer

SERVES 4-6
½ cup all-purpose flour
1 large egg, lightly beaten
⅔ cup whole milk
⅔ cup heavy whipping cream
1 tbsp butter
2-3 tbsp granulated sugar, depending
   on the sweetness of the apples
4 Pink Lady or other pink-skinned
   eating apples, sliced
vegetable oil
4½oz (125g) semisweet chocolate,
   grated or shaved

1 Sift the flour into a mixing bowl with a pinch of salt and make a well in the center. Put the egg and a little of the milk in the well. Using a wooden spoon, gradually stir the egg mixture, letting a little of the flour fall in as you go and adding the rest of the milk a little a time. When it's all incorporated, beat the mixture with an electric mixer to remove any lumps. Transfer to the refrigerator to rest for 15 minutes.

2 Meanwhile, put the cream in a mixing bowl and beat with an electric mixer until lightly whipped, then set aside. Put the butter and sugar in a pan over low heat and stir until the sugar has dissolved. Add the apple slices and toss well to coat. Cook for 5-10 minutes or until the apples are caramelized, then set aside and keep warm.

3 Heat a crêpe pan or small frying pan over medium-high heat. When hot, add a tiny amount of vegetable oil, then swirl it around the pan and pour the excess into a heatproof liquid-measure cup. Add 2 tablespoons of batter to the pan and swirl it around so it covers the bottom. Loosen the edges of the crêpe with a spatula and cook for 1 minute or until golden. Flip the crêpe and cook the other side for 30 seconds, or until set. Slide the crêpe onto a plate and repeat until all the batter has been used.

4 To serve, pile some of the apple mixture onto each crêpe and top with a dollop of cream, then fold to enclose the filling and sprinkle with chocolate.

VARIATION
Use sliced bananas instead of the apples. If you're feeling particularly indulgent, serve ice cream on the side, as well!

Crème caramel

PREP 20 MINS · **COOK 1 HR**

Resting • 15 minutes
Special equipment • electric mixer

SERVES 6

1¼ cups granulated sugar
2 cups whole milk
1 vanilla bean
3 large eggs, plus 3 large egg yolks

1 Put half the sugar in a saucepan with 4 tablespoons of water. Simmer, swirling the pan, until you have a rich golden caramel. Divide the hot caramel among 6 ramekins.

2 Put the milk in a saucepan. Split the vanilla bean in half lengthwise and scrape out most of the seeds with a knife. Add the seeds and bean to the milk, along with the remaining sugar. Heat gently, stirring occasionally, but do not allow to boil. Put the eggs and the egg yolks in a bowl and whisk with an electric mixer until creamy. Slowly pour in the milk, whisking the whole time until the mixture begins to thicken. Remove the vanilla bean. Preheat the oven to 350°F (180°C). Place the ramekins in a roasting pan, then divide the custard among them and leave to rest for 15 minutes.

3 Pour cold water into the pan so that it comes two-thirds of the way up the sides of the ramekins. Carefully transfer to the oven and bake for 45 minutes–1 hour, until the custards are set. Remove and leave to cool, then refrigerate until ready to serve.

4 To serve, loosen the edges if necessary and turn out onto plates or small bowls, so the caramel sauce streams down over the custards.

Mixed berries with white chocolate sauce

PREP 5 MINS · **COOK 5 MINS**

SERVES 4

1lb (450g) package frozen mixed berries, such as raspberries, strawberries, and blackberries
4½oz (125g) best-quality white chocolate, chopped, plus extra to grate (optional)
⅔ cup heavy whipping cream

1 Divide the berries among 4 dessert bowls. Combine the chocolate and cream in a small heavy saucepan. Cook over very low heat, stirring constantly, just until melted and smooth. Do not let the mixture boil.

2 Pour the warm chocolate mixture over the frozen berries and serve topped with grated white chocolate, if you wish.

COOK'S NOTES

Drizzle in some of your favorite liquor, such as whiskey, to the melted chocolate.

Chocolate and buttercream Swiss roll

Special equipment • electric mixer
• 8 x 12in (20 x 30cm) jelly roll pan

SERVES 8

3 large eggs

6 tbsp granulated sugar

½ cup all-purpose flour

¼ cup unsweetened cocoa powder,
  plus extra for dusting

5 tbsp butter, at room temperature

1 cup confectioners' (powdered)
  sugar, sifted, plus extra for
  dusting (optional)

1 Preheat the oven to 400°F (200°C). Place a large bowl over a pan of hot water, add the eggs and sugar, and beat with an electric mixer for 5–10 minutes, until the mixture is thick and creamy. Sift in the flour and cocoa powder and fold in with a spoon.

2 Line an 8 x 12in (20 x 30cm) jelly roll pan with parchment paper, then pour the mixture into the pan and level the top. Bake for 10 minutes, until the cake is springy to the touch. Remove from the oven, cover with a damp kitchen towel, and leave to cool.

3 Turn the cake out onto a sheet of parchment paper dusted with cocoa powder. Put the butter in a mixing bowl and beat with an electric mixer until creamy. Whisk in the confectioners' sugar a little at a time, then spread the mixture over the cake. Using the parchment paper to help you, roll the cake into a long cylinder, starting from one of the short sides. Dust with more cocoa powder, if desired, and serve.

COOK'S NOTES

Swiss rolls tend to go dry quite quickly, so it's best enjoyed on the same day it is made.

Baked stem ginger cheesecake

Cooling • 1 hour

Special equipment • electric mixer • 8in (20cm) springform pan

SERVES 8

1 x 7oz (200g) package British
  digestive biscuits or plain cookies,
  such as gingersnaps, vanilla wafers,
  or graham crackers

2 tbsp butter

4 large eggs, at room temperature,
  separated

1 cup granulated sugar

5½oz (150g) cream cheese, at
  room temperature

9oz (250g) mascarpone cheese

2 tbsp syrup from a jar of stem ginger

4–5 pieces stem ginger, thinly sliced
  and cut into thin strips

2 tbsp all-purpose flour

1 Preheat the oven to 350°F (180°C). Grease and line the bottom of an 8in (20cm) springform pan with parchment paper. Put the cookies in a plastic bag and crush with a rolling pin. Melt the butter in a saucepan, add the crumbs, and stir until evenly moistened. Spoon into the pan and press into the bottom to form a crust.

2 Put the egg yolks and sugar in a mixing bowl and beat with an electric mixer until thick and creamy. Stir in the cheeses, beat with a wooden spoon until smooth, and stir in the ginger syrup and sliced ginger. Sift in the flour and fold until no longer visible.

3 Put the egg whites in a bowl and beat until stiff peaks form. Fold into the yolk mixture and spoon over the crust. Bake for 50 minutes, until golden and almost set. Turn off the oven and leave the cake inside to cool for 1 hour. Loosen the edges with a blunt knife and release the springform. Cover and refrigerate until serving time.

COOK'S NOTES

Bring the eggs and cream cheese to room temperature before starting. Eggs take longer to whisk when they are cold.

Chocolate ice cream

PREP 15 MINS

Setting • overnight
Special equipment • electric mixer

SERVES 8

4½oz (125g) semisweet chocolate
1¾oz (50g) milk chocolate
4 large egg yolks
4 tbsp granulated sugar
4 cups (1.1 liters) heavy
   whipping cream

1 Break both of the chocolates into pieces and place in a heatproof bowl. Sit the bowl over a pan of simmering water and stir, just until the chocolate melts. Remove from the heat and allow to cool slightly.

2 Meanwhile, place the egg yolks in a mixing bowl and beat with an electric mixer for at least 2 minutes or until light and fluffy. Add the sugar a little at a time, whisking constantly until it is all combined. Gradually stir in the melted chocolate to blend well.

3 Place the cream in a mixing bowl and beat with an electric mixer until it forms soft peaks. Fold into the chocolate mixture. Spoon into a freezer-safe airtight container and freeze overnight to set.

4 Remove the ice cream from the freezer 5–10 minutes before serving so it has a chance to soften slightly.

COOK'S NOTES

Ice cream made sans ice cream maker becomes hard quickly, so it is best to eat within two days.

Cold lemon soufflé

PREP 30 MINS

Setting • 4 hours
Special equipment • electric mixer
• 1-quart (1.2-liter) soufflé dish

SERVES 6–8

1 x ¼oz (7g) envelope unflavored
   gelatin (about 2¼ tsp)
vegetable oil, for greasing
6 large eggs, separated
⅔ cup granulated sugar
juice and finely grated zest of 1 lemon
2 cups heavy whipping cream

1 Soften the gelatin in 3 tablespoons warm water for 5 minutes, then stir to dissolve. Meanwhile, cut a 4in (10cm) strip of parchment paper and grease lightly with vegetable oil. Wrap it around the top of a 1-quart (1.2-liter) soufflé dish, oiled-side facing inward, so it stands at least ¾in (2.5cm) higher than the rim of the dish. Secure with kitchen twine or tape.

2 Put the egg yolks, sugar, and lemon juice in a mixing bowl and beat with an electric mixer until the mixture is thick and creamy and leaves a trail when the beaters are lifted. Beat in the gelatin mixture and let stand for 10 minutes, until it begins to thicken.

3 Place the cream in a large bowl and beat until it forms soft peaks. Fold the whipped cream into the egg yolk mixture. Place the egg whites in a bowl and, using clean beaters, beat with an electric mixer until they form stiff peaks. Fold into the egg yolk mixture along with the lemon zest.

4 Spoon the mixture into the soufflé dish, then cover and transfer to the refrigerator to set for at least 4 hours or overnight. Carefully remove the parchment paper collar and serve.

VARIATION

Use 2 teaspoons of vanilla extract instead of the lemon zest and juice.

COOK'S NOTES

Due to salmonella, the USDA recommends that pregnant women and those with a weak immune system not consume raw eggs.

Peach and nectarine puff pastry tart

PREP 20 MINS | **COOK**

Cooling • 20 minutes
Special equipment • electric mixer

SERVES 8

1 large egg plus 1 large egg yolk
½ cup granulated sugar
¼ cup all-purpose flour
1¼ cups whole milk
juice of 1 lemon
half of a 17.3oz box (225g) frozen
    puff pastry thawed as directed
1 egg yolk, beaten
4 ripe peaches, halved and pitted
4 ripe nectarines, halved and pitted
confectioners' (powdered) sugar,
    for dusting

1 Put the egg, egg yolk, sugar and flour in a bowl and beat with an electric mixer until blended. Heat the milk in a saucepan until almost boiling, then slowly whisk into the egg mixture, along with the lemon juice. Return the mixture to the pan and slowly bring to a boil, stirring constantly. Cook for a few minutes until thickened, then transfer to a bowl. Place a piece of parchment paper on top, then leave to cool.

2 On a floured work surface, roll the pastry into a 9 x 12in (23 x 30cm) rectangle and transfer to a lightly oiled baking sheet. Score a rectangle on it, leaving a ¾in (2cm) border at the edge. Press the back of the knife into the border to make horizontal lines—these will ensure it rises evenly. Prick the base of the rectangle with a fork and refrigerate for 20 minutes. Preheat the oven to 400°F (200°C).

3 Brush the border of the pastry with the beaten egg yolk, then bake for 20 minutes or until the pastry is golden. Push the inner rectangle down slightly, so the border is elevated, then leave to cool for 30 minutes.

4 Spoon in the custard, then top with the fruit and dust with confectioners' sugar. Cut into squares to serve.

 VARIATION
Use 2 teaspoons of vanilla extract instead of the lemon juice.

COOK'S NOTES

If the custard becomes too firm as it cools, beat it well with a wooden spoon or pass it through a fine sieve.

Tiramisu bombe

PREP 20 MINS

Chilling • 6 hours
Special equipment • electric mixer
• 1-quart (1.2-liter) bowl or pudding mold

SERVES 8

vegetable oil, for greasing
7oz (200g) crisp Italian ladyfingers
2–3 tbsp brandy
½ cup brewed espresso
    or strong coffee
2 cups heavy whipping cream
2 tbsp unsweetened cocoa powder,
    plus extra for dusting
2 tbsp confectioners' (powdered)
    sugar, plus extra for dusting
10oz (300g) fresh cherries, stemmed,
    pitted, and halved, or 1 x 13–14oz
    (400g) can morello or black
    cherries, drained and halved,
    plus 3 whole cherries for garnish
4½oz (125g) semisweet chocolate

1 Grease a 1-quart (1.2-liter) bowl or pudding mold with vegetable oil and line the bottom with parchment paper. Dip all but five of the ladyfingers into the brandy, then into the coffee. Line the bottom of the bowl with a few ladyfingers, then line the sides as well, with sugared sides placed down.

2 In a bowl, beat the cream until soft peaks form. Transfer half of the whipped cream to another bowl. Sift the cocoa powder and confectioners' sugar into one of the bowls and fold to blend. Add the cherries to the other bowl. Layer the creams alternately in the mold, then top with the remaining ladyfingers. Cover and refrigerate for 6 hours or overnight, until firm.

3 To serve, uncover the bombe, invert onto a plate, and remove the mold. Dust with cocoa powder, top with the remaining whole cherries, and grate chocolate over all.

COOK'S NOTES

A well-chilled bombe is easiest to unmold without breaking, so it's best to make this decadent treat the day before serving.

CAKES AND BAKES

Gorgeous baked goodies, made quick and easy.

CAKES AND BAKES

Baking is an enjoyable experience, as long as you remember that it requires accuracy. A few dos and don'ts, a little discipline, and straightforward easy-to-follow recipes are the key to perfect baking. Classic baking recipes are often formulaic, but you can always be creative with flavorings and fillings.

FOOD FOR FRIENDS

Basic sponge cake This method will produce feather-light sponge.

Flavor the mixture

1 Preheat the oven to 350°F (180°C). Lightly grease and line 2 x 8in (20cm) round cake pans (see opposite). Put 16 tablespoons of softened butter in a mixing bowl, with 1 cup of granulated sugar and cream together, using an electric mixer or wooden spoon, until pale and fluffy.

2 Lightly beat 4 room-temperature eggs. Add them slowly, a little at a time, to the butter and sugar mixture, beating well after each addition. Add a tablespoon of sifted flour, taken from 1¾ cups of self-rising flour, to prevent it from curdling. Continue until all the egg has been added.

Once the basic cake recipe is mastered, you can experiment with different flavors.

Chocolate cake just requires a tablespoon of sieved cocoa powder (pictured above) added with the sifted flour.

Lemon zest or **orange zest** can be added into the creamed butter for a citrus cake.

Pumpkin pie spice or **nutmeg** will spice things up a little, if added with the sifted flour at the end.

Coffee is always a favorite. Add a teaspoon of ground coffee, mixed with water, to the creamed butter.

3 Using a metal or wooden spoon, fold in the rest of the flour. The mixture should drop off the spoon easily when it's ready. Add a tablespoon of water if the mixture is too thick.

4 Divide the mixture between the two pans and smooth out evenly. Put in the oven and bake for about 20 minutes, or until the cakes have risen, are golden, and feel springy if you lightly press the top with your fingertips. Remove and allow to cool in the pans for 5 minutes before turning out onto a wire rack to cool completely.

Psst...

If cake batter is left to sit for longer than 10 minutes before it's baked, it can curdle and turn frothy, and this won't make for a tasty cake. Always have the oven preheated and put the prepared mixture straight into the oven.

Line a pan
Turn out cakes and bakes cleanly and easily.

1 Sit the cake pan on a sheet of parchment paper, then draw around the outside of the base with a pencil.

2 Brush the base of the pan with a little vegetable or sunflower oil.

3 Neatly cut the circle out, just inside the pencil line, so the parchment paper will fit snugly inside the pan.

Easy toppings
Three simple ways to decorate your cake.

Apricot glaze
Melt 2 tablespoons of **apricot jam** in a pan over low heat. This will take 5–10 minutes. While it's still warm, brush liberally and evenly all over the top of the cake with a pastry brush. Leave to cool and fill with buttercream and apricot jam.

White chocolate drizzle
Place a handful of broken **white chocolate** in a bowl with a **2½ tbsp butter**. Sit the bowl over a pan of gently simmering water and stir the chocolate until it has melted. Heat 3 tablespoons of **heavy cream** until warm, and stir into the chocolate mixture until glossy. Spread or drizzle the mixture over the top of a cake filled with fresh summer fruit, such as strawberries and raspberries (see Easy fillings).

Mascarpone swirl
Mix 3 tablespoons of **mascarpone cheese** with 2–3 teaspoons of sieved **confectioners' (powdered) sugar**. Beat with a wooden spoon until it becomes a spreadable consistency. Add a drizzle of **Limoncello** (Italian lemon liqueur) and stir to combine. Taste and adjust the levels of Limoncello or confectioners' (powdered) sugar as desired. Spread the mixture over the top of a cake filled with lemon curd.

Easy fillings
Transform a basic cake into an indulgent treat.

Buttercream
Beat together 8 tablespoons of **softened butter** with 3oz (85g) of sieved **confectioners' (powdered) sugar** (you may need a little more or less; adjust according to taste). Add a drop or two of **vanilla extract a**nd beat until smooth. If it is too stiff, it will be difficult to spread. Add other flavors to the buttercream, such as maple syrup, almond essence, Amaretto, or espresso and chocolate for a mocha filling.

Summer fruits
Add a couple of handfuls of **raspberries (or summer berries of your choice)** to a pan, and sprinkle over a handful of **granulated sugar**. Simmer gently for about 5 minutes. Transfer to a bowl and, when cold, put in the refrigerator. Spoon over the bottom half of the cake, with a layer of **fresh raspberries (or summer berries of your choice)**, then cover with the top layer of sponge, dust with sieved confectioners' (powdered) sugar, and the white chocolate drizzle.

Chestnut cream
Whisk 4–5 tablespoons of **heavy cream** until it forms soft peaks. Spoon in 1–2 tablespoons of ready-made **sweetened chestnut purée** and stir until lightly marbled. Taste and add more purée if needed, or sweeten with sieved **confectioners' (powdered) sugar**. Spread over the first layer of cake and place the second layer on top. Dust with sieved confectioners' sugar and cocoa powder.

Basic cookie dough A simple recipe for vanilla cookies.

Flavor the mixture

1 Measure out 9 tablespoons butter, ¾ cup brown sugar, and 2¾ cups self-rising flour, allowing the butter to come to room temperature before you begin. Preheat the oven to 350°F (180°C).

2 In a bowl, mix the butter with the sugar. Add 1 egg and mix until combined. Add the flour and 2 teaspoons of vanilla extract and combine until the mixture forms a dough. Line 2 baking sheets with parchment paper.

Transform your basic cookie dough with these delicious flavors.

Hazelnuts and chocolate Add 1–2 teaspoons of cocoa powder to the flour and a handful of chopped hazelnuts (pictured) to the finished mixture.

Ginger Add 1–2 teaspoons of ground ginger to the flour.

Cinnamon Add a pinch of ground cinnamon to the flour.

Lemon Add lemon juice instead of vanilla extract to the buttercream for a zesty flavor.

Almond and orange Add 2–3 teaspoons of ground almonds to the finished mixture, with the zest and juice of half an orange.

Cranberry and white chocolate Mix a handful of finely chopped white chocolate pieces, and a handful of dried cranberries into the finished mixture.

3 Roll the dough into balls the size of walnuts and place on the baking sheets, then flatten with your fingers.

4 Bake in batches for 12–15 minutes, until golden, then remove from the oven and transfer to a wire rack to cool completely.

Psst...

Make sure you always leave a generous space between pieces of dough on the baking sheet, because they'll rise and spread slightly as they cook.

Baking ingredients What to choose, and how to use.

INGREDIENT	CHOOSE	USE
 **BUTTER**	Both **salted** or **unsalted butter** can be used for baking. It's all down to taste preference and whether you are reducing the salt in your diet. The amount of salt in salted butter varies, so check the label. Salted butter will keep for longer if you keep it in a butter dish out of the refrigerator.	Salted or unsalted, for cakes and bakes. Use softened butter (at room temperature). This means plenty of air will be held by the fat as you mix, making your cake or bake lighter.
SUGAR	**Granulated sugar** is commonly used for cakes and bakes. Demerara (raw) sugar is valued for its delicate flavor and coarse crystals. Although there is virtually no difference in the nutritional value of white sugar and demerara sugar, the latter is usually considered too coarse for baking. **Light and dark brown sugars** are plain white sugar with added molasses, and therefore have a slightly higher nutritional value.	Granulated sugar is most common for cakes and bakes.
BAKING POWDER	This is a rising agent used in baking. It is a mixture of baking soda and cream of tartar, a natural rising agent, and is different than **baking soda** or **sodium bicarbonate**, as they don't contain cream of tartar. The two cannot be interchanged. Check the sell-by date of baking powder, as it won't be effective if used when it's old.	Cakes and cookies. If a recipe calls for self-rising flour and you haven't got any, add baking powder to all-purpose flour (4 teaspoons per 1 cup).
 **FLOUR**	**All-purpose flour** and **self-rising flour** are quite low in gluten, unlike bread flour. There are many flours that are suitable for a wheat-free or gluten-free diet, such as **rice flour**, **chestnut flour**, and **potato flour**. If using, consult specialist recipes as they are not interchangeable with all-purpose flour.	All-purpose flour or self-rising flour, sifted, for cakes and bakes. Don't over-beat once flour has been added, as the gluten will strengthen and you'll get a tough texture. This is why recipes call for flour to be folded in.
 **EGGS**	Choose **medium organic** and/or **eggs from free-range hens**, as they will improve the flavor and quality of your finished cake.	Use at room temperature. If they are used cold from the refrigerator, they cool the butter down and the mixture can curdle.

Psst...

If you are switching your pans from square to round, go up 1in (2.5cm) in size. If your recipe calls for a round 7in (18cm) pan, you can use an 8in (20cm) square pan. And if switching the other way, from round to square, go down 1in (2.5cm).

Tools of the trade

Cake pans should be rigid and sturdy, so they don't buckle in the heat of the oven. A selection of sizes and shapes is useful. For making a 4-egg sponge cake, you will need 2 x 8in (20cm) round pans. Loose-bottomed cake pans are great–they make turning the cake out a lot easier. A springform cake pan is useful for larger cakes, or more fragile ones such as a baked cheesecake.

Baking sheets should be rigid and sturdy, so they don't buckle in the heat. Have a selection with and without lips.

Biscuit or cookie cutters often come in sets, so you have a variety of size and shapes. Metal are the best, and you can get straight-sided or fluted.

A wire rack is necessary for cooling all cakes and bakes. Choose a large one if you plan to do batch baking.

Ceramic baking beans are ideal for baking pastry blind, because they are heavy and can be used repeatedly. Take care though, as they get extremely hot. As an alternative, dried beans or rice can be used.

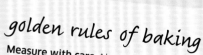
golden rules of baking

Measure with care Always measure everything accurately and stick to either metric or imperial (never switch between the two). Weigh out ingredients before you start baking.

Resist opening the oven door Don't be tempted to open the oven door while baking, at least for the first half of the cooking time. If you do need to peep, leave it as long as possible. Always set the oven temperature correctly, according to the recipe. Cakes and cookies don't need a particularly hot oven. If using a convection oven, adjust accordingly, or switch the fan off if you can.

Madeira cake

Special equipment • electric mixer
• 7in (18cm) round cake pan

SERVES 4-6

11 tbsp butter, at room temperature, plus extra for greasing

¾ cup sugar

3 eggs, lightly whisked

1¾ cups self-rising flour

juice of 1 lemon

1 Preheat the oven to 350°F (180°C). Put the butter and sugar in a mixing bowl and beat with an electric mixer for 5 minutes, or until pale and creamy.

2 Mixing all the time, add the eggs a little at a time, along with a little of the flour to stop the mixture from curdling. Stir in the lemon juice, then fold in the rest of the flour. Spoon the mixture into the lightly greased cake pan.

3 Bake for 1-1½ hours, or until cooked through. To test, pierce the center of the cake with a skewer–if it comes out clean, the cake is cooked. Remove from the oven and leave to cool for 10 minutes in the pan, then run a knife around the edge to loosen. Leave to cool completely, then turn out onto a plate and serve.

Cheat...
Instead of waiting for the butter to come to room temperature, use ready-softened butter from a tub.

Vanilla sponge cake

Freeze • before filling

Special equipment • electric mixer
• 7in (18cm) round cake pan

SERVES 4-6

2 eggs, lightly beaten

⅓ cup sugar

a few drops of vanilla extract

⅔ cup self-rising flour

3 tbsp butter, at room temperature, plus extra for greasing

1 cup confectioners' sugar

2 tbsp lemon curd

1 Preheat the oven to 350°F (180°C). Put the eggs and sugar in a mixing bowl and beat with an electric mixer for 5 minutes, or until pale and creamy. Add a few drops of the vanilla extract.

2 Sift in the flour, a little at a time, folding each batch in gently before adding more. Pour the mixture into the lightly greased cake pan. Bake in the oven for 30 minutes, or until lightly golden. To test, pierce the center of the cake with a skewer–if it comes out clean, the cake is cooked. Remove from the oven and leave to cool in the pan for 10-15 minutes, then loosen the edges with a knife and leave to cool completely.

3 Meanwhile, put the butter in a mixing bowl and beat with a wooden spoon for a few minutes until creamy. Sift in the confectioners' sugar, beat well, then add a few drops of vanilla extract and beat again. Remove the cake from the pan and slice in half horizontally. Cover the bottom half with the buttercream and the top half with the lemon curd. Sandwich together and serve.

Chocolate chip cookies

 PREP **10** MINS COOK **30** MINS ❄

Special equipment • electric mixer

MAKES ABOUT 30
14 tbsp butter, at room temperature
1½ cups sugar
1 large egg
1 tsp vanilla extract
2 cups self-rising flour
2 cups dark- or milk-
  chocolate chips

1 Preheat the oven to 350°F (180°C). Line two baking sheets with parchment paper. In a bowl, beat the butter and sugar together with an electric mixer until creamy, then mix in the egg and vanilla extract until completely combined.

2 Beat in the flour until the mixture forms a soft dough, then mix in the chocolate chips. Roll the dough into about 30 balls, each roughly the size of a walnut, and place on the baking sheets, leaving space around each one for it to spread. Flatten them slightly, then bake in two batches for 15 minutes, or until golden. Carefully transfer to a wire rack to cool completely.

VARIATION
Make double-chocolate-chip cookies by replacing ¼ cup of the flour with cocoa powder.

COOK'S NOTES
Don't worry if the golden cookies are still a little soft when you take them out of the oven—they will firm up as they cool to become deliciously chewy.

FOOD FOR FRIENDS

Rich chocolate cookies

 PREP **15** MINS COOK **20** MINS ❄

Special equipment • electric mixer

MAKES 16
7 tbsp butter, at room temperature
¼ cup sugar
1 cup all-purpose flour
¼ cup cocoa powder
melted dark or milk chocolate,
  to drizzle (optional)

1 Preheat the oven to 350°F (180°C). Line two baking sheets with parchment paper. In a bowl, mix the butter and sugar together with an electric mixer until pale and creamy. Sift in the flour and cocoa powder and beat until the mixture comes together to form a dough. You may need to bring it together with your hands at the end.

2 Roll the dough into 16 balls, each about the size of a walnut, and place on the baking sheets. Press the middle of each one with your thumb to flatten it, or use a fork, which will decorate it at the same time. Bake for 20 minutes, then transfer to a wire rack to cool completely. Drizzle with the melted chocolate (if using) and allow to set before serving.

COOK'S NOTES
Buy good-quality cocoa powder and chocolate (if using)—it will make all the difference.

Raspberry, lemon, and almond bake

PREP 20 MINS · **COOK 40 MINS**

Special equipment • 8in (20cm) square loose-bottomed cake pan

SERVES 8

1¼ cups all-purpose flour
1 tsp baking powder
1 cup ground almonds
11 tbsp butter, cubed
1 cup granulated sugar
3 tbsp fresh lemon juice
1 tsp vanilla extract
2 large eggs
1 cup fresh raspberries
confectioners' (powdered) sugar, for dusting (optional)

1 Preheat the oven to 350°F (180°C). Line the bottom and sides of an 8in (20cm) square loose-bottomed cake pan with parchment paper. Sift the flour and baking powder into a bowl and stir in the ground almonds. In a small saucepan, heat the butter, sugar, and lemon juice together, stirring until melted and smooth. Let cool slightly.

2 Stir the syrupy butter mixture into the dry ingredients, then mix in the vanilla extract and the eggs, one at a time, until the mixture is smooth and well blended. Scrape into the prepared pan, then scatter the raspberries over the top. Bake for 35–40 minutes or until golden and a skewer inserted into the cake comes out clean.

3 Cool in the pan for 10 minutes, then unmold and cool completely on a wire rack. Just before serving, dust with confectioners' sugar. To serve, cut into squares or bars.

VARIATION

This cake also works well with blueberries, or a mix of other soft berries.

Berry friands

PREP 15 MINS · **COOK 35 MINS**

Special equipment • electric hand whisk • 6-cup muffin pan

MAKES 6

1 cup confectioners' sugar
7 tbsp all-purpose flour
1 cup ground almonds
3 large egg whites
5 tbsp unsalted butter, melted
1 cup mixed fresh berries, such as blueberries and raspberries

1 Preheat the oven to 350°F (180°C). Sift the sugar and flour into a bowl, then stir in the ground almonds. In another bowl, whisk the egg whites with an electric mixer until they form soft peaks.

2 Gently fold the flour mixture and the melted butter into the egg whites until incorporated. Divide the batter equally between six muffin cups lined with paper liners. Scatter the berries evenly over the top of each one, gently pressing them into the batter. Bake for 30–35 minutes, or until golden brown and risen.

VARIATION

Use chopped stoned fruit such as apricots, peaches, or plums instead of the berries, but make sure they are really ripe and juicy.

All-in-one chocolate cake with fudge icing

PREP 20 MINS **COOK 40 MINS**

Special equipment • 2 x 8in (20cm) round sandwich pans • electric hand whisk or mixer

SERVES 8–12

16 tbsp butter, at room temperature, plus extra for greasing
1¾ cups self-rising flour
¼ cup unsweetened cocoa powder
1 tsp baking powder
4 large eggs
1 cup + 2 tbsp granulated sugar
1 tsp vanilla extract

For the chocolate fudge icing
½ cup unsweetened cocoa powder
1¼ cups confectioners' sugar
4 tbsp butter, melted
3 tbsp milk, plus little extra if needed

1 Preheat the oven to 350°F (180°C). Grease two 8in (20cm) round cake pans, then line with parchment paper. Sift the flour, cocoa, and baking powder into a large bowl. With an electric mixer, beat in the eggs, sugar, butter, and vanilla until well blended. Mix in 2 tablespoons hot tap water. If the batter is too firm to easily drop off the beaters, add up to 2 more tablespoons of hot water. Divide the batter evenly between the pans and smooth the tops.

2 Bake for 35–40 minutes, or until risen and firm. Let cool in the pans for 5 minutes before unmolding onto racks to cool completely.

3 Meanwhile, to make the icing, sift the cocoa powder and confectioners' sugar into a bowl, add the butter and milk, and beat until smooth. Add a little extra milk if the mixture is too thick to spread easily. Place one cooled cake layer on a serving plate and spread with half of the icing. Align the second layer on top of the first and spread with the remaining icing, leaving the sides unfrosted.

COOK'S NOTES

The cakes are cooked when they start to shrink away from the edge of the pan.

513

Apple streusel cake

PREP 20 MINS

COOK

Special equipment • 8in (20cm) round loose-bottomed or springform cake pan • electric hand whisk

SERVES 8

9 tbsp butter, at room temperature, plus extra for greasing
1¼ cups all-purpose flour
⅔ cup granulated sugar
1 tsp ground cinnamon
2 large eggs, lightly beaten
½ tsp vanilla extract
1 Granny Smith apple, peeled, cored, and cut into chunks
½ cup golden raisins

For the streusel topping
1 cup all-purpose flour
½ cup granulated sugar or light brown sugar (packed)
⅓ cup ground almonds
1 tsp ground cinnamon
5 tbsp butter, cubed

1 Preheat the oven to 350°F (180°C). Grease an 8in (20cm) round springform pan and line the bottom with parchment paper. Sift the flour into a bowl, add the butter, sugar, cinnamon, eggs, and vanilla and beat with an electric mixer until light and creamy. Scrape the mixture into the pan and scatter with the apple and raisins.

2 To make the topping: In another bowl, stir together the flour, sugar, ground almonds, and cinnamon. Rub the cubed butter into the mixture with your fingertips until it resembles coarse bread crumbs. Scatter an even layer of the topping over the fruit, pressing down gently. Bake for 1 hour 20 minutes or until a skewer inserted into the cake comes out clean or with only a bit of moist fruit clinging to it. Let cool in the pan for at least 20 minutes before releasing the sides of the springform.

Cheat...
Use store-bought crumble mixture, but add some ground cinnamon for extra flavor.

COOK'S NOTES

This cake also works well as a warm dessert served with ice cream, or cream.

Pecan, coffee, and maple cake

PREP 15 MINS

COOK 40

Special equipment • 2 x 8in (18cm) round cake pans • electric hand whisk

SERVES 8

1 cup granulated sugar
12 tbsp butter, at room temperature
3 large eggs, lightly beaten
½ cup sour cream
2 tbsp brewed espresso or strong coffee, or more as needed
2 cups self-rising flour
½ cup chopped pecans

For the icing
3½ tbsp butter
1 tbsp pure maple syrup
2 cups confectioners' sugar
2 tbsp brewed espresso or strong coffee
about 20 pecan halves or ⅓ cup chopped pecans, for garnish

1 Preheat the oven to 350°F (180°C). Lightly grease two 8in (18cm) round cake pans and line the bottoms with parchment paper. In a large bowl, beat the sugar and butter with an electric mixer until light and fluffy, about 2 minutes. Beat in the eggs one at time, beating well after each addition, then beat in the sour cream and espresso. Sift the flour into the bowl and add the pecans; fold until the flour is just incorporated and the pecans are mixed throughout. Divide the batter evenly between the pans and level the tops.

2 Bake for 35–40 minutes until risen, firm to the touch, and slightly shrunken from the sides of the pans. Let cool for 5 minutes in the pans, then unmold onto a wire rack to cool completely.

3 Meanwhile, make the icing. Melt the butter with the maple syrup in a small pan. Sift the sugar into a bowl, add the butter and syrup mixture along with the coffee, and beat with an electric mixer until thick and smooth. Spread the icing over the tops of the two cooled cakes, then sandwich together. Decorate the top of the cake with pecans.

VARIATION
This works just as well with walnuts instead of pecans.

Coconut and lime cake

PREP 20 MINS · **COOK 1¼ HRS**

Special equipment • 8in (18cm) round deep pan • electric hand whisk or mixer

SERVES 8

16 tbsp butter, at room temperature, plus extra for greasing

2 cups self-rising flour

1 cup + 2 tbsp granulated sugar

4 large eggs, lightly beaten

⅔ cup shredded coconut

finely grated zest of 1 lime

2 tbsp fresh lime juice

For the icing

1 cup confectioners' sugar, or more as needed

finely grated zest of 1 lime

2 tbsp fresh lime juice

10oz (300g) cream cheese, at room temperature

2 tbsp toasted shredded coconut

1 Preheat the oven to 350°F (180°C). Grease an 8in (18cm) round cake pan or springform pan that is at least 3in (7cm) deep. Line the bottom with parchment paper. Sift the flour into a large bowl, add the sugar, butter, and eggs and beat with an electric mixer until well blended. Stir in the coconut, lime zest, and lime juice. Scrape into the prepared pan and level the top.

Bake for 1 hour–1 hour 15 minutes or until risen and firm to the touch. Let cool for 5 minutes in the pan, then unmold onto a wire rack to cool completely. Using a serrated knife, carefully slice the cake horizontally into three equal layers.

2 To make the icing, sift the confectioners' sugar into a bowl, add the lime zest, lime juice, and cream cheese, and beat with an electric mixer until well blended. Taste, adding more sugar if needed. Spread the icing over the three layers of the cake, then sandwich them together. Scatter the toasted coconut over the top.

VARIATION Cut the cake into two rather than three layers. Spread the icing more thickly to use it up.

COOK'S NOTES

Toast the coconut in a small nonstick frying pan. There is no need for any fat, as it is already very oily, but this means it can burn easily and stick to the bottom of the pan, so shake the pan gently over the heat until the coconut is golden brown.

Orange and pistachio cake

PREP 15 MINS · **COOK 55 MINS**

Special equipment • electric hand whisk • 8in (20cm) round springform cake pan

SERVES 6

12 tbsp butter, at room temperature, plus extra for greasing

1 cup granulated sugar

2 large eggs

1½ cups self-rising flour

¾ cup Greek-style yogurt

½ cup pistachios, finely chopped

½ cup blanched almonds, finely chopped

finely grated zest and juice of 1 orange

finely grated zest and juice of 1 lemon

1 tsp baking powder

mascarpone cheese, to serve (optional)

1 Preheat the oven to 350°F (180°C). Put the butter and sugar in a large bowl and beat with an electric mixer for 5 minutes or until pale and creamy. Beat in the eggs one at a time, along with a few tablespoons of the flour to prevent the mixture from curdling.

2 Beat in the yogurt, pistachios-, almonds, orange zest and juice, and lemon zest and juice. Mix well to form a smooth batter. Sift in the remaining flour and the baking powder and carefully fold into the mixture. Pour into a lightly greased 8in (20cm) round springform pan.

3 Bake for 50–55 minutes, or until a skewer inserted into the center of the cake comes out clean. Remove from the oven and leave to cool in the pan for 10 minutes, then release the sides of the springform and leave on a wire rack to cool completely. Slice and serve with a dollop of mascarpone, if desired.

VARIATION Sift confectioners' sugar over the top of the cake before serving.

Toffee apple bake

PREP 20 MINS **COOK 45 MINS**

Special equipment • electric hand whisk or mixer • 9 x 13in (23 x 33cm) baking pan

MAKES 18 SQUARES
2 medium Granny Smith apples, peeled, cored, and thinly sliced
squeeze of lemon juice
3¼ cups self-rising flour
2 tsp baking powder
2 cups light brown sugar, packed
4 large eggs, lightly beaten
16 tbsp butter, melted
1 tbsp granulated sugar

For the toffee sauce
8 tbsp butter
⅔ cup light brown sugar, packed
1 tbsp fresh lemon juice
pinch of sea salt
crème fraîche, to serve (optional)

1 Preheat the oven to 350°F (180°C). Line the bottom and sides of a 9 x 13in (23 x 33cm) baking pan with parchment paper. Put the apple slices in a bowl and toss with the lemon juice to prevent browning.

2 Sift the flour and baking powder into a large mixing bowl and stir in the brown sugar. Beat in the eggs and the melted butter with an electric mixer to make a smooth batter. Pour into the prepared pan and smooth the top. Arrange the apple slices in three or four rows on top of the batter and sprinkle with the sugar. Bake for 45 minutes, or until the cake is firm to the touch and a skewer inserted into the center comes out clean.

3 Meanwhile, make the sauce by melting the butter and sugar in a saucepan over medium-low heat. Add the lemon juice and a pinch of salt, whisking until the mixture is melted and smooth. Let cool slightly. Pour the sauce over the cake while it is still in the pan, gently brushing over the top. Serve warm or at room temperature, with a dollop of crème fraîche.

Cheat...
Use a ready-made toffee sauce instead of making your own.

White chocolate and macadamia nut blondies

PREP 20 MINS **COOK 20 MINS**

Special equipment • 9 x 13in (23 x 33cm) baking pan

MAKES 24
10oz (300g) white chocolate, chopped
12 tbsp butter, cubed
1½ cups granulated sugar
4 large eggs
2 cups all-purpose flour
1 cup unsalted macadamia nuts, coarsely chopped

1 Preheat the oven to 400°F (200°C). Line the bottom and sides of a 9 x 13in (23 x 33cm) baking pan with parchment paper. In a bowl set over a saucepan of barely simmering water, melt the chocolate and butter together, stirring occasionally until smooth. Remove the bowl and set aside to cool for about 20 minutes.

2 Mix in the sugar (the mixture may become very thick and grainy, but the eggs will loosen it). Using a balloon whisk, stir in the eggs one at a time, making sure each is well incorporated before adding the next. Gradually sift in the flour, folding it in, and then stir in the nuts. Scrape the mixture into the prepared pan, gently spreading it into the corners. Bake for 20 minutes, or until just firm to the touch on top but still soft underneath. Place the pan on a wire rack to cool completely, then cut into squares.

VARIATION
Substitute walnuts or pecans for the macadamia nuts.

COOK'S NOTES
When melting the chocolate, be careful that no water splashes into it—it will ruin the chocolate.

Chocolate and hazelnut brownies

 PREP 25 MINS   **COOK** 15 MINS

Special equipment • 9 x 13 x 2in (23 x 30.5cm) pan

MAKES 24

10oz (300g) semisweet chocolate, chopped
12 tbsp butter, cubed
1½ cups granulated sugar
4 large eggs
1¾ cups all-purpose flour
¼ cup unsweetened cocoa powder
1 cup hazelnuts, toasted, skinned, and coarsely chopped

1 Preheat the oven to 400°F (200°C). Line the bottom and sides of a 9 x 13 x 2in (23 x 30.5cm) pan with parchment paper. In a large bowl set over a pan of barely simmering water, melt the chocolate and butter together until smooth, stirring occasionally. Remove the bowl from the pan and set aside to cool for about 20 minutes.

2 Mix in the sugar and then the eggs, one at a time, making sure each is well blended before adding the next. Sift in the flour and cocoa powder and fold in gently. Stir in the chopped nuts—the mixture should be thick and glossy. Scrape into the prepared pan, gently spreading it into the corners, then smooth the top.

3 Bake for 12–15 minutes, or until just firm to the touch on top but still gooey in the center. Transfer the pan to a wire rack to cool completely, then cut into squares.

 VARIATION
Chopped walnuts or pecans work well in place of hazelnuts. Or leave the nuts out altogether if you have an allergy.

COOK'S NOTES

Never overcook brownies or you will end up with chocolate cake. It is time to take them from the oven when they are just firm to the touch on top but still gooey in the center. They will firm up as they cool.

Strawberry and cream cake

 PREP 20 MINS   **COOK** 25 MINS   ❄

Special equipment • 2 x 8in (20cm) pans • electric hand whisk

SERVES 8

16 tbsp butter, at room temperature
1 cup + 2 tbsp granulated sugar
4 large eggs, lightly beaten
2 cups self-rising flour

For the strawberry and cream filling
½ cup heavy cream
¾ cup sliced strawberries
confectioners' sugar, to dust

1 Preheat the oven to 350°F (180°C). Line the bottom two 8in (20cm) round cake pans with parchment paper. In a bowl, beat the butter and sugar with an electric mixer until light and creamy. Beat in the eggs gradually, adding a little of the flour if the mixture begins to curdle. Sift in the remaining flour and fold in gently.

Divide the mixture evenly between the prepared pans and bake for 25 minutes, or until risen and firm to the touch. Let cool in the pans for 5 minutes, then unmold onto a wire rack to cool completely.

2 To make the filling, place the cream in a bowl and beat with an electric mixer until soft peaks form. Spread the whipped cream over one of the cakes, top with strawberries, then align the other cake layer on top. Dust generously with confectioners' sugar.

 VARIATION
For a more intense strawberry flavor, spread a layer of strawberry jam on the top of first cake before you cover it with cream.

Banana, date, and walnut loaf

Special equipment • electric mixer
• 8½ x 4½ x 2½in (18 x 9cm) loaf pan

SERVES 8–10

7 tbsp butter, at room
   temperature
½ cup granulated sugar
2 large eggs
2 cups self-rising flour, sifted
2 very ripe large bananas
1 cup pitted dates (preferably
   Medjool), chopped
1 cup walnut halves and pieces,
  coarsely chopped
1 tsp baking powder

1 Preheat the oven to 350°F (180°C).
Line the bottom of an 8½ x 4½ x 2½in
(18 x 9cm) loaf pan with parchment
paper. In a bowl, beat the butter and
sugar with an electric mixer until
pale, light, and fluffy. Add the eggs
one at a time, beating well and adding
1 tablespoon of the flour after each
addition. This will prevent the mixture
from curdling.

2 In a small bowl, mash the bananas
with a fork, then stir into the batter
along with the dates and walnuts.
Fold in the remaining flour and the
baking powder, then scrape the
mixture into the pan. Smooth the top,
pressing well into the corners. Bake
for 1 hour–1 hour 15 minutes, or until
risen and firm to the touch. If the top
of the cake starts to brown too much
before it is fully cooked, cover with
foil. Let cool in the pan, then remove
and cut into slices.

COOK'S NOTES

*For maximum sweetness,
use bananas with brown
speckled skins.*

Cherry and almond cake

Special equipment • electric mixer
• 8in (20.5cm) round springform pan

SERVES 8–10

11 tbsp butter, at room temperature,
   plus extra for greasing
¾ cup granulated sugar
2 large eggs, lightly beaten
2¼ cups self-rising flour, sifted
1 tsp baking powder
2 cups ground almonds
1 tsp vanilla extract
about ⅔ cup whole milk
1lb (450g) cherries, stemmed
   and pitted
¼ cup slivered almonds, chopped
confectioners' (powdered) sugar,
   for dusting (optional)

1 Preheat the oven to 350°F (180°C).
Lightly grease an 8in (20.5cm) round
springform pan and line the bottom
with parchment paper. In a bowl, beat
together the butter and sugar with an
electric mixer until pale and creamy.
Beat in the eggs one at a time, adding
1 tablespoon of the flour before
adding the second egg.

2 Mix in the remaining flour, baking
powder, ground almonds, and vanilla.
Stir in ⅓ cup of the milk. The batter
should drop easily from the beaters.
If the batter is too thick, gradually stir
in the remaining milk. Mix in half of the
cherries, then scrape the batter into the
pan. Scatter with the remaining cherries
and then the almonds.

3 Bake for 1 hour 30 minutes–1 hour
45 minutes or until golden and firm to
the touch. The exact cooking time will
depend upon how juicy the cherries
are. To test, insert a skewer into the
cake—if there is uncooked batter on it,
bake 5 minutes longer. If the surface
of the cake starts to brown too much
before it is fully baked, cover with
foil. Transfer the pan to a wire rack to
cool completely. Just before serving,
release the sides of the springform
and dust with confectioners' sugar.

Cheat...

*If fresh cherries are
not available, use frozen
pitted cherries, or a 16oz
(425g) can of cherries,
drained well.*

Light fruitcake

PREP 25 MINS · **COOK 1¾ HRS**

Special equipment • electric mixer • 8in (20cm) round cake pan

SERVES 8-12

12 tbsp butter, at room temperature
1 cup light brown sugar (packed)
3 large eggs
2¼ cups self-rising flour, sifted
2–3 tbsp whole milk
3 cups mixed dried fruit, coarsely chopped if needed

1 Preheat the oven to 350°F (180°C). Line the bottom and sides of an 8in (20cm) round cake pan with parchment paper. In a bowl, beat the butter and sugar together with an electric mixer until pale and creamy, then beat in the eggs, one at a time, adding 1 tablespoon of the flour after each one. Stir in the rest of the flour and the milk until well-blended–the mixture should drop easily off the beaters. Stir in the dried fruit.

2 Scrape the mixture into the prepared pan, level the top, and bake for 1 hour 30 minutes–1 hour 45 minutes, or until firm to the touch and a skewer inserted into the middle of the cake comes out clean. Leave in the pan to cool completely on a wire rack.

Lemon, lime, and poppy seed cake

PREP 15 MINS · **COOK 1 HR**

Special equipment • electric mixer • 8½ x 4½ x 2½in (21 x 11 x 6cm) loaf pan

SERVES 8-10

12 tbsp butter, at room temperature
1 cup granulated sugar
3 large eggs, lightly beaten
finely grated zest of 1 lemon
finely grated zest of 1 lime
2 tbsp fresh lemon juice
1⅔ cups self-rising flour
2 tbsp poppy seeds
1 tbsp fresh lime juice
1 cup confectioners' (powdered) sugar

1 Preheat the oven to 350°F (180°C). Line the bottom and sides of an 8½ x 4½ x 2½in (21 x 11 x 6cm) loaf pan with parchment paper. In a large bowl, beat the butter and granulated sugar with an electric mixer until light and fluffy. Gradually beat in the eggs until blended. Fold in the lemon zest, lime zest, and 1 tablespoon of the lemon juice. Sift in the flour, then fold into the batter with the poppy seeds.

2 Scrape into the prepared pan and smooth the top. Bake for 1 hour or until risen, golden, and firm to the touch. Let cool in the pan for 5 minutes, then unmold onto a wire rack and leave to cool completely.

3 Mix the remaining lemon juice with the lime juice in a saucepan. Sift in the confectioners' sugar and whisk to make a runny glaze. Place parchment paper under the rack to catch the drips, then spoon the warm glaze over the cake, letting it drizzle down the sides. Leave to set before serving.

COOK'S NOTES

If you prefer, omit the poppy seeds from the recipe and replace with finely chopped lemon peel.

Blueberry muffins

PREP 15 MINS
COOK 20 MINS

MAKES 12
2¼ cups self-rising flour
1 tsp baking powder
6 tbsp granulated sugar
finely grated zest of 1 lemon
   (optional)
salt
1 cup plain yogurt
2 large eggs, lightly beaten
3½ tbsp butter, melted and
   cooled slightly
1½ cups blueberries

1 Preheat the oven to 400°F (200°C). Line a 12-cup muffin pan with paper liners. Sift the flour and baking powder into a large bowl, then mix in the sugar, lemon zest, and a pinch of salt. Make a well in the center.

2 Mix the yogurt, eggs, and butter in a bowl, then pour into the dry ingredients, along with the blueberries. Fold together lightly, just until combined; don't overmix or the muffins will be heavy. Don't worry if a few lumps remain in the batter.

3 Spoon evenly into the muffin cups and bake for 20 minutes or until risen and golden. Cool in the pan for 5 minutes, then serve warm or let cool to room temperature.

VARIATION
Use raspberries instead of blueberries, or orange zest instead of lemon.

COOK'S NOTES
These muffins are best eaten the same day they're made, preferably when still warm from the oven.

Spiced honey cake

PREP 10 MINS
COOK 35 MINS

Special equipment • blender • 8½ x 4½ x 2½in (21 x 11 x 6cm) loaf pan

SERVES 8
1¼ cups self-rising flour
2 tsp pumpkin pie spice
1 tsp ground cinnamon
1 tsp ground ginger
½ tsp baking soda
½ cup honey
4 tbsp butter
⅓ cup dark or light brown sugar (packed)
1 large egg, lightly beaten
½ cup whole milk

1 Preheat the oven to 350°F (180°C). Line the bottom and sides of an 8½ x 4½ x 2½in (21 x 11 x 6cm) loaf pan with parchment paper. Sift the flour, spices, and baking soda into a bowl. Heat the honey, butter, and brown sugar in a pan until melted and smooth. Mix into the flour, then stir in the egg and milk until the mixture is well blended. The batter will be runny.

2 Pour into the prepared pan and bake for 30–35 minutes or until risen and firm to the touch. Transfer the pan to a wire rack to cool. To serve, unmold the cake and cut into slices.

VARIATION
Use a flavored honey, or substitute Lyle's Golden Syrup.

COOK'S NOTES
The cake can be stored for up to 1 week in an airtight container— the flavor will mature and the texture will become pleasantly, deliciously sticky.

Spiced carrot and orange cake

PREP 20 MINS   **COOK** 30 MINS

Special equipment • electric mixer
• 8in (20cm) square cake pan

MAKES 16 SQUARES

1½ cups self-rising flour
⅔ cup light or dark brown
   sugar (packed)
1 tsp ground cinnamon
1 tsp pumpkin pie spice
½ tsp baking soda
⅔ cup sunflower oil or light olive oil
2 large eggs
⅓ cup Lyle's Golden Syrup or light
   corn syrup
2 carrots (4½oz/125g), coarsely grated
finely grated zest of 1 orange

For the icing
1 cup confectioners' (powdered) sugar,
   or more, to taste
3½oz (100g) cream cheese, at
   room temperature
1–2 tbsp orange juice
finely grated zest of 1 orange, plus
   extra for garnish (optional)

1 Preheat the oven to 350°F (180°C).
Line the bottom and sides of an
8in (20cm) square cake pan with
parchment paper. In a large bowl,
stir together the flour, brown sugar,
cinnamon, pumpkin pie spice, and
baking soda. In another bowl, mix
together the oil, eggs, and syrup, then
combine with the dry ingredients. Stir
in the carrot and orange zest. Scrape
into the prepared pan and level the
top. Bake for 30 minutes or until firm
to the touch. Let cool in the pan for
5 minutes, then unmold onto a wire
rack to cool completely.

2 For the icing, sift the confectioners'
sugar into a bowl, add the cream
cheese, orange juice, and orange zest
and beat with an electric mixer until
thick and spreadable. When the cake
is cool, spread the icing over the top.
Garnish with extra orange zest and
cut into squares.

VARIATION
Add ½ cup chopped walnuts
to the cake batter and scatter
more over the icing, instead of
the orange zest.

Sticky date bar cookies

PREP 25 MINS   **COOK** 40 MINS

Special equipment • blender
• 8in (20.5cm) square baking pan

MAKES 16

2 cups pitted dates (preferably
   Medjool), chopped
½ tsp baking soda
1½ cups rolled oats
1 cup all-purpose flour
½ cup light brown sugar (packed)
½ tsp salt
12 tbsp butter, cut into pieces
2 tbsp Lyle's Golden Syrup or light
   corn syrup

1 Preheat the oven to 350°F (180°C).
Line the bottom of an 8in (20.5cm)
square baking pan with parchment
paper. Place the dates and baking
soda in a saucepan with enough water
to cover, simmer for 5 minutes, then
drain, reserving the liquid. Purée the
dates in a blender with 3 tablespoons
of the cooking liquid, then set aside.

2 In a bowl, combine the oats, flour,
brown sugar, and salt. Add the butter
and syrup. Blend the ingredients until
the mixture resembles coarse crumbs.
Press half of the mixture onto the
bottom of the pan. Spread the date
purée evenly over the top, then spoon
in the remaining oat mixture in an
even layer to cover the dates. Bake
for 45 to 55 minutes, or until golden
brown. Let cool for 10 minutes, then
mark into 16 squares with a knife.
Leave to cool completely before
removing the cookies with a spatula.

VARIATION
For plain bar cookies, simply
omit the dates and pack
the oat mixture into the
prepared pan.

Apricot crumble shortbread

PREP 20 MINS

Chilling • 1 hour
Special equipment • electric mixer

MAKES 20 BARS
7 tbsp butter, at room temperature
¼ cup granulated sugar
¾ cup + 2 tbsp all-purpose flour
6 tbsp cornstarch
1 x 12–14oz (400g) can
    apricot halves, drained
    and coarsely chopped

For the topping
2 tbsp butter, cubed
¾ cup all-purpose flour
3 tbsp raw or granulated sugar

1 Beat together the butter and sugar with an electric mixer until pale and creamy. Sift in the flour and cornstarch and combine so that the mix forms a dough. (You'll probably need to use your hands at the end.) Knead the dough lightly until smooth, then press evenly onto the bottom of the pan (see Cook's Notes). Refrigerate for at least 1 hour or until firm.

2 Preheat the oven to 350°F (180°C). Make the topping by rubbing the cubed butter into the flour in a bowl with your fingertips until the mixture resembles coarse bread crumbs. Stir in the sugar. Scatter the apricots evenly over the chilled dough, then top with the crumb mixture, pressing down firmly so that it is packed on. Bake for 1 hour 10 minutes or until a skewer inserted into the center of the cake comes out clean or with only a bit of moist fruit clinging to it. Transfer the pan to a wire rack to cool completely. Remove the shortbread from the pan and cut into bars or squares.

Use plums instead of apricots.

COOK'S NOTES

Use a rectangular tart pan with a removable bottom, approximately 13¾ x 4½in (35 x 11cm). Line the pan with parchment paper.

Tropical angel cake

PREP 15 MINS   **COOK 30 MINS**

Special equipment • electric mixer
• 9in (23cm) savarin ring mold

SERVES 6–8
4 large egg whites
½ tsp cream of tartar
¾ cup granulated sugar
½ cup all-purpose flour
4 tsp cornstarch
⅓ cup shredded coconut

For the topping
7oz (200g) Greek-style yogurt
1 cup mixed peeled and chopped
    tropical fruit, such as pineapple
    and mango
seeds and pulp from 2 passion fruits
finely grated lime zest, for garnish

1 Preheat the oven to 375°F (190°C). Put the egg whites, cream of tartar, and 1 tablespoon cold water in a mixing bowl and beat with an electric mixer until stiff peaks form. Beat in the sugar 1 tablespoon at a time until the mixture is stiff and shiny.

2 Sift the flour and cornstarch into the mixture, then fold in the coconut. Carefully spoon the batter into an ungreased 9in (23cm) savarin ring mold and smooth the top, pressing down gently to remove any air spaces. Bake for 15 minutes, then reduce the oven temperature to 350°F (180°C) and bake for another 15 minutes, until the top of the cake is firm to the touch and golden brown.

3 Place the pan on a wire rack and let cool completely. Carefully ease the cake out of the pan with a blunt knife and unmold onto a serving plate.

4 To make the topping, lightly beat the yogurt until smooth and creamy, then spoon into the center of the cake. Top with the fruit and drizzle with the passion fruit seeds. Scatter the lime zest over the top.

Cheat...
Use pre-cut fruit from the supermarket, or substitute well-drained canned fruit.

Ginger cookies

PREP 20 MINS · **COOK** 30 MINS

Special equipment • electric mixer

MAKES 24–30
8 tbsp butter, at room temperature
1 cup brown sugar (packed)
1 tbsp syrup from a jar of
   stem ginger
1 large egg
2 cups all-purpose flour
1 heaping tbsp ground ginger
2 tsp baking soda
¼ tsp salt
3 pieces stem ginger in syrup, drained
   and finely chopped

1 Preheat the oven to 350°F (180°C). Line two baking sheets with parchment paper. Beat the butter, sugar, and syrup with the mixer until creamy. Beat in the egg. In a separate bowl, combine the flour, ground ginger, baking soda and salt and whisk to blend. Add this to the butter mixture, then mix in the stem ginger.

2 Form the dough into walnut-size balls and place 2in (5cm) apart on the baking sheets. Flatten slightly with your fingers, then bake in two batches for 12–15 minutes or until golden brown. Carefully transfer to a wire rack to cool completely.

VARIATION
Omit the stem ginger and syrup and use 1 tablespoon of Lyle's Golden Syrup or molasses instead.

COOK'S NOTES

Jars of Chinese stem ginger can be found in Asian markets. These cookies will firm up a bit as they cool, so don't over-bake them.

Shortbread wedges

PREP 15 MINS · **COOK** 40 MINS

Chilling • 1 hour

Special equipment • electric mixer
• 8in (18cm) round cake pan

MAKES 8 WEDGES
7 tbsp butter, at room temperature,
   plus extra for greasing
¼ cup granulated sugar, plus extra
   for garnish
1 cup all-purpose flour
½ cup cornstarch

1 Lightly grease an 8in (18cm) round cake pan. In a bowl, beat the butter and sugar together with an electric mixer until pale and creamy. Sift in the flour and cornstarch and beat until the mixture forms coarse crumbs. Knead lightly to bring it together, then press the dough evenly into the pan and smooth the surface. Prick with a fork, then mark into 8 wedges. Refrigerate the dough for at least 1 hour or until firm. Preheat the oven to 325°F (160°C).

2 Bake for 40 minutes or until pale golden and firm to the touch. While still warm, mark the wedges again with a knife and sprinkle with a little sugar. Set the pan on a wire rack to cool. When cool, cut into wedges.

VARIATION

To make individual cookies, roll out the dough and cut with a round cookie cutter; arrange on a baking sheet.

COOK'S NOTES

Use high-quality butter to ensure your shortbread has the most delicious flavor.

Vanilla cupcakes

PREP 25 MINS | COOK 20 MINS | ❄

Special equipment • electric mixer

MAKES 12

9 tbsp butter, at room temperature
⅔ cup granulated sugar
2 large eggs
1¼ cups self-rising flour, sifted
1 tsp vanilla extract
1 tbsp whole milk, if needed

For the icing

1 cup confectioners' (powdered) sugar
3 tbsp unsweetened cocoa
   powder (optional)
7 tbsp butter, at room temperature
few drops of vanilla extract
2 tbsp whole milk, if needed
dark chocolate, shaved into curls
   with a vegetable peeler (optional)

1 Preheat the oven to 375°F (190°C). Line a 12-cup muffin pan with paper liners. Place the butter and sugar in a bowl and beat with an electric mixer until pale and fluffy. Beat in the eggs one at a time, adding 1 tablespoon of the flour after each addition. Beat in the vanilla extract and then the rest of the flour until smooth and blended—the mixture should drop easily off the beaters. If it doesn't, stir in the milk. Divide the mixture evenly between the muffin cups. Bake for 20 minutes or until risen, golden, and firm to the touch. Transfer the cupcakes to a wire rack to cool completely.

2 To make the icing, sift the confectioners' sugar and cocoa powder (if using) into a bowl. Beat in the butter and the vanilla with an electric mixer until the mixture is light and fluffy. If the icing is too thick, beat in the milk. Frost the cupcakes, swirling the icing decoratively. Scatter the dark chocolate shavings over the icing, if desired.

VARIATION

For lemon cupcakes, add the finely grated zest of ½ lemon to the batter; 1-2 tbsp fresh lemon juice to the icing; and omit the cocoa powder.

Swiss roll

PREP 20 MINS | COOK 15 MINS

Special equipment • electric mixer • 9 x 13 x 2in (23 x 33cm) jelly roll pan

SERVES 8-10

3 large eggs
½ cup granulated sugar, plus
   extra to sprinkle
pinch of sea salt
1 tsp vanilla extract
¾ cup self-rising flour
6 tbsp strawberry jam, raspberry jam,
   lemon curd, or Nutella

1 Preheat the oven to 400°F (200°C). Line the bottom and sides of a 9 x 13 x 2in (23 x 33cm) jelly roll pan with parchment paper. In a large bowl set over a saucepan of simmering water, beat the eggs, sugar, and a pinch of salt with an electric mixer for 5 minutes or until very thick and creamy—any batter that drips from the beaters should rest on the surface for a few seconds before sinking in.

2 Remove the bowl from the saucepan and place it on a work surface. Beat the mixture for about 2 minutes, or until cool to the touch. Add the vanilla and sift in the flour, folding it in gently. Scrape into the prepared pan and gently spread in an even layer, reaching into the corners.

Bake for 12-15 minutes or until the top is firm to the touch and the cake has shrunk from the sides of the pan.

3 Sprinkle a large sheet of parchment paper with granulated sugar, then invert the cake onto it. Let cool for 5 minutes, then carefully peel away the parchment that clings to the top of the cake. If the jam is too thick to spread, warm it in a saucepan, then spread it over the cake. Make a small indentation with the back of a knife along one of the short sides, about ¾in (2cm) in from the edge. With this side facing toward you, roll the cake into a cylinder, using the parchment paper to ease the process. When the cake is completely rolled up, leave to cool completely. Place the cake, seam-side down, on a serving plate. Dust with extra sugar before serving.

COOK'S NOTES

Swiss rolls are best eaten on the same day they are made. Serve with ice cream or whipped cream.

Chocolate marble cake

PREP 15 MINS **COOK** 55 MINS

Special equipment • electric mixer • 8½ x 4½ x 2½in (21 x 11 x 6cm) loaf pan

SERVES 8–10

1½ cups self-rising flour
1 tsp baking powder
12 tbsp butter, at room temperature
1 cup granulated sugar
3 large eggs, lightly beaten
1 tsp vanilla extract
1–2 tbsp milk
1 tbsp unsweetened cocoa powder

1 Preheat the oven to 350°F (180°C). Line the bottom of an 8½ x 4½ x 2½in (21 x 11 x 6cm) loaf pan with parchment paper. Sift the flour and baking powder into a large mixing bowl, and then add the butter, sugar, eggs, and vanilla. Beat with an electric mixer until well blended. Beat in enough milk so that the batter drops off easily from the beaters.

2 Spoon half of the mixture into a second bowl and mix in the cocoa powder. Layer the two batters alternately into the pan and swirl with a knife or skewer, making a figure-8 pattern to create the marbled effect.

3 Bake for 55 minutes or until risen and firm to the touch. Let cool in the pan for 5 minutes, then turn out onto a wire rack to cool completely. Cut into slices to serve.

VARIATION

For extra flavor, add the finely grated zest of 1 orange.

COOK'S NOTES

The marbled appearance of the cake depends on how carefully you swirl the two mixtures together. The more you swirl, the more intricate the pattern will be.

Marmalade and ginger loaf

PREP 15 MINS **COOK** 1¼ HRS

Special equipment • electric mixer • 9 x 5 x 3in (23 x 13 x 7cm) loaf pan

SERVES 8–10

2 cups self-rising flour
1 tsp baking powder
1 tsp ground cinnamon
1 tsp ground ginger
12 tbsp butter, at room temperature
1 cup granulated sugar
3 large eggs, lightly beaten
⅔ cup thick-cut Seville orange marmalade, coarsely chopped if needed, plus 2 tbsp extra for glazing

1 Preheat the oven to 350°F (180°C). Line the bottom and sides of a 9 x 5 x 3in (23 x 13 x 7cm) loaf pan with parchment paper. Sift the flour, baking powder, cinnamon, and ginger into a large bowl. Add the butter, sugar, eggs, and ⅔ cup marmalade and beat with an electric mixer until well blended.

2 Pour into the prepared pan and smooth the top. Bake for about 1 hour 15 minutes or until risen and firm to the touch. If the cake starts to brown too quickly, loosely cover the top with foil for the last 30 minutes. Let cool in the pan for 5 minutes, then carefully unmold onto a wire rack. Gently heat the remaining 2 tablespoons marmalade in a small saucepan and generously brush it over the warm cake. Let cool completely.

Dorling Kindersley would like to thank:

Kate Titford for contributing to the *Cakes and Bakes* chapter.

Guy Mirabella for contributing to the *Simple Starters*,
No-fuss Finger Food and Dips, and *Barbecue* chapters.

Editors Peggy Fallon, Michael Fullalove, Christy Lusiak, Lisa Masuda,
Nichole Morford, Siobhan O'Connor, Chrissa Yee, Kara Zuaro

Nutritionist Fiona Hunter

Designers Miranda Harvey, Mandy Earey

Thanks to Susan Downing for commissioning all of the book's photography,
including selection of photography teams and creation of the style brief.

Art Directors Nicky Collings, Luis Peral-Aranda, Lisa Pettibone, Sue Storey

Prop Stylists Sue Rowlands, Rachel Jukes

Food Stylists Annie Rigg, Fergal Connolly and Aya Nishimura, Cara Hobday,
Jenny White, Jane Lawrie, Penny Stephens

Presentation styling Nicola Powling

Indexer Marie Lorimer

Proofreader Sue Morony

Editor-in-Chief acknowledgments:

A very big thank you to Mary-Clare Jerram at Dorling Kindersley for giving me
the opportunity to be involved, and sharing her enthusiasm and excitement for
my ideas. And a massive thank you to my editor Laura Nickoll, who I have
enjoyed working with so much. She has had such passion for the project,
remained utterly calm throughout, and has been an infallible support.

Also to friends and family, that have tried, tested, suggested, and tasted recipes;
my mum for being a real home cook; my daughters Kim and Lorna for being good
eaters (but I wish they would cook more!); and Jos, my husband, for his invaluable
advice, and for being the most patient human being I've ever met.